Idaho, Mo... Y0-BCC-074
& Wyoming

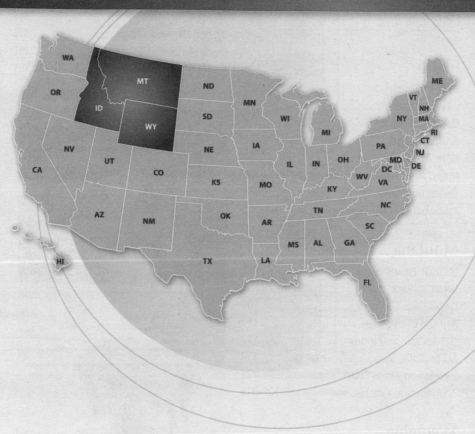

Published by AAA Publishing
1000 AAA Drive, Heathrow, FL 32746-5063
Copyright AAA 2014, All rights reserved

Advertising Rate and Circulation Information: (407) 444-8280

Printed in the USA by Quad/Graphics

This book is printed on paper certified by third-party standards for sustainably managed forestry and production.

 Printed on recyclable paper.
Please recycle whenever possible.

Stock #4611

CONTENTS

Attractions, hotels, restaurants and other travel experience information are all grouped under the alphabetical listing of the city in which those experiences are physically located—or the nearest recognized city.

Featured Information

Idaho

Montana

Wyoming

BEHIND-THE-SCENES
SNEAK PEEK

*AAA Inspectors:
On the Job for Members*

Curious about the experts behind AAA's reliable travel information? Get an inside look at the AAA professionals who inspect some 70,000 hotels, restaurants and attractions every year.

AAA inspectors travel anonymously to ensure a guest experience similar to yours—sometimes glamorous, occasionally awful and, often, just right for a particular travel experience.

That's where AAA's detailed guidelines and reliable ratings come in—ensuring the places you select provide the environment you expect... from simple to family friendly to world-class.

Scan to view an entertaining video.

A to Z City Listings

Cities and places are listed alphabetically within each state or province. Attractions, hotels and restaurants are listed once — under the city in which they are physically located.

Cities that are considered part of a larger destination city or area have an expanded city header. The header identifies the larger region and cross-references pages that contain shared trip planning resources:

- Destination map – outline map of the cities that comprise a destination city or area
- Attraction spotting map – regional street map marked with attraction locations
- Hotel/restaurant spotting map and index – regional street map numbered with hotel and restaurant locations identified in an accompanying index

Cities that are not considered part of a larger destination city or area but have a significant number of listings may have these resources within the individual city section:

- Attraction spotting map
- Hotel/restaurant spotting map and index

About Listed Establishments

AAA/CAA Approved attractions, hotels and restaurants are listed on the basis of merit alone after careful evaluation and approval by full-time, professionally trained AAA/CAA inspectors. An establishment's decision to advertise in the TourBook guide has no bearing on its evaluation or rating; nor does inclusion of advertising imply AAA endorsement of products and services.

Information in this guide was believed accurate at the time of publication. However, since changes inevitably occur between annual editions, please contact your AAA travel professional or visit AAA.com to confirm prices and schedules.

Location Abbreviations

Directions are from the center of town unless otherwise specified, using these highway abbreviations:

Bus. Rte.=business route
CR=county road
FM=farm to market
FR=forest road
Hwy.=Canadian highway
I=interstate highway
LR=legislative route
R.R.=rural route
SR/PR=state or provincial route
US=federal highway

Atlas Section

The Atlas Section provides navigable road maps from the AAA Road Atlas series. The overview map displays the entire coverage area. Corresponding, numbered detail maps offer a closer view for route planning and navigation.

Mobile Tags

Look for Microsoft Tags or QR codes throughout the TourBook guide and scan them with your smartphone to access special online offers, menus, videos and more.

To scan Microsoft Tags or QR codes:

- Download AAA's recommended scanning app to your smartphone at http://gettag.mobi.
- Start scanning Tags or QR codes.
- Link to featured content.

Some advertisers may use bar codes other than Microsoft Tags or QR codes. In those cases, please note any accompanying text that indicates where to download the required reader.

Attraction Listings

 SAVE **ATTRACTION NAME,** 3 mi. n. off SR 20A (Main Ave.), consists of 250 acres with Olmsted-designed gardens, a 205-foot marble and coquina bell tower and a Mediterranean-style mansion. One of the state's oldest attractions, the tower and gardens were dedicated to the American people in 1929 by President Calvin Coolidge on behalf of their founder, a Dutch immigrant.

Other features include daily concerts from the 60-bell carillon, a nature observatory and Nature Preserve Trail. The visitor center presents art exhibits, an orientation film and exhibits about the family legacy, the carillon and endangered plants and animals found on the property. **Hours:** Gardens daily 8-6. Last admission 1 hour before closing. Visitor center daily 9-5. Estate tours are given at noon and 2. Carillon concerts are given at 1 and 3. Phone ahead to confirm schedule. **Cost:** $10; $3 (ages 5-12). Gardens and estate $16; $8 (ages 5-12). **Phone:** (555) 555-5555.

⚡ 🍴 🛆 🚇 Dupont Circle, 13

AAA/CAA inspectors may designate an attraction of exceptional interest and quality as a AAA GEM — a *Great Experience for Members®.* See GEM Attraction Index (listed on CONTENTS page) for complete list of locations.

Adventure Travel

Activities such as air tours, hiking, skiing and white-water rafting are listed to provide member information and do not Imply AAA/CAA endorsement. For your safety, be aware of inherent risks and adhere to all safety instructions.

Cost

Prices are quoted without sales tax in the local currency (U.S. or Canadian dollars). Children under the lowest age specified are admitted free when accompanied by an adult. Most establishments accept credit cards, but a small number require cash, so please call ahead to verify.

Icons

SAVE Show Your Card & Save® member discount

⚡ Electric vehicle charging station on premises. Domestic station information provided by the U.S. Department of Energy. Canadian station information provided by Plug'n Drive Ontario.

🛆 Camping facilities

🍴 Food on premises

🚫 Recreational activities

🐾 Pets on leash allowed

🛆 Picnicking allowed

In select cities only:

🚇 Mass transit station within 1 mile. Icon is followed by station name and AAA/CAA designated station number within listing.

Information-Only Attraction Listings

Bulleted listings, which include the following categories, are listed for informational purposes as a service to members:

- **Gambling establishments** (even if located in a AAA/CAA Approved hotel)
- **Guided food tours**
- **Participatory recreational activities** (those requiring physical exertion or special skills)
- **Wineries that offer tours and tastings**

Hotel and Restaurant Listings

1 Diamond Rating – AAA/CAA Approved hotels and restaurants are assigned a rating of one to five Diamonds. Red Diamonds distinguish establishments that participate in the AAA/CAA logo licensing program. For details, see p. 11 or AAA.com/Diamonds.

fyi indicates hotels and restaurants that are not AAA/CAA Approved and/or Diamond Rated but are listed to provide additional choices for members:

- **Hotels** may be unrated if they are too new to rate, under construction, under major renovation or not evaluated; or if they do not meet all AAA requirements. Hotels that do not meet all AAA requirements may be included if they offer member value or are the only option; details are noted in the listing.
- **Restaurants** may be unrated if they have not yet been evaluated by AAA.

2 Classification or Cuisine Type – Noted after the Diamond Rating.

- **Hotel Classifications** indicate the style of operation, overall concept and service level. Subclassifications may also be added. (See p. 12 list.)
- **Restaurant Cuisine Types** identify the food concept from more than 100 categories. If applicable, a classification may also be added. (See p. 13 list.)

3 Dollar Amounts – Quoted without sales tax in the local currency (U.S. or Canadian dollars), rounded up to the nearest dollar. Most establishments accept credit cards, but a small number require cash, so please call ahead to verify.

- **Hotel Rates** indicate the publicly available two-person rate or rate range for a standard room, applicable all year.
- **Restaurant Prices** represent the minimum and maximum entrée cost per person. Exceptions may include one-of-a-kind or special market priced items.

4 Spotting Symbol – Ovals containing numbers correspond with numbered location markings on hotel and restaurant spotting maps.

5 Parking – Unless otherwise noted, parking is free, on-site self parking.

6 Hotel Value Nationwide – Blue boxes highlight member benefits available at AAA/CAA Approved locations across a hotel chain. (See Just For Members section for details.)

7 Hotel Unit Limited Availability – Unit types, amenities and room features preceded by "some" are available on a limited basis, potentially as few as one.

8 Hotel Terms – Cancellation and minimum stay policies are listed. Unless otherwise noted, most properties offer a full deposit refund with cancellations received at least 48 hours before standard check-in. Properties that require advance payment may not refund the difference for early departures. "Resort fee" indicates a charge may apply above and beyond the quoted room rate.

9 Hotel Check-in/Check-out – Unless otherwise noted, check-in is after 3 p.m. and check-out is before 10 a.m.

10 Restaurant Dress Code – Unless otherwise noted, dress is casual or dressy casual.

11 Restaurant Menu – Where indicated, menus may be viewed in a secure online environment at AAA.com or, if a mobile tag is provided, via the restaurant's website.

12 Hotel Icons – May be preceded by CALL and/or SOME UNITS.

Member Information:

SAVE Rate guarantee: discounted standard room rate or lowest public rate available at time of booking for dates of stay.

ECO Eco-certified by government or private organization. Visit AAA.com/eco for details.

Electric vehicle charging station on premises. Domestic station information provided by the U.S. Department of Energy. Canadian station information provided by Plug'n Drive Ontario.

Smoke-free premises

In select cities only:

Mass transit station within 1 mile. Icon is followed by station name and AAA/CAA designated station number within listing.

Services:

Airport transportation

Pets allowed (Call property for restrictions.)

Pets allowed (Call property for restrictions and fees.)

Restaurant on premises

Restaurant off premises

Room service for 2 or more meals

Full bar

Child care

HOTEL LISTING

RESTAURANT LISTING

BIZ Business area

&M Accessible features (Call property for available services and amenities.)

Activities:

🎰 Full-service casino

🏊 Pool

💪 Health club on premises

In-Room Amenities:

HS High-speed Internet service

sHS High-speed Internet service
   (Call property for fees.)

🛜 Wireless Internet service

s🛜 Wireless Internet service
   (Call property for fees.)

🛜 No wireless Internet service

🎬 Pay movies

🍴 Refrigerator

📺 Microwave

💻 Coffee maker

🚫 No air conditioning

📺 No TV

☎ No telephones

13 **Restaurant Icons**

SAVE Show Your Card & Save® member discount

ECO Eco-certified by government or private organization. Visit AAA.com/eco for details.

⚡ Electric vehicle charging station on premises. Domestic station information provided by the U.S. Department of Energy. Canadian station information provided by Plug'n Drive Ontario.

🚫 No air conditioning

&M Accessible features (Call property for available services and amenities.)

🚬 Designated smoking section

B Breakfast

L Lunch

D Dinner

24 Open 24 hours

LATE Open after 11 p.m.

🐾 Pet-friendly (Call property for restrictions.)

In select cities only:

🚇 Mass transit station within 1 mile. Icon is followed by station name and AAA/CAA designated station number within listing.

Just For Members

Understanding the Diamond Ratings

Hotel and restaurant evaluations are unscheduled to ensure our professionally trained inspectors encounter the same experience members do.

- When an establishment is Diamond Rated, it means members can expect a good fit with their needs. The inspector assigns a rating that indicates the type of experience to expect.
- While establishments at high levels must offer increasingly complex personalized services, establishments at every level are subject to the same basic requirements for cleanliness, comfort and hospitality. Learn more at AAA.com/Diamonds.

Hotels

Budget-oriented, offering basic comfort and hospitality.

Affordable, with modestly enhanced facilities, décor and amenities.

Distinguished, multi-faceted with enhanced physical attributes, amenities and guest comforts.

Refined, stylish with upscale physical attributes, extensive amenities and high degree of hospitality, service and attention to detail.

Ultimate luxury, sophistication and comfort with extraordinary physical attributes, meticulous personalized service, extensive amenities and impeccable standards of excellence.

Restaurants

Simple, familiar specialty food at an economical price. Often self-service, basic surroundings.

Familiar, family-oriented experience. Home-style foods and family favorites, often cooked to order, modestly enhanced and reasonably priced. Relaxed service, casual surroundings.

Fine dining, often adult-oriented. Latest cooking trends and/or traditional cuisine, expanded beverage offerings. Professional service staff and comfortable, well-coordinated ambience.

Distinctive fine-dining, typically expensive. Highly creative chefs, imaginative presentations and fresh, top-quality ingredients. Proficient service staff, upscale surroundings. Wine steward may offer menu-specific knowledge.

Luxurious and consistently world-class. Highly acclaimed chefs, artistic and imaginative menu selections using the finest ingredients. Maitre d' and unobtrusive, expert service staff.

What's the difference?

- Red Diamonds mark establishments that participate in the AAA/CAA logo licensing program for increased visibility to members.
- Black Diamonds identify all other AAA/CAA Approved and Diamond Rated establishments.

Hotel Classifications

Quality and comfort are usually consistent across each Diamond Rating level, but décor, facilities and service levels vary by classification.

1884 Paxton House Inn
Thomasville, GA

Bed & Breakfast – Typically owner-operated with a high degree of personal touches. Guests are encouraged to interact during evening and breakfast hours. A continental or full, hot breakfast is included in the room rate.

Barkwells
Mills River, NC

Cabin – Often located in wooded, rural or waterfront locations. Free-standing units are typically rustic and of basic design. As a rule, essential cleaning supplies, kitchen utensils and complete bed and bath linens are supplied.

Camelot by the Sea
Myrtle Beach, SC

Condominium – Apartment-style accommodations of varying design or décor, units often contain one or more bedrooms, a living room, a full kitchen and an eating area. As a rule, essential cleaning supplies, kitchen utensils and complete bed and bath linens are supplied.

The Red Horse Inn Cottages
Landrum, SC

Cottage – Often located in wooded, rural or waterfront locations. Free-standing units are typically home-style in design and décor. As a rule, essential cleaning supplies, kitchen utensils and complete bed and bath linens are supplied.

The Lodge at Moosehead
Lake, Greenville, ME

Country Inn – Although similar in definition to a bed and breakfast, country inns are usually larger in scale with spacious public areas and offer a dining facility that serves breakfast and dinner.

Grand America Hotel
Salt Lake City, UT

Hotel – Typically a multistory property with interior room entrances and a variety of guest unit styles. The magnitude of the public areas is determined by the overall theme, location and service level, but may include a variety of facilities such as a restaurant, shops, a fitness center, a spa, a business center and meeting rooms.

Windsor Palms Vacation
Rentals-All Star Vacation
Homes, Kissimmee, FL

House – Free-standing units of varying home-style design. Typically larger scale, often containing two or more bedrooms, a living room, a full kitchen, a dining room and multiple bathrooms. As a rule, essential cleaning supplies, kitchen utensils and complete bed and bath linens are supplied.

BEST WESTERN Bryson Inn
Mount Airy, NC

Motel – A one- or two-story roadside property with exterior room entrances and drive-up parking. Public areas and facilities are often limited in size and/or availability.

Lost Valley Ranch
Deckers, CO

Ranch – Typically a working ranch featuring an obvious rustic, Western theme, equestrian-related activities and a variety of guest unit styles.

Hotel Subclassifications

These additional descriptives may be added to the classification for more information:

- **Boutique** – Often thematic, typically informal yet highly personalized; may have a luxurious or quirky style that is fashionable or unique.
- **Casino** – Extensive gambling facilities are available, such as blackjack, craps, keno and slot machines.
- **Classic** – Renowned and landmark properties, older than 50 years, well known for their unique style and ambience.
- **Contemporary** – Overall theme reflects characteristics of present mainstream trends.
- **Extended Stay** – Offers a predominance of long-term accommodations with a designated full-service kitchen area within each unit.
- **Historic** – Over 75 years old with one of the following documented historical features: maintains the integrity of the historical nature, listed on the National Register of Historic Places, designated a National Historic Landmark or located in a National Register Historic District.

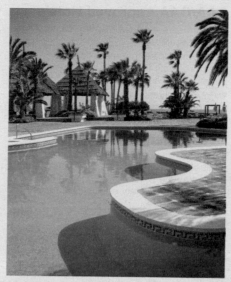

- **Resort** – Extensive recreational facilities and programs may include golf, tennis, skiing, fishing, water sports, spa treatments or professionally guided activities.
- **Retro** – Overall theme reflects a contemporary design that reinterprets styles from a past era.
- **Vacation Rental** – Typically houses, condos, cottages or cabins; these properties are "home away from home" self-catering accommodations.
- **Vintage** – Overall theme reflects upon and maintains the authentic traits and experience of a past era.

Restaurant Classifications

If applicable, in addition to the cuisine type noted under the Diamond Rating, restaurant listings may also include one or both classifications:

- **Classic** – Renowned and landmark operation in business for 25 plus years; unique style and ambience.
- **Historic** – Meets one of the following: Listed on National Register of Historic Places, designated a National Historic Landmark or located in a National Register Historic District.

Service Animals

Under the Americans with Disabilities Act (ADA), U.S. businesses that serve the public must allow people with disabilities to bring their service animals into all areas of the facility where customers are normally allowed to go.

Businesses may ask if an animal is a service animal and what tasks the animal has been trained to perform. Businesses may not ask about the person's disability, require special identification for the animal or request removal of the animal from the premises except in limited cases that require alternate assistance. Businesses may not charge extra fees for service animals, including standard pet fees, but may charge for damage caused by service animals if guests are normally charged for damage they cause.

Call the U.S. Department of Justice ADA Information Line: (800) 514-0301 or TTY (800) 514-0383, or visit ada.gov. Regulations may differ in Canada.

AAA/CAA Approved Hotels

For members, AAA/CAA Approved means quality assured.

- Only properties that meet basic requirements for cleanliness, comfort and hospitality pass inspection.
- Approved hotels receive a Diamond Rating that tells members the type of experience to expect.

Guest Safety

Inspectors view a sampling of rooms during evaluations and, therefore, AAA/CAA cannot guarantee the presence of working locks and operational fire safety equipment in every guest unit.

Member Rates

AAA/CAA members can generally expect to pay no more than the maximum TourBook listed rate for a standard room. Member discounts apply to rates quoted within the rate range and are applicable at the time of booking. Listed rates are usually based on last standard room availability. Within the range, rates may vary by season and room type. Obtain current AAA/CAA member rates and make reservations at AAA.com.

Exceptions

- Rates for properties operating as concessionaires for the U.S. National Park Service are not guaranteed due to governing regulations.
- Special advertised rates and short-term promotional rates below the rate range are not subject to additional member discounts.
- During special events, hotels may temporarily increase room rates, not recognize discounts or modify pricing policies. Special events may include Mardi Gras, the Kentucky Derby (including pre-Derby events), college football games, holidays, holiday periods and state fairs. Although some special events are listed in the TourBook guides and on AAA.com, it's always wise to check in advance with AAA travel professionals for specific dates.

If you are charged more than the maximum TourBook listed rate, question the additional charge. If an exception is not in effect and management refuses to adhere to the published rate, pay for the room and contact AAA/CAA. The amount paid above the stated maximum will be refunded if our investigation indicates an unjustified charge.

Reservations and Cancellations

When making your reservation, identify yourself as a AAA/CAA member and request written confirmation of your room type, rate, dates of stay, and cancellation and refund policies. At registration, show your membership card.

To cancel, contact the hotel or your AAA/CAA club office, depending on how you booked your reservation. Request a cancellation number or proof of cancellation.

If your room is not as specified and you have written confirmation of your reservation for a specific room type, you should be given the option of choosing a different room or receiving a refund. If management refuses to issue a refund, contact AAA/CAA.

Contacting AAA/CAA About Approved Properties

If your visit to a AAA/CAA Approved attraction, hotel or restaurant doesn't meet your expectations, please tell us about it — *during your visit or within 30 days*. Be sure to save your receipts and other documentation for reference.

Use the easy online form at AAA.com/TourBookComments to send us the details.

Alternatively, you can email your comments to: memberrelations@national.aaa.com or submit them via postal mail to: AAA Member Comments, 1000 AAA Dr., Box 61, Heathrow, FL 32746.

AAA/CAA Preferred Hotels

All AAA/CAA Approved hotels are committed to providing quality, value and member service. In addition, those designated as AAA/CAA Preferred Hotels also offer these extra values at Approved locations nationwide. Valid AAA/CAA membership required.

- **Best AAA/CAA member rates for your dates of stay.**
- **Seasonal promotions and special member offers.** Visit AAA.com to view current offers.
- **Member benefit.** See the blue boxes in hotel listings for the chains shown in the right-hand column below to find values offered at AAA/CAA Approved locations nationwide. Details valid at the time of publication may change without notice.

- **Total satisfaction guarantee.** If you book your stay with AAA/CAA Travel and your stay fails to meet your expectations, you can apply for a full refund. Bring the complaint to the hotel's attention during the stay and request resolution; if the complaint is not resolved by the hotel, ask your AAA/CAA travel agent to request resolution through the AAA/CAA Assured Stay program.

Preferred Hotels

Total Satisfaction Guarantee

Best Western, Best Western Plus and Best Western Premier

 TEN DISTINCT HOTEL BRANDS

Waldorf Astoria Hotels & Resorts, Conrad Hotels & Resorts, Hilton Hotels & Resorts, DoubleTree, Embassy Suites Hotels, Hilton Garden Inn, Hampton Hotels, Homewood Suites, Home2 Suites and Hilton Grand Vacations

Park Hyatt, Andaz, Grand Hyatt, Hyatt Regency, Hyatt Hotels & Resorts, Hyatt Place and Hyatt House

JW Marriott Hotels, EDITION, Autograph Collection Hotels, Renaissance Hotels, AC Hotels, Marriott Hotels & Resorts, Courtyard, SpringHill Suites, Fairfield Inn & Suites, Residence Inn, TownePlace Suites and Gaylord Hotels

Aloft, Element, Four Points, Le Meridien, Sheraton, St. Regis, The Luxury Collection, W Hotels and Westin

Show Your Card & Save®
Member Discounts

Visit AAA.com/searchfordiscounts to find local Show Your Card & Save discounts. Your AAA/CAA club may offer even greater discounts on theme park tickets. Amtrak and theme park discounts may be used for up to six tickets; restaurant savings may be used for up to six patrons. Other restrictions may apply. All offers subject to change. For complete restrictions, visit your AAA office or AAA.com/restrictions.

ATTRACTIONS

SeaWorld, Busch Gardens, Sesame Place

SEAWORLD PARKS & ENTERTAINMENT

- Save on admission at the gate, participating AAA/CAA offices or AAA.com/SeaWorld.
- Save 10% on up-close dining; visit Guest Relations for details.

Six Flags

- Save on admission at the gate, participating AAA/CAA offices or AAA.com/SixFlags.

SixFlags

- Save 10% on merchandise of $15 or more at in-park stores.

Universal Orlando Resort and Universal Studios Hollywood

- Save on admission at the gate, participating AAA/CAA offices or AAA.com/Universal.

The Entertainment Capital of L.A.

- Save on Blue Man Group tickets and at select food and merchandise venues in-park and at Universal CityWalk®.

BLUE MAN GROUP

DINING & SHOPPING

Hard Rock Cafe

- Save 10% on food, nonalcoholic beverages and merchandise at all locations in the U.S. and Canada and select international locations.

Landry's Seafood House, The Crab House, Chart House, Oceanaire, Saltgrass Steak House, Muer Seafood Restaurants and Aquarium Restaurants

- Save 10% on food and nonalcoholic beverages at all of the above restaurants.
- Save 10% on merchandise at Aquarium and Downtown Aquarium restaurants.
- Location information: AAA.com/Discounts.

Tanger Outlet Centers

- Simple present your AAA card in any Tanger Shopper Services Center or Management Office, and you'll receive a FREE coupon booklet filled with hundreds of dollars in savings from top brand names and designer outlet stores (a $5 value). Visit AAA.com/searchfordiscounts for locations.

TRANSPORTATION & TOURS

Amtrak

- Save 10% on rail fare booked at least 3 days in advance of travel date at AAA.com/Amtrak.

Hertz

- Save on daily, week-end, weekly and monthly rentals at AAA.com/hertz or 1-800-654-3080.

Pack your bags with
UNLIMITED AAA TRAVEL REWARDS

Take your travel farther with the AAA Member Rewards Visa® credit card

EXCLUSIVE OFFER FOR AAA MEMBERS!

Redeem unlimited rewards toward your next AAA vacation*

- **3X POINTS** on qualifying AAA and travel purchases
- **2X POINTS** on gas, grocery and drug store purchases
- **1 POINT PER $1** on purchases everywhere else
- **GET AAA BRANCH VOUCHERS FOR TRAVEL** worth up to 40% more than cash rewards"

VISIT AAA.com/creditcard | **STOP BY** any AAA branch

Reflection of the Sawtooth Mountains

Idaho

Visit Idaho and you'll need an oxygen mask; the scenery is that breathtaking. From the serrated granite peaks of the Sawtooth Mountains at the state's core to the towering Seven Devils flanking Hells Canyon, Idaho features some of the country's most stunning high-altitude panoramas. And if the views don't steal your breath away, the thin air at these lofty elevations just might.

Fortunately, there's no better place to deeply inhale than within the state's numerous unspoiled wilderness areas. Clean air and peaceful solitude attract pollution- and stress-weary urbanites from around the country to places like the Selway-Bitterroot Wilderness or Craters of the Moon National Monument and Preserve.

Expel that fresh air in a shout of triumph as you conquer exhilarating white water along the Snake, Selway or Salmon rivers. Whoop

Fly-fish the Boise River

with excitement flying down a powder-covered slope in Sun Valley or on Schweitzer Mountain. Scream with delight at the discovery of a star garnet near Coeur d'Alene, the only place outside of India you can find such treasure and just one reason Idaho's nickname—the Gem State—is appropriate.

The Call of the Wild West

Idaho remains one of the country's most isolated and rugged regions. To early explorers and entrepreneurs—from Meriwether Lewis and William Clark to adventurous traders and prospectors—the territory was practically impenetrable. But with a determination undaunted come Hells Canyon or high water, they journeyed west. Follow their lead, and you, too, will be struck by this land's power to inspire.

Idaho counts plenty of contemporary dreamers and doers on its dossier. The memorial marking one of Ernest Hemingway's favorite fly-fishing spots is half-hidden near a shady stream in Sun Valley's outskirts. And astronaut Alan Shepard and his crew trained for a lunar landing at Craters of the Moon National Monument and Preserve, an eerie volcanic landscape outside Arco.

As you shop and stroll in the resort towns of Ketchum and Hailey, keep a covert eye out for famous faces; a who's who of movie stars and Olympic athletes lives here part time. Still, Idaho's allure sways more than celebrities. The state is home to one of the world's largest concentrations of nesting hawks, falcons, owls and other raptors; spy on some of these magnificent birds at Boise's World Center for Birds of Prey.

Not For Your Eyes Only

So, what *is* all the fuss about? Mountains, mostly. Three of Idaho's borders wear crowns topping 9,000 feet. From Bruneau River Canyon's Goliath-like stone shoulders to the Precambrian pillars of City of Rocks National Reserve, grandiose mountain scenery dominates this state.

Not that less rugged diversions are lacking. State capital Boise offers a fine orchestra and opera. Coeur d'Alene reinforces its resort image with a fun theme park and a golf course featuring one offshore green. In Sandpoint, the focal point is a city bridge-turned-popular downtown market.

But it's the outdoors that beckon. Here you can watch the slow, mesmerizing spiral of a golden eagle poised on a canyon-channeled thermal of mountain air, or paddle through a fast, furious white-water spin cycle with a boatful of cohorts. The offerings are as vast as the mountains.

Recreation

An abundance of publicly held land and wilderness area is set aside in scenic Idaho—all the better for play in any season.

Thousands of miles of groomed trails—as well as millions of acres of forest land and backcountry—provide fast snowmobiling fun in the chilly winter air. Best bets include Clearwater, Idaho Panhandle and Nez Perce national forests.

For downhill skiing, Bogus Basin, 16 miles north of Boise; Silver Mountain, south of Kellogg; and Sun Valley will satisfy your need for speed. If you prefer cross-country skiing or snowshoeing, outfitters plan overnight treks through the Boulder, Pioneer, Sawtooth and Teton mountains. Skiers of moderate ability enjoy Fish Creek Meadows and Lolo Pass in Nez Perce National Forest; the scenic trails in Farragut State Park; and the paths winding throughout Sawtooth National Recreation Area.

Idaho's waterways provide thrills of their own. Class III and IV rapids, with names like Split Rock and Whiplash, may explain how the Salmon got its nickname as the "River of No Return." Rafting and kayaking also are wild and woolly on the Middle Fork of the Salmon and the Owyhee, Payette and Lochsa rivers, the last of which is a Nez Perce Indian word for "rough water." Jet boats zip along the Snake River through Hells Canyon.

Want to take it slowly? Go canoeing between the cliffs rising around the Snake River at Hagerman Fossil Beds National Monument in Hagerman, or watch eagles, ospreys and mink as you enjoy a leisurely float trip down the placid Boise River.

Dories and drift boats take anglers to favorite fishing waters on the Clearwater, Salmon and Snake rivers, where hardy steelhead thrive. Meanwhile, the upper St. Joe River is a haven for cutthroat.

Anglers find the northern lakes no less exciting. Coeur d'Alene, Pend Oreille and Priest lakes teem with chinook and kokanee salmon, Kamloops trout and northern pike.

Equestrian activities abound in the Grand Tetons and near Coeur d'Alene, Sun Valley and Yellowstone, while ridgelines across such ranges as the Bitterroot, Cougar and Salmon afford outstanding panoramas for mountain bikers.

Climbing expeditions tackle Slick Rock, near McCall; City of Rocks National Reserve, near Almo; and the state's highest peak, Mount Borah. For a less rugged experience, go hiking or backpacking or make your way up mountains around McCall and Sun Valley on a llama trek. Only pack trains and hikers penetrate the unspoiled terrain of the Frank Church-River of No Return, Sawtooth and Selway-Bitterroot wilderness areas, which blanket more than 2 million acres.

A skier hits some fresh powder

Historic Timeline

1805	Meriwether Lewis and William Clark explore what is now Idaho.
1860	Mormons establish Franklin, the first permanent white settlement in Idaho.
1874	The railroad first reaches Idaho at Franklin.
1890	Idaho becomes the 43rd state.
1951	An Atomic Energy Commission testing station near Idaho Falls first uses fission to generate electricity.
1968	Engineers complete three dams to harness the power of the Snake River.
1983	An earthquake registering 7.3 on the Richter scale shakes central Idaho.
1988	Congress establishes Hagerman Fossil Beds National Monument and the City of Rocks National Reserve.
1995	Idaho native Picabo Street becomes the first American to win a World Cup season title in a speed event.
1999	University of Idaho graduate Jeffrey S. Ashby pilots the space shuttle *Columbia*.
2009	Native American Larry EchoHawk, a former Idaho attorney general, becomes head of the U.S. Bureau of Indian Affairs.

What To Pack

Temperature Averages Maximum/Minimum	JANUARY	FEBRUARY	MARCH	APRIL	MAY	JUNE	JULY	AUGUST	SEPTEMBER	OCTOBER	NOVEMBER	DECEMBER
Boise	36/21	42/26	52/31	62/37	71/45	79/51	90/59	88/57	78/49	65/40	48/30	39/25
Idaho Falls	28/3	33/8	42/18	58/29	68/38	76/44	88/50	86/47	75/38	62/28	43/17	33/9
Lewiston	38/24	44/28	53/33	63/39	71/46	78/52	90/58	88/56	78/49	64/40	48/32	42/28
Pocatello	32/13	37/18	46/26	60/33	69/41	78/48	90/55	87/53	77/44	64/34	45/25	36/19
Salmon	28/9	37/15	50/25	60/32	69/40	78/46	87/51	86/48	75/40	60/30	41/21	29/11
Sandpoint	32/19	38/23	46/28	56/34	65/41	72/47	80/50	80/49	70/41	56/33	40/28	32/21

From the records of The Weather Channel Interactive, Inc.

Good Facts To Know

ABOUT THE STATE

POPULATION: 1,567,582.

AREA: 83,557 square miles; ranks 13th.

CAPITAL: Boise.

HIGHEST POINT: 12,662 ft., Borah Peak.

LOWEST POINT: 710 ft., Snake River at Lewiston.

TIME ZONE(S): Mountain/Pacific. DST.

GAMBLING

MINIMUM AGE FOR GAMBLING: 21.

REGULATIONS

TEEN DRIVING LAWS: No more than one passenger under age 17 (excluding family members) is permitted for the first 6 months. Driving is not permitted daily dusk-dawn. The minimum age for an unrestricted driver's license is 16. Phone (208) 334-8735 for more information about Idaho driver's license regulations.

SEAT BELT/CHILD RESTRAINT LAWS: Seat belts are required for driver and all passengers ages 7 and older. Children under age 7 are required to be in a child restraint. AAA recommends the use of seat belts and appropriate child restraints for the driver and all passengers.

CELL PHONE RESTRICTIONS: Text messaging while driving is prohibited for all drivers.

HELMETS FOR MOTORCYCLISTS: Required for riders under 18.

RADAR DETECTORS: Permitted.

MOVE OVER LAW: Driver is required to slow down and vacate lane nearest stopped police, fire and rescue vehicles using audible or flashing signals. The law also includes tow trucks.

FIREARMS LAWS: Vary by state and/or county. Contact Idaho Attorney General's Office, 700 W. Jefferson St., Suite 210, P.O. Box 83720, Boise ID 83720; phone (208) 334-2400.

HOLIDAYS

HOLIDAYS: Jan. 1 ▪ Martin Luther King Jr. Day, Jan. (3rd Mon.) ▪ Washington's Birthday/Presidents Day, Feb. (3rd Mon.) ▪ Memorial Day, May (last Mon.) ▪ July 4 ▪ Labor Day, Sept. (1st Mon.) ▪ Columbus Day, Oct. (2nd Mon.) ▪ Veterans Day, Nov. 11 ▪ Thanksgiving, Nov. (4th Thurs.) ▪ Christmas, Dec. 25.

MONEY

TAXES: Idaho's statewide sales tax is 6 percent. There is a 2 percent Travel & Convention Tax on lodgings, with local options to levy up to an additional 5 percent.

VISITOR INFORMATION

INFORMATION CENTERS: State welcome centers that provide details about state attractions, accommodations, historic sites, parks and events as well as road and ski reports are at Fruitland I-84E, Milepost 1 ▪ 6 miles south of Malad City on I-15N ▪ and along I-90E at Post Falls.

FURTHER INFORMATION FOR VISITORS:
Idaho Department of Commerce—Tourism Division
700 W. State St.
P.O. Box 83720
Boise, ID 83720
(208) 334-2470
(800) 847-4843

NATIONAL FOREST INFORMATION:
U.S. Forest Service, Idaho Panhandle National Forests
3815 Schreiber Way
Coeur d'Alene, ID 83815-8363
(208) 765-7223
(877) 444-6777 (reservations)
TTY (877) 833-6777
Intermountain Region, USDA Forest Service
507 25th St.
Ogden, UT 84401
(801) 625-5306
(877) 444-6777 (reservations)
(877) 833-6777 (TTY)

FISHING AND HUNTING REGULATIONS:
Idaho Department of Fish and Game
600 S. Walnut St.
Boise, ID 83712
(208) 334-3700

RECREATION INFORMATION:
Idaho Parks and Recreation Department
5657 Warm Springs Ave.
Boise, ID 83720
(208) 334-4199

Download eTourBook guides for
top destinations at AAA.com/ebooks

Idaho Annual Events

Please call ahead to confirm event details.

JANUARY

- Winter Carnival / McCall
  208-634-7631
- WinterFest / Island Park
  208-558-7755
- Soda Springs Winter
  Carnival, Fishing Derby and
  Cross Country Ski Race
  Soda Springs
  208-547-4516

FEBRUARY

- Pierce Winter Festival
  Pierce
  208-464-2171
- American Dog Derby
  Ashton
  208-652-7285
- Lionel Hampton Jazz
  Festival / Moscow
  208-885-6765

MARCH

- St. Patrick's Day Parade
  Coeur d'Alene
  208-415-0116
- Boise Flower and Garden
  Show / Boise
  503-335-3336
- Chrome in the Dome Car
  and Bike Show / Pocatello
  208-282-3605

APRIL

- Gene Harris Jazz Festival
  Boise
  208-426-1711
- Dogwood Festival of the
  Lewis-Clark Valley
  Lewiston
  208-743-3531
- Salmon River Jet Boat
  Races / Riggins
  208-628-3952

MAY

- Riggins Rodeo and Parade
  Riggins
  208-628-3971
- Sun Valley Wellness
  Festival / Sun Valley
  208-726-2777
- Lost in the '50s / Sandpoint
  208-263-9321

JUNE

- Meridian Dairy Days
  Festival and Marketplace
  Meridian
  208-888-2817
- Emmett Cherry Festival
  Emmett
  208-365-3485
- National Oldtime Fiddlers'
  Contest and Festival
  Weiser
  800-437-1280

JULY

- Snake River Stampede and
  Snake River Dayz / Nampa
  208-466-4641
- Hailey Days of the Old
  West 4th of July Celebration
  Hailey
  208-788-2700
- Salmon River Days
  Salmon
  208-756-2100

AUGUST

- Huckleberry Heritage
  Festival / Wallace
  208-753-7151
- Festival at Sandpoint
  Sandpoint
  208-263-6858
- Idaho International Dance
  and Music Festival
  Rexburg
  888-463-6880

SEPTEMBER

- Eastern Idaho State Fair
  Blackfoot
  208-785-2480
- Wagon Days Celebration
  Ketchum
  208-726-3423
- Idaho State Draft Horse
  and Mule International
  Show / Sandpoint
  208-263-8414

OCTOBER

- Trailing of the Sheep
  Ketchum
  800-634-3347
- Sun Valley Jazz Jamboree
  Sun Valley
  208-726-3423
- Fall Harvest Festival / Boise
  208-343-8649

NOVEMBER

- Boise Holiday Parade
  Boise
  208-433-5675
- Winter Garden aGlow at the
  Idaho Botanical Garden
  Boise
  208-343-8649
- Kootenai Health Foundation
  Festival of Trees
  Coeur d'Alene
  208-666-8733

DECEMBER

- Yuletide Celebration and
  Lighting Festival / Wallace
  208-753-7151
- Famous Idaho Potato Bowl
  Boise
  208-424-1011
- Winter Wonderland
  Festival / Sun Valley
  208-622-2800

Fresh potatoes, Sun Valley

State Capitol, Boise

Scenic lake near Coeur d'Alene

See elk in Nez Perce National Forest

Water ski in McCall

Index: Great Experience for Members

AAA editor's picks of exceptional note

Hells Canyon National Recreation Area

Craters of the Moon National Monument and Preserve

Discovery Center of Idaho

The Museum of Idaho

Make the Most of Your Trip
with AAA eTourBook® Guides

Maximize your travel experience when you take along AAA eTourBook guides for your ereader or smartphone. Each of the more than 100 available digital titles is packed with:

- Destination details
- AAA Approved and Diamond Rated hotel and restaurant listings
- Attraction and event information
- Preplanned itineraries
- Editor's don't-miss picks

Download now at
AAA.com/ebooks

Idaho
Atlas Section

ROADS/HIGHWAYS
- INTERSTATE
- CONTROLLED ACCESS
- CONTROLLED ACCESS TOLL
- TOLL ROAD
- PRIMARY DIVIDED
- PRIMARY UNDIVIDED
- SECONDARY DIVIDED
- SECONDARY UNDIVIDED
- LOCAL DIVIDED
- LOCAL UNDIVIDED
- UNPAVED ROAD
- UNDER CONSTRUCTION
- TUNNEL
- PEDESTRIAN ONLY
- AUTO FERRY
- PASSENGER FERRY
- SCENIC BYWAY
- DISTANCE BETWEEN MARKERS
- EXIT NUMBER–FREE/TOLL
- INTERCHANGE FULL/PARTIAL
- WELCOME CENTER
- REST AREA/ SERVICE CENTER

BOUNDARIES
- INTERNATIONAL
- STATE
- COUNTY
- TIME ZONE
- CONTINENTAL DIVIDE

ROAD SHIELDS
- INTERSTATE/BUSINESS
- U.S./STATE/COUNTY
- FOREST/INDIAN
- TRANS- CANADA
- PROVINCIAL AUTOROUTE
- MEXICO
- HISTORIC ROUTE 66

VT 41 — REFERENCE PAGE INDICATOR

AREAS OF INTEREST
- INDIAN
- MILITARY
- PARK
- FOREST
- GRASSLANDS
- HISTORIC
- INT'L REGIONAL AIRPORT
- INCORPORATED CITY

POINTS OF INTEREST
- TOWN
- NATIONAL CAPITAL
- STATE/PROVINCIAL CAPITAL
- AAA/CAA CLUB LOCATION
- FEATURE OF INTEREST
- COLLEGE/UNIVERSITY
- CAMPGROUND INFORMATION PROVIDED BY WOODALL'S ®
- CUSTOMS STATION
- HISTORIC
- LIGHTHOUSE
- MONUMENT/MEMORIAL
- STATE/PROVINCIAL PARK
- NATIONAL WILDLIFE REFUGE
- SKI AREA
- SPORTS COMPLEX
- DAM

CITIES/TOWNS are color-coded by size, showing where to find AAA Approved and Diamond rated lodgings or restaurants listed in the AAA TourBook guides and on AAA.com:
- Red - major destinations and capitals; many listings
- Black - destinations; some listings
- Grey - no listings

IDAHO
ONE INCH EQUALS APPROXIMATELY 20 MILES OR 32.74 KILOMETERS 1:2,471,040

ROAD Atlas 2014
OVER 100 YEARS OF NAVIGATION

Idaho
Orientation
NOT INTENDED FOR DRIVING.
SEE APPROPRIATE AAA SHEET MAP.

Only places listed in the Attractions
section appear on this map.

▽ See AAA GEM Index

◼1 See Recreation Areas Chart
on following page

Scale in Miles
50   0   50

© 2013 NAVTEQ

4016-14

Recreation Areas Chart

The map location numerals in column 2 show an area's location on the preceding map.

	MAP LOCATION	CAMPING	PICNICKING	HIKING TRAILS	BOATING	BOAT RAMP	BOAT RENTAL	FISHING	SWIMMING	PETS ON LEASH	BICYCLE TRAILS	WINTER SPORTS	VISITOR CENTER	LODGE/CABINS	FOOD SERVICE
NATIONAL FORESTS *(See place listings.)*															
Boise (E-2) 2,612,000 acres. South-central Idaho.		•	•	•	•	•		•	•	•	•		•	•	
Caribou-Targhee (F-5) 3,000,000 acres. Southeastern Idaho.		•	•	•	•	•	•	•	•	•	•	•	•	•	
Clearwater (C-2) 1.8 million acres. Northeastern Idaho.		•	•	•	•	•		•	•	•			•	•	
Idaho Panhandle (B-1) 2,495,517 acres. Northern Idaho.		•	•	•	•	•		•	•	•	•		•	•	
Nez Perce (D-2) 2,223,594 acres. North-central Idaho.		•	•	•	•	•		•	•	•			•	•	
Payette (E-1) 2,307,897 acres. West-central Idaho.		•	•	•	•	•		•	•	•	•		•		
Salmon-Challis (E-3) 4,300,000 acres. East-central Idaho.		•	•	•	•	•		•	•	•	•		•		
Sawtooth (F-3) 2,101,422 acres. South-central Idaho. Horse rental.		•	•	•	•	•	•	•	•	•	•	•	•	•	•
NATIONAL RECREATION AREAS *(See place listings.)*															
Hells Canyon (D-1) 652,977 acres in northeastern Oregon and western Idaho. Horse rental.		•	•	•	•	•		•		•			•	•	
Sawtooth (F-3) 756,000 acres in south-central Idaho.		•	•	•	•	•	•	•	•	•	•	•	•	•	
ARMY CORPS OF ENGINEERS															
Albeni Cove (A-1) 20 acres 1 mi. e. of Oldtown on a county road. Water skiing.	**1**	•	•	•	•	•		•	•	•					
Dworshak Reservoir (C-1) 19,823 acres 7 mi. n. of Orofino. Bird-watching, water skiing.	**2**	•	•	•	•	•		•	•	•			•		
Lucky Peak (G-2) 237 acres 9 mi. s.e. of Boise on SR 21. Water skiing.	**3**	•	•	•	•	•		•	•	•					•
STATE															
Bear Lake (H-6) 966 acres just e. of St. Charles on E. Shore Rd. Snowmobiling, water skiing. *(See St. Charles p. 93.)*	**4**	•	•		•	•		•	•			•			
Bruneau Dunes (G-2) 4,800 acres 5 mi. n. of Bruneau on SR 51/78, then 2 mi. e. on SR 78. Equestrian trails, sand dunes. No motorized boats. *(See Bruneau p. 52.)*	**5**	•	•	•	•			•	•	•			•		
Castle Rocks (H-4) 1,440 acres 2 mi. n. of Almo on Elba-Almo Rd., then 1.4 mi. w. on 2800 S. (Big Cove Ranch Rd.). Bird-watching, horseback riding, rock climbing, snowshoeing.	**6**	•	•	•				•	•	•	•	•	•	•	
Coeur d'Alene Parkway (B-1) 34 acres e. of Coeur d'Alene off I-90 exit 15 on Coeur d'Alene Lake Dr.	**7**		•	•	•	•		•		•	•	•	•		
Coeur d'Alene's Old Mission (B-1) 18 acres 11 mi. w. off I-90 exit 39. Historic. *(See Cataldo p. 55.)*	**8**		•	•				•		•	•	•	•	•	
Dworshak (C-1) 850 acres 26 mi. n.w. of Orofino.	**9**	•	•	•	•	•		•	•	•				•	
Farragut (B-1) 4,000 acres 4.9 mi. e. of Athol on SR 54. Historic. Cross-country skiing, snowmobiling. Museum. *(See Athol p. 35.)*	**10**	•	•	•	•	•		•	•	•	•	•	•		
Harriman (F-6) 11,000 acres 9 mi. s. of Island Park via US 20 at 3489 Green Canyon Rd. Cross-country skiing; horse rental. *(See Island Park p. 71.)*	**11**		•	•				•		•		•	•	•	•
Hells Gate (D-1) 360 acres 4 mi. s. of Lewiston off Snake River Ave. Water skiing. Interpretive centers. *(See Lewiston p. 76.)*	**12**	•	•	•	•	•		•	•	•	•		•		
Henry's Lake (F-6) 586 acres 15 mi. w. of West Yellowstone off US 20. Bird-watching, water skiing.	**13**	•	•	•	•	•		•		•		•			
Heyburn (C-1) 7,825 acres 5 mi. e. of Plummer on SR 5. Canoeing, cross-country skiing, horseback riding, ice fishing, water skiing. *(See Plummer p. 87.)*	**14**	•	•	•	•	•	•	•	•	•		•	•	•	•
Lake Cascade (F-1) 4,450 acres just n.w. of Cascade. Bird-watching, cross-country skiing, ice fishing, snowmobiling; horseshoe pits. *(See Cascade p. 55.)*	**15**	•	•	•	•	•		•	•	•	•	•	•		
Lake Walcott (H-4) 65 acres 11 mi. n.e. of Rupert off SR 24. *(See Rupert p. 93.)*	**16**	•	•	•	•	•		•		•	•				
Lucky Peak (G-2) 240 acres 10 mi. s.e. of Boise off SR 21.	**17**		•	•	•	•		•	•	•	•				•

Recreation Areas Chart

The map location numerals in column 2 show an area's location on the preceding map.

	MAP LOCATION	CAMPING	PICNICKING	HIKING TRAILS	BOATING	BOAT RAMP	BOAT RENTAL	FISHING	SWIMMING	PETS ON LEASH	BICYCLE TRAILS	WINTER SPORTS	VISITOR CENTER	LODGE/CABINS	FOOD SERVICE
Massacre Rocks (G-4) 990 acres 10 mi. s.w. of American Falls off I-86. Historic. Canoeing, disc golf, kayaking. *(See American Falls p. 34.)*	18	•	•	•	•	•		•		•	•		•	•	
Ponderosa (E-2) 1,470 acres 2 mi. n.e. of McCall via Park St. and Thompson Ave. at 1920 N. Davis Ave. Canoeing, cross-country skiing, snowshoeing. *(See McCall p. 78.)*	19	•	•	•	•	•	•	•	•	•	•	•	•	•	•
Priest Lake (A-1) 463 acres 11 mi. n. of Coolin. Cross-country skiing, ice fishing, snowmobiling.	20	•	•	•	•	•	•	•	•	•		•		•	
Round Lake (B-1) 142 acres 10 mi. s. of Sandpoint off US 95 on Dufort Rd. Cross-country skiing, ice fishing, ice-skating, sledding, snowshoeing. No motorized boats.	21	•	•	•	•			•	•	•		•			
Thousand Springs (H-3) 1,500 acres .2 mi. s. off I-84 exit 147, then .2 mi. w. following signs to the welcome kiosk at Malad Gorge. Canoeing, kayaking, horseback riding. *(See Hagerman p. 64.)*	22		•	•				•	•	•					
Three Island Crossing (G-2) 513 acres 1 mi. w. of Glenns Ferry via S. Commercial St. and W. Madison Ave. Historic. *(See Glenns Ferry p. 63.)*	23	•	•	•				•		•	•	•	•		
Winchester Lake (D-1) 318 acres .25 mi. s. of Winchester on US 95 Bus. Rte. Cross-country skiing, ice fishing, ice-skating, sledding. No motorized boats (except with electric motors).	24	•	•	•	•	•		•		•	•	•			
OTHER															
American Falls Reservoir (G-4) 59,893 acres .2 mi. n. of American Falls on I-15. Historic.	25	•	•	•	•	•		•	•	•			•		
Anderson Ranch Reservoir (G-2) 5,000 acres 30 mi. n.e. of Mountain Home on SR 20 and FR 61.	26	•	•	•	•	•	•	•	•	•			•	•	•
Arrowrock Reservoir (F-2) 4,000 acres 16 mi. e. of Boise on SR 21 and FR 268.	27	•	•	•	•	•		•	•	•					
Black Canyon Reservoir (F-1) 2,364 acres 8 mi. n.e. of Emmett on SR 52.	28	•	•	•	•	•		•		•					
Celebration Park (G-1) 84 acres 8.1 mi. s. of Melba at 6530 Hot Spot Ln. Historic. Scenic. Bird-watching, horseback riding; interpretive programs. *(See Melba p. 79.)*	29	•	•	•	•	•		•		•	•	•	•	•	
C.J. Strike Reservoir (G-2) 7,500 acres n.w. of Bruneau via SR 78. *(See Bruneau p. 52.)*	30	•	•	•	•	•		•	•	•			•		
Deadwood Reservoir (F-2) 3,000 acres 34 mi. n.e. of Garden Valley on FR 555.	31	•	•	•	•			•	•	•			•		
Island Park Reservoir (F-6) 7,800 acres 27 mi. n. of Ashton off US 20. Snowmobiling.	32	•	•		•	•		•	•	•		•		•	•
Lake Lowell (G-1) 10,587 acres 8 mi. s. of Caldwell via 10th Ave. or SR 55. Bird-watching; water skiing.	33		•		•	•		•	•	•			•		
Lake Pend Oreille (B-1) 94,600 acres s. and e. of Sandpoint. *(See Sandpoint p. 95.)*	34	•	•	•	•	•	•	•	•	•			•		
Lake Waha (D-1) 100 acres 18 mi. s.e. of Lewiston on Thain Rd.	35		•	•	•	•		•	•	•					
Little Wood River Reservoir (G-3) 976 acres 11 mi. n. of Carey on access road.	36	•	•		•	•		•	•	•					
Mann Creek Reservoir (F-1) 4 acres 9 mi. n. of Weiser on US 95. Water skiing.	37	•	•		•	•		•	•	•					
Palisades Reservoir (G-6) 27,845 acres 50 mi. s.e. of Idaho Falls on US 26.	38	•	•		•	•		•	•	•			•		•
Priest River (B-1) 20 acres .5 mi. e. of Priest River off US 2. Bird-watching, water skiing.	39	•	•	•	•	•		•	•	•					
Riley Creek (B-1) 45 acres 1 mi. s. of US 2 at Laclede on Riley Creek Rd. Water skiing.	40	•	•	•	•	•		•	•	•					
Ririe Reservoir (G-6) 6,069 acres 20 mi. n.e. of Idaho Falls on US 26.	41	•	•	•	•	•		•	•	•				•	

Recreation Areas Chart The map location numerals in column 2 show an area's location on the preceding map.	MAP LOCATION	CAMPING	PICNICKING	HIKING TRAILS	BOATING	BOAT RAMP	BOAT RENTAL	FISHING	SWIMMING	PETS ON LEASH	BICYCLE TRAILS	WINTER SPORTS	VISITOR CENTER	LODGE/CABINS	FOOD SERVICE
Springy Point (A-1) 13 acres 3.2 mi. w. of US 95 at Sandpoint on Lakeshore Dr. Water skiing.	42	•	•	•	•	•	•		•	•	•	•	•		•
Steck Park (F-1) 20 mi. n.w. of Weiser via SR 70 on the Snake River.	43	•	•		•	•		•		•			•		
Trestle Creek (B-1) 2 acres n.w. of Hope on SR 200. Water skiing.	44		•		•	•		•	•	•			•		
Veterans Memorial (F-1) 80 acres on SR 44 at 36th St. in Boise. Bird-watching. No motorized boats.	45		•	•	•			•			•	•			

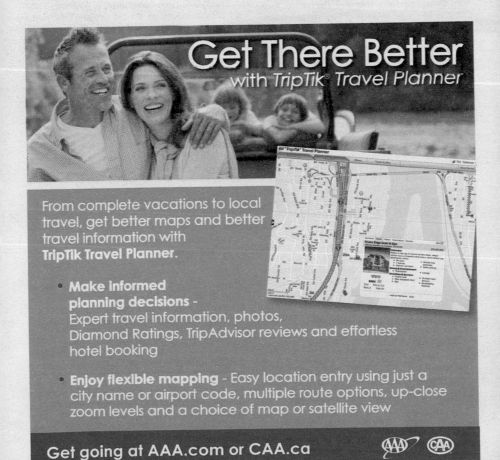

AHSAHKA (C-1) elev. 1,001'

CLEARWATER FISH HATCHERY is at 118 Hatchery Roe Dr. Interpretive panels throughout the complex describe the life cycles of steelhead, or rainbow trout, and chinook salmon, both of which are raised at the hatchery. A 1.8-mile pipeline delivers a constant flow of cool, clear water from Dworshak Dam to the facility. Smolts are released from mid-March through late April. Visitors can see adult chinook at the hatchery from mid-July to mid-September. A trout pond contains large steelhead.

Time: Allow 30 minutes minimum. **Hours:** Daily 7:30-4. Visitor center closed holidays; no fish in raceways the last 2 weeks in April. **Cost:** Free. **Phone:** (208) 476-3331. 🚻

DWORSHAK DAM VISITOR CENTER is 3 mi. e. on SR 7, following signs, on the North Fork of the Clearwater River. The visitor center overlooks the 717-foot dam, one of the highest straight-axis concrete gravity dams in North America. Behind the dam, Dworshak Reservoir *(see Recreation Areas Chart)* extends 54 miles into wild, rugged timberland.

Interpretive displays are available. Audiovisual presentations are shown in the theater upon request. **Hours:** Visitor center daily 8:30-4:30, Memorial Day weekend-Labor Day; Mon.-Fri. 8:30-4:30, rest of year. Closed holidays and Christmas-Jan. 1. Phone ahead to confirm schedule. **Cost:** Free. **Phone:** (208) 476-1255.

DWORSHAK NATIONAL FISH HATCHERY, s.e. on SR 7 at the confluence of the two forks of the Clearwater River, is one of the world's largest steelhead trout hatcheries. About 2 million steelhead trout and 1 million chinook salmon are raised in environmentally controlled ponds. The best time to see the adult steelhead is March through May; the returning salmon brood stock May through September.

Displays, a viewing balcony above the spawning room, incubators, nursery tanks and 126 outdoor ponds are on-site. A self-guiding tour map is available. **Time:** Allow 30 minutes minimum. **Hours:** Grounds daily dawn-dusk. Main building daily 7:30-4; hatchery building closed major holidays. **Cost:** Free. **Phone:** (208) 476-4591.

THE HIGH COUNTRY INN - OROFINO/AHSAHKA
(208)476-7570

Bed & Breakfast
$89-$400

Address: 70 High Country Ln 83520 **Location:** 0.5 mi w to Dworshak Visitors Center Rd, 2 mi n, then 1 mi w, follow signs. **Facility:** Located above a river valley midst ponderosa pines, this charming and inviting inn boasts sweeping views, is close to the Dworshak Reservoir recreation area and offers a nice selection of rooms and cabins. 6 units, some cabins. 1-2 stories (no elevator), interior/exterior corridors. **Terms:** 7 day cancellation notice, resort fee. **Activities:** hot tub. **Guest Services:** coin laundry. **Featured Amenity:** full hot breakfast.

[SAVE] [icons] / SOME UNITS [icons]

ALMO (H-4) elev. 5,390'

CITY OF ROCKS NATIONAL RESERVE is .25 mi. s. on Almo-Elba Rd. and 1 mi. w. on City Rocks Rd., on unpaved roads. Within the 14,407-acre reserve are massive granite rocks, some 2.5 billion years old, eroded into shapes resembling the ruins of an ancient city. Inscriptions written in axle grease and scratched into the rocks by pioneers traversing the Oregon and California trails afford insights into emigrant trail history. Rock climbing, sightseeing and hiking through high deserts are possible.

Hours: Visitor center daily 8-4:30, mid-Apr. to mid-Oct.; Mon.-Fri. 8-4:30, rest of year. Closed Jan. 1, Thanksgiving and Christmas. **Cost:** Day use free. Campsite fee $12. Only eight people and two tents per site are permitted. **Phone:** (208) 824-5901. 🏕️ 🚻

AMERICAN FALLS (G-5) pop. 4,457, elev. 4,330'

The "Idaho Gem Community" of American Falls, an early campsite on the old Oregon Trail, is the center of irrigation projects that enable the cultivation of thousands of acres of farmland. The American Falls Reservoir *(see Recreation Areas Chart)*, the largest on the Snake River, provides excellent opportunities for boating, sailing, water skiing and rainbow trout fishing.

American Falls Chamber of Commerce: P.O. Box 207, American Falls, ID 83211. **Phone:** (208) 226-5294.

MASSACRE ROCKS STATE PARK is off I-86 exit 28 at 3592 N. Park Ln. Once a popular stop along the Oregon Trail, this area along the Snake River is rich in pioneer and geological history. Travelers called the rocky gorge "Devil's Gate" and "Gate of Death" as it seemed a likely spot for an ambush. Inscriptions made by Oregon Trail emigrants can be seen at Register Rock, 2 miles west of I-86 exit 28.

The 1,000-acre state park offers six hiking trails. One leads beneath the freeway to Oregon Trail ruts. Guided interpretive programs are offered summer weekends. Canoe and kayak rentals are available, and two disc golf courses are on-site. *See Recreation Areas Chart.* **Time:** Allow 1 hour minimum. **Hours:** Daily dawn-dusk. **Cost:** $5 (per private vehicle). **Phone:** (208) 548-2672. 🏕️ 🎣 🚻 🚻

ARCO (G-4) pop. 995, elev. 5,320'

EXPERIMENTAL BREEDER REACTOR #1 is 20 mi. e. on US 20 at the Idaho National Laboratory. On Dec. 20, 1951, the reactor became the first nuclear reactor to generate a usable amount of electricity. Exhibits document the facility's history, and free 45- to 60-minute guided tours are conducted as needed by trained guides. Self-guiding tour pamphlets describing the nuclear reactors, a reactor control room and detection devices are available.

Time: Allow 1 hour minimum. **Hours:** Daily 9-5, Memorial Day weekend-Labor Day. Last tour begins 1 hour before closing. **Cost:** Free. **Phone:** (208) 526-2029 or (208) 526-0050.

ASHTON (F-6) pop. 1,127, elev. 5,259'

Located in the northeast corner of the Snake River Plain, Ashton was established in 1906 by the Oregon Short Line Railroad. The district is today the world's largest producer of seed potatoes and also grows wheat, barley, hay, peas and canola. Off to the southeast, the ragged profile of the Teton Range is visible on the horizon.

MESA FALLS RECREATION AREA is 15 mi. n.e. via SR 47 and Mesa Falls Scenic Byway. Henry's Fork of the Snake River carved a canyon here in tuff and basalt rock forming two scenic waterfalls. Upper Mesa Falls plunges 114 feet over a 200-foot-wide precipice. An interpretive boardwalk loops down for close-up views of the falls and canyon. Big Falls Inn, a 1916 roadhouse, serves as a visitor center that offers exhibits about plants and animals, the geology of the falls and the inn's history. Trails cut through the area, including one departing from a roadside pullout .8 miles south that leads to 65-foot Lower Mesa Falls.

Time: Allow 1 hour minimum. **Hours:** Recreation area daily 24 hours. Big Falls Inn daily 9:30-5:30, Memorial Day weekend to mid-Sept.; Sat.-Sun. 10-3, early Jan. to mid-Mar. Scenic byway typically closed late Oct.-Apr. 30. **Cost:** $5 (per private vehicle). **Phone:** (208) 652-7442.

ATHOL (B-1) pop. 692, elev. 2,391'
• Hotels p. 36

In a region rich with timber, Athol developed around a sawmill established at the turn of the 20th century. The town is in a popular summer recreation area centered on Lake Pend Oreille *(see Sandpoint p. 95).*

FARRAGUT STATE PARK is 4.9 mi. e. on SR 54. On the site of a former U.S. Navy training center built in 1942, the 4,000-acre park borders Lake Pend Oreille and is a popular boating, fishing and recreation area. Features include an extensive hiking and biking trail system, groomed trails for cross-country skiing and a visitor center with exhibits. Wildlife includes deer, bear, elk, mountain goats and a diverse bird population. *See Recreation Areas Chart.*

Time: Allow 1 hour minimum. **Hours:** Park open daily dawn-dusk. Visitor center open daily 8 a.m.-9 p.m. Phone ahead to confirm schedule. **Cost:** Park $5 (per private vehicle). Camping $10-$38.60. **Phone:** (208) 683-2425.

Museum at the Brig is 4.9 mi. e. on SR 54 in Farragut State Park. Exhibits housed in the former brig of Farragut Naval Training Station chronicle events of World War II and activities at the naval station during the period. Topics include boot camp, bunk quarters, health care and German prisoners of war. Displays feature memorabilia donated by military personnel. **Time:** Allow 30 minutes minimum. **Hours:** Daily 10-5, Memorial Day-Labor Day. **Cost:** Free with Farragut State Park admission of $5 (per private vehicle). **Phone:** (208) 683-2425.

SAVE **SILVERWOOD** is 2 mi. s. on US 95. One of the Northwest's largest theme parks, Silverwood covers 216 acres and offers more than 65 rides, shows and attractions. Aftershock is a 191-foot-tall steel roller coaster that travels forward and backward through a cobra loop at speeds exceeding 65 mph. SpinCycle, a 104-foot-tall thrill ride that swings upside down like a giant pendulum, tumbling riders at 3.5 times the normal gravitational pull, features cylindrical-shaped vehicles that rotate 360 degrees at 13 revolutions per minute.

Other rides include the 55-mph Timber Terror wooden coaster, the Corkscrew coaster, the 140-foot-tall Panic Plunge drop tower, the Thunder Canyon white-water ride and a 1915 steam-powered train. Tinywood is a miniature mining town for kids. The park also has dozens of traditional amusement rides. Entertainment includes a magic show, a staged train robbery, and appearances by Garfield and Odie.

Time: Allow 6 hours minimum. **Hours:** Open daily, late May-Labor Day; Sat.-Sun., May 1-late May and day after Labor Day-late Sept. Hours vary; phone ahead. **Cost:** One-day pass $43.99; $22.99 (ages 3-7 and 65+). One-day pass after 5 p.m. $21.99. Two-day pass $69.99; $35.99 (ages 3-7 and 65+). All passes include Boulder Beach Water Park when open. **Parking:** $4. **Phone:** (208) 683-3400.

Boulder Beach Water Park is 2 mi. s. on US 95 at Silverwood. Rides include two gigantic wave pools, four tube slides, three high-velocity body slides, two family raft rides, a lazy river and two play areas for children. **Time:** Allow 4 hours minimum. **Hours:** Opens daily at 11, early June-Labor Day. Closing times vary; phone ahead. **Cost:** (includes Silverwood) $43.99; $22.99 (ages 3-7 and 65+). Discounted admission is offered after 5 p.m. **Parking:** $4. **Phone:** (208) 683-3400.

LOG SPIRIT BED & BREAKFAST   208/683-4722

Bed & Breakfast
$140-$200

Address: 31328 N Tiara Ln 83801 **Location:** US 95, just e on SR 54 to Howard Rd, 1.8 mi n, then 0.5 mi e. **Facility:** The grounds of this log B&B offers a small bridge with a waterfall, gardens and small farm animals. You can play a game of croquet or sit on the porch enjoying the mountain views. 6 units. 2 stories, interior corridors. **Terms:** 2 night minimum stay - seasonal and/or weekends, 14 day cancellation notice-fee imposed. **Guest Services:** coin laundry. **Featured Amenity:** full hot breakfast.

BANKS (F-1) pop. 17, elev. 2,840'

At the confluence of the North and South forks of the Payette River, Banks is popular with kayakers and white-water rafters and lies along the 112-mile Payette River Scenic Byway (SR 55), which connects Boise, at the southern terminus, with New Meadows, to the north.

RECREATIONAL ACTIVITIES
White-water Rafting
- **Bear Valley Rafting Co.** meets downstairs from the Banks Store and Cafe on SR 55 for transportation to departure points. **Hours:** Daily 9-6, Memorial Day weekend-Sept. 30. **Phone:** (208) 793-2272 or (800) 235-2327.

BITTERROOT NATIONAL FOREST—See Montana p. 140.

BLACKFOOT (G-5) pop. 11,899, elev. 4,497'

At the northern end of the Snake River Valley, land is key. In the 19th century the fertile lava soil helped establish Blackfoot as an important agricultural center, with the russet potato eventually becoming the town's main crop. Visit the Idaho Potato Museum (see attraction listing) to learn why Blackfoot is known as the "Potato Capital of the World," then head next door to Depot Park for a self-guiding walking tour past antique potato harvesting devices. Remnants of the past also are exhibited at Veterans Park, which features army tanks and other military equipment.

Stemming from Blackfoot's agricultural roots, the Eastern Idaho State Fair attracts tens of thousands of revelers with livestock shows as well as mouth-watering foodstuffs—from Indian tacos to (what else?) loaded baked potatoes. The weeklong end-of-summer party takes place around Labor Day. Watch a bull riding competition or marvel over fine equestrian specimens; browse antiques and charming quilt displays; or sniff out the best recipes for such tasty bites as hash browns, brownies and peanut butter cookies.

Although residents have been tapping Blackfoot's natural resources since the late 1880s, the area still boasts striking, untouched terrain. You'll discover year-round recreational opportunities in and around town. In warm weather, you can hike, fish or get drenched white-water rafting at Wolverine Canyon, about 19 miles northeast. When temperatures drop there are still plenty of outdoor activities to enjoy, including cross-country skiing and snowmobiling.

Wildlife viewing is popular throughout the region. Blackfoot River Canyon—home to golden eagles, prairie falcons, red-tailed hawks and great horned owls—is especially breathtaking. In summer swimmers and boaters crowd 55-acre Jensen Lake at Jensen Grove; nearby you'll find such man-made recreational features as a skate park and a 2-mile paved walking path. Abutting Jensen Lake's northern bank at 3115 Teeples Dr. is the 18-hole Blackfoot Golf Course; phone (208) 785-9960.

Greater Blackfoot Area Chamber of Commerce: 130 N.W. Main St., P.O. Box 801, Blackfoot, ID 83221. **Phone:** (208) 785-0510.

BINGHAM COUNTY HISTORICAL MUSEUM, 190 N. Shilling Ave., is in a renovated 1905 Southern mansion built of lava rock and lumber. The museum displays period furnishings, clothing, photographs, dolls and other historical items. **Time:** Allow 30 minutes minimum. **Hours:** Thurs.-Sat. 10-5, June-Aug. **Cost:** Donations. **Phone:** (208) 785-9906.

IDAHO POTATO MUSEUM, 130 N.W. Main St., presents a variety of exhibits related to the potato, including antique machinery and tools, gunnysack clothing and, at 24 by 14 inches, the "Guinness World Records" world's largest potato crisp.

Each visitor is offered a free potato product. Videotapes about the potato industry and production processes are shown. Phone for special tour arrangements. **Time:** Allow 1 hour minimum. **Hours:** Mon.-Sat. 9:30-5, Apr.-Sept.; Mon.-Fri. 9:30-3, rest of year. **Cost:** $3; $2.50 (military with ID and senior citizens); $1 (ages 6-12). **Phone:** (208) 785-2517.

BEST WESTERN BLACKFOOT INN   (208)785-4144

Hotel
$72-$130

AAA Benefit: Members save 10% or more with Best Western!

Address: 750 Jensen Grove Dr 83221 **Location:** I-15 exit 93, 0.3 mi e to Parkway Dr, then 0.4 mi n. **Facility:** 60 units. 2 stories (no elevator), interior corridors. **Parking:** winter plug-ins. **Pool(s):** heated indoor. **Activities:** hot tub. **Guest Services:** coin laundry.

WHERE TO EAT

TOMMY VAUGHN'S GRILL   208/785-6400

American. Casual Dining. $9-$19 **AAA Inspector Notes:** Wood-framed flat-screen TVs adorn the walls throughout this comfortable eatery. Menu items include a tasty steak salad, a popular appetizer sampler, burgers, a few pasta selections, grilled shrimp skewers and beer-battered fish and chips. Do not hesitate to share a piece of red velvet cake. Gluten-free items are available. **Features:** full bar, patio dining, early bird specials, senior menu, happy hour. **Address:** 850 Jensen Grove Dr 83221 **Location:** I-15 exit 93, 0.3 mi e to Parkway Dr, then 0.7 mi ne. [L] [D]

BOISE (G-1) pop. 205,671, elev. 2,739'

• Hotels p. 44 • Restaurants p. 47
• Hotels & Restaurants map & index p. 41

The woods lining the Boise River were a welcome sight for French-Canadian trappers who were grateful to reach a forest again after trudging across the territory's semiarid plain. As a result, they named the area *Boisé*, meaning "wooded." The city, however, was not founded until 1863, a year after the gold rush reached the Boise Basin.

"The City of Trees," Boise is Idaho's capital and largest metropolitan area. The first sessions of the territorial government were held during 1863 in Lewiston, then moved to this population center the following year. The new territorial capital was the center of commerce and culture for miners and traders from nearby mountain boomtowns. Built in 1863, the O'Farrell Cabin on Fort Street is one of the city's oldest buildings.

The quality of life, low cost of living and liberal tax advantages as well as the city's role as state capital and transportation hub, account for Boise's steady economic growth. Many national and multinational firms have their headquarters in Boise, and light industry flourishes. The city also is the home of Boise State University *(see attraction listing)*, where the

Broncos play football on the blue field of Bronco Stadium from early September to early December; the Famous Idaho Potato Bowl takes place at the stadium after football season ends. In addition, the Boise Philharmonic plays in the university's Velma V. Morrison Center for the Performing Arts. Entertaining audiences since 1998, the Gene Harris Jazz Festival takes place at the college in April.

Boise is the southwest terminus of SR 21, the Ponderosa Pine Scenic Route. The route passes through part of Sawtooth National Forest before ending in Stanley; depending on weather conditions, portions of SR 21 may be closed in winter.

Protected from unduly harsh winter weather by the Owyhee Mountains, the capital enjoys year-round opportunities for leisure and recreation. Ann Morrison Park, 153 acres between Americana and Capital boulevards, offers picnicking, playgrounds, ball fields and tennis courts as well as the Spirit of Boise Balloon Classic, held in September.

A novel way to reach Ann Morrison Park is by floating down the Boise River on a rental raft or inner tube from Barber Park, which is on the southeast edge of town; at the junction of Warm Springs Avenue and SR 21 turn onto Eckert to reach the park. Rentals are available daily mid-June through Labor Day, river flows permitting; a return shuttle bus is available. Phone (208) 577-4584.

Kathryn Albertson Park is a 41-acre downtown wildlife sanctuary across Americana Boulevard from Ann Morrison Park. Paved footpaths meander past gazebos, ponds and fountains while offering glimpses of waterfowl and other wildlife. The park also provides nearby access to the Boise Greenbelt, a 25-mile path following the Boise River. A favorite place to walk, jog, skate or ride a bicycle, the greenbelt connects 12 area parks.

The Idaho Shakespeare Festival presents five plays in repertory June through September at an outdoor amphitheater at 5657 Warm Springs Ave.; phone (208) 336-9221.

Once used as a Native American lookout, Table Rock rises 1,100 feet above the valley east of Boise. Its flat summit, surmounted by an illuminated cross that can be seen for miles, affords a view of the city and a pioneer route south of the river.

In the 1921 St. Paul Baptist Church building at 508 Julia Davis Dr. in Julia Davis Park, the Idaho Black History Museum presents changing educational exhibits about the history and culture of African-Americans in Idaho; phone (208) 433-0017.

To the southeast, 12 miles south of Kuna, the Morley Nelson Snake River Birds of Prey National Conservation Area provides a 600,000-acre haven for two dozen species of raptors. The area represents one of the world's densest concentrations of birds of prey; phone (208) 384-3300.

(See map & index p. 41.)

Boise Convention & Visitors Bureau: 250 S. Fifth St., Suite 300, Boise, ID 83702. **Phone:** (208) 344-7777 or (800) 635-5240. *(See ad this page.)*

Self-guiding tours: A map showcasing downtown Boise's public art displays and historical points of interest is available from information kiosks at 8th and Idaho streets, 8th and Broad streets and the city hall front entrance.

Shopping areas: Boise Factory Outlets, I-84 exit Gowen Road, offers such factory stores as Eddie Bauer, Levi's Outlet and Reebok. Boise Towne Square Mall, Milwaukee and Franklin streets, features Dillard's, JCPenney, Macy's and Sears. Downtown shopping includes BoDo (short for Boise Downtown), a former late-1890s warehouse district at 8th and Front streets; Hyde Park on N. 13th Street; and Old Boise Historic District on Main Street between Capitol and 4th streets.

BASQUE MUSEUM AND CULTURAL CENTER, 611 Grove St., on the Basque block, celebrates the legacy of the Basques and is the only museum in the country dedicated to the ethnic group. Permanent and temporary exhibits focus on the history and culture of these modern people with ancient roots. Basque traditions are further depicted through a cultural center and a restored Basque boarding house. **Time:** Allow 30 minutes minimum. **Hours:** Tues.-Fri. 10-4, Sat. 11-3. Closed major holidays. **Cost:** $5; $4 (ages 65+ and students with ID); $3 (ages 6-12). **Phone:** (208) 343-2671.

BOISE STATE UNIVERSITY, 1910 University Dr. along the Boise River, is the state's largest institution of higher learning, with more than 200 fields of study in seven colleges. Established in 1932, the university has approximately 22,000 students enrolled in graduate and undergraduate programs.

Highlights of the campus include the Velma V. Morrison Center for the Performing Arts. Bronco Stadium is noted for its blue artificial turf. **Hours:** Public tours of the university are offered Mon.-Fri. at 10 and 1, during the academic year; at 10, in summer. **Cost:** Free. Reservations are recommended. **Phone:** (208) 426-1156.

BOISE TROLLEY TOURS departs from Joe's Crab Shack restaurant, 2288 N. Garden St., on the riverfront. The tour, aboard a replica open-air trolley car, includes a 75-minute historical narration covering downtown Boise, the State Capitol and other government buildings, Harrison Boulevard and Warm Springs-area mansions, Hyde Park and the Old Idaho Penitentiary State Historic Site. **Time:** Allow 1 hour minimum. **Hours:** Tours depart Mon.-Fri. at 11, Sat.-Sun. at 2, May-Sept. Phone ahead for holiday hours. **Cost:** $18; $16 (ages 65+ and students with ID); $8 (ages 3-12); $4 (ages 0-2). Reservations are required. **Phone:** (208) 433-0849.

GEM SAVE DISCOVERY CENTER OF IDAHO, 131 Myrtle St., is a hands-on museum with more than 160 exhibits relating to science, math and technology. Visitors can use the Whisper Dish exhibit to carry on a quiet conversation across the room; squeeze clay with 24,000 pounds of force at the Make a Rock exhibit; generate electricity using the Pedal Generator; and experiment with electric arcs at the Electric Flame exhibit.

Other displays designed to encourage interaction with natural science phenomena include Touch the Spring, Disappearing Glass Rods, Pedaling Legs and Air Brake. The center also brings in a variety of traveling exhibits throughout the year.

▼ *See AAA listing this page* ▼

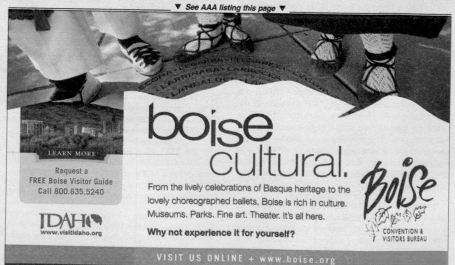

(See map & index p. 41.)

Time: Allow 1 hour minimum. Hours: Sun.-Thurs. 9:30-5:30, Fri.-Sat. 9:30-7:30. Closed Jan. 1, Easter, Thanksgiving and Christmas. Cost: $8; $6 (ages 4-17 and 60+). Phone: (208) 343-9895. ▇

FIRST UNITED METHODIST CHURCH occupies a city block bordered by 11th, 12th, Franklin and Hay sts.; the entrance is on 11th St. Known as the Cathedral of the Rockies, the church dates from 1872. The present Gothic structure, the third building used by the congregation, contains impressive stained glass windows and hand-painted murals. **Hours:** Mon.-Fri. 9-5. **Cost:** Free. **Phone:** (208) 343-7511.

IDAHO ANNE FRANK HUMAN RIGHTS MEMORIAL, at 777 S. 8th St. in a park behind the Boise Public Library, is dedicated to the importance of human rights. The life of Frank, the well-known Holocaust victim whose published diary became the basis for several plays and films, is highlighted. Benches are scattered throughout the memorial, which includes a life-size bronze statue of Frank, a wall engraved with more than 60 quotes from humanitarian leaders, and informational placards.

The site's water features are intended to mimic the canals of Amsterdam, where Frank and her family lived in hiding for many years. Other natural elements such as stone and native plants also are incorporated into the design. One-hour guided tours are available by appointment. **Time:** Allow 1 hour minimum. **Hours:** Daily dawn-dusk. **Cost:** Free. **Phone:** (208) 345-0304. ▇ ▇

▇ **IDAHO BOTANICAL GARDEN**, 2.5 mi. e. on Main St. and Warm Springs Ave., then n. on N. Penitentiary Rd., offers 14 specialty gardens on 33 acres of the former Idaho Penitentiary. The sandstone walls provide a historic backdrop for theme gardens, garden art and a labyrinth. The Lewis and Clark Native Plant Garden features a bronze likeness of Sacagawea and has examples of period plants catalogued by the explorers; it also offers views of Treasure Valley.

Time: Allow 1 hour minimum. **Hours:** Daily 9-dusk, mid-Mar. to mid-Nov. **Cost:** $5; $3 (ages 5-12 and 65+). **Phone:** (208) 343-8649.

THE IDAHO MILITARY HISTORY MUSEUM is at 4692 W. Harvard St. Weapons, photographs, artifacts, military guidons (flags) and small arms chronicle the participation of various Idaho military units in conflicts ranging from the Philippine Insurrection to Operation Iraqi Freedom and Operation Enduring Freedom. A collection of armored vehicles and aircraft is displayed outdoors. **Time:** Allow 1 hour minimum. **Hours:** Tues.-Sat. noon-4. Closed major holidays. **Cost:** Donations. **Phone:** (208) 272-4841.

IDAHO MUSEUM OF MINING & GEOLOGY (IMMG), 2455 Old Penitentiary Rd., documents the state's geologic history and mining heritage through models, dioramas, maps and other items. Rocks, minerals, fossils, photographs and historical artifacts are displayed in five themed exhibit areas. Topics discussed include mining districts of the Northwest, Ice Age floods and lakes, and the everyday uses of minerals. **Time:** Allow 45 minutes minimum. **Hours:** Wed.-Sun. and Mon. holidays noon-5, Apr.-Oct. **Cost:** Donations. **Phone:** (208) 368-9876.

JULIA DAVIS PARK, with entrances on Capitol Blvd. or Third St. off Myrtle St., contains within its 89-acre expanse the Boise Art Museum; the Idaho Historical Museum; the Idaho Black History Museum; Zoo Boise; and the Discovery Center of Idaho, which offers hands-on exhibits *(see attraction listing p. 38)*. A lagoon, a rose garden, a playground, a tennis complex and a band shell where concerts are given in the summer also are within the park; a portion of the Boise River Greenbelt runs through the park as well. **Hours:** Daily dawn-dusk. **Cost:** Free. **Phone:** (208) 608-7600, or (208) 577-4575 for boat rentals.

▇ **Boise Art Museum**, 670 Julia Davis Dr. at the Julia Davis Park entrance, displays more than 15 changing art exhibits annually, with a major exhibition each summer. **Time:** Allow 1 hour minimum. **Hours:** Tues.-Sat. 10-5 (also first Thurs. of the month 5-8), Sun. noon-5. Closed Jan. 1, Easter, Thanksgiving and Christmas. **Cost:** $6; $4 (ages 62+); $3 (students in grades 1-12 and college students with ID); donations (first Thurs. of the month). Special exhibition fees vary. **Phone:** (208) 345-8330.

▇ **Idaho Historical Museum**, 610 Julia Davis Dr., provides an overview of the state's history. Displays include a 19th-century saloon as well as artifacts of early Idaho. **Time:** Allow 1 hour minimum. **Hours:** Tues.-Fri. 9-5, Sat.-Sun. 10-5, May-Sept.; Tues.-Fri. 9-5, Sat. 10-5, rest of year. Closed Jan. 1, Thanksgiving and Christmas. Phone ahead to confirm schedule. **Cost:** $5; $4 (ages 60+); $3 (ages 6-12 and students with ID). **Phone:** (208) 334-2120.

Zoo Boise, .5 mi. s. off Capitol Blvd. in Julia Davis Park, has more than 200 animals from around the world, including Amur tigers, zebras, snow leopards, Magellanic penguins, lions, giraffes and red pandas. Small Animal Kingdom spotlights animals and plants indigenous to islands, deserts and rainforests. An education center offers wildlife exhibits. **Hours:** Daily 9-5, June 1-Labor Day; 10-5, rest of year. Closed Jan. 1, Thanksgiving and Christmas. **Cost:** May 1-Labor Day $10; $8 (ages 62+); $7 (ages 3-11). Rest of year $7.25; $4.50 (ages 62+); $4.25 (ages 4-11). Prices may vary; phone ahead. **Phone:** (208) 384-4260. ▇

MORRISON KNUDSEN NATURE CENTER is 2.5 mi. off I-84 exit 54 (Broadway Ave.); cross the Boise River, turn e. onto Park Blvd. then head .5 mi. e. to 600 S. Walnut St., following signs. This 4.5-acre area features a sampling of Idaho's ecosystems. Walking trails pass a mountain stream with logjams and waterfalls, a wetlands pond and a high desert plain with sagebrush and lava rock. Along the way are

(See map & index p. 41.)

plants and wildlife indigenous to each area. Windows along the stream walk offer "face-to-fish" viewing opportunities and lessons on stream ecology.

The visitor center features exhibits and offers educational programs. **Time:** Allow 1 hour minimum. **Hours:** Outdoor area daily dawn-dusk. Visitor center Tues.-Fri. 9-5, Sat.-Sun. 11-5. **Cost:** Free. **Phone:** (208) 334-2225.

[SAVE] **OLD IDAHO PENITENTIARY STATE HIS-TORIC SITE,** 1.5 mi. e. of Broadway and Warm Springs aves. at 2445 Old Penitentiary Rd., was used 1872-1973 as Idaho's state penitentiary. Additions to the complex were constructed by prisoners with sandstone they quarried and cut. Exhibits include historical weapons and vehicles; an explanation of the history of tattoos; and a video presentation recalling prison history, notorious inmates and conditions of prison life.

Guided tours are offered on weekends and during summer months. Visitors should wear comfortable shoes and dress for an outdoor experience. Picnicking is permitted outside the prison walls. **Time:** Allow 2 hours minimum. **Hours:** Daily 10-5, Memorial Day-Labor Day; noon-5, rest of year. Last admission 45 minutes before closing. Closed major holidays. Phone ahead to confirm schedule. **Cost:** $5; $4 (ages 60+); $3 (ages 6-12). **Phone:** (208) 334-2844.

STATE CAPITOL, bordered by Jefferson, W. State, 6th and 8th sts., is Boise's most treasured public building. The Idaho sandstone exterior base is carved to resemble logs—a tribute to pioneer cabins. Vermont and Georgian marble and hand-crafted scagliola (imitation marble) dominate the bright interior spaces of all four floors of the rotunda.

Begun in 1905, the five-part neoclassical building that motorists see while approaching from Capitol Boulevard was finished in 1920. A restored 5-foot-tall statue of a golden eagle sits atop the Capitol dome 208 feet above street level. **Hours:** Mon.-Fri. 6-6 (also 6-10 p.m., during legislative sessions), Sat.-Sun. 9-5. **Cost:** Free. **Phone:** (208) 332-1000 during legislative sessions, (208) 334-4860 in the interim between sessions or (800) 626-0471.

[SAVE] **WORLD CENTER FOR BIRDS OF PREY** is 7 mi. s. at 5668 W. Flying Hawk Ln.; take I-84 exit 50 to S. Cole Rd., then s. 6 mi. and w. on Flying Hawk Ln. to the top of the hill. The world headquarters of the Peregrine Fund—an organization dedicated to the conservation of birds of prey—includes a 7,200-square-foot interpretive center. Exhibits about wildlife, biology and ecology are featured, and live birds, such as falcons and eagles, can be seen. Docents are available to answer questions and to lead tours of the interpretive center.

Hours: Daily 10-5, June-Aug.; Tues.-Sun. 10-5, rest of year. Last admission 45 minutes before closing. Closed Jan. 1, Easter, Thanksgiving and Christmas. **Cost:** $7; $6 (ages 62+); $5 (ages 4-16). Prices may vary; phone ahead. **Phone:** (208) 362-8687.

RECREATIONAL ACTIVITIES
Skiing

- **Bogus Basin Mountain Recreation Area** is 16 mi. n. at 2600 N. Bogus Basin Rd. **Hours:** Mon.-Fri. 10-10, Sat.-Sun. and holidays 9 a.m.-10 p.m., Thanksgiving-late Mar. (weather permitting). Phone ahead to confirm schedule. **Phone:** (208) 332-5100 or (800) 367-4397.

Downtown Boise

© 2013 NAVTEQ

PEDESTRIAN WALKWAY

SEE BOISE INSET MAP FOR DETAIL

Boise
Hotels & Restaurants

Scale in Miles

SCENIC BYWAY

© AAA

1722-14

✈ Airport Hotels

Map Page	BOISE AIRPORT (Maximum driving distance from airport: 1.4 mi)	Diamond Rated	Rate Range	Page
27 p. 41	BEST WESTERN Airport Inn, 0.5 mi	◆◆	$70-$100 SAVE	44
29 p. 41	BEST WESTERN Vista Inn at the Airport, 0.5 mi	◆◆◆	$95-$129 SAVE	44
28 p. 41	Comfort Inn Airport, 0.6 mi	◆◆	$60-$116 SAVE	45
23 p. 41	Comfort Suites - Airport, 0.9 mi	◆◆	$85-$119	45
25 p. 41	Fairfield Inn by Marriott - Airport, 0.9 mi	◆◆	$70-$135	45
26 p. 41	Hampton Inn Boise - Airport, 0.6 mi	◆◆◆	$80-$155	45
24 p. 41	Holiday Inn Boise - Airport, 0.8 mi	◆◆◆	$79-$239	45
22 p. 41	Holiday Inn Express - Airport, 1.0 mi	◆◆	Rates not provided	46
30 p. 41	Inn America - Airport, 0.7 mi	◆◆	$49-$76 SAVE	46
31 p. 41	Shilo Inn Suites - Boise Airport, 1.4 mi	◆◆	Rates not provided	47

Boise

This index helps you "spot" where approved hotels and restaurants are located on the corresponding detailed maps. Hotel daily rate range is for comparison only. Restaurant price range is a combination of lunch and/or dinner. Turn to the listing page for more detailed rate and price information and consult display ads for special promotions.

BOISE

Map Page	Hotels	Diamond Rated	Rate Range	Page
1 p. 41	SpringHill Suites by Marriott - Boise	◆◆◆	$109-$139	47
2 p. 41	Hyatt Place - Boise Towne Square	◆◆◆	$84-$209 SAVE	46
3 p. 41	The Riverside Hotel	◆◆◆	Rates not provided	47
4 p. 41	La Quinta Inn & Suites Boise Towne Square	◆◆	Rates not provided	46
5 p. 41	Red Lion Hotel Boise Downtowner	◆◆◆	$69-$249	46
6 p. 41	Candlewood Suites - Boise Towne Square	◆◆◆	Rates not provided	44
7 p. 41	Residence Inn by Marriott Boise West	◆◆◆	$89-$129 SAVE	46
8 p. 41	Modern Hotel & Bar	◆◆	$99-$108	46
9 p. 41	Safari Inn Downtown	◆◆	$79-$109	47
10 p. 41	Hotel 43	◆◆◆	$109-$269 SAVE	46
11 p. 41	The Grove Hotel	◆◆◆	Rates not provided	45
12 p. 41	Hampton Inn & Suites Boise Downtown	◆◆◆	$109-$229	45
13 p. 41	Harrison Plaza Suite Hotel	◆◆	$79-$225	45
14 p. 41	Residence Inn by Marriott Downtown	◆◆◆	$99-$199	47
15 p. 41	Courtyard by Marriott - Downtown	◆◆◆	$89-$259	45
16 p. 41	TownePlace Suites by Marriott - Downtown	◆◆◆	$89-$189 SAVE	47
17 p. 41	Oxford Suites - Boise/Spectrum	◆◆◆	$105-$189 SAVE	46
18 p. 41	Hampton Inn & Suites - Boise/Spectrum	◆◆◆	$99-$219	45
19 p. 41	Homewood Suites by Hilton - Boise/Spectrum	◆◆◆	Rates not provided	46
20 p. 41	Hilton Garden Inn - Boise/Spectrum	◆◆◆	$99-$255	45
21 p. 41	SpringHill Suites by Marriott - Boise/ParkCenter	◆◆◆	$89-$189	47

BOISE (cont'd)

Map Page	Hotels (cont'd)	Diamond Rated	Rate Range	Page
22 p. 41	Holiday Inn Express - Airport	◇◇	Rates not provided	46
23 p. 41	Comfort Suites - Airport	◇◇	$85-$119	45
24 p. 41	Holiday Inn Boise - Airport	◇◇◇	$79-$239	45
25 p. 41	Fairfield Inn by Marriott - Airport	◇◇	$70-$135	45
26 p. 41	Hampton Inn Boise - Airport	◇◇◇	$80-$155	45
27 p. 41	**BEST WESTERN Airport Inn**	◇◇	$70-$100 SAVE	44
28 p. 41	**Comfort Inn Airport**	◇◇	$60-$116 SAVE	45
29 p. 41	**BEST WESTERN Vista Inn at the Airport**	◇◇◇	$95-$129 SAVE	44
30 p. 41	**Inn America - Airport**	◇◇	$49-$76 SAVE	46
31 p. 41	Shilo Inn Suites - Boise Airport	◇◇	Rates not provided	47
32 p. 41	**BEST WESTERN Northwest Lodge**	◇◇◇	$95-$129 SAVE	44

Map Page	Restaurants	Diamond Rated	Cuisine	Price Range	Page
1 p. 41	Flying Pie Pizzaria	◇	Pizza	$7-$30	49
2 p. 41	Highlands Hollow Brewhouse	◇◇	American	$7-$17	49
3 p. 41	Java Hyde Park	◇	American	$4-$10	49
4 p. 41	Flying Pie Pizzaria	◇	Pizza	$7-$30	49
5 p. 41	Cafe Vicino	◇◇◇	Mediterranean	$9-$29	48
6 p. 41	Big City Coffee & Cafe	◇	American	$4-$12	48
7 p. 41	The Cheesecake Factory	◇◇◇	International	$9-$30	48
8 p. 41	Cafe Ole Restaurant & Cantina	◇◇	Mexican	$8-$14	48
9 p. 41	Yen Ching	◇◇	Chinese	$7-$17	50
10 p. 41	Asiago's Restaurant & Winebar	◇◇◇	Italian	$7-$25	47
11 p. 41	Berryhill & Co.	◇◇◇	American	$8-$35	47
12 p. 41	Zeppole Downtown	◇	Sandwiches	$3-$7	50
13 p. 41	Cazba	◇◇	Eastern Mediterranean	$9-$30	48
14 p. 41	Bombay Grill	◇◇	Indian	$9-$20	48
15 p. 41	Bittercreek Alehouse	◇◇	Pacific Northwest	$8-$22	48
16 p. 41	Red Feather	◇◇◇	American	$7-$22	50
17 p. 41	Mai Thai Restaurant	◇◇◇	Thai	$8-$30	49
18 p. 41	Chandlers Steakhouse	◇◇◇	Steak Seafood	$27-$75	48
19 p. 41	Piper Pub & Grill	◇◇	American	$8-$19	49
20 p. 41	Moon's Kitchen Cafe	◇	American	$5-$12	49
21 p. 41	Shige Japanese Cuisine	◇◇	Japanese	$9-$24	50
22 p. 41	Java Downtown	◇	American	$3-$9	49
23 p. 41	Goldy's Breakfast Bistro	◇◇	American	$5-$13	49
24 p. 41	Flatbread Community Oven Pizzeria & Wine Bar - Downtown	◇◇	Pizza Sandwiches	$7-$17	49
25 p. 41	Bonefish Grill	◇◇◇	Seafood	$10-$29	48
26 p. 41	Happy Fish Sushi & Martini Bar	◇◇	Sushi	$13-$21	49
27 p. 41	Reef	◇◇	Polynesian	$8-$24	50
28 p. 41	Emilio's	◇◇◇	New American	$7-$29	48

Map Page	Restaurants (cont'd)	Diamond Rated	Cuisine	Price Range	Page
㉙ p. 41	Cafe Ole Restaurant & Cantina	◆◆	Mexican	$8-$13	48
㉚ p. 41	Bardenay	◆◆	International	$6-$23	47
㉛ p. 41	Leku Ona	◆◆	Basque	$7-$30	49
㉜ p. 41	Cottonwood Grille	◆◆◆	American	$10-$32	48
㉝ p. 41	Boise Fry Company	◆	Specialty Burgers	$4-$9	48
㉞ p. 41	Tucano's Brazilian Grill	◆◆	Brazilian	$8-$22	50
㉟ p. 41	Legends Pub & Grill	◆◆	American	$7-$18	49
㊲ p. 41	Cucina di Paolo	◆	Italian	$8-$11	48
㊳ p. 41	Willowcreek Grill	◆◆	American	$9-$27	50
㊴ p. 41	RAW Sushi	◆◆	Sushi	$8-$23	50
㊵ p. 41	Kopper Kitchen	◆◆	American	$6-$25	49
㊶ p. 41	Stubs Sports Pub	◆◆	American	$5-$13	50
㊷ p. 41	Bier: Thirty Bottle & Bistro	◆	German	$8-$10	47
㊸ p. 41	Tavern at Bown Crossing	◆◆	American	$10-$37	50
㊹ p. 41	Flatbread Community Oven Pizzeria & Wine Bar - Bown Crossing	◆◆	Pizza Sandwiches	$7-$17	48

BEST WESTERN AIRPORT INN
(208)384-5000 **27**

Motel
$70-$100

 AAA Benefit: Members save 10% or more with Best Western!

Address: 2660 Airport Way 83705 **Location:** I-84 exit 53 (Vista Ave), just s, then just e. **Facility:** 50 units. 2 stories (no elevator), exterior corridors. **Pool(s):** heated outdoor. **Guest Services:** coin laundry.

BEST WESTERN VISTA INN AT THE AIRPORT
(208)336-8100 **29**

Hotel
$95-$129

 AAA Benefit: Members save 10% or more with Best Western!

Address: 2645 Airport Way 83705 **Location:** I-84 exit 53 (Vista Ave), just s. **Facility:** 87 units. 2 stories (no elevator), interior/exterior corridors. **Pool(s):** heated indoor. **Activities:** hot tub, exercise room. **Guest Services:** valet and coin laundry.

BEST WESTERN NORTHWEST LODGE
(208)287-2300 **32**

Hotel
$95-$129

  AAA Benefit: Members save 10% or more with Best Western!

Address: 6989 Federal Way 83716 **Location:** I-84 exit 57 (Gowen Rd/Idaho City), just e, then just s. **Facility:** 69 units. 3 stories, interior corridors. **Parking:** winter plug-ins. **Pool(s):** heated indoor. **Activities:** hot tub, exercise room. **Guest Services:** valet and coin laundry.

CANDLEWOOD SUITES - BOISE TOWNE SQUARE
208/322-4300 **6**

◆◆◆ **Extended Stay Hotel.** Rates not provided. **Address:** 700 N Cole Rd 83704 **Location:** I-84 exit 50A westbound; exit 50B eastbound, 2 mi n on Cole Rd, then just w. **Facility:** 84 efficiencies. 3 stories, interior corridors. **Activities:** picnic facilities, exercise room. **Guest Services:** complimentary and valet laundry.

(See map & index p. 41.)

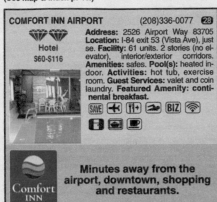

COMFORT INN AIRPORT   (208)336-0077 **28**
Hotel
S60-S116
Address: 2526 Airport Way 83705 **Location:** I-84 exit 53 (Vista Ave), just se. **Facility:** 61 units. 2 stories (no elevator), interior/exterior corridors. **Amenities:** safes. **Pool(s):** heated indoor. **Activities:** hot tub, exercise room. **Guest Services:** valet and coin laundry. **Featured Amenity:** continental breakfast.

Minutes away from the airport, downtown, shopping and restaurants.
Comfort INN

COMFORT SUITES - AIRPORT   (208)472-1222 **23**
Hotel $85-$119 **Address:** 2906 Vista Ave 83705 **Location:** I-84 exit 53 (Vista Ave), 0.5 mi n. **Facility:** 83 units. 3 stories, interior corridors. **Amenities:** safes. **Pool(s):** heated indoor. **Activities:** sauna, hot tub, exercise room. **Guest Services:** valet and coin laundry.

COURTYARD BY MARRIOTT - DOWNTOWN   (208)331-2700 **15**
Hotel $89-$259 **Address:** 222 S Broadway Ave 83702 **Location:** I-84 exit 54 (Broadway Ave), 3 mi n. **Facility:** 162 units. 4 stories, interior corridors. **Amenities:** video games. **Pool(s):** heated indoor. **Activities:** hot tub, exercise room. **Guest Services:** valet and coin laundry, boarding pass kiosk.

AAA Benefit: Members save 5% or more!

FAIRFIELD INN BY MARRIOTT - AIRPORT   (208)331-5656 **25**
Hotel $70-$135 **Address:** 3300 S Shoshone St 83705 **Location:** I-84 exit 53 (Vista Ave), just n to Elder St, then just w. **Facility:** 63 units. 3 stories, interior corridors. **Pool(s):** heated indoor. **Activities:** hot tub, limited exercise equipment. **Guest Services:** valet laundry.

AAA Benefit: Members save 5% or more!

THE GROVE HOTEL   208/333-8000 **11**
Boutique Contemporary Hotel. Rates not provided. **Address:** 245 S Capitol Blvd 83702 **Location:** At Front St and S Capitol Blvd; downtown. **Facility:** This downtown high-rise hotel features an upscale lobby, live piano music and well-appointed guest rooms. 250 units. 16 stories, interior corridors. **Parking:** on-site (fee) and valet. **Dining:** Emilio's, see separate listing. entertainment. **Pool(s):** heated indoor. **Activities:** sauna, hot tub, steamroom, massage. **Guest Services:** valet laundry.

HAMPTON INN & SUITES BOISE DOWNTOWN   (208)331-1900 **12**
Hotel $109-$229 **Address:** 495 S Capitol Blvd 83702 **Location:** I-84 exit 53 (Vista Ave), 2.2 mi n, then 0.8 mi ne; corner of W Myrtle St and S Capitol Blvd. **Facility:** 186 units. 11 stories, interior corridors. **Parking:** on-site (fee) and valet. **Terms:** 1-7 night minimum stay, cancellation fee imposed. **Amenities:** video games. **Pool(s):** heated indoor. **Activities:** hot tub, exercise room. **Guest Services:** valet and coin laundry.

AAA Benefit: Members save up to 10%!

HAMPTON INN & SUITES - BOISE/SPECTRUM   (208)323-2500 **18**
Contemporary Hotel $99-$219 **Address:** 7499 W Overland Rd 83709 **Location:** I-84 exit 50A westbound; exit 50B eastbound, just s. **Facility:** 133 units, some two bedrooms and efficiencies. 4 stories, interior corridors. **Terms:** 1-7 night minimum stay, cancellation fee imposed. **Pool(s):** heated indoor. **Activities:** hot tub, exercise room. **Guest Services:** valet and coin laundry.

AAA Benefit: Members save up to 10%!

HAMPTON INN BOISE - AIRPORT   (208)331-5600 **26**
Contemporary Hotel $80-$155 **Address:** 3270 S Shoshone St 83701 **Location:** I-84 exit 53 (Vista Ave), just n to Elder St, then just w. **Facility:** 63 units. 3 stories, interior corridors. **Terms:** 1-7 night minimum stay, cancellation fee imposed. **Pool(s):** heated indoor. **Activities:** hot tub, exercise room. **Guest Services:** valet laundry.

AAA Benefit: Members save up to 10%!

HARRISON PLAZA SUITE HOTEL   (208)375-7666 **13**
Hotel $79-$225 **Address:** 409 S Cole Rd 83709 **Location:** I-84 exit 50A westbound; exit 50B eastbound, 0.7 mi n. **Facility:** 38 units. 4 stories, interior corridors. **Terms:** cancellation fee imposed. **Pool(s):** heated indoor. **Guest Services:** valet laundry, area transportation.

HILTON GARDEN INN - BOISE/SPECTRUM   (208)376-1000 **20**
Contemporary Hotel $99-$255 **Address:** 7699 W Spectrum Way 83709 **Location:** I-84 exit 50A westbound; exit 50B eastbound, just s, then just w. **Facility:** 137 units. 4 stories, interior corridors. **Terms:** 1-7 night minimum stay, cancellation fee imposed. **Pool(s):** heated indoor. **Activities:** hot tub, exercise room. **Guest Services:** valet and coin laundry.

AAA Benefit: Members save up to 10%!

HOLIDAY INN BOISE - AIRPORT   (208)344-7444 **24**
Contemporary Hotel $79-$239 **Address:** 2970 W Elder St 83705 **Location:** I-84 exit 53 (Vista Ave), just n to Elder St, then just w. **Facility:** 119 units, some two bedrooms. 4 stories, interior corridors. **Amenities:** safes. **Pool(s):** heated indoor. **Activities:** hot tub, exercise room. **Guest Services:** valet and coin laundry.

(See map & index p. 41.)

HOLIDAY INN EXPRESS - AIRPORT   208/388-0800 22

💎💎 **Hotel.** Rates not provided. **Address:** 2613 S Vista Ave 83705 **Location:** I-84 exit 53 (Vista Ave), 0.6 mi n. Located in residential neighborhood. **Pool(s):** heated indoor. **Activities:** hot tub. **Guest Services:** valet and coin laundry.

HOMEWOOD SUITES BY HILTON - BOISE/SPECTRUM   208/375-8500 19

💎💎💎 **Extended Stay Contemporary Hotel.** Rates not provided. **Address:** 7957 W Spectrum Way 83709 **Location:** I-84 exit 50A westbound; exit 50B eastbound, just s, then just w. **Facility:** 110 efficiencies, some two bedrooms. 4 stories, interior corridors. **Parking:** winter plug-ins. **Amenities:** video games. **Pool(s):** heated indoor. **Activities:** hot tub, game room, picnic facilities, exercise room. **Guest Services:** valet and coin laundry.

AAA Benefit: Members save up to 10%!

HOTEL 43   (208)342-4622 10

Boutique Contemporary Hotel
$109-$269

Address: 981 W Grove St 83702 **Location:** Corner of 10th and W Grove sts; downtown. **Facility:** This northwest boutique hotel is on the 43rd parallel in the 43rd state and boasts artfully designed rooms and a variety of city views with a unique, modern décor style throughout. 112 units. 6 stories, interior corridors. **Parking:** on-site (fee) and valet. **Terms:** check-in 4 pm, cancellation fee imposed. **Dining:** Chandlers Steakhouse, see separate listing. **Activities:** exercise room. **Guest Services:** valet laundry.

HYATT PLACE - BOISE TOWNE SQUARE   (208)375-1200 2

Contemporary Hotel
$84-$209

HYATT PLACE
AAA Benefit: Members save 10%!

Address: 925 N Milwaukee St 83704 **Location:** I-84 exit 49 (Franklin St), just w, then 0.5 mi n. **Facility:** 127 units. 4 stories, interior corridors. **Terms:** cancellation fee imposed. **Amenities:** safes. **Pool(s):** heated indoor. **Activities:** exercise room. **Guest Services:** valet laundry, area transportation.

INN AMERICA - AIRPORT   (208)389-9800 30

Hotel
$49-$76

Address: 2275 Airport Way 83705 **Location:** I-84 exit 53 (Vista Ave), 0.3 mi se. **Facility:** 73 units. 3 stories, interior corridors. **Terms:** cancellation fee imposed, resort fee. **Pool(s):** heated outdoor. **Guest Services:** valet and coin laundry. **Featured Amenity:** continental breakfast.

LA QUINTA INN & SUITES BOISE TOWNE SQUARE   208/378-7000 4

💎💎 **Hotel.** Rates not provided. **Address:** 7965 W Emerald St 83704 **Location:** I-84 exit 49 (Franklin St), just w, 0.5 mi n on Milwaukee St to Emerald St, then just e. **Facility:** 124 units, some efficiencies. 4 stories, interior corridors. **Amenities:** video games. **Pool(s):** heated indoor. **Activities:** hot tub, exercise room. **Guest Services:** valet and coin laundry.

MODERN HOTEL & BAR   (208)424-8244 8

💎💎 **Motel** $99-$108 **Address:** 1314 W Grove St 83702 **Location:** At 13th and W Grove sts; downtown. **Facility:** 39 units. 2 stories (no elevator), interior/exterior corridors. **Parking:** on-site and street. **Terms:** cancellation fee imposed. **Activities:** bicycles. **Guest Services:** valet laundry.

OXFORD SUITES - BOISE/SPECTRUM   (208)322-8000 17

💎💎💎 **Hotel**
$105-$189

Address: 1426 S Entertainment Ave 83709 **Location:** I-84 exit 50A, just s to Spectrum Way, just w, then just n. **Facility:** 132 units, some efficiencies. 4 stories, interior corridors. **Terms:** 3 day cancellation notice-fee imposed. **Pool(s):** heated indoor. **Activities:** sauna, hot tub, steamroom, exercise room. **Guest Services:** valet and coin laundry, area transportation. **Featured Amenity:** breakfast buffet.

RED LION HOTEL BOISE DOWNTOWNER   (208)344-7691 5

💎💎💎 **Hotel** $69-$249 **Address:** 1800 Fairview Ave 83702 **Location:** I-184 exit 3 (Fairview Ave), 1 mi n. **Facility:** 182 units. 3-7 stories, interior corridors. **Terms:** cancellation fee imposed, resort fee. **Pool(s):** heated outdoor. **Activities:** hot tub, exercise room. **Guest Services:** valet laundry, area transportation.

RESIDENCE INN BY MARRIOTT BOISE WEST   (208)385-9000 7

Extended Stay Hotel
$89-$129

Residence Inn Marriott
AAA Benefit: Members save 5% or more!

Address: 7303 W Denton St 83704 **Location:** I-84 exit 50A westbound; exit 50B eastbound, 2 mi n on Cole Rd, then just w. **Facility:** 104 units, some two bedrooms, efficiencies and kitchens. 4 stories, interior corridors. **Pool(s):** heated indoor. **Activities:** hot tub, exercise room. **Guest Services:** valet and coin laundry.

(See map & index p. 41.)

RESIDENCE INN BY MARRIOTT DOWNTOWN
(208)344-1200 **14**

▼▼▼▼ **Extended Stay Hotel**
$99-$199 **Address:** 1401 S Lusk Ave
83706 **Location:** I-84 exit 53 (Vista Ave),
2.4 mi n, just w on Ann Morrison Park Dr,
then just s on Lois Ave. **Facility:** 104

AAA Benefit:
Members save 5%
or more!

kitchen units, some two bedrooms and efficiencies. 2-3 stories (no elevator), exterior corridors. **Pool(s):** heated outdoor. **Activities:** hot tub, exercise room. **Guest Services:** valet and coin laundry, area transportation.

🅿 🍴 🏊 BIZ 📶 ☒ 📶 📶 🖵
/SOME UNITS 🐾

THE RIVERSIDE HOTEL   208/343-1871 **3**

▼▼▼▼ **Hotel.** Rates not provided. **Address:** 2900 W Chinden Blvd 83714 **Location:** I-84 exit 49 (Franklin Rd/City Center), 2.7 mi ne on I-184 exit 3 (Fairview Ave), just n, then just w. Adjoining the Boise Greenbelt. **Facility:** 303 units, some two bedrooms. 2 stories, interior corridors. **Dining:** 2 restaurants. **Pool(s):** heated outdoor. **Activities:** hot tub, bicycles, trails, exercise room. **Guest Services:** complimentary and valet laundry, area transportation.

ECO 🅿 🍴 🖼 🍷 🏊 BIZ HS 📶 🖵
/SOME UNITS 🐾 📶 📶

SAFARI INN DOWNTOWN   (208)344-6556 **9**

▼▼▼ **Hotel** $79-$109 **Address:** 1070 Grove St 83702 **Location:** Corner of 11th and Grove sts. **Facility:** 103 units. 3 stories, interior corridors. **Amenities:** safes. **Pool(s):** heated outdoor. **Activities:** sauna, hot tub, exercise room. **Guest Services:** valet and coin laundry.

🅿 🍴 🏊 📶 ☒ 📶 📶 🖵
/SOME UNITS 🐾 HS

SHILO INN SUITES - BOISE AIRPORT   208/343-7662 **31**

▼▼▼ **Hotel.** Rates not provided. **Address:** 4111 Broadway Ave 83705 **Location:** I-84 exit 54 (Broadway Ave), just sw. Next to a truck stop. **Facility:** 126 units. 4 stories, interior corridors. **Pool(s):** heated outdoor. **Activities:** sauna, hot tub, steamroom, exercise room. **Guest Services:** coin laundry.

🅿 🍴 🏊 BIZ 📶 ☒ 🍴 📶
/SOME UNITS 🐾

SPRINGHILL SUITES BY MARRIOTT - BOISE
(208)939-8266 **1**

▼▼▼ **Contemporary Hotel**
$109-$139 **Address:** 6325 N Cloverdale
Rd 83713 **Location:** I-84 exit 46 (Eagle
Rd), 4.3 mi n in Chinden Blvd, 0.9 mi e,
then just s; in Boise Research Center.

AAA Benefit:
Members save 5%
or more!

Facility: 119 units. 4 stories, interior corridors. **Pool(s):** heated indoor. **Activities:** hot tub, exercise room. **Guest Services:** valet and coin laundry.

🅿 🍴 CALL 🅜 🏊 BIZ HS 📶 ☒ 🍴 📶
📶 🖵 /SOME UNITS 🐾

SPRINGHILL SUITES BY MARRIOTT - BOISE/PARKCENTER
(208)342-1044 **21**

▼▼▼▼ **Hotel** $89-$189 **Address:**
424 E Parkcenter Blvd 83706 **Location:**
I-84 exit 54 (Broadway Ave), 2.3 mi n to
Beacon St, 0.3 mi e, then 0.7 mi se. Located in a business park. **Facility:** 230

AAA Benefit:
Members save 5%
or more!

units. 3 stories, interior corridors. **Pool(s):** heated outdoor. **Activities:** hot tub, exercise room. **Guest Services:** valet and coin laundry, area transportation.

🅿 🍴 🏊 BIZ 📶 ☒ 📶 📶 🖵
/SOME UNITS 🐾

TOWNEPLACE SUITES BY MARRIOTT - DOWNTOWN
(208)429-8881 **16**

▼▼▼ **Extended Stay Contemporary Hotel**
$89-$189

TownePlace SUITES Marriott

AAA Benefit:
Members save 5%
or more!

Address: 1455 S Capitol Blvd 83706 **Location:** I-84 exit 53 (Vista Ave), 2.4 mi n. **Facility:** 121 efficiencies, some two bedrooms and kitchens. 4 stories, interior corridors. **Terms:** check-in 4 pm. **Pool(s):** heated indoor. **Activities:** hot tub, picnic facilities, exercise room. **Guest Services:** valet and coin laundry.

SAVE 🅿 🍴 CALL 🅜 🏊 BIZ
HS 📶 ☒ 📶 📶 🖵 /SOME UNITS 🐾

HOLIDAY INN EXPRESS BOISE DOWNTOWN   208/345-2002

fyi Not evaluated. **Address:** 475 W Parkcenter Blvd 83706 **Location:** I-84 exit 54 (Broadway Ave), 2.3 mi n to Beacon St, then 0.3 mi e. Facilities, services, and décor characterize a mid-scale property.

WHERE TO EAT

ASIAGO'S RESTAURANT & WINEBAR   208/336-5552 **10**

▼▼▼ Italian. Casual Dining. $7-$25 **AAA Inspector Notes:** The warm ambience found here mixes Old World designs with modern accents. The creative menu features walnut-pesto risotto cakes, marinated leg of lamb sautéed with sun-dried tomato, rosemary gnocchi with artichoke hearts and beef tenderloin with bacon-balsamic onion crust over whiskey-horseradish sauce. **Features:** beer & wine, patio dining. **Reservations:** suggested. **Address:** 1002 Main St 83701 **Location:** At 10th and Main sts; downtown. **Parking:** on-site (fee) and street. L D

BARDENAY   208/426-0538 **30**

▼▼▼ International. Casual Dining. $6-$23 **AAA Inspector Notes:** The first in the country licensed to operate its own distillery, this large, popular restaurant serves a wide variety of dishes. Vodka, rum and gin are produced on the premises. The restaurant is appropriately named: Bardenay is a term sailors use loosely in place of the word cocktail. **Features:** full bar, Sunday brunch. **Address:** 610 Grove St 83702 **Location:** Between Capitol and 6th sts; downtown. **Parking:** street only. L D

BERRYHILL & CO.   208/387-3553 **11**

▼▼▼ American. Fine Dining. $8-$35 **AAA Inspector Notes:** This restaurant began as a tasting room for the catering business, and after much positive response and some urging from clients, the restaurant was born. Fresh food focuses on as much local produce as possible. An extensive wine list pairs with creative and appealing dishes, ranging from quick lunches to special-occasion dinners. **Features:** full bar, patio dining, Sunday brunch. **Reservations:** suggested. **Address:** 121 N 9th St 83702 **Location:** Downtown; in Plaza 121. **Parking:** street only. L D

BIER: THIRTY BOTTLE & BISTRO   208/342-1916 **42**

▼ German. Gastropub. $8-$10 **AAA Inspector Notes:** In the East Side, this little gastropub offers more than 400 craft beers and imported bottles. Menu items include schnitzel tacos, bier broth mussels, barley pasta salad and an Alaskan amber hummus plate with olive salad and sun-dried tomato pesto—too good to share. Vegan and vegetarian items are available. **Features:** beer & wine, patio dining, happy hour. **Address:** 3073 S Bown Way 83706 **Location:** I-84 exit 54 (Broadway Ave), 1 mi n to Linden St, 1 mi e to Boise Ave, just se to Apple St, 0.3 mi n to Parkcenter Blvd, then 1 mi se to Bown Way. **Parking:** on-site and street. L D

(See map & index p. 41.)

BIG CITY COFFEE & CAFE · 208/345-3145 · 6
American. Quick Serve. $4-$12 AAA Inspector Notes: The epicenter of Boise culture, this eclectic cafe turns out freshly baked pastries, award-winning quiches and delicious wraps and sandwiches. The antiques and brightly colored walls and fixtures lend to a design that shows you something new with each visit. **Address:** 1416 W Grove St 83702 **Location:** Between 14th and 15th sts. **Parking:** street only. [B] [L]

BITTERCREEK ALEHOUSE · 208/345-1813 · 15
Pacific Northwest. Casual Dining. $8-$22 AAA Inspector Notes: From pasture-raised ground chuck to Alaskan salmon, Pacific cod or Idaho trout, this brew pub offers great Pacific Northwest entrees with just about any imaginable drink pairing. Street-side patio seating is available, weather permitting. **Features:** full bar, patio dining. **Address:** 246 N 8th St 83702 **Location:** Jct Idaho and 8th sts; downtown. **Parking:** street only. [L] [D] CALL[&M]

BOISE FRY COMPANY · 208/495-3858 · 33
Specialty Burgers. Quick Serve. $4-$9 AAA Inspector Notes: Fries are the main event here and they are treated with respect. Pick a potato (gold, purple, russet, sweet, white or yam) and then choose the cut (regular, whale or curly). Order a side, such as a bison burger, house vegan patty or quinoa salad, to go with it. You have to see the seasoning and dipping stations to believe it. Do not miss fry happy hour. Be advised in advance, this eatery is addictive. **Features:** beer only. **Address:** 111 S Broadway Ave, Suite 111 83702 **Location:** I-84 exit 54 (Broadway Ave), 3.1 mi n. [L] [D]

BOMBAY GRILL · 208/345-7888 · 14
Indian. Casual Dining. $9-$20 AAA Inspector Notes: Located near shops and a movie theater, this popular grill is inside the historic Idanha Building which served as a hotel in the early 1900s catering to guests such as Theodore Roosevelt and Ethel Barrymore. Menu highlights include a long list of chicken, lamb and tandoori specialties. **Features:** beer & wine. **Address:** 928 W Main St 83702 **Location:** At 10th St. **Parking:** street only. [L] [D]

BONEFISH GRILL · 208/433-1234 · 25
Seafood. Casual Dining. $10-$29 AAA Inspector Notes: Fish is the house specialty, and the menu and nightly specials offer a variety of choices. Well-prepared food is cooked to perfection. Service is casual in nature, and the staff is skilled and attentive. **Features:** full bar. **Reservations:** suggested. **Address:** 855 W Broad St 83702 **Location:** Jct Broad and 9th sts; downtown. **Parking:** street only. [D] CALL[&M]

CAFE OLE RESTAURANT & CANTINA · 208/344-3222 · 29
Mexican. Casual Dining. $8-$13 AAA Inspector Notes: Nestled in the urban BoDo corridor, this authentic Mexican restaurant is a local favorite. Great taste, value and traditional Mexican dishes have guests leaving with full tummies and happy hearts. **Features:** full bar. **Address:** 404 S 8th St 83702 **Location:** Between Broad and Myrtle sts; downtown. **Parking:** street only. [L] [D]

CAFE OLE RESTAURANT & CANTINA · 208/322-0222 · 8
Mexican. Casual Dining. $8-$14 AAA Inspector Notes: Set eyes on this white stucco, Spanish-style building and entry-way water fountain and you'll know immediately that you're about to experience authentic Mexican cuisine. Genuine dishes are served boasting loads of flavor. If you're in the mood for a margarita, be ready to choose from over 20 different types of tequila. **Features:** full bar. **Address:** 210 N Milwaukee Rd 83704 **Location:** I-84 exit 49 (Franklin Rd), just w, then just n. [L] [D]

CAFE VICINO · 208/472-1463 · 5
Mediterranean. Fine Dining. $9-$29 AAA Inspector Notes: Located in the historic North End, this quaint Mediterranean-style bistro serves up tasteful, innovative dishes. The menu changes seasonally and always features a variety of pasta, seafood and steak. **Features:** beer & wine, patio dining. **Reservations:** suggested. **Address:** 808 W Fort St 83702 **Location:** Between 7th and 8th sts; downtown. **Parking:** on-site and street. [L] [D]

CAZBA · 208/381-0222 · 13
Eastern Mediterranean. Casual Dining. $9-$30 AAA Inspector Notes: While Greek dishes are prominent here, the menu also lists a variety of original sauces and seasoning combinations offering subtle, distinctive and enjoyably flavor. In addition to more traditional items, there are numerous types of wraps. The artistic décor and ambience are light, airy and relaxing. **Features:** full bar. **Reservations:** suggested. **Address:** 211 N 8th St 83702 **Location:** Between Idaho and Bannock sts; downtown. **Parking:** street only. [L] [D]

CHANDLERS STEAKHOUSE · 208/383-4300 · 18
Steak Seafood. Fine Dining. $27-$75 AAA Inspector Notes: Specializing in steak and seafood dishes with a regional flair, this modern restaurant is known for its extensive wine list, creative cocktails and martinis and live nightly jazz performances. Patrons enjoy dinner at candlelit tables surrounded by bouquets of fresh flowers. Patio dining is available when the weather permits. **Features:** full bar, patio dining. **Reservations:** suggested. **Address:** 981 W Grove St 83702 **Location:** Corner of 10th and W Grove sts; downtown; in Hotel 43. **Parking:** valet and street only. [D] CALL[&M]

THE CHEESECAKE FACTORY · 208/377-4466 · 7
International. Family Dining. $9-$30 AAA Inspector Notes: A display case of mouthwatering cheesecakes is the first thing visitors see as they walk through the door. The extensive menu incorporates many types of cuisine, including Asian, Italian, Greek and Spanish. **Features:** full bar, Sunday brunch. **Address:** 330 N Milwaukee St 83704 **Location:** I-84 exit 49 (Franklin Rd), just w, then just n. [L] [D] CALL[&M]

COTTONWOOD GRILLE · 208/333-9800 · 32
American. Fine Dining. $10-$32 AAA Inspector Notes: This restaurant features riverfront dining in lush surroundings alongside the Boise River. Inside, the main dining room features an enormous stone fireplace. Menu items include a variety of elk, premium buffalo, grilled pheasant, rack of lamb, juicy steaks and a nice selection of fresh fish and shellfish. Diners may want to share the large seasonal and decadent desserts. **Features:** full bar, patio dining, Sunday brunch, happy hour. **Reservations:** suggested. **Address:** 913 W River St 83702 **Location:** I-84 exit 53 (Vista Ave), 2.8 mi n, then just w. [L] [D]

CUCINA DI PAOLO · 208/345-7150 · 37
Italian. Quick Serve. $8-$11 AAA Inspector Notes: Using as many local producers and farmers as possible, this cozy eatery offers tasty food in an adorable setting. Some menu items include a wide variety of lasagna, chicken pot pie, seasonal soups, attractively prepared salads and sandwiches. Try the triple crème Danish Brie and merlot wine jelly on grilled crostini. Mouth-watering desserts are lined up in a glass case just waiting to tempt guests. **Features:** beer & wine, patio dining. **Address:** 1504 S Vista Ave 83702 **Location:** I-84 exit 53 (Vista Ave), 1.4 mi n. [L] [D]

EMILIO'S · 208/333-8002 · 28
New American. Fine Dining. $7-$29 AAA Inspector Notes: Guests can relax in this upscale atmosphere that offers a European ambience while enjoying beef tenderloin brochettes, filet mignon, Jamaican jerk salmon, jumbo shrimp and sea scallops. **Features:** full bar. **Reservations:** suggested. **Address:** 245 S Capitol Blvd 83702 **Location:** At Front St and S Capitol Blvd; downtown; in The Grove Hotel. **Parking:** on-site and valet. [B] [L] [D] CALL[&M]

FLATBREAD COMMUNITY OVEN PIZZERIA & WINE BAR - BOWN CROSSING · 208/343-4177 · 44
Pizza Sandwiches. Casual Dining. $7-$17 AAA Inspector Notes: Tucked away in a quaint community, this certified Neapolitan pizzeria always is packed with returning fans. Choose from a variety of distinctive pizza, pasta and sandwich choices while enjoying the bright ambience that the patio fire pits and candlelit walls create. Gluten-free items are available. **Features:** full bar. **Address:** 3139 S Bown Way 83706 **Location:** I-84 exit 54 (Broadway Ave), 1.2 mi n, 1.1 mi e, then just n. **Parking:** street only. [L] [D]

(See map & index p. 41.)

FLATBREAD COMMUNITY OVEN PIZZERIA & WINE BAR - DOWNTOWN   208/287-4757   24
▼▼ Pizza Sandwiches. Casual Dining. $7-$17 **AAA Inspector Notes:** This certified Neapolitan pizzeria always is packed with returning fans. Choose from a variety of specialty pizza, salads and sandwiches while enjoying the bright ambience that this streetside location offers. **Features:** full bar, happy hour. **Address:** 615 W Main St 83702 **Location:** Between Capitol Blvd and 6th St. **Parking:** street only. L D

FLYING PIE PIZZARIA   208/345-0000   4
▼ Pizza. Casual Dining. $7-$30 **AAA Inspector Notes:** From its eclectic decor and unique pizza pies, it is no wonder this local favorite has become "whirled famous." Dining here is sure to be a new experience for each and every customer with a variety of contests and hands-on activities ranging from pizza tours to the rotating "It's Your Day" contest. **Features:** beer & wine. **Address:** 6508 Fairview Ave 83704 **Location:** I-184 exit 2 (Curtis Ave), just n, then 0.5 mi w. L D

FLYING PIE PIZZARIA   208/384-0000   1
▼ Pizza. Casual Dining. $7-$30 **AAA Inspector Notes:** From its eclectic decor and unique pizza pies, it is no wonder this local favorite has become "whirled famous." Dining here is sure to be a new experience for each and every customer with a variety of contests and hands-on activities ranging from pizza tours to the rotating "It's Your Day" contest. **Features:** beer & wine. **Address:** 4320 W State St 83703 **Location:** Jct Willow Ln. L D

GOLDY'S BREAKFAST BISTRO   208/345-4100   23
▼▼ American. Family Dining. $5-$13 **AAA Inspector Notes:** Within a few blocks of excellent shopping and a movie theater, this small, locally popular cafe features a wide variety of freshly prepared breakfast items and unique house dishes. Create-your-own combination plates offer a dizzying array of choices. The distinctive lighting fixtures add visual punch in the bi-level dining room. On the weekend, a long wait for a table is a given. **Address:** 108 S Capitol Blvd 83702 **Location:** At Main St; downtown. **Parking:** street only. B L

GOODWOOD BARBECUE COMPANY   208/658-7173
▼▼ Barbecue. Casual Dining. $9-$22 **AAA Inspector Notes:** This lively, casual, family-friendly restaurant specializes in traditional barbecue fare, as well as new twists on such old favorites as smoked prime rib. The menu lists comfort food at its best. Barbecue lovers should not miss this place. **Features:** full bar. **Address:** 7849 W Spectrum St 83709 **Location:** I-84 exit 50A westbound; exit 50B eastbound, just s, then just w. L D CALL 🄼

HAPPY FISH SUSHI & MARTINI BAR   208/343-4810   26
▼▼ Sushi. Casual Dining. $13-$21 **AAA Inspector Notes:** This eatery is located in the popular BoDo District, within walking distance of a comedy club, concert venue and movie theater. They serve a wide variety of nigiri, sashimi, traditional Japanese maki and specialty maki rolls. Along with great sushi, the contemporary restaurant is also known for their innovative martini creations. **Features:** full bar. **Address:** 855 Broad St, Suite 250 83702 **Location:** Downtown. **Parking:** street only. L D

HIGHLANDS HOLLOW BREWHOUSE   208/343-6820   2
▼▼ American. Casual Dining. $7-$17 **AAA Inspector Notes:** This eatery serves up traditional comfort food with a splash of Boise's North End eclectic style. Some favorites include the chicken cordon bleu sandwich, the North End Philly and the Highlands snow-capped cookie for dessert. Portions are hearty, so bring an appetite. Be sure to try one of their flavorful beers from the on-site brewery. **Features:** beer & wine. **Address:** 2455 Harrison Hollow Ln 83703 **Location:** I-184 exit River St, 0.8 mi n on 15th St, just w on Hays St, 1 mi n on Harrison Blvd, then just w. L D

JAVA DOWNTOWN   208/345-0777   22
▼ American. Quick Serve. $3-$9 **AAA Inspector Notes:** This casual eccentric cafe is located on one of the busiest street corners in downtown Boise, making dining in or taking your food to go both appealing options. They offer only fair trade certified organic coffee and homemade baked goods, soups, sandwiches and wraps made with fresh local ingredients. **Address:** 223 N 6th St 83702 **Location:** Jct Idaho St; downtown. **Parking:** street only. B L

JAVA HYDE PARK   208/345-4777   3
▼ American. Quick Serve. $4-$10 **AAA Inspector Notes:** Fair trade certified organic coffee couples with homemade baked goods, soups and entrees made from fresh local ingredients at this casual, eccentric cafe. **Address:** 1612 N 13th St 83702 **Location:** Jct 13th and Eastman sts; in Hyde Park District. **Parking:** on-site and street. B L

KOPPER KITCHEN   208/344-4271   40
▼▼ American. Casual Dining. $6-$25 **AAA Inspector Notes:** This restaurant appeals to travelers looking for a quick and convenient place to eat. The menu offers a full breakfast, sandwiches and several steak, chicken and pasta dishes. **Features:** full bar. **Address:** 2661 Airport Way 83705 **Location:** I-84 exit 53 (Vista Ave), just s. B L D

LEGENDS PUB & GRILL   208/377-1819   35
▼▼ American. Casual Dining. $7-$18 **AAA Inspector Notes:** This popular sports-themed restaurant offers a variety of steaks, poultry, pasta, seafood, salads, sandwiches and pizza. Patio seating overlooks a frequented sand volleyball court. **Features:** full bar. **Address:** 7609 W Overland Rd, Suite 100 83709 **Location:** I-84 exit 50A westbound; exit 50B eastbound, just s. L D

LEKU ONA   208/345-6665   31
▼▼ Basque. Casual Dining. $7-$30 **AAA Inspector Notes:** Meaning "good place," this eatery serves traditional fare from the Basque region of Spain. The dining room resembles a quaint country cottage with pictures of Basque cultural events adorning the walls, and menu items are hard to pronounce but deliciously identifiable. Favorites include red bean soup with chorizo and pork ribs, homemade meatballs, pork chops and grilled salmon. **Features:** full bar. **Reservations:** suggested. **Address:** 117 S 6th St 83702 **Location:** Corner of Grove St; center. **Parking:** street only. L D ◣

MAI THAI RESTAURANT   208/344-8424   17
▼▼◆ Thai. Casual Dining. $8-$30 **AAA Inspector Notes:** This contemporary Thai restaurant is known for a modern approach to traditional Thai cuisine and sushi. Guests can enjoy a meal surrounded by multiple calming water features, candlelight and distinctive and ornate wall appointments. **Features:** full bar, happy hour. **Reservations:** suggested. **Address:** 750 W Idaho St 83702 **Location:** Just nw of Capitol Blvd and W Idaho St; downtown. **Parking:** street only. L D

MCGRATH'S FISH HOUSE   208/375-6300
▼▼ Seafood. Casual Dining. $8-$29 **AAA Inspector Notes:** The popular chain specializes in fresh Pacific Northwest seafood, including dishes grilled over a wood fire and items from the daily fresh sheet. Also on the menu are steaks, chicken, pasta and gourmet burgers. **Features:** full bar. **Address:** 1749 S Cole Rd 83709 **Location:** I-84 exit 50A westbound; exit 50B eastbound, just s, then just w. L D CALL 🄼

MOON'S KITCHEN CAFE   208/385-0472   20
▼ American. Family Dining. $5-$12 **AAA Inspector Notes:** Guests can reminisce about the 1950s, when the traditional soda fountain and sandwich shop was a social gathering spot. This old-time eatery specializes in flavorful malts, shakes, sirloin burgers, chicken, sandwiches and big, home-style breakfasts. Guests should expect a wait during peak dining times. **Features:** beer & wine, early bird specials. **Address:** 712 W Idaho St 83702 **Location:** Between N Capitol Blvd and 8th St. **Parking:** street only. B L

PIPER PUB & GRILL   208/343-2444   19
▼▼ American. Casual Dining. $8-$19 **AAA Inspector Notes:** This congenial, nicely decorated downtown pub offers a large selection of appetizers, sandwiches and salads, along with two house specials: meatloaf sandwich and blue cheese/cracked pepper burgers. A bustling atmosphere predominates on Friday and Saturday with live music on most weekends. **Features:** full bar, patio dining, happy hour. **Address:** 150 N 8th St, Suite 200 83702 **Location:** Jct 8th and Main sts; downtown. **Parking:** street only. L D LATE

(See map & index p. 41.)

PROTO'S PIZZERIA NAPOLETANA   208/331-1400

◆◆ Pizza. Casual Dining. $5-$22 **AAA Inspector Notes:** Known for fresh ingredients, eclectic style and friendly service, this pizzeria always is bustling. Try the cannoli or tiramisu, but be prepared to wait in line for a table during peak dining hours. **Features:** full bar, patio dining. **Address:** 345 S 8th St 83702 **Location:** Downtown; in BoDo District. **Parking:** street only. [L] [D]

RAM RESTAURANT AND BREWERY   208/345-2929

◆◆ American. Casual Dining. $10-$24 **AAA Inspector Notes:** The enormous restaurant features high ceilings, huge television screens, large sports-themed banners and a brew pub area. The menu is equally enormous, with steaks, poultry, pasta, seafood, salads, sandwiches and pizza. The on-site brewery turns out a large selection of microbrews. **Features:** full bar, happy hour. **Address:** 709 E Park Blvd 83712 **Location:** I-84 exit 54 (Broadway Ave), 2.8 mi n. [L] [D] CALL [&M]

RAW SUSHI   208/343-0270   (39)

◆ Sushi. Casual Dining. $8-$23 **AAA Inspector Notes:** Relaxing, Zen-like decor surrounds diners at this eatery while the charming and entertaining servers add to this unique dining experience. The menu offers a wide variety of sushi, sashimi and maki. **Features:** beer & wine. **Address:** 2273 S Vista Ave 83705 **Location:** I-84 exit 53 (Vista Ave), 0.9 mi n. [L] [D]

RED FEATHER   208/429-6340   (16)

◆◆◆ American. Casual Dining. $7-$22 **AAA Inspector Notes:** This dimly lit, contemporary eatery offers innovative American cuisine ranging from flat-bread pizzas to short ribs and Asiago-encrusted calamari. Unique martinis along with a wide variety of wines can be found on the drink menu. **Features:** full bar, Sunday brunch, happy hour. **Reservations:** suggested. **Address:** 246 N 8th St 83702 **Location:** Between Idaho and Main sts; downtown. **Parking:** street only. [L] [D] CALL [&M]

REEF   208/287-9200   (27)

◆◆ Polynesian. Casual Dining. $8-$24 **AAA Inspector Notes:** Guests feel as though they are entering a Hawaiian luau as they arrive at this eatery. In a setting with tiki-adorned walls, thatch roofs and flowers, a wide variety of Hawaiian and Polynesian dishes are served here. On the patio, patrons can sit in personal tiki huts when the weather permits. **Features:** full bar, patio dining. **Address:** 105 S 6th St 83702 **Location:** Jct 6th and Main sts; downtown. **Parking:** street only. [L] [D]

SHIGE JAPANESE CUISINE   208/338-8423   (21)

◆◆ Japanese. Casual Dining. $9-$24 **AAA Inspector Notes:** Boise's original Japanese restaurant is still voted one of the best places for sushi and traditional Japanese cuisine. A variety of bento boxes, rice bowls and maki rolls are available. If fast sashimi is your style, try out Shige Express near the back of the restaurant. **Features:** beer & wine. **Address:** 100 N 8th St, Suite 215 83702 **Location:** At 8th and Main sts; center. **Parking:** street only. [L] [D]

SMOKY MOUNTAIN PIZZERIA GRILL   208/387-2727

◆◆ Italian. Family Dining. $7-$27 **AAA Inspector Notes:** Built into an old house in the city's historic district, this local favorite is adorned with eclectic decor from the past 40 years and is perfect for a family get-together. The patio opens when the weather permits. Worth noticing here are the rotating beer taps and creative seasonal drinks. **Features:** beer & wine. **Address:** 1805 W State St 83702 **Location:** Corner of 18th and State sts; downtown. [L] [D]

SMOKY MOUNTAIN PIZZERIA GRILL   208/429-0011

◆◆ Italian. Casual Dining. $7-$27 **AAA Inspector Notes:** This local favorite is perfect for a family get-together. Be sure to enjoy rotating beer taps, monthly pizza specials and creative seasonal salads and drinks. Gluten-free penne pasta items are available. **Features:** beer & wine, patio dining, happy hour. **Address:** 415 E Parkcenter Blvd 83706 **Location:** I-84 exit 54 (Broadway Ave), 2.4 mi s, then 0.7 mi e on Park Blvd (which becomes Parkcenter Blvd). [L] [D]

STUBS SPORTS PUB   208/336-7882   (41)

◆◆ American. Casual Dining. $5-$13 **AAA Inspector Notes:** Near Boise State University, this family favorite features meals named after well-known sports awards and legends. Sports memorabilia include autographed jerseys, antique ticket stubs and photographs. Diners have fun trying to answer the rotating sports trivia questions posted on the bulletin board. **Features:** beer & wine. **Address:** 3662 Findley Ave 83705 **Location:** I-84 exit 54 (Broadway Ave), just n to Federal Way, just e, then just s. [L] [D] CALL [&M]

TAVERN AT BOWN CROSSING   208/345-2277   (43)

◆◆ American. Casual Dining. $10-$37 **AAA Inspector Notes:** This popular eastside eatery features tasty USDA Prime steak, distinctive sushi rolls and fresh seafood. Enjoy a seat inside among the eclectic décor or, if the weather allows, enjoy the meal on the second floor patio with fire pits and amazing views of the mountains. The pot roast nachos are one of the favored appetizers. **Features:** full bar, patio dining, Sunday brunch. **Reservations:** suggested. **Address:** 3111 S Bown Way 83706 **Location:** I-84 exit 54 (Broadway Ave), 1.7 mi n, 2.3 mi e on Boise Ave, then just n. **Parking:** street only. [L] [D]

TUCANO'S BRAZILIAN GRILL   208/343-5588   (34)

◆◆ Brazilian. Casual Dining. $8-$22 **AAA Inspector Notes:** This eatery serves up fresh cuisine using the Brazilian tradition of grilling (churrasco). Be sure not to fill up on the extensive salad bar, as most entrées feature endless meats. **Features:** full bar. **Reservations:** suggested. **Address:** 1388 S Entertainment Ave 83709 **Location:** I-84 exit 50A eastbound; exit 50B westbound, just w on Overland Blvd. [L] [D] CALL [&M]

WILLOWCREEK GRILL   208/343-5544   (38)

◆◆ American. Casual Dining. $9-$27 **AAA Inspector Notes:** Tasty entrées at this grill include Idaho rib-eye, Atlantic salmon and seared ahi. Most dinners are coupled with Willowcreek twigs, also known as sweet potato fries. **Features:** beer & wine. **Address:** 2273 S Vista Ave, Suite 150 83705 **Location:** I-84 exit 53 (Vista Ave), 1 mi n. [L] [D]

YEN CHING   208/384-0384   (9)

◆◆ Chinese. Family Dining. $7-$17 **AAA Inspector Notes:** Located in the bustling downtown corridor, this popular eatery has been dubbed by locals as having some of the best Chinese food in town. Serving up traditional favorites, the menu features chow mein, egg foo yong, fried rice and a variety of chicken, pork, beef and seafood entrees. **Features:** full bar. **Address:** 305 N 9th St 83702 **Location:** Jct Bannock St; downtown. **Parking:** street only. [D]

ZEPPOLE DOWNTOWN   208/345-2149   (12)

◆ Sandwiches. Quick Serve. $3-$7 **AAA Inspector Notes:** Known for their wide variety of breads made from only the best all-natural and fresh ingredients, this soup and sandwich shop always is bustling during the lunch hour. In addition to sandwiches, their menu offers soups, salads and pastries. All menu items are made fresh daily. **Address:** 217 N 8th St 83702 **Location:** Between Bannock and Idaho sts; downtown. **Parking:** street only. [B] [L] [D]

BOISE NATIONAL FOREST (E-2)

Elevations in the forest range from 2,860 ft. at Lucky Peak Reservoir to 10,751 ft. at Thomason Peak. Refer to AAA maps for additional elevation information.

In south-central Idaho, lakes, abandoned mines and ghost towns amid ponderosa pine and Douglas fir dot the 2,612,000 acres of mountainous terrain that make up the Boise National Forest. Large areas of the forest serve as summer range for big game. Black bears, wolves, mountain goats, bighorn sheep, mule deer and elk inhabit the woods. Upland game birds including chukars, sage grouse, Hungarian partridges and turkeys roam the backcountry.

Salmon, trout and bass thrive in the cold, clear rivers, streams and reservoirs.

Deep canyons, rugged peaks exceeding 9,000 feet and high meadows offer an abundance of recreation opportunities year-round. Cross-country skiing and snowmobiling are popular during the winter. The forest offers more than 900 miles of hiking trails.

Scenic drives wind through the canyons and along the edge of the Sawtooth Wilderness; only trails enter the Frank Church-River of No Return Wilderness in the northeast section. Lake Cascade recreation facilities include camping; phone for more information about special facilities and amenities.

Additional information can be obtained from the Boise National Forest Visitor Center, 1387 S. Vinnell Way, Boise, ID 83709; phone (208) 373-4100, (208) 373-4039 or (208) 373-4007. *See Recreation Areas Chart.*

BONNERS FERRY (A-1) pop. 2,543, elev. 1,773'
• **Restaurants p. 52**

Although trappers David Thompson and Finan McDonald were drawn to the banks of the Kootenai River and established a fur trading post in 1808, it was not until 1864 that a permanent settlement was founded. It was in that year that E.L. Bonner's ferry replaced the canoes of Native Americans, who the previous year had carried gold miners rushing to the Canadian Wild Horse lode.

Trapping and river transportation no longer dominate the commerce of Bonners Ferry; today the town, 25 miles south of Canada, maintains a resource-oriented economy of lumbering and farming.

The mountainous terrain of northern Idaho and the gorge cut by the Kootenai River make the Bonners Ferry region popular for its beauty. Katka View Point, 9 miles east on CR 24, provides a view of the Kootenai Valley, the Selkirk Mountains and the proposed Selkirk Crest National Wilderness area. Another popular and easy-to-reach spot to enjoy mountain scenery is near the junction of US 95 and SR 1.

Greater Bonners Ferry Visitor Center: 6373 Bonner St., Bonners Ferry, ID 83805. **Phone:** (208) 267-5922.

BOUNDARY COUNTY HISTORICAL MUSEUM is at 7229 Main St. Themed exhibit areas showcase Native American and pioneer artifacts, an early post office, a doctor's office, household items, and logging equipment and tools. Historical photos and a digital photo display also are featured. Inside the main hall is a replica of the White Caribou Bar, a Main Street landmark that operated 1905-09 and was known for featuring a mounted white caribou in its storefront window. While the caribou has been at the museum for more than 20 years, it is now back in its rightful place in the bar's window.

Behind the museum, the Historic Railroad Courtyard includes a railway semaphore signal and interpretive plaques describing the three railroads that once served the area. **Time:** Allow 30 minutes minimum. **Hours:** Tues.-Sat. 10-4, Apr.-Sept.; Fri.-Sat. 10-4, rest of year. Closed major holidays. **Cost:** $2. **Phone:** (208) 267-7720.

KOOTENAI NATIONAL WILDLIFE REFUGE is 5 mi. w. on Riverside St. along the south shore of the Kootenai River. Almost 3,000 acres along the river provide feeding, resting and breeding areas for migratory birds. Tundra swans are common in spring; Canada geese and ducks are most numerous in fall. White-tailed and mule deer, moose, black bears and coyotes also use the refuge.

One vehicle route, foot trails and three observation areas are maintained for visitors. **Hours:** Refuge daily dawn-dusk. **Cost:** Free. **Phone:** (208) 267-3888.

GAMBLING ESTABLISHMENTS
• **Kootenai River Inn Casino & Spa** is at 7169 Plaza St. **Hours:** Daily 24 hours. **Phone:** (208) 267-8511 or (800) 346-5668.

BEST WESTERN PLUS KOOTENAI RIVER INN CASINO & SPA   (208)267-8511

Hotel
$129-$179

AAA Benefit: Members save 10% or more with Best Western!

Address: 7169 Plaza St 83805 **Location:** On US 95; City Center. **Facility:** The hotel's restaurant and all guest rooms overlook the Kootenai River. 65 units. 3 stories, interior corridors. **Amenities:** safes. **Pool(s):** heated indoor. **Activities:** sauna, hot tub, game room, exercise room, spa. **Guest Services:** coin laundry.

BONNERS FERRY LOG INN   208/267-3986

Motel
$78-$100

Address: 43 Tobe Way 83805 **Location:** 2.5 mi n on US 95. **Facility:** 22 units. 1 story, exterior corridors. *Bath:* shower only. **Parking:** winter plug-ins. **Activities:** hot tub. **Featured Amenity:** continental breakfast.

NORTHSIDE SCHOOL BED & BREAKFAST   208/267-1826

Historic Boutique Bed & Breakfast $80-$140 **Address:** 6497 Comanche St 83805 **Location:** US 95, w on Chinook St, just n on Bingham St, then just e. Located in a quiet rural area. **Facility:** In a historic schoolhouse, the charming inn's guest rooms are former classrooms and the principal's office, each with a unique theme. 9 units. 2 stories, interior corridors. **Terms:** resort fee. **Pool(s):** heated outdoor. **Activities:** hot tub.

PAPA BYRD'S BISTRO   208/267-0891
♥♥♥ Italian Pizza. Casual Dining. $8-$16 **AAA Inspector Notes:** If you want to take a break from the casino, stop by the bistro, just a short walk using the pedestrian tunnel. A local bakery makes the dough used for the pizza and sandwich bread. The pizza crust is pretty thick (thin crust is available) in order to hold all of the fresh veggies and thick-cut meats. I treated myself to the pecan salad, which was brimming with the in-house spiced pecans. **Features:** beer & wine. **Address:** 6371 Kootenai St 83805 **Location:** Center; in municipal parking lot across from visitor's center. [L] [D]

BRUNEAU (G-2) elev. 2,525'

Bruneau, the French name first given the brown-water river that skirts the northern edge of the Great Basin Desert, was founded by 19th-century French-Canadian trappers.

BRUNEAU CANYON OVERLOOK is 15 mi. s.e. via a paved and gravel road, then 3 mi. w. on a dirt road, following signs. The Bruneau River courses through a narrow canyon whose vertical walls consist of layers of volcanic rhyolite and basalt that are 800 feet high in places. The overlook provides a panoramic vista of this deep and rugged canyon.

BRUNEAU DUNES STATE PARK is 5 mi. n. on SR 51/78, then 2 mi. e. on SR 78 to 27608 Sand Dunes Rd. Windblown sands have collected in this swale for about 15,000 years. The relatively constant winds have formed what is said to be the tallest single-structured sand dune in North America; its peak towers 470 feet above a shallow lake at its base.

A visitor center features natural history displays, while The Bruneau Observatory, one of the largest public facilities of its kind in the Northwest, boasts a 25-inch reflector telescope. *See Recreation Areas Chart.*

Interpretive programs are available by appointment. **Note:** Summer temperatures in the park occasionally reach 110 F, and winter lows can fall below zero. Walking on the dunes is permitted, but vehicles must stay on the roads at all times. **Time:** Allow 1 hour minimum. **Hours:** Park open daily 7 a.m.-10 p.m. Visitor center open daily 9-5, Apr. 1 to mid-Oct.; hours vary rest of year. Observatory open Fri.-Sat. 7 p.m.-midnight, mid-Mar. to mid-Oct. Visitor center closed winter holidays. **Cost:** Park admission $5 (per private vehicle). Observatory $3; free (ages 0-5). **Phone:** (208) 366-7919.

C.J. STRIKE DAM AND RESERVOIR is n.w. via SR 78 on the Snake River. The 7,500-acre reservoir offers opportunities for boating, swimming and fishing. *See Recreation Areas Chart.* Guided tours are available by appointment and must be scheduled at least 1 week in advance of your visit. **Hours:** Daily 24 hours. **Cost:** Day-use access free. Camping Apr.-Oct. $8 (tent); $10 (RV). Camping rest of year $4 (tent); $5 (RV). **Phone:** (208) 388-6691 Mon.-Fri. 8-4, or (208) 736-3458 for tour appointments.

BUHL (H-3) pop. 4,122, elev. 3,800'

Buhl (BEWL) is on the Snake River, at the western end of a valley that grew little but sagebrush until 1906, when irrigation transformed the desert into lush farmland. Agriculture and aquaculture are the bases of Buhl's present economy. Tourism and the raising of sheep and beef and dairy cattle are important. The surrounding area produces barley, sugar beets, corn, dry beans, alfalfa, grains, sugar snap peas, seed crops and potatoes.

Buhl is said to be the rainbow trout capital of the United States, since the town is a leader in trout research and production. Trout farms raise and process rainbow trout that are shipped throughout the world; similar farms produce catfish, tilapia and salmon. The products of dirt farms and local craftsmen are available Wednesday 4:30-6 p.m., mid-July through early October, at the farmers market in the parking lot of the senior citizens' center at 1010 Main St.

An oddity of nature called the Balanced Rock can be seen by taking a short drive south to Castleford, then 6 miles west. The 40-foot-high rock is perched on a base only a few feet in diameter.

Buhl Chamber of Commerce: 716 US 30E, Buhl, ID 83316. **Phone:** (208) 543-6682.

BURLEY (H-4) pop. 10,345, elev. 4,165'

Hydroplanes, super stock and other powerful racing craft churn up Burley's Snake River waterfront during the month of June, when such national speedboat championships as the Idaho Regatta take place.

CASSIA COUNTY HISTORICAL SOCIETY MUSEUM, E. Main St. and Hiland Ave., contains collections of fossils; an early railroad car and caboose; local history items; a World War II exhibit; and tools and wagons of the miners, trappers, loggers and farmers who settled southern Idaho. Audiovisual displays chart the pioneer trails that led emigrants to the Pacific Northwest.

On the museum grounds are a replica sheepherder's wagon and furnished reproductions of a one-room cabin, a general store, a schoolhouse and a barbershop. **Time:** Allow 1 hour minimum. **Hours:** Tues.-Sat. 10-5, Apr. 15-Oct. 31. Closed major holidays. **Cost:** Donations. **Phone:** (208) 678-7172.

BEST WESTERN PLUS BURLEY INN & CONVENTION CENTER (208)678-3501

Hotel
$75-$100

AAA Benefit: Members save 10% or more with Best Western!

Address: 800 N Overland Ave 83318 **Location:** I-84 exit 208, just s. **Facility:** 124 units. 2 stories (no elevator), interior/exterior corridors. **Pool(s):** heated outdoor. **Activities:** hot tub, exercise room. **Guest Services:** valet and coin laundry.

FAIRFIELD INN & SUITES BY MARRIOTT (208)677-5000

Hotel
$94-$124

FAIRFIELD INN & SUITES Marriott.

AAA Benefit: Members save 5% or more!

Address: 230 W 7th St N 83318 **Location:** I-84 exit 208, just sw. **Facility:** 81 units. 3 stories, interior corridors. **Pool(s):** heated indoor. **Activities:** hot tub, exercise room. **Guest Services:** valet and coin laundry.

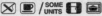

SUPER 8 BURLEY (208)678-7000

Hotel
$75-$116

Address: 336 S 600 W 83318 **Location:** I-84 exit 208, just n. **Facility:** 68 units. 3 stories, interior corridors. **Pool(s):** heated indoor. **Activities:** hot tub, exercise room. **Guest Services:** coin laundry. **Featured Amenity: continental breakfast.** *(See ad this page.)*

STEVO'S   208/679-3887
▼▼ American. Casual Dining. $6-$20 AAA Inspector Notes: In addition to popular burgers and sandwiches, this family-run restaurant offers thick lamb chops, juicy steaks, seven different types of Idaho super spuds and homemade pies. Features: beer & wine. Address: 290 S 600 W 83336 Location: I-84 exit 208, 0.3 mi n.
L D

CALDWELL (F-1) pop. 46,237, elev. 2,367'

On the Boise River, Caldwell was established in the late 19th century. The community, which began as a construction camp for the Oregon Short Line Railroad, is now associated with the processing and distribution of farm products. Boone Science Hall, near the corner of 20th and Fillmore streets on the 800-student College of Idaho campus, houses the Orma J. Smith Museum of Natural History, the Evans Gem and Mineral Collection and the Whittenberger Planetarium; phone (208) 459-5211.

Caldwell Chamber of Commerce: 704 Blaine St., Caldwell, ID 83606. **Phone:** (208) 459-7493.

WINERIES

• **Ste. Chapelle Winery** is 8 mi. s.w. on SR 55, then .5 mi. e., following signs. **Hours:** Mon.-Sat. 10-5, Sun. noon-5. Closed Easter, Thanksgiving and Christmas. **Phone:** (208) 453-7843.

BEST WESTERN PLUS CALDWELL INN & SUITES
                                       (208)454-7225
▼▼▼
Hotel
$74-$99

AAA Benefit: Members save 10% or more with Best Western!

Address: 908 Specht Ave 83605 Location: I-84 exit 29, just s. Across from truck stop. **Facility:** 69 units. 3 stories, interior corridors. **Pool(s):** heated indoor. **Activities:** hot tub, exercise room. **Guest Services:** valet and coin laundry.

LA QUINTA INN CALDWELL   (208)454-2222
▼▼ Hotel $72-$120 Address: 901 Specht Ave 83605 Location: I-84 exit 29, just s. Facility: 65 units, some kitchens. 3 stories (no elevator), interior corridors. Pool(s): heated indoor. Activities: hot tub, exercise room. Guest Services: coin laundry.

WILD ROSE MANOR BED & BREAKFAST   (208)454-3331
▼▼▼ Bed & Breakfast $139-$189 Address: 5800 Oasis Rd 83607 Location: I-84 exit 17 (Sand Hollow), just w, then 0.5 mi n, follow signs. Facility: This picturesque property offers beautifully appointed and themed guest rooms and is perfect for a single special night or a three-day weekend. 4 units. 2 stories (no elevator), interior corridors. Terms: check-in 4 pm, 3 day cancellation notice. Activities: hot tub.

MR. V'S FAMILY RESTAURANT   208/454-9778
▼▼ American. Family Dining. $7-$15 AAA Inspector Notes: Serving up traditional American favorites for more than 30 years, this family diner provides home-style favorites including pot roast, chicken-fried steak and roasted turkey, along with the friendliness and charm of a small town diner. Address: 407 N 10th Ave 83605 Location: I-84 exit 28 (10th Ave), just s. B L D

CAMBRIDGE (F-1) pop. 328, elev. 2,739'

CAMBRIDGE MUSEUM, jct. US 95 and SR 71, provides information about area heritage, from the arrival of the first settlers in 1869 through the 1930s. Displays focus on geology, farming, Native American life and the community's pioneer days. A blacksmith shop and a replica schoolroom with historical items can be seen. A reproduction of a mine entrance features illustrations demonstrating dynamiting techniques.

A genealogy library is available by appointment. **Time:** Allow 30 minutes minimum. **Hours:** Museum Wed.-Sat. 10-4, June-Aug. Phone ahead to confirm schedule. **Cost:** Donations. **Phone:** (208) 257-3485.

RECREATIONAL ACTIVITIES
White-water Rafting

• **Hughes River Expeditions** departs from various locations depending on trip. **Hours:** Schedule varies; phone ahead. **Phone:** (208) 257-3477 or (800) 262-1882.

• **ROW Adventures** departs from the Frontier Motel at 240 S. Superior St. **Hours:** Snake River trips are offered May-Sept. Schedule varies; phone ahead. **Phone:** (208) 765-0841 or (800) 451-6034.

CARIBOU-TARGHEE NATIONAL FOREST (F-5)

Elevations in the forest range from 4,700 ft. at Curlew Campground to 12,197 ft. at Diamond Peak. Refer to AAA maps for additional elevation information.

In southeast Idaho extending into Wyoming and Utah, Caribou-Targhee National Forest covers more than 3 million acres. The Caribou unit is noted for rugged scenery marked by towering mountain ranges and beautiful valleys. Drives along the Snake River and through the many canyons provide scenic vistas. A few traces of the ghost towns of Keenan and Caribou City recall the gold rush days.

Named for Tygee, a Bannock Indian chief, the Targhee section is in the Lemhi, Beaverhead, Teton, Centennial, Palisades and Caribou ranges and extends in a semicircle around the headwaters of Henry's Fork of the Snake River. The Continental Divide forms most of the northern boundary; Yellowstone and Grand Teton national parks make up most of the eastern border. Canyons, high peaks and desert add to the picturesque scenery.

Minnetonka Cave (see St. Charles p. 93) in St. Charles Canyon is one of two accessible caves and features interesting geological formations. Ice never melts in Paris Cave, a small, undeveloped cave in nearby Paris Canyon.

Water is abundant throughout the Targhee. Big Springs, one of the largest springs in the United States, is reached by SR 59 from US 20 at Macks Inn. It issues from the base of a high plateau at a constant 52 F and is the headwaters of Henry's Fork, which is the north fork of the Snake River.

A 3- to 5-hour canoe/float trip can be taken along a 5-mile national recreation water trail just below Big Springs. Moose, trumpeter swans, ospreys and bald eagles can often be seen. Further down Henry's Fork, boaters must portage around several sections of dangerous water between Macks Inn and Ashton.

Upper and Lower Mesa falls are east of US 20 and north of Ashton on Mesa Falls Scenic Byway. The Upper Mesa Falls is 114 feet high; the Lower Mesa Falls is 65 to 70 feet high.

Trout fishing is excellent, most notably at Palisades Reservoir, Henry's Lake, Island Park Reservoir, Henry's Fork and South Fork of the Snake River.

Winter sports activity areas near Ashton, Driggs, Helse, Island Park, Montpelier and Pocatello contain miles of groomed snowmobile and cross-country skiing trails as well as downhill ski resorts. More than 1,100 miles of hiking, horse and mountain bike trails provide a variety of summer backcountry experiences.

Camping is available from Memorial Day weekend to Labor Day (weather permitting). Fees for developed camping areas range from $10 to $36 at single-family campgrounds, depending on the level of service at each facility. Group camping facilities also are available. Phone (877) 444-6777 for campsite reservations.

Brochures are available at the visitor center, 420 Memorial Dr. in Idaho Falls, open year-round. For more information contact the Forest Supervisor's Office, Caribou-Targhee National Forest, 1405 Hollipark Dr., Idaho Falls, ID 83401; phone (208) 524-7500. See Recreation Areas Chart.

CASCADE (F-2) pop. 939

Though logging has historically been an important industry for Cascade, tourism has increasingly contributed to the local economy. The town is a jumping-off point for travel to millions of acres of mountainous backcountry and wilderness, where snowmobiling and Nordic skiing are popular cold weather pursuits.

In addition, the community is located in Long Valley near the southern end of Lake Cascade, a 30,000-acre reservoir formed in 1948. Boating, sailing, kayaking, water skiing and some of the state's best perch fishing can be enjoyed on the body of water, and in winter, ice fishing is added to the long list of recreational activities. Lake Cascade State Park, 4,450 acres off SR 55, offers camping facilities and six boat ramps (see Recreation Areas Chart).

Cascade Chamber of Commerce: P.O. Box 571, Cascade, ID 83611. Phone: (208) 382-3833.

KELLY'S WHITEWATER PARK is 1 mi. s. on SR 55. Stretching along 1,800 feet of the Payette River, the park features four sets of rapids suitable for kayaking, tubing and stand-up paddling enthusiasts of all ages and skill levels. A sloping lawn offers the perfect spot to dry off after a run on the river. Also on-site is a welcome center with changing displays that showcase various aspects of Valley County. Time: Allow 30 minutes minimum. Hours: Sun.-Fri. 10-8, Sat. 9-8, Memorial Day weekend-Labor Day. Phone: (208) 405-3000. 🍴 ☂

THE ASHLEY INN   (208)382-5621
▼▼▼ Boutique Hotel $132-$308 Address: 500 N Main St 83611 Location: 0.3 mi n of center on SR 55 (Main St). Facility: Located along a riverbend with panoramic mountain views, this well-appointed boutique-style hotel features a nice selection of themed-guest rooms, each with a fireplace. 67 units. 3 stories, interior corridors. Parking: winter plug-ins. Terms: cancellation fee imposed. Pool(s): heated indoor. Activities: hot tub, lawn sports, picnic facilities, exercise room. Guest Services: coin laundry.
🛗 CALL 🔒M 🛍 ℍⓈ 🛜 ✕ 🖥 / SOME UNITS 🎁 🖿

CATALDO (B-1) elev. 2,150'

COEUR D'ALENE'S OLD MISSION STATE PARK, off I-90 exit 39, is named for the restored Old Sacred Heart Mission, built 1848-53 by Coeur d'Alene Indians under the guidance of Jesuit priest Father Antonio Ravalli. It is reputedly the oldest standing structure in the state. The 18-inch-thick mission walls were built of woven grass and adobe mud without nails. The Sacred Encounters exhibit documents the meeting of the Jesuit missionaries and the Coeur d'Alene and Salish tribes and the effects the encounter had on both cultures.

Video presentations, mission tours and a visitor center are available. The park also is the headquarters for the state-run portion of the Trail of the Coeur d'Alenes; the 56-mile section runs between Mullan and Harrison. See Recreation Areas Chart. Hours: Daily 9-5, Apr.-Oct.; 10-3, rest of year. Closed Jan. 1, Thanksgiving and Christmas. Cost: Park admission $5 (per private vehicle). Sacred Encounters exhibit $5; $10 (family). Phone: (208) 682-3814.
✕ 🐾 ☂

CHALLIS (F-3) pop. 1,081, elev. 5,288'

LAND OF THE YANKEE FORK STATE PARK AND HISTORIC AREA has its interpretive center at jct. US 93 and SR 75. The center offers dioramas, artifacts and photographs of the mines and miners 1870-1920 as well as an audiovisual program about mining and ghost town history.

A 91-mile scenic loop, the Custer Motorway Adventure Road (FR 70), begins in Challis on a narrow, gravel and dirt road, and runs past stage stations, ghost towns and abandoned mines, the Yankee Fork Gold Dredge, the Custer Museum and Sunbeam Dam Interpretive Site. The loop's return road is paved SR 75 (the Salmon River Scenic Byway). Several recreational trails offer opportunities for hiking and biking; some are open to all-terrain vehicles and motorbikes. Bayhorse, a ghost town noted for its former silver mines, is a trailhead for a system of motorcycle/ATV trails. Access is via a well-maintained gravel road that accommodates trailers and motorhomes about 4 miles off SR 75.

Note: The Custer Motorway Adventure Road is not recommended for vehicles with low clearance, trailers or motor homes. Inquire locally for road conditions. Allow 30 minutes for the interpretive center. Allow 3 hours for the loop. **Hours:** Interpretive center open daily 9-5, May-Oct.; Wed.-Sat. 10-4, rest of year. The Custer Motorway Adventure Road is closed by snow late Oct. 1 to mid-June (weather permitting). Yankee Fork Gold Dredge open for tours Memorial Day-Labor Day. Custer Museum open Memorial Day-Labor Day. **Cost:** Park, interpretive centers and museum $2; $5 (family). Trails or ghost town $5. Gold dredge tour $5; $1 (ages 6-12). **Phone:** (208) 879-5244 or (208) 838-2529. 🎣

CHALLIS NATIONAL FOREST—See
Salmon-Challis National Forest p. 94.

CLARK FORK (B-1) pop. 536, elev. 2,084'

Clark Fork lies at the foot of the Cabinet Mountains, just northeast of Lake Pend Oreille. The town is on the lake's main tributary, the Clark Fork River, just before it flows into the lake. This location experiences unusually warm winters and cool summers.

The town sprang up in the 1880s when the main line of the Northern Pacific Railroad cut through the Bitterroot and Cabinet mountains. The railroad made lumbering profitable, and lumberjacks began arriving on the area's first steam tugboats. Soon nearby trappers were giving up their trade and joining the timber camps. Today the area attracts hikers, anglers and other outdoor enthusiasts.

Lake Pend Oreille is a focal point of the Pend Oreille Scenic Byway (SR 200), which runs northwest from the Montana border to Sandpoint.

Hope, Clark Fork & Trestle Creek Chamber of Commerce: 310 E. Fourth St., P.O. Box 159, Clark Fork, ID 83811. **Phone:** (208) 266-1800.

CABINET GORGE DAM, 8 mi. e. on SR 200, on the Clark Fork River, is a horseshoe-shaped dam in a scenic setting. A lookout point affords an excellent view of the project. **Hours:** Viewpoint open Apr.-Sept. (weather permitting).

CABINET GORGE HATCHERY, 8 mi. s.e. on River Rd., then n. on Cabinet Gorge Rd. following signs, raises up to 16 million kokanee salmon annually for release into Lake Pend Oreille in June. Self-guiding tours provide opportunities to see salmon and other fish species in various stages of development. Viewing is best November through June. **Tours:** Guided tours are available. **Time:** Allow 30 minutes minimum. **Hours:** Daily 8-4. Closed Jan. 1, Thanksgiving and Christmas. Phone ahead to confirm schedule. **Cost:** Free. **Phone:** (208) 266-1431.

CLARKIA (C-1)

The area surrounding Clarkia (CLAR-key) is rich in gemstones, particularly star garnets and fossils. Fossil digging is permitted at the Clarkia Miocene Site, south on SR 3.

EMERALD CREEK GARNET AREA is 7 mi. n. on SR 3, then 8 mi. w. on gravel FR 447. A .5-mile uphill trail leads to 281 Gulch, one of only two places in the world where star garnets exist (the other is in India). Visitors sluice for the 12-sided crystals using buckets, shovels and screen boxes furnished onsite. **Time:** Allow 2 hours minimum. **Hours:** Fri.-Tues. 9-5, Memorial Day weekend-Labor Day. **Cost:** $10; $5 (ages 6-12). **Phone:** (208) 245-2531 or (208) 245-1134. 🏕

CLEARWATER NATIONAL FOREST (C-2)

Elevations in the forest range from 1,200 ft. to 8,820 ft. at Ranger Peak. Refer to AAA maps for additional elevation information.

In the northeastern part of the state, large stands of tall trees and many miles of clear, fast-running streams and rivers characterize the rugged, mountainous Clearwater National Forest. Scenic Lewis and Clark Highway (US 12) runs a few miles south of but roughly parallel to the Lolo Trail, the Native American route across the Bitterroots to buffalo-hunting country.

A portion of the Selway-Bitterroot Wilderness, the second largest wilderness area in the continental United States, makes up part of Clearwater's 1.8 million acres. US 12 follows the rugged Lochsa Wild and Scenic River, where kayak and raft enthusiasts challenge the stream's white water. Recreation information is available at ranger stations in Kooskia, Orofino, Potlatch and Powell.

Lolo Pass Visitors Center, along US 12 at the crest of the Bitterroots on the Idaho-Montana border, and the restored Lochsa Historical Ranger Station, halfway between Powell and Kooskia on US 12, are open Memorial Day weekend through September 30. For further information contact the Supervisor's Office, Clearwater National Forest, 12730 US 12, Orofino, ID 83544; phone (208) 476-4541. *See Recreation Areas Chart.*

COEUR D'ALENE (B-1) pop. 44,137,
elev. 2,157'
• Restaurants p. 59

The largest city in northern Idaho takes its name from the local tribe of Native Americans. French trappers dubbed them Coeur d'Alene (CORE-dah-LANE), meaning "heart of the awl," a vernacular phrase describing them as shrewd traders.

Gen. William Tecumseh Sherman established an Army post in 1878 at the point where the Spokane River drains Lake Coeur d'Alene. Fort Sherman became the nucleus of a settlement that was named for the lake. The 1880s mining boom in the Silver Valley brought prosperity, as Coeur d'Alene became an important shipping point. For a period it was the busiest steamboat port west of the Mississippi River. By 1900 boats were carrying tourists on excursion cruises.

North Idaho College now occupies the old fort site, and Fort Sherman Chapel survives at the corner of Hubbard Street and Woodland Drive. The community college has an enrollment of 4,600; phone (208) 769-3300.

Idaho's "Lake City" remains a popular resort. In summer the city's beaches, parks and docks throng with outdoor enthusiasts. Boating, houseboating, swimming, water skiing, parasailing and fishing are popular activities.

Downtown on the shores of Lake Coeur d'Alene is forested Tubbs Hill, a 120-acre preserve featuring trails to secluded coves and beaches, and to the summit for panoramic views. Also along the waterfront, The Coeur d'Alene Resort Golf Course is a par 71 distinguished by its floating, 15,000-square-foot island green; phone (208) 667-4653 or (800) 935-6283.

What is said to be the world's longest floating boardwalk runs 3,300 feet from Independence Point in City Park to the foot of Third Street, around The Coeur d'Alene Resort. The park offers a large public beach as well as a playground designed after Fort Sherman. Here, walkers, bicyclists and skaters also find access to the North Idaho Centennial Trail. The paved pathway extends 24 miles from Higgens Point, east of Coeur d'Alene, west to the Idaho/Washington border, where it connects with Spokane's Centennial Trail.

Coeur d'Alene Visitor Bureau: 105 N. 1st St., Suite 100, Coeur d'Alene, ID 83814. **Phone:** (208) 664-3194 or (877) 782-9232.

Shopping areas: Silver Lake Mall, 3.5 miles north on US 95, offers JCPenney, Macy's and Sears. Antiques can be found at Coeur d'Alene Antique Mall, 408 Haycraft, and at Government Way Antique Mall, 3650 N. Government Way.

HUMAN RIGHTS EDUCATION INSTITUTE is at 414 W. Mullan Rd. in the historic 1902 Spokane & Inland Empire Electric Railway substation building in the northeast corner of Coeur d'Alene City Park. The cultural organization educates and raises awareness about various human rights issues; its exhibit galleries host changing displays that support these goals. The Peace Lives Here Gallery showcases artwork illustrating human rights principles and responsibilities. Interactive activities for children, including arts and crafts projects and story time sessions, are offered.

Tours: Guided tours are available. **Time:** Allow 30 minutes minimum. **Hours:** Mon.-Fri. 10-5, Sat. 10-2. Closed major holidays. **Cost:** Free. **Phone:** (208) 292-2359.

LAKE COEUR D'ALENE is s. of town. Once called one of the five most beautiful lakes in the world by *National Geographic*, it is surrounded by mountains and a lush forest. Twenty-five miles long, it averages 2.5 miles in width and has a 135-mile-long shoreline. It has one of the nation's largest populations of osprey, and bald eagles can be seen diving into the lake to catch salmon in winter. Power boating, sailing and fishing are popular summer sports.

LAKE COEUR D'ALENE CRUISES departs from the Coeur d'Alene city dock at Independence Point. A 90-minute, narrated lake cruise provides glimpses of wildlife and local scenery. Brunch, sunset, full-day and other cruises also are available. **Time:** Allow 2 hours minimum. **Hours:** Narrated lake cruises depart daily, late Apr.-late Oct. Departure times vary; phone ahead. **Cost:** $22.75; $20.75 (ages 55+); $14.75 (ages 6-12). **Phone:** (208) 765-4000, ext. 21.

MUSEUM OF NORTH IDAHO, 115 Northwest Blvd., explores the history of the Coeur d'Alene region. Exhibits about exploration, transportation, early settlers, firefighting, logging and lumbering are included. Rotating seasonal exhibits and a 20-minute video presentation relating the history of the Coeur d'Alene region also are offered. **Time:** Allow 30 minutes minimum. **Hours:** Tues.-Sat. 11-5, Apr.-Oct. Closed July 4. **Cost:** $3; $1 (ages 6-16); $7 (family, two adults and children ages 0-16). **Phone:** (208) 664-3448.

SILVERWOOD—see Athol p. 35.

RECREATIONAL ACTIVITIES
White-water Rafting

- **ROW Adventures** offers trips on the Grande Ronde, Owyhee and Snake rivers from various departure points. **Hours:** Trips are offered mid-May to mid-Sept. Schedule varies; phone ahead. **Phone:** (208) 765-0841 or (800) 451-6034.

THE COEUR D'ALENE RESORT   (208)765-4000

▼▼▼ ▼▼ Resort Hotel $129-$549 Address: 115 S 2nd St 83814 Location: Waterfront. I-90 exit 11 (Northwest Blvd), 2 mi s. Facility: Dominating the lake shore is this luxury resort, where you'll find lavishly decorated guest rooms, admirable service and stunning landscaped grounds. 338 units. 18 stories, interior/exterior corridors. Parking: on-site (fee) and valet. Terms: check-in 4 pm, 3 day cancellation notice-fee imposed. Amenities: video games. Some: safes. Dining: 5 restaurants, also, Beverly's, see separate listing, entertainment. Pool(s): heated outdoor, heated indoor. Activities: sauna, hot tub, steamroom, marina, fishing, regulation golf, tennis, recreation programs, bicycles, exercise room, spa. Guest Services: valet laundry, area transportation. Affiliated with A Preferred Hotel.

[icons] / SOME UNITS [icons]

COMFORT INN COEUR D'ALENE   (208)664-1649

▼▼ ▼▼ Hotel $63-$284 Address: 2303 N 4th St 83814 Location: I-90 exit 13 (4th St), just n. Facility: 69 units. 3 stories, interior corridors. Pool(s): heated indoor. Activities: hot tub. Guest Services: valet and coin laundry.

[icons] / SOME UNITS [icons]

DAYS INN-COEUR D'ALENE   (208)667-8668

▼▼ ▼▼ Hotel $65-$200 Address: 2200 Northwest Blvd 83814 Location: I-90 exit 11 (Northwest Blvd), just se. Located in a business park. Facility: 63 units, some efficiencies. 2 stories (no elevator), interior corridors. Parking: winter plug-ins. Amenities: safes. Activities: hot tub, exercise room. Guest Services: coin laundry.

CALL [icons] / SOME UNITS [icons]

FLAMINGO MOTEL   208/664-2159

▼▼ ▼▼ Motel $110-$180 Address: 718 E Sherman Ave 83814 Location: I-90 exit 15 (Sherman Ave), 1.1 mi s. Adjacent to city park. Facility: 13 units, some two bedrooms and kitchens. 1 story, exterior corridors. Terms: cancellation fee imposed.

[icons]

HAMPTON INN & SUITES COEUR D'ALENE   (208)769-7900

▼▼▼ ▼▼ Hotel $129-$249 Address: 1500 Riverstone Dr 83814 Location: I-90 exit 11 (Northwest Blvd), just sw. Facility: 124 units. 5 stories, interior corridors. Terms: 1-7 night minimum stay, cancellation fee imposed. Amenities: video games. Pool(s): heated indoor. Activities: hot tub, exercise room. Guest Services: valet and coin laundry.

AAA Benefit: Members save up to 10%!

[icons]

HOLIDAY INN EXPRESS HOTEL & SUITES COEUR D'ALENE
(208)667-3100

▼▼▼ ▼▼ Hotel $99-$300 Address: 2300 W Seltice Way 83814 Location: I-90 exit 11 (Northwest Blvd), just s. Facility: 101 units. 3 stories, interior/exterior corridors. Amenities: video games. Pool(s): heated indoor. Activities: hot tub, exercise room. Guest Services: valet and coin laundry.

[icons] / SOME UNITS [icons]

JAPAN HOUSE SUITES   (208)667-0600

▼▼ ▼▼ Hotel $69-$179 Address: 2113 E Sherman Ave 83814 Location: I-90 exit 15 (Sherman Ave), just s. Facility: 22 units. 2 stories (no elevator), interior corridors. Terms: cancellation fee imposed. [icons]

LA QUINTA INN & SUITES COEUR D'ALENE EAST
(208)667-6777

▼▼ ▼▼ Hotel $79-$184 Address: 2209 E Sherman Ave 83814 Location: I-90 exit 15 (Sherman Ave), just s. Facility: 62 units, some kitchens. 3 stories (no elevator), interior corridors. Pool(s): heated indoor. Activities: hot tub, exercise room. Guest Services: valet and coin laundry.

CALL [icons] / SOME UNITS [icons]

LA QUINTA INN COEUR D'ALENE APPLEWAY   (208)765-5500

▼▼ ▼▼ Hotel $79-$180 Address: 280 W Appleway Ave 83814 Location: I-90 exit 12, just ne. Facility: 51 units, some two bedrooms, efficiencies and kitchens. 3 stories (no elevator), interior corridors. Pool(s): heated indoor. Activities: hot tub, playground, exercise room. Guest Services: valet and coin laundry.

[icons] CALL [icons] / SOME UNITS [icons]

RESORT CITY INN   (208)676-1225
▼▼▼
Motel
$89-$129

Address: 621 Sherman Ave 83814 Location: I-90 exit 11 (Northwest Blvd), 2.5 mi e via Northwest Blvd and Sherman Ave; downtown. Facility: 18 units, some efficiencies. 2 stories (no elevator), exterior corridors. Terms: 3 day cancellation notice-fee imposed. Featured Amenity: continental breakfast.

[icons]

▼ See AAA listing p. 57 ▼

THE ROOSEVELT INN AND SPA
208/765-5200

WWWW **Historic Bed & Breakfast.** Rates not provided. **Address:** 105 E Wallace Ave 83814 **Location:** I-90 exit 13 (4th St), 2 mi s, then just w; downtown. **Facility:** Overshadowed by towering pines, The Roosevelt is housed in a converted 1905 red-brick schoolhouse complete with a bell tower. The three-story building hosted classes as recently as the 1960s. 12 units, some two bedrooms. 3 stories, interior corridors. **Activities:** sauna, hot tub, limited exercise equipment, massage.

[icons] BIZ ⊗ ✕ ♨ ⌐ / SOME UNITS 🐾

SHILO INN SUITES - COEUR D'ALENE
208/664-2300

WWW **Hotel.** Rates not provided. **Address:** 702 W Appleway Ave 83814 **Location:** I-90 exit 12, just n, then just w. **Facility:** 138 units. 4 stories, interior corridors. **Terms:** check-in 4 pm. **Amenities:** video games. **Pool(s):** heated indoor. **Activities:** sauna, hot tub, steamroom, exercise room. **Guest Services:** valet and coin laundry.

[icons] CALL M 🏊 BIZ ⊗ ✕ 🎥 🔲 / SOME UNITS 🐾

SPRINGHILL SUITES BY MARRIOTT COEUR D'ALENE
208/667-2212

[fyi] Not evaluated. **Address:** 2250 W Seltice Way 83814 **Location:** I-90 exit 11 (Northwest Blvd), just s. Facilities, services, and décor characterize a midscale property.

AAA Benefit: Members save 5% or more!

WHERE TO EAT

BARDENAY
208/765-1540

WW WW **American. Gastropub.** $7-$25 **AAA Inspector Notes:** The emphasis at this place is cocktails and microbrews, so I was skeptical that I could get a good meal. I was so wrong—ordering the spinach salad topped with grilled salmon turned out to be an excellent choice. The salmon was cooked perfectly with a light crust and juicy inside. A wall of windows overlooks the pond in Riverstone Village and there is a patio for al fresco dining. There is an age restriction after 10 pm, adults only. **Features:** full bar, patio dining, happy hour. **Address:** 1710 W Riverstone Dr 83814 **Location:** I-90 exit 11 (Northwest Blvd), just sw. L D

THE BEACHHOUSE
208/664-6464

WW WW **American. Casual Dining.** $11-$38 **AAA Inspector Notes:** This eatery offers excellent views of the lake and marina, creating somewhat of a boathouse ambience. Breaded halibut with Parmesan cheese, garlic mashed potatoes and a veggie medley is a signature dish, but there also is a full menu of steak and barbecue. The freestanding fireplace warms guests as they enjoy the views of the lake and marina. **Reservations:** suggested. **Address:** 3204 E Coeur d'Alene Lake Dr 83814 **Location:** I-90 exit 15 (Sherman Ave), just s, then 1 mi e. D

BEVERLY'S
208/765-4000

WWWWW **Pacific Rim. Fine Dining.** $10-$55 **AAA Inspector Notes:** The restaurant serves tantalizing food in a sleek, casually elegant dining room with panoramic views of pristine Lake Coeur d'Alene from its seventh-floor perch. The seasonal menu takes advantage of the freshest Northwest seafood and local produce and complementing the dining experience is one of the finest wine cellars in the world. **Features:** full bar. **Reservations:** suggested. **Address:** 115 S 2nd St 83814 **Location:** I-90 exit 11 (Northwest Blvd), 2 mi s; in The Coeur d'Alene Resort. **Parking:** on-site (fee). L D CALL M

BONSAI BISTRO
208/765-4321

WWWW **Asian. Fine Dining.** $8-$36 **AAA Inspector Notes:** The stylish Asian-inspired dining room ambles over two levels. On the lower level, some tables surround a koi pond, while outdoor seats are set amid rockwork and water features. The wide array of Asian dishes and sushi affords something for every taste. **Features:** full bar. **Address:** 101 E Sherman Ave 83814 **Location:** Downtown. L D

THE BREAKFAST NOOK
208/667-1699

WW WW **American. Family Dining.** $5-$10 **AAA Inspector Notes:** Serving up favorites including steak and eggs, eggs Benedict and waffles, this popular breakfast joint is frequented by locals and tourists alike. Burgers and sandwiches are offered during the lunch hour. Expect a wait during peak dining times. **Address:** 1719 N 4th St 83814 **Location:** I-90 exit 13 (4th St), 0.4 mi s on 3rd St, then just e on Poplar Ave. B L CALL M

THE CEDARS FLOATING RESTAURANT
208/664-2922

WWWW **Steak Seafood. Casual Dining.** $23-$69 **AAA Inspector Notes:** This seafood and steak restaurant floats on Lake Coeur d'Alene. Large windows offer expansive views of the lake and forest. The house specialty is Biergarten steak, a filet mignon basted with beer. **Features:** full bar, patio dining. **Reservations:** suggested. **Address:** 1 Marina Dr 83814 **Location:** I-90 exit 12, 1.5 mi s on US 95. D

CRICKET'S RESTAURANT & OYSTER BAR
208/765-1990

WWW **American. Casual Dining.** $10-$24 **AAA Inspector Notes:** A model train running on an overhead track contributes to the eclectic décor of this fun and lively establishment. The oyster bar offers up many variations for the oyster lover. Try the Port rib-eye with mushrooms or the homemade pizza. **Features:** full bar, patio dining. **Reservations:** suggested, in summer. **Address:** 424 Sherman Ave 83814 **Location:** Downtown. **Parking:** street only. L D

JAPAN HOUSE RESTAURANT
208/676-8889

WWWW **Japanese. Fine Dining.** $10-$25 **AAA Inspector Notes:** The stylish restaurant features authentic Japanese cuisine, including excellent nigiri sushi. **Features:** beer & wine. **Address:** 605 W Appleway Ave 83814 **Location:** I-90 exit 12, just n, then just w. D

JAVA ON SHERMAN
208/667-0010

WW **Coffee/Tea. Quick Serve.** $5-$10 **AAA Inspector Notes:** This spot offers only fair trade certified organic coffee and homemade baked goods, soups, and entrées. Try the lumpy muffins or apple, Brie and ham panini for lunch. This casual eccentric café is perfect for all types of diners. Happy hour menu is served after 4 pm. **Address:** 324 Sherman Ave 83814 **Location:** Downtown. **Parking:** street only. B L D

MOON TIME
208/667-2331

WW WW **American. Casual Dining.** $8-$14 **AAA Inspector Notes:** This informal restaurant has the feel of a neighborhood pub, complete with dartboards. With dishes ranging from gumbo and burritos to Caribbean pork sandwiches and vegetarian Anasazi bean burgers, the food is as eclectic as the restaurant itself. For something light, try the barbecue chicken quesadillas. **Features:** beer & wine. **Address:** 1602 Sherman Ave, Suite 116 83814 **Location:** I-90 exit 15 (Sherman Ave), 0.5 mi s. L D

THE OLYMPIA
208/666-9495

WW WW **Greek. Family Dining.** $6-$15 **AAA Inspector Notes:** Diners can enjoy authentic Greek comfort food at this family spot, just a short walk from the lakefront and shopping. The owner's father introduced gyros to the Northwest in 1970, so guests should try the requisite gyro—tender, flavorful and juicy. One of my favorites is the dolmades-grape leaves stuffed with meat and rice, covered with a lemon sauce. I also love the spanakopita (spinach pie made with flaky filo dough). The meal would not be complete without a slice of honey-kissed baklava and a cup of steaming Greek coffee. **Features:** beer & wine. **Address:** 301 E Lakeside Ave 83814 **Location:** Jct N 3rd St; downtown. **Parking:** street only. L D CALL M

THAI BAMBOO
208/667-5300

WW WW **Thai. Casual Dining.** $8-$19 **AAA Inspector Notes:** Offering a wide variety of traditional Thai dishes, this eatery offers a casual, vibrant atmosphere. Guests can enjoy the ever-changing colors of the celestial ceiling and distinctive bamboo textures while dining. **Features:** full bar. **Address:** 2010 N 4th St 83814 **Location:** I-90 exit 13 (4th St), just se. L D

TOMATO STREET   208/667-5000

♦♦♦♦ Italian. Family Dining. $8-$17 **AAA Inspector Notes:** This family-oriented, Italian market-style restaurant features brick-oven pizza, calzones, salad, sandwiches and traditional items. An attentive and efficient waitstaff cheerfully dons outlandish headgear, which sets this eatery apart from the norm. The canopied tables which occupy the center of the dining room give the feel of a sidewalk café. **Features:** full bar. **Address:** 221 W Appleway Ave 83814 **Location:** I-90 exit 13 (4th St) eastbound, just n, then just w; exit 12 westbound, just n, then just e. ⓛ Ⓓ

TONY'S ON THE LAKE   208/667-9885

♦♦♦♦ Italian. Casual Dining. $12-$32 **AAA Inspector Notes:** Enjoy views of Lake Coeur d'Alene from this warm and cozy restaurant as you dine on fine Italian cuisine. Select a pasta, veal, chicken or fish dish, then happily dig in. There is a dock available for those arriving by boat. **Features:** full bar, patio dining. **Reservations:** suggested. **Address:** 6823 Coeur d'Alene Lake Dr 83814 **Location:** I-90 exit 15 (Sherman Ave), just s, then 2.6 mi e. Ⓓ

TOP OF CHINA BUFFET   208/676-8888

♦♦♦ Chinese. Family Dining. $7-$12 **AAA Inspector Notes:** A near-staggering selection of Asian dishes makes all-you-can-eat dining popular in this comfortable, contemporary restaurant. Those who prefer something more familiar also can choose from among many American dishes, including the ever-popular children's favorite, pizza. **Features:** beer & wine. **Address:** 757 W Appleway Ave 83814 **Location:** I-90 exit 12, just n, then just w. ⓛ Ⓓ

THE WINE CELLAR   208/664-9463

♦♦♦♦ International. Casual Dining. $10-$45 **AAA Inspector Notes:** The cozy, inviting basement bistro features unobtrusive live music. Guests can enjoy the varied but predominantly Italian cuisine or just drop in for entertainment and a glass of wine from the extensive list. **Features:** full bar. **Address:** 317 E Sherman Ave 83814 **Location:** Downtown. ⓛ Ⓓ

COOLIN (A-1) elev. 2,147'

Coolin is the headquarters for the Priest Lake resort area. Priest Lake, with its 80-mile shoreline, is known for its big Mackinaw trout. The 25-mile-long lake is linked with smaller Upper Priest Lake via a channel called The Thorofare. Of the lake's seven islands, Kalispell, Bartoo, Four Mile and Eight Mile islands are available for camping.

The Roosevelt Grove of Ancient Cedars, a virgin forest, is on the west side of Priest Lake, 13 miles northwest of Nordman via FR 302 in Washington. Priest Lake State Park, on the east shore of Priest Lake, offers trails through cedar-hemlock forests *(see Recreation Areas Chart).*

Priest Lake Chamber of Commerce: P.O. Box 174, Coolin, ID 83821-0174. **Phone:** (208) 443-3191 or (888) 774-3785.

COTTONWOOD (D-1) pop. 900, elev. 3,411'

A way station constructed of cottonwood logs was established here in 1862 amid the rolling uplands of the Camas Prairie. During July 3-5, 1877, the area southeast of Cottonwood was the scene of several skirmishes between the Nez Perce and U.S. Cavalry troops and scouts. State interpretive markers give details of the battles. *See Nez Perce National Historical Park p. 85.*

The Camas Prairie Railroad's 66-mile Second Subdivision passes through Cottonwood. Opened in 1908 to transport the prairie's agricultural bounty, it was known as the "Railroad on Stilts" for its numerous

trestles, some of the nation's tallest. Many can be seen from US 95. The line was abandoned in 2000.

Near the northern entrance to the town is a structure shaped like a dog and known as the World's Biggest Beagle.

Cottonwood Chamber of Commerce: P.O. Box 15, Cottonwood, ID 83522. **Phone:** (208) 962-3231.

HISTORICAL MUSEUM AT ST. GERTRUDE is at 465 Keuterville Rd. Mining artifacts, Native American memorabilia, weapons and textiles are among the museum's 70,000-piece permanent collection covering such topics as the Chinese in Idaho, the monastery and local historical figures. A hand-carved wooden high altar in the monastery's chapel was constructed with mortise and glue; not a single nail was used. **Time:** Allow 30 minutes minimum. **Hours:** Tues.-Sat. 9:30-4:30. **Cost:** $5; $2 (ages 7-17). **Phone:** (208) 962-2050.

WEIS ROCKSHELTER is 7 mi. s. in Grave's Creek Canyon. Archeological excavations of this cliff recess have revealed almost continuous human occupation between 5500 B.C. and A.D. 1400.

COUNCIL (E-1) pop. 839, elev. 2,940'

COUNCIL VALLEY MUSEUM is at 100 S. Galena St. Area history is depicted through such structures as doctor's and dentist's offices, a jail, a dry goods store and a cowboy's cabin. Also displayed are Native American artifacts, including tools and weapons, and items related to local mining and fruit growing boom periods. **Time:** Allow 30 minutes minimum. **Hours:** Tues.-Sat. 10-4, Sun. 1-4, Memorial Day-Labor Day. **Cost:** Donations. **Phone:** (208) 253-4582.

▼ CRATERS OF THE MOON NATIONAL MONUMENT AND PRESERVE (G-4)

Eighteen miles west of Arco via US 20/26/93, Craters of the Moon National Monument and Preserve is at the base of the Pioneer Mountains.

This 1,100-square-mile area contains more basaltic volcanic features than any other area of its size in the continental United States. Lava rivers once flooded the surrounding countryside, leaving vast lava fields covered by cinder cones with large central vents that were thought by early observers to resemble the craters on the moon. The volcanic activity dates back about 15,000 years, with the last eruptions occurring about 2,000 years ago.

The area's variety of surface patterns and formations is typical of the world's other basaltic lava sites. Visitors should be cautious of sharp lava formations.

A 7-mile loop drive, open from mid-April to early November, leads past the monument's main points of interest and takes about 30 minutes to complete. The view from the summit of Inferno Cone takes in the cinder cone chain along the Great Rift, a weakened zone of fissures in the Earth's crust. In winter, when the snow is sufficiently deep, the loop road is closed to vehicular traffic and is groomed for cross-country skiing and snowshoeing.

The cones formed when fountains of molten, gas-charged rock shot into the air. The frothy lava then cooled and hardened into cinders that fell around the vent, producing symmetrical cones. Numerous lava bombs, ejected blobs of less frothy lava that range from an inch to several feet in diameter, are scattered over the slopes. Big Cinder, 700 feet high, is one of the world's largest purely basaltic cinder cones.

Nearby is the Big Craters-Spatter Cone Area. These cones formed when clots of pasty lava stuck together as they fell back to Earth. A trail leads from the drive to the Cave Area, a series of lava tubes that range up to 40 feet in diameter and hundreds of feet in length. The largest is 830-foot Indian Tunnel; Boy Scout Cave has a floor of ice, even in summer. Some of the tubes can be explored; wear sturdy shoes and carry a flashlight. Permits are required and are available at the visitor center.

Other trails lead to Devil's Orchard, cinder fields scattered with fragments of a crater wall, and the Tree Mold Area, where lava slowly enveloped a group of living trees.

More than 300 species of plants and many different species of animals live in this seemingly desolate terrain. In early summer, wildflowers burst into bloom on the cinder fields and slopes of the cones.

Note: Off-road vehicles may be needed on some undeveloped dirt roads. Inquire about road conditions in advance.

A visitor center and campground-picnic area are near the entrance. Guided walks and evening programs are provided during summer months; phone for schedule. The entrance fee is $8 (per private vehicle); $4 (per motorcycle or bicycle).

ROBERT LIMBERT VISITOR CENTER is at the start of the 7-mi. loop drive. Exhibits explain the geology, plants, animals and history of the monument. **Hours:** Daily 8-6, Memorial Day-Labor Day; 8-4:30, rest of year. Closed winter holidays. **Phone:** (208) 527-1335.

DONNELLY (E-2) pop. 152, elev. 4,865'

Donnelly nestles in a scenic 35-mile-long valley with Lake Cascade to the south and Payette Lake on the north. During winter, frozen Lake Cascade is used for ice fishing and cross-country skiing; summer activities include boating, kayaking, sailing and water skiing. The surrounding terrain is ideal for backcountry skiing and snowmobiling.

RECREATIONAL ACTIVITIES
Skiing and Snowboarding

- **Tamarack Resort** is at 311 Village Dr. Other activities, including golf, are offered seasonally. **Hours:** Open Thurs.-Sun., Thanksgiving weekend-Mar. 31 (weather permitting). Hours vary; phone ahead. **Phone:** (208) 325-1000.

DRIGGS (F-6) pop. 1,660, elev. 6,109'
- **Hotels & Restaurants map & index p. 295**
- **Part of Jackson Hole Including Grand Teton National Park area — see map p. 293**

Settled by Mormon pioneers in 1889, Driggs is the main trading center for the Teton Valley. The town center is an eclectic mix of Old West and contemporary, with specialty shops, art galleries, pubs, eateries and outdoor outfitters. Teton Valley Museum, 137 SR 33N, offers a glimpse into the area's history; phone (208) 354-6000.

If you're the outdoorsy type, embark on a horseback riding, hunting, mountain biking or skiing expedition. And if you can handle heights, why not check out the town from a hot air balloon? You can experience the oldest successful human-carrying flight technology during the Teton Valley Summer Festival, a 4-day event held in early July.

Teton Valley Chamber of Commerce: 57 S. Main St., P.O. Box 250, Driggs, ID 83422. **Phone:** (208) 354-2500.

RECREATIONAL ACTIVITIES
Horseback Riding

- **Dry Ridge Outfitters** departs from the Cabins at Moose Creek at the s. end of Teton Valley. **Hours:** One- to 4-hour trips by reservation, June 1-Sept. 15. Multiday trips by reservation mid-July through Labor Day. **Phone:** (208) 351-1796.

BEST WESTERN TETON WEST   (208)354-2363

Hotel
$100-$120

 AAA Benefit: Members save 10% or more with Best Western!

Address: 476 N Main St 83422 **Location:** 0.7 mi n on SR 33. **Facility:** 40 units. 2 stories (no elevator), interior corridors. **Terms:** closed 10/1-5/20. **Pool(s):** heated indoor. **Activities:** hot tub. **Guest Services:** coin laundry.

SUPER 8 DRIGGS   (208)354-8888

Hotel
$65-$182

 Address: 1361 N Hwy 33 83422 **Location:** 1.3 mi n. **Facility:** 46 units, some efficiencies and kitchens. 2 stories, interior corridors. **Parking:** winter plug-ins. **Pool(s):** heated indoor. **Activities:** hot tub. **Guest Services:** coin laundry. **Featured Amenity:** continental breakfast.

TETON VALLEY CABINS   (208)354-8153

 Motel $69-$99 **Address:** 388 Ski Hill Rd 83422 **Location:** 0.8 mi e on Little Ave from SR 33 E. Located in a rustic area. **Facility:** 20 units. 1 story, exterior corridors. **Parking:** winter plug-ins. **Terms:** check-in 4 pm, 7 day cancellation notice-fee imposed. **Activities:** hot tub. **Guest Services:** coin laundry.

(See map & index p. 295.)

WHERE TO EAT

TETON THAI   208/787-8424 ⓴
♥♥ Thai. Casual Dining. $9-$16 **AAA Inspector Notes:** This family-operated restaurant, a sibling to a Teton Village, WY, restaurant, lets guests savor Thai offerings in a contemporary full-service setting. **Features:** beer & wine, patio dining. **Address:** 18 N Main St 83422 **Location:** Center. **Parking:** street only. Ⓛ Ⓓ

EAGLE pop. 19,908

HILTON GARDEN INN - BOISE/EAGLE   (208)938-9600
♥♥♥ Hotel $104-$284 **Address:** 145 E Riverside Dr 83616 **Location:** I-84 exit 46 (Eagle Rd), 6 mi n to Riverside Dr, then just e. **Facility:** 98 units. 3 stories, interior corridors. **Terms:** 1-7 night minimum stay, cancellation fee imposed. **Pool(s):** heated indoor. **Activities:** hot tub, exercise room. **Guest Services:** valet and coin laundry.

AAA Benefit: Members save up to 10%!

➕ 🍴 🏊 BIZ HS 🛜 🔌 🖥 🖵

WHERE TO EAT

BARDENAY   208/938-5093
♥♥ International. Casual Dining. $6-$23 **AAA Inspector Notes:** Perched above the Boise River, this restaurant serves a wide variety of dishes such as cumin and chili-spiced calamari, red bean and chorizo stew and Kobe beef tacos. The pastry chef prepares seasonal desserts daily. Vodka, rum and gin are produced on the premises. Gluten-free items are available. **Features:** full bar, Sunday brunch. **Address:** 155 E Riverside Dr 83616 **Location:** I-84 exit 46 (Eagle Rd), 6.5 mi n, then just e. Ⓛ Ⓓ ⓁⒶⓉⒺ

THE GRIDDLE   208/939-9070
♥♥ American. Family Dining. $5-$14 **AAA Inspector Notes:** With made-from-scratch home-style cooking and hefty portions, it is no wonder this diner is such a favorite. The menu offers all of the traditional American breakfast favorites and a variety of sandwiches and burgers during lunch. **Address:** 177 Eagle River St 83616 **Location:** I-84 exit 46 (Eagle Rd), 6.3 mi n, then just ne.
Ⓑ Ⓛ CALL 🅜

REMBRANDT'S COFFEE HOUSE   208/938-1564
♥♥ Sandwiches Breads/Pastries. Quick Serve. $3-$11 **AAA Inspector Notes:** In a lofty building with a large patio, this local institution always is buzzing both inside and out. The menu lists seasonal soups, specialty sandwiches, gourmet salads and scores of breakfast favorites including delicious omelets and gourmet egg burritos. Local artists' pieces, most available for purchase, adorn the walls. Evening snacks are offered. **Address:** 93 S Eagle Rd 83616 **Location:** I-84 exit 46 (Eagle Rd), 7 mi n; just n of SR 44 and just s of State St. Ⓑ Ⓛ CALL 🅜

SMOKY MOUNTAIN PIZZERIA GRILL   208/939-0212
♥♥ Italian. Family Dining. $7-$27 **AAA Inspector Notes:** In the heart of downtown, this popular Italian eatery serves a wide variety of pasta dishes, pizzas, calzones and salads. **Features:** beer & wine, patio dining, happy hour. **Address:** 34 E State St 83616 **Location:** Jct Old State St and Eagle Rd. Ⓛ Ⓓ

ELK RIVER (C-1) pop. 125, elev. 2,854'

Potlatch Lumber Co. built a town for its electrically powered sawmill in 1909. Served by a railroad, Elk River's population peaked at nearly 1,200 in the 1920s. After the mill closed in 1936, the town declined. Relics of Elk River's halcyon days include a 1917 drugstore and an abandoned public school built in 1910. The former mill pond, south of town, is today a recreation area and a habitat for ospreys,

bald eagles and otters. On its west shore is the historic Clearwater-Potlatch Timber Protective Association's firefighters camp.

The Morris-Perkins Cedar Grove, 7 miles north on FR 382, then 3 miles west on winding FR 1969, has a 3/4-mile trail looping through an 80-acre stand of old growth western red cedar. Among the monarchs is Idaho's champion red cedar, a 177-foot giant more than 3,000 years old and measuring 18 feet in diameter. The grove is accessible from April to mid-December (weather permitting); phone (208) 875-1131.

The Elk River Back Country Byway is a 57-mile scenic route. It follows SR 8 19 miles from Bovill to Elk River, then 39 winding miles south to Orofino. The Elk River to Oroville section includes 17 miles of gravel and crosses Dworshak Reservoir via Dent Bridge, a graceful 1,550-foot suspension bridge.

ELK CREEK FALLS is 2 mi. w. on SR 8, then 2 mi. s. on FR 1452 (gravel road) to trailhead. Elk Creek tumbles over ancient lava flows to form three waterfalls with a collective drop of about 300 feet. The middle and lower falls are the highest at 70 and 50 feet, respectively. Outcrops of columnar basalt enhance the beauty of the canyon. A 1-mile trail, steep in places, leads down through the forest of pine, fir, cedar and larch to a viewpoint of the lower and middle falls. Side trails branch off to other vantage points.

Restrooms and picnic tables are available at the trailhead. **Time:** Allow 1 hour minimum. **Hours:** Daily dawn-dusk, mid-June to early Oct. (weather permitting). Phone ahead to confirm schedule. **Cost:** Free. **Phone:** (208) 875-1131.

EMMETT (F-1) pop. 6,557, elev. 2,362'

Located on the Payette River 30 miles northwest of Boise, Emmett was settled in the mid-1860s. Irrigation works began in the early 1900s and the district became noted for its orchard crops of peaches, apricots, apples and cherries. Freezeout Hill, 7 miles southeast on SR 16, on a ridge separating the Payette and Boise River valleys, offers a grand view of the town and its oasis-like setting.

GEM COUNTY VILLAGE MUSEUM is at 501 E. 1st St. The five-building complex includes a museum with a variety of historical displays as well as a blacksmith shop and a one-room school. A bunkhouse contains early ranching items and a natural history exhibit. The Hunt House showcases the furnishings and personal belongings of Frank W. Hunt, the fifth governor of Idaho. The first weekend in October, the museum features A River Through Time, a hands-on, living-history celebration of the people who settled Payette River Valley. **Time:** Allow 30 minutes minimum. **Hours:** Wed.-Sat. 1-5. Closed Thanksgiving and Christmas. **Cost:** Donations. **Phone:** (208) 365-9530.

FORT HALL (G-5) pop. 3,201, elev. 4,754'

One of the first permanent settlements in Idaho, Fort Hall was established as a trading post on the banks of the Snake River in 1834. Later owned by the Hudson's Bay Co., the trading post was abandoned in 1856 due to increased hostility with Native Americans and a decline in fur trading.

In 1864 a stage station was constructed a short distance southeast of Fort Hall. Built on the banks of Spring Creek with materials from this original fort, this post also was known as Fort Hall. In 1868 a treaty established the Fort Hall Indian Reservation, and agency offices some 20 miles east of the original post also were identified as Fort Hall. Today the Fort Hall Indian Reservation has its headquarters east of the town site on US 91. Guided tours of historic Fort Hall, which must be reserved in advance, can be arranged through the Shoshone-Bannock Tribal Museum *(see attraction listing).*

SHOSHONE-BANNOCK TRIBAL MUSEUM is on Simplot Rd. just w. of I-15 exit 80. Themed displays highlight the history of the Shoshone-Bannock Tribes, the Oregon Trail, the Fort Hall Indian Boarding School and Native American ranchers. Tribal beadwork, artwork, crafts, historical photographs and archeological artifacts are exhibited. **Time:** Allow 30 minutes minimum. **Hours:** Daily 9:30-5, June 1 to mid-Aug.; Mon.-Fri. 9:30-5, rest of year. Closed federal and tribal holidays. **Cost:** $2.50; $1 (ages 6-18); free (ages 0-5 and Native Americans with tribal ID). **Phone:** (208) 237-9791.

GAMBLING ESTABLISHMENTS

- **Fort Hall Casino** is on Simplot Rd. just w. of I-15 exit 80. **Hours:** Daily 24 hours. **Phone:** (208) 237-8778 or (800) 497-4231.

SHOSHONE-BANNOCK HOTEL & EVENT CENTER
(208)238-4800

Hotel $89 **Address:** 777 Bannock Tr 83203 **Location:** I-15 exit 80, just w. Adjacent to Fort Hall Casino. **Facility:** This hotel offers beautifully appointed public areas and guest rooms with stunning views. Some units include a fireplace, balcony or jetted tub. 156 units. 5 stories, interior corridors. **Terms:** cancellation fee imposed. **Amenities:** safes. **Dining:** 2 restaurants. **Pool(s):** heated indoor. **Activities:** hot tub, exercise room, spa. **Guest Services:** valet and coin laundry.

GLENNS FERRY (G-2) pop. 1,319, elev. 2,560'

Off I-84 on the Snake River, the community traces its beginnings to a ferry crossing established here in 1869. Housed in a former school building built in 1909, the Glenns Ferry Historical Museum exhibits artifacts that depict area history; for more information phone the Glenns Ferry City Hall at (208) 366-7418.

THREE ISLAND CROSSING STATE PARK, 1 mi. w. via S. Commercial St. and W. Madison Ave., preserves the site where Oregon Trail wagon trains were forced to ford the Snake River from the early 1840s until 1869, when a ferry began operating. The Oregon Trail History and Education Center features pioneer and Native American exhibits. *See Recreation Areas Chart.*

Time: Allow 1 hour minimum. **Hours:** Grounds daily dawn-dusk. History and education center Wed.-Sun. 9-4, Apr.-Oct. Phone ahead to confirm schedule. **Cost:** $5 (per private vehicle). Camping (includes water and electricity) $23.32-$40.28. Cabins $53. **Phone:** (208) 366-2394, or (888) 922-6743 for camping reservations.

WINERIES
- **Carmela Vineyards** is off I-84 Glenns Ferry exit at 1289 W. Madison Ave. next to Three Island

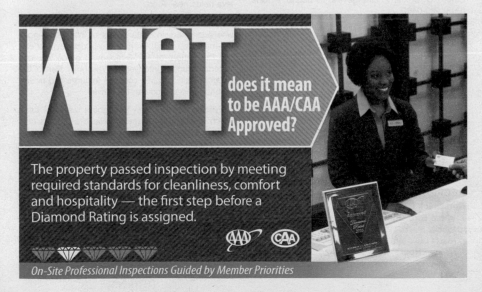

Crossing State Park, following signs. **Hours:** Mon.-Sat. 8 a.m.-9 p.m., Sun. 10-8. **Phone:** (208) 366-2313.

CARMELA VINEYARDS RESTAURANT   208/366-2313

♦♦ American. Casual Dining. $7-$25 **AAA Inspector Notes:** This castle-like restaurant sits on a bluff just off the river and is surrounded by picturesque grape arbors. The dining room is comfortable, bright and well appointed, and the food is tasty and fresh. Steak, pasta and seafood are dinner menu mainstays. **Features:** full bar, patio dining, Sunday brunch, happy hour. **Reservations:** suggested, weekends. **Address:** 1289 W Madison Ave 83623 **Location:** I-84 exit 120, 0.5 mi s to Bannock St, 0.4 mi e to Commercial St, 0.5 mi s to Madison Ave, then 0.7 mi w. 〔L〕 〔D〕 〔🐾〕

GRANGEVILLE (D-1) pop. 3,141, elev. 3,323'

A boomtown in gold rush days, Grangeville is a light industry and agricultural center and the largest town on the fertile Camas Prairie, one of the leading wheat-producing areas in the country. The prairie takes its name from *camassia esculenta*, an onion-like bulb common in the area and favored by the Nez Perce Indians. Today it is a site for an archeological excavation for mammoth bones.

A life-size replica of the giant mammoth unearthed in 1995 at nearby Tolo Lake, 6 miles west of town, can be seen in Eimers Park on US 95 at Pine Street. Grangeville also is an outfitting point for wilderness and float trips.

South of Grangeville US 95 descends 3,000 feet to the Salmon River Canyon via the White Bird Grade. This 7-mile section of the highway bypasses the dozens of switchbacks and hairpin curves of the original route, which can be seen to the east. White Bird Battlefield, a designated site of Nez Perce National Historical Park *(see place listing p. 85)*, is about 16 miles south on US 95.

Grangeville Chamber of Commerce: US 95 at N. Pine, P.O. Box 212, Grangeville, ID 83530. **Phone:** (208) 983-0460.

Self-guiding tours: A trail guide of White Bird Battlefield is available at the chamber of commerce and at the Nez Perce National Forest office in Grangeville.

BICENTENNIAL MUSEUM, 305 N. College St., chronicles the history of Idaho County and its residents. Exhibits include Nez Perce beadwork, basketry and clothing; historical photographs; and mining and military artifacts. Guided tours are available on request. **Time:** Allow 30 minutes minimum. **Hours:** Wed.-Fri. 1:30-5 (also July 4), June-Sept.; Thurs. 1:30-5, rest of year. **Cost:** Donations. **Phone:** (208) 983-2573.

RECREATIONAL ACTIVITIES
Horseback Riding
• **White Bird Summit Lodge** is 7 mi. s. on US 95 to mile marker 231, then 1 mi. e. on Old Hwy. 95 to 2141 Old White Bird Hill Rd. Other activities are offered. **Hours:** Trips are offered daily, June-Aug. Departure times vary; phone ahead. **Phone:** (208) 983-1802.

GATEWAY INN   208/983-2500

♦♦♦
Motel
$55-$99

Address: 700 W Main St 83530 **Location:** Jct US 95 and SR 13. **Facility:** 28 units, some efficiencies. 2 stories (no elevator), exterior corridors. **Pool(s):** heated outdoor. **Guest Services:** coin laundry. **Featured Amenity:** continental breakfast.

〔SAVE〕 〔📶+〕 〔🛏〕 〔📶〕 〔✕〕 〔🍴〕 〔🖥〕 〔💻〕 / SOME UNITS 〔🐾〕

WHERE TO EAT

SEASONS RESTAURANT   208/983-4203

♦♦ American. Casual Dining. $8-$20 **AAA Inspector Notes:** No matter the season, soup, burgers and sandwiches are the main stays for lunch while a nice selection of appetizers, pasta entrées, barbecued ribs and steak is offered in the evening. **Features:** beer & wine. **Address:** 124 W Main St 83530 **Location:** 0.5 mi e of jct US 95 and SR 13. **Parking:** street only. 〔B〕 〔L〕 〔D〕

HAGERMAN (G-3) pop. 872, elev. 2,959'

1000 SPRINGS TOURS, departing from Banbury Hot Springs, 11 mi. s. on US 30, offers 2-hour scenic boat trips through the Snake River Canyon and the Thousand Springs area. Waterfalls, wildlife and abundant waterfowl can be seen while guides relate area history and geography. Lunch and dinner tours also are available. **Hours:** Two-hour scenic boat tours depart daily. Departure times vary. **Cost:** $25. Reservations are required. **Phone:** (208) 837-9006.

THOUSAND SPRINGS STATE PARK is .2 mi. s. off I-84 exit 147, then .2 mi. w., following signs to the welcome kiosk at Malad Gorge. The highlight of this multi-unit state park are aquifer-fed springs that gush in beautiful cascades from the sides of Snake River Canyon. The springs are believed to be the reappearance of Lost River, which vanishes into the lava fields near Arco.

Park headquarters is at the Malad Gorge unit, where markers indicate points of interest along a 3.5-mile loop road. From a footbridge visitors can see the bottom of a 250-foot-deep gorge where a waterfall plunges into Devil's Washbowl. Part of the Oregon Trail, volcanic collapse features and underground springs also can be viewed.

Wildlife can be seen throughout the state park, which also encompasses the Niagara Springs unit, featuring 350-foot-high sheer basalt cliffs; the historic Kelton Trail, boasting pioneer wagon ruts; the Ritter Island unit, host to September's Thousand Springs Festival of the Arts; the Billingsley Creek unit, offering an indoor equestrian arena; and the Earl M. Hardy Box Canyon Springs Nature Preserve. *See Recreation Areas Chart.*

Tours: Guided tours are available. **Time:** Allow 45 minutes minimum. **Hours:** Park open daily 7 a.m.-10 p.m. Ritter Island unit open Fri.-Tues. 10-3, Memorial Day weekend-Labor Day. **Cost:** $5 (per private vehicle). **Phone:** (208) 837-4505.

〔✕〕 〔🐾〕 〔⛽〕

RECREATIONAL ACTIVITIES
White-water Rafting
- **High Adventure River Tours** is off I-84 exit 147 at 1211 East 2350 South. Other activities are offered. **Hours:** Rafting trips are offered daily, Apr.-Oct. Departure times vary; phone ahead. **Phone:** (208) 837-9005 or (208) 731-6673.

HAGERMAN VALLEY INN   (208)837-6196

Motel
$68-$108

Address: 661 Frog's Landing 83332 **Location:** South end of town on US 30. Located in Frog's Landing Business Complex. **Facility:** 16 units. 2 stories (no elevator), exterior corridors. **Terms:** cancellation fee imposed. **Dining:** Snake River Grill, see separate listing.

WHERE TO EAT

SNAKE RIVER GRILL   208/837-6227
American. Casual Dining. $5-$22 **AAA Inspector Notes:** This rustic restaurant is located in a small town near the Snake River and will appeal to the traveling family as well as the undaunted—the menu offers distinct wild game dinners where diners provide the game and the chef/owner prepares it. **Features:** beer & wine. **Address:** 611 Frog's Landing 83332 **Location:** South end of town on US 30, in Hagerman Valley Inn. B L D

HAGERMAN FOSSIL BEDS NATIONAL MONUMENT (G-2)

The monument is 4 mi. s. on US 30, then 3 mi. w. on Bell Rapids Rd., following signs. The 3.4-million-year-old fossil beds, one of the continent's best Pliocene freshwater fish and small-mammal fossil sites, have yielded more than 220 plant and animal species, including complete skeletons of the Hagerman horse. A 10.5-mile auto route provides insights into area geology and geography and access to the historic Owsley Bridge over the Snake River, the Upper Salmon Falls Dam, the Snake River Overlook, the 3-mile trailhead for the Emigrant Trail and the Oregon Trail Overlook.

VISITOR CENTER is at 221 N. State St., directly across US 30 from the high school. With exhibits, fossils, a discovery center, a DVD show, auto tour brochures and trail maps, the center is a good place to stop for information before touring the monument, as access to some trails and overlooks may be restricted. The visitor center also has information about Minidoka National Historic Site (see place listing p. 81). **Hours:** Daily 9-5, Memorial Day weekend-Aug. 31; Thurs.-Mon. 9-5, rest of year. Closed Jan. 1, Thanksgiving and Christmas. Phone ahead to confirm schedule. **Cost:** Free. **Phone:** (208) 933-4105.

HAILEY (G-3) pop. 7,960, elev. 5,330'

Hailey, laid out in the spring of 1881 by John Hailey, was the center of a rich mining district in its early days. An early Northwest pioneer, Hailey had previously taken part in the Boise Basin Gold Rush in 1862 and had established a name for himself as the owner of a stage and freight line. Fortunes in gold, silver and lead were extracted from mines with such names as Black Cinder, Star, Hope, Climax, Democrat and Big Camas until the mining boom played out in the late 1890s.

On May 7, 1883, Hailey residents witnessed the driving of the last spike of the Wood River branch of the Oregon Short Line. In October of that year the Idaho Territory's first telephone exchange went into use at Hailey. Hailey also was the first to have an electric light plant.

Passing through the community are the Big Wood River and a system of paved recreational trails. Surrounded by Sawtooth National Recreation Area (see place listing p. 97), Hailey offers a variety of outdoor activities, including hiking, bicycling and cross-country skiing.

Hailey Chamber of Commerce/Welcome Center: 781 Main St. S., P.O. Box 100, Hailey, ID 83333. **Phone:** (208) 788-3484.

Self-guiding tours: Brochures describing a self-guiding walking tour of Hailey's historic area are available at the chamber of commerce.

BLAINE COUNTY HISTORICAL MUSEUM, 218 N. Main St., displays early pioneer relics and memorabilia of local interest, including a replica of a mine tunnel. The American Political Items collection contains memorabilia from political campaigns since the late 1800s. **Time:** Allow 30 minutes minimum. **Hours:** Mon.-Sat. 11-5, Sun. 1-5, Memorial Day weekend-Oct. 31. **Cost:** Donations. **Phone:** (208) 788-1801.

AIRPORT INN   (200)788-2477
Motel $85-$140 **Address:** 820 S 4th Ave 83333 **Location:** 1 mi s of center to 4th Ave via Main St (SR 75); south end of town. Adjacent to Wood River Trail system. **Facility:** 29 units, some efficiencies. 1-2 stories (no elevator), exterior corridors. **Parking:** winter plug-ins. **Terms:** check-in 4 pm, 3 day cancellation notice. **Activities:** hot tub, picnic facilities. **Guest Services:** coin laundry.

AMERICINN LODGE & SUITES HAILEY/SUN VALLEY
                                       (208)788-7950
Hotel $99-$200 **Address:** 51 Cobblestone Ln 83333 **Location:** 0.5 mi n of center. **Facility:** 64 units. 3 stories, interior corridors. **Parking:** winter plug-ins. **Terms:** cancellation fee imposed. **Pool(s):** heated indoor. **Activities:** hot tub, steamroom, exercise room. **Guest Services:** coin laundry.

WOOD RIVER INN   (208)578-0600
Hotel $99-$159 **Address:** 601 N Main St 83333 **Location:** 0.3 mi n of center. **Facility:** 56 units, some efficiencies. 3 stories, interior corridors. **Parking:** winter plug-ins. **Terms:** cancellation fee imposed. **Pool(s):** heated indoor. **Activities:** hot tub, bicycles, exercise room. **Guest Services:** coin laundry.

WHERE TO EAT

CK'S REAL FOOD   208/788-1223

▼▼▼ Natural/Organic. Fine Dining. $9-$35 **AAA Inspector Notes:** This relaxed, yet upscale, eatery features globally-inspired food with a focus on local, organic and sustainable fare. Seasonal menu items include morel and watercress salad, country pate, grilled chicken over a Greek salad and grilled Idaho trout. Delicious sides consist of broccoli pancakes, antioxidant greens and roasted potatoes with smoked pork belly. Colorful desserts are beautifully presented. **Features:** beer & wine. **Reservations:** suggested. **Address:** 320 Main St S 83333 **Location:** On SR 75 at Main and Pine sts, 0.4 mi s of center. **Parking:** street only. [L] [D] CALL [&M]

SHORTY'S DINER   208/578-1293

▼ Comfort Food. Casual Dining. $5-$10 **AAA Inspector Notes:** This 1950s-style diner always is bustling with patrons. Serving up traditional American favorites, menu items range from omelets, skillets and pancakes to burgers, dogs, sandwiches and chicken-fried steak. **Features:** beer only. **Address:** 126 S Main St 83333 **Location:** On SR 75 at Main and Croy sts. **Parking:** street only. [B] [L] [D]

HAYDEN pop. 13,294

HOLIDAY INN EXPRESS HOTEL & SUITES   (208)772-7900

▼▼▼ Hotel $90-$399 **Address:** 151 W Orchard Ave 83835 **Location:** I-90 exit 12, 3.5 mi n. **Facility:** 95 units. 4 stories, interior corridors. **Terms:** check-in 4 pm. **Activities:** hot tub, miniature golf, game room, exercise room. **Guest Services:** valet and coin laundry.

[↑↓] CALL [&M] [BIZ] [HS] 🛜 [✕] 🔌 📷 💻 / SOME UNITS [S🛏]

HAYDEN LAKE pop. 574

THE PORCH PUBLIC HOUSE   208/772-7711

▼▼▼ American. Casual Dining. $9-$18 **AAA Inspector Notes:** This casual spot takes its name from its screened porch, which overlooks a golf course and is a favorite spot for seasonal dining. An eclectic menu offers choices to satisfy nearly every taste. For lunch, the marinated grilled lamb sandwich is superb. **Features:** full bar. **Address:** 1658 E Miles Ave 83835 **Location:** I-90 exit 12, 4.1 mi n to Miles Ave, then 1.4 mi e. [L] [D]

▰ HELLS CANYON NATIONAL RECREATION AREA (D-1)

Hells Canyon National Recreation Area is reached via SRs 82 and 86 in northeastern Oregon and US 95 in western Idaho. The 652,977-acre area straddles the Snake River Canyon and encompasses parts of national forests in both states.

Confined within steep, eroded black basalt walls, the surging Snake River has carved North America's deepest river gorge, measuring 7,913 feet from He Devil Mountain to Granite Creek below. White-water rapids alternating with deep pools characterize this 72-mile free-flowing portion of the Snake River as it races north to meet the Columbia River.

The varied elevations of Hells Canyon support mixed plant communities sheltering such wildlife as bears, bobcats, bighorn sheep, cougars, elk, mule deer, mountain goats and many smaller birds, mammals and reptiles. Sturgeon, reputedly growing up to 11 feet long, inhabit the Snake River, sharing it with bass, catfish, salmon, steelhead trout and rainbow trout.

From the desertlike canyon floor to the alpine lakes of the Seven Devils region, the area presents a variety of recreational opportunities including boating, float trips and backpacking. From Pittsburg Landing, the Kirkwood Historic Ranch and Museum, once the home of Idaho governor and U.S. senator Len B. Jordan, is accessible by powerboat, float boat or pack trail.

The Rapid River originates in the Seven Devils Mountains and eventually joins the Little Salmon River. The forks of the Rapid River provide quality water for raising chinook salmon and therefore house the Rapid River Fish Hatchery.

The 214,944-acre Hells Canyon Wilderness, with its extensive trail system, protects a large portion of the canyon along the Oregon-Idaho border. If you plan to fish the lakes and the Snake River shoreline, you must acquire the appropriate state licenses (see Good Facts To Know); both Oregon and Idaho licenses are valid for boat fishing on the river.

Scenic Hells Canyon All American Road/SR 86 is a series of routes to and through the Hells Canyon National Recreation Area. **On the Oregon side** the best route is a two-lane paved loop that originates in Baker City. From Baker City follow SR 86 to Richland for approximately 41 miles. From Richland continue on SR 86 north for 11 miles to Halfway. From Halfway follow SR 86 for 20 miles to Oxbow. Nine miles north off Halfway, SR 86 will intersect with FR 39N. Take FR 39N through the heart of the Wallowa Mountains, high mountain country and through the town of Joseph to Enterprise. One mile west of Enterprise on SR 82 is the Wallowa Mountain Visitor Center. Continue along SR 82 west for approximately 64 miles to arrive back on I-84 at La Grande. The higher elevation portions of FR 39 are closed in winter. The entire loop will take approximately 5 hours.

Another possible route from the Oregon side to the recreation area is via SR 82 to Enterprise and Joseph. From Joseph it is possible to go to Hat Point, a 6,982-foot ridge overlooking Hells Canyon, via Imnaha. The route to Hat Point, open summer through early fall, follows FR 4240, a gravel, narrow road with steep grades.

Another route from Imnaha, FR 3955, parallels the Imnaha River as it meanders through rims and benches similar to those along the Snake River. This route connects with the Wallowa Mountain Loop (FR 39), which leads back to Joseph or Halfway. FR 3955 and FR 39 are maintained for cars and trailers. FR 39 can be followed east to FR 3965, which leads to the Hells Canyon overlook. With an elevation of 6,000 feet, the overlook provides a spectacular view of the Wallowa Mountains in Oregon and Idaho. These roads are closed in winter.

Buckhorn Springs, a scenic area overlooking the Imnaha drainage, can be reached from FR 46 off SR 3, a mostly gravel logging road.

For maps and brochures of different drives contact the Baker County Chamber and Visitors Bureau, 490 Campbell St., Baker City, OR 97814; phone (541) 523-5855 or (888) 523-5855.

On the Idaho side there are two routes to the canyon. From Cambridge, SR 71 runs 29 miles northwest to Oxbow, Ore., crossing the Snake River near Brownlee Dam. It crosses back into Idaho at Oxbow, then follows the river north to Hells Canyon Dam. The total distance is about 55 miles. The other access point is Pittsburg Landing, 17 miles west of US 95 at White Bird via gravel FR 493. The drive from White Bird to Hells Canyon takes about 45 minutes.

Note: The majority of the Idaho side of the canyon is in the Mountain Time Zone; White Bird, Idaho, and the Oregon side of the canyon observe Pacific Time. It is advisable to check with the Hells Canyon National Recreation Area regarding road conditions and construction. Some roads are gravel and caution should be exercised. Phone (541) 426-5546.

More than 30 outfitters provide float and jet boat trips down the Snake River from Hells Canyon Dam and jet boat trips upstream from Lewiston and White Bird, Idaho, and from Asotin and Clarkston, Wash. For a list of local outfitters contact the Supervisor, Hells Canyon National Recreation Area, 2535 Riverside Dr., P.O. Box 699, Clarkston, WA 99403; phone (509) 758-0616, or (509) 758-0270 for powerboat reservations. See Recreation Areas Chart.

SAVE BEAMERS HELLS CANYON TOURS departs from the Beamers Tour Dock behind the Quality Inn at 700 Port Dr. in Clarkston, Wash. This tour company offers jet boat excursions through Hells Canyon—North America's deepest river gorge. The 1-day Snake River trip provides opportunities to view three mountain ranges, three states and three rivers. Half-day and other excursions also are available. Hours: Half- and full-day trips offered daily, May-Sept.; Sat.-Sun. only, Mar.-Apr. and in Oct. Departure times vary; phone ahead. Cost: One-day trip $209; free (ages 0-8). Half-day trip $139; free (ages 0-8). Phone: (509) 758-4800 or (800) 522-6966.

HELLS CANYON ADVENTURES is on SR 86 (All American Rd.), 1 mi. n. of Hells Canyon Dam and 23 mi. n. of Oxbow, Ore. Two-hour jet boat tours depart at 10 and at 2. Full-day jet boat tours depart at 10, traveling through the deepest part of Hells Canyon, navigating the largest rapids and visiting the Kirkwood Historical Ranch. Overnight jet boat tours and fishing charters on the Snake River also are available.

Hours: Tours depart daily May-Sept. Inquire about off-season tours. Departure times vary. Cost: Granite Creek Tour $80; $55 (ages 0-11). Wild Sheep Tour $60; $35 (ages 0-11). Kirkwood $172; $85 (ages 0-11). A fuel surcharge may apply; phone ahead for more information. Reservations are recommended. Phone: (541) 785-3352 or (800) 422-3568.

HELLS CANYON JET BOAT TRIPS & LODGING checks in guests at its office, 1 mi. s. on Old Hwy. 95 in White Bird, Idaho. The 65-mile, round-trip Wild River Tour through Class II to V rapids on the Snake River navigates the deepest and most rugged section of Hells Canyon, passing alongside Seven Devils Mountains en route to the dam. Other tours are available.

Time: Allow 6 hours minimum. **Hours:** Departures require a minimum of six people. Trips depart daily, Apr. 1 to mid-Oct. **Cost:** (includes a meal) $175; $110 (ages 1-11). Prices may vary. A shuttle to the departure point at Pittsburgh Landing marina, 17 mi. s.w. on a gravel road, is offered for a fee, or private vehicle parking is available at the marina. Reservations are required. **Phone:** (208) 839-2255 or (800) 469-8757. *(See ad p. 67.)*

HEYBURN   pop. 3,089

UPPER CRUST GRILL & BISTRO   208/679-0972
♦ Sandwiches Soup. Quick Serve. $7-$10 **AAA Inspector Notes:** Located above a popular attraction, this casual eatery's menu boasts a nice selection of salads, tasty sandwiches and artisan cheeses. Be sure to finish off the meal with a freshly baked cookie. **Address:** 1360 7th St 83336 **Location:** I-84 exit 211, 1.8 mi sw on US 30 to 7th St; exit 208, 0.5 mi s to 5th St, 1 mi e, then 0.8 mi s to US 30. [L] [D] CALL [&M]

HORSESHOE BEND   (F-1) pop. 707, elev. 2,630'

HORSESHOE BEND EXPRESS-THUNDER MOUNTAIN LINE departs from 120 Mill Rd. The nearly 3-hour Payette River Adventure parallels the Payette River and follows an old wagon trail to Banks, where a short stop is made. Four partially open-air cars and four enclosed cars are available to riders. Dinner, entertainment, holiday and themed excursions also are offered.

Hours: Depot open Fri. 4-7, Sat. 11-6, Sun. noon-4. Trips depart Apr.-Dec. Train ride schedule varies; phone ahead. **Cost:** Payette River Adventure $30; $27 (ages 61+); $20 (ages 3-12); $10 (ages 0-2). **Phone:** (208) 331-1184 or (877) 432-7245. [♦]

RECREATIONAL ACTIVITIES
White-water Rafting
- [SAVE] **Cascade Raft and Kayak** is at 7050 SR 55. Other activities are offered. **Hours:** Rafting trips depart daily at 9:30, 1:30 and 5, Apr.-Sept. **Phone:** (208) 793-2221 or (800) 292-7238.

IDAHO CITY   (F-2) pop. 485, elev. 4,000'

Soon after gold was discovered in the Boise Basin in 1862, Idaho City became one of the largest cities in the Pacific Northwest. By 1865 it was home to some 7,000 gold seekers; nearly one quarter were Chinese. At its peak the basin was home to 15,000-20,000 miners. The mining district around Idaho City, including nearby Placerville and Centerville, was one of the largest sources of gold ever discovered.

More than 20 pioneer buildings from the 1860s and miles of dredge workings are still visible. The First Masonic Hall, built in 1865 to house Idaho's first Grand Lodge of Masons, displays Masonic items. Idaho City was the site of the territory's first prison, a portion of which has been restored. Guided town walking tours are available from the Boise Basin Museum *(see attraction listing)* by appointment; there is a $30 minimum per group.

Boise National Forest *(see place listing p. 50)* surrounds the town. Idaho City lies on scenic SR 21, also known as the Ponderosa Pine Scenic Route. SR 21 heads northeast through Sawtooth National Forest *(see place listing p. 96)* and ends in Stanley.

Idaho City Chamber of Commerce: 100 Main St., P.O. Box 507, Idaho City, ID 83631. **Phone:** (208) 392-4159.

BOISE BASIN MUSEUM, Montgomery St. at Wall St., was erected as a post office in 1867 and served as a stage and freight company station before being renovated for its present use. Exhibits, which commemorate the town's origin with memorabilia from its days as a mining boomtown, include a working stamp mill model. A video presentation about basin history is shown.

Hours: Daily 11-4 or by appointment, Memorial Day-Labor Day; Fri.-Sun. 11-4 or by appointment, May 1-day before Memorial Day and day after Labor Day-Oct. 31. Phone ahead to confirm schedule. **Cost:** $2; $1.50 (ages 65+ and students with ID); $5 (family, two adults and two children ages 0-17). **Phone:** (208) 392-4550.

A ONE STEP AWAY BED & BREAKFAST   208/392-4938
♦ Historic Bed & Breakfast $50-$90 **Address:** 112 Cottonwood St 83631 **Location:** At SR 21 and Cottonwood St; just w of center. **Facility:** This 102-year-old building in a small mountain community began as a dredging company's workplace. The small guest rooms are comfortably appointed. 4 units. 1-2 stories (no elevator), exterior corridors. **Terms:** cancellation fee imposed. **Activities:** fishing, cross country skiing, snowmobiling.
[♦] [⚲] [✕] [⚱] [▤] [▣] [▬]

IDAHO FALLS   (G-5) pop. 56,813, elev. 4,742'
- Restaurants p. 70

Although it lies miles from the silver and gold lodes discovered in the region during the mid-1800s, Idaho Falls owes its formation to these riches. The settlement—originally called Taylor's Crossing—was established about 1860 along one of the few fording points on the upper Snake River. J.M. Taylor's ferry attracted many miners en route to Montana from Salt Lake City.

As the veins of precious metal diminished, transients and disillusioned residents abandoned the area. The few remaining settlers, faced with either adopting a new livelihood or adding the community to the growing list of Western ghost towns, dug channels to irrigate the arid land. Soon the town flourished along with the newly established agriculture. The irrigation system that saved the town now provides water to more than 1 million acres of farmland.

Tautphaus Park has sports facilities, picnic grounds, amusement rides and a zoo *(see attraction listing)*. Sandy Downs, 2 miles south of 17th Street on St. Clair Road, is the site of various recreational activities.

Greater Idaho Falls Chamber of Commerce & Visitors Center: 425 N. Capital Ave., Idaho Falls, ID 83402. **Phone:** (208) 523-1010 or (866) 365-6943.

THE ART MUSEUM OF EASTERN IDAHO, 300 S. Capitol Ave., is the only art museum in southeastern Idaho. Changing exhibitions featuring local and regional art are offered. **Time:** Allow 30 minutes minimum. **Hours:** Tues.-Sat. 11-5. Closed major holidays. **Cost:** $4; $2 (ages 6-18 and college students with ID); free (ages 0-5, senior citizens first Tues. of the month and to all first Sat. of the month); $10 (family). **Phone:** (208) 524-7777.

IDAHO FALLS is .5 mi. e. off I-15 Broadway exit 118, then n. on River Pkwy. The low but picturesque and turbulent waterfall in the Snake River is 1,200 feet wide. Next to the scenic falls is a 2.5-mile river walk. 🏞

THE MUSEUM OF IDAHO is off I-15 exit 118 (Broadway) at 200 N. Eastern Ave. It features such exhibits as Race for Atomic Power, which documents important milestones in the history of nuclear energy that occurred in southeastern Idaho; Lewis and Clark in Idaho; Bonneville County, 1911-2011: A Centennial Celebration; and Eagle Rock USA, a replica of the 19th-century community that later became Idaho Falls.

Temporary exhibitions also are offered. **Time:** Allow 1 hour minimum. **Hours:** Mon.-Tues. 9-8, Wed.-Sat. 9-5. Closed Jan. 1, Thanksgiving and Christmas. Phone ahead to confirm schedule. **Cost:** $8; $7 (ages 62+); $6 (ages 4-17); $25 (family); $20 (family, Mon. 5-8 p.m.). Prices may vary. **Phone:** (208) 522-1400.

TAUTPHAUS PARK ZOO is at Rogers St. and Carnival Way. Housed in regional habitats representing North and South America, Africa, Asia, Australia and New Guinea, more than 400 creatures inhabit Idaho's largest zoo. Animal encounter shows are scheduled daily in summer. Also popular is the Penguin Interaction Program in which participants meet a zookeeper, interact with the birds and learn about the fascinating lives of penguins. A children's zoo and plant identification gardens are on-site.

Time: Allow 1 hour minimum. **Hours:** Zoo daily 9-5 (also holiday Mon. and fourth Mon. of the month 5-7), Memorial Day weekend-Labor Day; 9-4, mid-Apr. through day before Memorial Day weekend and day after Labor Day-early Oct. Penguin Interaction Program is offered Thurs.-Sun. at 11, late May-early Oct. **Cost:** Zoo $6; $4.50 (ages 62+); $3 (ages 4-12). Penguin Interaction Program $20; $10 (ages 4-12). Prices may vary; phone ahead. Reservations

for the Penguin Interaction Program are strongly recommended. **Phone:** (208) 612-8552.

BEST WESTERN PLUS COTTONTREE INN
(208)523-6000

Hotel
$80-$140

AAA Benefit: Members save 10% or more with Best Western!

Address: 900 Lindsay Blvd 83402 **Location:** I-15 exit 119, just e. **Facility:** 94 units, some efficiencies. 3 stories, interior corridors. **Parking:** winter plug-ins. **Pool(s):** heated indoor. **Activities:** hot tub, exercise room. **Guest Services:** valet and coin laundry.

BEST WESTERN PLUS DRIFTWOOD INN   (208)523-2242

Motel
$79-$149

AAA Benefit: Members save 10% or more with Best Western!

Address: 575 River Pkwy 83402 **Location:** I-15 exit 118, 0.5 mi e, then 0.3 mi n. **Facility:** 75 units, some efficiencies and kitchens. 2 stories (no elevator), exterior corridors. **Parking:** winter plug-ins. **Pool(s):** heated outdoor. **Activities:** hot tub, bicycles, exercise room. **Guest Services:** valet and coin laundry.

CANDLEWOOD SUITES   208/525-9800

Extended Stay Hotel. Rates not provided. **Address:** 665 Pancheri Dr 83402 **Location:** I-15 exit 118, 1 mi e (cross bridge), then 0.5 mi s on S Capital Ave. **Facility:** 81 kitchen units. 4 stories, interior corridors. **Activities:** picnic facilities, exercise room. **Guest Services:** complimentary laundry.

FAIRFIELD INN & SUITES BY MARRIOTT   (208)552-7378

Contemporary Hotel
$109-$149

FAIRFIELD INN & SUITES Marriott
AAA Benefit: Members save 5% or more!

Address: 1293 W Broadway St 83402 **Location:** I-15 exit 118, just e. Next to a shopping area. **Facility:** 81 units. 3 stories, interior corridors. **Pool(s):** heated indoor. **Activities:** hot tub, exercise room. **Guest Services:** valet and coin laundry.

HAMPTON INN   (208)529-9800

Contemporary Hotel $89-$119 **Address:** 2500 Channing Way 83404 **Location:** I-15 exit 118, 1 mi e, 0.5 mi s on Yellowstone Hwy, 2.7 mi e on 17th St, then 0.3 mi s. Adjacent to a shopping mall. **Facility:** 79 units. 3 stories, interior corridors. **Terms:** 1-7 night minimum stay, cancellation fee imposed. **Pool(s):** heated indoor. **Activities:** hot tub, exercise room. **Guest Services:** valet and coin laundry, area transportation.

AAA Benefit: Members save up to 10%!

HAMPTON INN AIRPORT (208)523-1400

WWW Contemporary Hotel $74-$129 **Address:** 645 Lindsay Blvd 83402 **Location:** I-15 exit 118, 0.4 mi e, then just n; exit 119, 0.4 mi se. **Facility:** 127 units, some efficiencies. 4 stories, interior corridors. **Terms:** 1-7 night minimum stay, cancellation fee imposed. **Pool(s):** heated indoor. **Activities:** hot tub, exercise room. **Guest Services:** valet and coin laundry, area transportation.

AAA Benefit:
Members save up to 10%!

HILTON GARDEN INN IDAHO FALLS (208)522-9500

WWW Hotel $109-$189 **Address:** 700 Lindsay Blvd 83402 **Location:** I-15 exit 118, 0.5 mi e, then just n. **Facility:** 119 units. 4 stories, interior corridors. **Parking:** winter plug-ins. **Terms:** 1-7 night minimum stay, cancellation fee imposed. **Amenities:** video games. **Pool(s):** heated indoor. **Activities:** hot tub, exercise room. **Guest Services:** valet and coin laundry.

AAA Benefit:
Members save up to 10%!

HOLIDAY INN EXPRESS & SUITES (208)542-9800

WWW Contemporary Hotel $109-$149 **Address:** 2270 Channing Way 83404 **Location:** I-15 exit 118, 1 mi e, 0.5 mi s on Yellowstone Hwy, 2.7 mi e on 17th St, then 0.3 mi s. Adjacent to a shopping mall. **Facility:** 79 units. 3 stories, interior corridors. **Parking:** winter plug-ins. **Pool(s):** heated indoor. **Activities:** hot tub, exercise room. **Guest Services:** valet and coin laundry, area transportation.

HOTEL ON THE FALLS (208)523-8000

WW Hotel $75-$220 **Address:** 475 River Pkwy 83402 **Location:** I-15 exit 118, 0.5 mi e, then just n. **Facility:** 140 units. 8 stories, interior/exterior corridors. **Pool(s):** heated outdoor. **Activities:** sauna, hot tub, exercise room. **Guest Services:** valet and coin laundry, area transportation.

LA QUINTA INN & SUITES IDAHO FALLS (208)552-2500

WWW Hotel $109-$154 **Address:** 2501 S 25th St E 83406 **Location:** I-15 exit 118, 1 mi e, 0.5 mi s on Yellowstone Hwy, 3.8 mi e on 17th St to Hitt Rd, then just s. Located near shopping area. **Facility:** 84 units, some efficiencies. 3 stories, interior corridors. **Pool(s):** heated indoor. **Activities:** hot tub, exercise room. **Guest Services:** valet and coin laundry.

LE RITZ HOTEL & SUITES (208)528-0880

WW Hotel $69-$129 **Address:** 720 Lindsay Blvd 83402 **Location:** I-15 exit 118, 0.5 mi e, then 0.4 mi n. **Facility:** 116 units. 2 stories, interior corridors. **Parking:** winter plug-ins. **Pool(s):** heated indoor. **Activities:** hot tub, exercise room. **Guest Services:** valet and coin laundry.

RESIDENCE INN BY MARRIOTT (208)542-0000

WWW Extended Stay Hotel $129-$179 **Address:** 635 W Broadway 83402 **Location:** I-15 exit 118, 0.4 mi e. **Facility:** 108 efficiencies, some two bedrooms and kitchens. 5 stories, interior corridors. **Pool(s):** heated indoor. **Activities:** hot tub, picnic facilities, exercise room. **Guest Services:** valet and coin laundry, boarding pass kiosk.

AAA Benefit:
Members save 5% or more!

SLEEP INN & SUITES (208)821-3647

WWW Contemporary Hotel $81-$99 **Address:** 3200 Outlet Blvd 83405 **Location:** I-15 exit 116, just w. **Facility:** 75 units. 3 stories, interior corridors. **Amenities:** safes. **Pool(s):** heated indoor. **Activities:** hot tub, exercise room. **Guest Services:** valet and coin laundry.

WHERE TO EAT

BLUE HASHI 208/525-2583

WW Japanese. Casual Dining. $7-$15 **AAA Inspector Notes:** Translated, the name of this casual spot means chopsticks. Voted best Japanese food for 3 years by locals in Idaho Falls, the chefs here create a few distinctive sushi rolls, and if they are received well, they become a regular menu item. Along with popular sashimi, maki and sushi there are a few yakisoba noodle dishes and fully cooked entrées with rice and vegetables. **Features:** beer & wine. **Address:** 2894 S 25th E 83401 **Location:** I-15 exit 116, 5 mi e on Sunnyside Rd, just n on S Hitt Rd, then just w. [L] [D]

JALISCO'S MEXICAN RESTAURANT 208/612-0102

WW Mexican. Casual Dining. $7-$15 **AAA Inspector Notes:** Across from the falls, this colorful eatery has a varied menu including four choices of soup, traditional beef, chicken and pork entrées and combinations for one, two or three items. All dishes are thoughtfully presented. The background music is festive. **Features:** beer & wine. **Address:** 325 River Pkwy 83401 **Location:** I-15 exit 118, 0.4 mi e, then just n. [L] [D]

THE SANDPIPER 208/524-3344

WW American. Casual Dining. $11-$27 **AAA Inspector Notes:** Adjacent to the Snake River, this small-town, locally popular restaurant serves immense amounts of food. For starters, try the tasty pan-fried oysters, then move on to an entree of hearty barbecued ribs. Seasonal patio dining with views of the river also is available. **Features:** full bar. **Address:** 750 Lindsay Blvd 83402 **Location:** I-15 exit 118, 0.5 mi e, then 0.4 mi n. [D]

THE SNAKEBITE RESTAURANT 208/525-2522

WW American. Casual Dining. $7-$26 **AAA Inspector Notes:** The comfortable décor and notable food are nice departures from the endless supply of fast food outlets in the area. There is a nice selection of gourmet burgers and salads, sandwiches and pasta. Dinner entrées include bourbon chicken, osso buco and tequila salmon, to name a few. **Features:** beer & wine. **Address:** 401 Park Ave 83402 **Location:** I-15 exit 118, 0.6 mi e, just n on Shoup Ave, then just w; corner of A St and Park Ave; in historic downtown. **Parking:** street only. [L] [D]

IDAHO PANHANDLE NATIONAL FORESTS (B-1)

Elevations in the forests range from 2,060 ft. at Lake Pend Oreille to 7,705 ft. at Northwest Peak. Refer to AAA maps for additional elevation information.

In northern Idaho and adjoining parts of Montana and Washington, the many-segmented Idaho Panhandle National Forests have rugged peaks, canyons and valleys. The approximately 2.5-million-acre area includes the former St. Joe, Kaniksu and Coeur d'Alene national forests.

Of particular interest are the stands of old-growth cedars at Hanna Flats and Roosevelt Grove near Priest Lake, the Settlers Grove of Ancient Cedars near Prichard and the Hobo Cedar Grove near Clarkia. Among the nearly 400 species of wildlife are wolves and grizzly bears.

Fishing is available at Priest Lake, Lake Coeur d'Alene and Lake Pend Oreille; nature trails traverse these areas. Float trips are popular on the Coeur d'Alene, St. Joe and Priest rivers. Winter sports areas are off SR 6 between St. Maries and Moscow, at Lookout Pass just off I-90 on the Idaho-Montana border and at 4th of July Pass off I-90.

Information is available at the headquarters in Coeur d'Alene and at ranger stations at Avery, Bonners Ferry, Priest River, St. Maries, Sandpoint and Smelterville. For additional information contact the Forest Supervisor's Office, Idaho Panhandle National Forests, 3815 Schreiber Way, Coeur d'Alene, ID 83815-8363; phone (208) 765-7223. *See Recreation Areas Chart.*

ISLAND PARK (F-6) pop. 286, elev. 6,293'

The scattered settlement of Island Park lies at the northern edge of Henry's Fork Caldera, also known as the Mesa Falls Caldera, an ancient volcanic feature. Millions of years ago, this was an active supervolcano. When the volcano collapsed some 1.3 million years ago, it left behind a giant, circular crater with a diameter of 18 to 23 miles. The caldera is known for its beautiful forests, clear streams, waterfalls, springs, lakes, marshes, wildlife and fishing.

HARRIMAN STATE PARK is 9 mi. s. on US 20 to 3489 Green Canyon Rd., following signs. Occupying the site of the 11,000-acre Railroad Ranch, owned by Union Pacific Railroad investors 1902-77, the park is today a wildlife refuge within the greater Yellowstone ecosystem.

Free 1-hour ranger-led walking tours visit several of the historic ranch buildings on-site. More than 20 miles of hiking, mountain biking and equestrian trails traverse the park, which is known for its spectacular summer wildflower displays. Dry Ridge Outfitters offers guided horseback rides in summer and fall, and winter draws Nordic skiers and snowshoers. *See Recreation Areas Chart.*

Pets must be leashed and are allowed in day-use parking lots only. **Time:** Allow 1 hour minimum. **Hours:** Park open daily dawn-dusk. Visitor center open daily 8-4, June-Aug. Ranch walking tours are given Sat.-Sun. and holidays, Memorial Day-Labor Day. Trail rides are available daily, Memorial Day weekend-Oct. 31 (weather permitting). **Cost:** Day-use fee $5 (per private vehicle). Trail rides $35-$55. **Phone:** (208) 558-7368. ⊗ ⛱

JEROME pop. 10,890

BEST WESTERN SAWTOOTH INN & SUITES
(208)324-9200

Hotel
$90-$110

AAA Benefit: Members save 10% or more with Best Western!

Address: 2653 S Lincoln Ave 83338 **Location:** I-84 exit 168, just n. Across from shopping center and next to gas station. **Facility:** 67 units. 2 stories (no elevator), interior corridors. **Terms:** check-in 4 pm. **Pool(s):** heated indoor. **Activities:** hot tub, exercise room. **Guest Services:** valet and coin laundry. **Featured Amenity: full hot breakfast.** *(See ad p. 100.)*

SAVE ⊷ BIZ 🛜 ⊗ 🛏 🖥 🖵 / SOME UNITS 🔧 HS

COMFORT INN & SUITES   (208)644-1200
Hotel $99-$119 **Address:** 379 Crossroads Point Blvd 83338 **Location:** I-84 exit 173, 0.3 mi n. **Facility:** 103 units. 3 stories, interior corridors. **Amenities:** safes. **Pool(s):** heated indoor. **Activities:** hot tub, exercise room. **Guest Services:** valet and coin laundry.
⊷ BIZ HS 🛜 ⊗ 🛏 🖥 🖵 / SOME UNITS 🔧

DAYS INN TWIN FALLS/JEROME   (208)324-6400
Hotel $69-$110 **Address:** 1200 Centennial Spur 83338 **Location:** I-84 exit 173, just n on US 93. Next to truck stop. **Facility:** 72 units. 3 stories, interior corridors. *Bath:* shower only. **Activities:** hot tub, limited exercise equipment. **Guest Services:** coin laundry.
🛜 🖵 / SOME UNITS 🔧 🛏 🖵

KAMIAH (D-2) pop. 1,295, elev. 1,196'
• Hotels p. 72 • Restaurants p. 72

Meriwether Lewis and William Clark camped on the north bank of the Clearwater River just north of Kamiah (KAM-ee-eye) in the spring of 1806 on their homeward journey. Today a sawmill occupies the site of their monthlong encampment.

A pasture about a half mile northwest of Kamiah is supposedly the location of the mission that Asa and Sarah Smith started in 1839. They stayed only 2 years, and their work in this area was not resumed until 30 years later.

The 1871 First Presbyterian Church is said to be the oldest Native American church in continuous use in Idaho. The Northwest Passage Scenic Byway (US 12) also passes through town. It's considered one of the top 10 motorcycle roads in the nation.

Kamiah Chamber of Commerce: 518 Main St., P.O. Box 1124, Kamiah, ID 83536. **Phone:** (208) 935-2290.

EAST KAMIAH, 2 mi. e. on US 12, has a volcanic rock formation, Heart of the Monster, the place of creation in Nez Perce mythology. Folklore says that in the prehuman years a monster was devouring the animals. Coyote, the chief animal, slew the monster, cut him into pieces and scattered these bits to the winds. Where each bit landed a new Indian tribe arose. The

Nez Perce tribe came from blood from the monster's heart. East Kamiah is a designated site of Nez Perce National Historical Park *(see place listing p. 85)*. An interpretive display is available. **Hours:** Daily dawn-dusk. **Phone:** (208) 843-7001, ext. 7020.

CLEARWATER 12 MOTEL   208/935-2671
▼▼ **Motel.** Rates not provided. **Address:** 108 E 3rd St (Hwy 12) 83536 **Location:** On US 12, just e of center. **Facility:** 29 units, some kitchens. 2 stories (no elevator), exterior corridors.
[ↂ] [🛜] [🅱] [🖥] [💵] / SOME UNITS [💲]

HEARTHSTONE ELEGANT LODGE ON THE RIVER
                                          (208)935-1492

Bed & Breakfast
$125-$235

Address: 3250 Hwy 12 at Milepost 64 83536 **Location:** 2.2 mi w of center. **Facility:** Spacious, artistically appointed rooms have fine linens on canopied king-size beds with beautiful antique headboards, vaulted ceilings, fireplaces and covered deck entrances with skylights. 5 units, some cottages. 1-2 stories (no elevator), exterior corridors. **Terms:** check-in 4 pm, 3 day cancellation notice. **Activities:** beach access, fishing, massage. **Featured Amenity: full hot breakfast.**
[SAVE] [BIZ] [🛜] [✕] [🅱] [🖥]

WHERE TO EAT

HEARTHSTONE RESTAURANT BAKERY   208/935-1912
▼▼ American. Casual Dining. $5-$20 **AAA Inspector Notes:** *Historic.* This charming restaurant has the feel of a Victorian tea room. Salads, sandwiches and soups are all made in-house and taste great with freshly baked breads of several varieties. Desserts abound and range from cookies and cinnamon rolls to fruit and cream pies. Dinner service is offered Thursday through Saturday. **Features:** beer & wine. **Address:** 502 Main St 83536 **Location:** Downtown.
[B] [L] CALL [💲M]

KELLOGG (B-1) pop. 2,120, elev. 2,305'

Kellogg, the Silver Valley's largest town, celebrates its heritage as a longtime mining community. The Coeur d'Alene mining district has yielded more than a billion dollars in silver, lead, gold and zinc; the Lucky Friday, Sunshine Silver Mine and Galena Mine are a few of the largest mines that still operate. The Shoshone County Mining and Smelting Museum, also known as The Staff House Museum *(see attraction listing)*, chronicles the colorful history of Silver Valley. The Sunshine Mine Disaster Memorial, off I-90 exit 54, commemorates the 1972 mine fire that claimed 91 lives. It was one of the nation's worst metal and nonmetal mine disasters.

The Kellogg area also is known for outdoor recreation, particularly its biking trails, which range from easy to "What was I thinking?" Accessible here is the Trail of the Coeur d'Alenes, a 72-mile paved path that runs from the Montana border to the Washington state line. Hardy cyclists also can take their bikes up the Silver Mountain Gondola *(see attraction listing)* to enjoy 40 miles of trails, including some that descend 3,000 feet.

Historic Silver Valley Chamber of Commerce: 10 Station Ave., Kellogg, ID 83837. **Phone:** (208) 784-0821.

CRYSTAL GOLD MINE is off I-90 exit 54 (Big Creek Rd.) westbound or I-90 exit 51 (N. Division St.) eastbound at 51931 Silver Valley Rd. The guided underground tours conducted by experienced miners provide an interesting glimpse into the hand-labor, hard-rock mining of the late 1800s. Gold, silver and smithsonite are visible inside the mine. The temperature inside the mine is 48 F; visitors should dress appropriately.

Time: Allow 30 minutes minimum. **Hours:** Tours depart every 15 to 30 minutes daily 9-6, Apr. 1-Sept. 15; 10-4, rest of year. Closed Jan. 1, Easter, Thanksgiving and Christmas. **Cost:** (includes 1 hour of gold panning Apr.-Sept.) $12; $11 (ages 65+); $8.50 (ages 4-16); $45 (family, two adults and three children, $5 for each additional child). **Phone:** (208) 783-4653. [▲]

SILVER MOUNTAIN GONDOLA is .25 mi. e. off I-90 exit 49 to 610 Bunker Ave. Riders travel 3.1 miles in what is said to be North America's longest single-stage gondola. The ride takes 24 minutes to go 3,400 feet from the base to the Mountain House upper terminal. Mountain House features include mountain biking and hiking trails, a children's play area, a nature trail and an amphitheater where concerts are staged.

Time: Allow 2 hours minimum. **Hours:** Sun.-Tues. 9:30-4, Fri. 2-8, Sat. 9:30-5, July-Aug.; Sat. 9:30-5, Sun. 9:30-4, in June and Sept. Last departure up the mountain is 30 minutes before closing. **Cost:** $17; $13 (ages 4-17); $54 (family, four people, $11 for each additional person). Prices vary on weekends. **Phone:** (208) 783-1111, ext. 8240, or (800) 204-6428.

THE STAFF HOUSE MUSEUM, 820 McKinley Ave., is in a 1906 house built for the Bunker Hill Mine's top executive. The museum has geological, mining, smelting, medical and Boy Scout exhibits. Displays include mineral collections, mine models and photographs. An outdoor display features an 1895 Nordberg compressor once used to pump air underground into mines. **Time:** Allow 30 minutes minimum. **Hours:** Wed.-Mon. 10-6, late May-late Sept. **Cost:** $4; $3 (ages 55+); $1 (ages 6-18); $6 (family). **Phone:** (208) 786-4141.

RECREATIONAL ACTIVITIES
Skiing
- **Silver Mountain Resort** is off I-90 exit 49 at 610 Bunker Ave. Other activities are offered. **Hours:** Winter activities are available Thurs.-Mon. 9-4, late Nov. to mid-Apr. Schedule varies during holiday weeks; phone ahead. **Phone:** (208) 783-1111 or (800) 204-6428.

GUESTHOUSE INN & SUITES   208/783-1234
▼▼ **Hotel.** Rates not provided. **Address:** 601 Bunker Ave 83837 **Location:** I-90 exit 49, 0.5 mi se. **Facility:** 60 units. 2 stories (no elevator), interior corridors. **Parking:** winter plug-ins. **Pool(s):** heated indoor. **Activities:** hot tub, bicycles, exercise room. **Guest Services:** coin laundry.
[ↂ+] CALL [💲M] [🍽] [🛜] [🅱] [🖥] [💵] / SOME UNITS [💲]

MORNING STAR LODGE (208)783-0202

 Resort Condominium $101-$720 **Address:** 602 Bunker Ave 83837 **Location:** I-90 exit 49, 0.5 mi se. **Facility:** The condos at this ski resort are spacious and feature upscale décor. On the property and included in the room rate is an elaborate water park and nearby is the famous Route of the Hiawatha trail. 215 condominiums. 4-5 stories, interior corridors. **Parking:** winter plug-ins. **Terms:** check-in 4 pm, cancellation fee imposed, resort fee. **Dining:** 3 restaurants. **Activities:** hot tub, regulation golf, downhill skiing, bicycles, exercise room, massage. **Guest Services:** complimentary laundry, area transportation.

⊕ 🍴 🍸 BIZ HS 🐾 ⊠ 🔋 🖼 💻 / SOME UNITS 💲🐾

SILVERHORN MOTOR INN 208/783-1151

🔷 **Hotel** $69-$120 **Address:** 699 W Cameron Ave 83837 **Location:** I-90 exit 49, just ne. **Facility:** 40 units. 2 stories (no elevator), interior corridors. **Parking:** winter plug-ins. **Activities:** hot tub, limited exercise equipment. **Guest Services:** complimentary laundry.

🍴 BIZ 🛜 🔋 🖼 / SOME UNITS 🐾

KETCHUM (G-3) pop. 2,689, elev. 5,821'
• **Restaurants p. 74**

In the late 19th century Ketchum sprang up almost overnight as a shipping and smelting center for the remote mountain mines surrounding the Wood River Valley. Ores and supplies were transported by the giant ore wagons of the Horace Lewis Fast Freight Line. These relics of the area's past are displayed in the Ore Wagon Museum on East Avenue next to City Hall and once again appear on the streets during the Wagon Days Celebration Labor Day weekend. The history and culture of Wood River Valley's sheep industry is spotlighted in October during the 🐑 Trailing of the Sheep festival. The Ketchum Cemetery includes the grave of Ernest Hemingway.

As the gateway to the Sun Valley *(see place listing p. 99)* resort area and the Sawtooth National Recreation Area *(see place listing p. 97)*, the town offers an abundance of activities year-round. Such outdoor recreational activities as swimming, moun-

tain biking and bicycling, hiking, horseback riding, cross-country skiing, snowshoeing and camping are foremost among Ketchum's attractions. For the spectator Ketchum offers some 30 art galleries and the nexStage Theatre, where local theater companies perform year-round. For theater information phone (208) 726-4857.

Sun Valley Visitors Center: 491 Sun Valley Rd., Ketchum ID 83340. **Phone:** (208) 726-3423 or (800) 634-3347.

Self-guiding tours: The Heritage & Ski Museum, 1st Street and Washington Avenue, has a booklet about the history of Ketchum that includes a walking tour through the downtown area; phone (208) 726-8118.

Shopping areas: Downtown Ketchum offers more than 70 shops and restaurants offering everything from antiques and books to children's toys and specialty gifts.

RECREATIONAL ACTIVITIES
Horseback Riding
• **Galena Stage Stop Corrals-Trail Rides** is 24 mi. n. on SR 75. Other activities are offered. **Hours:** Horseback riding trips daily 8-5, mid-June through Labor Day. **Phone:** (208) 726-1735.

BEST WESTERN PLUS KENTWOOD LODGE
(208)726-4114

 Hotel $100-$230

 AAA Benefit: Members save 10% or more with Best Western!

Address: 180 S Main St 83340 **Location:** On SR 75, at Main and Rivers sts. **Facility:** 57 units, some efficiencies. 3 stories, interior corridors. **Terms:** 2 night minimum stay - seasonal, 7 day cancellation notice-fee imposed. **Pool(s):** heated indoor. **Activities:** hot tub, exercise room. **Guest Services:** valet and coin laundry.

SAVE 🍴 🏊 BIZ 🛜 ⊠ 🔋

🖼 💻

▼ *See AAA listing p. 74* ▼

RESORTQUEST - CHRISTOPHE CONDOMINIUMS
208/726-5601

Condominium. Rates not provided. **Address:** 351 2nd Ave S 83340 **Location:** Just w of Main St (SR 75) on Rivers St; south end of town. **Facility:** These condominiums offer comfortable guest rooms. 15 condominiums. 3 stories, exterior corridors. **Terms:** off-site registration, check-in 4 pm. **Pool(s):** heated outdoor. **Activities:** hot tub. **Guest Services:** coin laundry.

TAMARACK LODGE
208/726-3344

Motel $101-$179 **Address:** 291 Walnut Ave N 83340 **Location:** 0.3 mi e on Sun Valley Rd. **Facility:** 26 units. 2-3 stories (no elevator), interior/exterior corridors. **Parking:** winter plug-ins. **Terms:** check-in 4 pm, cancellation fee imposed. **Pool(s):** heated indoor. **Activities:** hot tub, bicycles.

WHERE TO EAT

CRISTINA'S RESTAURANT & BAKERY
208/726-4499

European. Casual Dining. $10-$19 **AAA Inspector Notes:** This popular eatery is located in a charming salmon-colored house. The seasonally-inspired menu includes an assortment of hot and cold appetizers and entrées, salads, homemade pasta, thin crust pizza and truly mouth-watering desserts, breads and pastries. **Features:** beer & wine, Sunday brunch. **Reservations:** suggested. **Address:** 520 2nd St E 83340 **Location:** Just e on 3rd St, s on East Ave to 2nd St, then just e. B L

DESPO'S
208/726-3068

Mexican. Casual Dining. $8-$15 **AAA Inspector Notes:** This modern Mexican restaurant specializes in sustainable practices when attaining their tasty ingredients. Supporting local and regional farms, the menu is comprised of only the freshest ingredients. **Features:** full bar. **Address:** 211 4th St E 83340 **Location:** Jct Washington Ave; downtown. **Parking:** on-site and street. L D

GLOBUS RESTAURANT & WINE BAR
208/726-1301

Asian. Fine Dining. $15-$38 **AAA Inspector Notes:** The ambience is colorful, intimate and inviting. Creative, seasonal and flavorful starters, salads and entrées are meticulously prepared and may include watermelon terrine, steamed clay pot mussels, Korean style pork baby back ribs or pomegranate seared duck breast in celery root purée. The roasted chicken breast in cauliflower-miso purée with glazed carrots, grapefruit and frisée is beautifully presented. An extensive wine list and a nice selection of teas also are offered. **Features:** beer & wine. **Reservations:** suggested. **Address:** 291 6th St 83340 **Location:** At 6th St and Warm Springs Rd, just w of 6th and Main sts. D

JAVA ON FOURTH
208/726-2882

American. Quick Serve. $4-$9 **AAA Inspector Notes:** This quaint and eclectic cafe always is bustling with locals and tourists alike. From soup and sandwiches to delicious granola and fresh pastries, the menu offers something for everyone. **Address:** 191 4th St 83340 **Location:** North end of town; on SR 75 (Main St), just w. **Parking:** on-site and street. B L

KETCHUM GRILL
208/726-4660

American. Casual Dining. $6-$20 **AAA Inspector Notes:** This casual, rustic restaurant, located in a converted house, offers seasonal appetizers, entrées and desserts, all creatively presented. **Features:** full bar, patio dining. **Reservations:** suggested. **Address:** 520 East Ave N 83340 **Location:** At East Ave and 5th St; downtown. **Parking:** street only. D

MICHEL'S CHRISTIANIA RESTAURANT & OLYMPIC BAR
208/726-3388

French. Fine Dining. $20-$38 **AAA Inspector Notes:** This casually elegant restaurant serves a variety of fresh dishes in one of the country's premier ski and summer resort communities. The lounge is a local favorite and draws a lively, conversational crowd. Seasonal patio dining also is available. **Features:** full bar. **Reservations:** suggested. **Address:** 303 N Walnut Ave 83340 **Location:** 0.3 mi e on Sun Valley Rd. **Parking:** street only. D

SAWTOOTH CLUB
208/726-5233

American. Casual Dining. $14-$32 **AAA Inspector Notes:** This rustic - and, at times, loud and energetic - but always popular watering hole appeals to the casual après-ski crowd as well as the summer tourist. The distinctive flavor of mesquite grilling infuses large cuts of beef and the house specialty, Idaho rack of lamb. Signature potato skin appetizers are produced at a near-constant pace. **Features:** full bar, patio dining. **Reservations:** suggested. **Address:** 231 N Main St 83340 **Location:** Corner of 2nd Ave and SR 75 (Main St); downtown. **Parking:** street only. D

SMOKY MOUNTAIN PIZZERIA GRILL
208/622-5625

Italian. Family Dining. $7-$27 **AAA Inspector Notes:** Situated in the Sawtooth Mountains, this local favorite offers the perfect setting for a get-together, with a game room to entertain the kids and a rotating beer tap for the adults. **Features:** beer & wine, happy hour. **Address:** 200 Sun Valley Rd 83340 **Location:** North end of town; SR 75 (Main St), just w. **Parking:** street only. L D

WHISKEY JACQUES'
208/726-5297

American. Casual Dining. $9-$18 **AAA Inspector Notes:** This favorite watering hole is the place to experience all of the local flavor in the Ketchum and Sun Valley area. With live music multiple evenings per week, the atmosphere is always fun-filled, lively and bustling. The menu offers a variety of pizza, salads, sandwiches, wraps and burgers. **Features:** full bar, happy hour. **Address:** 251 N Main St 83340 **Location:** On SR 75 (Main St); downtown. **Parking:** street only. D LATE

KOOSKIA (D-2) pop. 607, elev. 1,261'

Kooskia (KOOS-key), founded in 1895 at the confluence of the Middle and South Forks of the Clearwater River, takes its name from a Nez Perce phrase meaning "where the waters meet."

Kooskia Chamber of Commerce: P.O. Box 310, Kooskia, ID 83539. **Phone:** (208) 926-4362.

KOOSKIA NATIONAL FISH HATCHERY is 2 mi. s.e. on Clear Creek County Rd. Chinook salmon eggs are collected, incubated and hatched, and the young fish are reared. The best times to visit are in early March before the young chinook are set free or during June and July when the adults return to spawn. An interpretive trail passes a historic mill and an Indian village site. **Hours:** Daily 8-3. Closed major holidays. **Cost:** Free. **Phone:** (208) 926-4272.

REFLECTIONS INN   208/926-0855

▼▼▼▼▼ **Bed & Breakfast** $99-$149 **Address:** 6873 Hwy 12 83539 **Location:** 11 mi e of Kooskia on US 12; between MM 84 and 85. Located in a quiet secluded area. **Facility:** In true ranch style, guest units are separate from the main house, dining and extensive indoor and outdoor common areas. The property is set on 10 wooded acres surrounded by a mountain and river. 8 units, some kitchens. 2 stories (no elevator), exterior corridors. **Terms:** 7 day cancellation notice-fee imposed, resort fee. **Activities:** hot tub, picnic facilities. **Guest Services:** coin laundry.

🛜 ⊠ 🛗 🖼 🔋 💻

RIVER DANCE LODGE   (208)926-4300

▼▼▼▼▼ **Vacation Rental Cabin** $109-$419 **Address:** 7743 Hwy 12 83539 **Location:** On US 12, 16 mi e of Kooskia at MM 89. Located in Syringa. **Facility:** Ideally located for outdoor enthusiasts, this lodge is set back above the banks of the Clearwater River and features hand-crafted custom log cabins, each with a large deck and hot tub. 8 cabins. 2 stories (no elevator), exterior corridors. **Terms:** closed 10/13-4/17, check-in 4 pm, 2-3 night minimum stay - seasonal and/or weekends, 45 day cancellation notice-fee imposed. **Activities:** limited beach access, fishing, snorkeling, bicycles.

🛏 🍽 🛜 🛗 🖼 🔋 🖼 💻
/SOME 🔋
/UNITS

KOOTENAI NATIONAL FOREST—See
Montana p. 186.

LAPWAI (D-1) pop. 1,137, elev. 891'

Lapwai (LAP-way) is the site of the first military fort in Idaho, built in 1862 to prevent clashes between pioneers and Native Americans in the area. The U.S. Army occupied the fort until 1884. Some of the old buildings around the parade ground are still in use. The Old Fort Lapwai Cemetery is located on the ridge just south of the fort.

NORTHERN IDAHO INDIAN AGENCY, 99 Agency Rd. near Fort Lapwai, is the Bureau of Indian Affairs headquarters of Idaho's Nez Perce, Coeur d'Alene and Kootenai Indians. Established in 1862, the agency is a component of Nez Perce National Historical Park *(see place listing p. 85).* The 1883 Officer's Quarters is one of the fort's few original buildings. The Nez Perce Tribal Community Building and Bureau of Indian Affairs Office are .25-mile north of Old Fort Lapwai. **Hours:** Agency open Mon.-Fri. 7:30-4. Closed federal holidays. **Phone:** (208) 843-9410.

LAVA HOT SPRINGS (H-5) pop. 407, elev. 5,151'

Lava Hot Springs was named for the mineral springs that boil out of lava rocks at the base of massive cliffs along the Portneuf River. Geologists believe that the pools have remained at the same temperature—110 F—for 50 million years. Lava Hot Springs is a popular health and pleasure resort offering hiking, bicycling, tubing and swimming.

For centuries the Shoshone and Bannock Indians regarded the springs as a neutral site. But the tribes camp was disrupted during the 19th century when the springs were discovered by Oregon-bound travelers and Utah pioneers who founded a settlement called Dempsey. By 1902 the Native Americans had ceded their rights to the springs, selling the land to the U.S. government, which in turn gave the area to the state.

Pioneer Country Travel Council: P.O. Box 669, Lava Hot Springs, ID 83246. **Phone:** (208) 776-5221 or (888) 201-1063. *(See ad p. 333.)*

IDAHO WORLD FAMOUS HOT POOLS AND OLYMPIC SWIMMING COMPLEX, on US 30E, is a resort that consists of hot mineral pools on the eastern edge of the village and outdoor Olympic-size swimming pools with tube slides on the western edge. The Sunken Gardens bloom on terraces that cling to the walls of an extinct volcano. Snowmobiling and skiing, subject to local weather conditions, are possible on the surrounding mountains.

Hours: Mineral baths daily 8 a.m.-11 p.m., May-Sept.; Sun.-Thurs. 9 a.m.-10 p.m., Fri.-Sat. 9 a.m.-11 p.m., rest of year. Swimming pool daily 11-8, May 1-Labor Day. Closed Thanksgiving and Christmas.

Cost: Mineral bath Fri.-Sun. and holidays $7; $6.50 (ages 3-11 and 60+). Mineral bath Mon.-Thurs. $5.50; $5 (ages 3-11 and 60+). Swimming pool Fri.-Sun. and holidays $9; $8 (ages 3-11); $1.50 (ages 0-2). Swimming pool Mon.-Thurs. $7; $6.50 (ages 3-11); $1.50 (ages 0-2). A combination mineral bath and swimming pool pass is available, as are discounted family rates and all-day passes some days. Prices may vary; phone ahead. **Phone:** (208) 776-5221 or (800) 423-8597.

SOUTH BANNOCK COUNTY HISTORICAL CENTER AND MUSEUM, off US 30 at 110 E. Main St., contains a collection of Native American and pioneer artifacts as well as a permanent exhibit showing the effects of transportation on the area and the six communities of south Bannock County. An interpretive exhibit details the interaction of Native Americans with the natural hot waters. Also featured are A Photographic History of 100 Years of Southeastern Idaho, exhibited through digital media, and a DVD documenting the history of past influential female residents. Also explored is the history of Charles and Nellie Ball, who were immortalized as characters in Owen Wister's "The Virginian," the first western romantic novel. **Hours:** Daily noon-5. Closed Thanksgiving and Christmas. **Cost:** Donations. **Phone:** (208) 776-5254.

LIONS GATE MANOR BED & BREAKFAST   (208)776-5118

▼▼▼▼ **Bed & Breakfast** $119-$229 **Address:** 10376 S Dempsey Creek Rd 83246 **Location:** US 30, just s on Center St, just w on Main St, then 0.7 mi s on 4th Ave to Dempsey Creek Rd, follow signs. **Facility:** The property is set up on a hillside with a community balcony for enjoying striking views of the mountains and valleys. Culturally themed, modern and spacious guest rooms offer luxurious appointments. 8 units. 2 stories (no elevator), interior corridors. **Terms:** check-in 4 pm, cancellation fee imposed. 🛜 ⊠

LEWISTON (D-1) pop. 31,894, elev. 738'

At the confluence of the Clearwater and Snake rivers, Lewiston is on a site where Meriwether Lewis and William Clark camped in 1805 and again in 1806. Following the discovery of gold nearby, the settlement became a supply point for mining camps and, subsequently, the state's first territorial capital 1863-65.

Large quantities of grain and other cargo are shipped from Lewiston, known as "Idaho's Seaport," by barge 465 miles down the Snake and Columbia rivers to the Pacific. Boats reach the port by passing through locks at eight dams.

In April the city celebrates the arrival of spring with the ♥ Dogwood Festival of the Lewis-Clark Valley. Lewiston lies on an especially scenic section of US 95 that extends north to Plummer and south to Banks. North of the city US 95 climbs 2,000 feet to the top of Lewiston Hill, where a viewpoint overlooks the valley. The original road up the hill, known as the Spiral Highway for its 64 curves, opened in 1917. The old road is still open but was replaced in 1979 by the long, easier grade of the new alignment.

Shopping areas: Lewiston Center Mall, 1 mile south of US 12 via 18th or 21st streets, features JCPenney, Macy's and Sears.

BOAT TRIPS UP HELLS CANYON OF THE SNAKE RIVER,

departing from various locations, are spectacular journeys into the main part of Hells Canyon, the deepest river gorge in North America. Most trips, by aluminum jet boat, return the same day; multiday tours also are available. All include one or more meals and offer refreshments. Inquire about age restrictions, refund and weather policies. **Hours:** Jet boat trips depart daily; phone ahead for details. **Cost:** Prices vary. **Phone:** (509) 758-7489 or (877) 774-7248.

HELLS GATE STATE PARK

is 4 mi. s. of US 12 off Snake River Ave. This 360-acre riverside park offers fishing, boating, hiking and other outdoor activities. Boat trips to Hells Canyon depart from docks within the park. *See Recreation Areas Chart.* **Time:** Allow 1 hour minimum. **Hours:** Park open daily dawn-dusk. **Cost:** $5 (per private vehicle). **Phone:** (208) 799-5015. 🏕 🍴 ⊠ 🐾 🌲

Jack O'Connor Hunting Heritage and Education Center

is 4 mi. s. on US 12 to Snake River Ave. in Hells Gate State Park. This museum features exhibits about wildlife resource management and the achievements of outdoor writer, magazine editor and sportsman Jack O'Connor. Displays include shotguns and 65 big game trophies from three continents. An 8-minute orientation video about Idaho wildlife is available. **Time:** Allow 30 minutes minimum. **Hours:** Mon.-Fri. 10-5, Sat.-Sun. 1-5, Labor Day-Memorial Day; Tues.-Fri. 10-4, Sat.-Sun. 1-4, rest of year. **Cost:** Free. **Phone:** (208) 743-5043.

Lewis and Clark Discovery Center is 4 mi. s. on US 12 to Snake River Ave. in Hells Gate State Park. Exhibits focusing on Meriwether Lewis' and William Clark 's journey through Idaho are complemented by a 32-minute video shown hourly in the auditorium. A 2-acre interpretive plaza overlooks the Snake River. **Time:** Allow 45 minutes minimum. **Hours:** Daily 8-6, June-Aug.; 8-4, rest of year. Closed Jan. 1, Thanksgiving and Christmas. Phone ahead to confirm schedule. **Cost:** Free. **Phone:** (208) 799-5015.

River Quest Excursions departs from the marina in Hells Gate State Park, 4 mi. s. on Snake River Ave. Jet boat trips into Hells Canyon include narration about early exploration, mining, wildlife, geology and Native American history. Overnight trips also are available. **Time:** Allow 6 hours minimum. **Hours:** Full-day trips depart daily at 8 a.m., May-Sept. Half-day trips depart daily at 10 a.m., May-Sept. Arrive 30 minutes prior to departure. **Cost:** Full-day trip $165; $65 (ages 0-11). Half-day trip $110; $52 (ages 0-11). **Phone:** (208) 746-8060 or (800) 589-1129.

LEWIS & CLARK INTERPRETIVE CENTER

is at the w. end of D St. between 1st St. and US 12 bypass. An open-air pavilion overlooks the confluence of the Snake and Clearwater rivers, where Meriwether Lewis and William Clark camped in 1805, and features interpretive panels about the explorers' expedition, the Nez Perce Indians and the U.S. Army Corps of Engineers' levee system. Exhibits include a replica of a dugout canoe and a sculpture symbolizing the meeting of the waters. **Time:** Allow 30 minutes minimum. **Hours:** Daily dawn-dusk. **Cost:** Free. **Phone:** (509) 751-0240.

LEWIS-CLARK STATE COLLEGE CENTER FOR ARTS AND HISTORY,

415 Main St., features a rotating schedule of exhibitions that showcase the works of local, regional and national artists. Also highlighted are Nez Perce tribal artifacts and an exhibit about Lewiston's Beuk Aie Temple that relates the history of a late 19th-century Chinese community. **Hours:** Tues.-Sat. 11-4. Closed major holidays. **Cost:** Donations. **Phone:** (208) 792-2243.

NEZ PERCE COUNTY HISTORICAL SOCIETY AND MUSEUM

is at 3rd and Capital sts. Built in the 1930s, the Art Deco-style building features a chronology of area history with displays of Nez Perce Indian and pioneer artifacts. **Hours:** Tues.-Sat. 10-4, early Mar. to mid-Dec. Closed major holidays. **Cost:** $2; $1 (ages 7-17). **Phone:** (208) 743-2535.

GAMBLING ESTABLISHMENTS

- **Clearwater River Casino** is 4 mi. e. on US 12 at 17500 Nez Perce Rd. **Hours:** Daily 24 hours. **Phone:** (208) 746-0723 or (877) 678-7423.

CLEARWATER RIVER CASINO & LODGE — 208/298-1400

▼▼▼▼ **Resort Hotel** $90-$200 **Address:** 17500 Nez Perce Rd 83501 **Location:** US 12/95, 4 mi e. **Facility:** Located near the Snake River and adjacent to an RV park, this hotel has spacious guest rooms nicely appointed with Native American décor. 50 units. 3 stories, interior corridors. **Parking:** winter plug-ins. **Terms:** check-in 4 pm, cancellation fee imposed, resort fee. **Dining:** 2 restaurants. **Pool(s):** heated indoor. **Activities:** hot tub. **Guest Services:** coin laundry, area transportation.

⊗ ⊀ ⑪ ⊻ CALL ⅃M ⇌ BIZ HS 🛜 ✕
🖾 🖾 / SOME UNITS 🔌

HOLIDAY INN EXPRESS — (208)750-1600

▼▼▼▼
Hotel
$119-$269

Address: 2425 Nez Perce Dr 83501 **Location:** 1.2 mi s on US 12 from jct US 95, 1.2 mi s on 21st St, just e. **Facility:** 100 units. 3 stories, interior corridors. **Pool(s):** heated indoor. **Activities:** hot tub, exercise room. **Guest Services:** valet and coin laundry. **Featured Amenity:** continental breakfast.

SAVE ⊀ ⑪⁺ CALL ⅃M ⇌ BIZ
HS 🛜 ✕ 🔌 🖾 🖾
/ SOME UNITS 🔌

INN AMERICA — 208/746-4600

▼▼ ▼ **Hotel.** Rates not provided. **Address:** 702 21st St 83501 **Location:** 1.2 mi s on US 12 from jct US 95, just s. **Facility:** 61 units. 3 stories, interior corridors. **Pool(s):** heated outdoor. **Guest Services:** coin laundry.

⑪⁺ CALL ⅃M ⇌ 🛜 🔌 🖾 🖾 / SOME UNITS 🔌

WHERE TO EAT

ANTONIO'S — 208/746-6262

▼▼ ▼ Italian. Casual Dining. $7-$19 **AAA Inspector Notes:** This popular Italian restaurant buzzes with tourists and locals alike. The hearty menu features traditional pasta dishes and pizza, along with steak and seafood preparations. Diners can start off a great meal with a run through the extensive salad bar. **Features:** beer & wine. **Address:** 1407 Main St 83501 **Location:** On US 12. L D

MAIN STREET GRILL — 208/746-2440

▼▼ ▼ American. Casual Dining. $7-$15 **AAA Inspector Notes:** This classic diner has walls decorated with historical photos of the community and baseball players. While the signature basket dishes are chunks of chicken, steak or shrimp battered and fried, they also serve a varied selection of hand-formed burgers, quesadillas, salads, sandwiches and wraps. **Features:** beer & wine, patio dining. **Address:** 625 Main St 83501 **Location:** In historic downtown. L D

WAFFLES N' MORE — 208/743-5189

▼▼ ▼ American. Casual Dining. $6-$10 **AAA Inspector Notes:** Servers are energetic and friendly at this favorite breakfast and lunch spot. In addition to excellent waffles, the menu lists varied good-value breakfast items, including the iron man or iron woman for hearty appetites. Lighter fare also is available. **Address:** 1421 Main St 83501 **Location:** 1.3 mi e of Snake River. B L

WAYBACK CAFE — 208/743-2396

▼▼ ▼ American. Family Dining. $7-$18 **AAA Inspector Notes:** Guests can return to the Eisenhower era and dine in a classic 1950s-themed diner, complete with a jukebox, fuzzy dice and servers in poodle skirts. **Features:** beer & wine. **Address:** 2138 13th Ave 83501 **Location:** 1.2 mi s on US 12 from jct US 95, 0.6 mi s on 21st St, just e. B L D

ZANY'S HOLLYWOOD GRILL — 208/746-8131

▼▼ ▼ American. Family Dining. $5-$18 **AAA Inspector Notes:** Burgers, sandwiches, salads and steaks are featured at this casual family restaurant, where a lively 1950s decor is simply chock-full of odd little treasures that are sure to delight the eye. Seasonal patio dining also is available. **Features:** beer & wine. **Address:** 2004 19th Ave 83501 **Location:** 1.2 mi s on US 12 from jct US 95, 1 mi s on 21st St. L D CALL ⅃M

LOWER STANLEY

BRIDGE STREET GRILL — 208/774-2208

▼▼ ▼ American. Casual Dining. $6-$30 **AAA Inspector Notes:** Large portions of grilled foods, such as burgers, seafood, chicken and out-of-this-world ribs can be found at this grill. Casual decor is featured inside, with al fresco dining overlooking the Salmon River. **Features:** beer & wine. **Address:** SR 75 83278 **Location:** On SR 75, 1 mi n of jct SR 21. L D 🅰

MALAD CITY (H-5) pop. 2,095, elev. 4,550'

The area's name came about in the early 19th century, when French trappers who believed they had become ill after drinking water from the valley's principal stream called it *malade,* meaning "sickly."

In the mid-1850s Brigham Young dispatched 15 families to the upper Malad Valley to establish a Latter-day Saint agricultural outpost. Many other early settlers were Welsh; the community celebrates this heritage during the Malad Valley Welsh Festival in late June.

ONEIDA COUNTY PIONEER MUSEUM is at 27 Bannock St. The ground floor of this 1914 building, which once housed a drugstore, contains artifacts and historical photographs illustrating the history of Malad City and Oneida County. Among the items displayed are a stove, an upright piano, an early telephone switchboard and the drugstore's original safe. The mezzanine features displays of period clothing. **Time:** Allow 30 minutes minimum. **Hours:** Tues.-Sat. 1-5, Sat. before Memorial Day-Sat. after Labor Day and by appointment. Closed major holidays. **Cost:** Donations. Under 12 must be with an adult. **Phone:** (208) 766-4010 or (208) 766-2649.

McCALL (E-1) pop. 2,991, elev. 5,025'
• Hotels p. 78 • Restaurants p. 78

At the southern end of beautiful Payette Lake, McCall is a year-round recreational resort with a municipal airport. Fishing, boating, water skiing, horseback riding, white-water rafting, golf, camping and hunting are available. Skiing, snowboarding, snowshoeing and snowmobiling are popular winter sports. Manchester Ice and Event Centre is open year-round for indoor ice-skating and curling.

Firefighting facilities at the Forest Service's Smokejumper Headquarters feature smokejumping equipment, a fire retardant mixing plant and communications services. Tours are offered twice daily; phone (208) 634-0378.

McCall lies on an especially scenic section of SR 55, also called the Payette River Scenic Byway. The highway heads north, merges with US 95 and continues toward Coeur d'Alene. The southern terminus of the route is Boise.

McCall Area Chamber of Commerce: 301 E. Lake St., P.O. Box 350, McCall, ID 83638. **Phone:** (208) 634-7631 or (800) 260-5130.

CENTRAL IDAHO HISTORICAL MUSEUM is at 1001 State St. The 4-acre complex features seven structures erected by the Civilian Conservation Corps (CCC) in 1937 for the Southern Idaho Timber Protective Association (SITPA). A self-guiding tour highlights the buildings, including The Pump House and The Machine Shop, as well as mining equipment, a lookout tower and a statue honoring the CCC.

Guided tours of the seven-bedroom Fire Warden's House, entirely completed using hand tools, also are offered. **Time:** Allow 45 minutes minimum. **Hours:** Wed.-Sat. 11-3, June-Aug. Phone ahead to confirm schedule. **Cost:** Museum free. Fire Warden's House tour $3. **Phone:** (208) 634-4497. ⌖

PONDEROSA STATE PARK is 2 mi. n.e. via Park St. and Thompson Ave. at 1920 N. Davis Ave. Embracing most of a 1,000-acre peninsula on the shores of Payette Lake, the park is named for its old-growth forest of ponderosa pines, some upwards of 150 feet tall. More than 12 miles of trails lead hikers and mountain bikers through the diverse landscape, which ranges from dense woods and sagebrush flats to marsh and lakeside cliffs.

On Saturdays in summer, rangers conduct guided walks and evening campfire programs. Winter activities include snowshoeing on 5 miles of trials and Nordic skiing. Cabins are open year-round. *See Recreation Areas Chart.* **Time:** Allow 1 hour minimum. **Hours:** Park open daily dawn-dusk. Visitor center open daily 9-9, Memorial Day weekend-Labor Day; Tues.-Sat. 10-4, rest of year. **Cost:** Day-use fee $5 (per private vehicle). **Phone:** (208) 634-2164. 🅰 ⊠ ⌖ ⌖

RECREATIONAL ACTIVITIES
Skiing
• **Brundage Mountain Resort** is 4 mi. n. on SR 55 to Goose Lake Rd., then 4 mi. n. Other activities, including mountain biking, are offered in summer. **Hours:** Skiing daily 9:30-4:30, early Dec. to mid-Apr. **Phone:** (208) 634-4151.

BEST WESTERN PLUS MCCALL LODGE & SUITES
(208)634-2230

▼▼▼
Hotel
$100-$160

AAA Benefit: Members save 10% or more with Best Western!

Address: 211 S 3rd St 83638 **Location:** 1 mi s of center on SR 55. **Facility:** 66 units, some efficiencies. 3 stories, interior corridors. **Parking:** winter plug-ins. **Pool(s):** heated indoor. **Activities:** sauna, hot tub, exercise room. **Guest Services:** coin laundry. **Featured Amenity: full hot breakfast.**

 🆓 🍴 CALL 📳 ➰ BIZ 📶 ⊠ 🖥 🖨 🖥 /SOME UNITS 🍳

HOLIDAY INN EXPRESS HOTEL & SUITES - THE HUNT LODGE
(208)634-4700

▼▼▼▼ **Hotel** $119-$159 **Address:** 210 N 3rd St 83638 **Location:** 0.7 mi s of center on SR 55. **Facility:** 85 units. 3 stories, interior corridors. **Terms:** cancellation fee imposed, resort fee. **Pool(s):** heated indoor. **Activities:** hot tub, exercise room. **Guest Services:** coin laundry.

🔀 🍴 CALL 📳 ➰ BIZ HS 📶 ⊠ 🖥 /SOME UNITS 🖥 🖨

SHORE LODGE
(208)634-2244

▼▼▼ ▼▼▼
Resort Hotel
$104-$409

Address: 501 W Lake St 83638 **Location:** Waterfront. 1 mi w of center on SR 55. **Facility:** Spring, summer, fall or winter, the picture-perfect postcard views of Payette Lake are stunning at this property offering a beautifully appointed lobby and well-appointed rooms and suites, most with lake views. 77 units. 3 stories, interior corridors. **Parking:** on-site and valet. **Terms:** check-in 4 pm, 2-4 night minimum stay - seasonal and/or weekends, 14 day cancellation notice, resort fee. **Amenities:** *Some:* safes, also, The Narrows at Shore Lodge, see separate listing. **Pool(s):** heated outdoor. **Activities:** sauna, hot tub, limited beach access, marina, tennis, recreation programs in summer, bicycles, game room, exercise room, spa. **Guest Services:** area transportation.

🆓 🔀 🍴 ⌖ 🍸 ➰ BIZ 📶 ⊠ 🖥 /SOME UNITS 🍳 🖨 🖥

WHERE TO EAT

BISTRO 45 WINE BAR & CAFE   208/634-4515

▼ American. Quick Serve. $6-$12 **AAA Inspector Notes:** This café is frequented by locals and tourists alike. Favorites include the tomato, mozzarella and basil grilled sandwich, quiche, baked Brie topped with roasted garlic, steamed blue mussels or clams and a variety of seasonal bottled beer, drafts and wine offerings. Smaller plates and a children's menu are available. **Features:** beer & wine. **Address:** 1101 N 3rd St 83638 **Location:** Downtown. **Parking:** on-site and street. B L D 🐾

THE MILL STEAKS & SPIRITS   208/634-7683

▼▼▼ American. Casual Dining. $15-$45 **AAA Inspector Notes:** Widely known prime rib is served in large portions at this eatery, so bring a healthy appetite when you visit. Surrounded in a casual setting with antiques and nostalgic mining memorabilia, appointments are coordinated with heavy wooden beams and supports, log slab tables in the lounge, and a carnival resort town atmosphere. **Features:** full bar. **Reservations:** suggested. **Address:** 324 N 3rd St 83638 **Location:** 0.3 mi s on SR 55. D

MY FATHER'S PLACE   208/634-4401

▼ Burgers. Quick Serve. $4-$10 **AAA Inspector Notes:** Serving up delicious burgers, fries and milkshakes, this local institution within walking distance from Payette Lake, always is bustling with locals and tourists alike. Expect a wait during peak seasons. Patio dining is available when the weather is nice. **Features:** patio dining. **Address:** 901 N 3rd St 83638 **Location:** Just s on SR 55; downtown. **Parking:** on-site and street. L D 🍷

THE NARROWS AT SHORE LODGE   208/634-2244

▼▼▼ American. Fine Dining. $18-$36 **AAA Inspector Notes:** Seasonal menu offerings here feature such starters as hamachi sashimi with pineapple salsa and corn and shrimp chowder, while main courses include Dungeness crab-crusted Alaskan halibut, grilled veal T-bone steak, potato-crusted Idaho trout, dry-aged filet mignon and beef prime rib for two. **Features:** full bar, happy hour. **Reservations:** suggested. **Address:** 501 W Lake St 83638 **Location:** 1 mi w of center on SR 55; in Shore Lodge. D

THE PANCAKE & CHRISTMAS HOUSE   208/634-5849

▼▼ American. Casual Dining. $6-$19 **AAA Inspector Notes:** This warm and inviting restaurant always is loaded with happy and hungry guests that have remained busy since the restaurant's opening in the 1950s. The themed gift shop sharing the building brings Christmas cheer year round. Menu offerings consist of popular breakfast items, hearty sandwiches, soups, steak and turkey dinners. **Features:** beer & wine. **Address:** 209 N 3rd St 83638 **Location:** 0.8 mi s of center on SR 55. B L D

SI BUENO SOUTHSIDE GRILL & CANTINA 208/634-2128

 Mexican. Casual Dining. $8-$25 **AAA Inspector Notes:** This colorful and friendly eatery offers a wide variety of menu items including salads, tostadas, sandwiches, burritos, Baja fish tacos, steaming chile verde, sizzling fajitas, hand-carved rib-eye steak, racks of plump St. Louis ribs, charbroiled chicken seasoned in lemon-pepper and hearty Mexican or combo platters available in one or two servings. Thirst quenching and fun-named margaritas are available slushy or chilled on the rocks and can be enjoyed in the dining room or the spacious cantina. **Features:** full bar. **Address:** 339 Deinhard Ln 83638 **Location:** 1 mi s of center via SR 55; across from McCall Airport. [L] [D]

STEAMERS STEAK & SEAFOOD RESTAURANT & WINE BAR 208/634-1411

 Seafood Steak. Casual Dining. $19-$33 **AAA Inspector Notes:** This restaurant features a cozy wine bar and offers a wide array of tempting seafood and steak dishes such as steamed clams, pan-fried oysters, a popular walnut and pear salad, poached wild sockeye salmon, filet mignon served with port-cranberry demi-glace and rack of tender lamb. **Features:** full bar, happy hour. **Reservations:** suggested. **Address:** 308 E Lake St 83638 **Location:** Just w of SR 55; downtown. **Parking:** street only. [D]

MELBA (G-1) pop. 513, elev. 2,667'

CELEBRATION PARK is .7 mi. e. on Baseline Rd., 3 mi. s. on Can Ada Rd., 1.6 mi. w. on Warren Spur Rd., 2.8 mi. s. on Sinker Rd., then just e., following signs to 6530 Hot Spot Ln. Located along the Snake River, this area was once used by the Paiute Indians as wintering grounds. Thousands of petroglyphs, some of which are 12,000 years old, can be seen

The park affords a variety of recreational activities, such as bird-watching and horseback riding. Visitors also can traverse the historic Guffy Bridge, which is appointed with informational placards. Educational programs, including lectures and guided tours, relate the site's features and history; phone ahead for schedules. *See Recreation Areas Chart.*

Time: Allow 1 hour, 30 minutes minimum. **Hours:** Daily 9-4. Visitor center staffed daily 10-2. Closed Thanksgiving and Christmas. **Cost:** Day-use fee $2. Camping fee $5. Annual pass $15; $5 (senior citizens). Cash only. **Phone:** (208) 455-6022.

[A] [X] [⛱]

MERIDIAN (G-1) pop. 75,092, elev. 2,600'
• Restaurants p. 80

[SAVE] **ROARING SPRINGS WATERPARK** is off I-84 exit 44, then w. at 400 W. Overland Rd. The water park features more than 20 attractions, including the Super Loop, two family raft rides, a wave pool, an endless river, tube slides, a bowl slide, a four-lane racing slide and a children's play area. The adjacent Wahooz Family Fun Zone offers miniature golf, laser tag, go-carts, bumper boats, an arcade and a bowling center.

Time: Allow 4 hours minimum. **Hours:** Water park daily 11-8, June-Aug.; Sat.-Sun. 11-7, mid-May through May 31 and Sept. 1 to mid-Sept. Wahooz Family Fun Zone and Pinz Bowling Center daily 10-10, June-Aug.; 11-9, rest of year. Phone ahead to confirm schedule. **Cost:** Water park

$29.99; $24.99 (under 48 inches tall). Water park after 3 p.m. $21.99. Fun zone and bowling center prices vary. **Phone:** (208) 884-8842 for water park, or (208) 898-0900 for fun zone. [▯]

BEST WESTERN PLUS RAMA INN (208)887-7888

Hotel
$100-$135

AAA Benefit: Members save 10% or more with Best Western!

Address: 1019 S Progress Ave 83642 **Location:** I-84 exit 44 (Meridian/Kuna), just ne. **Facility:** 61 units. 2 stories (no elevator), interior corridors. **Pool(s):** heated indoor. **Activities:** hot tub, limited exercise equipment. **Guest Services:** valet and coin laundry.

CANDLEWOOD SUITES - MERIDIAN/WEST BOISE 208/888-5121

 Extended Stay Contemporary Hotel. Rates not provided. **Address:** 1855 S Silverstone Way 83642 **Location:** I-84 exit 46 (Eagle Rd), 0.6 mi s, just e on Overland Rd, then just s. **Facility:** 120 efficiencies. 3 stories, interior corridors. **Activities:** hot tub, picnic facilities, exercise room. **Guest Services:** complimentary and valet laundry.

COUNTRY INN & SUITES BY CARLSON-BOISE WEST 208/639-3300

Hotel
Rates not provided

Address: 3355 E Pine Ave 83642 **Location:** I-84 exit 46 (Eagle Rd), 0.7 mi n, then just e. **Facility:** 82 units. 4 stories, interior corridors. **Pool(s):** heated indoor. **Activities:** hot tub, exercise room. **Guest Services:** valet and coin laundry. **Featured Amenity:** breakfast buffet.

COURTYARD BY MARRIOTT - MERIDIAN/WEST BOISE (208)888-0800

Contemporary Hotel $99-$179 **Address:** 1789 S Eagle Rd 83642 **Location:** I-84 exit 46 (Eagle Rd), just s. **Facility:** 145 units. 4 stories, interior corridors. **Pool(s):** heated indoor. **Activities:** hot tub, exercise room. **Guest Services:** valet and coin laundry.

AAA Benefit: Members save 5% or more!

HAMPTON INN & SUITES - MERIDIAN/WEST BOISE (208)887-3600

Contemporary Hotel $109-$129 **Address:** 875 S Allen St 83642 **Location:** I-84 exit 46 (Eagle Rd), just nw. **Facility:** 128 units. 3 stories, interior corridors. **Terms:** 1-7 night minimum stay, cancellation fee imposed. **Pool(s):** heated indoor. **Activities:** hot tub, exercise room. **Guest Services:** valet and coin laundry, area transportation.

AAA Benefit: Members save up to 10%!

HOLIDAY INN EXPRESS & SUITES BOISE WEST - MERIDIAN   (208)288-2060

Hotel
$95-$170

Address: 2610 E Freeway Dr 83642 **Location:** I-84 exit 46 (Eagle Rd), just n, then 0.3 mi w. **Facility:** 76 units. 3 stories, interior corridors. **Terms:** check-in 4 pm, cancellation fee imposed. **Pool(s):** heated indoor. **Activities:** hot tub, game room, exercise room. **Guest Services:** valet and coin laundry. **Featured Amenity: full hot breakfast.**

LA QUINTA INN & SUITES MERIDIAN BOISE   (208)288-2100

Hotel $84-$129 **Address:** 800 S Allen St 83642 **Location:** I-84 exit 46 (Eagle Rd), just nw. **Facility:** 67 units. 3 stories, interior corridors. **Pool(s):** heated indoor. **Activities:** hot tub, exercise room. **Guest Services:** valet and coin laundry.

TOWNEPLACE SUITES BY MARRIOTT - MERIDIAN/ WEST BOISE   (208)884-8550

Extended Stay
Contemporary
Hotel
$98-$116

TownePlace SUITES Marriott

AAA Benefit: Members save 5% or more!

Address: 1415 S Eagle Rd 83642 **Location:** I-84 exit 46 (Eagle Rd), just sw. **Facility:** 100 units, some efficiencies and kitchens. 4 stories, interior corridors. **Terms:** check-in 4 pm. **Pool(s):** heated indoor. **Activities:** hot tub, picnic facilities, exercise room. **Guest Services:** valet and coin laundry.

WHERE TO EAT

FLATBREAD COMMUNITY OVEN PIZZERIA & WINE BAR
208-0969

Italian. Casual Dining. $7-$17 **AAA Inspector Notes:** Located in downtown Meridian, this certified Neapolitan pizzeria is always packed with returning fans. Choose from a variety of unique pizza, pasta and sandwiches while enjoying the bright ambience that the garage door wall and intimate lighting create. **Features:** beer & wine. **Address:** 830 N Main St, Suite A 83642 **Location:** I-84 exit 44 (Meridian/Kuna), 1.1 mi n. **Parking:** street only. [L] [D]

GOODWOOD BARBECUE COMPANY   208/884-1021

Barbecue. Family Dining. $9-$24 **AAA Inspector Notes:** Buzzing with energy, this welcoming restaurant is home to traditional barbecue favorites including prime rib, pulled pork, brisket, and a variety of full and half-racks of beef and pork ribs. **Features:** full bar. **Address:** 1140 N Eagle Rd 83642 **Location:** I-84 exit 46 (Eagle Rd), 1.4 mi n. [L] [D] CALL

THE GRIDDLE   208/288-1848

American. Family Dining. $5-$14 **AAA Inspector Notes:** With made-from-scratch home-style cooking and hefty portions, it is no wonder this diner is such a favorite. The menu offers all of the traditional American breakfast favorites as well as a variety of sandwiches and burgers served during the lunch hour. **Address:** 2310 E Overland Rd, Suite 130 83642 **Location:** I-84 exit 46 (Eagle Rd), 0.5 mi s, then 0.5 mi w. [B] [L]

KAHOOTZ STEAK & ALE HOUSE   208/895-9861

American. Casual Dining. $8-$26 **AAA Inspector Notes:** Known for its great-tasting food, this brew pub offers a broad selection of draft beers with 43 taps. On the menu are steak sandwiches, pasta and high-grade meat including pork loin and filet mignon. Bread pudding is an absolute must. **Features:** full bar. **Address:** 1603 N Main St 83642 **Location:** I-84 exit 44 (Meridian/Kuna), 1.7 mi n. [L] [D]

LOUIE'S PIZZA & ITALIAN RESTAURANT   208/884-5200

Italian. Family Dining. $8-$20 **AAA Inspector Notes:** Serving traditional pizza, pasta, sandwiches, calzones and salads, this Italian eatery infuses its dishes with a distinctive flair. Diners can eat in the open dining room, which is appointed with murals of the Italian countryside, or on the patio if the weather permits. A lunch buffet is an affordable favorite. **Features:** full bar, patio dining, Sunday brunch. **Address:** 2500 E Fairview Ave 83642 **Location:** I-84 exit 46 (Eagle Rd), 1.6 mi n, then 0.5 mi w. [L] [D]

MISS TAMI'S COTTAGE & TEA ROOM   208/888-6829

American. Casual Dining. $6-$14 **AAA Inspector Notes:** This Victorian decorated cottage features full afternoon tea service and offers such menu favorites as tea sandwiches, quiche, meatloaf, fish and chips, stuffed salmon and chicken pot pie. A breakfast buffet brunch is offered on Saturdays. **Features:** beer & wine. **Reservations:** suggested. **Address:** 1031 N Main St 83642 **Location:** I-84 exit 44 (Meridian/Kuna), 1.3 mi n. **Parking:** on-site and street. [L]

RAM RESTAURANT AND BREWERY   208/888-0314

American. Casual Dining. $10-$24 **AAA Inspector Notes:** The enormous restaurant features high ceilings, huge television screens, large sports-themed banners and a brew pub area. The menu is equally enormous, with steaks, poultry, pasta, seafood, salads, sandwiches and pizza. The on-site brewery turns out a large selection of microbrews. **Features:** full bar, happy hour. **Address:** 3272 E Pine St 83642 **Location:** I-84 exit 46 (Eagle Rd), 1.2 mi n. [L] [D] [LATE]

RUDY'S PUB & GRILL   208/884-4453

American. Casual Dining. $9-$17 **AAA Inspector Notes:** This popular sports bar usually is full of casual diners and sports fans alike, so expect a wait at peak times. The menu offers up burgers, sandwiches and salads. Be sure to sample their signature mushroom and brie soup. **Features:** full bar. **Address:** 2310 E Overland Rd, Suite 150 83642 **Location:** I-84 exit 46 (Eagle Rd), 0.5 mi s, then 0.5 mi w. [L] [D] CALL

SA-WAD-DEE THAI RESTAURANT   208/884-0701

Thai. Casual Dining. $8-$21 **AAA Inspector Notes:** With a name that means "Hello" in Thai, this restaurant offers guests not only hospitable service, but also the many delicious traditional Thai dishes that their loyal guests have come to love. With a lunch menu offering variety and value, the place is always bustling during the lunch hour. Sushi is offered Monday through Saturday. **Features:** full bar. **Address:** 1890 E Fairview Ave 83642 **Location:** I-84 exit 46 (Eagle Rd), 1.8 mi n, then 0.8 mi w. [L] [D]

SMOKY MOUNTAIN PIZZERIA GRILL   208/884-1067

Italian. Family Dining. $7-$27 **AAA Inspector Notes:** This local favorite is adorned with eclectic decor representing Idaho's history. Perfect for a family get-together, business luncheon or romantic dinner, the eatery's menu offers a wide variety of pizza, pasta and grilled meats, all with an Italian flare. **Features:** beer & wine, patio dining. **Address:** 980 E Fairview Ave 83642 **Location:** I-84 exit 46 (Eagle Rd), 1.6 mi n, then 1.4 mi w. [L] [D] CALL

WHITEWATER PIZZA & PASTA   208/888-6611

Italian. Family Dining. $6-$22 **AAA Inspector Notes:** Appointed with whitewater adventure decor, this open and airy restaurant located in a popular shopping district, offers a variety of pizza, sandwiches and salads. **Features:** beer & wine. **Address:** 1510 N Eagle Rd 83642 **Location:** I-84 exit 46 (Eagle Rd), 1.6 mi n. [L] [D] CALL

MINIDOKA NATIONAL HISTORIC SITE (G-3)

Minidoka, the site of a relocation camp used for the detainment of Japanese persons living in the United States after the attack on Pearl Harbor, is northeast of Twin Falls via US 93 and SR 25; from the intersection of I-84 and US 93, head 5 miles north on US 93, 9.5 miles east on SR 25 to the Hunt Road exit, then 2.2 miles east on Hunt Road. President Franklin D. Roosevelt ordered the opening of 10 such facilities in February 1942, displacing more than 100,000 Japanese and Japanese Americans until 1945.

Originally comprising 33,000 acres with more than 600 buildings, the Minidoka site now encompasses roughly 300 acres. It features interpretive signs as well as remains of an entry station, a waiting room, a root cellar and an ornamental rock garden. Those who died after leaving the camp to serve in the U.S. military during World War II are commemorated on plaques. More than 900 names of Minidoka residents are listed on the Honor Roll at the entrance to the site.

Note: Visitors should inquire about road conditions before going to the historic site. Exhibits about Minidoka and maps are available at the visitor center at Hagerman Fossil Beds National Monument *(see place listing p. 65);* phone (208) 933-4100. The historic site is open daily dawn to dusk. Admission is free.

MONTPELIER (H-6) pop. 2,597, elev. 5,934'

Montpelier, one of the state's oldest towns, is at the junction of US 89 and US 30N, the historic Old Oregon Trail. Brigham Young established a Mormon community and named the town for the capital of his home state, Vermont. In 1896 Butch Cassidy relieved the Bank of Montpelier of $7,000. Bear Lake resort is about 17 miles south on US 89.

Bear Lake Convention and Visitors Bureau: 69 N. Paradise Pkwy., Bldg. A, P.O. Box 471, Garden City, UT 84028. **Phone:** (435) 946-2197 or (800) 448-2327.

SAVE **NATIONAL OREGON/CALIFORNIA TRAIL CENTER** is at jct. US 30 and US 89 at 320 N. 4th St. This living-history center, which sits directly on the site of the historic Clover Creek Encampment on the Oregon Trail, depicts the pioneers' journey across the continent. A wagon master guides visitors through the experience of riding the trail in a covered wagon courtesy of a computer simulation. Displays and artifacts about the history of the Bear Lake valley and the railroad era can be seen in the Rails and Trails Museum.

Time: Allow 30 minutes minimum. **Hours:** Guided tours Sun.-Thurs. 9-5, Fri.-Sat. 9-6, May-Sept.; Tues.-Sat. 10-3, Sun.-Mon. by appointment, in Oct.; by appointment rest of year. **Cost:** $10; $9 (ages 60+); $7 (ages 8-17); $3 (ages 4-7). Prices may vary; phone ahead. **Phone:** (208) 847-3800.

CLOVER CREEK INN & SUITES   (208)847-1782

Motel
$75-$125

Address: 243 N 4th St 83254 **Location:** On US 30, just n of jct US 89. **Facility:** 64 units. 2 stories (no elevator), exterior corridors. **Parking:** winter plug-ins. **Activities:** hot tub, exercise room. **Guest Services:** coin laundry. **Featured Amenity: full hot breakfast.**

[SAVE] [Y] [HS] [📶] [🛏] [📺] [🖥] / SOME UNITS [🐾]

SUPER 8   (208)847-8888

Hotel $69-$180 **Address:** 276 N 4th St 83254 **Location:** On US 30, just n of jct US 89. **Facility:** 61 units. 2 stories (no elevator), interior corridors. **Parking:** winter plug-ins. **Terms:** cancellation fee imposed. **Pool(s):** heated indoor. **Activities:** hot tub, exercise room. **Guest Services:** coin laundry.

[⛨] [🛁] [BIZ] [📶] [🛏] [📺] [🖥]

WHERE TO EAT

LOTT'S RESTAURANT   208/847-1090

American. Casual Dining. $6-$16 **AAA Inspector Notes:** This restaurant offers a popular salad bar and a nice variety of homemade soups, sandwiches, burgers and dinner specials served nightly. **Address:** 690 N 4th St 83254 **Location:** On US 30, 0.7 mi n of center. [B] [L] [D]

MOSCOW (C-1) pop. 23,800, elev. 2,574'
• Hotels p. 82 • Restaurants p. 82

Moscow (MOSS-co) lies on an especially scenic section of US 95, which heads north toward Coeur d'Alene and south to Banks. The area to the west is rolling, fertile Palouse country where black volcanic ash soil, ample rainfall and warm autumn temperatures combine to produce bountiful crops of lentils, dry peas, canola, wheat and barley.

Home to the University of Idaho *(see attraction listing),* Moscow is a quintessential college town with an emerging arts community. The annual arts scene includes February's Lionel Hampton Jazz Festival; the Idaho Repertory Theatre; and the Moscow Renaissance Fair, which is held the first weekend in May.

Moscow Chamber of Commerce: 411 S. Main St., Moscow, ID 83843. **Phone:** (208) 882-1800 or (800) 380-1801.

Shopping areas: Macy's anchors Palouse Mall, 1.5 miles west on SR 8.

APPALOOSA MUSEUM AND HERITAGE CENTER, w. on SR 8 in the Appaloosa Horse Club building at 2720 W. Pullman Rd., contains Nez Perce regalia and artifacts, cowboy tack, photographs and artwork illustrating Appaloosa history. A children's activity area also is available. **Time:** Allow 1 hour minimum. **Hours:** Mon.-Fri. 11-4, Sat. 10-4 or by appointment. Closed major holidays. **Cost:** Donations. **Phone:** (208) 882-5578, ext. 279.

McCONNELL MANSION, 110 S. Adams St., was built in the late 19th century by Gov. William J. McConnell. Operated by the Latah County Historical

Society, the mansion displays relics and Victorian-style furniture from the late 1800s as well as exhibits about area history. A backyard garden and a research library are available. Children's activities are offered. **Time:** Allow 1 hour minimum. **Hours:** Mansion Tues.-Sat. 1-4. Research library Tues.-Fri. 9-5. Closed major holidays. **Cost:** Donations. **Phone:** (208) 882-1004.

PRICHARD ART GALLERY is at 414 S. Main St. Hosting between nine and 11 changing exhibitions each year, the two-level gallery showcases the contemporary works of both professional artists and University of Idaho students. Included are fine arts pieces, photographs, ceramics, computer-generated art, sculpture, folk art and architectural displays. **Time:** Allow 30 minutes minimum. **Hours:** Tues.-Sat. 10-8, Sun. 10-6, Sept.-May; Tues.-Thurs. 1-6, Fri. 1-7, Sat. 9-3, rest of year. Closed major holidays. **Cost:** Donations. **Phone:** (208) 885-3586.

UNIVERSITY OF IDAHO is on the s.w. side of town, w. of US 95 via 6th St. Established in 1889, UI sprawls across 1,580 landscaped acres and has around 12,000 students. An 80-foot clock tower atop the Collegiate Gothic-style administration building overlooks a lawn containing the President's Grove and a Spanish-American War statue.

Shattuck Arboretum, on a hill between Rayburn Street and Nez Perce Drive, is a 14-acre tract of trees planted in 1910. Trails loop through groves of mature beech, incense-cedar, maple, hemlock and others. Among these specimens is a giant sequoia. The UI Arboretum and Botanical Garden *(see attraction listing)* is home to a larger collection of trees on the south side of campus.

Guided campus tours lasting an hour depart from the Office of Admissions and Campus Visits at 709 Deakin Ave. **Time:** Allow 1 hour minimum. **Hours:** Office Mon.-Fri. 7:30-4:30, late May-late Aug.; Mon.-Fri. 8-5, rest of year. Campus tours are offered Mon.-Fri. at 9:30 and 1:30, Sat. at 9. Closed major holidays. **Cost:** Free. **Parking:** $2 (free if tour is registered online). **Phone:** (208) 885-6163 or (888) 884-3246.

University of Idaho Arboretum and Botanical Garden is on the s. side of the campus at 1200 W. Palouse River Dr. The 63-acre arboretum features gravel and bark trails leading through plantings grouped into four geographical areas: Asia, Europe, Eastern North America and Western North America. A display garden, showing off irises, daylilies, heather and xeriscape techniques, is at the arboretum's southern end. Hosta gardens are located at the north end. **Time:** Allow 1 hour minimum. **Hours:** Daily dawn-dusk. **Cost:** Free. **Phone:** (208) 885-5978.

WINERIES

- **Camas Prairie Winery** is at 110 S. Main St. Free tours are available by request. **Hours:** Mon.-Sat. noon-6:30. Closed Jan. 1, Thanksgiving and Christmas. **Phone:** (208) 882-0214.

BEST WESTERN PLUS UNIVERSITY INN   (208)882-0550

Hotel
$99-$219

AAA Benefit: Members save 10% or more with Best Western!

Address: 1516 Pullman Rd 83843 **Location:** Jct US 95, 1 mi w on SR 8. Adjacent to a university and shopping mall. **Facility:** 173 units. 2 stories (no elevator), interior corridors. **Terms:** check-in 4 pm, resort fee. **Amenities:** video games. **Dining:** 2 restaurants. **Pool(s):** heated indoor. **Activities:** sauna, hot tub, game room, exercise room. **Guest Services:** valet and coin laundry, area transportation.

LA QUINTA INN & SUITES MOSCOW PULLMAN
(208)882-5365

Hotel $109-$154 **Address:** 185 Warbonnet Dr 83843 **Location:** 1.6 mi w on SR 8 from jct US 95, just n. **Facility:** 76 units. 3 stories, interior corridors. **Parking:** winter plug-ins. **Pool(s):** heated indoor. **Activities:** hot tub, exercise room. **Guest Services:** coin laundry.

SUPER 8   (208)883-1503

Hotel $66-$185 **Address:** 175 Peterson Dr 83843 **Location:** Jct US 95, 0.8 mi w on SR 8, just n. **Facility:** 60 units. 3 stories (no elevator), interior corridors. **Guest Services:** coin laundry.

FAIRFIELD INN & SUITES BY MARRIOTT MOSCOW
208/882-4600

fyi Not evaluated. **Address:** 1000 W Pullman Rd 83843 **Location:** Jct US 95, 1 mi w on SR 8. Facilities, services, and décor characterize a mid-scale property.

AAA Benefit: Members save 5% or more!

WHERE TO EAT

SANGRIA GRILLE   208/882-2693

Peruvian. Casual Dining. $9-$23 **AAA Inspector Notes:** The chef/owner here pays homage to his varied heritage—Peruvian and Greek. The meats are cut in house. The menu is extensive and full of specialties like paella, Peruvian curry, Greek lamb chops and many gluten-free items. Home-made desserts such as tres leches cake are offered. Also open for lunch Friday through Sunday. **Features:** full bar, happy hour. **Reservations:** suggested. **Address:** 2124 W Pullman Hwy 83843 **Location:** 1.5 mi w on SR 8 from jct US 95; in front of Palouse Mall. D

SMOKY MOUNTAIN PIZZERIA GRILL   208/892-8000

Italian. Family Dining. $7-$27 **AAA Inspector Notes:** This popular Italian restaurant is a great place to meet for a quick lunch, corporate meeting or family dinner. The menu offers up a variety of entrees including pasta, salads, sandwiches, pizza and delicious desserts. A lunch buffet is offered Monday through Friday. **Features:** beer & wine. **Address:** 1838 W Pullman Rd 83843 **Location:** Jct US 95, 1.1 mi w on SR 8. L D CALL

MOUNTAIN HOME pop. 14,206

BEST WESTERN FOOTHILLS INN (208)587-8477

Motel
$109-$149

AAA Benefit: Members save 10% or more with Best Western!

Address: 1080 Hwy 20 83647 **Location:** I-84 exit 95, just n. **Facility:** 77 units, some kitchens. 2 stories (no elevator), exterior corridors. **Parking:** winter plug-ins. **Pool(s):** heated outdoor. **Activities:** hot tub, picnic facilities, exercise room. **Guest Services:** valet and coin laundry.

[SAVE] [TI+] [⌘] [BIZ] [📶] [🔌] [📷]
[💻] / SOME UNITS [S⌐] [HS]

HAMPTON INN & SUITES (208)587-7300

▼▼▼ Contemporary Hotel $99-$149 **Address:** 3175 NE Foothills Ave 83647 **Location:** I-84 exit 95, just n. **Facility:** 74 units. 3 stories, interior corridors. **Terms:** 1-7 night minimum stay, cancellation fee imposed. **Amenities:** video games. **Pool(s):** heated indoor. **Activities:** hot tub, exercise room. **Guest Services:** valet and coin laundry.

AAA Benefit: Members save up to 10%!

[TI+] [⌘] [BIZ] [📶] [🎬] [💻] / SOME UNITS [🔌] [📷]

MOUNTAIN HOME INN (208)587-9743

▼▼ Hotel $84-$99 **Address:** 1180 Hwy 20 83647 **Location:** I-84 exit 95, just n. **Facility:** 60 units. 2 stories (no elevator), interior corridors. *Bath:* shower only. **Terms:** cancellation fee imposed.

[TI+] [BIZ] [📶] [🔌] [📷] [💻] / SOME UNITS [S⌐]

DUSTY ROSE INN 208/580-2460

[fyi] Not evaluated. **Address:** 815 N 3rd St E 83647 **Location:** I-84 exit 95, 2 mi w, then 0.4 mi n. Facilities, services, and décor characterize a mid-scale property. This 1904 Victorian charmer overlooks extensive gardens and is a great place for weddings, family gatherings or just an overnight visit.

WHERE TO EAT

CARLOS' MEXICAN STYLE FAMILY DINING 208/587-2966

▼ Mexican. Casual Dining. $6-$12 **AAA Inspector Notes:** For those looking for a casual restaurant with a menu featuring traditional Mexican fare, this is it. **Features:** beer & wine. **Address:** 1500 Sunset Strip 83647 **Location:** I-84 exit 90, 2.9 mi se on I-84 business route. [L] [D]

MULLAN (B-2) pop. 692, elev. 3,277'

Silver Valley's easternmost mining town was established in 1885 and named for John Mullan, an Army captain credited with blazing a 624-mile road across Montana, Idaho and Washington in the early 1860s. The Lucky Friday Mine, dating back to 1899, still produces silver.

Mullan nestles below Lookout Pass in the Bitterroot Mountains, a popular year-round recreation area for skiing, snowboarding, hiking and mountain biking. The paved Trail of the Coeur d'Alenes follows a former Union Pacific railway path 73 miles west from Mullan to Plummer; phone (208) 682-3814 for additional information. With 10 tunnels and seven trestles, the gravel, 15-mile Route of the Hiawatha runs south of Lookout Pass along another

repurposed railroad right-of-way. Shuttles are available at trailheads from late May to early October; phone (208) 744-1301.

CAPTAIN JOHN MULLAN MUSEUM, 229 Earle St., occupies the 1930 Independent Order of Odd Fellows (I.O.O.F.) Building, which also once served as the town's theater. Historical photos, ladies' wear, school items, work tools and I.O.O.F. regalia are displayed in themed areas, including a drugstore, a nursery and a sitting room. **Time:** Allow 30 minutes minimum. **Hours:** Mon.-Fri. 10-4 or by appointment, June-Aug. **Cost:** Donations. **Phone:** (208) 744-1155.

RECREATIONAL ACTIVITIES

Skiing and Snowboarding

• **Lookout Pass Ski and Recreation Area** is 6 mi. e. on I-90. Other activities are offered, including mountain biking. **Hours:** Winter activities are available daily 9-4, Dec. 19-Jan. 6; Mon. and Wed.-Fri. 9-4, Sat.-Sun. 8:30-4:30, Jan. 7-Feb. 28; Mon. and Thurs.-Fri. 9-4, Sat.-Sun. 8:30-4, Mar.-Apr. and Thanksgiving-Dec. 18. **Phone:** (208) 744-1301.

NAMPA (G-1) pop. 81,557, elev. 2,492'
• Hotels p. 84 • Restaurants p. 84

Col. W.H. Dewey moved his fortune during the 1890s to Nampa, an agricultural hamlet just north of the Great Basin Desert. Dewey brought prosperity to Nampa by attracting several railway branches and constructing the Dewey Palace hotel, which was a town landmark for several decades until it was damaged by fire and torn down. Nampa's name comes from Nampuh, or "Bigfoot," a Shoshone chief who was so large that his feet were supposedly 17 inches long.

Nampa is a central location from which to explore southwestern Idaho's natural wonders and historical sites. Givens Hot Springs is 17 miles south on SR 45, then 8 miles west on SR 78 on the south side of the Snake River. There are steam baths, an indoor natural hot-water pool and a picnic area.

Silver City and DeLamar, high in the Owyhee Mountains, can be reached by taking SR 45 south to Walter's Ferry, then turning east on SR 78 4.5 miles past Murphy. The towns, at one time thriving mining communities in one of the greatest silver-producing areas in the nation, are on a rough gravel and earth road *(see Silver City p. 97)*. DeLamar has been abandoned.

Nampa Chamber of Commerce: 315 11th Ave. S., Nampa, ID 83651. **Phone:** (208) 466-4641.

DEER FLAT NATIONAL WILDLIFE REFUGE is 4 mi. s.w. The refuge consists of two sections: Lake Lowell, an irrigation reservoir, and 101 islands in the Snake River, from Walter's Ferry downstream to Farewell Bend in Oregon. The islands are accessible only by boat.

The refuge harbors waterfowl as well as other birds and mammals. In winter the lake attracts ducks and geese as well as bald eagles that come to feed; in spring and summer, western grebes, great blue herons and black-crowned night herons come to nest. **Hours:** Refuge daily dawn-dusk. Visitor center Mon.-Fri. 8-4, Sat. 10-4. Closed major holidays. **Cost:** Free. **Phone:** (208) 467-9278.

NAMPA TRAIN DEPOT MUSEUM is at 1200 Front St. The 1903 Baroque Revival-style building, formerly the Oregon Short Line Depot, houses changing exhibits that illustrate Nampa's importance as a railway town. Highlights include Canyon County and Union Pacific Railroad history, model train layouts and a caboose from the 1940s. **Time:** Allow 30 minutes minimum. **Hours:** Thurs.-Fri. 11-4, Sat. 9-2, last Sat. in Apr.-last Sat. in Oct.; Thurs.-Fri. 11-4, Sat. 11-2, rest of year. Closed Jan. 1, July 4, Thanksgiving and Christmas. **Cost:** $3; $2 (ages 13-18 and 65+); $1 (ages 6-12); $7 (family, four people). **Phone:** (208) 467-7611.

[SAVE] **WARHAWK AIR MUSEUM** is at 201 Municipal Dr. next to Nampa Municipal Airport. The museum features restored and flyable aircraft from World War II, including a Curtiss P-40E Kittyhawk, a P-51 Mustang, a Curtiss P-40N Warhawk and a 1940 Navy N3N biplane trainer. Other World War II items displayed are a restored 1940 DeSoto staff car, period poster art, trench art, uniforms and home-front memorabilia.

Time: Allow 2 hours minimum. **Hours:** Tues.-Sat. 10-5, Sun. 11-4. Closed Jan. 1, Easter, Mother's Day, July 5, Thanksgiving and Christmas. Phone ahead to confirm schedule. **Cost:** $10; $8 (ages 65+ and military with ID); $4 (ages 5-12). **Phone:** (208) 465-6446.

FAIRFIELD INN & SUITES BY MARRIOTT (208)467-5888

▼▼▼ Contemporary Hotel $84-$139

FAIRFIELD INN & SUITES Marriott

AAA Benefit: Members save 5% or more!

Address: 16150 N Midland Blvd 83687 **Location:** I-84 exit 33B westbound; exit 33 eastbound, just e. Located in a commercial area. **Facility:** 88 units. 3 stories, interior corridors. **Pool(s):** heated indoor. **Activities:** hot tub, exercise room. **Guest Services:** valet and coin laundry.

[SAVE] [♂] CALL [&M] [≈] [BIZ] [HS] [🛜] [✕] [▯] / SOME UNITS [🔌] [🗄]

HAMPTON INN & SUITES AT THE IDAHO CENTER (208)442-0038

▼▼▼ **Hotel** $109-$169 **Address:** 5750 E Franklin Rd 83687 **Location:** I-84 exit 38, 0.5 mi n to Franklin Rd, then just e. **Facility:** 101 units. 4 stories, interior corridors. **Terms:** 1-7 night minimum stay, cancellation fee imposed. **Pool(s):** heated indoor. **Activities:** hot tub, exercise room. **Guest Services:** valet and coin laundry.

AAA Benefit: Members save up to 10%!

[♂] [≈] [BIZ] [HS] [🛜] [✕] [▯] / SOME UNITS [🔌] [🗄]

HOLIDAY INN EXPRESS HOTEL & SUITES 208/466-4045

▼▼▼ **Contemporary Hotel.** Rates not provided. **Address:** 4104 E Flamingo Ave 83687 **Location:** I-84 exit 38, just s, then just w. **Facility:** 74 units, some efficiencies. 3 stories, interior corridors. **Pool(s):** heated indoor. **Activities:** hot tub, exercise room. **Guest Services:** valet and coin laundry.

CALL [&M] [≈] [BIZ] [HS] [🛜] [✕] [🔌] [🗄] [▯] / SOME UNITS [🔋]

SLEEP INN (208)463-6300

▼▼ **Hotel** $65-$98 **Address:** 1315 Industrial Rd 83687 **Location:** I-84 exit 36 (Franklin Blvd), just s. Located in a commercial area. **Facility:** 81 units. 3 stories, interior corridors. **Pool(s):** heated indoor. **Activities:** hot tub. **Guest Services:** coin laundry.

[≈] [BIZ] [🛜] [🔌] [▯] / SOME UNITS [🐾] [🔌] [🗄]

WHERE TO EAT

BRICK 29 BISTRO 208/468-0029

▼▼▼ American. Casual Dining. $7-$25 **AAA Inspector Notes:** By placing an emphasis on ingredients from local farmers and vendors, this eatery offers some of the most flavorful food in the valley. From the all-natural pork chop to the delicious shiitake mushroom soup or tomato bisque, there is something for everyone. Diners will not be disappointed when ordering the brick, the signature dessert. **Features:** full bar, Sunday brunch. **Address:** 320 11th Ave S, Suite 101 83687 **Location:** I-84 exit 36 (Franklin Blvd), 0.9 mi s, 0.8 mi s on 11th Ave N, just e on 3rd St S, 1 mi s on 12th Ave S, then just w. **Parking:** on-site and street. [L] [D] CALL [&M]

COPPER CANYON RESTAURANT 208/466-1114

▼▼▼ Seafood Steak. Casual Dining. $9-$28 **AAA Inspector Notes:** Located in the Broadmore Golf Course Country Club, this Northwestern contemporary dining establishment offers an expanded wine list and serves a variety of attractively presented menu items including smoked salmon chowder, warm duck salad, Basque-style penne pasta, seafood linguine and broiled five-spice pork tenderloin. **Features:** full bar, patio dining, Sunday brunch. **Address:** 103 Shannon Dr S 83687 **Location:** I-84 exit 35 (Northside Blvd), just s, then just w. [L] [D]

THE EGG FACTORY 208/466-2728

▼▼ Breakfast. Family Dining. $5-$9 **AAA Inspector Notes:** Serving up the home-style cooking that your grandma used to make, this quaint diner offers hearty portions and make-yourself-at-home hospitality. The menu features all of the breakfast favorites as well as sandwiches and burgers. Just look for the gigantic white hen. **Features:** Sunday brunch. **Address:** 820 Caldwell Blvd 83651 **Location:** I-84 exit 35 (Northside Blvd), 1 mi s, then 1.2 mi w. [B] [L]

EL RINCONCITO 208/466-6963

▼▼ Mexican. Family Dining. $4-$10 **AAA Inspector Notes:** Known as the Rincon by locals, this traditional Mexican restaurant is a favorite for many. With an expansive menu that offers almost any Mexican dish that one can imagine, the eatery features bright colors and upbeat music to keep diners smiling throughout their meal. **Features:** beer only. **Address:** 824 1st St S 83651 **Location:** I-84 exit 36 (Franklin Blvd), 1.6 mi s, 0.7 mi s on 11th Ave N, then just w. **Parking:** on-site and street. [L] [D]

JALAPENO'S BAR & GRILL 208/442-6355

▼▼ Mexican. Casual Dining. $6-$15 **AAA Inspector Notes:** Serving up authentic Mexican cuisine, this colorful eatery is a favorite for tourists and locals alike. The large menu features all of the traditional favorites including burritos, enchiladas, fajitas, chimichangas and tamales. The bar serves more than 80 types of tequila. **Features:** full bar, patio dining, happy hour. **Address:** 1921 Nampa-Caldwell Blvd 83651 **Location:** I-84 exit 33 eastbound; exit 33A westbound, 0.6 mi sw, then just e. [L] [D]

SMOKY MOUNTAIN PIZZERIA GRILL   208/461-7333
▼▼▼ Italian. Casual Dining. $7-$24 **AAA Inspector Notes:** This is a great place to meet for a quick lunch, corporate meeting or family dinner. Located near a movie theater complex, it makes a great stop for a bite before the flick. The menu offers up a variety of entrées including a nice selection of pasta, salads, sandwiches and pizza. Gluten-free menu items are available. **Features:** full bar, patio dining, happy hour. **Address:** 2007 N Cassia St 83651 **Location:** I-84 exit 33 eastbound; exit 33A westbound, 0.4 mi w, then just s.

[L] [D]

NEZ PERCE NATIONAL FOREST (D-2)

Elevations in the forest range from 1,350 ft. in Hells Canyon to 9,393 ft. at Devil's Peak. Refer to AAA maps for additional elevation information.

In the north-central part of the state, Nez Perce National Forest was named for the Nez Perce Indians, whose ancestral lands once included this rugged area of 2,223,594 acres. The forest contains the Gospel-Hump Wilderness and portions of the Selway-Bitterroot Wilderness, Frank Church-River of No Return Wilderness, Hells Canyon Wilderness and Hells Canyon National Recreation Area *(see place listing p. 66)*. Portions of the forest are close to parts of Nez Perce National Historical Park *(see place listing)*.

More than 150 miles of the Rapid, Salmon and Selway rivers and the Middle Fork of the Clearwater River are classified as wild and scenic rivers. Elk, moose, deer, cougars, mountain goats, bighorn sheep and bears inhabit the forest, while steelhead trout, white sturgeon and small-mouth bass can be found in the rivers and streams.

The historic Magruder Corridor Road (FR 468) is open to forest visitors July through October. The primitive road, rough but passable to two-wheel-drive, high-clearance vehicles, begins at the Red River Ranger Station and ends in Darby, Mont. The wilderness areas adjoining the route together form the largest tract of roadless land in the U.S. outside Alaska. Other roads, many unpaved, lead to such mining ghost towns as Dixie, Florence and Orogrande.

Ranger stations are located in Elk City, Kooskia and White Bird. For information contact the Forest Supervisor, Nez Perce National Forest, 104 Airport Rd., Grangeville, ID 83530; phone (208) 983-1950. *See Recreation Areas Chart.*

NEZ PERCE NATIONAL HISTORICAL PARK (C-1)

Encompassing 38 sites scattered across 12,000 square miles of north-central Idaho as well as 10 sites in Oregon, Washington and Montana, each part of Nez Perce National Historical Park reflects a portion of the history and culture of the Nez Perce Indians and their relationships with white explorers, missionaries, miners, settlers and soldiers.

Some sites are scenic views, some are geologic formations and others contain historic places and buildings. They include the Lolo Trail, Native American battlefields and former campsites of Meriwether Lewis and William Clark.

For thousands of years the Nez Perce lived in the valleys of the Clearwater and Snake rivers and their tributaries. Their first documented meeting with white settlers in Nez Perce territory took place in September 1805, when the Lewis and Clark expedition encountered them, and the Indians gave supplies and assistance. In 1855 the Nez Perce reluctantly signed a treaty setting aside their ancestral home as a reservation.

A new treaty was negotiated in 1863 with some of the Nez Perce bands after gold was discovered within the reservation; this treaty reduced the reservation to one-tenth of its original size.

The first major battle of the Nez Perce War was on June 17, 1877, near White Bird *(see place listing p. 104)*. The U.S. Army pursued the bands of Nez Perce who had not signed the 1863 treaty across the Nez Perce Trail to Montana. After many battles the Nez Perce surrendered only 40 miles from the Canadian border. They were exiled for 8 years to Oklahoma Territory; the survivors eventually returned to the Pacific Northwest. Today the Nez Perce National Historic Trail parallels much of the original 1877 route. A brochure for a self-guiding driving tour of White Bird Battlefield is available.

The Weippe (WEE-ipe) Prairie, 18 miles east of US 12 on SR 11, is part of Nez Perce National Historical Park. The Idaho section of the Nez Perce Trail and Pass climbs through 150 miles of rough terrain east of Weippe as it ascends the 5,187-foot Lolo Pass through the Bitterroot Mountains.

The park's headquarters and visitor center are in Spalding *(see place listing p. 98)*. Also see Cottonwood, Grangeville, Kamiah, Lapwai, Nez Perce National Forest and Orofino.

Spalding Visitor Center open daily 8-5, Memorial Day weekend-Labor Day; 8-4:30, mid-Mar. through day before Memorial Day weekend and day after Labor Day to mid-Nov.; 9-4, rest of year. Closed Jan. 1, Thanksgiving and Christmas. Free. Phone (208) 843-7001, ext. 7020.

NORTH FORK (E-3) elev. 3,620'

RECREATIONAL ACTIVITIES
White-water Rafting
- **North Fork Guides** trips meet at the North Fork Store, Motel and Campground at 2046 US 93N. Other activities are offered. **Hours:** Rafting trips are offered mid-Apr. through Nov. 30. Schedule varies; phone ahead. **Phone:** (208) 865-2534.

OLDTOWN (B-1) pop. 184, elev. 2,180'

Oldtown is separated from Newport, Wash., by State Avenue and is the site of the original settlement from which the two towns evolved.

Greater Newport Area Chamber of Commerce: 325 W. 4th St., Newport, WA 99156. **Phone:** (509) 447-5812 or (877) 818-1008.

ALBENI FALLS DAM, 2 mi. e. on US 2 on the Pend Oreille River, offers a scenic viewpoint and visitor center. One-hour guided tours to the powerhouse overlook, offered in the summer, provide information about the dam and powerhouse. The films "The Power and Play of the Pend Oreille" and "The Bonneville Power System" are shown in the visitor center, which also has exhibits.

Hours: Visitor center daily 7:30-6, June-Aug.; Mon.-Fri. 7:30-5, rest of year. Tours are available daily at 10, 11, 1 and 2, Memorial Day weekend-Labor Day. **Cost:** Free. **Phone:** (208) 437-4617.

OROFINO (C-1) pop. 3,142, elev. 1,027'

In 1805 members of Meriwether Lewis' and William Clark's expedition passed near the present site of Orofino on their way west. The first gold miners swarmed into the area 60 years later from California, and soon Idaho's first permanent settlements began to take shape. Orofino is on the Nez Perce Indian Reservation, and the Clearwater River runs through the town's boundaries. The Clearwater National Forest *(see place listing p. 56)* and Nez Perce National Forest *(see place listing p. 85)* are nearby.

Orofino's economy relies on lumbering, farming and government employment. A long growing season, ample precipitation and fertile soil contribute to the prosperity of this agricultural community. Northwest of Orofino, near Ahsahka *(see place listing p. 34)*, is the Dworshak National Fish Hatchery and Dworshak Dam and Reservoir.

Orofino Chamber of Commerce: 217 1st St., P.O. Box 2346, Orofino, ID 83544. **Phone:** (208) 476-4335.

CLEARWATER HISTORICAL MUSEUM is at 315 College Ave. Exhibits describe the Nez Perce culture; the Lewis and Clark expedition; early mining, logging and railroads; achievements of the Civilian Conservation Corps (CCC) in the 1930s; and the construction of the Dworshak Dam. **Time:** Allow 30 minutes minimum. **Hours:** Tues.-Sat. 12:30-5:30, June-Sept.; Tues.-Sat. 1:30-4:30, rest of year. Closed Jan. 1, Thanksgiving and Christmas. **Cost:** Donations. **Phone:** (208) 476-5033.

LEWIS AND CLARK CANOE CAMP, 4 mi. w. on US 12, is part of the Nez Perce National Historical Park *(see place listing p. 85)*. After crossing the Bitterroot Mountains on horseback, Meriwether Lewis' and William Clark's expedition camped here and built five dugout canoes for the remainder of their journey to the Pacific Ocean. **Hours:** Daily dawn-dusk. **Cost:** Free. **Phone:** (208) 843-7001, ext. 7020.

BEST WESTERN PLUS LODGE AT RIVER'S EDGE (208)476-9999

Hotel
$116

AAA Benefit: Members save 10% or more with Best Western!

Address: 615 Main St 83544 **Location:** US 12, 0.3 mi e to Main St, 0.3 mi s. **Facility:** 49 units. 3 stories, interior corridors. **Terms:** check-in 4 pm. **Amenities:** *Some:* safes. **Pool(s):** heated indoor. **Activities:** hot tub, fishing, exercise room. **Guest Services:** coin laundry. **Featured Amenity: full hot breakfast.**

HELGESON HOTEL SUITES (208)476-5729

Extended Stay Hotel $63-$85 **Address:** 125 Johnson Ave 83544 **Location:** US 12, 0.3 mi e; downtown. **Facility:** 20 kitchen units, some two bedrooms. 3 stories, interior corridors. **Parking:** on-site and street. **Activities:** hot tub, exercise room.

KONKOLVILLE MOTEL (208)476-5584

Motel $57-$82 **Address:** 2600 Michigan Ave 83544 **Location:** US 12, 3 mi e. **Facility:** 40 units. 2 stories (no elevator), exterior corridors. **Terms:** cancellation fee imposed. **Pool(s):** heated outdoor. **Activities:** hot tub. **Guest Services:** coin laundry.

WHERE TO EAT

DINING ON THE EDGE 208/476-7805

American. Fine Dining. $9-$35 **AAA Inspector Notes:** On the Clearwater River, this restaurant offers diners upscale dining while basking in nature. Be sure to ask for a seat on the deck overlooking the river. They are known for prime rib which comes with fresh-baked rosemary garlic focaccia bread with whipped rosemary butter. Vegetarian items are available. Crème brûlée is a popular dessert. **Features:** full bar, patio dining. **Address:** 625 Main St 83544 **Location:** At Main and 4th sts; downtown.

PARIS (H-6) pop. 513, elev. 5,964'

Seat of Bear Lake County, Paris was settled in 1863 by Mormon pioneers who believed they were in Utah until the boundary was surveyed in 1872. The City of Paris Museum, 34 Main St., displays local artifacts, memorabilia and historical photographs; phone the Bear Lake County office, (208) 945-2212, for more information.

The Bear River Range west of town has several remote points of interest. Six miles down the gravel Paris Canyon Road is Paris Springs; Paris Ice Cave is another 6 miles up the canyon. The cave is usually accessible by mid-July; contact the ranger station in Montpelier, (208) 847-0375, for more information.

PARIS TABERNACLE, 109 S. Main St., is a Romanesque-style Mormon place of worship dedicated in 1889. Designed by Brigham Young's son Joseph Don Carlos, this impressive sandstone edifice is considered to be one of the pioneer landmarks of the Intermountain Region. The interior, which can hold 1,500 worshipers, features hardwood floors and pine pews. The distinctive ceiling reflects a style common to sailing ships of the time.

Pioneer artifacts are displayed, and guided tours are available on request. Ninety-minute recitals are offered on an early 20th-century pipe organ made by Austin Organs Inc., one of the oldest U.S. organ manufacturers still in operation. **Time:** Allow 30 minutes minimum. **Hours:** Daily 9:30-5, Memorial Day-Labor Day. Organ recitals are given Mon.-Fri. at 11. **Cost:** Free. **Phone:** (800) 448-2327.

PAYETTE NATIONAL FOREST (E-1)

Elevations in the forest range from 1,464 ft. in Hells Canyon to 9,545 ft. at Mormon Mountain. Refer to AAA maps for additional elevation information.

Bounded by the Snake and Salmon rivers and the Middle Fork of the Salmon River in the west-central part of the state, Payette National Forest contains 2,307,897 acres ranging in elevation from 1,400 to 9,000 feet above sea level. More than 1,800 miles of both motorized and non-motorized trails include Lava Ridge National Recreation Trail and Sheep Rock Nature Trail. The forest's remote rivers and mountains offer exceptional fishing, hiking, hunting, climbing and boating opportunities during summer and fall months.

Winter sports include alpine skiing at Brundage Mountain Resort and the smaller Payette Lakes Ski Hill as well as cross-country skiing and snowmobiling in many other areas. Thousands of burned forest acres continue to regenerate as part of the natural cycle after major fires in 1994, 2000 and 2007.

A small portion of the Hells Canyon Wilderness and Hells Canyon National Recreation Area *(see place listing p. 66)* and a large portion of the Frank Church-River of No Return Wilderness are within the forest. These primitive mountainous areas overlap several national forests and contain extensive non-motorized trail networks. For more information write Payette National Forest, 800 W. Lakeside Ave., McCall, ID 83638; phone (208) 634-0700. *See Recreation Areas Chart.*

PIERCE (C-2) pop. 508, elev. 3,094'

Gold was found here in 1860, triggering a rush of some 6,000 prospectors, many of whom were Chinese. In 1861 the rough mining camp became seat of Shoshone County and the first established town in what was to become Idaho Territory 3 years later. After mining played out in the 1880s, Pierce re-emerged as a forest products center in the 1900s. Its population peaked at over 1,200 in 1970.

Idaho's oldest government building, a courthouse built in 1862, still stands 1 block east of SR 11 on Court Street. It became a private residence after the

county seat was moved to Murray in 1885. The J. Howard Bradbury Memorial Logging Museum, 103 S. Main St., has historical photographs, indoor and outdoor displays of mining and logging relics, and a 1920 log cabin; phone (208) 464-2677. An interpretive pavilion, on SR 11 at the north end of town, features 15 panels describing the history of the area.

Pierce is on the Gold Rush Historic Byway, a 43-mile route following SR 11 from Greer up to Weippe *(see place listing p. 104)* and Pierce and ending at Headquarters. Numerous roadside plaques describe points of interest along the byway.

RECREATIONAL ACTIVITIES
Skiing
• **Bald Mountain Ski Area** is 6 mi. n. on SR 11. **Hours:** Sat.-Sun. and holidays 9:30-3:30, mid-Dec. to late Mar. (weather permitting). **Phone:** (208) 464-2311 or (208) 435-4272.

PLUMMER (C-1) pop. 1,044, elev. 2,743'

Plummer is the commercial center of the Coeur d'Alene Indian Reservation and the surrounding farms and timberlands. The town also is the western trailhead of the Trail of the Coeur d'Alenes, a paved walking and bicycling route extending 72 miles east to Mullan.

HEYBURN STATE PARK, 5 mi. e. on SR 5, brackets the south end of Lake Coeur d'Alene. Established in 1908, it is the oldest state park in the Pacific Northwest as well as Idaho's largest state park at 7,825 acres. Heyburn is home to bears, deer, elk and heron and boasts one of the largest concentrations of nesting osprey in North America. A visitor center at Hawleys Landing off SR 5 contains exhibits about area wildlife and tribal history as well as historical photographs documenting the Civilian Conservation Corps' role in the park's development.

Heyburn also offers 20 miles of multiuse trails. A section of the 72-mile, paved Trail of the Coeur d'Alenes passes through the northern part of the park; it is accessible from the Chatcolet Day Use Area 2.5 miles north of the visitor center. You can hike or bike across the trail's 3,100-foot bridge/trestle, which spans the lake.

Cottonwood Point, 2 miles east of the main park entrance on SR 5, offers an excellent view of the "river flowing through a lake." This unusual feature formed in 1904, when the Post Falls Dam on the Spokane River raised the lake level, drowning the lowlands flanking the lower reaches of the St. Joe River, but leaving its natural, tree-lined levees above the waters. *See Recreation Areas Chart.*

Time: Allow 1 hour minimum. **Hours:** Park open daily 24 hours. Visitor Center open daily 8:30-6, Memorial Day weekend-Labor Day; Mon.-Fri. 7-3:30, rest of year. Phone ahead to confirm schedule. **Cost:** $5 (per private vehicle). **Phone:** (208) 686-1308.

POCATELLO (G-5) pop. 54,255, elev. 4,365'

Originally part of the Fort Hall Indian Reservation, Pocatello is named for a 19th-century Shoshone chief who granted the Utah & Northern a right-of-way for a Salt Lake City-to-Butte railroad line. The subsequent arrival in 1882 of the Union Pacific Railway, which linked the Midwest and Pacific Northwest, spawned a makeshift community—a congregation of tents at the meeting of the two lines—that was first called Pocatello Junction.

Pocatello maintains its position as one of the region's leading industrial, distribution and transportation centers. Education also is a principal concern; Idaho State University, with 12,000 students, is one of the state's leading 4-year institutions. The school's state-of-the-art L.E. and Thelma E. Stephens Performing Arts Center, 1002 Sam Nixon Ave., entertains lovers of music, dance and theater; phone (208) 282-3595.

The town is the northern terminus of an especially scenic section of I-15, which heads south into Utah. Just off Main Street visitors can see the Union Pacific Depot, a three-story passenger station designed in the late 1800s. Train passengers of the era stayed overnight across the street at the historic Yellowstone Hotel.

Greater Pocatello Convention & Visitors Bureau: P.O. Box 626, Pocatello, ID 83204. **Phone:** (208) 479-7659.

DON ASLETT MUSEUM OF CLEAN is at 711 S. 2nd Ave. This five-story green building, a renovated 20th-century brick warehouse, is filled with captivating themed displays that relate the history of cleaning. More than 5,000 items are exhibited, including art, appliances, tools and products. How-to videos, such as "How to Clean Your Bathroom in 2-3 Minutes," offer quick and easy cleaning tips to visitors. The three-story Kids' Cleaning World teaches children about cleanliness and responsibility and features mops, buckets and other supplies for wee ones to try out.

Fast-paced workshops discussing various cleaning topics are offered weekly. **Time:** Allow 1 hour, 30 minutes minimum. **Hours:** Tues.-Sat. 10-5. Closed Jan. 1, Thanksgiving and Christmas. Phone ahead to confirm schedule. **Cost:** $5; $3 (ages 3-15); $15 (family). **Phone:** (208) 236-6906.

IDAHO MUSEUM OF NATURAL HISTORY is on the main floor of the museum building at the corner of 5th Ave. and Dillon St. on the Idaho State University campus. Among the permanent exhibits is Living Off the Land, which features an extensive collection of Shoshone-Bannock tribal basketry; the ISU Tree Walk; and a natural history garden. The Discovery Room allows children hands-on encounters with fossils and other specimens.

Time: Allow 30 minutes minimum. **Hours:** Tues.-Sat. 11-5. Closed major holidays. **Cost:** Donations. **Phone:** (208) 282-3317.

ROSS PARK is between 2nd and 5th aves. With such amenities as a skate park and horseshoe and volleyball areas on-site, a variety of recreational activities can be enjoyed. The community park also comprises a museum, a re-created historical trading post and a zoo. In addition its stellar aquatic complex offers a 50-meter swimming pool, a waterslide, a lazy river and an interactive wading area.

Time: Allow 1 hour minimum. **Hours:** Park open daily dawn-dusk. Aquatic complex open daily noon-8, Memorial Day weekend-Labor Day (weather permitting). Phone ahead to confirm schedule. **Cost:** Park admission free. Aquatic complex (excludes waterslide) $6; $5 (ages 7-17); $4 (ages 60+); $2 (ages 1-6). Half-price admission Mon. and Wed. 5-8 p.m. Aquatic complex unlimited waterslide pass $3. **Phone:** (208) 234-0472. 🛣

Bannock County Historical Museum is off I-15 exit 67, then 1 mi. n. on N. 5th Ave. (US 30/91) to 3000 Alvord Loop in Upper Ross Park. The museum contains Native American and railroad displays, a restored stagecoach, a 1915 La France fire truck and a history/donor mural wall. Other displays include a 1900s parlor, a country store, an early dental office and a 1947 Linotype press. **Hours:** Daily 10-6, Memorial Day weekend-Labor Day; Tues.-Sat. 10-4, rest of year. Closed major holidays. **Cost:** Memorial Day weekend-Labor Day (includes Fort Hall Replica) $4; $3 (senior citizens); $2 (ages 6-12). Rest of year (does not include Fort Hall Replica) $2; $1 (ages 6-12). **Phone:** (208) 233-0434.

Fort Hall Replica, off I-15 exit 67, then 1 mi. n. on N. 5th Ave. (US 30/91) to 2990 Avenue of the Chiefs in Upper Ross Park, re-creates the fur-trading post that operated nearby 1834-60. Original Hudson's Bay Co. plans were used to create the full-scale replica. Buffaloes, elk, deer and pronghorn antelopes are kept in a field next to the fort.

Time: Allow 1 hour minimum. **Hours:** Mon.-Sat. 10-6, Sun. 1-5, day after Memorial Day-Labor Day. Phone ahead to confirm schedule. **Cost:** $4; $3 (senior citizens); $2 (ages 6-12). **Phone:** (208) 234-1795.

Pocatello Zoo, 2900 S. 2nd Ave. in the lower level of Ross Park, features native North American wildlife including elk, bison, grizzly and black bears, bighorn sheep, pronghorn, mountain lions and waterfowl in 23 acres of natural habitats. Children can play in a 900-square-foot tree house or a 30-foot tipi. **Time:** Allow 1 hour minimum. **Hours:** Daily 10-6, June 16-Labor Day; daily 9-5, May 1-June 15; Sat.-Sun. 10-5, Apr. 15-30; Sat.-Sun. 10-4, day after Labor Day-Oct. 31. **Cost:** $5.25; $4 (ages 60+); $3.25 (ages 3-11). **Phone:** (208) 234-6196.

AMERITEL INN   (208)234-7500
▼▼▼ Hotel $80-$160 **Address:** 1440 Bench Rd 83201 **Location:** I-15 exit 71, just e. **Facility:** 148 units, some efficiencies. 3 stories, interior corridors. **Pool(s):** heated indoor. **Activities:** hot tub, exercise room. **Guest Services:** valet and coin laundry.

BEST WESTERN POCATELLO INN   (208)237-7650

Hotel
$100-$110

AAA Benefit: Members save 10% or more with Best Western!

Address: 1415 Bench Rd 83201 **Location:** I-15 exit 71, just e. **Facility:** 149 units, some kitchens. 2-3 stories (no elevator), interior corridors. **Parking:** winter plug-ins. **Amenities:** *Some:* safes. **Pool(s):** heated indoor. **Activities:** hot tub. **Guest Services:** valet and coin laundry, area transportation.

CLARION INN   (208)237-1400

Hotel $89-$119 **Address:** 1399 Bench Rd 83201 **Location:** I-15 exit 71, just e. **Facility:** 196 units. 2 stories (no elevator), interior/exterior corridors. **Pool(s):** heated indoor. **Activities:** sauna, hot tub, game room, picnic facilities, exercise room. **Guest Services:** valet and coin laundry.

COMFORT INN   (208)237-8155

Hotel
$75-$110

Address: 1333 Bench Rd 83201 **Location:** I-15 exit 71, just e. **Facility:** 52 units. 2 stories (no elevator), interior corridors. **Amenities:** safes. **Pool(s):** heated indoor. **Activities:** hot tub. **Guest Services:** valet laundry. **Featured Amenity. full hot breakfast.**

HAMPTON INN & SUITES   208/233-8200

Contemporary Hotel. Rates not provided. **Address:** 151 Vista Dr 83201 **Location:** I-15 exit 69 (Clark St), just e. **Facility:** 89 units. 4 stories, interior corridors. **Pool(s):** heated indoor. **Activities:** hot tub, exercise room. **Guest Services:** valet and coin laundry.

AAA Benefit: Members save up to 10%!

RED LION HOTEL   (208)233-2200

Hotel $79-$95 **Address:** 1555 Pocatello Creek Rd 83201 **Location:** I-15 exit 71, just e. **Facility:** 150 units. 2 stories (no elevator), interior corridors. **Terms:** cancellation fee imposed. **Pool(s):** heated indoor. **Activities:** hot tub, exercise room. **Guest Services:** valet and coin laundry, area transportation.

SUPER 8   (208)234-0888

Motel
$60-$90

Address: 1330 Bench Rd 83201 **Location:** I-15 exit 71, just e. **Facility:** 80 units. 3 stories, interior corridors. **Guest Services:** coin laundry. **Featured Amenity: continental breakfast.**

THUNDERBIRD MOTEL   (208)232-6330

Motel $46-$59 **Address:** 1415 S 5th Ave 83201 **Location:** I-15 exit 67 (5th Ave), 1.3 mi n; just s of Idaho State University. **Facility:** 43 units. 2 stories (no elevator), exterior corridors. **Parking:** winter plug-ins. **Terms:** resort fee. **Pool(s):** heated outdoor.

TOWNEPLACE SUITES BY MARRIOTT   (208)478-7000

Extended Stay Hotel
$109-$139

TownePlace SUITES *Marriott*

AAA Benefit: Members save 5% or more!

Address: 2376 Via Caporatti Dr 83201 **Location:** I-15 exit 69 (Clark St), 0.3 mi e. **Facility:** 93 units, some two bedrooms, efficiencies and kitchens. 4 stories, interior corridors. **Parking:** winter plug-ins. **Pool(s):** heated indoor. **Activities:** hot tub, picnic facilities, exercise room. **Guest Services:** valet and coin laundry.

BLACK SWAN INN LUXURIOUS THEME SUITES
208/233-3051

fyi Not evaluated. **Address:** 746 E Center St 83201 **Location:** I-15 exit 69 (Clark St), 1.1 mi w, just s on 7th Ave, then just w; downtown. Facilities, services, and décor characterize a mid-scale property.

WHERE TO EAT

BUDDY'S   208/233-1172

Italian. Casual Dining. $5-$16 **AAA Inspector Notes:** The locals love the bustling atmosphere and good food at this family-owned restaurant-in business for more than 40 years. Italian fare dominates the menu, right up to the handmade ravioli, a house specialty, and the famous salad dressing. Vegetarian zesty non-meat marinara sauce is available upon request. The atmosphere is warm and friendly. **Features:** beer & wine. **Address:** 626 E Lewis St 83201 **Location:** I-15 exit 69 (Clark St), 1 mi w, just s on 7th Ave, then just w.

EL HERRADERO   208/233-6747

Mexican. Casual Dining. $5-$10 **AAA Inspector Notes:** This charming family-run eatery serves an array of combos, appetizers, enchiladas, nachos, burritos, and chicken, beef or shrimp fajitas. Visitors will appreciate the a la carte menu which features more than 11 items. Vegetarian items are available upon request. I opted for the chicken rollitos and beef sopitos, which were delicious and attractively presented. **Features:** beer only. **Address:** 123 Jefferson Ave 83201 **Location:** I-15 exit 67 (5th Ave), 2.2 mi n to Center St, 0.5 mi e to 13th Ave, then 0.5 mi n to Oak St; corner of Oak St and Jefferson Ave.

PORTNEUF VALLEY BREWING   970/232-1644

American. Casual Dining. $7-$28 **AAA Inspector Notes:** Some popular favorites served here are the salads and sandwiches, veggie or meat lasagna, teriyaki bowl stir-fry, wacky macaroni and cheese, made-to-order fresh baked pizza and craft-brewed beverages. The Bavarian bun and giant salty pretzel are addictive. Many items are available in smaller portions. **Features:** full bar. **Address:** 615 S 1st Ave 83201 **Location:** I-15 exit 69 (Clark St), 1.2 mi sw to 4th Ave, 0.3 mi se to Whitman St, 0.3 mi sw to S 1st Ave, then just se. **Parking:** street only.

THE SANDPIPER   208/233-1000

Seafood Steak. Casual Dining. $11-$32 **AAA Inspector Notes:** Good choices are the house salad with shrimp and creamy garlic dressing and the prime rib entrée at this informal, bustling restaurant. Deck dining is available in season. **Features:** full bar. **Reservations:** suggested, weekends. **Address:** 1400 Bench Rd 83201 **Location:** I-15 exit 71, just e, then just n.

PONDERAY   pop. 1,137

GUESTHOUSE LODGE-SANDPOINT   (208)263-2210
◆◆◆ Hotel $47-$155 Address: 476841 Hwy 95 N 83852 Location: 0.7 mi n on US 95 from jct SR 200. Facility: 59 units. 2 stories (no elevator), interior corridors. Terms: 3 day cancellation notice-fee imposed, resort fee. Activities: hot tub. Guest Services: coin laundry.
CALL ⓜ 🛜 ⊠ 🖥 🖨 💻 / SOME UNITS 🅂🄿

HOLIDAY INN EXPRESS & SUITES   208/255-4500
◆◆◆ Hotel. Rates not provided. Address: 477326 Hwy 95 N 83852 Location: 0.7 mi n on US 95 from jct SR 200. Facility: 83 units, some two bedrooms. 3 stories, interior corridors. Parking: winter plug-ins. Pool(s): heated indoor. Activities: hot tub, exercise room. Guest Services: valet and coin laundry.
🛗 CALL ⓜ 🖐 🅱🄸🅉 🛜 ⊠ 🖥 🖨 💻 / SOME UNITS 🅂🄿 🄷🅂

HOWARD JOHNSON SANDPOINT/PONDERAY   (208)263-5383
◆◆ Hotel $55-$135 Address: 477255 Hwy 95 N 83852 Location: 1.2 mi n on US 95 from jct SR 200. Facility: 70 units. 2 stories (no elevator), interior corridors. Parking: winter plug-ins. Amenities: safes. Activities: hot tub. Guest Services: coin laundry.
🛗 CALL ⓜ 🛜 💻 / SOME UNITS 🅂🄿 🖥 🖨

WHERE TO EAT

SWEET LOU'S   208/263-1381
◆◆◆ Barbecue. Gastropub. $8-$23 AAA Inspector Notes: Sports bar or gastropub, guests are sure to enjoy the succulent ribs or hangar steak sandwiches, along with the buckets of beer found here. Hand-cut fries and homemade fry sauce complement the meal. There is a seasonal sister restaurant in the northwestern town of Hope. Features: full bar, happy hour. Address: 477272 Hwy 95 N 83852 Location: 0.7 mi n on US 95 from jct SR 200; adjacent to Holiday Inn Express & Suites. Ⓛ Ⓓ CALL ⓜ

POST FALLS   (B-1) pop. 27,574, elev. 2,169'

On the Spokane River at the Washington-Idaho state line, Post Falls was founded in the late 1800s by Frederick Post when he harnessed the falls to generate power for his sawmill.

Stateline Speedway, off I-90 exit 2 at 1349 N. Beck Rd., features stock car racing Wednesdays and Saturdays from mid-April through September; phone (208) 773-5019.

Post Falls/Coeur d'Alene Visitor Center: 201 E. Fourth Ave., Post Falls, ID 83854. Phone: (208) 773-5016 or (800) 292-2553.

FALLS PARK, off I-90 Spokane St. exit, 2 blks. s. on Spokane St., then 1.5 blks. w. to 305 W. 4th St., offers visitors picturesque views of Post Falls and the gorge. The best viewing is during spring runoff. Children also can fish in a stocked pond. Trails lead to nearby Treaty Rock Historic Site *(see attraction listing)*, which marks the location of Post Falls' founding. Hours: Daily dawn-dusk (weather permitting). Cost: Free. Phone: (208) 773-0539. 🎌

Q'EMILN PARK AND TRAILS is off I-90 exit 5, .9 mi. s. on Spokane St., then .2 mi. w. on Parkway Dr. Twelve connected trails wind along the south bank of the Spokane River. The pathways lead to historic sites, abandoned homesteads, mining camps, logging areas and scenic spots above and below Post Falls Dam. The park is known for its rock climbing, with opportunities that appeal to all skill levels. A boat launch, picnic areas and seasonal community events are offered. Swimming is permitted in designated areas. Time: Allow 1 hour minimum. Hours: Daily dawn-dusk. Cost: Free. Parking: Memorial Day weekend-Labor Day $3.50. Phone: (208) 773-0539. ⊠ 🎌

TREATY ROCK HISTORIC SITE, jct. 7th and Compton sts., commemorates the spot where Coeur d'Alene Indian Chief Andrew Seltice transferred land to Frederick Post, the founder of Post Falls. A trail with interpretive signage features Native American petroglyphs and paintings. Time: Allow 30 minutes minimum. Hours: Daily dawn-dusk. Cost: Free. Phone: (208) 773-0539. 🎌

RED LION TEMPLIN'S HOTEL ON THE RIVER - POST FALLS   (208)773-1611
◆◆◆ Hotel $109-$229

Address: 414 E 1st Ave 83854 Location: I-90 exit 5 eastbound, just s to 1st Ave; exit 6 westbound, 0.7 mi w on Seltice Way to Spokane St, 0.5 mi s, then just e. Facility: 163 units. 2-3 stories, interior corridors. Parking: winter plug-ins. Terms: cancellation fee imposed. Pool(s): heated indoor. Activities: sauna, hot tub, marina, fishing, tennis, exercise room. Guest Services: valet and coin laundry.
🆂🅰🆅🅴 🔙 🛗 🍽 CALL ⓜ 🏊 🅱🄸🅉 🄷🅂 🛜 ⊠ 🖥 🖨 💻 / SOME UNITS 🅂🄿

RIVERBEND INN   (208)773-3583
◆◆◆ Hotel $59-$99

Address: 4100 W Riverbend Ave 83854 Location: I-90 exit 2, just s. Adjacent to outlet mall. Facility: 71 units, some efficiencies. 2 stories (no elevator), interior corridors. Parking: winter plug-ins. Pool(s): heated outdoor. Activities: hot tub. Guest Services: valet and coin laundry.
🆂🅰🆅🅴 🛗 🏊 🛜 / SOME UNITS 🖥 🖨

SLEEP INN   (208)777-9394
◆◆ Hotel $61-$169 Address: 157 S Pleasant View Rd 83854 Location: I-90 exit 2, just s. Adjacent to outlet mall. Facility: 84 units. 2 stories (no elevator), interior corridors. Parking: winter plug-ins. Pool(s): heated indoor. Activities: hot tub. Guest Services: valet and coin laundry.
🛗 CALL ⓜ 🏊 🅱🄸🅉 🛜 ⊠ 💻 / SOME UNITS 🅂🄿 🖥 🖨

WHERE TO EAT

FLEUR DE SEL   208/777-7600
◆◆◆ French. Fine Dining. $9-$24 AAA Inspector Notes: Fleur De Sel means flower of salt and not just any salt—the salt on the tables has been hand-raked from the Mediterranean Sea. The chef/owner, Laurent, creates delectable French food that changes seasonally. Many items on the menu are modestly priced, encouraging tasting and sharing. Features: full bar, patio dining. Reservations: suggested. Address: 4365 Inverness Dr 83854 Location: I-90 exit 7 (SR 41 N), just e on E Seltice Way, just n on SR 41 N/ Ross Point Rd, just e on E Mullan Rd, then just e on Sterling Rd; in Highlands Day Spa. Ⓓ CALL ⓜ

OLD EUROPEAN RESTAURANT   208/777-2017

♦♦ ♦♦ European Breakfast. Family Dining. $6-$12 **AAA Inspector Notes:** Join the crowds who pile into this place at breakfast-as well as other times of the day-for European comfort foods. Guests can sample tasty homemade soups and such made-from-scratch baked goods as Swedish cream-filled crepes, Danish aebleskivers (a ball-like pancake), Belgian waffles, German potato pancakes, Hungarian breakfast goulash and Irish shepherd's pie. Plentiful portions ensure that no one will leave hungry. **Address:** 1710 E Schneidmiller Ave 83854 **Location:** I-90 exit 5, just n, 1 mi e on E Seltice Way, then just ne on 5th Ave. [B] [L] CALL [M]

THE WHITE HOUSE GRILL   208/777-9672

♦♦ ♦♦ Mediterranean. Casual Dining. $9-$20 **AAA Inspector Notes:** Not for the faint of heart or those who worry about their breath, the restaurant is a virtual shrine to garlic. The intimate and casual setting incorporates outdoor seating when the weather permits. The primarily Mediterranean menu highlights Chilean sea bass, lamb kabobs as well as desserts that range from sweet baklava to light tiramisu. **Features:** full bar, patio dining. **Reservations:** suggested. **Address:** 712 N Spokane St 83854 **Location:** I-90 exit 5, just n. [L] [D]

PRIEST LAKE—See Coolin p. 60.

PRIEST RIVER (B-1) pop. 1,751, elev. 2,082'

Priest River, at the junction of the Pend Oreille and Priest rivers and 30 miles south of Priest Lake via SR 57, is the gateway to the Idaho Panhandle National Forests (see place listing p. 70). The 1895 Keyser House contains historical displays.

Priest River Chamber of Commerce: 119 Main St., Suite 203B, P.O. Box 929, Priest River, ID 83856. **Phone:** (208) 448-2721.

EAGLE'S NEST MOTEL   208/448-2000

♦♦ Motel $59-$125 **Address:** 5722 Hwy 2 83856 **Location:** US 2, 0.5 mi w. **Facility:** 30 units. 1 story, exterior corridors. **Terms:** 3 day cancellation notice.

CALL [M] [HS] 🛜 🔲 🖼 /SOME UNITS S🔲

REXBURG (F-6) pop. 25,484, elev. 4,861'
• Restaurants p. 92

In the late 1870s many miners heading into Montana in search of gold stopped along the west side of the Snake River and claimed land under the Homestead Act of 1862. Many of these first homesteaders were Mormons. In 1883 another influx of settlers drove their sleighs to the banks of the Snake River and established the present town site of Rexburg.

In June 1976 the nearby Teton Dam collapsed, sending 8 billion gallons of flood water into the valley below. To see the site, travel 20 miles northeast on SR 33.

Rexburg plays host to the ♦♦ Idaho International Dance and Music Festival in late July and early August. The Centennial Carousel, which took 5 years to restore, is in Porter Park. Located at 2nd West 2nd South in downtown Rexburg, the park offers picnic tables; a playground; and recreational facilities for baseball, volleyball, tennis and basketball.

Rexburg Area Chamber of Commerce: 127 E. Main St., Rexburg, ID 83440. **Phone:** (208) 356-5700 or (888) 463-6880.

LEGACY FLIGHT MUSEUM, 400 Airport Rd., features a dozen operational aircraft. A working hanger displays World War II planes, including a rare P-63 Kingcobra, three P-51 Mustangs and an L-2 Grasshopper, along with aircraft used during the Vietnam and Korean wars. A small museum displays artifacts from the Civil War to present-day conflicts in the Middle East. Orientation flights are available by reservation.

Tours: Guided tours are available. **Time:** Allow 1 hour minimum. **Hours:** Mon.-Sat. 9-5, Memorial Day-Labor Day; Fri.-Sat. 9-5, rest of year. The Annual Air Show takes place Father's Day weekend on even-numbered years. **Cost:** $6; $5 (students, veterans and active military with ID and senior citizens); $3 (ages 8-18); $15 (family). **Phone:** (208) 359-5905.

TETON FLOOD MUSEUM is at 51 N. Center St. Shows and picture displays document the 1976 break in the Teton Dam and the subsequent flooding. A film about the flood is shown by request. Other exhibits include pioneer relics, a collection of North American animal mounts, and items related to World War I and II. **Hours:** Mon.-Sat. 10-5 (also Mon. 5-7), May 1-late Sept.; Mon.-Fri. 11-5 (also Mon. 5-7), rest of year. Closed major holidays. **Cost:** $2; $1 (ages 12-18); 50¢ (ages 2-11). **Phone:** (208) 359-3063.

[SAVE] **YELLOWSTONE BEAR WORLD** is 7 mi. s. on US 20. From the comfort of your automobile, you'll experience up-close encounters with black and grizzly bears at this drive-through wildlife park. Elk, deer and timber wolves also roam the 120-acre grounds.

Guided curator tours and bottle-feeding tours are available. **Time:** Allow 1 hour minimum. **Hours:** Daily 9-6, Memorial Day weekend-Labor Day; 9-5, early May-day before Memorial Day weekend and day after Labor Day to mid-Oct. **Cost:** $15.95; $14.95 (ages 65+); $9.95 (ages 3-10); $69.95 (family, per private vehicle with up to seven people). Prices may vary; phone ahead. **Phone:** (208) 359-9688. [T]

AMERICINN LODGE & SUITES OF REXBURG   (208)356-5333

♦♦ ♦♦ Hotel $89-$210 **Address:** 1098 Golden Beauty Dr 83440 **Location:** US 20 exit 332 (S Rexburg). **Facility:** 66 units. 3 stories, interior corridors. **Parking:** winter plug-ins. **Pool(s):** heated indoor. **Activities:** hot tub, exercise room. **Guest Services:** coin laundry.

🏊 [BIZ] [HS] 🛜 ✕ 🔲 🖼 💻 /SOME UNITS S🔲

QUALITY INN   (208)359-1311

♦♦♦ ♦♦♦
Hotel
$79-$138

Address: 885 W Main St 83440 **Location:** US 20 exit 333 (Salmon), just e. **Facility:** 52 units. 2 stories (no elevator), interior corridors. **Parking:** winter plug-ins. **Pool(s):** heated indoor. **Activities:** hot tub. **Guest Services:** coin laundry. **Featured Amenity:** continental breakfast.

[SAVE] 🏊 [BIZ] [HS] 🛜 ✕ 💻 /SOME UNITS 🐾 🔲 🖼

SPRINGHILL SUITES BY MARRIOTT REXBURG
(208)356-3003

🔷🔷🔷 **Hotel** $99-$190 **Address:** 1177 S Yellowstone Hwy 83440 **Location:** US 20 exit 332 (S Rexburg). **Facility:** 97 units, some two bedrooms. 4 stories, interior corridors. **Pool(s):** heated indoor. **Activities:** hot tub, exercise room. **Guest Services:** valet and coin laundry.

AAA Benefit: Members save 5% or more!

CALL

SUPER 8
(208)356-8888

🔷🔷
Hotel
$65-$137

Address: 215 W Main St 83440 **Location:** US 20 exit 333 (Salmon), 1 mi e on SR 33 (Main St). **Facility:** 45 units. 2 stories (no elevator), interior corridors. **Parking:** winter plug-ins. **Terms:** cancellation fee imposed. **Pool(s):** heated indoor. **Activities:** hot tub, limited exercise equipment. **Guest Services:** coin laundry. **Featured Amenity:** continental breakfast.

WHERE TO EAT

DA PINEAPPLE GRILL
208/356-4398

🔷🔷 Hawaiian Sushi. Casual Dining. $9-$18 **AAA Inspector Notes:** Diners can see mahi mahi, teriyaki and pulled pork sandwiches along with traditional sushi on the menu at this casual spot. The owner's artistic background not only is reflected in the gorgeous murals of Hawaiian scenes that adorn the walls, but also in the signature sauces and sushi rolls on the menu. **Address:** 383 S 2nd W 83440 **Location:** US 20 exit 333 (Salmon), 1 mi e on SR 33 (Main St), then 0.6 mi s. ⓛ ⓓ CALL 🅶🅼

FRONTIER PIES RESTAURANT & BAKERY
208/356-3600

🔷🔷 American. Family Dining. $6-$18 **AAA Inspector Notes:** Choose from sandwiches, soup or chicken-fried steak at this eatery. However, don't budge before savoring a slice of any one of 25 varieties of made-from-scratch pie. The delicious strawberry pie is worth the splurge. **Features:** early bird specials, senior menu. **Address:** 460 W 4th S 83440 **Location:** US 20 exit 332 (S Rexburg), 1 mi e.

Ⓑ Ⓛ Ⓓ

ORIGINAL THAI
208/359-9660

🔷🔷 Thai. Casual Dining. $10-$14 **AAA Inspector Notes:** As is usually the case with college town ethnic restaurants, the food here is fantastic, but the decor leaves a lot to be desired. The service is friendly and the location is convenient on the main street in town. **Address:** 10 E Main St 83440 **Location:** US 20 exit 333 (Salmon), 1.5 mi e on SR 33 (Main St). **Parking:** street only. Ⓛ Ⓓ

RIGBY (F-5) pop. 3,945, elev. 4,850'

JEFFERSON COUNTY HISTORICAL SOCIETY AND FARNSWORTH TV PIONEER MUSEUM, 118 West 1st South, highlights Jefferson County history and includes displays about the city's role in the birth of television. Philo Farnsworth, who conceived the world's first all-electronic television, formulated his ideas about the electronic transmission of visual images while a Rigby resident. The museum's varied collection includes vintage TV sets as well as an early barbershop and military memorabilia. Also featured are World War I and World War II uniforms, weapons and mementos.

Time: Allow 30 minutes minimum. **Hours:** Tues.-Sat. 1-5 and by appointment. Closed major holidays. **Cost:** $2; $1 (ages 7-18). **Phone:** (208) 745-8423.

BLUE HERON INN
(208)745-9922

🔷🔷🔷 Bed & Breakfast $109-$199 **Address:** 706 N Yellowstone Hwy 83442 **Location:** US 20 exit 325, just e, then 0.4 mi ne just before railroad tracks; at end of road. **Facility:** Perfect for a romantic visit, this beautiful property is located in a peaceful country setting with breathtaking mountain and river views. Some of these well-appointed rooms feature a fireplace and balcony. 7 units. 2 stories (no elevator), interior/exterior corridors. **Terms:** age restrictions may apply, 7 day cancellation notice-fee imposed. **Activities:** hot tub, massage.

RIGGINS (E-1) pop. 419, elev. 1,800'

Riggins, where the Little Salmon pours into the main Salmon River, is a starting point for a drive north along US 95 through the scenic gorge of the Salmon River. The town is considered a white-water capital and features opportunities for white-water rafting, boating and fishing.

East of town lies the wilderness of the Payette National Forest *(see place listing p. 87)*. To the west rise the 9,000-foot Seven Devils Mountains, which form a semicircle above the Snake River's chasm, Hells Canyon; some 30 alpine lakes are clustered around the peaks. To the south is the Rapid River Fish Hatchery, one of the Northwest's most successful chinook salmon-breeding operations.

Salmon River Chamber of Commerce: P.O. Box 289, Riggins, ID 83549. **Phone:** (208) 628-3320.

RECREATIONAL ACTIVITIES
Fishing

- **River Adventures Ltd.** trips depart from various locations, including Riggins City Park on US 95. Other activities are offered. **Hours:** Trips are offered daily, Apr.-Sept. Departure times vary; phone ahead. **Phone:** (208) 628-3952 or (800) 524-9710.

White-water Rafting

- **Epley's Whitewater Adventures** is on US 95 at the n. end of town. **Hours:** Trips are offered daily, June-Sept. Departure times vary; phone ahead. **Phone:** (208) 628-3586 or (800) 233-1813.

- **Mountain River Outfitters** is at 411 N. Main St. (US 95). Other activities, including fishing excursions, are offered. **Hours:** Rafting trips are offered daily, May-Sept. Departure times vary; phone ahead. **Phone:** (208) 628-3733 or (888) 547-4837.

- **Northwest Voyageurs** is 9 mi. s. on US 95. Other activities are offered. **Hours:** Rafting trips are offered daily, late Mar. to mid-Oct. Departure times vary; phone ahead. **Phone:** (208) 628-3022 or (800) 727-9977.

- **Salmon River Challenge** is on US 95 at Milepost 197. Other activities are offered. **Hours:** Rafting trips depart daily at 7:30 (2- and 3-day trips), 9 (full-day trips) and 12:30 (half-day trips), May 1-late Sept. **Phone:** (208) 628-3264 or (800) 732-8574.

PINEHURST RESORT CABINS & RV   (208)628-3323

▼▼ **Cabin** $65-$95 **Address:** 5604 Hwy 95 83654 **Location:** Waterfront. 12 mi s of Riggins; MM 182. Located on the Little Salmon River. **Facility:** 7 cabins. 1 story, exterior corridors. *Bath:* shower only. **Terms:** cancellation fee imposed. **Activities:** fishing, picnic facilities.

SALMON RAPIDS LODGE   (208)628-2743

▼▼▼ **Hotel** $90-$127 **Address:** 1010 S Main St 83549 **Location:** 0.3 mi s of center. **Facility:** 55 units. 2 stories (no elevator), interior corridors. **Pool(s):** heated indoor. **Activities:** hot tub, limited exercise equipment. **Guest Services:** coin laundry.

WHERE TO EAT

RIVER ROCK CAFE   208/628-3434

▼▼ American. Casual Dining. $7-$25 **AAA Inspector Notes:** Undoubtedly popular with locals, this café is a favorite stop for patrons passing through the area. Varied menu selections include pizza, calzones, burgers, hot and cold sandwiches and a nice selection of salads. The dinner menu features pasta, steak, chicken and seafood. Boxed lunches to go are perfect for those rafting on the river, fishing, hunting or sightseeing. Blackberry cobbler is a great meal-ender. **Features:** beer & wine. **Reservations:** suggested. **Address:** 1149 S Main St 83549 **Location:** Just s of center. B L D

RUPERT (H-4) pop. 5,554, elev. 4,158'

Rupert was platted by the Bureau of Reclamation, which accounts for its business district being built around a square that is now a public park. Irrigation from dam projects on the Snake River has transformed the surrounding area from semiarid land to one of Idaho's principal agricultural areas. Potatoes and sugar beets are important crops.

Camping, picnicking, birding, hiking and other recreational opportunities are available in nearby Lake Walcott State Park. *See Recreation Areas Chart.*

MINIDOKA NATIONAL WILDLIFE REFUGE extends 20 mi. up the Snake River from Minidoka Dam; refuge headquarters is 12 mi. n.e. via SR 24 and CR 400N. As many as 100,000 waterfowl stop at the refuge as they migrate along the Pacific flyway. Some 200 species of birds plus mule deer, pronghorn antelopes and various predators inhabit the 20,721-acre refuge.

Fishing, boating and picnicking are permitted on the western end of Lake Walcott, though boating is prohibited October through February. A 1.2-mile hiking trail loop with interpretive signs is accessible via Lake Walcott State Park, 11 mi. n.e. of Rupert off SR 24. Roads are primitive. **Hours:** Refuge open daily dawn-dusk. Office open Mon.-Fri. 7-4:30. Closed major holidays. **Phone:** (208) 436-3589.

SAGLE (B-1) elev. 2,149'

BIRD AVIATION MUSEUM AND INVENTION CENTER is 12 mi. e. of US 95 on Sagle Rd., following signs to 500 Bird Ranch Rd. The museum hangar exhibits six mint-condition aircraft (1927-72) and motor vehicles from the same period. Additional displays include military uniforms, models, artwork and items from NASA.

The Imagination Room honors inventors who perfected products ranging from Kitty Litter and Barbie dolls to microprocessors and the artificial heart. An upstairs gallery displays a respiratory ventilator and an Anti-"G" Suit used by high-altitude pilots, both invented by museum co-founder Dr. Forrest Bird.

Time: Allow 1 hour minimum. **Hours:** Mon.-Sat. 8-4, mid-May to mid-Oct.; Mon.-Fri. 8-4, rest of year. Closed Jan. 1, Easter, Thanksgiving, Christmas and Dec. 31. **Cost:** Donations. **Phone:** (208) 255-4321.

THE LODGE AT SANDPOINT   (208)263-2211

▼▼▼ **Hotel** $129-$459 **Address:** 41 Lakeshore Dr 83860 **Location:** 1 mi s of Sandpoint on US 95; just s of Long Bridge. **Facility:** 33 units, some cabins. 4 stories, interior corridors. **Terms:** check-in 4 pm, 14 day cancellation notice-fee imposed. **Dining:** 2 restaurants. **Activities:** hot tub, limited beach access, boat dock, fishing, bicycles, exercise room, massage. **Guest Services:** valet laundry. **Featured Amenity: continental breakfast.**

ST. ANTHONY pop. 3,542

GUESTHOUSE INTERNATIONAL HENRY'S FORK INN   (208)624-3711

▼▼ **Motel** $60-$98 **Address:** 115 S Bridge St 83445 **Location:** US 20 exit 346, just e. **Facility:** 30 units. 2 stories (no elevator), exterior corridors. **Terms:** cancellation fee imposed. **Activities:** hot tub. **Guest Services:** coin laundry.

ST. CHARLES (H-6) pop. 131, elev. 5,944'

This small town near the northwest corner of Bear Lake was the birthplace of Gutzon Borglum (1867-1941), the artist and sculptor who carved the Mount Rushmore National Memorial in South Dakota.

Bear Lake straddles the Idaho-Utah border south and east of St. Charles. Known as the "Caribbean of the Rockies" for its turquoise hue, the result of soluble microscopic carbonates suspended in the water, the 120-square-mile lake is popular with fishermen seeking cutthroat trout, sculpin and whitefish. In winter anglers use nets to catch the Bonneville cisco, a species of fish endemic to the lake.

Bear Lake National Wildlife Refuge, a 19,000 acre tract of wetlands north of Bear Lake, provides habitat for migratory birds and small mammals. Bear Lake State Park *(see Recreation Areas Chart)*, just e. of St. Charles at 5637 E. Shore Rd., has two units. The North Beach unit has a boat launch and a 2-mile-long shorefront; the East Beach unit, with its 1.5-mile-long beach, offers a campground. Phone (208) 945-2565.

MINNETONKA CAVE is s.w. via US 89 to St. Charles, then 10 mi. w. to St. Charles Canyon. The cave, 7,700 feet above sea level, contains nine rooms of stalactites, stalagmites and banded travertine originally discovered by grouse hunters. **Note:**

The temperature is a constant 40 F; jackets are recommended. The tour involves climbing 444 steps. **Hours:** Guided 1.25-hour tours are given daily on the half-hour 10-5:30, early June-Labor Day (weather permitting). Last tour begins at closing. **Cost:** $8; $6 (ages 6-15); $32 (family). **Phone:** (435) 245-4422.

SALMON (E-4) pop. 3,112, elev. 4,040'

Once the winter campsite of fur trappers, including Jim Bridger and Kit Carson, Salmon is at the fork of the Salmon and Lemhi rivers near the edge of the Salmon Valley, a prosperous livestock and mining area. Permanent settlement of this region began with the discovery of gold in 1866. The town is a favorite starting point for pack trips into the Frank Church-River of No Return Wilderness and for float trips down the Salmon River and its wildest branch, the Middle Fork.

Salmon lies on a scenic section of US 93, which heads north to the Montana border and southwest toward Sawtooth National Forest (see place listing p. 96).

Salmon Valley Chamber of Commerce: 200 Main St., Salmon, ID 83467. **Phone:** (208) 756-2100.

LEMHI COUNTY HISTORICAL MUSEUM, 210 Main St., exhibits the largest collection of Lemhi Shoshone (or, Agaideka, the people of Sacagawea) artifacts in the world. Also featured are interpretive exhibits portraying life in the American West and the Ray Edwards Asian Collection. **Hours:** Mon.-Sat. 10-5, May-Oct.; Wed. 11-4, rest of year. Phone ahead to confirm schedule. **Cost:** $2; free (ages 0-11). **Phone:** (208) 756-3342.

SACAJAWEA INTERPRETIVE, CULTURAL AND EDUCATIONAL CENTER, 1 mi. e. on SR 28 (Main St.), is in the Lemhi River Valley, the homeland of the Agaidika Shoshone and Sacajawea (Sacagawea). The 71-acre park commemorates Sacajawea's role in the Lewis and Clark expedition and features a visitor center, an outdoor amphitheater, a monument, kiosks, displays and a 1-mile interpretive trail with a tipi encampment, riverside sweat lodge and wildlife exhibits.

Time: Allow 1 hour minimum. **Hours:** Park open daily dawn-dusk. Interpretive center open Mon.-Sat. 9-5, Sun. 12:30-5, Memorial Day-Labor Day; Sat. 9-5, Sun. 12:30-5, May 1-day before Memorial Day and day after Labor Day-Oct. 31. **Cost:** $5; free (ages 0-6); $12 (family). **Phone:** (208) 756-1188.
🎟

RECREATIONAL ACTIVITIES
White-water Rafting

• **Idaho Adventures** trips traverse the Salmon River. Other activities are offered, including steelhead fishing. **Hours:** Rafting trips are offered Mar.-Nov. Schedule varies; phone ahead. **Phone:** (208) 756-2986 or (800) 789-9283.

• **Kookaburra Rafting Trips** is at 1115 US 93S. Other activities are offered, including fishing. **Hours:** One-day rafting trips are offered daily, Apr.-Sept. Three-day rafting trips also are offered June-Sept. Schedules vary; phone ahead. **Phone:** (208) 756-4386 or (888) 654-4386.

• **Rawhide Outfitters** trips traverse the Salmon River. Other activities are offered, including fishing and horseback riding excursions. **Hours:** Rafting trips are offered Sun.-Fri., May-Oct. Departure times vary; phone ahead. **Phone:** (208) 756-4276.

STAGECOACH INN   208/756-2919

♥♥♥ **Motel.** Rates not provided. **Address:** 201 Riverfront Dr (US 93 N) 83467 **Location:** Just n on US 93 from jct SR 28. **Facility:** 101 units, some kitchens. 2 stories, interior corridors. **Parking:** winter plug-ins. **Pool(s):** heated outdoor. **Activities:** hot tub. **Guest Services:** coin laundry, area transportation.
➕ 🛗 ➜ 📶 💳 / SOME UNITS 🍽 🔒 📺

WHERE TO EAT

SHADY NOOK STEAKHOUSE   208/756-4182

♥♥ ♥♥
American
Casual Dining
$10-$33

AAA Inspector Notes: Experience the relaxed atmosphere of this local landmark restaurant. Enjoy watching the Salmon River while dining on the patio during the summer. Nightly specials and desserts made in-house are sure to delight. **Features:** full bar. **Reservations:** suggested, in summer. **Address:** 501 Riverfront Dr (US 93 N) 83467 **Location:** Jct SR 28, 0.8 mi n. [D]

SALMON-CHALLIS NATIONAL FOREST (E-3)

Elevations in the forest range from 2,200 ft. in the lower canyon of the Salmon River to 12,662 ft. at Borah Peak. Refer to AAA maps for additional elevation information.

From the headwaters of the Salmon River, down the Lost River, Pahsimeroi and Lemhi Mountain Ranges, to the western slope of the Continental Divide, the Salmon-Challis National Forest covers 4.3 million acres. Over 300,000 acres are in the Frank Church-River of No Return Wilderness (see Payette National Forest p. 87).

The historic Lewis and Clark Trail passes through part of the forest, where several monuments to the explorers have been erected. The Custer Motorway Loop and Salmon River Road provide glimpses of historic mining towns and native wildlife.

Because of swift currents the Salmon River west of Salmon is known as the "River of No Return." Now, however, it is possible to navigate this river upstream via jet boats. Boat trips down the river can be arranged in Salmon (see place listing).

More than 2,800 miles of trail stripe the forest floor. Hiking season is generally between April and October; hunting, fishing, camping and wildlife viewing also are excellent.

The section of the river between Corn Creek and Riggins can be traveled by kayaks, jet boats or rubber rafts. Skiing is available nearby on the Idaho-Montana border at Lost Trail Pass. For more information write the Salmon-Challis National Forest Headquarters, 1206 S. Challis St., Salmon, ID 83467; phone (208) 756-5100. *See Recreation Areas Chart.*

SANDPOINT (B-1) pop. 7,365, elev. 2,086'
• Hotels p. 96 • Restaurants p. 96

Sandpoint, at the north end of Lake Pend Oreille, is a year-round resort town and artists' community that offers a wide variety of land- and water-based recreational opportunities. Park facilities at City Beach, west of First Avenue via Bridge Street, include beaches, two marinas, a boat launch and a pedestrian bridge over Sand Creek that links the park with downtown. Lake Pend Oreille Cruises offers a variety of tours; phone (208) 255-5253.

One of the West's great railroad towns, Sandpoint is known as "The Funnel" for the major rail lines that converge here. More than 40 trains a day draw rail fans to the city. A brochure "A Rail Fan's Guide to Sandpoint, Idaho" is available from the chamber of commerce.

Greater Sandpoint Chamber of Commerce: 1202 Fifth Ave., P.O. Box 928, Sandpoint, ID 83864. **Phone:** (208) 263-0887 or (800) 800-2106.

Shopping areas: One of downtown Sandpoint's focal points is the Cedar Street Bridge Public Market. Formerly a city bridge over Sand Creek, this renovated two-level structure is patterned after the famed Ponte Vecchio bridge in Florence, Italy, and contains two levels of restaurants and shops. Coldwater Creek, nationally known catalog merchandiser, operates its flagship store at 311 N. First St.

BONNER COUNTY HISTORICAL MUSEUM, 611 S. Ella Ave. in Lakeview Park, uses pioneer relics and other exhibits to chronicle the history of the county, with emphasis on the Kalispel Indians, the local timber industry, and steamboat and railroad transportation. The grounds feature an arboretum with indigenous plants. **Time:** Allow 30 minutes minimum. **Hours:** Tues.-Fri. 10-4. Closed major holidays. **Cost:** $3; $1 (ages 6-18). **Phone:** (208) 263-2344.

INTERNATIONAL SELKIRK LOOP is a 280-mile National Scenic Byway in northern Idaho, northeastern Washington and adjoining British Columbia. Starting at Sandpoint the 89-mile Idaho segment follows US 2 west to the Washington border at Oldtown. North from Sandpoint the byway takes US 2/95 to Bonners Ferry, then US 95 and SR 1 to the Canadian border at Porthill.

West from Sandpoint the loop follows the Pend Oreille (pond-ah-RAY) River, which drains Lake Pend Oreille. Several recreation sites offer access to the river, and there are numerous roadside pull-outs. At Priest River, SR 57 runs 30 miles north to

jewel-like Priest Lake, a paradise for kayaking, canoeing and fishing set amid cedars and pines in the heart of the Selkirks. Public campgrounds and lodging options are numerous.

North of Sandpoint the route runs along the Purcell Trench, a long, narrow trough between the Selkirk, Cabinet and Purcell Mountains. The trench is a natural funnel for migratory birds. Between Bonners Ferry and Priest Lake, the Selkirks are a rugged wilderness with peaks in excess of 7,000 feet. The Kootenai National Wildlife Refuge, 5 miles west of Bonners Ferry, offers a 4-mile auto-tour route and numerous hiking trails.

Chambers of commerce and visitor centers along the loop provide maps and information. Visitors also can order a free copy of the visitor travel guide online or write to International Selkirk Loop, P.O. Box 920, Bonners Ferry, ID 83805. **Phone:** (208) 267-0822 or (888) 823-2626.

LAKE PEND OREILLE, s. and e. of town, was formed by glaciers and is encircled by lofty mountain peaks. At 43 miles long, Lake Pend Oreille (pond-ah-RAY) is one of the largest freshwater lakes in the Pacific Northwest. Swimming, boating and tennis are popular. Noted for its scenic coves and 1,150-foot depth, the lake is stocked with Kamloops rainbow trout. A special fishing season runs from early May to late November. *See Recreation Areas Chart.*

Facilities for other types of recreation are found at Clark Fork *(see place listing p. 55),* Athol *(see place listing p. 35)* and numerous lakeside communities. **Time:** Allow a full day. **Phone:** (208) 263-2161 or (800) 800-2106. 🅰 🗙 🐄 🎴

RECREATIONAL ACTIVITIES
Horseback Riding
• **Mountain Horse Adventures** is at 10000 Schweitzer Mountain Rd. **Hours:** Horseback riding trips lasting 2.5 hours depart daily at 9 and 1, May 1 to mid-Oct. Under 8 are not permitted. **Phone:** (208) 263-8768 or (208) 255-3081.

Skiing
• **Schweitzer Mountain Resort** is 11 mi. n. via US 2/95 at 10000 Schweitzer Mountain Rd. **Hours:** Daily 9-8, day after Christmas-early Jan.; Sun.-Thurs. 9-4, Fri.-Sat. 9-7, early Jan. to mid-Mar.; daily 9-4, mid-Mar. to early Apr. and Thanksgiving-Christmas. **Phone:** (208) 263-9555, (208) 263-9562 for a recorded snow report or (877) 487-4643.

WINERIES
• **Pend d'Oreille Winery** is at 301 Cedar St. Guided tours are available. **Hours:** Mon.-Sat. 10-6 (also Thurs.-Sat. 6-9 p.m.), Sun. 11-9. Closed Jan. 1, Thanksgiving and Christmas. Phone ahead to confirm schedule. **Phone:** (208) 265-8545 or (877) 452-9011.

BEST WESTERN PLUS EDGEWATER RESORT
(208)263-3194

Hotel
$99-$299

AAA Benefit: Members save 10% or more with Best Western!

Address: 56 Bridge St 83864 **Location:** Just e of US 95; downtown. **Facility:** 54 units. 2-3 stories (no elevator), interior corridors. **Parking:** winter plug-ins. **Dining:** Trinity at City Beach, see separate listing. **Pool(s):** heated indoor. **Activities:** sauna, hot tub, limited beach access, boat dock, fishing, exercise room.

LA QUINTA INN SANDPOINT
(208)263-9581

Hotel $94-$209 **Address:** 415 Cedar St 83864 **Location:** Jct US 2 and 95; downtown. **Facility:** 68 units, some efficiencies. 2-3 stories, interior/exterior corridors. **Parking:** winter plug-ins. **Pool(s):** heated outdoor. **Activities:** hot tub, exercise room. **Guest Services:** coin laundry, area transportation.

QUALITY INN SANDPOINT
(208)263-2111

Hotel $64-$199 **Address:** 807 N 5th Ave 83864 **Location:** US 2 and 95, just s of jct SR 200. **Facility:** 62 units. 2 stories (no elevator), interior corridors. **Parking:** winter plug-ins. **Pool(s):** heated indoor. **Activities:** hot tub. **Guest Services:** coin laundry.

SELKIRK LODGE AT SCHWEITZER MOUNTAIN RESORT
(208)265-0257

Resort Hotel $117-$605 **Address:** 10000 Schweitzer Mountain Rd 83864 **Location:** 2 mi n on US 95, 10 mi w, follow signs. **Facility:** A combination of European and Northern Idaho influences combine to create a unique décor. This hotel condominium property is ideally located near the ski slopes. 76 units, some condominiums. 4 stories, interior corridors. **Terms:** check-in 4 pm, 14 day cancellation notice, resort fee. **Pool(s):** heated outdoor. **Activities:** hot tub, tennis, downhill & cross country skiing, snowmobiling, sledding, bicycles, exercise room, massage. **Guest Services:** coin laundry.

WHITE PINE LODGE AT SCHWEITZER MOUNTAIN RESORT
(208)265-0257

Condominium $169-$1078 **Address:** 145 Village Ln 83864 **Location:** 2 mi n on US 95, 10 mi w, follow signs. **Facility:** Convenient to the ski slopes, this property features a modern, mountain-influenced design throughout. 26 condominiums. 5 stories, interior corridors. **Terms:** check-in 4 pm, 14 day cancellation notice, resort fee. **Activities:** hot tub, tennis, exercise room. **Guest Services:** complimentary laundry.

WHERE TO EAT

HYDRA STEAKHOUSE
208/263-7123

American. Casual Dining. $9-$34 **AAA Inspector Notes:** Dinners feature prime rib, steak and seafood specialties and creative pasta dishes served in a casual atmosphere. This comfortable, intimate eatery boasts a pleasant decor of stained glass, natural wood and greenery. **Features:** full bar, patio dining. **Address:** 115 Lake St 83864 **Location:** Just w of US 95 at 2nd and Lake sts; center.
[L] [D]

IVANO'S RISTORANTE & CAFFE
208/263-0211

Regional Italian. Fine Dining. $9-$27 **AAA Inspector Notes:** Italian cuisine is served in comfortable, casual surroundings enhanced by distinctive artwork and oak accents. Pasta, veal, chicken, beef and seafood all make a good showing, but it's the chocolate mousse that wins rave reviews. Seasonal outdoor seating is an option at the busy downtown location. **Features:** full bar, patio dining. **Address:** 102 S 1st Ave 83864 **Location:** Downtown. [D]

JALAPENOS
208/263-2995

Mexican. Casual Dining. $10-$15 **AAA Inspector Notes:** Colorful, hand-painted murals and large, potted plants give this restaurant a tropical feel. Friendly service, good food and specialty drinks make it a favorite of tourists and locals alike. Patio seating is available, weather permitting. **Features:** full bar, patio dining, happy hour. **Address:** 314 N 2nd Ave 83864 **Location:** Downtown. **Parking:** street only. [L] [D]

LITTLE OLIVE
208/597-7499

Mediterranean. Casual Dining. $8-$25 **AAA Inspector Notes:** The chef here focuses on Mediterranean-influenced delectables including lamb kebabs, gyros and hummus. **Features:** beer & wine, patio dining. **Address:** 124 S 2nd Ave 83864 **Location:** Jct Lake St; center. **Parking:** street only. [L] [D]

TRINITY AT CITY BEACH
208/255-7558

American. Family Dining. $8-$35 **AAA Inspector Notes:** Seating at this eatery is available on the patio overlooking Sand Creek or in the quietly elegant dining room. From gumbo to crawfish etouffee, menu selections are reminiscent of New Orleans. All the scrumptious desserts are made in house. **Features:** full bar, patio dining. **Address:** 56 Bridge St 83864 **Location:** Just e of US 95 N; downtown; in BEST WESTERN PLUS Edgewater Resort.
[B] [L] [D]

SAWTOOTH NATIONAL FOREST (F-3)

Elevations in the forest range from 4,514 ft. at Rock Creek Drain to 12,009 ft. at Hyndman Peak. Refer to AAA maps for additional elevation information.

In south-central Idaho, the Sawtooth National Forest embraces approximately 2.1 million acres. Offering a wide range of recreational opportunities and spectacular scenery, the forest consists of a northern division containing the Sawtooth National Recreation Area and a southern division along the Nevada and Utah borders.

Adjacent to Sun Valley (see place listing p. 99), the northern division is bisected by the Sawtooth Scenic Byway (SR 75) and provides hundreds of miles of hiking and horseback-riding trails in the Smoky, Pioneer, Sawtooth, Boulder and White Cloud mountains. The Baumgartner Nature Trail, near Baumgartner Campground in the Fairfield District, is a popular hiking area.

The southern division contains the Rock Creek Canyon, Howell Canyon, Black Pine, Raft River and Sublett areas. Alpine and cross-country skiing as well as snowmobiling are available in areas near Twin Falls (see place listing p. 100), Burley (see place listing p. 52), Fairfield and Sun Valley (see place listing p. 99).

Information about campgrounds and recreational opportunities is available at the forest supervisor's office in Twin Falls and the district ranger stations. For further information write Sawtooth National

Forest, 2647 Kimberly Rd. E., Twin Falls, ID 83301; phone (208) 737-3200. *See Recreation Areas Chart.*

SAWTOOTH NATIONAL RECREATION AREA (F-3)

In south-central Idaho, the Sawtooth National Recreation Area comprises 756,000 acres of the northern division of the Sawtooth National Forest. The recreation area features three mountain ranges of peaks exceeding 11,000 feet, deep forests and high mountain lakes. The recreation area includes the Sawtooth Wilderness, the White Cloud-Boulder Mountains, portions of the Smokey Mountains, the Salmon River and five major lakes. The backcountry has 750 miles of hiking trails and more than 300 lakes.

Nature trails in the forest include the Fishhook Creek Nature Trail, adjacent to Redfish Lake Visitor Center, and the Wood River Adventure Trail, bordering the Wood River Campground.

The Stanley Ranger Station is open Mon.-Fri. 8:30-4:30. A visitor center on the northern shore of Redfish Lake, 5 miles south of Stanley on SR 75, is open daily 10-5, mid-June to mid-Sept. The North Fork visitor center and national recreation area headquarters is open Mon.-Sat. 8:30-5.

A free audio tour explaining the area's history and features can be borrowed at the Sawtooth National Recreation Area headquarters, Stanley Ranger Station or the Ketchum Ranger District. For more information write Sawtooth National Recreation Headquarters, 5 North Fork Canyon Rd., Ketchum, ID 83340; phone (208) 727-5000 for headquarters, (208) 774-3000 for the Stanley Ranger Station or (208) 774-3376 for the Redfish Lake Visitors Center. *See Recreation Areas Chart.*

SHOSHONE (G-3) pop. 1,461, elev. 3,968'

Shoshone, in an irrigated farming belt and sheep-raising area, was settled in 1882. Many buildings, including the Community Methodist Church at Apple and C streets, are made from local dark, porous lava rock.

SHOSHONE INDIAN ICE CAVES, 17 mi. n. on SR 75, are caves of ice that maintain a temperature of 18 to 28 F, while a few feet away on the surface the thermometer might register more than 100. Visitors should wear sturdy shoes and a coat. The 3/4-mile tour includes 100 feet of stairs. A museum features collections of gems, minerals and rocks. **Time:** Allow 1 hour minimum. **Hours:** Tour schedule varies; phone ahead. **Cost:** $10; $8 (ages 62+); $6 (ages 4-12). Prices may vary. **Phone:** (208) 886-2058.

SILVER CITY (G-1) elev. 6,179'

Silver City, high in the Owyhee Mountains of southwestern Idaho, became an important gold and silver mining center after prospectors struck it rich near the headwaters of Jordan Creek in 1862. A 500-pound solid silver crystal from the nearby Poorman mine on War Eagle Mountain won a prize at the 1866 exposition in Paris.

Mining remained a force until 1912, then continued sporadically through the 1930s. In its heyday Silver City boasted a courthouse, hotels, Idaho's first daily newspaper and a population of 3,000. By 1920 its population had fallen to 100.

A walk down Silver City's unpaved streets is a living-history tour. Some 75 buildings remain of this once boisterous mining town. The 1892 schoolhouse and drugstore are now museums. On the knoll near the school is Our Lady of Tears Catholic Church. The 20-bedroom Idaho Hotel, which is also a museum, dominates Main Street and was once the finest in the territory. Several historic cemeteries are in the community.

Note: The 21-mile road leading to Silver City from SR 78 south of Murphy is paved for only the first 8 miles (the rest is graveled) and is not recommended for oversize vehicles. The road is not maintained in winter and is normally closed early October to late May. Phone (208) 583-4104 (Idaho Hotel) or write P.O. Box 75, Murphy, ID 83650-0075, for weather and road conditions.

The first 8 miles of the 25-mile road leading west from Silver City to Jordan Valley, Ore., are rough, winding and narrow. There are no automobile service facilities in the vicinity.

SODA SPRINGS (H-6) pop. 3,058, elev. 5,777'

Since pioneer days Soda Springs has been known for its 30 mineral salt springs. Early trappers called Hooper Spring, a mile north of town, "Beer Spring" because of its natural soda water, which visitors can sample today.

Nearby Captive Geyser is a carbon dioxide geyser controlled to erupt hourly, winds permitting. Foot-deep wagon ruts from the Old Oregon Trail that date from the mid-1800s provide an unusual hazard on the local golf course. The Pioneer Museum downtown displays mementos reflecting area history.

Soda Springs Chamber of Commerce: 9 West 2nd South, P.O. Box 697, Soda Springs, ID 83276. **Phone:** (208) 547-2600.

SPALDING (D-1) elev. 840'

Catholic, Protestant and Mormon missionaries occupied much of central Idaho during the mid- and late 1800s in an attempt to convert the Native Americans. Spalding, now within the boundaries of the Nez Perce National Historical Park *(see place listing p. 85)*, is named for the Rev. Henry H. Spalding, who built a mission near the present town of Lapwai *(see place listing p. 75)* in 1836.

Two years later he moved the mission 2 miles north to the Clearwater River, where the headquarters of the Nez Perce National Historical Park is today.

Several geologic formations near Spalding have significance in Nez Perce tradition. Coyote's Fishnet, about 4 miles west, is a formation on the bluffs of the Clearwater River's south shore. A talus slope known as The Bear is high on the north side of the river. Ant and Yellowjacket is a rock arch 1.5 miles west off US 12 just before its junction with US 95.

Idaho's first homestead, the Craig Donation Land Claim, is about 8 miles south along US 95. In 1840 mountain man William Craig settled on 630 acres given to him by the Nez Perce. He is buried in the nearby town of Jacques. St. Joseph's Mission, 4 miles south of Jacques in the village of Slickpoo, was dedicated in 1874 and was the first Catholic church in Nez Perce country.

NEZ PERCE NATIONAL HISTORICAL PARK VISITOR CENTER, on US 95, contains exhibits and audiovisual programs about Nez Perce culture. Area history also is chronicled. A park folder is available for a self-guiding driving tour of the 38 sites included in the park. **Time:** Allow 30 minutes minimum. **Hours:** Daily 8-5, Memorial Day weekend-Labor Day; 8-4:30, mid-Mar. through day before Memorial Day weekend and day after Labor Day to mid-Nov.; 9-4, rest of year. Ranger-led programs are offered daily at 11, 1 and 3, Memorial Day-Labor Day. Closed Jan. 1, Thanksgiving and Christmas. **Cost:** Donations. **Phone:** (208) 843-7001, ext. 7020.

SPALDING SITE, .2 mi. e., is the location of the second mission built by the Rev. Henry H. Spalding and his wife in 1838. The Presbyterian mission included the territory's first printing press, sawmill and gristmill; it was later used as Indian Agency headquarters. The Spaldings and many Nez Perce are buried in the Spalding Mission Cemetery. The Spaldings' first homesite, 2 miles south at Thunder Hill, was built in 1836, the year they arrived in the Northwest. **Time:** Allow 30 minutes minimum.

STANLEY (F-3) pop. 63, elev. 6,260'

On the Salmon River (the "River of No Return"), Stanley is within the Sawtooth National Recreation Area *(see place listing p. 97)*, Sawtooth Valley and the spectacular Sawtooth Basin. Most float trips on the Middle Fork of the Salmon River and the main Salmon River are outfitted at this site. The town lies on two exceptionally scenic highways, SRs 21 and 75.

The Ponderosa Pine Scenic Byway (SR 21) passes through part of the Sawtooth National Forest *(see place listing p. 96)* and ends in Boise; motorists should check for possible temporary closures due to snow. The northeastern segment of SR 75, the Salmon River Scenic Byway, passes through the Sawtooth National Recreation Area and then merges with US 93. The southeastern segment of SR 75, the Sawtooth Scenic Byway, heads south toward Twin Falls and Sun Valley.

Stanley-Sawtooth Chamber of Commerce: P.O. Box 8, Stanley, ID 83278. **Phone:** (208) 774-3411 or (800) 878-7950.

SAWTOOTH FISH HATCHERY, 5 mi. s. on SR 75, is used for trapping and holding spring chinook salmon and steelhead trout. The hatchery produces chinook and collects steelhead eggs for later transport to the Hagerman and Magic Valley hatcheries. The fish trap is emptied daily at 9 a.m. in season. An observation deck is on the premises. **Hours:** Visitor center daily 8-5. Guided 45-minute tours departing from the visitor center are given daily beginning at 1:30, Memorial Day weekend-Labor Day. **Cost:** Free. **Phone:** (208) 774-3684.

RECREATIONAL ACTIVITIES
Horseback Riding

- **Mystic Saddle Ranch** is on SR 75 in the Sawtooth National Recreation Area. **Hours:** Trips are offered daily, June-Sept. Departure times vary; phone ahead. **Phone:** (208) 774-3591.

- **Pioneer Outfitters** is 9 mi. s. on SR 75 at the Idaho Rocky Mountain Ranch. **Hours:** Departure days and times vary; phone ahead. **Phone:** (208) 774-3737 June-Oct., or (208) 324-7171 rest of year.

- **Redfish Lake Corrals-Trail Rides** is off SR 21. **Hours:** Trips are offered daily 9-3, Memorial Day to mid-Sept. **Phone:** (208) 774-3311.

White-water Rafting

- **Middle Fork River Expeditions** offers trips on the Middle Fork of the Salmon River and the main Salmon River near Sun Valley. Other activities are offered. **Hours:** Four-, 6- and 10-day rafting trips are offered June-Sept. Schedule varies; phone ahead. **Phone:** (800) 801-5146.

- **The River Co.** is .7 mi. w. on SR 21. Other activities are offered. **Hours:** Day rafting trips are offered mid-May to early Sept. Schedule varies; phone ahead. **Phone:** (208) 788-5775 or (800) 398-0346.

- **Rocky Mountain River Tours** offers trips on the Middle Fork, the wild and main section of the Salmon River. **Hours:** Four- to 6-day trips are offered mid-May to mid-Sept. Schedule varies; phone ahead. **Phone:** (208) 345-2400.

- **ROW Adventures** offers trips on the Middle Fork of the Salmon River. Other activities are offered. **Hours:** One- to 6-day rafting trips are offered mid-May to mid-Sept. Schedule varies; phone ahead. **Phone:** (208) 765-0841 or (800) 451-6034.

- **Sawtooth Adventure Co.** is 1 mi. n. on US 75. Other activities are offered. **Hours:** Trips are offered May 20-Sept. 15. Schedule varies; phone ahead. **Phone:** (866) 774-4644.

- **White Cloud Rafting Adventures** is at jct. US 75 and SR 21. **Hours:** Half- and full-day trips are offered daily, late May-early Sept. Schedule varies; phone ahead. **Phone:** (208) 774-7238 or (800) 571-7238.

POT BELLY CAFE   208/774-2202

▽ American. Casual Dining. $5-$16 **AAA Inspector Notes:** This rustic restaurant serves homemade pies and comfort foods such as barbecue ribs, burgers and camp beans made in cast iron. **Features:** beer & wine, patio dining. **Address:** SR 21 83278 **Location:** Jct SR 75, 4 mi w; Milepost 126.5; at Elk Mountain RV Resort.

B L D ⟨ℵ⟩

STANLEY BAKING CO. & CAFE   208/774-6573

▽▽ Sandwiches Soup. Casual Dining. $7-$10 **AAA Inspector Notes:** It will only take one visit and travelers always will plan their trip around a mandatory stop here for breakfast or lunch. The creative menu features beautifully presented soups, salads and delicious sandwiches. Scones, cinnamon rolls, sticky buns, croissants, muffins, coffee cake and cookies are baked fresh daily and a full tea and espresso menu is available. **Features:** beer & wine, Sunday brunch. **Address:** 250 Wall St 83278 **Location:** 0.3 mi w of jct SR 21 and 75 to Wall St, just s. B L ⟨ℵ⟩

SUN VALLEY (F-3) pop. 1,406, elev. 5,926'

Sun Valley got its start in 1935 when Union Pacific Railroad Chairman Averell Harriman hired Austrian Count Felix Shaffgotsch to find the most scenic snow spot in the country for a huge ski resort. Passing up places that would become Aspen, Jackson Hole and Mount Hood, Shaffgotsch chose Sun Valley. Soon stars from all across the country came to ski down Dollar Mountain (chairlifts were not installed on 9,150-foot-tall Bald Mountain until Sun Valley's fourth operating season) and hobnob in the huge lodge Harriman built. Gary Cooper and Clark Gable were frequent visitors; novelist Ernest Hemingway spent his last years in the area, and a memorial to him stands alongside Trail Creek.

Today nearly a quarter-million persons visit the area, which somehow still manages to maintain an uncrowded, non-tourist atmosphere. Sun Valley, along with the neighboring town of Ketchum *(see place listing p. 73)*, offers heated outdoor pools, saunas and indoor and outdoor ice-skating rinks. The list of local summer activities includes golf, tennis, swimming, white-water rafting, camping, bicycling, hiking, horseback riding, skeet shooting, trapshooting, fishing, mountaineering and kayaking. Offering respite from the great outdoors, The Sun Valley Pavilion, 1 Sun Valley Rd., hosts the Sun Valley Summer Symphony for 3 weeks in July and August. Admission is free; phone (208) 622-2135 or (888) 622-2108 for the schedule.

Winter brings sleigh rides, snowmobiling and ice-skating as well as downhill, cross-country and helicopter skiing. Saturday nights are reserved for hockey games in winter and professional ice shows in summer. Skiing begins on Thanksgiving.

RECREATIONAL ACTIVITIES
Horseback Riding

• **Sun Valley Stables** is off Sun Valley Rd., just n. of the Sun Valley Resort. Other activities are offered. **Hours:** One-hour and 90-minute trips are offered daily 9-4, early June-late Sept. Phone ahead to confirm schedule. **Phone:** (208) 622-2391 for reservations.

Skiing

• **Bald Mountain** is off SR 75; take Serenade Ln. w. to 3rd Ave., then s. to River Run Access. **Hours:** Daily 9-4, Thanksgiving to mid-Apr. **Phone:** (208) 622-6136.

• **Dollar Mountain** is adjacent to Sun Valley. **Hours:** Daily 9-4, Thanksgiving-early Apr. **Phone:** (208) 622-2241 or (208) 622-6136.

SUN VALLEY LODGE & SUN VALLEY INN   (208)622-4111

▽▽ ▽▽▽ Resort Hotel $149-$604 **Address:** 1 Sun Valley Rd 83353 **Location:** 1.2 mi ne of Main St (SR 75) and Sun Valley Rd. **Facility:** This famous resort, situated on beautiful grounds and with extensive public facilities, offers a very nice selection of luxurious guest rooms and one- to three-bedroom apartments. 254 units, some kitchens. 1-4 stories, interior corridors. **Parking:** on-site and valet, winter plug-ins. **Terms:** check-in 4 pm, 30 day cancellation notice-fee imposed, resort fee. **Amenities:** video games, safes. **Dining:** 3 restaurants, also, Gretchen's, see separate listing, entertainment. **Pool(s):** heated outdoor. **Activities:** sauna, hot tub, fishing, regulation golf, tennis, downhill & cross country skiing, snowmobiling, sledding, ice skating, recreation programs, bicycles, game room, exercise room, spa. **Guest Services:** valet and coin laundry.

🍴 🛎 🍸 ➰ BIZ HS 📶 ✕ 🐾 🛗 ▣ / SOME UNITS 🖨

WHERE TO EAT

GRETCHEN'S   208/622-4111

▽▽▽ American. Casual Dining. $9-$22 **AAA Inspector Notes:** This restaurant features a nice selection of game, pasta dishes, seafood and freshly baked desserts. Dine on the terrace to enjoy the views of the famous ice skating rink. **Features:** full bar, patio dining. **Reservations:** suggested. **Address:** 1 Sun Valley Rd 83353 **Location:** 1.2 mi ne of Main St (SR 75) and Sun Valley Rd; in Sun Valley Lodge & Sun Valley Inn. **Parking:** on-site and valet.

B L D

SWAN VALLEY pop. 204
• **Part of Jackson Hole Including Grand Teton National Park area — see map p. 293**

SLEEPY J CABINS   208/483-0411

fyi Not evaluated. **Address:** 19 Hwy 31 83449 **Location:** Just ne of jct US 26. Facilities, services, and décor characterize a mid-scale property.

SYRINGA (D-2) elev. 1,440'

Syringa is named for Idaho's state flower, a variety of mock orange whose creamy white blooms fill the forest in early summer. The town is nestled along the Middle Fork of the Clearwater River, a designated National Wild & Scenic River.

Lowell/Syringa Chamber of Commerce: 115 Selway Rd., Kooskia, ID 83539. **Phone:** (888) 926-4430.

RECREATIONAL ACTIVITIES
White-water Rafting

• **ROW Adventures** departs from the ROW office on US 12. Other activities are offered. **Hours:** Rafting trips are offered daily, mid-May to early Sept. Departure times vary; phone ahead. **Phone:** (208) 765-0841 or (800) 451-6034.

TARGHEE NATIONAL FOREST—See
Caribou-Targhee National Forest p. 54.

TWIN FALLS (H-3) pop. 44,125, elev. 3,745'

Twin Falls is in the center of 500,000 acres of prime farmland irrigated by the waters of the Snake River. Since the turn of the 20th century, the "Magic Valley" area has been known as one of the nation's most prolific crop-producing regions. Twin Falls also is on the edge of the Snake River Canyon, which was gouged out some 30,000 years ago by the Great Bonneville Flood.

From Bliss, the 67.8-mile Thousand Springs Scenic Byway runs southeast, following US 30 through Hagerman *(see place listing p. 64)*, Buhl *(see place listing p. 52)* and Twin Falls, and SR 50 north to the junction of I-84; a spur road (US 93) juts due north from Twin Falls to I-84. Cascading from the sides of Snake River Canyon, the lovely natural springs are fed by the Snake River Plain Aquifer, one of the world's largest groundwater systems. The scenic byway affords access to the five units of Thousand Springs State Park *(see attraction listing p. 64)* as well as three hot mineral pools: Banbury Hot Springs, 10 miles west of Buhl, Miracle Hot Springs, 9 miles south of Hagerman, and Thousand Springs Resort, 5 miles south of Hagerman.

Just northeast of Twin Falls, the white waters of the Snake River plunge more than 212 feet at Shoshone Falls, known as the "Niagara of the West." The best time to view the falls is late April through early June, since irrigation waters are retained upstream during the summer months. **Note:** During periods of drought, the falls may be dry; phone ahead to confirm the status.

Twin Falls Area Chamber of Commerce: 858 Blue Lakes Blvd. N., Twin Falls, ID 83301. **Phone:** (208) 733-3974.

THE HERRETT CENTER FOR ARTS & SCIENCE, on the north side of the College of Southern Idaho campus, contains artifacts from pre-Columbian civilizations of the Western Hemisphere. The center features contemporary art, a mammoth skeleton and changing exhibits. Visitors can see educational and entertainment shows in a planetarium. The observatory has a research-grade 24-inch telescope. A rain forest exhibit is home to live reptiles and features interactive displays.

Time: Allow 30 minutes minimum. **Hours:** Museum Tues.-Fri. 9:30-4:30 (also Tues. and Fri. 4:30-9), Sat. 1-9. Planetarium and observatory show times vary; phone for schedule. Closed major holidays. **Cost:** Museum and galleries free. Planetarium $4.50; $3.50 (ages 60+); $2.50 (ages 3-18). **Phone:** (208) 732-6655.

PERRINE MEMORIAL BRIDGE, on the northern edge of town, spans the Snake River Gorge 486 feet above the water. The four-lane bridge has pedestrian walkways with views of sheer cliffs, the Blue Lakes, waterfalls, a park and two golf courses. A road descends to these areas. The Buzz Langdon Visitor Center is next to the bridge.

Daredevil Evel Knievel attempted to leap across the Snake River Canyon a mile east of the bridge in 1974; the dirt ramp used to launch his rocket-powered vehicle remains. The bridge is reputedly the only U.S. location where BASE jumping is permitted year-round without a permit. Spectators can view this extreme sport from overlooks. **Hours:** Bridge open year-round. Visitor center open daily 9-dusk, mid-Mar. to mid-Oct. Phone ahead to confirm schedule. **Phone:** (208) 733-9458.

▼ See AAA listing p. 71 ▼

BEST WESTERN PLUS TWIN FALLS HOTEL
(208)736-8000

Hotel
$99-$149

AAA Benefit: Members save 10% or more with Best Western!

Address: 1377 Blue Lakes Blvd N 83301 **Location:** I-84 exit 173, 4 mi s on US 93. **Facility:** 118 units. 3 stories, interior corridors. **Terms:** 3 day cancellation notice-fee imposed. **Pool(s):** heated indoor. **Activities:** hot tub, limited exercise equipment. **Guest Services:** valet and coin laundry, area transportation.

HAMPTON INN
(208)734-2233

Hotel $99-$159 Address: 1658 Fillmore St N 83301 **Location:** I-84 exit 173, 3.5 mi s to Pole Line Rd, then just w. **Facility:** 75 units. 3 stories, interior corridors. **Terms:** 1-7 night minimum stay, cancellation fee imposed. **Pool(s):** heated indoor. **Activities:** hot tub, exercise room. **Guest Services:** valet and coin laundry.

AAA Benefit: Members save up to 10%!

HILTON GARDEN INN
(208)733-8500

Hotel $109-$179 Address: 1741 Harrison St N 83301 **Location:** I-84 exit 173, 3 mi s to Pole Line Rd, then 0.3 mi w. **Facility:** 107 units. 3 stories, interior corridors. **Terms:** 1-7 night minimum stay, cancellation fee imposed. **Pool(s):** heated indoor. **Activities:** hot tub, exercise room. **Guest Services:** valet and coin laundry.

AAA Benefit: Members save up to 10%!

HOLIDAY INN EXPRESS & SUITES
(208)732-6001

Hotel $104-$179 Address: 1554 Fillmore St N 83301 **Location:** I-84 exit 173, 3.5 mi s to Pole Line Rd, just w, then just s. **Facility:** 91 units. 3 stories, interior corridors. **Amenities:** safes. **Pool(s):** heated indoor. **Activities:** hot tub, exercise room. **Guest Services:** valet and coin laundry.

LA QUINTA INN & SUITES
(208)736-9600

Hotel $109-$150 Address: 539 Pole Line Rd 83301 **Location:** I-84 exit 173, 3 mi s to Pole Line Rd, then 0.3 mi w. **Facility:** 101 units, some two bedrooms. 3 stories, interior corridors. **Pool(s):** heated indoor. **Activities:** hot tub, exercise room. **Guest Services:** valet and coin laundry.

QUALITY INN & SUITES
(208)734-7494

Hotel $79-$159 Address: 1910 Fillmore St N 83301 **Location:** I-84 exit 173, 3.1 mi s to Fillmore St, then 0.5 mi sw. **Facility:** 111 units. 3 stories, interior corridors. **Pool(s):** heated indoor. **Activities:** hot tub, exercise room. **Guest Services:** valet and coin laundry.

RED LION HOTEL CANYON SPRINGS
(208)734-5000

Hotel $79-$129 Address: 1357 Blue Lakes Blvd N 83301 **Location:** I-84 exit 173, 4 mi s on US 93. **Facility:** 112 units. 2 stories (no elevator), interior corridors. **Terms:** cancellation fee imposed. **Pool(s):** heated outdoor. **Activities:** exercise room. **Guest Services:** valet laundry.

SUPER 8 TWIN FALLS
(208)734-5801

Hotel $62-$110 Address: 1260 Blue Lakes Blvd N 83301 **Location:** I-84 exit 173, 4 mi s, then just s of College Rd. **Facility:** 94 units. 3 stories (no elevator), interior corridors. **Activities:** limited exercise equipment. **Guest Services:** coin laundry.

WHERE TO EAT

ANCHOR BISTRO & BAR
208/733-6566

American. Casual Dining. $7-$17 **AAA Inspector Notes:** This cozy bistro and bar features comfortable seating inside and an outdoor patio. Menu item favorites include freshly-made Bermuda onion rings, house beer-battered mahi mahi and French fries, sirloin steak sandwich, Italian grilled sandwiches and for dessert-fried chocolate brownies topped with vanilla ice cream. **Features:** full bar, Sunday brunch. **Address:** 334 Blue Lakes Blvd N 83301 **Location:** I-84 exit 173, 5 mi s, then just s of Filer Ave.

CANYON CREST DINING & EVENT CENTER
208/733-9392

American. Casual Dining. $7-$32 **AAA Inspector Notes:** Overlooking the breathtaking Snake River Canyon, this well-appointed restaurant is home to some of the best views in the Magic Valley. Beautiful wood, stone and glass detail create an exquisite ambience. The open veranda is sure to create an unforgettable experience for diners. **Features:** full bar. **Address:** 330 Canyon Crest Dr 83301 **Location:** I-84 exit 173, 3.9 mi s to Pole Line Rd, 1 mi w, then just n.

ELEVATION 486 FOOD & SPIRITS
208/737-0486

American. Casual Dining. $10-$28 **AAA Inspector Notes:** With postcard-picture views, this restaurant is perched 486 vertical feet above the south rim of the Snake River. Menu items include appetizers, salads and such entrées as fire-grilled artichoke, Northwest steamer clams, hand-cut steaks, tomahawk-cut Idaho pork chops, pan-broiled fresh Alaskan halibut and seared Alaskan scallops. **Features:** full bar, patio dining. **Address:** 195 River Vista Pl 83301 **Location:** I-84 exit 173, 3.5 mi s to Pole Line Rd, 1 mi w to N 2900 E, 0.3 mi n to Canyon Crest Dr, just e, then just n on Pinnacle Pl; in Magic Valley Arts Complex.

IDAHO JOE'S
208/734-9403

American Casual Dining $5-$14

AAA Inspector Notes: The atmosphere is rustic at this local favorite. In addition to generous portions and satisfying breakfasts, there are many fruit and cream pies. The Navajo taco is one of the house specials. **Features:** beer & wine, Sunday brunch. **Address:** 598 Blue Lakes Blvd N 83301 **Location:** I-84 exit 173, 5 mi s; in Lynwood Shopping Center.

JAKERS BAR & GRILL
208/733-8400

American. Casual Dining. $10-$29 **AAA Inspector Notes:** Diners can find a wide variety of steak and seafood at this pleasant restaurant featuring halibut rolled in almonds, miso-citrus glazed salmon, slow-roasted baby back ribs, boneless short ribs and almond-crusted chicken. Five soups are featured daily at the buffet along with an enormous selection of fruit and salads. Be sure to try one of the decadent desserts. **Features:** full bar, patio dining, Sunday brunch. **Address:** 1598 Blue Lakes Blvd 83301 **Location:** I-84 exit 173, 4 mi s on US 93.

LA CASITA MEXICAN RESTAURANT
208/734-7974

Mexican. Casual Dining. $5-$12 **AAA Inspector Notes:** Dine on classic Mexican cuisine featuring a variety of fresh-cooked shredded meat and chicken dishes—all hearty and tasty. This casual, local favorite offers quite a bang for your buck. **Features:** beer & wine. **Address:** 111 S Park Ave W 83301 **Location:** I-84 exit 173, 6.5 mi s on US 93 to Addison Ave, then 1.3 mi sw on Shoshone St.

TWIN FALLS SANDWICH COMPANY   208/734-8372

▼ Deli Coffee/Tea. Quick Serve. $6-$9 **AAA Inspector Notes:** This downtown eatery serves hot and cold sandwiches with a nice selection of sides, such as chips made in house and tasty pasta salad. Menu items are named after local attractions such as Balanced Rock and the Perrine Bridge. Microbrews are available. **Features:** beer & wine, patio dining. **Address:** 128 Main Ave N 83301 **Location:** Just w of Main Ave and Shoshone St; downtown. **Parking:** street only. [B] [L]

WOK'N GRILL RESTAURANT   208/734-6898

▼▼ Chinese. Casual Dining. $8-$29 **AAA Inspector Notes:** This restaurant serves lobster fresh from the lobster tank. Other menu highlights include traditional appetizers along with beef, pork, chicken and seafood dishes, as well as sandwiches and steak. Whether visiting or traveling through the area, the popular luncheon specials and family dinners can be enjoyed by everyone. **Features:** beer & wine, Sunday brunch. **Address:** 1188 Blue Lakes Blvd N 83301 **Location:** I-84 exit 173, 5 mi s. [L] [D]

VICTOR (G-6) pop. 1,928, elev. 6,214'

• **Hotels & Restaurants map & index p. 295**
• **Part of Jackson Hole Including Grand Teton National Park area — see map p. 293**

BAGLEY'S TETON MOUNTAIN RANCH is at 2655 West 8000 South (Cedron Rd.). The ranch offers tours featuring up-close encounters with elk and buffalo herds. Stops are afforded for photos. In addition 1- and 2-hour horseback riding trips as well as half-day, 1-day and overnight trail rides are available.

Time: Allow 1 hour, 30 minutes minimum. **Hours:** Tours Mon.-Sat. 9-5, June-Sept. **Cost:** Tour $10; free (ages 0-3). Reservations are required. **Phone:** (208) 787-9005 or (866) 787-9005.

YELLOWSTONE-GRAND TETON SCENIC LOOP is an approximately 263-mile scenic drive in eastern Idaho, northwestern Wyoming and a small portion of south-central Montana. The route encompasses the Teton and Mesa Falls scenic byways as well as Yellowstone and Grand Teton national parks.

Starting in Victor, Idaho, the 47-mile first segment follows SRs 33 and 32 northwest to Ashton, Idaho (see place listing p. 35), along the Teton Scenic Byway, from which the Teton Mountains can be viewed to the east.

As you take the Mesa Falls Scenic Byway north to Island Park, Idaho (see place listing p. 71), on the 35-mile second segment, you'll pass Upper Mesa Falls (see Mesa Falls Recreation Area attraction listing p. 35) and Harriman State Park (see attraction listing p. 71), both to the west.

Following US 20 north on the 28-mile third segment, you'll reach Henry's Lake State Park (see Recreation Areas Chart) and then head east through touristy West Yellowstone, Mont. (see place listing p. 208), which is situated at Yellowstone National Park's west entrance (hence the name).

Most of the 98-mile fourth segment traverses the western side of Yellowstone National Park (see place listing p. 326). After exiting the park via the south entrance (which is also the north entrance to Grand Teton National Park), you'll drive over the Continental Divide, through pine and fir forests and

past Jackson Lake. Recreational opportunities abound at Jackson Lake and throughout Grand Teton National Park (see place listing p. 266).

The 30-mile fifth segment begins at the Moran junction. US 26/191, with the Tetons on the northern side and pastures with buffalo and elk on the southern side, has numerous pull-offs with informational plaques. The route passes the National Elk Refuge (see attraction listing p. 276), where you can observe elk from boardwalks and decks, and then enters Jackson Hole.

On the 25-mile final segment of the trip, you'll head back to Victor via SR 33, which winds through Caribou-Targhee National Forest (see place listing p. 54) over dramatic mountains with hairpin turns.

Note: Mesa Falls Scenic Byway is closed from mid-November to late April; take US 20 toward Island Park as an alternate route. The road between Yellowstone National Park's west and south entrances also is closed from mid-November to late April. **Phone:** (208) 354-2500 (Teton Valley Chamber of Commerce).

HEADWATERS GRILLE   208/787-3600 ㉕

▼▼▼ Regional American. Fine Dining. $7-$30 **AAA Inspector Notes:** Adjacent to the golf course, this grill offers a golf décor blended with an upscale Western setting complete with leather and wood. Menu highlights include bison, elk, locally-harvested steaks and Alaskan halibut. Upscale presentations and large portions are featured in this casual, club-like atmosphere. **Features:** full bar. **Reservations:** suggested. **Address:** 10 Warm Creek Ln 83455 **Location:** 1 mi s on SR 33, follow signs. [B] [L] [D] CALL[M]

THE KNOTTY PINE BAR & RESTAURANT   208/787-2866 ㉔

▼▼ American. Casual Dining. $8-$25 **AAA Inspector Notes:** This popular restaurant also serves as this small community's most popular entertainment venue with a stage located just off the dining floor. Their intriguing menu offers a variety of beef, seafood and pork entrees. A large patio allows for al fresco dining if the weather permits. **Features:** full bar. **Address:** 58 S Main St 83455 **Location:** Center. **Parking:** street only. [D]

SCRATCH   208/787-5678 ㉓

▼▼ American. Casual Dining. $8-$18 **AAA Inspector Notes:** As the name suggests, this eatery offers innovative recipes made from scratch. The decor is done in pastels and has retro chrome tables and chairs. **Features:** beer & wine, Sunday brunch. **Address:** 185 W Center St (SR 31) 83455 **Location:** Just w of jct SR 33. **Parking:** on-site and street. [D] [Ⓚ]

WALLACE (B-2) pop. 784, elev. 2,744'

The center of a great lead- and silver-mining region, Wallace is at the junction of four major canyons, three of which lead to important active mining districts. This region claims several of the world's largest and deepest silver mines; some of the mines founded in the late 1800s have 200 miles of tunnels.

Among the historic buildings still standing in town are the railroad depot with its original Chinese bricks; the Smokehouse Building, which was once the courthouse; and the Rossi Building with its Queen Anne-style turret. The turret is a characteristic architectural feature seen on most of the corner buildings throughout the historic district.

Pulaski Trail, 1 mile south, features interpretive signs describing the 1910 fire that consumed 3 million acres and is said to be one of the largest fires in U.S. history.

At the east end of Wallace, SR 4 leads north from I-90 exit 62 into Burke Canyon, one of the district's historic mining areas. The 7-mile road passes tailings, abandoned mines, derelict buildings and the once bustling towns of Gem and Burke. The latter town, in a narrow canyon, was renowned for the 150-room Tiger Hotel, which was not only built over a creek, but also had a rail line tunneling through its center and a street running under its west end; the hotel was razed in 1964.

Area back roads attract all-terrain vehicle enthusiasts in summer and snowmobilers in winter.

Historic Wallace Chamber of Commerce Visitor Center: 10 River St., Wallace, ID 83873. **Phone:** (208) 753-7151.

Self-guiding tours: A brochure describing driving and walking tours of the mining and historic districts is available at the visitor center.

NORTHERN PACIFIC DEPOT RAILROAD MUSEUM, 219 Sixth St., occupies a restored station that was built in 1901 and operated until 1980. Exhibits include a re-creation of an early 1900s railroad depot as well as photographs and railway relics recalling the history of the Coeur d'Alene mining district. Changing exhibits also are featured. **Time:** Allow 30 minutes minimum. **Hours:** Daily 9-5, Mar.-Oct.; by appointment rest of year. **Cost:** $2; $1.50 (ages 60+); $1 (ages 6-16); $6 (family). **Phone:** (208) 752-0111.

[SAVE] **SIERRA SILVER MINE TOUR,** at the corner of Fifth and Bank sts., takes visitors into an underground mine where they can view exhibits, equipment in operation and techniques used in hard-rock silver mining. Retired miners conduct the 75-minute guided tour, which includes a ride through town aboard a vintage-style trolley and anecdotes about the mining days. Led by a costumed interpreter portraying a 19th-century miner, a 45-minute tour to Burke, a nearby ghost town, also is offered.

Time: Allow 1 hour, 30 minutes minimum. **Hours:** Mine tours depart every 30 minutes daily 10-4, June-Aug.; 10-2 in May and Sept. Ghost town tours depart Wed.-Sat. on the hour 11-1, July-Aug. **Cost:** Mine tour $14; $12.50 (ages 60+); $8.50 (ages 4-16); $45 (family, two adults and children). Trolley ride only $6. Ghost town tour $10; $6 (ages 4-16). **Phone:** (208) 752-5151.

SIXTH STREET MELODRAMA is at 212 Sixth St. Audience participation is encouraged each summer during a family-style melodrama that reflects the area's mining background. The play, staged in the 1899 Lux Building, is followed by the Kelly's Alley Revue, during which visitors can enjoy old-fashioned music and humor. Other plays and musicals also are produced during the rest of the year; phone for schedule and rates.

Time: Allow 2 hours minimum. **Hours:** Summer performances are given Wed.-Sat. at 7 p.m., Sun. at 2, early July-late Aug. **Cost:** Summer show $10; $30 (family, two adults and two children, $5 for each additional child). Rest of year $15; $13 (ages 55+ and students with ID); $30 (family, two adults and two children, $5 for each additional child). Prices may vary; phone ahead. **Phone:** (208) 752-8871 or (877) 749-8478.

WALLACE DISTRICT MINING MUSEUM, 509 Bank St., displays local mining equipment and photographs. A 20-minute video depicts the life of early miners and the development of one of the richest silver mining districts in the world. Archives are available. **Time:** Allow 1 hour minimum. **Hours:** Daily 9-5, July-Aug.; daily 10-5, May-June and in Sept.; Mon.-Sat. 10-5, rest of year. Closed Jan. 1, Martin Luther King Jr. Day, Presidents Day, Easter, July 4, Thanksgiving and Christmas. Phone ahead to confirm schedule. **Cost:** $3; $1 (ages 6-15); $7 (family). **Phone:** (208) 556-1592.

RECREATIONAL ACTIVITIES
Ziplines
• **Silver Streak Zipline Tours** departs from The Wallace Inn at 516 Pine St. **Note:** Participants must weigh between 95 and 270 pounds. **Hours:** Open daily May-Oct. (weather permitting). Schedule varies; phone ahead. **Phone:** (208) 556-1690.

THE WALLACE INN   (208)752-1252

Hotel
$72-$175

Address: 100 Front St 83873 **Location:** I-90 exit 61 (Business Rt 90), just se. **Facility:** 63 units. 2 stories (no elevator), interior corridors. **Parking:** winter plug-ins. **Terms:** 3 day cancellation notice-fee imposed. **Dining:** Trailside Restaurant, see separate listing. **Pool(s):** heated indoor. **Activities:** sauna, hot tub, steamroom, exercise room. **Guest Services:** valet laundry.

[SAVE] [icons] CALL [icons] / SOME UNITS [icons]

WHERE TO EAT

1313 CLUB   208/752-9391

American
Casual Dining
$6-$22

AAA Inspector Notes: The historic mining town's classic old-time bar and grill has an eclectic decor heavy on taxidermists' mounts and collectible items. Try beer-battered french fries with a certified Angus hamburger or steak. **Features:** full bar, patio dining, happy hour. **Address:** 608 Bank St 83873 **Location:** Downtown. **Parking:** street only. *Menu on AAA.com* [B] [L] [D] [icon]

TRAILSIDE RESTAURANT   208/752-1252

American. Casual Dining. $9-$18 **AAA Inspector Notes:** Patrons can enjoy casual dining in bright and contemporary surroundings with friendly and attentive service. The menu's varied selection includes something for nearly every taste and member of the family. Dining room hours may vary during the winter months. **Features:** full bar. **Address:** 100 Front St 83873 **Location:** I-90 exit 61 (Business Rt 90), just se; in The Wallace Inn. [B] [L] [D]

WEIPPE (D-2) pop. 441, elev. 3,015'

Weippe (WEE-ipe) sits on its namesake prairie, a 9-by-20-mile upland area of mixed grassland and forest, today given over to grain cultivation and forestry. In spring blue blossoms of camas carpet the expanse. The edible bulb was an important food for the Nez Perce Indians, who had several summer encampments on the prairie. Just south of Weippe, members of the Lewis and Clark expedition, nearing starvation after their arduous crossing of the Bitterroot Mountains, were welcomed and sustained by the Nez Perce in 1805.

Weippe is on the 43-mile Gold Rush Historic Byway, which follows SR 11 from Greer to Headquarters. Roadside plaques describe points of interest along the scenic route.

Pierce-Weippe Chamber of Commerce: 204 Wood St., P.O. Box 378, Weippe, ID 83553. **Phone:** (208) 435-4406.

WEIPPE DISCOVERY CENTER, on SR 11 at Wood St., features interpretive murals on its exterior walls that relate the meeting of Meriwether Lewis and William Clark with the Nez Perce Indians in 1805. A trail loops through the Living Lewis & Clark Landscape, which showcases local vegetation used by the Nez Perce and documented by members of the Lewis and Clark expedition. The center also displays mounted native animals.

Time: Allow 30 minutes minimum. **Hours:** Outdoor displays and trail open daily dawn-dusk. Center open Mon.-Fri. 10-5 (also Tues.-Wed. 5-7), Sat. 10-1. Closed major holidays. **Cost:** Free. **Phone:** (208) 435-4406.

WEISER (F-1) pop. 5,507, elev. 2,114'

Named for Sgt. Peter Weiser (WEE-zer) of the Lewis and Clark expedition, Weiser is on the Idaho-Oregon border at the confluence of the Weiser and Snake rivers. Since 1953, the city has been home to the ⚜ National Oldtime Fiddlers' Contest and Festival, which takes place the third full week in June.

Scenic views of Hells Canyon are afforded from viewpoints north of Weiser; open only in summer, the viewpoints can be reached via US 95 and SR 71. Closer looks at the canyon are made possible by the float trips and jet boat tours that are available from Hells Canyon Dam. The minimum age for most float trips is 6 years; inquire about refund and weather policies.

The southern trailhead of the Weiser River Trail, converted from the banks of the former Pacific & Idaho Northern (PIN) railroad grade, is in Weiser off Main Street. The 84-mile route also passes through Midvale, Cambridge and Council. Wildlife including deer, elk, heron, bear, waterfowl, raptors and wild turkeys can be seen. While hiking, bicycling or horseback riding along the trail, visitors view rolling hills and black lava cliffs in the southern portion of the canyon; the northern portion is forested. Cross-country skiing also can be enjoyed in winter.

Fifteen miles northeast of Weiser, just east of the Snake River, four-wheelers kick up lots of down and dirty fun at the Weiser Sand Dunes.

Greater Weiser Area Chamber of Commerce: Vendome Event Center, 309 State St., Weiser, ID 83672. **Phone:** (208) 414-0452.

INDIANHEAD MOTEL & RV   208/549-0331

⬥⬥ **Motel** $65-$95 **Address:** 747 Hillcrest Ave 83672 **Location:** 1 mi n of center; jct US 95 and Indianhead Rd. **Facility:** 8 units. 1 story, exterior corridors. **Terms:** cancellation fee imposed. **Activities:** picnic facilities. 🛗➡ 📶 ☒

WHITE BIRD (D-1) pop. 91, elev. 1,560'
See also Hells Canyon National Recreation Area p. 66

White Bird, near the Salmon River, provides direct access to outdoor recreational activities—including white-water rafting, jet boating and hiking—in the heart of Hells Canyon National Recreation Area. FR 493, a gravel road, is the only way in and out of the area. A boat launch is available, as is a 26-mile trail system that borders the Snake River. Sturgeon fishing is popular on both the Snake and Salmon rivers.

White Bird Battlefield, just north on Old Hwy. 95, was the site of the first confrontation of the Nez Perce War. It is one of the designated historical sites of Nez Perce National Historical Park (see place listing p. 85).

White Bird Chamber of Commerce: 128 White Bird Rd., White Bird, ID 83554. **Phone:** (208) 839-2777.

Self-guiding tours: A trail guide of White Bird Battlefield is available at the chamber of commerce.

HELLS CANYON JET BOAT TRIPS & LODGING   (208)839-2255

⬥ **Motel** $70-$80 **Address:** 3252 Waterfront Dr 83554 **Location:** US 95 exit White Bird, 1.5 mi s of center. **Facility:** 6 units. 1 story, exterior corridors. *Bath:* shower only. **Terms:** 7 day cancellation notice-fee imposed. **Activities:** limited beach access, fishing, picnic facilities. **Guest Services:** coin laundry. (See ad p. 67.)
📶 ☒ 🍴 💲 /SOME UNITS 🅢 🎛 🖼

WINCHESTER (D-1) pop. 340, elev. 3,968'

Early settlers allegedly named this former logging town for the famous firearm. A replica of a Winchester rifle hangs above Main Street. Winchester Lake State Park, just south on US 95 Bus. Rte., occupies the site of the 1910 Craig Mountain Lumber Co., whose 103-acre millpond is today the centerpiece of the park (see Recreation Areas Chart). Remains of the mill can be seen on the hill near the city water tower.

THE WOLF EDUCATION AND RESEARCH CENTER is at 1721 Forest Rd. The center's 300 acres of timberland are home to two resident packs of gray wolves. Visitors have a chance to observe these animals in their natural habitat, courtesy of a .3-mile trail that comes within 50 yards of the wolves' enclosure, though sightings cannot be guaranteed. A visitor center, built to resemble a Nez Perce tribal long house, has displays about wolves.

Time: Allow 30 minutes minimum. **Hours:** Daily 9-5, Memorial Day weekend-Labor Day; by appointment rest of year. Two-hour guided tours are given Tues.-Sat. at 7:30 a.m. and 6 p.m., Mon. at 6 p.m., Sun. at 7:30 a.m., Memorial Day-Labor Day. **Cost:** $5; $2 (ages 6-13). Guided tour (includes admission) $10; $3 (ages 6-13). Reservations are required for guided tours and must be made at least 24 hours in advance. **Phone:** (208) 924-6960.

WORLEY (C-1) pop. 257, elev. 2,650'

GAMBLING ESTABLISHMENTS

- **Coeur d'Alene Casino** is on US 95. **Hours:** Daily 24 hours. **Phone:** (800) 523-2464.

COEUR D'ALENE CASINO RESORT HOTEL   208/769-2600

🔷🔷🔷 **Resort Hotel.** Rates not provided. **Address:** 37914 S Nukwalqw Rd 83876 **Location:** On US 95, 3 mi n. **Facility:** Located just outside of Coeur d'Alene, this casino-style property offers guests a variety of entertainment options. 300 units. 3-4 stories, interior corridors. **Parking:** on-site and valet. **Terms:** check-in 4 pm. **Amenities:** safes. **Dining:** 5 restaurants, also, Chinook Steak & Pasta, High Mountain Buffet, see separate listings. **Pool(s):** heated indoor. **Activities:** hot tub, regulation golf, exercise room, spa. **Guest Services:** area transportation.

WHERE TO EAT

CHINOOK STEAK & PASTA   208/769-2600

🔷🔷🔷 Regional Steak Seafood. Fine Dining. $14-$35 **AAA Inspector Notes:** With a name meaning stand before the fire, this steakhouse uses that technique to grill its 28-day aged beef. The menu is diverse and the presentation creative. Highlights include local steelhead trout, succulent Alaskan black cod and juicy porterhouse steak for two carved tableside. Most food is homemade, including the butter for the popovers and the custard for the ice cream. The contemporary décor reflects the natural beauty of the Palouse Prairie with the use of natural materials. **Features:** full bar, patio dining, happy hour. **Address:** 37914 S Nukwalqw Rd 83876 **Location:** On US 95, 3 mi n; in Coeur d'Alene Casino Resort Hotel. **Parking:** on-site and valet. D CALL 🖪M

HIGH MOUNTAIN BUFFET   208/686-0248

🔷🔷 American. Casual Dining. $8-$19 **AAA Inspector Notes:** This casual restaurant is somewhat remote. Specializing in buffet service for the busy gambler, the eatery also offers cooked-to-order steak and seafood. The most eye-catching aspect of the Western-style décor is the large rock waterfall and museum-quality diorama depicting a canoe beached amid the cattails on the shore of a lake. **Features:** full bar. **Address:** 37914 S Nukwalqw Rd 83876 **Location:** On US 95, 3 mi n; in Coeur d'Alene Casino Resort Hotel. **Parking:** on-site and valet. B L D

🔷 **YELLOWSTONE NATIONAL PARK**—See Wyoming p. 326.

Glacier National Park

Montana

Under a giant sky varying between shades of azure, turquoise and peacock blue, Montana's landscape—encompassing golden wheat fields, timber-covered mountains, flowing trout streams, rocky bluffs and canyon-carved lakes—is a love affair for the eyes.

The state enjoys the best of both worlds. The Continental Divide in western Montana gave rise to the name *montaña,* Spanish for "mountainous." And although the craggy peaks of the northern Rocky Mountains dominate the west, wide open space is the name of the game in the east: Expansive, dizzying prairie grasslands in this region coined the state's nickname, Big Sky Country.

While there are differences between Montana's agriculture- and ranching-based Great Plains and its lumber-dominated west, residents have one thing in common: appreciation for the beauty of their surroundings. Still,

National Bison Range, Moiese

with a harsh climate and sparse population, no one will argue that living in Montana is a piece of cake. But the view from a ranch window seems to make it worthwhile.

The Treasure State

Vast fortunes were made in Montana, but many would assert they came at the expense of people and land, a notion that doesn't sit well with residents. Many Montanans believe that state resources historically have been exploited in the interests of outsiders.

At Little Bighorn Battlefield National Monument, crooked headstones on a grassy hill attest to the passion that thousands of Lakota, Cheyenne and Arapaho warriors exhibited in an attempt to save their homeland.

And the unearthing of copper ores in Butte began a bitter battle between the "copper kings"—entrepreneurs William A. Clark and Marcus Daly. Today, mining relics are displayed downtown in old mine shafts, cabins and such stately homes as Clark's lavish Copper King Mansion.

Colorful Virginia City sports reminders of its gold mining past with restored buildings. And Helena is home to baroque, Gothic and Italianate mansions recalling the city's golden days.

More recently, locals have exhibited an overwhelming drive to preserve Montana's natural blessings. In the early 1970s, residents amended the state constitution to include strict environmental protection laws, setting a national example.

Spectacular Settings

Take in the snowy peaks, ice-sculpted valleys, and twinkling lakes and waterfalls of Glacier National Park, a majestic region so awe-inspiring the Blackfeet Indians deemed it sacred ground. If the area's resident grizzlies, mountain lions and wolves could talk, they would probably agree.

Your heart will skip a beat on Going-to-the-Sun Road, a mind-boggling scenic byway that snakes around cliffs and climbs 6,646 feet to the summit of Logan Pass.

But save some time for the nation's *first* national park, Yellowstone, which Congress established in 1872. You'll also want to visit the National Bison Range in Moiese, where some 500 buffalo roam the plains.

And, along what is now the Upper Missouri National Wild and Scenic River, you can follow the path of the Lewis and Clark expedition. Journal notes suggest that these explorers were enamored with Montana's scenery as well.

Recreation

What's in the perfect Montana recreation kit? Bear bells. Quick-dry nylon shorts. Ski poles. Maybe some chest waders. Definitely some dry socks. And, of course, a size 2 Sofa Pillow.

The quick-dry shorts will come in handy if you immerse yourself in one of this state's top recreation draws—river rafting. At Glacier National Park you can drift down placid portions of the wild and scenic Flathead River, savoring arching canyon walls and wildflower-filled meadows. Or, you might tackle the bucking, boulder-studded rapids of the Flathead's Middle Fork. And Bear Creek is one of the few runs where mountain goats are regularly sighted, thanks to Goat Lick, a cliff on the waterway's north side that excretes mineral salts irresistible to the horned animals.

As any good fly fisher knows, Montana is trout territory, and that's where the chest waders come in. The best catch must be coaxed out with a deft flick of the wrist and an enticing fly on the end of the line. Such flies can have kind of funny names—hence the Sofa Pillow. For top casting sites, head to Bozeman's outskirts and take your pick of such trout-filled rivers as the Madison, Yellowstone and Gallatin. You'll find plenty of rental boats here, too, complete with guides who will do the rowing for you.

Fly-fishing may be out if you hit Bozeman mid-winter, but that doesn't mean you're too late to have fun. Excellent downhill skiing is just around the corner at Big Sky Resort, which averages 400 inches of powder annually. And locals rave about the bowl and chute skiing available at 1,200-acre Bridger Bowl Ski Area. Six cross-country skiing trails rim the region as well, notably the 10-mile Bozeman Creek to Mystic Lake trail and the 4-mile Hyalite Reservoir Ski Loop.

In addition you'll find superb ski venues close to many other Montana towns, including Big Mountain near Whitefish, Red Lodge Mountain near Red Lodge and Snowbowl near Missoula. All make great places to put those ski poles you packed to good use.

Plus, ski poles can often be helpful when hiking Montana's rugged terrain. Such "walking sticks" are especially useful when the only way to follow your trail is to ford a frigid, knee-high creek. The dry socks are for when you get to the other side.

Montana has several great hiking trails, but try not to miss Cinnamon Mountain Lookout Trail in the Gallatin National Forest, or Stoney Indian Pass in Glacier National Park's Belly River Country. Both reward hikers with sudden, stunning vistas of Montana's treasured mountains. One caveat—while such spectacular scenery can be a pleasant surprise, startling an 800-pound grizzly is just plain hazardous. And *that's* why bear bells are number one on any Montana recreational equipment list.

Cycling in Bozeman

Historic Timeline

1805	Meriwether Lewis and William Clark arrive in what is now the state of Montana.
1862	Miners strike gold at Grasshopper Creek and later at Diamond City and Virginia City.
1876	Lt. Col. George Armstrong Custer and troops are defeated at the Battle of the Little Bighorn.
1880	Irish immigrant Marcus Daly purchases the Anaconda, a mine with a rich copper reserve that will make him wealthy.
1916	Montana Republican Jeannette Rankin becomes the first U.S. congresswoman; she later voted against both world wars.
1955	The Anaconda Aluminum Co. opens a $65 million plant in northwestern Montana.
1972	Montana's electorate approves a new state constitution.
1984	Launched in 1967, the Libby Dam hydroelectric project is finally completed.
1988	Forest fires sweep through Montana for nearly 3 months, wiping out trees and wildlife in Yellowstone National Park.
1998	Montana Freemen leaders involved in a 1996 armed standoff with FBI agents are convicted of various charges.
2000	Judy Martz is elected governor and becomes the state's first female chief executive.

What To Pack

Temperature Averages Maximum/Minimum	JANUARY	FEBRUARY	MARCH	APRIL	MAY	JUNE	JULY	AUGUST	SEPTEMBER	OCTOBER	NOVEMBER	DECEMBER
Billings	33/13	36/15	43/23	57/34	68/43	76/51	89/58	86/55	75/46	63/37	46/26	39/19
Great Falls	32/14	34/15	41/21	55/33	66/42	72/49	84/56	81/54	70/46	59/38	44/26	37/20
Havre	26/6	29/8	40/18	57/32	69/43	75/51	86/57	83/54	72/44	60/35	42/21	33/12
Kalispell	26/9	32/12	40/19	55/30	65/39	72/46	83/49	80/46	69/39	55/31	37/21	29/16
Medicine Lake	18/-2	27/7	40/18	56/30	68/42	77/51	83/54	82/53	70/42	58/31	36/16	23/3
Miles City	27/6	32/9	42/19	59/33	71/44	79/53	90/60	88/58	75/47	62/36	44/22	34/12

From the records of The Weather Channel Interactive, Inc.

Good Facts To Know

ABOUT THE STATE

POPULATION: 989,415.

AREA: 147,138 square miles; ranks 4th.

CAPITAL: Helena.

HIGHEST POINT: 12,799 ft., Granite Peak.

LOWEST POINT: 1,862 ft., Kootenai River.

TIME ZONE(S): Mountain. DST.

REGULATIONS

TEEN DRIVING LAWS: No more than one unrelated passenger under 18 for the first 6 months and no more than three unrelated passengers under 18 for the second 6 months. Driving is not permitted 11 p.m.-5 a.m. The minimum age for an unrestricted driver's license is 16. Phone (406) 444-3933 for more information about Montana driver's license regulations.

SEAT BELT/CHILD RESTRAINT LAWS: Seat belts are required for driver and all passengers ages 6 and over and at least 60 pounds. Children under age 6 and less than 60 pounds are required to be in a child restraint. AAA recommends the use of seat belts and appropriate child restraints for the driver and all passengers.

HELMETS FOR MOTORCYCLISTS: Required for riders under 18.

RADAR DETECTORS: Permitted.

MOVE OVER LAW: Driver is required to slow down and vacate the lane nearest stopped police, fire and rescue vehicles using audible or flashing signals. The law also includes tow trucks. If on a highway with a speed limit of 50 mph or greater, the driver must slow down by at least 20 mph below the posted speed limit.

FIREARMS LAWS: Vary by state and/or county. Contact the Montana Department of Justice, Help Desk, 3013 N. Roberts, Room 470, Helena, MT 59601; phone (406) 444-2800.

HOLIDAYS

HOLIDAYS: Jan. 1 ▪ Martin Luther King Jr. Day, Jan. (3rd Mon.) ▪ Lincoln's and Washington's Birthday/Presidents Day, Feb. (3rd Mon.) ▪ Memorial Day, May (last Mon.) ▪ July 4 ▪ Labor Day, Sept. (1st Mon.) ▪ Columbus Day, Oct. (2nd Mon.) ▪ Election Day, Nov. (1st Tues. following 1st Mon.) ▪ Veterans Day, Nov. 11 ▪ Thanksgiving, Nov. (4th Thurs.) ▪ Christmas, Dec. 25.

MONEY

TAXES: Montana does not have a statewide sales tax. Designated resort communities may enact a resort tax of up to 3 percent for goods and services. There is a 7 percent statewide Lodging Tax.

VISITOR INFORMATION

INFORMATION CENTERS: State welcome centers are on US 2 just 1 mile east of Culbertson ▪ at jct. Main St. and US 2 in Shelby ▪ off I-94 in Wibaux ▪ on I-90 southbound a half-mile east of Hardin ▪ at jct. US 191 and US 20N in West Yellowstone ▪ and off I-15 southbound in Dillon.

ROAD CONDITIONS: The Montana Department of Transportation provides information about highway conditions and construction; phone (406) 444-6201 or (800) 226-7623.

FURTHER INFORMATION FOR VISITORS:
Montana Office of Tourism
301 S. Park
Helena, MT 59601
(406) 841-2870
(800) 847-4868

NATIONAL FOREST INFORMATION:
U.S. Forest Service
Lolo National Forest
24 Fort Missoula Rd.
Missoula, MT 59804
(406) 329-3750
(877) 833-6777 (TTY)

FISHING AND HUNTING REGULATIONS:
Montana Department of Fish, Wildlife & Parks
1420 E. 6th Ave.
P.O. Box 200701
Helena, MT 59620
(406) 444-2535
(406) 444-1200 (TTY)

Montana Annual Events

Please call ahead to confirm event details.

JANUARY

- Montana PRCA Pro Rodeo Circuit Finals / Great Falls
  406-727-8900
- Montana Winter Fair Lewistown
  406-538-3007
- Seeley Lake Area Winterfest / Seeley Lake
  406-677-2880

FEBRUARY

- Cowtown Beef Breeders Show, Craft Expo and Ag Trade Show / Miles City
  406-234-2893
- Wild West Winterfest Bozeman
  406-582-3270
- Whitefish Winter Carnival Whitefish
  406-862-3501

MARCH

- St. Patrick's Day Events Butte
  406-723-3177
- West Yellowstone Snowmobile EXPO West Yellowstone
  406-647-7701
- St. Patrick's Day Parade Anaconda
  406-563-2400

APRIL

- Rendezvous Days / Eureka
  406-889-4636
- Ice Breaker Road Race Great Falls
  406-771-1265
- Montana Storytelling Roundup / Cut Bank
  406-873-2295

MAY

- Bigfork Whitewater Festival Bigfork
  406-270-1551
- International Migratory Bird Day / Moiese
  406-644-2211, ext. 207
- MSU-Billings Wine and Food Festival / Billings
  888-430-6782

JUNE

- Custer's Last Stand Re-enactment / Hardin
  406-665-3577
- Lewis and Clark Festival Great Falls
  406-452-5661
- Libby Logger Days / Libby
  406-293-8585

JULY

- Montana Folk Festival Butte
  406-497-6464
- Wolf Point Wild Horse Stampede / Wolf Point
  406-653-2012
- Montana State Fair Great Falls
  406-727-8900

AUGUST

- Montana Cowboy Poetry Gathering and Western Music Rendezvous Lewistown
  406-538-4575
- Sweet Pea Festival Bozeman
  406-586-4003
- MontanaFair / Billings
  800-366-8538

SEPTEMBER

- Havre's Festival Days Havre
  406-265-4383
- Libby Nordicfest / Libby
  406-293-6430
- Miner's Union Day Philipsburg
  406-859-5125

OCTOBER

- Northern International Livestock Exposition Stock Show, Pro Rodeo and Western Expo / Billings
  406-256-2495
- McIntosh Apple Day Hamilton
  406-363-3338
- Humanities Montana Festival of the Book Missoula
  406-243-6022

NOVEMBER

- Parade of Lights / Forsyth
  406-347-5656
- Seasonal Bazaar and Parade of Lights / Cut Bank
  406-873-4041
- Holiday Parade / Billings
  406-259-5454

DECEMBER

- A Montana Country Christmas / Stevensville
  406-777-3773
- First Night Missoula Missoula
  406-549-4755
- Montana Ballet Company's Nutcracker / Bozeman
  406-582-8702

The Cathedral of St. Helena, Helena

Native American cultural celebration

Hike in Glacier National Park

Rafting on the Gallatin River

Roosevelt Arch, north gate to Yellowstone National Park

Index: Great Experience for Members

AAA editor's picks of exceptional note

Virginia City

Glacier National Park

Little Bighorn
Battlefield National
Monument

State Capitol

Montana Atlas Section

ROADS/HIGHWAYS

	INTERSTATE
	CONTROLLED ACCESS
	CONTROLLED ACCESS TOLL
	TOLL ROAD
	PRIMARY DIVIDED
	PRIMARY UNDIVIDED
	SECONDARY DIVIDED
	SECONDARY UNDIVIDED
	LOCAL DIVIDED
	LOCAL UNDIVIDED
	UNPAVED ROAD
	UNDER CONSTRUCTION
	TUNNEL
	PEDESTRIAN ONLY
	AUTO FERRY
	PASSENGER FERRY
	SCENIC BYWAY
10	DISTANCE BETWEEN MARKERS
	EXIT NUMBER-FREE/TOLL
	INTERCHANGE FULL/PARTIAL
	WELCOME CENTER
	REST AREA/ SERVICE CENTER

BOUNDARIES

	INTERNATIONAL
	STATE
	COUNTY
	TIME ZONE
	CONTINENTAL DIVIDE

ROAD SHIELDS

	INTERSTATE/BUSINESS
22 22 22	U.S./STATE/COUNTY
	FOREST/INDIAN
	TRANS- CANADA
1	PROVINCIAL AUTOROUTE
1	MEXICO
66	HISTORIC ROUTE 66
VT 41	REFERENCE PAGE INDICATOR

AREAS OF INTEREST

	INDIAN
	MILITARY
	PARK
	FOREST
	GRASSLANDS
	HISTORIC
✈	INT'L/REGIONAL AIRPORT
	INCORPORATED CITY

POINTS OF INTEREST

○	TOWN
⊛	NATIONAL CAPITAL
★	STATE/PROVINCIAL CAPITAL
	AAA/CAA CLUB LOCATION
■	FEATURE OF INTEREST
	COLLEGE/UNIVERSITY
▲	CAMPGROUND INFORMATION PROVIDED BY WOODALL'S®
	CUSTOMS STATION
	HISTORIC
⛬	LIGHTHOUSE
	MONUMENT/MEMORIAL
	STATE/PROVINCIAL PARK
	NATIONAL WILDLIFE REFUGE
	SKI AREA
⊗	SPORTS COMPLEX
—	DAM

CITIES/TOWNS are color-coded by size, showing where to find AAA Approved and Diamond rated lodgings or restaurants listed in the AAA TourBook guides and on AAA.com:

● **Red** - major destinations and capitals; many listings

● **Black** - destinations; some listings

● Grey - no listings

MONTANA

Montana
Orientation

NOT INTENDED FOR DRIVING.
SEE APPROPRIATE AAA SHEET MAP.

Scale in Miles
0   40
40   40

Only places listed in the Attractions
section appear on this map.

▽ See AAA GEM Index
1 See Recreation Areas Chart
on following page

© 2013 NAVTEQ

© AAA

4017-14

Recreation Areas Chart

The map location numerals in column 2 show an area's location on the preceding map.

	MAP LOCATION	CAMPING	PICNICKING	HIKING TRAILS	BOATING	BOAT RAMP	BOAT RENTAL	FISHING	SWIMMING	PETS ON LEASH	BICYCLE TRAILS	WINTER SPORTS	VISITOR CENTER	LODGE/CABINS	FOOD SERVICE
NATIONAL PARKS *(See place listings.)*															
Glacier (A-2) 1,000,000 acres. Horse rental.		•	•	•	•	•	•	•	•	•			•	•	•
NATIONAL FORESTS *(See place listings.)*															
Beaverhead-Deerlodge (E-2) 3,392,930 acres. Southwestern Montana. Horse rental.		•	•	•	•	•		•	•	•	•	•		•	
Bitterroot (D-2) 1,577,883 acres. Western Montana.		•	•	•	•	•		•	•	•	•	•			
Custer (E-4) 1.3 million acres. Southeastern Montana and north-western South Dakota.		•	•	•	•	•		•	•	•	•	•			
Flathead (A-2) 2,330,029 acres. Northwestern Montana. Horse rental.		•	•	•	•	•		•	•	•	•	•			
Gallatin (E-4) 1,735,239 acres. South-central Montana. Horse rental.		•	•	•	•	•	•	•	•	•	•	•		•	•
Helena (D-3) 976,000 acres. West-central Montana.		•	•	•	•	•		•	•	•		•		•	
Kootenai (A-1) 2.2 million acres. Northwestern Montana. Horse rental.		•	•	•	•	•	•	•	•	•	•	•		•	
Lewis and Clark (B-3) 1,843,397 acres. West-central Montana.		•	•	•	•	•		•	•	•		•		•	
Lolo (B-1) 2,100,000 acres. Western Montana. Horse rental.		•	•	•	•	•		•	•	•	•	•		•	•
NATIONAL RECREATION AREAS *(See place listings.)*															
Bighorn Canyon (E-6) 120,000 acres in southern Montana and northern Wyoming.		•	•	•	•	•	•	•	•	•			•		•
ARMY CORPS OF ENGINEERS															
Fort Peck Lake (B-7) off SR 24 in Fort Peck. Bird-watching. *(See Fort Peck p. 158.)*	**1**	•	•	•	•	•	•		•	•	•	•		•		•
Downstream (B-7) 347 acres 1 mi. e. of Fort Peck off SR 117. Museum, playground.	**2**	•	•	•	•	•			•		•				
Dredge Cuts (B-7) 650 acres .5 mi. n. of Fort Peck off SR 117. Playground.	**3**		•		•	•		•	•	•					
Fourchette Bay (C-6) 80 acres 60 mi. s.e. of Malta off SR 191.	**4**	•	•		•	•		•	•	•					
Nelson Creek (C-7) 468 acres 45 mi. s. of Fort Peck off SR 24.	**5**	•	•		•	•		•	•	•					
The Pines (B-6) 927 acres 4.5 mi. n.w. of Fort Peck on SR 24, 14 mi. s.w. via a gravel road, then 12 mi. s.e. via a gravel road. Playground.	**6**	•	•		•	•		•	•	•					
Rock Creek (C-7) 345 acres 32 mi. s.e. of Fort Peck off SR 24.	**7**	•	•		•	•		•	•	•					
Libby Dam (Lake Koocanusa) (B-1) 46,000 acres 13.5 mi. e. of Libby on SR 37, then 3.5 mi. n. on FR 228, following signs. *(See Libby p. 188.)*	**8**	•	•	•	•	•		•	•	•		•	•	•	•
STATE															
Bannack (F-2) 1,529 acres 17 mi. w. of Dillon on SR 278, then 4 mi. s. on Bannack Rd., following signs. Historic. *(See Dillon p. 154.)*	**9**	•	•	•				•		•	•	•	•		
Beartooth Wildlife Management Area (D-3) 27,000 acres 10 mi. s.e. of Wolf Creek via a gravel road.	**10**	•	•		•	•		•	•	•					
Black Sandy (D-3) 55 acres 14 mi. n.e. of Helena via I-15 and CR 415.	**11**	•	•	•	•	•		•	•	•				•	
Canyon Ferry Lake (D-3) e. of Helena.	**12**	•			•	•	•								
Canyon Ferry (D-3) 5,000 acres s.e. of Helena off US 287 on Canyon Ferry Lake. Hunting.	**13**	•	•		•	•	•	•	•	•					•
Cave Bay (D-4) 19 mi. e. of Helena via US 287 and CR 284.	**14**		•		•	•	•	•	•	•					
Chinaman (D-4) 19 mi. e. of Helena via US 287 and CR 284.	**15**		•		•	•		•	•	•					
Court Sheriff (D-4) 18 mi. e. of Helena via US 287 and CR 284.	**16**	•	•		•			•	•	•					
Hellgate (D-3) 27 mi. e. of Helena via US 287 and CR 284.	**17**	•	•		•	•		•	•	•					
Indian Road (D-3) 1 mi. n. of Townsend on US 287.	**18**	•	•		•	•		•		•					

Recreation Areas Chart

The map location numerals in column 2 show an area's location on the preceding map.

	MAP LOCATION	CAMPING	PICNICKING	HIKING TRAILS	BOATING	BOAT RAMP	BOAT RENTAL	FISHING	SWIMMING	PETS ON LEASH	BICYCLE TRAILS	WINTER SPORTS	VISITOR CENTER	LODGE/CABINS	FOOD SERVICE
Riverside (D-4) 18 mi. e. of Helena via US 287 and CR 284.	19	•	•		•	•		•		•					
Silos (D-3) 8 mi. n.w. of Townsend off US 287.	20	•	•		•	•		•		•					•
White Earth (D-3) 5 mi. e. of Winston.	21	•	•		•	•		•		•					
Cooney Reservoir (E-5) 304 acres 5 mi. w. of Boyd via a gravel road.	22	•	•	•	•	•		•	•	•					•
Deadman's Basin (D-5) 500 acres 29 mi. e. of Harlowton off US 12.	23	•	•		•	•		•	•	•					
Flathead Lake (C-2) n. of Polson on US 93 (see Polson p. 199.)	24				•	•	•	•	•	•					
Big Arm (C-1) 55 acres 15 mi. n. of Polson on US 93.	25	•	•		•	•		•	•	•					
Finley Point (C-2) 24 acres about 12 mi. n.e. of Polson off SR 35.	26	•	•		•	•		•	•	•	•				
Wayfarers (B-2) 68 acres 1 mi. s. of Bigfork off SR 35.	27	•	•		•	•		•	•	•					
West Shore (B-1) 146 acres about 20 mi. s. of Kalispell on US 93.	28	•	•	•	•	•		•	•	•					
Yellow Bay (B-2) 10 acres 20 mi. n.e. of Polson off SR 35.	29	•	•		•	•		•	•	•					
Hell Creek (C-6) 172 acres 26 mi. n. of Jordan via a gravel road on Fort Peck Reservoir.	30	•	•		•	•	•	•						•	•
Lake Mary Ronan (B-1) 76 acres 7 mi. n.w. of Dayton off US 93.	31	•	•		•	•		•	•	•					
Logan (B-1) 18 acres 45 mi. w. of Kalispell off US 2.	32	•	•	•	•	•		•	•	•					
Makoshika (C-8) 11,531 acres 1 mi. s. of Glendive at 1301 Snyder Ave. (See Glendive p. 172.)	33	•	•	•						•		•	•		
Medicine Rocks (D-8) 320 acres 24 mi. s. of Baker on SR 7. Historic. (See Baker p. 128.)	34	•	•	•						•		•	•		
Missouri Headwaters (E-4) 527 acres 3 mi. e. of Three Forks, then 3 mi. n. of US 10 at 1585 Trident Jct. (See Three Forks p. 206.)	35	•	•	•	•	•		•		•			•		
Painted Rocks (E-2) 263 acres 20 mi. s.w. of Conner off SR 473.	36	•	•		•	•		•	•	•					
Placid Lake (C-2) 32 acres 6 mi. s.w. of Seeley Lake via CR 83.	37	•	•		•	•		•	•	•	•				
Rosebud (D-6) 32 acres e. of Forsyth off I-94.	38	•	•	•	•	•				•	•				
Salmon Lake (C-2) 42 acres 5 mi. s. of Seeley Lake on SR 83.	39	•	•	•	•	•		•	•	•					
Thompson Falls (C-1) 36 acres 3 mi. w. of Thompson Falls off SR 200.	40	•	•	•	•	•		•		•	•				
Tongue River Reservoir (F-6) 640 acres 6 mi. n. of Decker on CR 314, then 1 mi. e.	41	•	•		•	•		•	•	•					•
Whitefish Lake (A-2) 10 acres 5 mi. w. of Whitefish on US 93.	42	•	•		•	•	•	•	•	•				•	•
OTHER															
Barretts Park (F-3) 38 acres 8 mi. s.w. of Dillon off I-15.	43	•	•		•			•	•	•					
Beaver Creek (B-5) 10,000 acres 11 mi. s. of Havre on CR 234. Bird-watching. (See Havre p. 179.)	44	•	•	•	•	•		•	•	•		•			
Bitterroot Lake (B-1) 36 acres 5 mi. n. of US 2 at Marion.	45	•	•		•	•		•	•					•	
Clark Canyon Reservoir (F-2) 4,131 acres 20 mi. s.w. of Dillon on I-15. Hunting.	46	•	•		•	•	•	•	•	•					
Fresno Reservoir (B-4) 25,668 acres n.w. of Havre. Hunting, water skiing.	47	•	•		•	•		•	•	•					
Georgetown Lake (D-2) 2,850 acres 15 mi. w. of Anaconda on SR 1. Water skiing; playground. (See Beaverhead-Deerlodge National Forest p. 129.)	48	•	•	•	•	•		•	•	•		•		•	
Holter Lake (C-3) 22 acres 2 mi. e. of Wolf Creek on Missouri River Rd., then 3 mi. s. via a gravel road. (See Wolf Creek p. 215.)	49	•	•		•	•		•	•	•				•	•
Hungry Horse Reservoir (B-2) 6,836 acres 10 mi. e. of Columbia Falls on SR 40, then s. 5 mi. via a gravel road. Hunting. (See Glacier National Park p. 166.)	50	•	•	•	•	•		•	•			•	•	•	
Hyalite Canyon (E-3) 35,000 acres 14 mi. s. of Bozeman on SR 85.	51	•	•	•	•	•		•	•	•		•	•		

Recreation Areas Chart

The map location numerals in column 2 show an area's location on the preceding map.

	MAP LOCATION	CAMPING	PICNICKING	HIKING TRAILS	BOATING	BOAT RAMP	BOAT RENTAL	FISHING	SWIMMING	PETS ON LEASH	BICYCLE TRAILS	WINTER SPORTS	VISITOR CENTER	LODGE/CABINS	FOOD SERVICE
James Kipp (C-5) 465 acres 65 mi. n.e. of Lewistown off US 191.	52	•	•		•	•		•							
Judith Landing (C-5) 44 mi. s.e. of Big Sandy on CR 236.	53	•			•	•		•							
Lake Blaine (B-2) 13 acres 7 mi. e. of Kalispell.	54		•		•	•		•	•	•	•				•	•
Lake Elwell (B-4) 6,197 acres 18 mi. s.w. of Chester.	55	•	•		•	•		•	•	•					•
Nelson Reservoir (B-6) 7,702 acres 18 mi. n.e. of Malta off US 2.	56	•	•		•	•		•	•	•					
Riverfront Park (E-5) 1 mi. s. of Billings on CR 416.	57		•	•	•			•					•	•	
Swan Lake (B-2) 10 acres 14 mi. s.e. of Bigfork on SR 83. Water skiing.	58	•	•		•	•		•	•	•					

ABSAROKEE (E-5) pop. 1,150, elev. 4,039'

RECREATIONAL ACTIVITIES
Horseback Riding
- [SAVE] **Paintbrush Adventures** is in Stillwater Valley n. of Yellowstone National Park. Other activities are offered. **Hours:** Horseback riding trips are offered daily year-round. Departure times vary; phone ahead. **Phone:** (406) 328-4158.

White-water Rafting
- **Absaroka River Adventures** is at 113 Grove St. Other activities are offered. **Hours:** Rafting trips daily 7 a.m.-10 p.m., May-Aug. **Phone:** (406) 328-7440 or (800) 334-7238.

ALBERTON (C-1) pop. 420, elev. 3,029'

RECREATIONAL ACTIVITIES
White-water Rafting
- **Montana River Guides** departs from Missoula and the Alberton Gorge. **Hours:** Full- and half-day white-water rafting trips depart daily at 9 and 2, mid-Apr. to mid-Oct. **Phone:** (406) 722-7238 or (800) 381-7238.

ANACONDA (D-2) elev. 5,288'

Because it had ample water and was surrounded by one of the world's richest copper deposits, Anaconda was chosen for the site of a copper smelter by the originator of Montana's copper industry, Marcus Daly. Daly, an Irish immigrant who was a manager of a mine in Utah, bought the mine when it was thought worthless after the silver lode ran out. Daly saw the mine's potential in its copper reserves—with the invention of the telephone and telegraph, copper wire was in high demand. By the time Daly died in 1900, he was one of the world's richest men.

Daly also founded the nearby town of Hamilton (see place listing p. 178), where he spent summers with his family. Today all that is left of Daly's smelter is the 585-foot smokestack. The Stack Interpretive Center on 4th Street has exhibits about copper production.

A number of buildings from the 1800s remain, including the Deer Lodge County Courthouse, 800 S. Main St.; City Hall Center at 401 E. Commercial St.; Hearst Free Library at Fourth and Main streets; and St. Mark's Episcopal Church, corner of Fifth and Main streets. Anaconda's architecture spans Romanesque to Victorian styles. At 305 Main St. is the Art Deco, neoclassical 1936 Washoe Theatre.

A popular scenic highway, SR 1, begins in Anaconda and heads west over Flint Creek Pass.

Anaconda Chamber of Commerce: 306 E. Park St., Anaconda, MT 59711. **Phone:** (406) 563-2400.

Self-guiding tours: The chamber of commerce offers a map describing a walking tour of the historic district; the fee is $2.

COPPER VILLAGE MUSEUM AND ARTS CENTER is at 401 E. Commercial in Anaconda's former city hall. The ornate building houses archives and the Marcus Daly Historical Society Museum, which chronicles the area's heritage through pioneer and smelting relics. Temporary art exhibitions highlight the work of international artists. Regularly scheduled special events and educational activities also are offered.

Tours: Guided tours are available. **Time:** Allow 30 minutes minimum. **Hours:** Tues.-Sat. 10-4. Closed major holidays. **Cost:** Free. **Phone:** (406) 563-2422. 🅷

VINTAGE BUS TOUR departs from the Anaconda Visitor's Center, 306 E. Park St. Highlights of the sightseeing trip in a 1936 touring bus include the historic business district, several churches, the Washoe Theatre, the smokestack interpretive site, a Jack Nicklaus-designed golf course on reclaimed smelter property and one of the state's oldest fish hatcheries. **Time:** Allow 1 hour minimum. **Hours:** Tours are given Mon.-Sat. at 10 and 2, mid-May to mid-Sept. **Cost:** $8; $4 (ages 0-5). **Phone:** (406) 563-2400.

BARCLAY II SUPPER CLUB & LOUNGE   406/563-5541
▼▼ Steak Seafood. Casual Dining. $15-$35 **AAA Inspector Notes:** At this Montana supper club, all meals include a relish tray, salad or soup, a side of spaghetti and a scoop of ice cream for dessert. Patrons dine on large portions, including locally purchased and in-house cut steaks—most notably the tenderloin entrée. In an informal setting just 6 miles from Fairmont Hot Springs, the crowd enjoys good food and pleasant service. **Features:** full bar. **Reservations:** suggested, weekends. **Address:** 1300 E Commercial Ave 59711 **Location:** I-90 exit 208 (Anaconda), 7.5 mi sw on SR 1 (E Commercial Ave). [D]

MAY PALACE   406/563-3388
▼▼ Chinese. Casual Dining. $8-$12 **AAA Inspector Notes:** This very popular restaurant, with an attached casino, serves tasty, authentic food. The mu shu is quite flavorful and the portion is large. **Features:** full bar. **Address:** 1520 E Commercial Ave 59711 **Location:** I-90 exit 208 (Anaconda), 7 mi sw on SR 1 (E Commercial Ave). [L] [D]

BAKER (D-8) pop. 1,741

Named for the superintendent of construction of the Milwaukee Road, Baker is near the middle of vast oil and gas fields. Until 1915 Baker was solely a grazing and farming town. Then, a driller in search of water struck a natural-gas pocket, setting fire to his well, which burned as a natural torch for 6 years. Baker is now a center for local petroleum and agricultural interests.

Baker Chamber of Commerce: 121 S. Main St., P.O. Box 849, Baker, MT 59313. **Phone:** (406) 778-2266 or (866) 862-2537.

MEDICINE ROCKS STATE PARK is 24 mi. s. on SR 7. The 320-acre park contains huge sandstone formations once used by Native Americans for ceremonies. An interpretive trail describes the site's history. In summer hiking and bicycling can be enjoyed, and in winter snowshoeing is a popular activity. See Recreation Areas Chart. **Cost:** $5 (nonresidents per private vehicle); $3 (nonresidents arriving by other means); free (residents). **Phone:** (406) 234-0926. 🅰 ⊠ ⛲

BEAVERHEAD-DEERLODGE NATIONAL FOREST (E-2)

Elevations in the forest range from 4,075 ft. in the valleys to 11,361 ft. on Hilgard Peak. Refer to AAA maps for additional elevation information.

Beaverhead-Deerlodge National Forest is part of the huge complex of national forests occupying most of southwestern Montana. In 1996, Deerlodge National Forest's 1,194,124 acres (nearly 100 square miles) were combined with Beaverhead National Forest to form an outdoor recreation area encompassing more than 3.3 million acres.

Glaciated peaks rise from broad valleys in the area to form some of Montana's most majestic ranges—the Anaconda, Bitterroot, Beaverhead, Flint Creek, Gravelly, Highland, Madison, Tobacco Root and Sapphire. Mountains in these ranges are among the loftiest in the state; more than 40 surpass 10,000 feet. Mount Evans rises to 10,604 feet, and several more, including Hilgard Peak, exceed 11,000 feet.

From the snowpack of these ranges spring the Big Hole, Beaverhead and Ruby rivers, which form three major tributaries of the Jefferson River. The high country also supplies some of the tributaries of the Madison River. The Clark Fork River flows from its headwaters west of the Continental Divide to Idaho's Lake Pend Oreille.

Through this maze of mountains and river valleys Sacagawea led Meriwether Lewis and William Clark in their search for a passage to the Pacific. This was the land of Sacagawea's people, the Shoshones, who re-provisioned and led the expedition over Lemhi Pass in 1805 and north to a final passage to the West. Despite the inroads of progress—lumbering, mining and ranching—much of the forest's lands have changed little since Lewis and Clark's visit.

Within the forest are portions of the Anaconda-Pintler and Lee Metcalf wilderness areas and a large number of roadless tracts. Typical features of roadless areas are glacial lakes, trout streams and rugged mountain vistas.

The Anaconda-Pintler Wilderness straddles 30 miles of the Anaconda Range and the Continental Divide. The land gradually rises from dense stands of lodgepole pine to open parks dotted with lakes, culminating in jagged peaks in the heart of the range. Anglers prize the clear mountain streams and alpine lakes for their abundance and variety of trout.

Another major area is the Taylor-Hilgard portion of the Lee Metcalf Wilderness. This unit is one of the four portions of wilderness along the spine of the Madison Range, which lies just northwest of Yellowstone National Park. Soaring peaks, knife-edged ridges and alpine lakes are characteristics of this popular area. Bird-watchers will find more than 260 species frequenting a variety of habitats in the forest. The region provides winter range for bighorn sheep and mountain goats and a home to grizzly and black bears, mule deer, mountain lions, elk and moose.

The bald eagle, formerly on the endangered species list, nests in the southeastern Gravelly Range and winters along the Red Rock, Ruby, Jefferson, Madison, Big Hole and Beaverhead rivers. Most migration and wintering activities occur in the large river valleys adjoining the forest. The endangered gray wolf is an occasional visitor to parts of the Continental Divide southwest of Dillon. Grizzly bears occupy portions of the Madison Range within the Lee Metcalf Wilderness and are occasional visitors to the Tobacco Root Mountains and the Gravelly Range.

The forest offers fishing streams, hiking trails, groomed snowmobile trails, developed campgrounds and sites for motorized boating. Visitors can explore many old mines near Deer Lodge, plus the ghost town of Elkhorn, near Boulder, an 1880s mining town with a few corporeal residents. Fifteen miles west of Anaconda on SR 1 is Georgetown Lake *(see Recreation Areas Chart),* one of the area's busiest recreation sites, partly due to its excellent fishing. Snowmobiling and cross-country and downhill skiing are available at Discovery Basin, north of Georgetown Lake, and at Maverick Mountain near Dillon.

The forest's most unusual feature is Sheepshead Recreation Area, a site designed for the physically impaired. In addition to meadows, forests and a 15-acre lake, the setting offers paved trails, a picnic area and a fishing pier.

Detailed information about campgrounds and recreational opportunities is available at the district ranger stations in Butte, Deer Lodge, Dillon, Ennis, Philipsburg, Sheridan, Whitehall, Wisdom and Wise River. For further information contact the Beaverhead-Deerlodge National Forest Supervisor's Office, USDA Service Center, 420 Barrett St., Dillon, MT 59725; phone (406) 683-3900 or (406) 683-3913 for the park's 24-hour information line. *See Recreation Areas Chart.*

BELGRADE   pop. 7,389
• Restaurants p. 130

GALLATIN RIVER LODGE   (406)388-0148

▼▼▼ **Country Inn** $170-$400 **Address:** 9105 Thorpe Rd 59718 **Location:** I-90 exit 298, 2.7 mi s on SR 85, 1 mi w on Valley Center Rd (gravel), then 0.5 mi s, follow signs. **Facility:** This angler's lodge offers a pond stocked with rainbow trout. Guest rooms feature gas fireplaces, Mission-style furniture and Tiffany-style lamps. The lodge is off the beaten path. 12 units. 2 stories (no elevator), interior/exterior corridors. **Parking:** winter plug-ins. **Terms:** 3 night minimum stay - seasonal, 7 day cancellation notice-fee imposed. **Dining:** Gallatin River Grill, see separate listing. **Activities:** fishing, massage.

🅰 🍴 🍸 📶 ⊠ 💻 / SOME UNITS 🆓

LA QUINTA INN & SUITES BELGRADE / BOZEMAN
(406)388-2222

▼▼▼ **Hotel** $72-$164 **Address:** 6445 Jackrabbit Ln 59714 Location: I-90 exit 298, just s on SR 85. **Facility:** 65 units, some efficiencies. 3 stories, interior corridors. **Parking:** winter plug-ins.
Pool(s): heated indoor. **Activities:** sauna, hot tub, exercise room.
Guest Services: coin laundry.

QUALITY INN
(406)388-0800

▼▼
Hotel
$69-$139

Address: 6261 Jackrabbit Ln 59714 Location: I-90 exit 298, just s on SR 85.
Facility: 67 units. 3 stories, interior corridors. **Parking:** winter plug-ins. **Activities:** exercise room. **Guest Services:**
coin laundry. **Featured Amenity: continental breakfast.**

SUPER 8-BELGRADE/BOZEMAN AIRPORT
(406)388-1493

▼▼ **Hotel** $70-$99 **Address:** 6450 Jackrabbit Ln 59714 Location: I-90 exit 298, just s on SR 85. **Facility:** 72 units. 4 stories, interior corridors. **Parking:** winter plug-ins. **Pool(s):** heated indoor.
Activities: hot tub, exercise room. **Guest Services:** coin laundry.

WHERE TO EAT

FIESTA MEXICANA
406/388-8887

▼▼ Mexican. Casual Dining. $8-$18 **AAA Inspector Notes:**
The homemade salsas, sauces (including my fave, chili verde),
beans and dips will transport you to Mexico. Heat levels are optional
and the staff will allow your choice for the sides on the platters. Wood
floors, comfy booth seats and Mexican décor add to the appeal.
Sister restaurants in Bozeman and Butte have the same menus. **Features:** beer & wine. **Address:** 6220 Jackrabbit Ln 59714 **Location:**
I-90 exit 298, just s. Ⓛ Ⓓ

GALLATIN RIVER GRILL
406/388-0148

▼▼▼ Regional American. Casual Dining. $22-$28 **AAA Inspector Notes:** Patrons find quality in the regional meats and fish
and in the creative preparations. Views of the surrounding mountains
from the casual dining room contribute to a Big Sky adventure. **Features:** full bar, patio dining. **Reservations:** suggested. **Address:**
9105 Thorpe Rd 59718 **Location:** I-90 exit 298, 2.7 mi s on SR 85,
1 mi w on Valley Center Rd (gravel), then 0.5 mi s, follow signs; in
Gallatin River Lodge. Ⓓ

MACKENZIE RIVER PIZZA
406/388-0016

▼▼ Pizza. Casual Dining. $8-$20 **AAA Inspector Notes:**
Known for its eclectic Western decor, the restaurant lets patrons
choose from several microbrews to accompany a specialty pizza or
large, innovative sandwich. Pizza crusts are wonderful and offer the
choice of sourdough, natural grain, deep dish or thin crust. **Features:**
beer & wine, patio dining. **Address:** 409 W Main St 59714 **Location:**
I-90 exit 298, 1 mi s, then just e. Ⓛ Ⓓ

RIO SABINAS SOUTHWESTERN GRILL
406/388-9200

▼▼ Southwestern. Casual Dining. $9-$20 **AAA Inspector
Notes:** The new concept restaurant from the owners of the highly
successful regional Rib and Chop House restaurants flavors dishes
with original sauces and homemade salsas. In the newly remodeled
Mercantile Building, the dining area features Western decor, beautiful
reclaimed wood beams and rough-hewn wood accents. **Features:**
full bar. **Address:** 11 W Main St 59714 **Location:** Jct Broadway;
center; in Belgrade Mercantile Building. **Parking:** street only.
Ⓓ CALL Ⓜ

THE WOK
406/388-2838

▼▼ Chinese. Casual Dining. $8-$13 **AAA Inspector Notes:**
Just like the owner's other location in Bozeman, the menu here offers
traditionally prepared cuisine. Set in a small strip mall on the west end
of town, with modern decor. **Features:** beer & wine. **Address:** 312 W
Main St, Suite B-10 59714 **Location:** I-90 exit 298, 1 mi n, then 0.5
mi w. Ⓛ Ⓓ

BIGFORK (B-2) pop. 4,270, elev. 2,968'

On the bay formed by the Swan River on the
northeastern shore of Flathead Lake, Bigfork once
was a small fishing village and trade center for
nearby orchards and farms. Its reputation as an artists' and writers' colony now makes it a popular cultural retreat. Among recreational pursuits are
snowmobiling and skiing in winter and a host of
water sports in summer.

Glacially formed Flathead Lake *(see place listing
p. 156)* is the largest natural body of fresh water
west of the Mississippi River; at points along its 38-
mile length the lake stretches 15 miles wide. Jewel
Basin, one of the country's most popular hiking
areas with 35 miles of trails, is 11 miles north. A Flathead National Forest *(see place listing p. 156)*
ranger station provides information about recreational opportunities in the nearby mountains.

Cultural highlights in Bigfork include the Riverbend Concert Series, which stages Sunday performances throughout the summer. From mid-May
through Labor Day, Bigfork Summer Playhouse
presents a regular repertory of Broadway musicals;
phone (406) 837-4886 for ticket information.

Bigfork Area Chamber of Commerce: 8155 Hwy.
35, P.O. Box 237, Bigfork, MT 59911. **Phone:** (406)
837-5888.

QUESTA SAIL BOAT departs from Bigfork 4. This
1929 restored 51-foot racing sloop offers 2-hour tours
on Flathead Lake. A sister ship is available in case the
Questa is filled. **Hours:** Tours depart daily at 1:30 and
7, mid-June to mid-Sept. **Cost:** Day fare $39; $32
(ages 0-11 and 65+). Sunset fare $44. Reservations
are recommended. **Phone:** (406) 837-5569.

BRIDGE STREET COTTAGES
(406)837-2785

▼▼▼
Cottage
$85-$295

Address: 309 Bridge St 59911 **Location:** Downtown. **Facility:** Unique cottages are set in a grove of mature trees
next to the Swan River and on the edge
of Bigfork Village. 12 cottages. 1 story,
exterior corridors. **Parking:** winter plug-
ins. **Terms:** 3 night minimum stay - seasonal and/or weekends, 30 day
cancellation notice-fee imposed, resort
fee. **Amenities:** safes.

MOUNTAIN LAKE LODGE (406)837-3800

▼▼▼▼

Hotel

$239-$285

Address: 14735 Sylvan Dr 59911 **Location:** On SR 35, 5 mi s. Located in a quiet area. **Facility:** 30 units, some kitchens. 1-3 stories (no elevator), exterior corridors. **Parking:** winter plug-ins. **Terms:** check-in 4 pm, 7 day cancellation notice-fee imposed. **Dining:** 2 restaurants. **Pool(s):** heated outdoor. **Activities:** hot tub, exercise room. **Guest Services:** coin laundry.

[SAVE] [❌] [☒] CALL [☒] [☒] [BIZ]
[☎] [🄳] [🄳] [🄳] / SOME UNITS [🄳]

TIMBERS MOTEL 406/837-6200

▼▼ ▼▼ **Motel.** Rates not provided. **Address:** 8540 Hwy 35 59911 **Location:** Just n on SR 35 from jct SR 209. **Facility:** 40 units. 2 stories (no elevator), exterior corridors. **Amenities:** safes. **Pool(s):** heated outdoor. **Activities:** sauna, hot tub.

[❌] [🄳] [☎] [🄳] [🄳] [🄳] / SOME UNITS [🄳]

WHERE TO EAT

ECHO LAKE CAFE 406/837-4252

▼▼ ▼▼ Breakfast. Casual Dining. $6-$10 **AAA Inspector Notes:** Always trust the locals. Based on a tip from a resident, I tried this café at the foothills of the Mission Mountains and was blown away by the high quality of ingredients. Fresh-squeezed orange juice, wagon-wheel-sized pancakes, real maple syrup, fresh fruits, oh, the list goes on and on. Voted number one for breakfasts in Flathead Valley, the café's lunches are excellent, too. It's very popular and extremely busy; your wait may be long as they do not accept reservations. **Features:** patio dining. **Address:** 1195 Swan Hwy (SR 83) 59911 **Location:** 2.7 mi w on SR 35, 2.1 mi e. [B] [L]

EL TOPO 406/837-2114

▼▼ ▼▼ Mexican. Casual Dining. $8-$15 **AAA Inspector Notes:** The wildly popular, lively gathering spot serves what many consider to be some of the area's best Mexican food. Fresh ingredients, careful preparation and friendly service are hallmarks. For a true taste treat, don't pass up the fish tacos. **Features:** full bar. **Address:** 7987 SR 35 59911 **Location:** On north end of town. [D]

MOSAIC 406/837-2923

▼▼ ▼▼ Fusion. Casual Dining. $8-$10 **AAA Inspector Notes:** This small bistro-style restaurant serves panini sandwiches, baguettes and wraps. Sit on the patio or at the custom-made mosaic-tiled bar to try one of their specialty cocktails. **Features:** full bar. **Reservations:** suggested. **Address:** 408 Bridge St 59911 **Location:** Downtown. **Parking:** street only. [L]

MOSAIC FRENCH DELI 406/837-2923

▼▼ French. Quick Serve. $6-$11 **AAA Inspector Notes:** Patrons can expect delicatessen-style service at this spot, which serves gourmet sandwiches, soups, quiches and fresh pastries for either take-out or eating on the new enclosed deck. **Features:** beer & wine. **Address:** 408 Bridge St 59911 **Location:** Downtown. **Parking:** street only. [L]

SHOWTHYME! 406/837-0707

▼▼ ▼▼ ▼▼ American. Fine Dining. $14-$28 **AAA Inspector Notes:** The top-notch staff treats every diner with special enthusiasm at this casual, fun eatery, where imaginative fare is the norm. Seasonal menus feature creative entrees and desserts, such as truffle torte on crème anglaise. Summer deck seating is available. **Features:** full bar, patio dining. **Reservations:** suggested. **Address:** 548 Electric Ave 59911 **Location:** Downtown. **Parking:** street only. [D]

WHEN IN ROME 406/837-7663

▼▼ ▼▼ Mediterranean Pizza. Casual Dining. $7-$23 **AAA Inspector Notes:** Pizza is their specialty, but you'll find some pasta dishes as well, including traditional lasagna. The homemade whole-wheat thin crust is topped with fresh meats and veggies, then baked Roman style for a light and crispy result. Gourmet panini sandwiches are the star at lunch. The chef recently won a pizza competition in Las Vegas, so the word's out. This is a very popular place and a reservation is a must. A sister restaurant in Kalispell is open for lunch also. **Features:** beer & wine, patio dining. **Reservations:** suggested. **Address:** 8270 Hwy 35 59911 **Location:** 1 mi n on SR 35 from jct SR 209. [D]

BIG HOLE NATIONAL BATTLEFIELD (E-2)

Big Hole National Battlefield is 10 miles west of Wisdom on SR 43. Covering 655 acres of Nez Perce National Historical Park *(see place listing in Idaho p. 85)*, the site commemorates the battle fought Aug. 9-10, 1877, when U.S. troops aided by civilian volunteers staged a surprise attack against several bands of Nez Perce Indians. The Nez Perce were attempting to escape confinement to a reservation by fleeing to Idaho Territory.

Although victorious at Big Hole, the Nez Perce sustained severe losses—approximately 90 men, women and children were killed. These losses forced their surrender 2 months later on Oct. 5, 1877, in the Bear Paw Mountains. Some 250 Nez Perce escaped to Canada.

The battlefield became a military reserve in 1883, a national monument in 1910 and a national battlefield in 1963. The visitor center displays Native American and military items and presents an audio-visual program about the battle. An observation deck features scopes for wildlife viewing. Interpretive trails traverse the battlefield to the areas where the soldiers retreated and the Nez Perce camped.

Allow 30 minutes minimum for the visitor center and 1 hour, 30 minutes for the battlefield. Battlefield open daily dawn-dusk. Visitor center open daily 9-5, mid-May through Sept. 30; 10-5, rest of year. A hands-on tipi-raising session takes place daily at 10, and guided tours are offered daily, June-Aug. Visitor center closed Jan. 1, Martin Luther King Jr. Day, Presidents Day, Columbus Day, Veterans Day, Thanksgiving and Christmas. Battlefield Road is closed to automobile traffic in winter; skiing and snowshoeing are permitted. Free. Phone (406) 689-3155.

BIGHORN CANYON NATIONAL RECREATION AREA (E-6)

In Montana and northern Wyoming, Bighorn Canyon National Recreation Area centers on a 71-mile-long lake bounded by steep canyon walls. Covering about 120,000 acres, the area features facilities for boat launching, picnicking and camping at Ok-A-Beh Marina, 42 miles southwest of Hardin via SR 313.

Horseshoe Bend in Wyoming, 14 miles north of Lovell, Wyo., via SR 37, and Barry's Landing in Montana, 32 miles south of Yellowtail Dam by boat or north of Lovell via SR 37, have areas for swimming, camping, picnicking and boat launching (personal watercraft are permitted). Hunting and fishing also are available.

Admission to the recreation area is $5 for a daily pass. Yellowtail Dam Visitor Center in Fort Smith offers an orientation film about the area as well as exhibits about wildlife, Native American culture and the construction of Yellowtail Dam, said to be the highest dam in the Missouri River Basin. The center is open daily 9-5, Memorial Day-late September. Phone (406) 666-3218.

The Bighorn Canyon Visitor Center, at the junction of US 310 and US 14A in Lovell is open daily 8-6, Memorial Day-Labor Day; 8:30-4:30, rest of year. Closed Jan. 1, Thanksgiving and Christmas. Phone (307) 548-5406.

For further information, contact Bighorn Canyon National Recreation Area, P.O. Box 7458, Fort Smith, MT 59035 or 20 US 14A E., Lovell, WY 82431; to verify schedule phone (406) 666-2412 or (307) 548-5406. *See Recreation Areas Chart.*

BIG SKY (E-3) pop. 2,308
- **Hotels & Restaurants map & index p. 336**
- **Part of Yellowstone National Park area — see map p. 326**

Surrounded by the mountain meadows and forested slopes of Gallatin National Forest *(see place listing p. 159)* and the Spanish Peaks Wilderness, Big Sky is an all-year resort community. Lone Mountain serves as the centerpiece for this village conceived and developed by newsman Chet Huntley.

Skiing and snowmobiling are popular in winter, while summer activity revolves around hiking, horseback riding, white-water rafting and mountain biking.

RECREATIONAL ACTIVITIES
Skiing
- **Big Sky Resort** is at 150 Big Sky Resort Rd. Other activities are offered. **Hours:** Skiing is available daily mid-Nov. to late Apr. Hours vary; phone ahead. **Phone:** (406) 995-5000 or (800) 548-4486.

BUCK'S T-4 LODGE   (406)995-4111 (9)
▼▼ ▼ **Hotel** $129-$169 **Address:** 46625 Gallatin Rd 59716 **Location:** US 191, 1 mi s of Big Sky entrance. **Facility:** 72 units, some two bedrooms and efficiencies. 2 stories (no elevator), interior/exterior corridors. **Parking:** winter plug-ins. **Terms:** closed 4/16-5/27 & 10/6-11/25, check-in 4 pm, 7 day cancellation notice. **Dining:** Buck's T-4, see separate listing. **Activities:** hot tub, fishing, cross country skiing, snowmobiling, game room.
[icons]

THE LODGE AT BIG SKY   (406)995-7858 (8)
▼▼▼ **Hotel** $130-$320 **Address:** 75 Sitting Bull Ln 59716 **Location:** Jct US 191 and SR 64, 9 mi w on SR 64. Located in Big Sky Mountain Village. **Facility:** 90 units, some efficiencies. 4 stories, interior corridors. **Parking:** winter plug-ins. **Terms:** closed 10/1-12/15, check-in 4 pm, 30 day cancellation notice-fee imposed. **Pool(s):** heated indoor. **Activities:** hot tub, game room, exercise room. **Guest Services:** coin laundry, area transportation.
[icons]

RAINBOW RANCH LODGE   (406)995-4132 (10)
▼▼▼▼ **Resort Hotel** $150-$450 **Address:** 42950 Gallatin Rd 59730 **Location:** 5 mi s on US 191. Located on Gallatin River. **Facility:** In the Gallatin National Forest, this riverside property offers relaxation and an infinity hot tub on the deck. 21 units, some two bedrooms. 2 stories, exterior corridors. **Parking:** winter plug-ins. **Terms:** 14 day cancellation notice. **Dining:** restaurant, see separate listing. **Activities:** hot tub, fishing, massage.
[icons]

WHERE TO EAT

BUCK'S T-4   406/993-5222 (6)
▼▼▼ Regional American. Fine Dining. $24-$32 **AAA Inspector Notes:** Such features as a warm, comfy blaze in the stone hearth, game trophies, wildlife pictures and welcoming staff members might make guests feel like lords of a country estate. The chef creates beautiful and delicious meals featuring wild game and other regional delectables. More than 140 wines are on the award-winning list. **Features:** full bar. **Reservations:** suggested. **Address:** 46225 Gallatin Rd 59716 **Location:** US 191, 1 mi s of Big Sky entrance; in Buck's T-4 Lodge. [icons]

THE CABIN BAR & GRILL   406/995-4244 (4)
▼▼▼ Regional American. Casual Dining. $10-$38 **AAA Inspector Notes:** After a day on the slopes, snow lovers can stop in for an après-ski snack, but it's well worth the trip to come back for a delicious, creatively prepared dinner. The varied menu focuses on regional cuisine. The Cabin is open only for dinner during the summer months. **Features:** full bar. **Address:** Big Sky's Mountain Village 59716 **Location:** Jct US 191 and SR 64; 9 mi w on SR 64; in Big Sky Resort, 3rd floor of Arrowhead Mall. [icons]

THE CORRAL STEAKHOUSE   406/995-4249 (7)
▼▼ ▼
Steak
Casual Dining
$9-$35
AAA Inspector Notes: This local favorite serves comfort good in a rustic Western setting, replete with mounted heads, posters and pictures of the old days. The dining room and lounge are in a large wood-accented room. **Features:** full bar. **Address:** 42895 Gallatin Rd 59730 **Location:** 5 mi s on US 191. [icons]

LOTUS PAD   406/995-2728 (5)
▼▼ ▼ Thai. Casual Dining. $14-$20 **AAA Inspector Notes:** The owners have tried to replicate the street foods of Thailand, and for the most part have succeeded. Variations of well known dishes include the larb (a spicy mixture of meat wrapped in a lettuce leaf), known here as "larp" and spiced a bit differently than the traditional dish; I was expecting meat marinated in lime juice. This version was still quite good. An open kitchen dominates the dining area, which only has six tables. There's also counter seating. **Features:** full bar. **Reservations:** required. **Address:** 3090 Pine Dr 59716 **Location:** Jct US 191 and SR 64 (Lone Mountain Tr), 3 mi w on SR 64, just s. [icons]

RAINBOW RANCH LODGE   406/995-4132 (8)
▼▼▼ Regional American. Fine Dining. $23-$41 **AAA Inspector Notes:** Patrons can enjoy the view of the Gallatin River and surrounding mountains of Big Sky while dining on expertly prepared gourmet cuisine. The chef always has special offerings that focus on regional favorites and wild game. Choices on the extensive award-winning wine list will complement a wide selection of meals. **Features:** full bar, patio dining, happy hour. **Reservations:** suggested. **Address:** 42950 Gallatin Rd 59736 **Location:** 5 mi s on US 191. [icons]

BIG TIMBER (E-4) pop. 1,641, elev. 4,075'

BIG TIMBER WATERSLIDE is 9 mi. e.; take I-90 exit 377 then e. .2 mi. on Frontage Rd. Seven large waterslides, a Junior Olympic-size pool, wading pools and a moat featuring a lazy river ride are some of the amusements offered. **Hours:** Daily 10-6, early June-Labor Day. **Cost:** $15.95; $11.95 (ages 4-12). After 3 p.m. $12.95; $9.95 (ages 4-12). **Phone:** (406) 932-6570 in season. 🍽 🎡

CRAZY MOUNTAIN MUSEUM is off I-90 exit 367, s. to Frontage Rd., then e. to Cemetery Rd. Displays relate the history of the Sweet Grass area. Featured are a one-room schoolhouse; a Norwegian *stabbur* (storehouse); a model of the area as it appeared in 1907; a 1915 Ford; paintings by Jessica Zemsky and Jack Hines; photographs; printed history and memorabilia from the 1900s; and displays about the Leo Cremer Rodeo, Meriwether Lewis and William Clark, and archeology. Changing exhibits also are offered. **Hours:** Mon.-Sat. 10-4:30, Sun. 1-4:30, Memorial Day-Oct. 31. Phone ahead to confirm schedule. **Cost:** Donations. **Phone:** (406) 932-5126.

BIG TIMBER SUPER 8   (406)932-8888
🚩🚩 Hotel $84-$109 **Address:** 20A Big Timber Loop Rd 59011 **Location:** I-90 exit 367. **Facility:** 41 units. 2 stories (no elevator), interior corridors. **Parking:** winter plug-ins. **Guest Services:** coin laundry.
📶➕ CALL 📠 BIZ 📶 🍴 ☕ /SOME UNITS 📶 HS 📷

RIVER VALLEY INN   (406)932-4943
🚩 Hotel $68-$100 **Address:** 600 W 2nd St 59011 **Location:** I-90 exit 367, just n, then 0.6 mi e. **Facility:** 22 units. 2 stories (no elevator), interior corridors. **Parking:** winter plug-ins. **Terms:** closed 12/26-3/1. ✈ 📶 /SOME UNITS 📶 🍴

WHERE TO EAT

THE GRAND   406/932-4459
🚩🚩 Regional American. Casual Dining. $9-$31 **AAA Inspector Notes:** *Historic.* "Offering beautiful accommodations, fine dining and spirits to travelers, fishermen, cowboys and sheepherders since 1890." The motto says it all. Listed on the National Register of Historic Places, The Grand Hotel has been restored to her original state, showcasing wood accents that highlight the Western décor. The restaurant serves locally raised beef and lamb and fresh seafood flown in daily. An inexpensive menu is offered in the 1890 Saloon. Lunch is not served on Saturday. **Features:** full bar, Sunday brunch. **Address:** 139 McLeod St 59011 **Location:** Jct E 2nd Ave. **Parking:** street only. L D CALL 📠

BILLINGS (E-5) pop. 104,170, elev. 3,124'
• Hotels p. 135 • Restaurants p. 139

In 1823 at Alkali Creek, the site of present-day Billings, 400 Blackfeet attacked American Fur Co. trappers. Some pelts taken by the Blackfeet were traded to Hudson's Bay Co. and later appeared on the London market. An American recognized the stolen pelts, touching off an international incident.

The Northern Pacific Railroad arrived in 1882, literally putting Billings on the map. Refusing to pay the exorbitant prices the landowners in Coulson were demanding, Northern Pacific Railroad laid out a new city 2 miles upriver and named it in honor of its president, Frederick Billings. In 5 months the town grew from a single building to 250 buildings and 2,000 citizens.

The Rimrocks, Billings' most striking natural feature, rise 500 feet above the Yellowstone Valley, running the length of the city and beyond. Legend has it that Crow warriors once rode over Sacrifice Cliff to appease their gods and to halt the spread of smallpox among their people. At the bottom of Chief Black Otter Trail is Boothill Cemetery. The only vestige of the town of Coulson, the cemetery is the final resting place of two dozen individuals, including peace officers, massacre victims and Muggins Taylor, the scout who brought the world the news of Lt. Col. George Armstrong Custer's last stand.

Pictograph Cave State Park, 7 miles southeast at the I-90 Lockwood exit, features caverns that have sheltered people of many Native American cultures. Pictorial records adorn the walls of one cave.

🚩 MontanaFair is a 9-day agricultural celebration beginning the second week in August. Exhibits, music, food, entertainment, a carnival and petting zoo add to the experience. One of the region's largest events, the fair is held annually in MetraPark.

Billings Chamber of Commerce/Convention and Visitors Bureau: 815 S. 27th St., P.O. Box 31177, Billings, MT 59107-1177. **Phone:** (406) 252-4016 or (800) 735-2635.

Self-guiding tours: A map of historic sites can be obtained at the chamber of commerce.

Shopping areas: Rimrock Mall, at the junction of Central Avenue and 24th Street West, includes Dillard's and JCPenney among its 95 stores.

CHIEF BLACK OTTER TRAIL follows the edge of the Rimrocks north of the city. Swords Park, the area along the Rimrocks from Billings Logan International Airport to Boothill Cemetery, includes the unmarked grave of Crow Indian Chief Black Otter, who was killed in a battle with the Sioux. Yellowstone Kelly, renowned army scout, explorer and frontiersman, also is buried along the route. While the road is difficult to traverse, some of the best views of Sacrifice Cliff can be had here.

Range Rider of the Yellowstone stands at the entrance of Billings Logan International Airport. Cowboy motion picture star William S. Hart posed for this bronze statue of a cowboy and his horse.

MONTANA FUN ADVENTURES TOURS departs the Moss Mansion at 914 Division Ave. for downtown tours, and picks up passengers at area hotels and campgrounds for other tours. Among the trips offered are the 2-hour Historic Billings tour highlighting local landmarks and a narrated 3-hour tour tracing Meriwether Lewis' and William Clark's route along the Yellowstone River to Pompeys Pillar National Monument. A 6-hour trip to Little Bighorn Battlefield also is available. A jeep tour featuring wild mustangs also is offered.

Time: Allow 2 hours minimum. **Hours:** Historic Billings tour departs Mon.-Sat. at 11 and 7 p.m., Sun. at 2, June 1-Sept. 1; by request rest of year. Lewis and Clark tour departs daily at 7:30 and 5:30, Apr.-Sept. Little Bighorn tour departs daily at 8:30 and 5:30, June-Sept.; daily at 8:30 rest of year. **Cost:** Historic Billings tour $25; $35 (with hotel pickup). Lewis and Clark tour $65. Little Bighorn tour $152.50. Reservations are required. **Phone:** (406) 254-7180.

MOSS MANSION is at 914 Division St. An Old World-style house designed by architect H.J. Hardenbergh, this massive red sandstone mansion completed in 1903 features an eclectic decor with original carpet and drapes, ornate ceilings and handmade light fixtures. The Moss family occupied the house until 1984 and left the interior intact. The three-story mansion is an unusually complete example of early 20th-century decorative arts.

Hours: Guided 1-hour tours are given on the hour Tues.-Sat. 10-3, Sun. 1-3, Memorial Day-Labor Day; Tues.-Sun. 1-3, rest of year. Closed Jan. 1, Easter, July 4, second week in Nov., Thanksgiving and Christmas. Last tour begins at closing. **Cost:** $10; $7 (ages 62+ and military with ID); $6 (ages 6-17). **Phone:** (406) 256-5100 to confirm schedule.

PETER YEGEN JR. YELLOWSTONE COUNTY MUSEUM is at 1950 Terminal Cir., across from Billings Logan International Airport. Exhibits depict the history of Montana and the northern Plains, including the arrival of Meriwether Lewis and William Clark. More than 20,000 artifacts relate to the military, the railroad, Native Americans and the history of the Yellowstone area. **Time:** Allow 30 minutes minimum. **Hours:** Tues.-Sat. 10:30-5:30. Closed Jan. 1, Thanksgiving and Christmas. **Cost:** Donations. **Phone:** (406) 256-6811.

WESTERN HERITAGE CENTER, at 2822 Montana Ave. in the historic 1901 Parmly Billings Library Building, features changing exhibits about the history and culture of the Yellowstone Valley region. Audiovisual programs are presented regularly. **Time:** Allow 1 hour minimum. **Hours:** Tues.-Sat. 10-5. Closed major holidays. **Cost:** $5; $3 (ages 55+ and students with ID); $1 (ages 6-11). **Phone:** (406) 256-6809.

SAVE **YELLOWSTONE ART MUSEUM** is at 401 N. 27th St. Housed in the original Yellowstone County jail, the museum offers changing exhibitions of historic and contemporary art. Boundless Visions tells the story of art in Montana with interactive exhibits and works from the permanent collection. Guided tours are available by appointment. **Time:** Allow 30 minutes minimum. **Hours:** Tues.-Sat. 11-5 (also Thurs.-Fri. 5-8 p.m.), Sun. 11-4. **Cost:** $6; $4 (ages 65+); $3 (ages 6-18 and college students with ID); $12 (family, two adults and three children). **Phone:** (406) 256-6804.

ZOOMONTANA is off I-90 exit 443, .9 mi. w. on Zoo Dr., then just s. to 2100 S. Shiloh Rd. This 72-acre site is home to northern latitude temperate creatures. Eagles, grizzly bears, otters, deer, red pandas, Siberian tigers, wolves and river otters can be seen. Also featured are various gardens, an amphitheater and a playground.

Time: Allow 1 hour minimum. **Hours:** Daily 10-4, May 1-Oct. 1; 10-2, rest of year. The zoo may be closed due to inclement weather during fall and winter. Closed Thanksgiving and Christmas. Phone ahead to confirm schedule. **Cost:** $7; $5 (ages 65+ and military with ID); $4 (ages 3-15). **Phone:** (406) 652-8100.

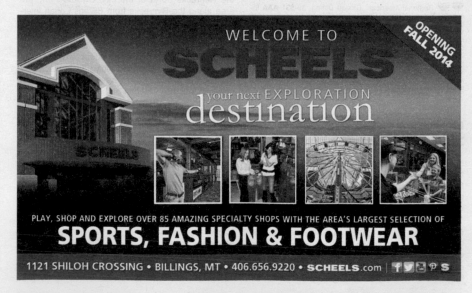

BEST WESTERN PLUS CLOCKTOWER INN

(406)259-5511

Hotel
$100-$180

Best Western PLUS

AAA Benefit: Members save 10% or more with Best Western!

Address: 2511 1st Ave N 59101 **Location:** On I-90 business loop; downtown. **Facility:** 126 units, some kitchens. 1-3 stories, interior/exterior corridors. **Parking:** winter plug-ins. **Pool(s):** heated outdoor. **Activities:** sauna, exercise room. **Guest Services:** valet and coin laundry.

BEST WESTERN PLUS KELLY INN & SUITES

(406)256-9400

Hotel
$120-$170

Best Western PLUS

AAA Benefit: Members save 10% or more with Best Western!

Address: 4915 Southgate Dr 59101 **Location:** I-90 exit 447, just w. Across from family fun park. **Facility:** 89 units. 3 stories, interior/exterior corridors. **Parking:** winter plug-ins. **Pool(s):** heated indoor. **Activities:** exercise room. **Guest Services:** valet and coin laundry. **Featured Amenity:** continental breakfast.

BIG HORN RESORT, AN ASCEND HOTEL COLLECTION MEMBER

(406)839-9300

Hotel $129-$275 **Address:** 1801 Majestic Ln 59102 **Location:** I-90 exit 443 (Zoo Dr), just n, then just s. Adjacent to Big Horn Resort Water Park. **Facility:** 108 units. 3 stories, interior corridors. **Parking:** winter plug-ins. **Amenities:** video games, safes. **Activities:** hot tub, game room, exercise room, massage. **Guest Services:** valet and coin laundry, area transportation.

BILLINGS INN BY RIVERSAGE (406)252-6800

Hotel
$85-$95

Address: 880 N 29th St 59101 **Location:** I-90 exit 450, 2 mi n on 27th St, then just w on 9th Ave. Across from Deaconess Hospital. **Facility:** 59 units. 4 stories, interior corridors. **Parking:** winter plug-ins. **Terms:** cancellation fee imposed, resort fee. **Activities:** exercise room. **Guest Services:** valet and coin laundry. **Featured Amenity: continental breakfast.** *(See ad p. 135.)*

BOOTHILL INN & SUITES (406)245-2000

Hotel
$93-$145

Address: 242 E Airport Rd 59105 **Location:** I-90 exit 452, 1.8 mi n on US 87. **Facility:** 69 units. 4 stories, interior corridors. **Terms:** cancellation fee imposed. **Pool(s):** heated indoor. **Activities:** hot tub, exercise room. **Guest Services:** coin laundry, area transportation. **Featured Amenity: full hot breakfast.**

BILLINGS SUPER 8 (406)248-8842

Hotel
$79-$89

Address: 5400 Southgate Dr 59102 **Location:** I-90 exit 447, just n on S Billings Blvd, 0.8 mi w on King Ave, then just s on Parkway Ln. **Facility:** 106 units. 3 stories, interior corridors. **Parking:** winter plug-ins. **Amenities:** safes. **Activities:** exercise room. **Guest Services:** coin laundry.

CHERRY TREE INN (406)252-5603

Hotel
$73-$76

Address: 823 N Broadway 59101 **Location:** I-90 exit 450, 2 mi n on 27th St, then just w on 9th Ave. Opposite Deaconess Hospital. **Facility:** 65 units, some two bedrooms, efficiencies and kitchens. 2 stories, interior corridors. **Parking:** winter plug-ins. **Activities:** sauna, limited exercise equipment. **Guest Services:** valet and coin laundry. **Featured Amenity: continental breakfast.** *(See ad this page.)*

C'MON INN
(406)655-1100

Hotel
$115-$135

Address: 2020 Overland Ave 59102 **Location:** I-90 exit 446, 0.5 mi n, then just s. **Facility:** 82 units. 2 stories (no elevator), interior corridors. **Parking:** winter plug-ins. **Terms:** cancellation fee imposed. **Pool(s):** heated indoor. **Activities:** hot tub, game room, exercise room. **Guest Services:** valet and coin laundry. **Featured Amenity:** full hot breakfast.

COMFORT INN BY CHOICE HOTELS
(406)652-5200

Hotel $110-$140 **Address:** 2030 Overland Ave 59102 **Location:** I-90 exit 446, 0.5 mi n, then just s. **Facility:** 60 units. 2 stories (no elevator), interior corridors. **Parking:** winter plug-ins. **Pool(s):** heated indoor. **Activities:** hot tub. **Guest Services:** valet laundry.

COUNTRY INN & SUITES BY CARLSON, BILLINGS AT METRA PARK
(406)245-9995

Hotel
$120-$220

Address: 231 Main St 59105 **Location:** I-90 exit 452, 2 mi n, then follow Metra signs. **Facility:** 67 units. 3 stories, interior corridors. **Pool(s):** heated indoor. **Activities:** hot tub, exercise room. **Guest Services:** valet and coin laundry. **Featured Amenity:** breakfast buffet.

CROWNE PLAZA
(406)252-7400

Hotel
$119-$499

Address: 27 N 27th St 59101 **Location:** I-90 business loop and SR 3. **Facility:** 289 units. 23 stories, interior corridors. **Terms:** cancellation fee imposed. **Activities:** exercise room. **Guest Services:** valet and coin laundry, luggage security pick-up, area transportation.

DAYS INN
(406)252-4007

Hotel $73-$125 **Address:** 843 Parkway Ln 59101 **Location:** I-90 exit 447, just n on S Billings Blvd, 0.8 mi w on King Ave, then just s. **Facility:** 61 units. 2 stories (no elevator), interior corridors. **Parking:** winter plug-ins. **Activities:** hot tub. **Guest Services:** coin laundry.

ECONO LODGE
(406)252-2700

Hotel $80-$140 **Address:** 5425 Midland Rd 59101 **Location:** I-90 exit 446, just se. **Facility:** 86 units. 2 stories (no elevator), interior/exterior corridors. **Parking:** winter plug-ins. **Pool(s):** heated outdoor. **Activities:** hot tub. **Guest Services:** coin laundry.

EXTENDED STAY AMERICA-BILLINGS-WEST END
(406)245-3980

Extended Stay Hotel $65-$105 **Address:** 4950 Southgate Dr 59101 **Location:** I-90 exit 447, just w. **Facility:** 104 efficiencies. 3 stories, interior corridors. **Parking:** winter plug-ins. **Terms:** cancellation fee imposed. **Guest Services:** coin laundry.

FAIRFIELD INN & SUITES BY MARRIOTT-BILLINGS
(406)652-5330

Hotel $109-$159 **Address:** 2026 Overland Ave 59102 **Location:** I-90 exit 446, 0.5 mi n, then just s. **Facility:** 60 units. 3 stories, interior corridors. **Parking:** winter plug-ins. **Pool(s):** heated indoor. **Activities:** hot tub, exercise room. **Guest Services:** valet and coin laundry.

AAA Benefit: Members save 5% or more!

HAMPTON INN
(406)248-4949

Hotel $109-$169 **Address:** 5110 Southgate Dr 59101 **Location:** I-90 exit 447, just w. **Facility:** 120 units, some efficiencies. 4 stories, interior corridors. **Parking:** winter plug-ins. **Terms:** check-in 4 pm, 1-7 night minimum stay, cancellation fee imposed. **Amenities:** video games. **Pool(s):** heated indoor. **Activities:** hot tub, exercise room. **Guest Services:** valet and coin laundry.

AAA Benefit: Members save up to 10%!

HAMPTON INN & SUITES
(406)656-7511

Hotel $109-$149 **Address:** 3550 Ember Ln 59102 **Location:** I-90 exit 443 (Zoo Dr), just n. **Facility:** 101 units. 4 stories, interior corridors. **Parking:** winter plug-ins. **Terms:** check-in 4 pm, 1-7 night minimum stay, cancellation fee imposed. **Pool(s):** heated indoor. **Activities:** hot tub, exercise room. **Guest Services:** valet and coin laundry.

AAA Benefit: Members save up to 10%!

HILLTOP INN BY RIVERSAGE
(406)245-5000

Hotel
$85-$95

Address: 1116 N 28th St 59101 **Location:** I-90 exit 450, 2 mi n on 27th St, just w on 11th Ave, then just n. Adjacent to St. Vincent Hospital. **Facility:** 56 units. 3 stories, interior corridors. **Parking:** winter plug-ins. **Terms:** cancellation fee imposed, resort fee. **Activities:** exercise room. **Guest Services:** valet and coin laundry. **Featured Amenity:** continental breakfast. (See ad p. 138.)

HILTON GARDEN INN BILLINGS
(406)655-8800

Hotel $109-$189

AAA Benefit: Members save up to 10%!

Address: 2465 Grant Rd 59102 **Location:** I-90 exit 446, 1.5 mi w, just s on S 24th St W, then just w. **Facility:** 128 units. 5 stories, interior corridors. **Parking:** winter plug-ins. **Terms:** 1-7 night minimum stay, cancellation fee imposed. **Pool(s):** heated indoor. **Activities:** hot tub, exercise room. **Guest Services:** valet and coin laundry.

HOLIDAY INN EXPRESS BILLINGS   (406)259-8600
▼▼▼ **Hotel** $119-$179 **Address:** 430 Cole St 59101 **Location:** I-90 exit 455, just s, then just e. **Facility:** 66 units. 3 stories, interior corridors. **Parking:** winter plug-ins. **Pool(s):** heated indoor. **Activities:** hot tub, exercise room. **Guest Services:** valet laundry.

HOLIDAY INN GRAND MONTANA BILLINGS
(406)248-7701
▼▼▼
Hotel
$119-$149
Address: 5500 Midland Rd 59101 **Location:** I-90 exit 446. **Facility:** 316 units. 7 stories, interior corridors. **Parking:** winter plug-ins. **Terms:** check-in 4 pm, cancellation fee imposed, resort fee. **Amenities:** video games. **Pool(s):** heated indoor. **Activities:** sauna, hot tub, exercise room. **Guest Services:** valet and coin laundry.

KELLY INN   406/248-9800
▼▼ **Hotel.** Rates not provided. **Address:** 5610 S Frontage Rd 59101 **Location:** I-90 exit 446, just s. **Facility:** 80 units. 3 stories, interior/exterior corridors. **Parking:** winter plug-ins. **Pool(s):** heated indoor. **Activities:** hot tub, exercise room. **Guest Services:** valet and coin laundry.

LEXINGTON INN & SUITES   (406)294-9090
▼▼▼ **Hotel** $109-$169 **Address:** 3040 King Ave W 59102 **Location:** I-90 exit 446, 3 mi n. **Facility:** 87 units. 4 stories, interior corridors. **Parking:** winter plug-ins. **Terms:** check-in 4 pm, resort fee. **Pool(s):** heated indoor. **Activities:** hot tub, exercise room. **Guest Services:** valet and coin laundry.

MOTEL 6 #1150 BILLINGS NORTH   (406)248-7551
▼ **Motel** $71-$81 **Address:** 5353 Midland Rd 59102 **Location:** I-90 exit 446, just se. **Facility:** 116 units. 2 stories (no elevator), interior corridors. **Parking:** winter plug-ins. **Pool(s):** heated indoor. **Guest Services:** coin laundry.

MOTEL 6 #178 BILLINGS SOUTH   (406)252-0093
▼ **Motel** $55-$75 **Address:** 5400 Midland Rd 59101 **Location:** I-90 exit 446, just se. **Facility:** 99 units. 2 stories (no elevator), exterior corridors. *Bath:* shower only. **Guest Services:** coin laundry.

QUALITY INN HOMESTEAD   (406)652-1320
▼▼ **Hotel** $79-$129 **Address:** 2036 Overland Ave 59102 **Location:** I-90 exit 446, 0.5 mi n, then just s. **Facility:** 119 units. 2 stories (no elevator), interior corridors. **Parking:** winter plug-ins. **Amenities:** safes. **Pool(s):** heated indoor. **Activities:** sauna, hot tub. **Guest Services:** valet and coin laundry.

▼ See AAA listing p. 137 ▼

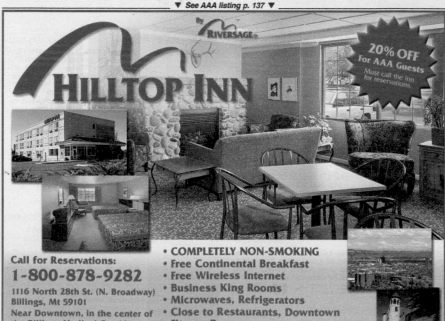

RESIDENCE INN BY MARRIOTT
(406)656-3900

Extended Stay Hotel
$149-$279

AAA Benefit: Members save 5% or more!

Address: 956 S 25th St W 59102 **Location:** I-90 exit 446, 1.5 mi w, just s on S 24th St, then just s; behind Home Depot. **Facility:** 92 kitchen units, some two bedrooms. 4 stories, interior corridors. **Parking:** winter plug-ins. **Pool(s):** heated indoor. **Activities:** hot tub, exercise room. **Guest Services:** valet and coin laundry. **Featured Amenity:** breakfast buffet.

WESTERN EXECUTIVE INN
406/294-8888

Hotel
$80-$210

Address: 3121 King Ave W 59102 **Location:** I-90 exit 446, 2.5 mi w. **Facility:** 40 units, some kitchens. 2 stories (no elevator), interior corridors. **Parking:** winter plug-ins. **Terms:** cancellation fee imposed. **Guest Services:** valet laundry. **Featured Amenity:** full hot breakfast.

WESTWOOD'S RIMVIEW INN
406/240-2022

Motel
Rates not provided

Address: 1025 N 27th St 59101 **Location:** I-90 exit 450, 2 mi n. **Facility:** 54 units, some efficiencies. 3 stories (no elevator), interior/exterior corridors. **Parking:** winter plug-ins. **Guest Services:** coin laundry, area transportation. **Featured Amenity:** continental breakfast.

WHERE TO EAT

THE ATHENIAN RESTAURANT
406/248-5681

Greek. Casual Dining. $6-$25 **AAA Inspector Notes:** The family-run restaurant entices guests with the chef/owner's dishes, which combine spices, feta cheese, olives and cooking wines imported from Greece. **Features:** wine only. **Address:** 18 N 29th St 59101 **Location:** Between Montana Ave (I-90 business route) and 1st Ave N; downtown. **Parking:** street only.

BISTRO ENZO
406/651-0999

Mediterranean. Casual Dining. $10-$28 **AAA Inspector Notes:** The menu at this bistro includes an array of delicious pasta, sandwiches and meats prepared with a European flair. There is a daily special of fish, pork and beef. Try a warm chocolate popover for dessert. **Features:** beer & wine. **Reservations:** suggested. **Address:** 1502 Rehberg Ln 59102 **Location:** West side of town; jct Grand Ave.

BRUNO'S A TASTE OF ITALY
406/652-4416

Italian. Casual Dining. $8-$18 **AAA Inspector Notes:** In the mood for something authentic? Head to this newly constructed, Italian villa-style eatery for traditional favorites. Enjoy homemade pastas and sauces and hand-rolled meatballs. Even the sausage is prepared in house. **Features:** beer & wine. **Address:** 1911 King Ave W 59101 **Location:** I-90 exit 446, after overpass, then just e on Carbon St; in King Ave West Plaza.

CAFÉ DECAMP
406/256-7285

Regional American. Casual Dining. $7-$26 **AAA Inspector Notes:** The name loosely means, in French, "to take leave." The chef-owner makes an effort to depart from conventional creations and the results are delectable. Savory or sweet crêpes filled with such items as home-cured pork belly or port-poached figs are just a few scrumptious choices. This is a true farm-to-table café, and by purchasing regionally the owner supports local ranches and farmers. **Features:** full bar. **Address:** 2905 Montana Ave N 59101 **Location:** Between N 29th and 30th sts; downtown.

CHAM THAI CUISINE
406/256-1812

Thai. Casual Dining. $8-$13 **AAA Inspector Notes:** The décor isn't much, but the food is classic. The fresh spices make the food pop. There also are some Chinese dishes. A buffet is offered on Fridays. **Address:** 2916 1st Ave N 59101 **Location:** Between 29th and 30th sts; downtown. **Parking:** street only.

CIAO MAMBO
406/325-5100

Italian. Casual Dining. $11-$28 **AAA Inspector Notes:** Just like its sister restaurants in Whitefish and Missoula, Mont., and Spokane Wash., this family-owned place serves traditional and inventive dishes in casual and comfortable surroundings. This location is in a converted warehouse. The marinara, with slivers of garlic, is fragrant and delicious. Have a seat at the counter and watch the chefs hand toss your pizza. **Features:** full bar. **Reservations:** required. **Address:** 2301 Montana Ave 59101 **Location:** Jct N 23rd St, downtown; across from historic Billings Depot. **Parking:** street only.

C J'S BAR & GRILL
406/656-1400

American. Casual Dining. $10-$29 **AAA Inspector Notes:** Diners enjoy a great selection of ribs, steaks and seafood cooked over mesquite, oak and apple wood and served in a relaxed, contemporary atmosphere. The service is pleasant and prompt. The nice lounge area has a fireplace and leather couches. **Features:** full bar. **Reservations:** suggested. **Address:** 2455 Central Ave 59102 **Location:** I-90 exit 446, 1 mi w on King Ave, 1 mi n on 24th St, 0.3 mi w, then just n at light.

DOS MACHOS RESTAURANT
406/652-2020

Mexican. Casual Dining. $10-$16 **AAA Inspector Notes:** In business for 30 years, the popular restaurant is known for its large Mexican/American menu, which lists sizzling fajitas, San Lucas scampi and an 8-ounce top sirloin. **Features:** full bar. **Address:** 980 S 24th St W 59102 **Location:** I-90 exit 446, 1.3 mi nw on King Ave, then just s.

GOLDEN PHOENIX RESTAURANT
406/256-8319

Chinese. Casual Dining. $8-$22 **AAA Inspector Notes:** The décor is pretty typical of most Chinese restaurants with large tanks of koi, colorful lanterns and Chinese art in a large dining area. Food is consistently tasty. The family-run establishment is in a standalone building. A lunch buffet is offered on weekdays. **Features:** beer & wine. **Address:** 279 Swords Ln 59105 **Location:** I-90 exit 452, 2 mi n, follow Metra signs; jct Main St and Airport Rd.

JAKE'S BAR & GRILL
406/252-9375

American. Casual Dining. $9-$29 **AAA Inspector Notes:** One of the newest additions to the rapidly growing west end of town, this informal contemporary restaurant is a sibling of its downtown namesake and includes many of the menu items from that location. A 1930s urban-Western ambience complements the varied menu. Locals and tourists flock here for steak, chicken and homemade desserts, along with made-to-order vegetarian dishes. A limited menu is presented in the lounge from 2 to 5 pm and from 10 pm to midnight. **Features:** full bar, happy hour. **Address:** 2425 Gabel Rd 59102 **Location:** I-90 exit 446, 0.5 mi nw, then 0.7 mi w on Overland Ave.

JAKES OF BILLINGS
406/259-9375

▼▼ American. Casual Dining. $8-$34 **AAA Inspector Notes:** A 1930s urban-Western ambience complements the varied menu at the informal, contemporary eatery. Locals and tourists flock here for steak, chicken and homemade desserts, along with made-to-order vegetarian dishes. **Features:** full bar, happy hour. **Reservations:** suggested, weekends. **Address:** 2701 1st Ave N 59101 **Location:** I-90 business loop and SR 3; downtown. **Parking:** on-site (fee).

L D

MACKENZIE RIVER PIZZA

▼▼ Pizza. Casual Dining. $8-$20 **AAA Inspector Notes:** Known for its eclectic Western decor, the restaurant lets patrons choose from several microbrews to accompany a specialty pizza or large, innovative sandwich. Pizza crusts are wonderful and offer the choice of sourdough, natural grain, deep dish or thin crust.

L D

For additional information, visit AAA.com
LOCATIONS:
Address: 3025 E Grand Ave 59102 **Location:** 4.5 mi w of City Center. **Bar:** full bar, patio dining. **Phone:** 406/651-0068
Address: 405 Main St 59105 **Location:** I-90 exit 452, 1.3 mi w on I-90 business loop, then 0.9 mi e; in Heights Target Complex. **Bar:** full bar, patio dining. **Phone:** 406/254-0066

MCCORMICK CAFE
406/255-9555

▼ American. Casual Dining. $6-$10 **AAA Inspector Notes:** Banana-stuffed French toast, grilled portobello sandwiches and moist, double-layer carrot cake are just a few of the excellent, made-from-scratch choices at the popular, sunny cafe. Mouthwatering aromas of roasted coffee beans and freshly squeezed fruit and vegetable juices fill the dining area. Breakfast is served until 10 am. **Address:** 2419 Montana Ave 59101 **Location:** I-90 exit 450, 1.5 mi n on 27th St, then just e. B L

MONTANA'S RIB & CHOP HOUSE
406/839-9200

▼▼ American. Casual Dining. $9-$22 **AAA Inspector Notes:** Specialties include 24-hour marinated baby back ribs and an 8-ounce Montana tenderloin, hand-cut, beef fillet. Diners also can sink their teeth into a variety of chicken, seafood and other steak entrées. The restaurant serves sushi on select days, so be sure to phone ahead. **Features:** full bar, Sunday brunch, happy hour. **Reservations:** suggested. **Address:** 1849 Majestic Ln 59102 **Location:** I-90 exit 443 (Zoo Dr), just n, just e on Gabel Rd, then just s.

L D CALL &M

NA RA RESTAURANT SUSHI BAR
406/245-8866

▼ Asian. Casual Dining. $10-$32 **AAA Inspector Notes:** It may be a bit awkward to find this restaurant as it's on the point of three streets—Custer, Montana and Division—but please try because the food is very good. Korean and Japanese dishes are available in the evenings, along with sushi. Lunch has a limited menu with sushi only. This is a friendly, family-run restaurant. **Features:** beer & wine. **Address:** 3 Custer Ave 59101 **Location:** Jct Montana Ave and Division St; east of downtown. L D CALL &M

THE REX
406/245-7477

▼▼ American. Casual Dining. $10-$40 **AAA Inspector Notes:** Among choices on the diverse menu are Montana-raised roasted buffalo, Tuscan pork loin, Cajun barbecued shrimp and the popular blackened prime rib. There are many smoked meats, including baby back ribs and smoked chicken, to try. A patio bar and grill offers lighter fare and outside seating, weather permitting. **Features:** full bar, patio dining. **Address:** 2401 Montana Ave 59101 **Location:** I-90 exit 450, 1.5 mi n on 27th St, then just e. L D

SIAM THAI
406/652-4315

▼▼ Thai. Casual Dining. $9-$21 **AAA Inspector Notes:** Well-prepared food made with authentic spices is served in an upscale atmosphere at the family-operated eatery. **Address:** 3210 Henesta Dr, Suite G 59102 **Location:** I-90 exit 446, 3.9 mi n on W King St; jct 32nd St; in King's Plaza. L D CALL &M

TASTE OF INDIA
406/281-8001

▼▼ Indian. Casual Dining. $10-$18 **AAA Inspector Notes:** Serving mostly Southern Indian comfort foods, this family-run restaurant also has belly dancers for your entertainment. Specialties include entrées cooked in the tandoori oven and vegetarian dishes. **Features:** beer & wine. **Address:** 216 N 28th St 59101 **Location:** Between 1st and 2nd aves N; downtown. **Parking:** street only.

L D

WALKER'S GRILL
406/245-9291

▼▼▼ Regional American. Fine Dining. $11-$37 **AAA Inspector Notes:** One visit to the restaurant makes it clear why this place is an area institution. Dining in an upscale atmosphere can be found in Billings! With a distinctly Western motif, diners will be pleasantly treated to creative presentations using the freshest ingredients. The eatery employs knowledgeable, friendly servers. A delectable tapas menu is offered starting at 4 pm. **Features:** full bar. **Reservations:** suggested. **Address:** 2700 1st Ave N 59101 **Location:** Jct N 27th St; in Securities Building. **Parking:** on-site and street.

D CALL &M

THE WINDMILL
406/252-8100

▼▼ American. Casual Dining. $11-$50 **AAA Inspector Notes:** A Billings institution for more than 20 years. The original windmill in front of the building is from an old barn, and the inside carries the western theme through with a copper tin-type ceiling, exposed beam rafters, etched-glass accents, large pictures of windmills and a large stone fireplace. A back wall of windows overlooks a large patio dining area and a pond. Dinner only on Sunday. **Features:** full bar, happy hour. **Address:** 3429 Trans Tech Way 59102 **Location:** I-90 exit 443 (Zoo Dr), just n, 0.7 mi e on Gabel Rd, then just n.

L D CALL &M

BITTERROOT NATIONAL FOREST (D-2)

Elevations in the forest range from 3,500 ft. at the Kootenai Creek Trail to 10,175 ft. on Trapper Peak. Refer to AAA maps for additional elevation information.

Bitterroot National Forest is in Montana and Idaho. The Montana section curves around the headwaters of the Bitterroot River, reaching into the Sapphire and Bitterroot ranges. This is a region of strong contrasts, with rolling subalpine woodland, open parks and lakes, and jagged, glaciated peaks and canyons.

The national forest takes its name from the bitterroot plant, whose pink flowers carpet the valleys and foothills from late April to July. Meriwether Lewis, on his journey through the region, added the bitterroot flower to his botanical collection and sampled the meal that the Native Americans ground from its root. A British botanist later honored Lewis' contribution by using his name as the basis of the flower's Latin name, *Lewisia rediviva*.

As one of the first forest reserves, Bitterroot National Forest also is the site of the first Forest Service ranger station, at Alta. The forest's Idaho portion encompasses the headwaters of the Selway River and a stretch of the Salmon River. Both rivers are components of the National Wild and Scenic River system. Portions of the Frank Church-River of No Return Wilderness, the Selway-Bitterroot Wilderness and the Anaconda-Pintler Wilderness occupy about half of the forest's 1.6 million acres. For further information contact Bitterroot National Forest, 1801 N. First St., Hamilton, MT 59840; phone (406) 363-7100. *See Recreation Areas Chart.*

BLACK EAGLE pop. 904

3D INTERNATIONAL   406/453-6561

▼▼ ▼▼ International. Casual Dining. $9-$21 **AAA Inspector Notes:** *Classic.* 3D equals "Dine, Drink, Dance," and it has been a Great Falls institution since 1946. While it used to promote big-name acts and dancing, renovations in 1998 transformed it into the setting it is today. The neon lighting and original lounge seating were retained, creating an unique atmosphere in which to enjoy Italian food, Mongolian buffet or Asian cuisine. **Features:** full bar. **Reservations:** suggested. **Address:** 1825 Smelter Ave 59414 **Location:** Jct 9th St and Smelter Ave, 0.5 mi e. **Parking:** on-site and street.

L   D

BORRIES   406/761-0300

▼▼ ▼▼ American. Casual Dining. $10-$30 **AAA Inspector Notes:** In an older industrial neighborhood of a small mill town, the casual dining establishment prepares simple, hearty food and serves it in generous portions. In addition to steaks, the menu lists Southern Italian pasta dishes, including spaghetti and the signature ravioli. Many pictures and photographs highlight the history of the community when it was a center of the world's copper industry. **Features:** full bar. **Reservations:** suggested, weekends. **Address:** 1800 Smelter Ave 59414 **Location:** Jct 9th St and Smelter Ave, 0.5 mi e. D

BOULDER pop. 1,183

BOULDER HOT SPRINGS INN & SPA   406/225-4339

fyi Not evaluated. **Address:** 31 S Hot Springs Rd 59632 **Location:** I-90 exit 164, 3 mi s on SR 69. Facilities, services, and décor characterize an economy property. This historic building has been an inn since 1863. The property offers a large outdoor hot springs pool and two indoor pools. Sit on one of the 50 rocking chairs on the veranda overlooking Peace Valley.

BOX ELDER (B-4) pop. 87, elev. 2,686'

ROCKY BOY INDIAN RESERVATION is on US 87 in the Bear Paw Mountains. Established in 1916, the Chippewa Cree reservation is named for a Chippewa leader whose Indian name, meaning "Stone Child," later was changed to "Rocky Boy." Tours of historical sites are offered. Fishing is permitted in a number of well-stocked streams and ponds; a tribal license is required. Hiking trails are available. Bear Paw Ski Bowl is on the reservation. **Hours:** Ski area open mid-December to early April. **Cost:** Fishing license (valid for 3 consecutive days) $10; $5 (1-day license); $25 (season pass), a conservation license may also be required. Rates may vary; phone ahead. **Phone:** (406) 395-4207.

BOZEMAN (E-4) pop. 37,280, elev. 4,755'
• Restaurants p. 143

Bozeman was named for John Bozeman, who brought the first wagon train of pioneers to settle the Gallatin Valley. The trail he blazed became not only a highway for settlers and miners but also a flashpoint between the Native Americans and the settlers. Three years after bringing settlers to the valley, Bozeman was killed by the Sioux, and his trail remained unused for 9 years because of repeated attacks upon wayfarers.

The valley that Bozeman helped settle once was a neutral and sacred hunting ground known to Native Americans as the "Valley of the Flowers." The area has blossomed into one of the state's more agriculturally productive regions.

Bozeman Area Chamber of Commerce: 2000 Commerce Way, Bozeman, MT 59715. **Phone:** (406) 586-5421 or (800) 228-4224.

GALLATIN PIONEER MUSEUM is at 317 W. Main St. Housed in a 1911 county jail, the museum contains old photographs, Native American artifacts, and exhibits about early settlement and 20th-century history. **Hours:** Mon.-Sat. 10-5, Memorial Day-Labor Day; Tues.-Sat. 11-4, rest of year. **Cost:** $5; free (ages 0-12). **Phone:** (406) 522-8122.

MUSEUM OF MODERN HUMAN PROGRESS (AMERICAN COMPUTER & ROBOTICS MUSEUM) is at 2023 Stadium Dr., Suite 1A. Exhibits chronicle the evolution of the information age, from abacus to microchips. **Tours:** Guided tours are available. **Time:** Allow 30 minutes minimum. **Hours:** Daily 10-4, June-Aug.; Tues.-Sun. noon-4, rest of year. Closed Jan. 1, Easter, July 4, Thanksgiving and Christmas. **Cost:** Donations. **Phone:** (406) 582-1288.

▼▼ GEM SAVE **MUSEUM OF THE ROCKIES** is on the Montana State University campus at S. Seventh Ave. and W. Kagy Blvd. Home to the largest dinosaur fossil collection in the United States, the museum's Siebel Dinosaur Complex features Tyrannosaurus rex, triceratops, dinosaur eggs, nests and sculptures. Other exhibits include the Paugh History Hall with a vast array of regional artifacts; the Enduring Peoples exhibit that examines the life and culture of American Indians of the Northern Plains and the Rockies; the Living History Farm (closed in winter) which is a historically accurate, late-1800s Montana homestead; and the Martin Children's Discovery Center. The museum also features the Taylor Planetarium, offering a breathtaking journey through the cosmos.

Hours: Daily 8-8, Memorial Day weekend-Labor Day; Mon.-Sat. 9-5, Sun. 12:30-5, rest of year. Planetarium shows are given daily. Closed Jan. 1, Thanksgiving and Christmas. **Cost:** Museum (includes planetarium) $14; $13 (ages 65+); $9.50 (ages 5-17). **Phone:** (406) 994-3466 or (406) 994-2251.

BEST WESTERN PLUS GRANTREE INN   (406)587-5261

▼▼ ▼▼ ▼▼
Hotel
$99-$199

AAA Benefit: Members save 10% or more with Best Western!

Address: 1325 N 7th Ave 59715 **Location:** I-90 exit 306, just s. **Facility:** 120 units. 2 stories (no elevator), interior corridors. **Parking:** winter plug-ins. **Amenities:** video games, safes. **Pool(s):** heated indoor. **Activities:** hot tub, exercise room. **Guest Services:** valet and coin laundry, area transportation.

BOZEMAN DAYS INN & SUITES (406)587-5251

◆◆ **Hotel** $60-$135 **Address:** 1321 N 7th Ave 59715 **Location:** I-90 exit 306, just s. **Facility:** 114 units. 2-3 stories, interior corridors. **Parking:** winter plug-ins. **Amenities:** safes. **Pool(s):** heated indoor. **Amenities:** sauna, hot tub, exercise room. **Guest Services:** valet and coin laundry, area transportation.

[icons]

BOZEMAN INN (406)587-3176

Motel
$60-$99

Address: 1235 N 7th Ave 59715 **Location:** I-90 exit 306, just s. **Facility:** 49 units, some two bedrooms. 2 stories (no elevator), exterior corridors. **Parking:** winter plug-ins. **Pool(s):** heated outdoor. **Activities:** sauna, hot tub. **Guest Services:** coin laundry.

[icons]

BOZEMAN'S WESTERN HERITAGE INN (406)586-8534

◆◆ **Hotel** $78-$179 **Address:** 1200 E Main St 59715 **Location:** I-90 exit 309, 0.5 mi w. **Facility:** 37 units, some efficiencies and kitchens. 3 stories (no elevator), interior corridors. **Parking:** winter plug-ins. **Terms:** cancellation fee imposed. **Activities:** hot tub, steamroom. **Guest Services:** coin laundry.

[icons]

CITY CENTER INN 406/587-3158

◆ **Hotel. Rates not provided. Address:** 507 W Main St 59715 **Location:** Center. **Facility:** 64 units. 3 stories, interior corridors. **Parking:** winter plug-ins. **Amenities:** safes. **Pool(s):** heated indoor. **Activities:** hot tub, exercise room.

[icons]

C'MON INN (406)587-3555

Hotel
$89-$180

Address: 6139 E Valley Center Rd 59718 **Location:** I-90 exit 305, just s on CR 41 (19th St), then just w. **Facility:** 125 units. 3 stories, interior corridors. **Terms:** check-in 4 pm. **Amenities:** video games. **Pool(s):** heated indoor. **Activities:** hot tub, game room, exercise room. **Guest Services:** valet and coin laundry. **Featured Amenity:** continental breakfast.

[icons]

COMFORT INN OF BOZEMAN (406)587-2322

◆◆ **Hotel** $85-$130 **Address:** 1370 N 7th Ave 59715 **Location:** I-90 exit 306, just s. **Facility:** 122 units, some efficiencies. 3 stories, interior corridors. **Parking:** winter plug-ins. **Pool(s):** heated indoor. **Activities:** hot tub, exercise room. **Guest Services:** valet and coin laundry, area transportation.

[icons]

FAIRFIELD INN BY MARRIOTT (406)587-2222

◆◆ **Hotel** $79-$259 **Address:** 828 Wheat Dr 59715 **Location:** I-90 exit 306, just nw. **Facility:** 57 units. 3 stories, interior corridors. **Parking:** winter plug-ins. **Pool(s):** heated indoor. **Activities:** hot tub. **Guest Services:** valet laundry.

AAA Benefit:
Members save 5% or more!

[icons]

FOX HOLLOW BED AND BREAKFAST (406)582-8440

◆◆◆ **Bed & Breakfast** $119-$189 **Address:** 545 Mary Rd 59718 **Location:** I-90 exit 305, just s on SR 412 (N 19th St), 3.1 mi w on SR 235 (Valley Center Rd), then 0.6 mi n. **Facility:** This B&B offers gourmet breakfasts and spectacular mountain and meadow views. After a day on the hiking trails, sit on the beautiful wraparound porch while sampling fresh baked goods. 5 units, some kitchens. 2 stories (no elevator), interior corridors. **Parking:** winter plug-ins. **Terms:** 14 day cancellation notice-fee imposed. **Activities:** hot tub.

[icons]

HAMPTON INN (406)522-8000

◆◆◆
Hotel
$99-$179

AAA Benefit:
Members save up to 10%!

Address: 75 Baxter Ln 59715 **Location:** I-90 exit 306, just s, then just n. **Facility:** 70 units. 2 stories, interior corridors. **Parking:** winter plug-ins. **Terms:** 1-7 night minimum stay, cancellation fee imposed. **Pool(s):** heated indoor. **Activities:** hot tub, exercise room. **Guest Services:** valet and coin laundry. **Featured Amenity:** breakfast buffet.

[icons]

HILTON GARDEN INN (406)582-9900

◆◆◆ **Hotel** $109-$229 **Address:** 2023 Commerce Way 59715 **Location:** I-90 exit 305, just s, then just e on Baxter Ln. **Facility:** 123 units. 3 stories, interior corridors. **Parking:** winter plug-ins.

AAA Benefit:
Members save up to 10%!

Terms: check-in 4 pm, 1-7 night minimum stay, cancellation fee imposed. **Amenities:** video games. **Pool(s):** heated indoor. **Activities:** hot tub, exercise room. **Guest Services:** valet and coin laundry, area transportation.

[icons]

HOLIDAY INN BOZEMAN (406)587-4561

◆◆◆ **Hotel** $79-$179 **Address:** 5 E Baxter Ln 59715 **Location:** I-90 exit 306, just s. **Facility:** 177 units. 2 stories (no elevator), interior corridors. **Parking:** winter plug-ins. **Terms:** check-in 4 pm, cancellation fee imposed, resort fee. **Pool(s):** heated indoor. **Activities:** hot tub, exercise room. **Guest Services:** valet and coin laundry, area transportation.

[icons]

HOLIDAY INN EXPRESS & SUITES (406)582-4995

◆◆◆ **Hotel** $99-$189 **Address:** 2305 Catron St 59718 **Location:** I-90 exit 305, just s on CR 41 (19th St), then just w on E Valley Center Rd. **Facility:** 86 units. 3 stories, interior corridors. **Parking:** winter plug-ins. **Terms:** check-in 4 pm. **Amenities:** video games, safes. **Pool(s):** heated indoor. **Activities:** hot tub, exercise room. **Guest Services:** valet and coin laundry.

[icons]

HOMEWOOD SUITES BY HILTON BOZEMAN (406)587-8180

◆◆◆ **Extended Stay Hotel** $99-$229 **Address:** 1023 Baxter Ln 59715 **Location:** I-90 exit 306, just s, then just n. **Facility:** 102 units, some two bedrooms and efficiencies. 4 stories, interior corridors. **Parking:** winter plug-ins. **Terms:** 1-7 night minimum stay, cancellation fee imposed. **Pool(s):** heated indoor. **Activities:** hot tub, exercise room. **Guest Services:** valet and coin laundry, area transportation.

AAA Benefit:
Members save up to 10%!

[icons]

HOWLERS INN BED & BREAKFAST
406/587-5229

Bed & Breakfast $110-$195 Address: 3185 Jackson Creek Rd 59715 Location: I-90 exit 319 (Jackson Creek Rd), 3.1 mi n, then just e. Facility: A wolf sanctuary is on the grounds of this inn, which offers scenic views as well as a location 15 minutes from downtown that is also close to ski areas and a national forest. 4 units, some two bedrooms and kitchens. 2-3 stories (no elevator), interior/exterior corridors. Parking: winter plug-ins. Terms: check-in 4 pm, 2 night minimum stay - seasonal, 10 day cancellation notice. Activities: sauna, hot tub, playground, exercise room. Guest Services: complimentary laundry.

LA QUINTA INN & SUITES
(406)585-9300

Hotel $79-$164 Address: 620 Nikles Dr 59715 Location: I-90 exit 306, just ne. Facility: 56 units. 4 stories, interior corridors. Parking: winter plug-ins. Pool(s): heated indoor. Activities: hot tub, exercise room. Guest Services: valet and coin laundry.

MICROTEL INN & SUITES BY WYNDHAM BOZEMAN
(406)586-3797

Hotel $60-$140 Address: 612 Nikles Dr 59715 Location: I-90 exit 306, just ne. Facility: 61 units. 3 stories, interior corridors. Parking: winter plug-ins. Pool(s): heated indoor. Activities: hot tub. Guest Services: valet laundry.

MOTEL 6 BOZEMAN #4818
406/585-7888

Hotel. Rates not provided. Address: 817 Wheat Dr 59718 Location: I-90 exit 306, just n. Facility: 56 units. 2 stories (no elevator), interior corridors. Parking: winter plug-ins. Pool(s): heated indoor. Activities: sauna, hot tub. Guest Services: coin laundry.

MOUNTAINVIEW LODGE & SUITES
(406)522-8686

Hotel $89-$179 Address: 1121 Reeves Rd W 59718 Location: I-90 exit 305, just n. Facility: 52 units, some kitchens. 2 stories (no elevator), interior corridors. Parking: winter plug-ins. Pool(s): heated indoor. Activities: hot tub, game room, exercise room. Guest Services: coin laundry.

RAINBOW MOTEL
(406)587-4201

Motel
$75-$95

Address: 510 N 7th Ave 59715 Location: I-90 exit 306, 0.8 mi s. Facility: 42 units, some two bedrooms and efficiencies. 1-2 stories (no elevator), exterior corridors. Parking: winter plug-ins. Terms: cancellation fee imposed. Pool(s): heated outdoor.

RAMADA LIMITED
(406)585-2626

Hotel $60-$140 Address: 2020 Wheat Dr 59715 Location: I-90 exit 306, just n, then just w. Facility: 50 units. 2 stories (no elevator), interior/exterior corridors. Parking: winter plug-ins. Terms: 3 day cancellation notice-fee imposed. Pool(s): heated indoor. Activities: hot tub, exercise room. Guest Services: valet and coin laundry.

ROYAL "7" BUDGET INN
(406)587-3103

Motel
$50-$75

Address: 310 N 7th Ave 59715 Location: I-90 exit 306, 0.8 mi s. Facility: 47 units, some two bedrooms. 1 story, exterior corridors. Parking: winter plug-ins. Guest Services: coin laundry. Featured Amenity: continental breakfast.

SUPER 8
(406)586-1521

Hotel $59-$159 Address: 800 Wheat Dr 59715 Location: I-90 exit 306, just n, then just w. Facility: 107 units. 3 stories (no elevator), interior corridors. Parking: winter plug-ins. Guest Services: coin laundry.

WHERE TO EAT

CAFE FRANCAIS DES ARTS
406/209-7490

French. Casual Dining. $5-$10 AAA Inspector Notes: Try a little bit of France in Montana! Specialties include scrumptious sweets loaded with real sweet-cream butter, eggs, imported chocolate and even imported flour. Favorite savories include croque monsieur on homemade bread, French onion soup topped with Gruyère, assorted quiches and crêpes. This is a family-run café where you'll find the mother's art decorating the walls and her sons in the kitchen hard at work. Address: 24 S Tracy Ave 59715 Location: Between Main and Babcock sts; downtown. Parking: on-site and street.

CAFÉ ZYDECO
406/994-0188

Cajun. Quick Serve. $9-$16 AAA Inspector Notes: Traditionally prepared Cajun goodies are served with a smile in the casual eatery. Breakfast is served Saturday and Sunday. Beignets are served all day Sunday. There is another location in Helena. Address: 2711 W College St 59715 Location: Just e of Huffine Ln/W Main St; in Old Hatchery Winery building.

CHICKPEA CAFE
406/551-2007

Mediterranean. Casual Dining. $5-$26 AAA Inspector Notes: The focus of this little restaurant is Middle Eastern salads and meats, such as hummus, tabbouleh, falafel and shwarma. You also can find dolmades (stuffed grape leaves), gyros and Greek salads. The salads are made fresh and the shwarma is continually turning on the rotisserie. Crispy and buttery pistachio baklava served with mint or cardamom tea rounds out the meal. Address: 25 N Willson Ave, Suite A 59715 Location: Jct W Mendenhall St; downtown. Parking: street only.

CHINATOWN RESTAURANT
406/587-5168

Chinese. Casual Dining. $9-$18 AAA Inspector Notes: Patrons can choose from more than 100 entrées prepared in the Peking, Hunan, Szechuan and Cantonese styles. The quick lunch menu is popular for those in a hurry. Address: 1228 W Main St 59715 Location: West of historic downtown; across from Bozeman High School.

FERRARO'S
406/587-2555

Italian. Casual Dining. $14-$45 AAA Inspector Notes: Locals frequent this place for its authentic cuisine, daily-made pasta and extensive wine list. The lounge offers wine flights of exceptional value and features overstuffed leather furnishings and a cozy fireplace. There's a new wood oven and pizza bar. Features: full bar, patio dining. Reservations: suggested. Address: 726 N 7th Ave 59772 Location: I-90 exit 306, 0.6 mi s.

THE GARAGE
406/585-8558

▼▼ American. Casual Dining. $8-$19 **AAA Inspector Notes:** First-timers can expect to be pleasantly surprised when they step into the converted retro-era garage. The soup counter allows for a choice between at least seven innovative homemade selections with varied toppings. Because sampling is encouraged, the signature clam chowder is a must-try. Contributing to the funky yet casual décor are the restaurant's menus, which are sandwiched between old license plates. Weather permitting, sit on the deck to enjoy the downtown scene. **Features:** beer & wine, patio dining. **Address:** 451 E Main St 59715 **Location:** Jct Church St; center. **Parking:** street only.

L D 🅺

I-HO'S KOREAN GRILL
406/522-0949

▼ Korean. Casual Dining. $7-$15 **AAA Inspector Notes:** You will love the authentic food prepared in a traditional manner. The homey café is a big hit with the local college students and teachers alike. Specials range from Korean teriyaki chicken to daily soups. If you're feeling bold, try the kimchi. Outdoor seating is popular during summer months. **Features:** patio dining. **Address:** 1216 W Lincoln St 59715 **Location:** I-90 exit 306, 1 mi se, 0.5 mi w on W Main St, 1 mi se on 11th St, then just w; adjacent to Montana State University Campus. L D

JOHN BOZEMAN'S BISTRO
406/587-4100

▼▼▼ American. Casual Dining. $9-$36 **AAA Inspector Notes:** The locals' favorite bistro provides eye-candy décor and a creative menu. Eclectic choices include inventive local lamb, buffalo, fish, tenderloin, poultry and vegetarian dishes. Seating in booths and on stools at the counter help provide a casual feel, and the service is attentive, knowledgeable and friendly. **Features:** beer & wine. **Address:** 125 W Main St 59715 **Location:** Center. **Parking:** street only. L D CALL 🅜

LA PARILLA
406/582-9511

▼ Fusion. Quick Serve. $7-$10 **AAA Inspector Notes:** The fusion menu includes Cajun, Thai and Indian cuisine, and features gourmet burritos and fresh salmon. **Features:** beer only. **Address:** 1424 W Babcock St 59771 **Location:** Jct N 7th Ave and W Main St, 0.5 mi w, just s on S 11th Ave, then just w. L D

LEMONGRASS THAI
406/551-2168

▼▼ Thai. Casual Dining. $11-$15 **AAA Inspector Notes:** Finally! Authentic Thai food in Bozeman. In one of the newer buildings close to the university, this is a great place to get tom yum soup (which the chef assures me is made from scratch), ginger beef—yummy with slivers of fresh ginger—pad thai and freshly rolled spring rolls. The café adds specials here and there, so be sure to check back often. **Features:** beer & wine. **Reservations:** required. **Address:** 290 W Kagy Blvd, Suite C 59715 **Location:** From Main St, 1.3 mi s on S Willson Ave; near Montana State University.

L D CALL 🅜

MACKENZIE RIVER PIZZA
406/587-0055

▼▼ Pizza. Casual Dining. $8-$20 **AAA Inspector Notes:** Known for its eclectic Western decor, the restaurant lets patrons choose from several microbrews to accompany a specialty pizza or large, innovative sandwich. Pizza crusts are wonderful and offer the choice of sourdough, natural grain, deep dish or thin crust. **Features:** beer & wine. **Address:** 232 E Main St 59715 **Location:** Center. **Parking:** street only. L D

MAIN STREET OVEREASY
406/587-3205

▼▼ American. Family Dining. $7-$15 **AAA Inspector Notes:** A hot spot for breakfast, the restaurant prepares homemade biscuits and gravy, home fries, pancakes and gourmet omelets. Excellent coffee and great service are other reasons for its loyal clientele. **Address:** 9 E Main St 59715 **Location:** Downtown. **Parking:** street only. B L

THE NAKED NOODLE
406/585-4501

▼
**Noodles
Specialty
Quick Serve
$7-$13**

AAA Inspector Notes: This place offers a great concept. Diners pick from seven varieties of pasta, including a gluten-free option, then choose sauces, meats, vegetables, seafood and toppings to create a delicious meal. Can't decide? Choose one of the many tried-and-true combinations or salads posted on the board. It's a self-serve, but orders are taken by a patient and friendly staff. An extensive healthy children's menu is available. **Address:** 27 S Willson Ave 59715 **Location:** Just s; center. **Parking:** on-site and street. L D

PHO REAL
406/404-1075

▼ Soup. Quick Serve. $7-$12 **AAA Inspector Notes:** The limited menu highlights some of the more popular staples of soup and sandwiches. The cafeteria-style ordering is convenient; you choose your broth and meat, then move on to the vegetables and spices that will top your soup. **Address:** 242 E Main St 59715 **Location:** Between Rouse and Bozeman aves; downtown. **Parking:** street only.

L D CALL 🅜

SANTA FE RED'S
406/587-5838

▼▼ Mexican. Casual Dining. $8-$18 **AAA Inspector Notes:** The upbeat, bustling and popular Mexican restaurant serves such homemade Southwestern cuisine as fajitas, burritos and tacos. Guests can top off any meal with the signature dessert: fried ice cream. **Features:** full bar, patio dining. **Address:** 1235 N 7th Ave 59715 **Location:** I-90 exit 306, just s; adjacent to Bozeman Inn. L D

SOLA CAFE
406/922-7652

▼ Deli. Quick Serve. $7-$21 **AAA Inspector Notes:** More than a typical deli, you can enjoy made from scratch delectables using regionally available fresh fruits, veggies, meats and cheeses. Each day brings a new creation for the specials board. The day I was there, I had cauliflower curry soup and a smoked turkey panini. They offer vegetarian, gluten free or low carb for those with special dietary needs. Drive through is available for those on the go. **Features:** beer & wine, Sunday brunch. **Address:** 290 W Kagy Blvd 59715 **Location:** From Main St, 1.3 mi s on S Willson Ave; near Montana State University and Museum of the Rockies.

B L D CALL 🅜

SWEET CHILI - ASIAN BISTRO
406/582-1188

▼▼ Asian. Casual Dining. $9-$19 **AAA Inspector Notes:** Even though the owners/chefs are Chinese, they spent quite a few years under the tutelage of the Siam Thai restaurant in Billings. On the menu you'll find many classic Thai dishes, including tom yum soup, pad Thai, basil chicken and fresh rolls. There are also a few classic Chinese dishes offered. The restaurant space is open. Along with tables, there are many seats that face each other along a long counter. Parking is available in the city garage. **Features:** beer & wine. **Reservations:** required. **Address:** 101 E Main St, Unit 1 59715 **Location:** Jct Black St; downtown. **Parking:** street only. L D

THE WOK
406/585-1245

▼▼ Chinese. Casual Dining. $7-$18 **AAA Inspector Notes:** A popular favorite for family-style Asian dining, this place offers both tasty food and hearty portions. The staff is friendly and helpful. It's a good thing the dining room is large, as this place can get busy at the dinner hour. **Features:** beer & wine. **Address:** 319 N 7th Ave 59715 **Location:** I-90 exit 306, 1 mi s. L D CALL 🅜

COMMUNITY FOOD CO-OP
406/587-4039

fyi Not evaluated. Located inside a community organic foods market, this deli counter and soup bar offers a wide variety of healthy organic choices. There is another convenient location downtown on Main Street. **Address:** 908 W Main St 59715 **Location:** Between 9th and 10th aves.

LA CHATELAINE CHOCOLAT CO
406/522-5440

fyi Not evaluated. The local chocolate makers specialize in French chocolates with five global regional beans used for production. Selections can change daily and are prepared in small batches on site. There also is a satellite location in the Baxter Hotel (downtown). **Address:** 1516 W Main St 59715 **Location:** Between 15th and 16th aves; behind Café Zydeco.

THE PICKLE BARREL   406/587-2411
[fyi] Not evaluated. This eatery serves large, fresh deli sandwiches with dill pickles. **Address:** 809 W College St 59715

BROWNING (B-2) pop. 1,016, elev. 4,366'
• Part of Glacier National Park area — see map p. 163

Founded in 1895, Browning is the hub of the Blackfeet Nation and a center for reservation activities. It also is the site of the Blackfeet Tribal Headquarters, which includes a nine-member business council, the governing board of the Blackfeet Tribe. Fifteen miles east on the reservation, a monument marks the northernmost point reached by the Lewis and Clark expedition on July 23, 1806. About 10,000 Native Americans live on the Blackfeet Indian Reservation, which covers 1.5 million acres.

MUSEUM OF THE PLAINS INDIAN is at jct. US 2 and US 89W. Murals, dioramas, historical and contemporary Native American arts and artifacts of the Northern Plains region are displayed. Changing exhibits also are offered. **Time:** Allow 1 hour minimum. **Hours:** Tues.-Sat. 9-4:45, June-Sept.; Mon.-Fri. 10-4:30, rest of year. Closed major holidays. **Cost:** June-Sept. $4; $1 (ages 6-12). Rest of year free. **Phone:** (406) 338-2230.

GOING TO THE SUN INN & SUITES   (406)338-7572

♦♦♦
Motel
$88-$174

Address: 121 Central Ave E 59417 **Location:** On US 2; center. **Facility:** 15 units. 1 story, exterior corridors. **Parking:** winter plug-ins. **Terms:** 4 day cancellation notice-fee imposed. **Guest Services:** area transportation. **Featured Amenity:** continental breakfast. (SAVE) 📶 ✕ 🅱 🖥 /SOME UNITS 🅢🇲

BUTTE (E-3) elev. 5,716'
• Hotels p. 146 • Restaurants p. 148

Silver Bow Creek's gold and silver first brought the mineral wealth of remote Butte to the attention of the world. But it was copper that made Butte's reputation as "the richest hill on Earth," producing more than 20 billion pounds of the metal. "Copper kings" fought for control of Butte's wealth; Marcus Daly's Anaconda Copper Mining Co. eventually gained ownership of every mine in Butte and became the dominant power in Montana.

By 1955 the high-grade copper ore was almost played out, and excavation began on Berkeley Open Pit Mine to extract low-grade ore. The mine was one of the larger truck-operated pit mines in the world. The Berkeley Pit Viewing Stand, open daily dawn to dusk from March to mid-November, is $2 for adults and $1 for children and provides an excellent view of the old open mine. As a transportation hub, the city has become one of the nation's larger inland ports, with containerized cargo from the Orient being cleared and routed to points throughout the Midwest.

The Anselmo Mine Yard, uptown at Caledonia and Excelsior streets, is a fine example of surface support facilities that once served the miners. An interpretive center and tours are offered during the summer. The Granite Mountain Mine Memorial, 1308 N. Main St., is dedicated to the 168 men who died in a 1917 mine disaster.

Butte's historic district contains a large concentration of late 19th- and early 20th-century residential and commercial buildings as well as mining relics such as the steel headframes used to lower miners to a network of more than 2,000 miles of tunnels under "the hill." The Piccadilly Transportation Memorabilia Museum, 20 W. Broadway St., has a replica of a 1930s service station as well as collections of signs and license plates; phone (406) 723-3034.

Butte is surrounded by Beaverhead-Deerlodge National Forest *(see place listing p. 129)*, which offers varied recreational opportunities. Sheepshead Recreation Area, about 10 miles north via I-15, was designed for the physically impaired. Visitors can experience the beauty of the nearby rugged mountains, verdant forests and meadows by driving either north to Helena or south to Monida on I-15.

Butte-Silver Bow Chamber of Commerce and Visitor Center: 1000 George St., Butte, MT 59701. **Phone:** (406) 723-3177 or (800) 735-6814.

Self-guiding tours: Brochures detailing two walking tours of the historic district are available at the chamber of commerce and visitor center.

BUTTE TROLLEY TOUR departs from the chamber of commerce; take I-90 exit 126 to 1000 George St. Narrated tours explain the city's mining history. Visitors are transported through the historic district, with stops that include the Berkeley Pit and some of the headframes (steel mining structures).

Time: Allow 1 hour, 30 minutes minimum. **Hours:** Tours are given Mon.-Sat. at 10:30, 1 and 3:30, Sun. at 10:30 and 1, day after Memorial Day-day before Labor Day; daily at 10:30 and 1, day after Labor Day-Sept. 30. Phone ahead to confirm schedule. **Cost:** $15; $13 (ages 65+); $10 (ages 12-17); $6 (ages 4-11). Fares may vary; phone ahead. **Phone:** (406) 723-3177 or (800) 735-6814.

(SAVE) **CHARLES W. CLARK CHATEAU** is at 321 W. Broadway. Built in 1898, the residence of Charles W. Clark, eldest son of "copper king" William A. Clark, was modeled after a French château. Today the building contains the works of Montana artists. Exhibits change periodically. An antique furniture collection from the University of Montana and the first piano in Montana also are displayed. **Time:** Allow 1 hour minimum. **Hours:** Tours are given Tues.-Sat. 10-5, June 1-Labor Day; Tues.-Thurs. 11-4, rest of year. Phone ahead to confirm schedule. **Cost:** $4; $3 (senior citizens); $2 (ages 0-15); $10 (family). **Phone:** (406) 723-7600.

COPPER KING MANSION is at 219 W. Granite St. The 37-room Victorian house was the residence of William A. Clark, a U.S. senator and "copper king." Now a national historic landmark and bed and breakfast, the restored 1884-88 mansion is furnished in period and serves as a showcase for numerous collections. **Time:** Allow 1 hour minimum. **Hours:** Guided tours are given daily 9-4, May-Sept.; Sat.-Sun. 9-4, in Apr.; by appointment rest of year. **Cost:** $7.50; $3.50 (ages 6-14); $25 (family). **Phone:** (406) 782-7580.

MINERAL MUSEUM, at 1300 W. Park St. in the Museum Building of Montana Tech, exhibits more than 1,500 specimens, including fluorescent minerals, a gold nugget considered to be the largest in Montana and a 400-pound quartz crystal found near Butte. Other features are a geological relief map and an earthquake studies laboratory. **Hours:** Daily 9-5, June 15-Sept. 15; Mon.-Fri. 9-4, rest of year. Closed major holidays. **Cost:** Donations. **Phone:** (406) 496-4414.

OUR LADY OF THE ROCKIES is e. atop the Continental Divide; tours to the site depart from the Plaza Mall, 3100 Harrison Ave. The 90-foot-high statue of the Virgin Mary—a nondenominational tribute to motherhood—took 6 years to build and was airlifted into place in 1985. Visitors may step inside the metal structure. The road to the statue is not open to public traffic. A chapel observatory is available.

Hours: Bus tours lasting 2.5 hours depart Mon.-Sat. at 10 and 2, Sun. at 11, June-Oct. (weather permitting). **Cost:** $15; $13 (ages 55+); $11 (ages 13-17); $7 (ages 5-12); $2 (ages 0-4). **Phone:** (406) 782-1221 or (800) 800-5239.

WORLD MUSEUM OF MINING & HELL ROARING GULCH is at 155 Museum Way. The museum is on the grounds of the Orphan Girl mine, a silver mine in operation 1875-1956. The mine yard contains the original headframe, hoist house, timber slide and hose house. More than 50 buildings comprise Hell Roaring Gulch, a reconstructed 1890s mining town with mining and regional history exhibits. A 75- to 90-minute guided mine tour is offered.

Time: Allow 2 hours minimum. **Hours:** Complex open daily 9-6, with mine tours at 10:30, 12:30 and 3, Apr.-Oct. Last admission at 4:30. **Cost:** Museum $8.50; $7.50 (ages 66+); $6 (ages 13-18); $3 (ages 5-12). Mine tour $12; $10 (ages 66+); $8 (ages 13-18); $5 (ages 5-12). A combination museum and mine tour ticket is available. Under 5 are not permitted on mine tours. A maximum of 14 people are allowed on the mine tour, so reservations are suggested. **Phone:** (406) 723-7211.

▼ See AAA listing p. 146 ▼

A full service hotel, close to Montana Tech, REC Silicon and St. James Hospital

- Complimentary Hot Breakfast
- Free Wireless Internet
- Indoor Pool, Hot Tub & Sauna
- Hops Pub and Casino on-site
- Perkins Family Restaurant with Room Service Available

BEST WESTERN PLUS
Butte Plaza Inn

2900 Harrison Ave, Butte, MT 59701
406.494.3500
1-800-543-5814
bestwestern.com/aaa

▼ See AAA listing p. 148 ▼

Hamptonality with a Local Flavor!

- Relaxing Pool & Spa
- On the House! Free, Hot Breakfast
- Butte's Best 24-Hour Fitness Center
- Free Wireless Internet throughout Hotel
- 2 Business Centers
- 24-Hour Hot Coffee Bar with Freshly-Baked Cookies
- Hampton's Clean & Fresh Bedding
- Hilton HHonors Rewards

$119 – 169
1-4 Adults
Based on Availability
* Must Present Proof of Membership

3499 Harrison Ave
Butte, MT 59701

www.butte.hamptoninn.com   406-494-2250

Savings for Your Inner Child

Save on entertainment and dining, coast to coast.

AAA.com/searchfordiscounts

HAMPTON INN
(406)494-2250

Hotel
$119-$169

AAA Benefit: Members save up to 10%!

Address: 3499 Harrison Ave 59701 **Location:** I-90/15 exit 127 (Harrison Ave), 0.6 mi s. **Facility:** 91 units. 3 stories, interior corridors. **Terms:** 1-7 night minimum stay, cancellation fee imposed. **Amenities:** video games. **Pool(s):** heated indoor. **Activities:** hot tub, exercise room. **Guest Services:** valet and coin laundry, area transportation. **Featured Amenity:** full hot breakfast. *(See ad p. 147.)*

LA QUINTA INN & SUITES
(406)494-6999

Hotel $104-$154 **Address:** 1 Holiday Park Dr 59701 **Location:** I-90/15 exit 127 (Harrison Ave), just n to Cornell St, then just e, follow signs. Across from a park and Greenway Walking Trail. **Facility:** 83 units. 5 stories, interior corridors. **Parking:** winter plug-ins. **Activities:** hot tub, exercise room. **Guest Services:** valet and coin laundry.

QUALITY INN & SUITES BUTTE
(406)494-7800

Hotel $80-$150 **Address:** 2100 Cornell Ave 59701 **Location:** I-90/15 exit 127B (Harrison Ave), just n, then just e. **Facility:** 128 units. 2 stories (no elevator), interior corridors. **Parking:** winter plug-ins. **Terms:** check-in 4 pm. **Pool(s):** heated indoor. **Activities:** sauna, hot tub, exercise room. **Guest Services:** valet laundry.

SUPER 8 OF BUTTE
(406)494-6000

Hotel
$72-$115

Address: 2929 Harrison Ave 59701 **Location:** I-90/15 exit 127 (Harrison Ave), just s. Opposite a shopping mall. **Facility:** 106 units. 3 stories (no elevator), interior corridors. **Parking:** winter plug-ins. **Guest Services:** valet and coin laundry. **Featured Amenity:** continental breakfast.

WHERE TO EAT

BROADWAY CAFE
406/723-8711

Pizza Natural/Organic. Family Dining. $7-$17 **AAA Inspector Notes:** *Historic.* Gourmet pizzas are served in a converted historic building. Organic ingredients are used in sauces, pizza toppings and salads. Local bands play weekly in the casual eatery. The back room overlooks the city and offers wonderful views of the mountains. **Features:** beer & wine. **Address:** 302 E Broadway 59701 **Location:** I-90/15 exit 126, 1.4 mi n on Montana St, then 2 mi e. **Parking:** street only.

CASAGRANDA'S STEAKHOUSE
406/723-4141

American. Casual Dining. $15-$29 **AAA Inspector Notes:** In a circa 1900s distribution warehouse, the family-run restaurant has wood floors, beamed ceilings and old paper invoices tacked to the walls. Steak and seafood are served in large portions. Included in the meal price are appetizers and dessert. **Features:** full bar. **Address:** 800 S Utah Ave 59701 **Location:** I-90 exit 126, just n, 1 mi e on Front St, then just n; in Bertoglio Warehouse.

CHRISTINA'S COCINA CAFE
406/723-8444

Mexican. Casual Dining. $8-$19 **AAA Inspector Notes:** The very popular neighborhood restaurant is in a residential district and offers an extensive menu of Tex-Mex cuisine, including slow-cooked beans instead of refried and in-house made taco chips and sauces. **Features:** full bar. **Address:** 2201 Silver Bow Blvd 59701 **Location:** I-90/15 exit Continental Dr, 4 mi w, then 1 mi s on Howard St.

FRED'S MESQUITE GRILL
406/723-4440

American. Casual Dining. $9-$26 **AAA Inspector Notes:** The eatery's focal point is the huge wood-fired grill. Those who choose to sit at the counter can watch and smell the kebabs, steaks, chicken, vegetables and seafood sizzling before being served to them piping hot. The chef does it the right way, with homemade onion rings, freshly prepared salads and choice cuts of meat. **Features:** full bar, patio dining. **Address:** 205 S Arizona St 59701 **Location:** Jct Mercury St; in Historic Uptown.

MATT'S PLACE DRIVE IN
406/782-8049

American. Family Dining. $6-$10 **AAA Inspector Notes:** *Historic.* This classic diner is on the historic registry. In business since 1930, this place serves classic, made-from-scratch food and homemade ice cream. Thick, rich milkshakes come in a variety of flavors. Distinctive equipment and period furniture are part of the décor. They still have car-hop service. **Address:** 2339 Placer St 59701 **Location:** I-90 exit 126, 0.5 mi s; jct Rowe Rd and Montana Ave.

METALS SPORTS BAR & GRILL
406/782-5534

American. Casual Dining. $7-$22 **AAA Inspector Notes:** *Historic.* In the historic Metals Bank building, the eatery sports no fewer than 24 TVs. The old vault is used as a wine cave, which offers one intimate table, and the original marble teller counter serves as the bar. The menu features meats from a local butcher. **Features:** full bar. **Address:** 8 W Park St 59701 **Location:** Jct Main St; in Historic Uptown. **Parking:** street only.

THE MONTANA CLUB
406/494-1400

Regional American. Casual Dining. $7-$22 **AAA Inspector Notes:** Sister restaurants are in Missoula and Kalispell. This new construction has a wood interior. Fresh Alaskan salmon, halibut and house-cut meats are on the menu. The family-friendly restaurant has large portions and is next to a casino. **Features:** full bar, senior menu. **Address:** 3540 Harrison Ave 59701 **Location:** I-90/15 exit 127 (Harrison Ave), 0.7 mi s.

SOHO ASIAN CUISINE
406/221-7288

Chinese. Casual Dining. $7-$16 **AAA Inspector Notes:** A few steps up from the Acoma, this restaurant has a wall of windows and a skylight. You'll have lots of light during the day, but at night, the lights of Butte sparkle. Drinks may be ordered from the Acoma only during the evening. The owners create Chinese comfort food to go along with the comfortable décor. Recently, sushi has been added to the diverse menu. **Features:** full bar, senior menu. **Address:** 60 1/2 E Broadway 59701 **Location:** Jct Wyoming St; in Historic Uptown. **Parking:** street only.

TRIMBO'S "OFF THE HOOK" PIZZA
406/782-1700

Eastern Pizza. Family Dining. $7-$24 **AAA Inspector Notes:** *Historic.* "Off the hook" is an expression used by New Yorkers to mean fantastic, super, et cetera. And that's just what this New York-style pizza is. The dough is made from scratch daily, then hand-tossed to stretch it out. And believe me, it needs to be stretched in order for all of those fresh ingredients to fit. The veggies are fresh and the meats and cheeses are imported. But for me, the crust is it—just a bit chewy but mostly crispy with a wonderful fresh taste, just like "back East." **Features:** beer & wine. **Address:** 43 E Park St 59701 **Location:** Just e of jct Main St; in Historic Uptown. **Parking:** street only.

UPTOWN CAFE   406/723-4735

Continental
Casual Dining
$7-$32

AAA Inspector Notes: *Historic.* An informal, modern decor and art gallery complement house specials of fresh seafood, steak, poultry and pasta. Gourmet desserts include tortes and cakes, and the homemade bread is excellent. A convenient, upscale luncheon buffet is offered. **Features:** full bar. **Reservations:** suggested, for dinner. **Address:** 47 E Broadway 59701 **Location:** I-90/15 exit 126, 1.5 mi n on Montana St, then just e. **Parking:** street only. [L] [D]

BYNUM (B-3) pop. 31, elev. 3,972'

TWO MEDICINE DINOSAUR CENTER is at 120 Second Ave. S. Guided 3-hour walking tours of an active dinosaur dig site along the front range of the Rocky Mountains include a discussion about paleontology and an opportunity to search for fossil specimens. Transportation to the field is provided. Hands-on paleontology programs are offered.

Note: The walk may cover up to 2 miles and involve some stooping and bending. Comfortable clothing and shoes are recommended. **Hours:** Departures require a minimum of three people. Tours are given daily 9-6, Memorial Day weekend-Sept. 15; Wed.-Sun. 10-5, May 1-day before Memorial Day weekend and Sept. 16-30; by appointment rest of year. Phone ahead to confirm schedule. **Cost:** Tour $75. Gallery only $5; $4 (ages 55+); $3 (ages 3-12). Reservations are required. **Phone:** (406) 469-2211 or (800) 238-6873.

CARDWELL pop. 50

LAHOOD PARK   406/287-3281

American. Casual Dining. $7-$25 **AAA Inspector Notes:** Only 100 yards from where Lewis and Clark camped along the Jefferson River and 4 miles from Lewis and Clark Caverns, the restaurant offers good cuts of steak, made-in-house sauces and homemade sourdough bread. The portions are nicely sized. Popular with locals, the budget, rustic-style restaurant gets crowded during the summer, so reservations are necessary. **Features:** full bar. **Reservations:** suggested. **Address:** 960 E Hwy 2 59721 **Location:** I-90 exit 256, 2 mi e. [L] [D] [AC]

CHARLO (C-2) pop. 379, elev. 2,936'

NINEPIPES MUSEUM OF EARLY MONTANA is at 40962 US 93. The extensive and in-depth collections include examples of antique and contemporary beadwork and quillwork, photographs dating from the late 1800s, Western artwork by such notables as Charles M. Russell and E.S. Paxson, and period Western and native clothing. A large diorama includes mounted specimens. **Time:** Allow 1 hour minimum. **Hours:** Mon.-Sat. 10-5, Memorial Day-Labor Day; Thurs.-Sat. 10-4, day after Labor Day-Oct. 31 and early Apr.-day before Memorial Day. Phone ahead to confirm the end of the fall season. **Cost:** $5; $4.50 (ages 65+); $4 (students with ID); $2.50 (ages 5-11). **Phone:** (406) 644-3435.

CHESTER (B-4) pop. 847

LIBERTY COUNTY MUSEUM is at 230 Second St. E. Housed in a former Methodist church, the museum contains artifacts, photographs and other items depicting the homesteading days on the High Plains. Archives and genealogy records are available for research. **Time:** Allow 30 minutes minimum. **Hours:** Daily 1-5 and 7-9, late May-Labor Day. **Cost:** Donations. **Phone:** (406) 759-5256.

CHICO HOT SPRINGS (E-4) elev. 5,274'

RECREATIONAL ACTIVITIES
Dog Sledding
• **Absaroka Dogsled Treks** departs from the Chico Hot Springs Resort at 1 Old Chico Rd. **Hours:** Trips are offered daily, day after Thanksgiving-late Mar. Departure times vary; phone ahead. **Phone:** (406) 333-4933 after hours.

Horseback Riding
• **The Chico Horse Barn** is at the Chico Hot Springs Resort at 1 Old Chico Rd. **Hours:** Horseback riding trips are offered daily, Mar.-Nov. (weather permitting). Departure times vary; phone ahead. **Phone:** (406) 333-4933 or (406) 333-4505.

CHINOOK (B-5) pop. 1,203, elev. 2,405'
• Hotels p. 150

Chinook was named after the Native American word for the winds that often whip through this area during January and February, causing the temperature to rise as much as 70 degrees in a few hours. Melting the snow and exposing the grass, chinooks have saved many cattle herds from disaster. Charles M. Russell captured the significance of these winds to the range cattleman in his picture of a starving cow titled "Waiting for a Chinook."

Chinook Area Chamber of Commerce: P.O. Box 744, Chinook, MT 59523.

BEAR PAW BATTLEFIELD-NEZ PERCE NATIONAL HISTORICAL PARK is off US 2, 16 mi. s. on CR 240, following signs. Chief Joseph, leader of the Nez Perce Indians, surrendered to Col. Nelson A. Miles on this site Oct. 5, 1877. A 1.5-mile walking trail is available. Blaine County Museum *(see attraction listing)* serves as the park's visitor center. **Tours:** Guided tours are available. **Hours:** Daily dawn-dusk. **Cost:** Free. **Phone:** (406) 357-3130, or (406) 357-2590 for the Blaine County Museum.

BLAINE COUNTY MUSEUM is 4 blks. s. of US 2 at 501 Indiana St. In addition to fossil exhibits and Native American and pioneer artifacts, the museum features re-creations of a tar paper homestead, a schoolroom, medical offices and a church. A multimedia account of the Battle of Bear Paw and information about Bear Paw Battlefield-Nez Perce National Historical Park *(see attraction listing)* also are offered.

Tours: Guided tours are available. **Time:** Allow 1 hour minimum. **Hours:** Daily 8-noon and 1-5, Memorial Day-Labor Day; Mon.-Fri. 8-noon and 1-5, May 1-day before Memorial Day and day after Labor Day-Sept. 30; Mon.-Fri. 1-5, rest of year. Closed

Jan. 1, Thanksgiving and Christmas. **Cost:** Free. **Phone:** (406) 357-2590.

CHINOOK MOTOR INN   406/357-2248

Motel
$69-$79

Address: 100 Indiana St 59523 **Location:** On US 2. **Facility:** 37 units. 2 stories (no elevator), interior corridors. **Parking:** winter plug-ins. **Terms:** cancellation fee imposed.

SAVE 🍴 🍽 🛜 ✕ 🖥 /SOME UNITS 💲

CHOTEAU (C-3) pop. 1,684, elev. 4,000'

Choteau (SHO-toe) was named after French fur trader Pierre Chouteau; the name is spelled with one "u" to distinguish it from the adjoining county, also named after the Frenchman.

Choteau Chamber of Commerce: 815 Main Ave. N., P.O. Box 897, Choteau, MT 59422. **Phone:** (406) 466-5316.

OLD TRAIL MUSEUM is at 823 N. Main Ave. Set in a Western village, this local history and paleontology museum chronicles the history of the Rocky Mountain Front beginning with the dinosaur era. **Hours:** Daily 9-5, Memorial Day-Labor Day. **Cost:** $2; free (ages 0-2). **Phone:** (406) 466-5332.

CHOTEAU STAGE STOP INN   (406)466-5900

Hotel
$82-$125

Address: 1005 N Main Ave 59422 **Location:** On US 89, north of town center. **Facility:** 43 units. 2 stories (no elevator), interior corridors. **Parking:** winter plug-ins. **Terms:** cancellation fee imposed. **Pool(s):** heated indoor. **Activities:** hot tub, exercise room. **Guest Services:** coin laundry. **Featured Amenity: full hot breakfast.** *(See ad p. 331, p. 171.)*

SAVE 🅿 BIZ 🛜 ✕ 🖥
📷 🖨

WHERE TO EAT

ELK COUNTRY GRILL   406/466-3311

🔷🔷 American. Casual Dining. $7-$27 **AAA Inspector Notes:** The roomy dining area has wood accents. Good ribs and chops are offered. Hear the elk bugle when an order is ready in the kitchen. Elk antlers decorate the restaurant. Rib-eye steaks are fresh cut when you order. You will want to try the home-baked breads and desserts. **Features:** beer & wine. **Address:** 925 N Main Ave 59422 **Location:** On US 89, north of town center. L D

JOHN HENRY'S   406/466-5642

🔷🔷 American. Casual Dining. $7-$19 **AAA Inspector Notes:** You'll find affordable, tasty pizzas, burgers and family fare served in a casual, friendly atmosphere. **Features:** beer & wine. **Address:** 215 N Main St 59422 **Location:** On US 89; center. **Parking:** street only.
B L D

CIRCLE (C-7) pop. 615, elev. 2,424'

Circle takes its name from a cattle ranch that once stood near this site. In the late 19th century the area around Circle was booming cattle country, but the devastation caused by the winter of 1886-87 put many

---

ranchers out of business. Circle remains an agricultural community and the seat of McCone County.

Circle Chamber of Commerce and Agriculture: 219 Main St., P.O. Box 321, Circle, MT 59215. **Phone:** (406) 485-4782.

McCONE COUNTY MUSEUM is at 801 SR 200S. Featured are a large collection of mounted birds and animals as well as artifacts, farm machinery, tools and guns from the homestead era. Dinosaur bones also are displayed. **Time:** Allow 1 hour minimum. **Hours:** Mon.-Fri. 9-noon and 1-5, May-Sept. **Cost:** $2; $1 (ages 0-11). **Phone:** (406) 485-2414.

CLINTON   pop. 1,052

EKSTROM'S STAGE STATION   406/825-3183

🔷🔷 American. Casual Dining. $7-$21 **AAA Inspector Notes:** Dine in what was once the stable of a stagecoach station. Recipes have been handed down between generations in a family that has been in the hospitality business since 1883. Home-baked goods and trout are specialties and they are served amid rustic décor comprised of antique wood tables and mismatched antique chairs of different styles. The walls are adorned with mounted heads of big-game animals and birds as well as farm tools and interesting, century-old objects. May be open weekends in April. **Features:** beer & wine. **Address:** 81 Rock Creek Rd 59825 **Location:** I-90 exit 126 (Rock Creek Rd), 0.5 mi s. B L D

COLUMBIA FALLS (B-2) pop. 4,688, elev. 3,098'

• **Hotels & Restaurants map & index p. 168**
• **Part of Glacier National Park area — see map p. 163**

The union of the North and Middle forks of the Flathead River has carved out Bad Rock Canyon, at the entrance of which lies Columbia Falls. The abundance of water and timber in the area supports Columbia Falls Aluminum Co. and Plum Creek Timber Co., the town's major industries.

Numerous recreational opportunities are available along scenic CR 486, which follows the North Fork of the Flathead River 20 miles north to the Camas Creek entrance to Glacier National Park. Hungry Horse Dam *(see Glacier National Park p. 166)* and the Great Bear and Bob Marshall wilderness areas also are nearby.

SAVE **BIG SKY WATERPARK** is 2 blks. w. of jct. US 2 and SR 206 at 7211 US 2 E. Among the park's amusements are a game arcade, a miniature golf course, bumper cars, a carousel, a water-wars game and several waterslides. **Time:** Allow 2 hours minimum. **Hours:** Daily 11-7 (twilight rate begins at 3), July 1 to mid-Aug.; 11-6 (twilight rate begins at 3), Memorial Day-June 30 and mid- to late Aug. and Labor Day weekend. Phone to confirm June schedule. **Cost:** $24.99; $19.99 (ages 60+ and under 48 inches tall). Twilight rate $19.99; $14.99 (ages 60+ and under 48 inches tall). Miniature golf $6. **Phone:** (406) 892-5026. 🍴 🎡

(See map & index p. 168.)

BAD ROCK BED & BREAKFAST   (406)892-2829

Bed & Breakfast
$125-$225

Address: 480 Bad Rock Dr 59912 **Location:** Jct US 2 and SR 206, 2.4 mi s on SR 206, 0.9 mi w. Located in a quiet area. **Facility:** This B&B on 30 acres of manicured grounds offers sweeping mountain views. The grounds surround a large main house built to recreate the grand old farm houses of the turn of the century. 8 units, some cabins. 1-2 stories (no elevator), interior/exterior corridors. **Parking:** winter plug-ins. **Terms:** 2 night minimum stay - seasonal, 30 day cancellation notice-fee imposed. **Activities:** cross country skiing, bicycles, game room, exercise room, massage. **Guest Services:** complimentary laundry. **Featured Amenity:** full hot breakfast.

GLACIER PARK SUPER 8   (406)892-0888 5

Hotel
$53-$180

Address: 7336 US 2 E 59912 **Location:** Jct SR 206, just ne. **Facility:** 32 units. 2 stories (no elevator), interior/exterior corridors. **Parking:** winter plug-ins. **Featured Amenity:** continental breakfast.

MEADOW LAKE RESORT   (406)892-8700 4

Vacation Rental Condominium
$119-$520

Address: 100 St Andrews Dr 59912 **Location:** Jct US 2 and SR 40, 1.4 mi e on US 2, 1.1 mi n on Meadow Lake Blvd. **Facility:** A destination in itself, the resort is located on a world-class golf course and offers accommodations including single hotel rooms, large condo units and homes capable of housing entire families. 62 units, some houses and condominiums. 1-3 stories, interior/exterior corridors. **Parking:** winter plug-ins. **Terms:** check-in 4 pm, 30 day cancellation notice-fee imposed. **Pool(s):** heated outdoor, heated indoor. **Activities:** sauna, hot tub, steamroom, regulation golf, tennis, cross country skiing, recreation programs, playground, game room, exercise room, spa. **Guest Services:** area transportation.

WHERE TO EAT

THE BACK ROOM/NITE OWL RESTAURANTS
    406/892-2191 5

American Casual Dining
$10-$20

AAA Inspector Notes: The casual eatery prepares excellent barbecue, steaks and seafood with few frills. Dedicated carnivores can sample any of three styles of ribs served with fry bread. **Features:** full bar, patio dining. **Address:** 522 9th St W 59912 **Location:** Just w of downtown. *Menu on AAA.com* D

CIMARRON CAFE   406/892-9000 4

American. Casual Dining. $6-$19 **AAA Inspector Notes:** The small, unassuming log restaurant serves breakfast and lunch, in addition to dinner four nights a week. On the menu is an array of sandwiches, salads, wraps and a daily quiche special, as well as homemade desserts. **Address:** 700 9th St W 59912 **Location:** Just w of downtown. B L D

COLUMBUS (E-5) pop. 1,893, elev. 3,600'

In 1875 travelers stopped at Countryman stage station on the north bank of the Yellowstone River. The hardy travelers referred to the settlement as Eagle's Nest, or as Sheep Dip, because of its vile whiskey. With the coming of the Northern Pacific Railroad in 1882 the town became a livestock and agricultural center. Initially called Stillwater by the railroad because it lay at the confluence of the Stillwater and Yellowstone rivers, it was renamed Columbus in 1893 to avoid confusion with Stillwater, Minn.

Today the town's economy still rests upon farming and ranching, but the area also is home to the only platinum and palladium mine in the United States. The town manufactures laminated structural wood beams and Western-style buckles, jewelry and saddle trim.

MUSEUM OF THE BEARTOOTHS is off I-90 exit 408, w. on Fourth Ave., then n. on Fifth St. to the corner of Fifth Ave. Displays illustrate the history of Stillwater County, mining and homesteading. The museum also pays tribute to local Congressional Medal of Honor winner Donald J. Ruhl, in whose name SR 78 was designated a Memorial Highway.

An additional building on the grounds displays outdoor machinery. **Time:** Allow 30 minutes minimum. **Hours:** Mon.-Fri. 10-5, Sat. 11-3, Memorial Day-Labor Day; Mon.-Fri. 10-5, Apr. 1-day before Memorial Day and day after Labor Day-Dec. 31. **Cost:** Donations. **Phone:** (406) 322-4588.

SUPER 8 OF COLUMBUS   (406)322-4101

Hotel
$73-$120

Address: 602 8th Ave N 59019 **Location:** I-90 exit 408, just s on SR 78. **Facility:** 72 units, some kitchens. 2 stories (no elevator), interior corridors. **Parking:** winter plug-ins. **Guest Services:** coin laundry. **Featured Amenity:** continental breakfast.

CONRAD pop. 2,570

SUPER 8   (406)278-7676

Hotel $86-$103 **Address:** 215 N Main St 59425 **Location:** I-15 exit 339, just w. **Facility:** 46 units. 2 stories (no elevator), interior corridors. **Parking:** winter plug-ins. **Guest Services:** coin laundry.

COOKE CITY (F-4) pop. 75, elev. 7,675'
• Hotels & Restaurants map & index p. 336
• Part of Yellowstone National Park area — see map p. 326

Gold miners settled Cooke City in the early 1870s, and by 1880 the town numbered 7,000 fortune-seeking souls. Gold mining continued until the late 1950s, when commercial mining finally ceased. Gold-panning in area streams remains popular.

Cooke City is 4 miles from Yellowstone National Park's northeast gate. Beartooth Scenic Highway (see Red Lodge p. 201), the town's eastern access, usually is open May through September. Cooke City can be reached all year via the road from Gardiner through Yellowstone.

Cooke City Area Chamber of Commerce: 206 W. Main St., P.O. Box 1071, Cooke City, MT 59020. **Phone:** (406) 838-2495.

ELK HORN LODGE   406/838-2332   28
Motel $105-$125 **Address:** 103 Main St 59020 **Location:** US 212; center. **Facility:** 8 units, some cabins. 2 stories (no elevator), exterior corridors. **Terms:** 7 day cancellation notice. **Activities:** hot tub.

CULBERTSON (B-8) pop. 714, elev. 1,919'

THE KINGS INN   406/787-6277
Motel $95-$115 **Address:** 408 E 6th St 59218 **Location:** Jct US 2 and SR 16, 0.3 mi e. **Facility:** 20 units. 1 story, interior corridors. **Parking:** winter plug-ins. **Terms:** cancellation fee imposed.

CUSTER NATIONAL FOREST (E-4)

Elevations in the forest range from 1,035 ft. in the grasslands of South Dakota to 12,799 ft. at Granite Peak in Montana. Refer to AAA maps for additional elevation information.

Scattered across counties in Montana and South Dakota, Custer National Forest encompasses nearly 1.3 million acres in three unique districts. The mountainous section, or Beartooth District, includes a portion of the Absaroka-Beartooth Wilderness and Granite Peak, the highest point in Montana. The eastern portions range from the pine-clad hills and rough break country of southeastern Montana to the rolling grassland of northwestern South Dakota and the badlands of western North Dakota.

Beartooth Scenic Highway, usually open May to mid-October, traverses the mountain country. Other good routes provide access to campgrounds and trailheads. Guide and pack services are available in nearby towns.

Trail information, which can be obtained from Forest Service offices, should be checked and updated at Beartooth Ranger Station before a trip into Absaroka-Beartooth Wilderness is attempted. The ranger station, south of Red Lodge, Mont., on US 212, is open daily 8-4:30, Memorial Day-Labor Day; Mon.-Fri. 8-4:30, rest of year.

For further information contact the Forest Supervisor, 1310 Main St., Billings, MT 59105; phone (406) 255-1400 or Beartooth Ranger Station, (406) 446-2103. See Recreation Areas Chart.

CUT BANK pop. 2,869

CUT BANK SUPER 8   (406)873-5662

Motel
$95-$215

Address: 609 W Main St 59427 **Location:** On US 2, 0.3 mi w. **Facility:** 61 units. 3 stories (no elevator), interior corridors. **Parking:** winter plug-ins. **Terms:** check-in 4 pm. **Pool(s):** heated indoor. **Activities:** limited exercise equipment. **Guest Services:** coin laundry. **Featured Amenity: continental breakfast.**

GLACIER GATEWAY PLAZA   (406)873-2566
Motel
$69-$90
Address: 1130 E Main St 59427 **Location:** US 2, just e from town center. **Facility:** 19 units. 1 story, interior corridors. **Parking:** winter plug-ins. **Terms:** resort fee. **Pool(s):** heated indoor. **Activities:** hot tub, exercise room. **Guest Services:** coin laundry, area transportation. **Featured Amenity: continental breakfast.**

DARBY pop. 720

RYE CREEK LODGE   (406)821-3366
Vacation Rental Cabin $250-$750 **Address:** 458 Rye Creek Rd 59829 **Location:** US 93, 4.5 mi s, 1.5 mi e. Located in a quiet, secluded setting. **Facility:** Spend a weekend relaxing in front of the fire or take an ATV ride. Cabins are spaced to give maximum privacy and you may see elk, moose or a deer from your porch. Each cabin has a hot tub. 6 cabins. 1-2 stories (no elevator), exterior corridors. **Parking:** winter plug-ins. **Terms:** check-in 4 pm, 60 day cancellation notice-fee imposed, resort fee. **Activities:** fishing, snowmobiling, bicycles. **Guest Services:** complimentary laundry.

DEER LODGE (D-3) pop. 3,111, elev. 4,519'
• Hotels p. 154

The second oldest city in Montana, Deer Lodge is on the Clark Fork River midway between Yellowstone and Glacier national parks. The city was established in 1862 as the result of a nearby gold discovery. With fresh food and a blacksmith as drawing cards, Deer Lodge was a welcome stop for the many settlers and miners who passed through the area.

Southwest Montana: 1105 Main St., Deer Lodge, MT 59722. **Phone:** (800) 879-1159.

Self-guiding tours: Driving tour maps for the surrounding area are available from the Powell County Chamber of Commerce at 1109 Main St.; phone (406) 846-2094.

GRANT-KOHRS RANCH NATIONAL HISTORIC SITE is off I-90 exit 184 or 187. Established in the early 1860s, the ranch had grown to 27,000 acres by the early 1900s, and the owners controlled more than a million acres of public range in four states and Canada. Though much reduced, the 1,500-acre ranch still has livestock and more than 80 buildings, from bunkhouse row to the 23-room ranch house.

Hours: Daily 9-5:30, Memorial Day-Labor Day; 9-4:30, rest of year. Guided historic house tours are given on the hour in the morning and on the half-hour in the afternoon. Closed Jan. 1, Thanksgiving and Christmas. Phone ahead to confirm schedule. **Cost:** Free. **Phone:** (406) 846-2070.

OLD MONTANA PRISON is off I-90 exit 184 or 187 at 1106 Main St. Self-guiding tours of the cell house, maximum-security areas, hole, tunnel and walled prison grounds together with an exhibit of photographs provide insight into early prison life and area history. The facility served as a prison 1871-1979.

Time: Allow 45 minutes minimum. **Hours:** Daily 8-6, mid-May to mid-Sept.; otherwise varies. Last admission 50 minutes before closing. Closed Jan. 1, Thanksgiving and Christmas. Phone ahead to confirm schedule. **Cost:** (includes Frontier Montana Museum, Montana Auto Museum and Yesterday's Playthings Doll & Toy Museum) $10; $9 (ages 62+ and military with ID); $6 (ages 10-15). **Phone:** (406) 846-3111 or (406) 846-3114.

Frontier Montana Museum is at 1106 Main St. An extensive private collection of Western memorabilia from the 1800s is a highlight of this museum. Also featured are Civil War items, a gun collection comprising 250 weapons, Native American artifacts, a railroad saloon diorama, railroad artifacts and a display of "gambler's essentials." **Hours:** Daily 10-5, mid-May to mid-Sept.; otherwise varies rest of year.**Cost:** Entrance included with Old Montana

Prison admission of $10; $9 (ages 62+ and military with ID); $6 (ages 10-15). **Phone:** (406) 846-3111.

Montana Auto Museum is at 1106 Main St. The museum houses a representative collection of vintage automobiles from the 1800s through the 1970s. Included are a 1903 Model A Ford, a 1914 Detroit Electric Car, 1950s Chevrolets and muscle cars from the late 1960s and early '70s. Interpretive displays and photographs enhance the collection.

Hours: Daily 8-6, mid-May to mid-Sept.; otherwise varies. Last admission 30 minutes before closing. Closed Jan. 1, Thanksgiving and Christmas. Phone ahead to confirm schedule. **Cost:** Entrance included with Old Montana Prison admission of $10; $9 (ages 62+ and military with ID); $6 (ages 10-15). **Phone:** (406) 846-3111.

Powell County Museum is at 1193 Main St. Permanent and changing exhibits depict the history of Powell County and Deer Lodge Valley. Displays include a woodcarving collection, mining and ranching equipment and household and school items. **Hours:** Daily noon-5, in summer. Phone ahead to confirm schedule. **Cost:** Free. **Phone:** (406) 846-3111.

Yesterday's Playthings Doll & Toy Museum is at 1097 Main St. The history of children's toys from the 19th century to the present is the focus of this museum. The collection includes an extensive Raggedy Ann and Andy display, dolls from different cultures and dolls made from materials ranging from papier-mâché to china. A model railroad collection also is displayed. **Time:** Allow 30 minutes minimum. **Hours:** Daily 10-5, mid-May to mid-Sept. **Cost:** Entrance included with Old Montana Prison admission of $10; $9 (ages 62+ and military with ID); $6 (ages 10-15). **Phone:** (406) 846-3111.

TRAVELODGE (406)846-2370

Motel
$80-$200

Address: 1150 N Main St 59722 **Location:** I-90 exit 184, 0.3 mi s. **Facility:** 57 units. 2 stories (no elevator), interior corridors. **Parking:** winter plug-ins. **Featured Amenity: continental breakfast.**

WESTERN BIG SKY INN 406/846-2590

Motel. Rates not provided. **Address:** 210 N Main St 59722 **Location:** I-90 exit 184, 1 mi w. **Facility:** 20 units, some two bedrooms. 2 stories (no elevator), exterior corridors. **Parking:** winter plug-ins.

DILLON (E-3) pop. 4,134, elev. 5,102'

Dillon was established in 1880 by a group of businessmen who bought out a rancher who refused to give up his land to the railroad. Named for the president of Union Pacific Railroad, Dillon is today a focal point for five rich stock-raising valleys, including Big Hole, Grasshopper and Beaverhead. Beaverhead County is among the top cattle- and hay-producing regions in the state.

West of Dillon is Bannack State Park *(see attraction listing)*, on the site of a former mining town. In 1863 Sidney Edgerton, a lawyer from Ohio, arrived in the vicinity and stayed throughout the winter season. When he visited Washington, D.C., in the spring, he advocated the creation of a new territory; President Abraham Lincoln named Edgerton governor and Bannack the temporary capital. The following year the territory's seat was moved to the boomtown of Virginia City.

Fishing is a popular recreational pursuit in the area. Some of Montana's higher mountains can be seen from scenic I-15, which follows the Beaverhead and Red Rock rivers to the Idaho border.

Beaverhead Chamber of Commerce: 10 W. Reeder St., P.O. Box 425, Dillon, MT 59725. **Phone:** (406) 683-5511.

Self-guiding tours: A brochure outlining a walking tour of historic Dillon is available from the chamber of commerce and the Beaverhead County Museum *(see attraction listing).*

BANNACK STATE PARK is 17 mi. w. on SR 278, then 4 mi. s. on Bannack Rd., following signs. Montana's first territorial capital and one of the original gold-rush towns of this area, the park includes weathered remains of the first capitol, jail, hotel and log cabins. The visitor center offers 19th-century photographs of the region and videotapes about mining and local history. Primitive camping facilities are $23 (nonresidents); $18 (nonresidents with a Montana State Park passport); $15 (residents). *See Recreation Areas Chart.*

Time: Allow 1 hour minimum. **Hours:** Park daily 8 a.m.-9 p.m., Memorial Day-Labor Day; 8-dusk, May

1-day before Memorial Day; 8-5, rest of year. Visitor center daily 10-6, May-Sept.; Sat.-Sun. 11-6, in Oct. Closed Christmas Eve and Christmas. **Cost:** $5 (nonresidents per private vehicle); $3 (nonresidents arriving by other means); free (residents). **Phone:** (406) 834-3413.

BEAVERHEAD COUNTY MUSEUM is at 15 S. Montana St. Included are a native birds exhibit and items pertaining to Native American and pioneer life in Beaverhead County. An outdoor interpretive area features a 1,300-foot boardwalk, an 1885 homesteader's cabin and sheep wagon, and a 1910 one-room schoolhouse. **Hours:** Mon.-Fri. 8-5. Closed major holidays. **Cost:** $3; $2 (ages 12-17 and 55+); $6 (family). **Phone:** (406) 683-5027.

THE UNIVERSITY OF MONTANA WESTERN ART GALLERY/MUSEUM is in Main Hall at 710 S. Atlantic St. Featured are changing art exhibits; a permanent art collection that includes works by Charles M. Russell, Edgar Paxson and Monte Dolack; and the Seidensticker Wildlife Collection, featuring mounted animal trophies from around the world. **Hours:** Mon.-Thurs. 9-4. Phone ahead to confirm schedule. **Cost:** Free. **Phone:** (406) 491-1444.

BEST WESTERN PARADISE INN (406)683-4214

Hotel
$68-$180

AAA Benefit: Members save 10% or more with Best Western!

Address: 650 N Montana St 59725 **Location:** I-15 exit 63, 0.3 mi s on SR 41. **Facility:** 63 units, some two bedrooms. 2 stories (no elevator), exterior corridors. **Parking:** winter plug-ins. **Pool(s):** heated indoor. **Activities:** hot tub, exercise room. **Guest Services:** coin laundry.

COMFORT INN OF DILLON (406)683-6831

Hotel $109-$134 **Address:** 450 N Interchange 59725 **Location:** I-15 exit 63. **Facility:** 48 units. 2 stories (no elevator), interior corridors. **Parking:** winter plug-ins. **Pool(s):** heated indoor. **Guest Services:** coin laundry.

GUESTHOUSE INTERNATIONAL INN & SUITES (406)683-3636

Hotel $69-$199 **Address:** 580 Sinclair St 59725 **Location:** I-15 exit 63. **Facility:** 58 units. 2 stories (no elevator), interior corridors. **Parking:** winter plug-ins. **Pool(s):** indoor. **Activities:** hot tub, exercise room. **Guest Services:** coin laundry.

EAST GLACIER PARK (B-2) elev. 4,795'

- Hotels & Restaurants map & index p. 168
- Part of Glacier National Park area — see map p. 163

In the Two Medicine Valley, East Glacier Park is the recreational center and eastern gateway to Glacier National Park (see place listing p. 163). The community maintains an Old West appearance.

DANCING BEARS INN & SUITES (406)226-4402 ⑪

Motel
$8B-$174

Address: 40 Montana Ave 59434 **Location:** Just off US 2, follow signs; center. **Facility:** 18 units, some efficiencies, houses and cabins. 1 story, interior/exterior corridors. **Parking:** winter plug-ins. **Terms:** 4 day cancellation notice-fee imposed. **Featured Amenity: continental breakfast.**

JACOBSON'S SCENIC VIEW COTTAGES 406/226-4422 ⑨

Cottage $70-$105 **Address:** 1204 Hwy 49 59434 **Location:** On SR 49, 0.8 mi n. Adjacent to Glacier National Park. **Facility:** 12 cottages. 1 story, exterior corridors. **Terms:** closed 10/6-4/30. **Activities:** playground.

MOUNTAIN PINE MOTEL 406/226-4403 ⑩

Motel $61-$92 **Address:** SR 49 N 59434 **Location:** On SR 49, 0.6 mi n. Adjacent to Glacier National Park. **Facility:** 27 units, some houses and cottages. 1 story, exterior corridors. **Terms:** closed 10/1-4/30, resort fee. **Activities:** lawn sports.

GLACIER PARK LODGE 406/226-5600

[fyi] Not evaluated. **Address:** SR 49 59434 **Location:** On SR 49, jct US 2; across from Amtrak station. Facilities, services, and décor characterize a mid-scale property. This property features spacious, beautifully landscaped grounds and cozy, charming guest units. The expansive public areas reflect the pioneer railroad era of yesteryear.

WHERE TO EAT

SERRANO'S 406/226-9392 ⑧

Mexican. Casual Dining. $9-$19 **AAA Inspector Notes:** This restaurant is inside the historic former Dawson House where the atmosphere is intimate but bustling. Expect a wait. You can't go wrong with the sautéed red snapper or the strip steak. The Indian taco is always a favorite. Patio seating is offered in July and August. **Features:** full bar. **Address:** 29 Dawson Ave 59434 **Location:** Center. **Parking:** street only.

EMIGRANT pop. 488

- Hotels & Restaurants map & index p. 336
- Part of Yellowstone National Park area — see map p. 326

JOHNSTAD'S BED & BREAKFAST & LOG CABIN
406/333-9003

Bed & Breakfast $125-$175 **Address:** 03 Paradise Ln 59027 **Location:** I-90 exit 333 (US 89), 17 mi s; between MM 36 and 37. **Facility:** Surrounded by views of the Paradise Valley and the Beartooth/Absaroka mountain ranges, the B&B offers private access to the Yellowstone River. 3 units, some cabins. 1 story, exterior corridors. **Terms:** check-in 4 pm, 2 night minimum stay - seasonal and/or weekends, 30 day cancellation notice-fee imposed, resort fee. **Activities:** fishing.

MOUNTAIN SKY GUEST RANCH (406)333-4911 ⑤

Resort Hotel $720-$1146 **Address:** Big Creek Rd 59027 **Location:** I-90 exit 333 (US 89), 27 mi s; 6 mi s of town, 4.5 mi w. **Facility:** Nestled in the Gallatin Mountain Range, the ranch offers modern guest rooms and one- to three-bedroom rustic cabins. All are supplied with baskets of fruit, coffee and tea. 31 units, some two bedrooms, three bedrooms, houses and cabins. 1 story, exterior corridors. **Terms:** closed 11/1-4/30, 3-7 night minimum stay - seasonal, cancellation fee imposed. **Pool(s):** heated outdoor. **Activities:** sauna, hot tub, fishing, regulation golf, tennis, recreation programs, kids club, game room, exercise room, massage. **Guest Services:** complimentary laundry.

PARADISE GATEWAY BED & BREAKFAST & GUEST CABIN 406/333-4063

Bed & Breakfast
$85-$400

Address: 2644 Hwy 89 S 59027 **Location:** I-90 exit 333 (US 89), 4.5 mi s of town; between MM 26 and 27, 0.3 mi e on gravel road. **Facility:** Nestled in the majestic Absaroka Mountains along the banks of the pristine Yellowstone River, the B&B is just minutes away from scenic Yellowstone National Park. It's a great spot for avid fishermen. 3 units, some two bedrooms and cabins. 1-2 stories (no elevator), interior/exterior corridors. **Terms:** check-in 4 pm, 2 night minimum stay - weekends, age restrictions may apply, 14 day cancellation notice-fee imposed. **Activities:** fishing. **Featured Amenity: full hot breakfast.**

ENNIS (E-3) pop. 838, elev. 4,939'

Ennis is in the broad, rolling Madison Valley, flanked on both sides by mountain ranges. Built along the Madison River, the town is convenient to the historic gold-mining towns of Virginia City and Nevada City as well as to the trout-filled lakes and streams of the Beaverhead-Deerlodge and Gallatin national forests (see place listings p. 129 and p. 159).

Ennis Chamber of Commerce: P.O. Box 291, Ennis, MT 59729. **Phone:** (406) 682-4388.

FAN MOUNTAIN INN 406/682-5200

Motel
$65-$90

Address: 204 N Main St 59729 **Location:** US 287, just nw of City Center. **Facility:** 27 units. 2 stories (no elevator), exterior corridors. **Parking:** winter plug-ins. **Terms:** 10 day cancellation notice-fee imposed.

WHERE TO EAT

CONTINENTAL DIVIDE 406/682-7600

Regional Continental. Fine Dining. $18-$39 **AAA Inspector Notes:** The chef/owner of this little gem of a bistro splits his creative talents seasonally. In the winter, his creative bent is jazz trombone, and for our eating pleasure in the summer, his artistry shines through in dishes such as sautéed Manila clams in an Asian-style broth or lobster cannelloni. His warm and approachable manner is also evident during his visits with patrons. While the dining room in the cabin is intimate and comfortable, dining al fresco is available. **Features:** beer & wine, patio dining. **Reservations:** suggested. **Address:** 47 Geyser St 59729 **Location:** 1.3 mi n on US 287, just e.

ESSEX

- Hotels & Restaurants map & index p. 168
- Part of Glacier National Park area — see map p. 163

GLACIER HAVEN INN   (406)888-5720 ㉙

Motel
$75-$149

Address: 14305 US Hwy 2 E 59916 **Location:** Between MM 173 and 174; 20 mi e of West Glacier; 35 mi w of East Glacier. **Facility:** 8 units. 1 story, exterior corridors. **Parking:** winter plug-ins. **Terms:** 31 day cancellation notice-fee imposed. **Guest Services:** coin laundry.

SAVE 🍴 CALL 📶 📶 🐾 📠
📶 📠 📄

IZAAK WALTON INN   (406)888-5700 ㉚

🔻🔻 **Historic Country Inn** $109-$359 **Address:** 290 Izaak Walton Inn Rd 59916 **Location:** On US 2; between MM 179 and 180. **Facility:** One of the original hotels built by railroad magnate J.J. Hill to provide lodging for turn-of-the-century visitors from the East wishing to explore Glacier National Park. Today it serves the same purpose. 49 units, some two bedrooms, kitchens, cabins and cottages. 1-3 stories (no elevator), interior/exterior corridors. **Parking:** winter plug-ins. **Terms:** 30 day cancellation notice-fee imposed. **Dining:** The Dining Car, see separate listing. **Activities:** sauna, cross country skiing, bicycles, game room, lawn sports, picnic facilities, trails. **Guest Services:** coin laundry.

🍴 📶 📶 ✕ 🐾 📠
/SOME UNITS 📺 📶 📠 📄

WHERE TO EAT

THE DINING CAR   406/888-5700 ㉗

🔻🔻🔻 American. Casual Dining. $8-$24 **AAA Inspector Notes:** This restaurant is set up like you're on a train — complete with observation windows overlooking the train line, while a model train circles the room overhead. The seasonal menu features fresh seafood, regional meats and veggies. For dessert try the heavenly cake — a flour-less chocolate cake topped with huckleberry ice cream and surrounded by meringue. **Features:** full bar, patio dining. **Address:** 290 Izaak Walton Inn Rd 59916 **Location:** On US 2; between MM 179 and 180; in Izaak Walton Inn.

B L D LATE

HEALTHY HAVEN CAFE   406/888-5720 ㉖

🔻 American. Casual Dining. $10-$26 **AAA Inspector Notes:** This is a true multi-generational endeavor. Grandma is the pie baker, Mom is the cook and grandchildren round out the service. A limited menu of healthy choices, such as bison steak or tilapia, is offered in the evening, while an extensive breakfast buffet is available in the morning. **Address:** 14305 US 2 E 59916 **Location:** Between MM 173 and 174; 20 mi e of West Glacier; 35 mi w of East Glacier.

B D CALL 📶

EUREKA (A-1) pop. 1,037

Located in the Tobacco River Valley 7 miles south of the Canadian border, Eureka was settled in the 1880s. Fur trader and explorer David Thompson passed through the valley in the early 1880s, an event commemorated each April during Rendezvous Days. Recreational activities, including fishing, kayaking, swimming, water skiing and ice-skating, are available on 90-mile-long Lake Koocanusa *(see Libby p. 188)*, 4 miles west of town, as well as on numerous smaller lakes in the vicinity. Huckleberries abound in the clearings of area forests.

Seven-mile Flathead Tunnel, the second longest railroad tunnel in the country, is 16 miles south of US 93 on Fortine Creek Road (FR 36). The tunnel was built in 1970 when the rising waters of Lake Koocanusa behind Libby Dam forced the railroad to relocate.

Eureka Chamber of Commerce and Visitors Center: 2 Dewey Ave., P.O. Box 186, Eureka, MT 59917. **Phone:** (406) 889-4636.

TOBACCO VALLEY HISTORICAL VILLAGE, 4 Dewey Ave., features a collection of late 19th- and early 20th-century buildings, each of which contains historical displays and artifacts. Among the structures assembled in this parklike setting are a general store; a log house; a church; a railroad depot; a one-room school; a library; a fire tower; and Eureka's first log cabin, built in 1891. Also on the grounds are a covered wagon, antique farm equipment and a Great Northern caboose.

Walking trails lead visitors along the banks of the Tobacco River. **Time:** Allow 1 hour minimum. **Hours:** Grounds daily dawn-dusk. Buildings daily 1-5, Memorial Day-Labor Day. **Cost:** Donations. **Phone:** (406) 297-7654. 🎫

FLATHEAD LAKE (B-2)

A recreational mecca, Flathead Lake appeals to those who enjoy a wide array of activities ranging from water skiing and fishing to sailing and sightseeing. The 28-mile-long, 15-mile-wide lake boasts several islands; sheep, deer, bears, eagles and ospreys inhabit Wild Horse. Nearby communities include Bigfork, Kalispell, Lakeside and Polson *(see individual place listings).*

FLATHEAD NATIONAL FOREST (A-2)

Elevations in the forest range from 3,500 ft. at the valley floor to 9,289 ft. on Swan Peak in the Swan Valley. Refer to AAA maps for additional elevation information.

Flathead National Forest stretches along the spine of the Rocky Mountains south from the Canadian border for more than 120 miles. With parts of its eastern and northern boundaries bordering Glacier National Park *(see place listing p. 163)*, the forest shares much of the park's spectacular scenery of high ridges and mountains. Its principal rivers are the Swan, Stillwater and the three forks of the Flathead—the North Fork, Middle Fork and South Fork, all in the National Wild and Scenic River system. This is augmented by 3,400 miles of streams and many small lakes.

Almost half the national forest's approximately 2.3 million acres lies within the Bob Marshall Wilderness complex, which includes the Bob Marshall, Great Bear and Scapegoat wilderness areas. The combined 1.5 million acres attracts those who seek out a challenging recreation experience in a natural setting where mechanized travel and equipment are prohibited.

Popularly known as the "Bob," the Bob Marshall Wilderness straddles the Continental Divide. There are many rugged peaks, alpine lakes, mountain valleys, meandering streams, wildflower-strewn meadows and waterfalls. Sunsets often are highlighted by long streamers of wave-shaped clouds, a phenomenon created partly by strong winds blowing perpendicular to a mountain range.

For those seeking utter solitude, winter use of the "Bob" is almost nil. This vast reserve, appropriately named for the man who helped preserve millions of acres of the wilderness system, shelters one of the country's largest wildlife populations, including elk, bighorn sheep, black bears and several hundred grizzly bears. About 50 outfitting and guiding businesses serve the area.

Other areas of interest in the forest are Mission Mountain Wilderness and Hungry Horse Reservoir *(see Recreation Areas Chart and Hungry Horse Dam in Glacier National Park p. 166)*, along the shores of which are almost half of the forest's camping and picnic areas. The 15,000-acre Jewel Basin Hiking Area, reached by forest roads from SRs 83 or 35, is a scenic area of rushing waterways, open meadows and subalpine forests; mechanized vehicles and pack animals are not permitted. Hiking, fishing and floating the three forks of the Flathead River are popular activities.

Information about the forest's 31 campgrounds and recreational opportunities is available at the forest headquarters in Kalispell and at district ranger stations. For further information contact the Supervisor's Office, Flathead National Forest, 650 Wolfpack Way, Kalispell, MT 59901; phone (406) 758-5204. *See Recreation Areas Chart.*

FORSYTH pop. 1,777

MAGNUSON HOTELS SUNDOWNER INN   (406)346-2115

Motel
$95-$130

Address: 1018 Front St 59327 **Location:** I-94 exit 95, 0.5 mi nw. **Facility:** 40 units. 2 stories (no elevator), exterior corridors. **Parking:** winter plug-ins. **Guest Services:** coin laundry. **Featured Amenity:** continental breakfast.

 / SOME UNITS

RAILS INN MOTEL   (406)346-2242
Hotel
$65-$80

Address: 290 Front St 59327 **Location:** I-94 exit 93, just n, then 0.5 mi e. **Facility:** 50 units. 2 stories (no elevator), interior corridors. **Parking:** winter plug-ins. **Terms:** 3 day cancellation notice.
Featured Amenity: continental breakfast.

 / SOME UNITS

RESTWEL MOTEL   406/346-2771
Motel
$72-$88

Address: 810 Front St 59327 **Location:** I-94 exit 95, 0.8 mi nw. **Facility:** 20 units, some efficiencies. 1 story, exterior corridors. **Parking:** winter plug-ins.

 / SOME UNITS

WESTWIND MOTOR INN   (406)346-2038
Motel
$65-$80

Address: 225 Westwind Ln 59327 **Location:** I-94 exit 93, 0.3 mi n. **Facility:** 32 units, some two bedrooms. 2 stories (no elevator), interior corridors. **Parking:** winter plug-ins. **Terms:** 3 day cancellation notice. **Featured Amenity:** continental breakfast.

 / SOME UNITS

FORT BENTON (C-4) pop. 1,464, elev. 2,632'
• Hotels p. 158 • Restaurants p. 158

At the head of navigation on the Missouri River, Fort Benton is one of Montana's oldest communities and was the link between east and west. Thousands of immigrants and miners marked this landing as the beginning of the way west along Mullan Road or north along WhoopUp Trail. Fort Benton also was their chief means of supply, as all goods were brought by steamboat from St. Louis. In 1868, 39 steamboats unloaded 8,000 tons of freight and 10,000 passengers; one steamboat returned to St. Louis with $1.5 million in gold.

The Lewis and Clark Memorial overlooks the Missouri River from the levee not far from the old fort; the memorial stands as a reminder of the explorers' stay in the area and the role they and Fort Benton played in opening the West. A statue of Lt. John Mullan, the first white man to pave the way west from Fort Benton to Walla Walla, Wash., and for whom the Mullan Trail is named, also stands on the levee.

Fort Benton is on the western fringe of the Upper Missouri River Breaks National Monument, and its corridor traces the Upper Missouri River 149 miles east into the Charles M. Russell National Wildlife Refuge. Recreation information can be obtained from the Upper Missouri River Breaks National Monument Interpretive Center *(see attraction listing).*

Fort Benton Chamber of Commerce: 1421 Front St., P.O. Box 12, Fort Benton, MT 59442. **Phone:** (406) 622-3864.

Self-guiding tours: A brochure outlining a walking and driving tour of Fort Benton is available from the Museum of the Upper Missouri *(see attraction listing)* and from the Fort Benton Visitor Information Center on Front Street.

MUSEUM OF THE NORTHERN GREAT PLAINS is at 1205 20th St. This museum contains the mounted remains of the Hornaday bull, the bovine model for the buffalo nickel; a 1920s village exhibit; and displays relating to agriculture. **Time:** Allow 1 hour minimum. **Hours:** Mon.-Sat. 10:30-4:30, Sun. noon-4, Memorial Day weekend-Sept. 30; by appointment rest of year. **Cost:** (includes Museum of the Upper Missouri and Upper Missouri River Breaks National Monument Interpretive Center) $10; $1 (ages 6-12). **Phone:** (406) 622-5316.

MUSEUM OF THE UPPER MISSOURI is in Old Fort Park at 1900 River St. Dioramas and exhibits about early trading and river steamers are offered and visitors can take a self-guiding tour of Old Fort Benton. **Hours:** Mon.-Sat. 10:30-4:30, Sun. noon-4, Memorial Day weekend-Sept. 30; by appointment rest of year. **Cost:** (includes Museum of the Northern Great Plains and Upper Missouri River Breaks National Monument Interpretive Center) $10; $1 (ages 6-12). **Phone:** (406) 622-5316.

UPPER MISSOURI RIVER BREAKS NATIONAL MONUMENT INTERPRETIVE CENTER is at 701 7th St. Through displays highlighting the region's resources and a 20-minute overview about the monument, the center documents the cultural and natural history of the Fort Benton area. Planning assistance with self-guiding river trips is available. **Time:** Allow 30 minutes minimum. **Hours:** Daily 8-5, Memorial Day weekend-Sept. 30; Mon.-Fri. 8-5, rest of year. **Cost:** (includes Museum of the Northern Great Plains and Museum of the Upper Missouri) $10; $1 (ages 6-12). **Phone:** (406) 622-4000.

GRAND UNION HOTEL   (406)622-1882

Historic Hotel
$100-$205

Address: 1 Grand Union 59442 **Location:** Center. **Facility:** This fully restored 1882 hotel commands picturesque views of the Missouri River. All guest units are richly appointed. A seasonal riverside dining deck, a brewpub and a fine dining room are offered. 26 units. 3 stories, interior corridors. **Parking:** street only, winter plug-ins. **Terms:** check-in 4 pm, 7 day cancellation notice-fee imposed, resort fee. **Dining:** Union Grille Restaurant, see separate listing. **Activities:** trails.

WHERE TO EAT

UNION GRILLE RESTAURANT   406/622-1882

Regional American Fine Dining
$19-$32

AAA Inspector Notes: *Historic.* Traditional and innovative cuisine will give your taste buds something to sing about. Inside this historic hotel dining room you'll find cozy wood-accent décor, which sets the stage for an intimate and impressive evening. The chef expertly chooses and prepares the freshest locally available ingredients, utilizing a farm-to-table philosophy. Some items are flown in, for example, striped bass from Maryland or black cod from Alaska. **Features:** beer & wine, patio dining. **Reservations:** suggested. **Address:** 1 Grand Union 59442 **Location:** Center; in Grand Union Hotel. **Parking:** street only. *Menu on AAA.com* (D)

FORT PECK (B-7) pop. 233, elev. 2,100'

The federal government developed Fort Peck in the early 1930s as a support community for the construction of Fort Peck Dam. Built by the U.S. Army Corps of Engineers, the dam harnesses the Missouri River, providing electric power, irrigation and recreation.

Fort Peck Summer Theatre, 201 Missouri Ave., presents contemporary productions from mid-June to early September; phone the box office at (406) 526-9943.

Glasgow Area Chamber of Commerce and Agriculture-Fort Peck: 23 US 2E, P.O. Box 832, Glasgow, MT 59230. **Phone:** (406) 228-2222.

FORT PECK DAM & LAKE is on SR 24. The construction of one of the largest hydraulic earth-filled dams in the world created Fort Peck Lake *(see Recreation Areas Chart)*, which offers excellent fishing, camping, boating, hiking, bird-watching and other recreation along its 130-mile length.

A testament to the human spirit, the dam was originally authorized in 1933 by President Franklin D. Roosevelt, who believed it would provide jobs for thousands of Depression-era people and serve as flood protection-a concern since the 1860s. Today, a hard-surfaced highway follows the crest of the dam 250 feet above the tunnel outlets. **Tours:** Guided tours are available. **Phone:** (406) 526-3411.

Fort Peck Interpretive Center & Museum, adjacent to the dam powerhouses, offers exhibits depicting the wildlife of the Charles M. Russell National Wildlife Refuge, along with information about the history of the Fort Peck Dam & Lake. In addition a cast of Peck's Rex, a Tyrannosaurus rex specimen found in the area, and two large aquariums housing native and game fish of Fort Peck Lake and the Missouri River can be seen. Interpretive programs and theater presentations are offered in summer.

Time: Allow 2 hours minimum. **Hours:** Daily 9-5, May-Sept.; Tues.-Sun. 10-4, in Oct.; Tues.-Fri. 10-4, rest of year. Closed major holidays, except Memorial Day, July 4 and Labor Day. **Cost:** Free. **Phone:** (406) 526-3493.

Powerhouse Tour departs from the Fort Peck Interpretive Center & Museum adjacent to the dam powerhouses. The tour describes how the power plants at Fort Peck Dam transform flowing water into electricity. Generators, surge tanks and turbines are displayed.

Note: Adult visitors must present a valid, government-issued photo ID. **Time:** Allow 1 hour minimum. **Hours:** Tours depart Mon.-Fri. at 9, 11, 1 and 3, Sat.-Sun. and holidays on the hour 9-4, Memorial Day-Labor Day; by appointment, Apr. 1-day before Memorial Day and day after Labor Day-Sept. 30. Visitors must sign up at least 15 minutes prior to the tour. **Cost:** Free. **Phone:** (406) 526-3493.

FORT UNION TRADING POST NATIONAL HISTORIC SITE (B-8)

Fort Union Trading Post National Historic Site, reached via US 2 and SR 1804, is 25 miles southwest of Williston, N.D., and 24 miles northeast of Sidney, Mont. Founded by John Jacob Astor for his American Fur Co. in 1828, the trading post became the center for the fur trade on the Upper Missouri River. The fort was 1,800 miles by river from St. Louis, the nearest supply point.

Excavators have unearthed the stone foundations of the Bourgeois House, palisades, an Indian trade house, an icehouse and other structures. The trade house has been rebuilt and furnished as it might have been in the early 1850s. The fort's walls and bastions also have been reconstructed. A visitor center at the Bourgeois House features exhibits about the fur trade.

Allow 30 minutes minimum. Daily 8-6:30 CST, Memorial Day weekend-Labor Day; 9-5:30 CST, rest of year. Closed Jan. 1, Thanksgiving and Christmas. Trade house open 10-5:45 CST, Memorial Day weekend-Labor Day. Free. Phone (701) 572-9083.

GALLATIN GATEWAY (E-4) pop. 856, elev. 4,941'

RECREATIONAL ACTIVITIES
White-water Rafting
- **Geyser Whitewater Expeditions** is on US 191 1 mi. s. of the entrance to Big Sky Resort *(see attraction listing p. 132)* at 46651 Gallatin Rd. **Hours:** Trips are offered daily, May 1 to mid-Sept. Departure times vary; phone ahead. **Phone:** (406) 995-4989 or (800) 914-9031.
- **Montana Whitewater Rafting and ZipLine Company** is on US 191 at Milepost 64. Other activities are offered. **Hours:** Trips are offered daily, May-Sept. Departure times vary; phone ahead. **Phone:** (406) 995-4613 or (800) 799-4465.

GALLATIN NATIONAL FOREST (E-4)

Elevations in the forest range from 4,300 ft. at Derby Gulch to 12,799 ft. on Granite Peak. Refer to AAA maps for additional elevation information.

Gallatin National Forest is in south-central Montana. Some of the most rugged mountains in the state can be found in the 1,735,239-acre forest. On the western side are the Madison and Gallatin ranges; to the east, the Absaroka and Beartooth; and to the north, the Bridger Mountains and the isolated block encompassing the Crazy Mountains.

To some, such as the Crow Indians who sought their visions in the Crazies, these mountains inspire a mystical reverence; to others, such as the mountain men who thought the Beartooth Range resembled the teeth of a familiar predator, they inspire a sense of awe. Much of this region remains unchanged, protected in the forest's two wilderness units, the Lee Metcalf and the Absaroka-Beartooth.

Absaroka-Beartooth Wilderness is named for its two very different mountain ranges. Rugged mountains, broad forested valleys and a variety of plant life characterize the Absaroka Range, which receives precipitation that is unusually abundant for this region. In contrast, the Beartooths present a jagged silhouette of monumental walls and spires soaring to heights of more than 12,000 feet. Forming the roof of these massive peaks are broad plateaus of alpine tundra carpeted with summer wildflowers and hundreds of lakes. The ranges are an integral part of the Yellowstone ecosystem, offering shelter to grizzlies, moose, deer, eagles and turkeys.

The Yellowstone, Gallatin, Madison and Boulder, which are the principal rivers, are renowned for excellent fishing. Natural Bridge State Monument, 28 miles south of Big Timber via SR 289, features a 100-foot waterfall at the mouth of Boulder River Canyon. Several short trails lead from the parking area to observation sites of the falls.

Hikers favor Lee Metcalf Wilderness *(see Beaverhead-Deerlodge National Forest p. 129)* and the Hyalite area of the Gallatin Range. Also scenic are the trails in the Bridger Mountains near Bozeman. To experience the region's beauty by car travel Beartooth Scenic Highway *(see Red Lodge p. 201)* or US 191 from West Yellowstone to Gallatin Gateway; or take a self-guiding tour of the Madison River Canyon Earthquake Area.

Information about the forest's numerous campgrounds and picnic areas is available at district ranger stations. For further information write Bozeman Ranger District, 3710 Fallon St., Ste. C, Bozeman, MT 59718; phone (406) 522-2520. *See Recreation Areas Chart.*

MADISON RIVER CANYON EARTHQUAKE AREA—see West Yellowstone p. 209.

GARDINER (F-4) pop. 875, elev. 5,267'
• Restaurants p. 162
• Hotels & Restaurants map & index p. 336
• Part of Yellowstone National Park area — see map p. 326

The northern entrance to Yellowstone National Park *(see place listing p. 326)*, Gardiner is the only approach open all year. The Devil's Slide, an unusual rock formation 5 miles northwest on US 89, is visible from the highway. A mile north of town by gravel road is a travertine rock quarry. Theodore Roosevelt dedicated Roosevelt Arch in 1903.

Gardiner Chamber of Commerce: 222 Park St., P.O. Box 81, Gardiner, MT 59030. **Phone:** (406) 848-7971.

SAVE **WILD WEST RAFTING** departs from 906 W. Scott St. in the Yellowstone Outpost Mall. Passengers may view and photograph Montana wildlife on a leisurely 5-mile float trip on the Yellowstone River. A guide rows the vessel through Paradise Valley. Other activities as well as white-water rafting excursions also are available.

Time: Allow 2 hours minimum. **Hours:** Scenic float trips depart daily at 9:30, 1, 4 and 6, May 1-Sept. 15. Half-day white-water rafting trips depart daily at 9, 10, 12:30, 3:30 and 5:30, May 1-Sept. 15. **Cost:** Scenic float trip or half-day white-water rafting trip $41; $31 (ages 3-12). **Phone:** (406) 848-2252 or (800) 862-0557.

RECREATIONAL ACTIVITIES

White-water Rafting

• **Montana Whitewater Rafting and ZipLine Company** is at 603 Scott St. Other activities are offered. **Hours:** Trips are offered daily, May-Sept. Departure times vary; phone ahead. **Phone:** (406) 848-7398 or (800) 799-4465. *(See ad this page.)*

• **Yellowstone Raft Co.** is .5 mi. s. of Yellowstone River bridge on US 89. **Hours:** Trips are offered daily, May 15-Sept. 30. Departure times vary; phone ahead. **Phone:** (406) 848-7777 or (800) 858-7781.

Get more from your membership with an upgrade to Plus or Premier

(See map & index p. 336.)

COMFORT INN YELLOWSTONE NORTH   (406)848-7536
♦♦ Hotel $95-$245 **Address:** 107 Hellroaring St 59030 **Location:** North entrance, just s on US 89. **Facility:** 77 units, some two bedrooms. 3 stories, interior corridors. **Terms:** check-in 4 pm, 3 day cancellation notice. **Dining:** The Antler Pub & Grill, see separate listing. **Activities:** game room, limited exercise equipment. **Guest Services:** coin laundry.

YELLOWSTONE BASIN INN   406/848-7080
♦♦ Motel $95-$425 **Address:** 4 Maiden Basin Dr 59030 **Location:** 5 mi n on US 89 at MM 5. **Facility:** 11 units, some two bedrooms, three bedrooms and kitchens. 2 stories (no elevator), exterior corridors. **Terms:** check-in 4 pm, 10 day cancellation notice-fee imposed, resort fee. **Activities:** hot tub.

YELLOWSTONE RIVER MOTEL   (406)848-7303
Motel $65-$118   **Address:** 14 E Park St 59030 **Location:** Just e of US 89. **Facility:** 38 units, some two bedrooms and kitchens. 1-2 stories (no elevator), exterior corridors. **Terms:** closed 11/1-4/14, cancellation fee imposed, resort fee. **Activities:** fishing.

YELLOWSTONE SUPER 8-GARDINER   (406)848-7401
♦♦ Hotel $50-$210 **Address:** Hwy 89 S 59030 **Location:** On US 89. **Facility:** 66 units, some two bedrooms and kitchens. 2-3 stories (no elevator), interior corridors. **Parking:** winter plug-ins. **Terms:** check-in 4 pm. **Pool(s):** heated indoor. **Guest Services:** coin laundry.

▼ See AAA listing p. 160 ▼

(See map & index p. 336.)

YELLOWSTONE VILLAGE INN   406/848-7417 **14**

◆◆◆ **Hotel.** Rates not provided. **Address:** Yellowstone Park North Entrance 59030 **Location:** 0.8 mi n on US 89. **Facility:** 45 units, some two bedrooms and kitchens. 1-2 stories (no elevator), interior/exterior corridors. **Parking:** winter plug-ins. **Terms:** check-in 3:30 pm. **Pool(s):** heated indoor. **Guest Services:** coin laundry.

WHERE TO EAT

THE ANTLER PUB & GRILL   406/848-7536 **11**

◆◆ American. Casual Dining. $9-$28 **AAA Inspector Notes:** A large dining room featuring wild game trophy mounts and rustic decor is the setting for this family restaurant, which offers comfort food from a limited menu. Call ahead for seasonal hours. **Features:** full bar. **Address:** 107 Hellroaring St 59030 **Location:** North entrance, just s on US 89; in Comfort Inn Yellowstone North.

D

THE RAVEN GRILL   406/848-7600 **13**

◆◆ American. Casual Dining. $9-$26 **AAA Inspector Notes:** Favorites are rib-eye, salmon and pastas. The chef/owner makes a delicious fennel and lemon preserve slaw as an accompaniment to some seafood dishes. The decadent chocolate cake is worth the extra calories. They are closed for lunch Saturday and Sunday. **Features:** beer & wine, patio dining. **Address:** 220 W Park St 59030 **Location:** Center. **Parking:** street only. **L** **D** **AC**

YELLOWSTONE MINE RESTAURANT

406/848-7336 **12**

◆◆ American Casual Dining $9-$22

AAA Inspector Notes: Entering this eatery is like walking into an Old West mine, chock-full of Old West artifacts on the walls. Chicken, steak and seafood are all good menu choices. **Features:** full bar, happy hour. **Address:** 905 Scott St W 59030 **Location:** 0.5 mi n; in BEST WESTERN PLUS By Mammoth Hot Springs. **B** **D**

GARRYOWEN (E-6) elev. 3,114'

SAVE **CUSTER BATTLEFIELD MUSEUM** is at 4185 Garryowen Road, on the site of the Battle of the Little Bighorn, which pitted the U.S. Army's seventh cavalry against Lakota, Cheyenne and Arapaho Indians in 1876. The tomb of an unknown soldier killed in the battle as well as photographs and artifacts pertaining to Plains Indian culture and the seventh cavalry are displayed. Personal effects of Lt. Col. George Armstrong Custer and Lakota leaders Crazy Horse and Sitting Bull may be seen.

Time: Allow 1 hour minimum. **Hours:** Daily 8-6, May-Sept.; 8-4:30, rest of year. Closed major holidays. **Cost:** $7.50; free (ages 0-12). **Phone:** (406) 638-1876.

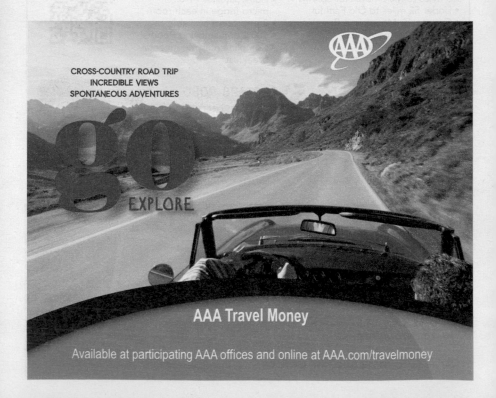

GLACIER NATIONAL PARK (A-2)

• **Hotels p. 171** • **Restaurants p. 172**
• **Attractions map p. 165**
• **Hotels & Restaurants map & index p. 168**

Elevations in the park range from a low of 3,100 ft. in the West Glacier Area to 10,466 ft. on Mt. Cleveland. Refer to AAA maps for additional elevation information.

Glacier National Park is in northwestern Montana. Geologic processes formed and sculpted the peaks, leaving about 25 glaciers and 750 lakes. The mountains are a result of an overthrust of the Earth's crust. Rock layers about a billion years old lie above layers millions of years younger. Some of the finest mountain scenery in America is within this 1-million-acre national park, which marked its centennial in 2010.

The U-shaped valleys, as well as most of the lakes, are the legacy of the last ice age. Most glaciers are accessible only by trail; a few can be viewed from the road. Glacier National Park and Waterton Lakes National Park, in Alberta, together form Waterton-Glacier International Peace Park, although each is administered separately. Scenic Going-to-the-Sun Road *(see attraction listing p. 166)* connects the east and west sections of Glacier National Park.

Though Glacier is a refuge for many large mammals, most of the animals seek the undisturbed areas, and few are seen along the roads during the travel season. The park also is a haven for more than 260 species of birds.

The brilliance and diversity of its floral life is one of Glacier's outstanding features; July marks the height of bloom for many of the alpine species of vascular plants. In the valleys on the east side are dense stands of Engelmann spruce, subalpine fir and lodgepole pine. The western valleys present a different picture with their many dense stands of western red cedars, hemlocks and other conifers.

This map shows cities in Glacier National Park where you will find attractions, hotels and restaurants. Cities are listed alphabetically in this book on the following pages.

(See map & index p. 168.)

General Information and Activities

The park's peak travel season is roughly from mid-June to mid-September; however, the park is open year-round. Visitors can use the park's shuttle system for unlimited one-way or round-trip travel to various park locations from 7 a.m.-7 p.m. early July through Labor Day. The last shuttle buses leave Logan Pass at 7 p.m. for both Apgar Transit Center and St. Mary Visitor Center. Check the shuttle schedule upon arrival. The shuttle is free with park admission. Canoe and motor boat rentals are available at Apgar dock; phone (406) 892-2525. Other docks include ones at Lake McDonald Lodge, Two Medicine and Rising Sun.

Note: Vehicles and vehicle combinations longer than 21 feet or wider than 8 feet (including mirrors) are prohibited from traveling the section of the Going-to-the-Sun Road between the Avalanche Creek picnic area and Sun Point parking areas, where they may park.

More than 700 miles of trails penetrate the park, and many points of interest are within easy walking distance of the hotels and chalets. Swan Mountain Outfitter offers guided horseback rides through the park. Tours depart from Lake McDonald Corral near Lake McDonald Lodge, Apgar Corral and Many Glacier Corral; phone (406) 888-5121 or (406) 732-4203.

There are more than 60 campsites for backpackers; backcountry camping permits are required ($5 per person per night, June-Sept.) and can be obtained at Apgar backcountry office, St. Mary Visitor Center and the Two Medicine, Many Glacier or Polebridge ranger stations. For more information about permits phone (406) 888-7857. Topographic maps can be purchased at the park visitor centers or ordered by mail from Glacier Association, West Glacier, MT 59936.

Mountain whitefish and cutthroat trout are the most common fish. Lake trout are taken from the larger lakes, principally McDonald, St. Mary and Waterton lakes. Grayling thrive in Elizabeth Lake. A fishing license is not required inside the park; regulations are available at the visitor centers. When fishing or participating in any activity in or near park water, watch for slippery rocks at the water's edge.

Several concessionaires within the park provide tours. Glacier Park Inc. offers trips aboard historic buses. Glacier Wilderness Guides arranges guided backpacking trips. Glacier Park Boat Co. *(see attraction listing p. 164)* operates guided lake cruises on McDonald, St. Mary, Two Medicine, Swiftcurrent and Josephine lakes. Boats and canoes can be rented at Two Medicine, Swiftcurrent and McDonald lakes and at the Many Glacier Hotel on Swiftcurrent Lake. Shuttle services are available at Upper Waterton Lake.

CCInc. Auto Tape Tours of the park are available at Glacier Gift Shop in West Glacier or St. Mary's Lodge in St. Mary; phone (201) 236-1666.

Trail rides ranging from 1 hour to all day depart from Lake McDonald Lodge and Many Glacier Hotel. Daily schedules of ranger-led hikes, junior ranger activities, boat trips and campfire programs are printed as a supplement to the *Waterton-Glacier Guide,* the park's newspaper, which is handed out at the visitor centers. *See Recreation Areas Chart.*

Note: Although the animals in the park might appear tame, they are wild and potentially dangerous. Do not approach, feed, molest or tease them in any manner. Bears and mountain lions especially should be avoided; if one approaches, stay in your closed vehicle. Sightings should be reported to park rangers.

ADMISSION May-Nov. is $25 (per private vehicle); $12 (per motorcyclist or person arriving by other means). Admission rest of year is $15 (per private vehicle); $10 (per motorcyclist or person arriving by other means). The above fees permit entrance to the park for 7 calendar days from date of purchase.

PETS are permitted in the park only if they are leashed, crated or otherwise physically restrained at all times. They are not allowed on park trails or in the water.

ADDRESS inquiries to the Superintendent, Glacier National Park, P.O. Box 128, West Glacier, MT 59936; phone (406) 888-7800.

AVALANCHE CREEK is on Going-to-the-Sun Rd. A deep, narrow gorge cut through brilliant red mudstone is filled with potholes scoured out by stones swirled in the foaming torrent. From the gorge a 2-mile trail travels to Avalanche Basin and Lake, a semicircular amphitheater with walls more than 2,000 feet high, over which plunge a half-dozen waterfalls. A nature trail with a boardwalk for physically impaired visitors leads to the gorge. **Time:** Allow 30 minutes minimum. **Phone:** (406) 888-7800.

BELLY RIVER COUNTRY is accessible by trail from Many Glacier through Ptarmigan Tunnel, from Waterton Lake over Stoney Indian Pass, or from Chief Mountain customs station on Chief Mountain International Rd. Spurs are available to Helen, Cosley, Glenns, Mokowanis and Elizabeth lakes and Gros Ventre and Dawn Mist falls. The region is wild and heavily forested in some places.

A 33-mile drive through the Chief Mountain area to Waterton Lakes National Park of Canada offers scenic views. Waterton Inter-Nation Shoreline Cruise Co. operates a launch on Waterton Lake early May to mid-October (weather permitting). **Time:** Allow 2 hours minimum. **Cost:** Round-trip launch fare (in Canadian dollars) $42; $21 (ages 13-17); $14 (ages 4-12).

CUT BANK, at the s.e. portion of Glacier National Park off US 89, is a primitive, densely wooded valley. At the head of the valley is 8,020-foot Triple Divide Peak.

© AAA

Waterton-Glacier International Peace Park
Attractions

Scale in Miles

4.9   0   4.9

To Pincher Creek

Waterton Lakes National Park

BRITISH COLUMBIA CAN
MONTANA USA

ALBERTA
BRITISH COLUMBIA

Crandell Mountain

TOWNSHIP ROAD 20A

Waterton River

River

To Cardston

MT CRANDALL EL 2,381 FT

Lower Waterton Lake

Waterton Park Townsite

Mountain View

PARKE PEAK EL 9,038 FT

AGASSIZ GLACIER

Upper Waterton Lake

Middle Waterton Lake

Lee Creek

Glacier

KINTLA GLACIER

CHAPMAN PEAK EL 9,406 FT

ALBERTA CAN
MONTANA USA

Chief Mountain

Kintla Lake
Kintla Lake

North

INSIDE

THUNDERBIRD GLACIER

DIXON GLACIER

Bowman Lake

RAINBOW PEAK EL 9,891 FT

MT CLEVELAND EL 10,466 FT

BELLY RIVER COUNTRY

CHIEF MOUNTAIN EL 9,080 FT

17

To Cardston

Bowman Lake

Quartz Lake

VULTURE PEAK EL 9,638 FT

KOOTENAI PEAK EL 8,542 FT

89

Pole-bridge

BOWMAN LAKE RD

Bowman Creek

LOGGING MOUNTAIN EL 8,566 FT

North Fork

Quartz Creek

TRAPPER PEAK EL 7,702 FT

Belly

River

ROAD CLOSED IN WINTER

Kennedy

Logging Lake

Flathead

Logging Creek

Quartz Creek

Logging Cr.

FLATTOP MOUNTAIN EL 6,872 FT

CONTINENTAL

MANY GLACIER REGION

Babb

Flathead

National

LONGFELLOW PEAK EL 8,904 FT

Granite Park

Many Glacier

MANY GLACIER RD

Lower St Mary Lake

National

CAMAS RD

Logging Creek

Big Creek

Camas Creek

Logging

ROAD CLOSED IN WINTER

TUN Avalanche Creek

GRINNELL GLACIER

Lake Sherburne

LOGAN PASS EL 6,646 FT

MT SIYEH EL 10,014 FT

ROAD CLOSED IN WINTER

St Mary Visitor Center

St Mary

National

Camas

Lake McDonald

Sprague Creek

Avalanche

GOING-TO-THE-SUN MOUNTAIN EL 9,642 FT

89

Forest

Fish Creek

GOING TO THE SUN RD

SPERRY GLACIER

Logan Pass Visitor Center

St Mary Lake

Rising Sun

Blackfeet

Apgar Visitor Center

Sperry Chalet

JACKSON GLACIER

LITTLE CHIEF MOUNTAIN EL 9,541 FT

Red Eagle Lake

89

BLANKENSHIP RD

Apgar

Glacier Nat'l Park Headquarters

MT JACKSON EL 10,052 FT

HARRISON GLACIER

BLACKFOOT GLACIER

DIVIDE MOUNTAIN EL 8,603 FT

Indian

486

West Glacier

Harrison Lake

PUMPELLY GLACIER

MOUNT JAMES EL 9,375 FT

Cut Bank

2

Coram

Great

2

MT THOMPSON GLACIER EL 8,527 FT

TRIPLE DIVIDE PEAK EL 8,020 FT

CUT BANK CREEK RD

To Kalispell

Martin City

Middle

LONEMAN MTN EL 7,181 FT

MT STIMSON EL 10,142 FT

Kiowa

89

Hungry Horse

WEST SIDE SOUTH FORK RD

Nyack

MT PINCHOT EL 9,310 FT

MT MORGAN EL 8,781 FT

ROAD CLOSED IN WINTER

TWO MEDICINE RD

To Browning

Bear

N

Fork

EAGLEHEAD MTN EL 9,140 FT

RISING WOLF MTN EL 9,513 FT

Two Medicine

Lower Two Medicine Lake

Lost Johnny Point

FLATHEAD

Park

DIVIDE

Two Medicine Lake

MT HENRY EL 8,847 FT

49

Hungry

MT SAINT NICHOLAS EL 9,376 FT

GRIZZLY MTN EL 9,067 FT

BEARHEAD MTN EL 8,406 FT

2

To Browning

Horse

RD

Murray Bay

CHURCH BUTTE EL 8,808 FT

East Glacier Park

Res

Reservoir

Flathead

SUMMIT MTN EL 8,770 FT

2

Lewis and Clark

SCENIC BYWAY

Essex

Ole

SNOWSLIP MTN EL 7,290 FT

Summit

National

CAMPGROUND SITE WITHIN NAT'L. PARK. INFORMATION PROVIDED BY WOODALL'S ®.

Wilderness

Creek

Devil Creek

Forest

© 2013 NAVTEQ

2126-14

166   GLACIER NP, MT

(See map & index p. 168.)

GLACIER PARK BOAT CO. departs from Lake Mc-Donald, Many Glacier, Rising Sun and Two Medicine. The company offers scenic cruises aboard classic wooden boats that have plied the lakes here since the park's early days. Narrated trips offer views of wilderness areas, glacial formations, waterfalls and rugged cliffs. Tours last between 45 minutes and 1.5 hours. Guided hikes also are available.

Hours: Tours depart from Lake McDonald Lodge daily at 11, 1:30, 3, 5:30 and 7, late May-Labor Day; at 1:30, 3 and 5:30, day after Labor Day-late Sept. Tours depart from Many Glacier daily at 8:30, 9, 11, 2 and 4:30, mid-June to mid-Sept. (also at 1 and 3, July 1-Labor Day). Tours depart from Rising Sun daily at 10, noon, 2, 4 and 6:30, mid-June to early Sept. Tours depart from Two Medicine daily at 10:30, 1, 3 and 5, early June-early Sept. (also at 9 a.m., July 1-Labor Day). Phone ahead to confirm schedule.

Cost: Fares $12-$24.25; $6-$12 (ages 4-12). Rates may vary. Reservations are recommended. **Phone:** (406) 257-2426.

GOING-TO-THE-SUN ROAD joins US 89 at St. Mary and US 2 at West Glacier. Acclaimed as one of the outstanding scenic roadways of the world, the 50-mile route traverses the width of the park, crossing the Continental Divide through Logan Pass at an elevation of 6,646 feet while affording magnificent views of some of the park's loveliest scenery. Several miles of the two-lane highway had to be cut out of steep mountainsides and consequently it took more than a decade to complete.

At its official dedication on July 15, 1933, the road was given its current whimsical name, which comes from a mountain looming over the route east of Logan Pass. The source of the mountain's name is open to debate. It may have originated in a Blackfeet Indian legend or simply been made up by a white explorer with an active imagination.

You could drive Going-to-the-Sun Road from one end to the other in around 2 hours without stopping, but take your time because pulling over at one or more of the road's many scenic overlooks is an essential Glacier National Park experience. Some of the classic photo ops you should look for, from east to west: tiny Wild Goose Island in the midst of St. Mary Lake; Jackson Glacier, one of the few glaciers visible from the road; Bird Woman Falls, a silver ribbon of water falling hundreds of feet down the face of Mount Oberlin; the Weeping Wall, a waterfall that actually splashes onto the roadway; and McDonald Creek, a picturesque boulder-strewn stream.

Several trailheads are just off Going-to-the-Sun Road. Some paths go for miles into the backcountry while others offer short hikes to beauty spots. At Avalanche Creek (see attraction listing), the Trail of the Cedars offers a pleasant .7-mile boardwalk loop among moisture-loving cedars and hemlocks. At Logan Pass, the Hidden Lake Overlook Trail is a 3-mile roundtrip journey through alpine meadows

filled with wildlife and ending with a spectacular view high above a mountain lake.

Note: Logan Pass closes for the season no later than November 1 and reopens in mid-June (weather permitting). *For vehicle restrictions, see General Information and Activities p. 164.* The park's optional, free Going-to-the-Sun Road shuttle stops at various points along the road July through Labor Day. **Phone:** (406) 888-7800 for road closure information.

GRANITE PARK is reached from Waterton by the northern portion of the Highline Trail, from Logan Pass along the Highline Trail and from Many Glacier over Swiftcurrent Pass Trail. Exposed is a great mass of lava that once spread over the region. Trails radiate into the surrounding mountains. Granite Park Chalet, operated by a concessioner, is open from late June to mid-Sept.; reservations are required. **Phone:** (888) 345-2649 for chalet information.

HUNGRY HORSE DAM is 15 mi. s.e. of Glacier National Park. One of the world's largest concrete dams, Hungry Horse's 2,115-foot crest is crossed by a 39-foot-wide roadway. A visitor center 4 miles east of US 2 has interactive displays and a video. *See Recreation Areas Chart.* **Hours:** Visitor center Wed.-Sun. 7:30-4, Memorial Day-Labor Day. Guided dam tours depart on the hour 8-3. Phone ahead to confirm schedule. **Cost:** Free. **Phone:** (406) 387-5241, ext. 361.

LAKE McDONALD is reached via Going-to-the-Sun Road, which runs along the eastern shore. Ten miles long and 1 mile wide, the lake is the largest in the park. Its shores are heavily forested, and impressive rocky summits rise 6,000 feet above. Lake McDonald Lodge, near the upper end of the lake, is the focal point for trails to Sperry Chalet, Gunsight Pass, Sperry Glacier, Upper McDonald Valley and the summit of Mount Brown. A cruise boat operates from the lodge Memorial Day weekend through Labor Day. Boat rentals and naturalist programs are available at the lodge and at Apgar.

LOGAN PASS lies between the headwaters of Logan and Reynolds creeks. At an elevation of 6,646 feet, it straddles the Continental Divide and carries Going-to-the-Sun Road from St. Mary to West Glacier. Though there are no overnight stopping places, other than campgrounds along the road, easy access by automobile makes it a favorite starting point for several walks, including the trail to Hidden Lake Overlook. Naturalist-led day trips and orientation talks are offered. **Note:** Parking is limited during peak visiting hours, generally mid-morning to late afternoon.

MANY GLACIER REGION is in the n.e. sector of the park. The area encompasses Swiftcurrent Lake, from which branch many deep, glaciated valleys. It can be reached by road 13 miles from US 89 at Babb or by trail from Siyeh Bend, Granite Park, Belly River and Waterton Lake. Launch trips on Swiftcurrent and Josephine lakes depart daily, Memorial Day through Labor Day.

(See map & index p. 168.)

RED EAGLE LAKE is in Red Eagle Valley. Access to the valley is by trail from the St. Mary park entrance, from Sun Point via Red Eagle Trail and from Cut Bank over Triple Divide Pass.

ST. MARY LAKE lies at the foot of the Lewis Range. Peaks of the front barrier of the Rockies soar a mile above lake waters. A trail radiating from Sun Point is the shortest and best trail to Baring Falls. Red Eagle Trail along the south shore leads to Red Eagle Lake. Programs are presented nightly in summer at the visitor center and at Rising Sun campground. Launch trips and boat tours are available at the boat landing at Rising Sun from mid-June to early September.

SPERRY CHALET can be reached only by foot or on horseback from Lake McDonald and by foot from the St. Mary Valley via Gunsight and Lincoln passes. In a high, steep hollow at the upper end of a mountain valley, the chalet is hemmed in on three sides by precipitous peaks. Hiking and exploring the Sperry Glacier and fishing in nearby Lake Ellen Wilson are the chief diversions. Mountain goats frequently are seen on the cirque walls, usually during the late afternoon. **Hours:** Open July-Sept. **Phone:** (888) 345-2649.

TWO MEDICINE VALLEY is 11 mi. from East Glacier and 7 mi. off SR 49. Features include a lake surrounded by majestic peaks separated by deep, glaciated valleys. Trails for hikers and saddle horse parties radiate to adjacent points of interest; one short trail leads through dense evergreen forest to the foot of Twin Falls. Launch trips across Two Medicine Lake depart daily, early July-early September.

A readily accessible .3-mile scenic trail is at Running Eagle Falls, 2 miles below the lake near the road bridge across Two Medicine Creek. A portion of the falls' waters flows from a cave beneath the brink of the main falls. Early in the year it appears to be an ordinary waterfall, but late in the season water issues from the cave alone, and the waterfall above it is dry.

Glacier National Park

This index helps you "spot" where approved hotels and restaurants are located on the corresponding detailed maps. Hotel daily rate range is for comparison only. Restaurant price range is a combination of lunch and/or dinner. Turn to the listing page for more detailed rate and price information and consult display ads for special promotions.

GLACIER NATIONAL PARK

Map Page	Hotel	Diamond Rated	Rate Range	Page
⚫1 p. 168	Apgar Village Lodge	◆	$95-$309	171

Map Page	Restaurant	Diamond Rated	Cuisine	Price Range	Page
① p. 168	Eddie's Restaurant	◆	American	$9-$20	172

COLUMBIA FALLS

Map Page	Hotels	Diamond Rated	Rate Range	Page
⚫4 p. 168	Meadow Lake Resort	◆◆◆	$119-$520 SAVE	151
⚫5 p. 168	Glacier Park Super 8	◆◆	$53-$180 SAVE	151
⚫6 p. 168	Bad Rock Bed & Breakfast	◆◆◆	$125-$225 SAVE	151

Map Page	Restaurants	Diamond Rated	Cuisine	Price Range	Page
④ p. 168	Cimarron Cafe	◆◆	American	$6-$19	151
⑤ p. 168	The Back Room/Nite Owl Restaurants	◆◆	American	$10-$20	151

EAST GLACIER PARK

Map Page	Hotels	Diamond Rated	Rate Range	Page
⚫9 p. 168	Jacobson's Scenic View Cottages	◆	$70-$105	155
⚫10 p. 168	Mountain Pine Motel	◆	$61-$92	155
⚫11 p. 168	Dancing Bears Inn & Suites	◆	$88-$174 SAVE	155

Map Page	Restaurant	Diamond Rated	Cuisine	Price Range	Page
⑧ p. 168	Serrano's	◆◆	Mexican	$9-$19	155

WHITEFISH

Map Page	Hotels	Diamond Rated	Rate Range	Page
⚫14 p. 168	Kristianna Mountain Homes	◆◆	Rates not provided	212
⚫15 p. 168	Whitefish Mountain Resort	◆◆	Rates not provided	213
⚫16 p. 168	The Lodge at Whitefish Lake	◆◆◆◆	$115 SAVE	213
⚫17 p. 168	Bay Point on the Lake	◆◆	$133-$211	212
⚫18 p. 168	Grouse Mountain Lodge	◆◆◆	Rates not provided SAVE	212
⚫19 p. 168	Pine Lodge	◆◆	$79-$170 SAVE	213
⚫20 p. 168	BEST WESTERN Rocky Mountain Lodge	◆◆◆	$107-$210 SAVE	212
⚫21 p. 168	Chalet Motel	◆	$60-$125 SAVE	212
⚫22 p. 168	North Forty Resort	◆◆	$119-$289	213

Map Page	Restaurants	Diamond Rated	Cuisine	Price Range	Page
⑪ p. 168	Whitefish Lake Restaurant	◆◆◆	American	$9-$39	214
⑫ p. 168	The Naked Noodle	◆	Noodles	$7-$12	213
⑬ p. 168	Tupelo Grille and Wine Bar	◆◆◆	Continental	$16-$36	213
⑭ p. 168	Logan's Grill	◆◆◆	American	$9-$35	213
⑮ p. 168	Amazing Crêpes & Catering	◆	Specialty	$6-$9	213
⑯ p. 168	Mambo Italiano	◆◆	Italian	$11-$28	213
⑰ p. 168	Loula's	◆◆	American	$6-$16	213

Map Page	Restaurants (cont'd)	Diamond Rated	Cuisine	Price Range	Page
⑱ p. 168	Wasabi Sushi Bar & The Ginger Grill	◆◆◆	Asian	$8-$45	214
⑲ p. 168	Buffalo Cafe	◆◆	American	$8-$25	213
⑳ p. 168	The Shak	◆	Southern Barbecue	$7-$16	213

HUNGRY HORSE

Map Page	Hotels	Diamond Rated	Rate Range	Page
㉕ p. 168	**Historic Tamarack Lodge & Cabins**	◆◆	$63-$320 SAVE	183
㉖ p. 168	**Mini Golden Inns Motel**	◆	$86-$160 SAVE	183

ESSEX

Map Page	Hotels	Diamond Rated	Rate Range	Page
㉙ p. 168	**Glacier Haven Inn**	◆	$75-$149 SAVE	156
㉚ p. 168	Izaak Walton Inn	◆◆	$109-$359	156

Map Page	Restaurants	Diamond Rated	Cuisine	Price Range	Page
㉖ p. 168	Healthy Haven Cafe	◆	American	$10-$26	156
㉗ p. 168	The Dining Car	◆◆◆	American	$8-$24	156

WEST GLACIER

Map Page	Hotels	Diamond Rated	Rate Range	Page
㉝ p. 168	**Glacier Raft Company Cabins at Glacier Outdoor Center**	◆◆	$126-$600 SAVE	208
㉞ p. 168	Glaciers' Mountain Resort, LLC	◆◆	$119-$245	208
㉟ p. 168	**Silverwolf Log Chalets**	◆◆	$125-$179 SAVE	208

KALISPELL

Map Page	Hotels	Diamond Rated	Rate Range	Page
㊳ p. 168	Holiday Inn Express & Suites	◆◆◆	$99-$249	185
㊴ p. 168	Americas Best Value Inn	◆◆	$60-$135	184
㊵ p. 168	La Quinta Inn & Suites Kalispell	◆◆◆	$94-$194	185
㊶ p. 168	**Hampton Inn Kalispell**	◆◆◆	$93-$239 SAVE	185
㊷ p. 168	**Comfort Inn**	◆◆	$89-$239 SAVE	185
㊸ p. 168	Red Lion Hotel Kalispell	◆◆◆	Rates not provided	185
㊹ p. 168	Kalispell Grand Hotel	◆◆	$85-$155	185
㊺ p. 168	Kalispell/Glacier Int'l Airport area Super 8	◆◆	$53-$120	185
㊻ p. 168	**Aero Inn**	◆	$49-$104 SAVE	184
㊼ p. 168	**Hilton Garden Inn Kalispell**	◆◆◆	$89-$259 SAVE	185

Map Page	Restaurants	Diamond Rated	Cuisine	Price Range	Page
㉚ p. 168	Spencer & Co	◆◆	Steak	$12-$29	186
㉛ p. 168	Cislo's	◆◆	American	$7-$18	186
㉜ p. 168	Nickel Charlie's Casino & Eatery	◆◆	American	$8-$24	186
㉝ p. 168	Bojangles Diner	◆◆	American	$4-$13	185
㉞ p. 168	Julie's Center Street Cafe	◆◆	American	$6-$13	186
㉟ p. 168	Montana Coffee Traders	◆	Coffee/Tea	$6-$10	186
㊱ p. 168	Rising Sun Bistro	◆◆	French	$7-$19	186
㊲ p. 168	Bonelli's Bistro	◆◆	Mediterranean	$6-$10	185
㊳ p. 168	The Alley Connection	◆◆	Chinese	$6-$18	185
㊴ p. 168	ScottiBelli's Ristorante Italiano	◆◆	Italian	$10-$28	186

Map Page	Restaurants (cont'd)	Diamond Rated	Cuisine	Price Range	Page
㊵ p. 168	Hops Downtown Grill	◈◈◈	Western Burgers	$9-$20	186
㊶ p. 168	Genki	◈◈	Asian Sushi	$7-$17	186
㊷ p. 168	Thai Palace Restaurant	◈◈	Thai	$12-$22	186
㊸ p. 168	Wheat Montana Bakery & Deli	◈	Deli	$5-$10	186
㊹ p. 168	The Montana Club	◈◈	Western Steak Seafood	$8-$24	186
㊺ p. 168	Blue Canyon Kitchen & Tavern	◈◈◈	American	$10-$26	185

ST. MARY

Map Page	Restaurant	Diamond Rated	Cuisine	Price Range	Page
㉓ p. 168	Two Sisters Cafe	◈◈	American	$13-$24	203

GLACIER NATIONAL PARK

- Restaurants p. 172
- Attractions map p. 165
- Hotels & Restaurants map & index p. 168

APGAR VILLAGE LODGE   406/888-5484   **1**

 Cabin $95-$309 **Address:** 200 Going to the Sun Rd 59936 **Location:** 2 mi nw of West Glacier from jct US 2; in park at Apgar Village. **Facility:** 48 units, some cabins. 1 story, exterior corridors. *Bath:* shower only. **Terms:** closed 9/29-5/22, 2 night minimum stay, 3 day cancellation notice-fee imposed. **Activities:** fishing.

MANY GLACIER HOTEL   406/892-2525

fyi Not evaluated. **Address:** Swiftcurrent Lake 59434 **Location:** East side of Glacier National Park; 12 mi e of Babb Jct. Facilities, services, and décor characterize an economy property. Swiss chalet-style buildings are set among the backdrop of stunning glacial peaks and a mountain lake. Find boat rentals on site, as well as numerous trail heads into the backcountry wilderness.

▼ See AAA listing p. 150 ▼

(See map & index p. 168.)

WHERE TO EAT

EDDIE'S RESTAURANT   406/888-5361 (1)
American. Family Dining. $9-$20 **AAA Inspector Notes:** The friendly staff serves sandwiches, salad, soup and several dinner entrees such as pan-fried trout and broasted chicken. Named for one of the earliest settlers, this is one of a handful of eateries inside the park and the only one privately owned. **Features:** beer & wine. **Address:** 1 Fish Creek Rd 59936 **Location:** 2 mi nw of West Glacier from jct US 2; in park at Apgar Village. (B) (L) (D)

GLASGOW (B-6) pop. 3,250, elev. 2,090'

In the midst of the Milk and Missouri River valleys, Glasgow began as a railroad station. It is now an agricultural and commercial center for northeastern Montana, and the surrounding area is known for its hunting, fishing and outdoor recreation.

Glasgow Area Chamber of Commerce and Agriculture: 23 US 2E, P.O. Box 832, Glasgow, MT 59230. **Phone:** (406) 228-2222.

VALLEY COUNTY PIONEER MUSEUM is at 816 US 2. Displays include 19th-century Native American and pioneer artifacts, Lewis and Clark expedition memorabilia, paleontology specimens, photographs and agricultural tools. Mounted wildlife and a historic barroom exhibit also are featured. **Time:** Allow 1 hour minimum. **Hours:** Daily 9-5, May 1-Labor Day; Tues.-Fri. 1-5, day after Labor Day-Oct. 31; Tues. and Sat. 1-4, Nov.-Dec. and Feb.-Apr. Closed major holidays. Phone ahead to confirm schedule. **Cost:** $3; $2 (ages 7-21). **Phone:** (406) 228-8692.

COTTONWOOD INN   406/228-8213
Hotel $87-$112 **Address:** 45 1st Ave NE 59230 **Location:** 0.5 mi e on US 2. **Facility:** 145 units. 2 stories (no elevator), interior corridors. **Parking:** winter plug-ins. **Pool(s):** heated indoor. **Activities:** hot tub, exercise room. **Guest Services:** valet and coin laundry.

WHERE TO EAT

DURUM RESTAURANT   406/228-2236
American. Casual Dining. $6-$33 **AAA Inspector Notes:** This restaurant, which specializes in steak and pasta, is known as one of the best in town. Casual but also a little up-market, they also offer grilled entrees of pork, chicken, fish and some simpler things like burgers. Staff is accommodating and helps make your night out complete. Lunch includes a range of salads, sandwiches and stir-frys. **Features:** full bar. **Reservations:** suggested, for dinner. **Address:** 803 US Hwy 2 59230 **Location:** Just w on US 2; across from Pamida. (L) (D) CALL (M)

GLENDIVE (C-8) pop. 4,935, elev. 2,070'

Once a center for cattle ranches, Glendive is now a distribution point for diverse agricultural products. The surrounding area is rich in petroleum, natural gas and coal. Another natural resource, the boneless paddlefish, roams the bottom of the Yellowstone River in such numbers that Glendive has assumed the title of "Paddlefish Capital." Paddlefish

season is mid-May to late June. Besides anglers, Glendive attracts rockhounds in search of moss agates and fossils, which are plentiful in the area.

Glendive Area Chamber of Commerce and Agriculture: 808 N. Merrill, Glendive, MT 59330. **Phone:** (406) 377-5601.

Self-guiding tours: Brochures of a walking tour of the downtown historic district are available from the chamber of commerce and agriculture.

FRONTIER GATEWAY MUSEUM is 1 mi. e. off I-94 exit 215 on Belle Prairie Rd. This museum contains dinosaur fossils, Native American artifacts, farm machinery and other items depicting eastern Montana from prehistoric times to the present. Among buildings on the grounds are a rural schoolhouse, log cabin and smithy. **Hours:** Mon.-Sat. 9-noon and 1-5, Sun. and holidays 1-5, June-Aug.; daily 1-5, last week in May and in Sept. Phone ahead to confirm schedule. **Cost:** Donations. **Phone:** (406) 377-8168.

MAKOSHIKA DINOSAUR MUSEUM is at 104 W. Bell St. Dioramas depict dinosaurs in their natural habitat. Exhibits include fossils, sculptures and casts. The Cretaceous Forest, Ages of the Sea and Abyss displays add to the interactive experience. The museum is one of several stops along the Montana Dinosaur Trail. **Time:** Allow 1 hour minimum. **Hours:** Mon.-Sat. 10-5, June-Aug. **Cost:** $5; $3 (ages 6-17). **Phone:** (406) 377-1637.

MAKOSHIKA STATE PARK is 1 mi. s. at 1301 Snyder Ave. Makoshika comes from the Lakota word meaning "bad earth" or "badlands." The area encompasses 11,531 acres of eroded and vividly colored buttes and gullies, which can be viewed along the Kinney Coulee, Cap Rock and Diane Gabriel nature trails. A visitor center displays fossils and a triceratops skull. *See Recreation Areas Chart.*

Time: Allow 2 hours minimum. **Hours:** Park open daily 24 hours (weather permitting). Visitor center open daily 10-6, Memorial Day-Labor Day; 9-5, rest of year. **Cost:** $5 (nonresidents per private vehicle); $3 (nonresidents arriving by other means); free (residents). Camping fee $23 (nonresidents); $18 (nonresidents with a Montana State Park passport); $15 (residents). **Phone:** (406) 377-6256.

ASTORIA HOTEL & SUITES   (406)377-6000
Hotel
$143-$179
Address: 201 California St 59330 **Location:** I-94 exit 215. **Facility:** 89 units. 4 stories, interior corridors. **Pool(s):** heated indoor. **Activities:** hot tub, exercise room. **Guest Services:** coin laundry. **Featured Amenity:** continental breakfast.

GREAT FALLS (C-4) pop. 58,505, elev. 3,312'
• Hotels p. 174 • Restaurants p. 177

Meriwether Lewis and William Clark visited the Great Falls of the Missouri River in 1805. Clark mapped the area while the other expedition members portaged around a series of five falls. The party returned to this site on its trip from the Pacific coast a year later. In 1882 Paris Gibson visited the site; he returned in the spring of 1883 with a surveyor and an attorney, and a townsite soon was plotted and named Great Falls. Important contributors to the economy are Malmstrom Air Force Base, agriculture and tourism.

River's Edge Trail, which begins north of US 89 on River Drive and stretches along the Missouri River, is popular with pedestrians and bicyclists. The trail's 40-plus miles include both paved and graveled sections.

A large American flag marks the visitor center on the Broadwater Overlook; follow directional signs on the approach and throughout the city. The center can provide information about guided tours; phone (406) 771-0885. An audio tour tracing 34 miles of the Lewis and Clark National Historic Trail is available from The History Museum, 422 Second St. S.; phone (406) 452-3462.

The ☙ Lewis and Clark Festival features historic re-enactments, foods that were typically eaten on the expedition, tours, exhibits and demonstrations. Other events also include outdoor art, a dinner gala, and live and silent auctions. The 3-day celebration in late June takes place at various locations, including the Lewis and Clark National Historic Trail Interpretive Center (see attraction listing) and Giant Springs State Park.

Great Falls Area Chamber of Commerce: 100 First Ave. N., Great Falls, MT 59401. **Phone:** (406) 761-4434 or (800) 735-8535.

Shopping areas: Holiday Village Mall, 2.5 miles east of US 15 at 1200 10th Ave. S., houses 95 stores including Herberger's, JCPenney and Sears.

CHILDREN'S MUSEUM OF MONTANA is at 22 Railroad Sq. The museum's hands-on exhibits are designed to encourage a lifetime interest in math, science and culture. **Time:** Allow 1 hour minimum. **Hours:** Mon.-Sat. 9:30-5. Closed Jan. 1, July 4, Thanksgiving, Christmas Eve and Christmas. **Cost:** $4; free (ages 0-2). **Phone:** (406) 452-6661.

◆ GEM SAVE **C.M. RUSSELL MUSEUM,** 400 13th St. N., pays homage to the cowboy artist Charles Marion Russell. The complex contains a museum, original Russell home and log studio, and sculpture garden. Russell's observation of life, personal philosophy and love of Montana greatly influenced his paintings and sculpture. Though Russell was an established artist at the time of his death in 1926, creating art was not always his ambition. Rather, he was attracted to the exciting life of a cowboy.

Just days after celebrating his 16th birthday, Russell moved from St. Louis to Judith Basin in Montana where he tended sheep for a brief stint. He spent 2 years learning from a hunter. His experience led him to become a night wrangler and he seized the time and opportunity to closely observe and sketch all the daily and nightly activities of the camp. After 11 years of being a ranch hand, he retired to pursue his life as a full-time artist.

Russell's great admiration of Native Americans, especially those of the Northern Plains, is quite evident in his detailed works on the subject. The cowboy's life is romanticized in many works. In addition, images of bison, wolves, elk and other wild animals also feature in his paintings and reflect his life in Montana.

A visit to the museum reveals five galleries of Russell's watercolors, sculptures, oil paintings and illustrated cards and letters. Also featured are historical photographs of the Old West, a collection of Browning firearms and works by other Western artists. Changing exhibits showcase Russell contemporaries including Henry Famy and J.H. Sharp.

Guided tours are available by appointment. **Time:** Allow 2 hours minimum. **Hours:** Tues.-Sun. 10-5, Memorial Day-Labor Day; Wed.-Sat. 10-5, rest of year. Closed Jan. 1, Easter, Thanksgiving and Christmas. Phone ahead to confirm schedule. **Cost:** (includes C.M. Russell Home and Log Studio of C.M. Russell) $9; $7 (ages 60+); $4 (students with ID); free (ages 0-5 and military with ID). Additional fees may be charged for special exhibitions. **Phone:** (406) 727-8787.

C.M. Russell Home is at 400 13th St. N., next to the Log Studio of C.M. Russell. Russell's permanent residence was built in 1900 and is furnished in period. **Hours:** Tues.-Sun. 11-4, Memorial Day-Labor Day. Phone ahead to confirm schedule. **Cost:** Included in C.M. Russell Museum admission of $9; $7 (ages 60+); $4 (students with ID); free (ages 0-5 and military with ID). Additional fees may be charged for special exhibitions. **Phone:** (406) 727-8787.

Log Studio of C.M. Russell is next to the C.M. Russell Home at 400 13th St. N. Built in 1903, the studio contains Russell's pallet and brushes, cowboy memorabilia and Native American artifacts he used as models. **Hours:** Tues.-Sun. 11-4, Memorial Day-Labor Day; Wed.-Sat. 11-4, rest of year. Phone ahead to confirm schedule. **Cost:** Included in C.M. Russell Museum admission of $9; $7 (ages 60+); $4 (students with ID); free (ages 0-5 and military with ID). Additional fees may be charged for special exhibitions. **Phone:** (406) 727-8787.

GIANT SPRINGS FISH, WILDLIFE AND PARKS VISITOR CENTER AND FISH HATCHERY is 2.5 mi. n.e. off US 87 on 4600 Giant Springs Rd. The regional headquarters visitor center has wildlife displays, photographs about park history and film presentations. Across the street is the hatchery for six strains of rainbow trout and two species of salmon;

a visitor center explains fish raising. The park preserves one of the largest freshwater springs in the world. Scenic overlooks are available from two dams within 2 miles of the site.

Time: Allow 1 hour minimum. **Hours:** Park daily 8 a.m.-dusk. Park visitor center Mon.-Fri. 8-5. Hatchery visitor center daily 8-4:30. **Cost:** Park admission $2. Visitor centers free. **Phone:** (406) 454-5840 for the regional headquarters visitor center, or (406) 452-5734 for the hatchery.

GREAT FALLS HISTORIC TROLLEY departs from the visitor center at 15 Overlook Dr. and picks up passengers at area select lodgings. Highlights of the 1-hour City Tour are the historic downtown business district, the railroad area, the historic home district, a waterfall, parks, museums and churches. The 2-hour Historic Tour includes Lewis and Clark Trail sites, four waterfalls, Giant Springs, museums, historic homes and downtown districts, saloons, churches, the railroad area and parks.

Tours are available on a first come, first serve basis. **Hours:** City Tour departs Mon.-Thurs. at 4, Fri.-Sun. at 1 and 4, June-Sept.; by appointment rest of year. Historic Tour departs Mon.-Sat. at 10, June-Sept.; by appointment rest of year. Phone ahead to confirm schedule. **Cost:** One-hour City Tour $13; $5 (ages 2-12). Two-hour Historic Tour $22; $5 (ages 2-12). **Phone:** (406) 564-0539 or (406) 453-6151.

LEWIS AND CLARK NATIONAL HISTORIC TRAIL INTERPRETIVE CENTER is at 4201 Giant Springs Rd. Exhibits detail the 1804-06 Lewis and Clark expedition, particularly the portion that took place in what is now Montana. Highlighted are the Indian tribes of the Plains and Pacific Northwest who aided the explorers. Rangers demonstrate skills used on the journey. A 30-minute introductory film by Ken Burns sets the stage for the visitor's own discovery journey. A second 20-minute movie depicts the arduous journey around the Great Falls of the Missouri River.

The interpretive center, managed by the USDA Forest Service, overlooks the Missouri River. Onsite features include walking trails, scenic overlooks and grounds landscaped with plants described in the explorers' journals. Outdoor living-history programs are presented in the summer. Audio tours are available in several languages.

Time: Allow 2 hours minimum. **Hours:** Daily 9-6, Memorial Day weekend-Sept. 30; Tues.-Sat. 9-5, Sun. noon-5, rest of year. Closed Jan. 1, Thanksgiving and Christmas. **Cost:** $8; free (ages 0-15). **Phone:** (406) 727-8733.

MALMSTROM AIR FORCE BASE MUSEUM AND AIR PARK is on Malmstrom Air Force Base, just inside the base's main gate at the east end of Second Ave. N. The museum displays uniforms, Minuteman Missile Launch equipment and photographs relating to base history. An outdoor air park contains aircraft

that date from the mid-20th century. **Note:** Adult visitors must present a valid, government-issued photo ID. **Time:** Allow 1 hour minimum. **Hours:** Mon.-Fri. 10-4. Closed major holidays. **Cost:** Free. **Phone:** (406) 731-2705 for museum information, or (406) 731-4050 for Malmstrom AFB Public Affairs.

MEHMKE STEAM TRACTOR MUSEUM is 10 mi. e. on US 87/89. Operable antique steam engines and gas tractors are exhibited along with various farming artifacts. **Time:** Allow 1 hour minimum. **Hours:** Daily dawn-dusk. **Cost:** Donations. **Phone:** (307) 751-2051.

PARIS GIBSON SQUARE MUSEUM OF ART is at jct. 14th St. and First Ave. N. in the Norman Architectural Building. The museum contains contemporary art exhibits. **Time:** Allow 1 hour, 30 minutes minimum. **Hours:** Mon.-Fri. 10-5 (also Tues. 7-9 p.m.), Sat. noon-5. Closed major holidays. **Cost:** Free. **Phone:** (406) 727-8255.

TOUR DE GREAT FALLS picks up passengers at area hotels. Guided bus tours to museums, parks and natural sites are conducted. Other tours are available. **Time:** Allow 2 hours, 30 minutes minimum. **Hours:** Trips are offered daily, June-Sept.; by appointment rest of year. **Cost:** $22; $20 (ages 65+ and active military with ID); $12 (ages 2-12). Attraction admissions are not included in fare. Reservations are required. **Phone:** (406) 771-1100 or (888) 707-1100.

RECREATIONAL ACTIVITIES
White-water Rafting

- **ROW Adventures** departs from a local lodging. **Hours:** White-water rafting trips are offered early June to mid-Sept. Departure days and times vary; phone ahead. **Phone:** (208) 765-0841 or (800) 451-6034.

COMFORT INN & SUITES (406)455-1000

   Hotel $99-$164 **Address:** 1801 Market Place Dr 59404 **Location:** I-15 exit 278, just sw. **Facility:** 88 units, some two bedrooms. 4 stories, interior corridors. **Parking:** winter plug-ins. **Activities:** exercise room. **Guest Services:** valet and coin laundry, area transportation.

COMFORT INN BY CHOICE HOTELS (406)454-2727

Hotel
$89-$149

Address: 1120 9th St S 59405 **Location:** I-15 exit 278, 3 mi e on 10th Ave S, US 87/89 and SR 3/200, then just s. Next to a mall. **Facility:** 64 units. 3 stories, interior corridors. **Parking:** winter plug-ins. **Amenities:** safes. **Pool(s):** heated indoor. **Activities:** hot tub. **Guest Services:** valet laundry. **Featured Amenity:** full hot breakfast.

DAYS INN OF GREAT FALLS (406)727-6565

 Hotel $78-$93 **Address:** 101 14th Ave NW 59404 **Location:** I-15 exit 280 (Central Ave), 1.3 mi e on Central Ave/Business Rt I-15, 0.8 mi n on 3rd St NW, then just w. Adjacent to a high school. **Facility:** 60 units. 2 stories (no elevator), interior corridors. **Parking:** winter plug-ins. **Activities:** exercise room. **Guest Services:** valet and coin laundry.

EXTENDED STAY AMERICA-GREAT FALLS-MISSOURI RIVER (406)761-7524

  Extended Stay Hotel $55-$109 **Address:** 800 River Dr S 59405 **Location:** I-15 exit 278, 1.7 mi e on 10th Ave S, then 0.7 mi n. Located along the river. **Facility:** 104 kitchen units. 3 stories, interior corridors. **Terms:** cancellation fee imposed. **Activities:** fishing. **Guest Services:** coin laundry.

FAIRFIELD INN BY MARRIOTT (406)454-3000

  Hotel $79-$199 **Address:** 1000 9th Ave S 59405 **Location:** I-15 exit 278, 3 mi e on 10th Ave S, US 87/89 and SR 3/200, then just n. Across from a mall. **Facility:** 63 units. 3 stories, interior corridors. **Parking:** winter plug-ins. **Pool(s):** heated indoor. **Activities:** hot tub. **Guest Services:** valet and coin laundry.

AAA Benefit:
Members save 5% or more!

THE GREAT FALLS INN BY RIVERSAGE (406)453-6000

Hotel
$75-$95

Address: 1400 28th St S 59405 **Location:** I-15 exit 278, 5.3 mi e on 10th Ave S, 0.3 mi s on 26th St S, then just e on 15th Ave S. Next to a medical facility. **Facility:** 60 units. 4 stories, interior corridors. **Parking:** winter plug-ins. **Activities:** limited exercise equipment. **Guest Services:** valet and coin laundry. **Featured Amenity:** continental breakfast. (See ad p. 176.)

▼ See AAA listing p. 174 ▼

HAMPTON INN
(406)453-2675

▼▼▼▼ Hotel $129-$210 **Address:** 2301 14th St SW 59404 **Location:** I-15 exit 278, just sw. **Facility:** 97 units. 4 stories, interior corridors. **Parking:** winter plug-ins. **Terms:** check-in 4 pm, 1-7 night minimum stay, cancellation fee imposed. **Pool(s):** heated indoor. **Activities:** hot tub, exercise room. **Guest Services:** valet and coin laundry, area transportation.

AAA Benefit: Members save up to 10%!

Amenities: video games.

HILTON GARDEN INN
(406)452-1000

▼▼▼ Hotel $129-$159 **Address:** 2520 14th St SW 59404 **Location:** I-15 exit 278, just sw. **Facility:** 118 units. 4 stories, interior corridors. **Terms:** check-in 4 pm, 1-7 night minimum stay, cancellation fee imposed. **Amenities:** *Some:* safes. **Pool(s):** indoor. **Activities:** hot tub, exercise room. **Guest Services:** valet and coin laundry, area transportation.

AAA Benefit: Members save up to 10%!

HOLIDAY INN
(406)727-7200

Hotel
$89-$169

Address: 400 10th Ave S 59405 **Location:** I-15 exit 278, 2 mi e on 10th Ave S, then just s. Located in a commercial area. **Facility:** 168 units, some two bedrooms. 7 stories, interior corridors. **Parking:** winter plug-ins. **Pool(s):** heated indoor. **Activities:** hot tub, exercise room. **Guest Services:** valet and coin laundry.

HOLIDAY INN EXPRESS & SUITES
(406)453-4000

▼▼▼ Hotel $109-$189 **Address:** 1625 Market Place Dr 59404 **Location:** I-15 exit 278, just sw. **Facility:** 85 units. 4 stories, interior corridors. **Parking:** winter plug-ins. **Terms:** cancellation fee imposed, resort fee. **Pool(s):** heated indoor. **Activities:** hot tub, exercise room. **Guest Services:** valet and coin laundry.

LA QUINTA INN & SUITES GREAT FALLS
(406)761-2600

▼▼▼▼ Hotel $94-$156 **Address:** 600 River Dr S 59405 **Location:** I-15 exit 278, 1.7 mi e on 10th Ave S, then 0.8 mi n. Located along the river. **Facility:** 92 units, some kitchens. 3 stories, interior corridors. **Parking:** winter plug-ins. **Pool(s):** heated indoor. **Activities:** sauna, hot tub, bicycles, trails, exercise room. **Guest Services:** valet and coin laundry.

▼ See AAA listing p. 175 ▼

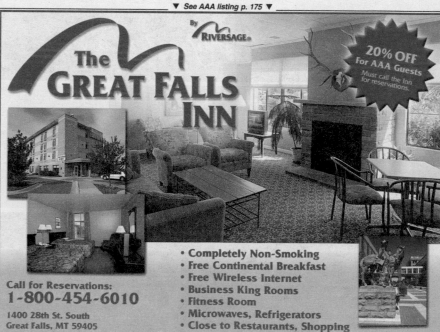

MOTEL 6 #4238 (406)453-1602

◆
Motel
$67-$95

Address: 2 Treasure State Dr 59404 **Location:** I-15 exit 278, 0.8 mi e on 10th Ave S and US 87/89 and SR 3/200. **Facility:** 59 units. 2 stories (no elevator), interior corridors. **Parking:** winter plug-ins. **Guest Services:** area transportation.

SAVE ⊬ ⍾ 🛜 / SOME UNITS 🐾 📠

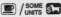

Free high-speed internet and airport transportation.

ACCOR hotels

O'HAIRE MOTOR INN (406)454-2141

◆ Motel $65-$75 **Address:** 17 7th St S 59403 **Location:** Center of downtown. **Facility:** 67 units, some two bedrooms. 3 stories, interior/exterior corridors. **Parking:** winter plug-ins. **Pool(s):** heated indoor. **Guest Services:** valet laundry.

⊬ ⍾ 🍸 ⊿ BIZ HS 🛜 💻 / SOME UNITS 🐕 📠

QUALITY INN (406)761-3410

◆◆◆
Hotel
$64-$114

Address: 220 Central Ave 59401 **Location:** Downtown. **Facility:** 105 units. 4 stories, interior/exterior corridors. **Parking:** winter plug-ins. **Pool(s):** heated outdoor. **Guest Services:** coin laundry. **Featured Amenity:** continental breakfast.

SAVE ⍾ 🍸 ⊿ BIZ 🛜 💻 / SOME UNITS 🐕 📠 🖨

STAYBRIDGE SUITES (406)761-4903

◆◆◆ Extended Stay Hotel $99-$199 **Address:** 201 3rd St NW (US 87) 59404 **Location:** I-15 exit 280 (Central Ave), 1.2 mi w, then just n. Located along the river. **Facility:** 113 kitchen units, some two bedrooms. 4 stories, interior corridors. **Parking:** winter plug-ins. **Terms:** check-in 4 pm. **Pool(s):** heated indoor. **Activities:** hot tub, exercise room. **Guest Services:** complimentary and valet laundry.

⊬ CALL 🔐 ⊿ BIZ HS 🛜 ✕ 🐾 📠 🖨 💻 / SOME UNITS 🐕

TOWNHOUSE INN OF GREAT FALLS (406)761-4600

◆◆◆
Motel
$85-$140

Address: 1411 10th Ave S 59405 **Location:** I-15 exit 278, 2.6 mi e on 10th Ave S, US 87/89 and SR 3/200. **Facility:** 108 units. 2 stories (no elevator), interior corridors. **Parking:** winter plug-ins. **Terms:** resort fee. **Pool(s):** heated indoor. **Activities:** sauna, hot tub, game room. **Guest Services:** valet and coin laundry, area transportation. **Featured Amenity:** full hot breakfast.

SAVE ⊬ ⍾ ⊿ BIZ HS 🛜 ✕ 📠 🖨 💻 / SOME UNITS 🐕

THE CATTLEMAN'S CUT SUPPER CLUB BAR & CASINO
406/452-0702

◆◆ Steak Seafood. Casual Dining. $8-$29 **AAA Inspector Notes:** This seems like an unlikely place to find quality prepared steaks, but here it is! Not only does the meat cut like butter, the taste is exquisite. The owner does it right--a bottomless salad bar, dessert and the entree, all for one affordable price. **Features:** full bar. **Reservations:** suggested. **Address:** 369 Vaughn Frontage Rd 59404 **Location:** I-15 exit 286, just w, then just n. [D] CALL 🔐

DANTE'S CREATIVE CUISINE 406/453-9599

◆◆ Italian. Casual Dining. $10-$29 **AAA Inspector Notes:** In an imposing red-brick structure that was built in 1908 as an ironworks, this casual dining restaurant offers good variety. The menu lists many traditional Italian selections, as well as Mexican and Southwestern dishes, steaks, prime rib and seafood. Signature fare includes the Gorgonzola salad and sourdough bread served with olive oil and roasted garlic. The dining room has extensive oak woodwork and a pressed-tin ceiling. **Features:** full bar. **Address:** 1325 8th Ave N 59401 **Location:** Jct 14th St and 8th Ave N. [L] [D]

DIMITRI'S 406/452-5774

◆ Greek. Casual Dining. $8-$23 **AAA Inspector Notes:** A family-run restaurant with delicious traditional favorites such as homemade salad dressings, tzatiki sauce, Aegean shrimp and baklava. Not open for dinner on Sunday. Be sure to check when the belly dancers are scheduled to entertain. Opa! **Features:** beer & wine. **Address:** 1919 3rd St NW 59404 **Location:** I-15 exit 280 (Central Ave), 1.3 mi e on Central Ave/Business Rt I-15, then 1 mi n. [L] [D] CALL 🔐

FASTEST BASSET COFFEE & CREPE HAUS 406/868-6089

◆ Coffee/Tea. Quick Serve. $5-$8 **AAA Inspector Notes:** Mostly American-influenced versions of the French crepe can be enjoyed with your favorite form of coffee. The owner loves his Basset Hound, Beatrice and pays homage to her in the form of pictures and even in the name of some of the savory crepe specialties. Dessert crepes are also on the menu. **Address:** 215 3rd St NW (US 87) 59404 **Location:** I-15 exit 280 (Central Ave), 1.2 mi w, then just n. [B] [L] CALL 🔐

LITTLE ATHENS 406/453-1430

◆ Greek. Quick Serve. $6-$12 **AAA Inspector Notes:** This is not typical mall fast food. The owner and his family prepare true Greek food with authentic ingredients. A splurge on a piece of baklava (or two) is a must. **Address:** 1200 10th Ave S 59404 **Location:** I-15 exit 278, 2.5 mi e; in Holiday Village Mall, lower level. [L] [D] CALL 🔐

MACKENZIE RIVER PIZZA 406/761-0085

◆◆ Pizza. Casual Dining. $8-$20 **AAA Inspector Notes:** Known for its eclectic Western decor, the restaurant lets patrons choose from several microbrews to accompany a specialty pizza or large, innovative sandwich. Pizza crusts are wonderful and offer the choice of sourdough, natural grain, deep dish or thin crust. **Features:** beer & wine, patio dining. **Address:** 500 River Dr S 59405 **Location:** I-15 exit 278, 1.7 mi e on 10th Ave S, then 0.8 mi n. [L] [D]

RIKKI'S PIZZA & PASTA 406/761-8052

◆◆ American. Casual Dining. $9-$14 **AAA Inspector Notes:** Ask anyone around town where to eat and Rikki's is at the top of the list. They make their own salad dressings and pasta sauces. Thai street noodles with spicy sauce and loads of vegetables is one of the favorites. Save room for gooey butter cake—the name says it all. **Features:** full bar. **Address:** 1220 9th St S 59405 **Location:** I-15 exit 278, 3 mi e on 10th Ave S, US 87/89 and SR 3/200, then just s; next to mall. [L] [D] CALL 🔐

SUKI CAFE 406/770-3038

◆◆ Thai Sushi. Casual Dining. $9-$17 **AAA Inspector Notes:** She's from Thailand, he's from Japan. A married couple share their respective cuisines in this unique café. The Thai dishes stray a bit from the traditional, but the flavors mesh. The sushi is traditional, very fresh and displayed creatively. **Features:** beer & wine. **Address:** 1229 10th Ave S 59405 **Location:** Jct 12th St. [L] [D]

HAMILTON (D-2) pop. 4,348, elev. 3,572'

The seat of Ravalli County and headquarters of Bitterroot National Forest, Hamilton was founded by 19th-century copper magnate Marcus Daly.

Bitterroot Valley Chamber of Commerce: 105 E. Main St., Hamilton, MT 59840. **Phone:** (406) 363-2400.

[SAVE] **DALY MANSION** is at 251 Eastside Hwy. (CR 269). The riverside estate of Montana copper baron Marcus Daly contains original furniture and Italian marble fireplaces. The Georgian Revival house is on the grounds of the 27-acre Margaret Daly Memorial Arboretum and is surrounded by a 22,000-acre stock farm where Daly raised Thoroughbred racehorses. **Time:** Allow 1 hour minimum. **Hours:** Guided mansion tours depart daily on the hour 10-3, mid-May to late Sept.; by appointment rest of year. Phone ahead to confirm schedule. **Cost:** $9; $8 (ages 60+); $6 (ages 6-17). Grounds free. **Phone:** (406) 363-6004.

RAVALLI COUNTY MUSEUM, at 205 Bedford St., is in the original Ravalli County Courthouse, which once served as the meeting spot for social and political activity in the Bitter Root Valley. The museum includes a collection of Native American artifacts, a miner and trapper exhibit, a Lewis and Clark expedition display, a natural history room and historical photographs and newspapers. A Walk Through Bitter Root is a period room that depicts life in the valley during the late 1800s, with rotating exhibits, events and educational programs throughout the year.

Time: Allow 1 hour minimum. **Hours:** Tues.-Fri. 10-4 (also Thurs. 4-8), Sat. 9-1. Closed major holidays. Phone ahead to confirm schedule. **Cost:** $3 (adults); $1 (senior citizens and students with ID); $6 (family). **Phone:** (406) 363-3338.

BITTERROOT RIVER INN & CONFERENCE CENTER
(406)375-2525
[WW] **Hotel** $69-$139 **Address:** 139 Bitterroot Plaza Dr 59840 **Location:** US 93, 1 mi n, then just w. Adjacent to city park, bird sanctuary and river. **Facility:** 65 units. 3 stories, interior/exterior corridors. **Terms:** resort fee. **Pool(s):** heated indoor. **Activities:** sauna, hot tub, exercise room. **Guest Services:** coin laundry.
[icons]

MOTEL 6 HAMILTON BLACK BEAR INN
(406)363-2142
[WW] **Motel** $77-$89 **Address:** 409 S 1st St (US 93) 59840 **Location:** On US 93, s of City Center, jct Madison St. **Facility:** 39 units. 1-2 stories (no elevator), exterior corridors. **Parking:** winter plug-ins. **Activities:** hot tub.
[icons]

TOWN HOUSE INNS
(406)363-6600
[WW] **Hotel** $65-$100 **Address:** 1113 N 1st St 59840 **Location:** On US 93, n of City Center. **Facility:** 62 units. 2 stories (no elevator), interior corridors. **Parking:** winter plug-ins. **Activities:** sauna, exercise room. **Guest Services:** coin laundry.
[icons]

WHERE TO EAT

2ND STREET SUSHI & ASIAN GRILL
406/363-0600
[WW] Asian Sushi. Casual Dining. $10-$29 **AAA Inspector Notes:** This quaint grill flies in seafood from Seattle. Fresh choices range from the yokisoba noodle bowl to the maki rolls. **Features:** beer & wine. **Address:** 322 S 2nd St 59840 **Location:** On US 93, s of City Center, just w on Madison St; in shared building with American Legion. **Parking:** on-site and street. [icons]

SPICE OF LIFE
406/363-4433
[WW] American. Casual Dining. $8-$22 **AAA Inspector Notes:** The cafe's eclectic menu runs from Jamaican to Italian to Thai, and also includes good old American burgers. Organic greens and vegetables, as well as locally produced meats and handcrafted breads, are used when available. Dinner is only Wednesday through Saturday. Phone ahead for hours. **Features:** beer & wine. **Address:** 163 S 2nd St 59840 **Location:** Just s of Main St; downtown. **Parking:** street only. [icons]

HARDIN (E-6) pop. 3,505, elev. 2,902'

Hardin borders Crow Indian Reservation and serves as a trading center for its people. The town was named after Samuel Hardin, a rancher from Wyoming who leased land on the reservation. Nearby is the former site of Fort Custer, a military garrison said to have been one of the finest cavalry posts in the world. It was established in 1877, just after Lt. Col. George Armstrong Custer's defeat at the Battle of the Little Bighorn.

The 4-day Little Big Horn Days celebration takes place in June. Festivities include a grand ball with period music, costumes and dances; [icon] Custer's Last Stand Re-enactment; a powwow; arts and crafts shows; and dancing.

Hardin Area Chamber of Commerce: 10 E. Railway St., P.O. Box 446, Hardin, MT 59034. **Phone:** (406) 665-1672.

BIG HORN COUNTY HISTORICAL MUSEUM AND STATE VISITOR CENTER is 1 mi. e. off I-90 exit 497 to 1163 3rd St. E. The 35-acre complex features 26 historic buildings, including a 1911 farmhouse and barn, a Native American log cabin, a railroad depot, a doctor's building, the Will James studio and a church. Exhibits about Fort Custer, Plains Indians, and restored tractors and automobiles also are on display. The main building contains a library, educational rooms, a gallery and a state visitor center. **Hours:** Museum open daily 8-6, May-Sept.; Mon.-Fri. 9-5, rest of year. Outbuildings open only May-Sept. **Cost:** $5; $4 (ages 62+); $3 (ages 12-17). **Phone:** (406) 665-1671. [icon]

[icon] **LITTLE BIGHORN BATTLEFIELD NATIONAL MONUMENT**—see place listing p. 188.

RODEWAY INN
(406)665-1870
[W] **Motel** $80-$221 **Address:** 1324 N Crawford Ave 59034 **Location:** I-90 exit 495, just s on SR 47. **Facility:** 42 units. 2 stories (no elevator), exterior corridors. **Parking:** winter plug-ins. **Pool(s):** heated outdoor. **Activities:** hot tub. **Guest Services:** coin laundry.
[icons]

WESTERN MOTEL   406/665-2296

Motel. Rates not provided. **Address:** 830 W 3rd St 59034 **Location:** I-90 exit 495 eastbound, 1.3 mi s on SR 47 and CR 313, then just e; exit 497 westbound, 0.3 mi w on I-90 business loop, continue on 3rd St for 0.7 mi. **Facility:** 12 units, some two bedrooms. 2 stories (no elevator), exterior corridors. **Parking:** winter plug-ins.

HARLOWTON (D-4) pop. 997

UPPER MUSSELSHELL MUSEUM is at 11 S. Central Ave. Life in the early 1900s is depicted through replicas of a general store, schoolroom, kitchen and living room. Supplementing these exhibits are displays of period clothing, farm tools and other artifacts. Also displayed is a replica of an avaceratops dinosaur whose remains were found north of town on Careless Creek. **Time:** Allow 30 minutes minimum. **Hours:** Mon.-Sat. 10-5, Memorial Day-Labor Day; by appointment rest of year. **Cost:** $5; $2.50 (ages 55+); free (ages 0-15). **Phone:** (406) 632-5519.

COUNTRYSIDE INN   406/632-4119

Motel $55-$65 **Address:** 309 3rd St NE 59036 **Location:** US 12 E. **Facility:** 19 units. 1 story, exterior corridors. **Parking:** winter plug-ins.

HAVRE (B-5) pop. 9,310, elev. 2,493'

Havre's beginnings as a transportation hub were forged by the railroad, which brought supplies to trappers, miners and the military at nearby Fort Assinniboine. The town was named by railroad officials after the French city Le Havre, but its citizens gave it a different pronunciation: HAV-er.

Departing from the H. Earl Clack Museum *(see attraction listing)*, guided tours of Fort Assinniboine, 8 miles southwest off US 87, are offered for a fee daily at noon and 5 (weather permitting), June-Labor Day. High Line Heritage Resources Walking Tours offers 1-hour tours of the downtown area departing from 132 Third St. A separate hour-long walking tour leaving from the corner of Third Avenue and Main Street explores a 36-block residential historic district. High Line's tours are available by appointment year-round (weather permitting); phone (406) 265-6233.

Area geography can best be described as dichotomous. Here, rolling plains meet the Bear Paw Mountains, providing unlimited summer and winter recreation opportunities. Beaver Creek Park, a 17-mile-long, 1-mile-wide strip park 11 miles south on CR 234, encases Beaver Creek and two lakes and offers a variety of activities including camping, fishing, hiking, cross-country skiing and snowshoeing *(see Recreation Areas Chart)*.

Havre Area Chamber of Commerce: 130 Fifth Ave., P.O. Box 308, Havre, MT 59501. **Phone:** (406) 265-4383.

Self-guiding tours: Free brochures for self-guiding walking tours of the 36-block historic district are available from the chamber of commerce.

HAVRE BENEATH THE STREETS is at 120 Third Ave. This guided walking tour takes visitors through the city's historical underground. Many of the original buildings built in 1904 are now beneath the city streets. Included are a Chinese laundry, post office, bordello, meat market, bakery, opium den, barbershop and saloon. **Time:** Allow 1 hour minimum. **Hours:** Tours depart daily 9:30-3:30, Memorial Day-Sept. 30; Mon.-Sat. 10:30-2:30, rest of year. Closed major holidays. **Cost:** $12; $10 (ages 65+); $8 (ages 6-12). Prices may vary; phone ahead. Reservations are recommended. **Phone:** (406) 265-8888.

H. EARL CLACK MUSEUM is at 1753 US 2 N.W., #30, in the Holiday Village Mall. Local history is chronicled through artifacts, dioramas and exhibits. **Time:** Allow 1 hour minimum. **Hours:** Mon.-Sat. 10-5, Sun. noon-5, Memorial Day-Labor Day; Tues.-Sat. 1-5, rest of year. Phone ahead to confirm schedule. **Cost:** Donations. **Phone:** (406) 265-4000.

Wahkpa Chu'gn Buffalo Jump is on US 2 behind the Holiday Village Mall. Pronounced "walk-paw chew-gun," an Assinniboine name for the Milk River, this prehistoric buffalo jump site was occupied by three separate cultures from 600 to 2,000 years ago. A 45-minute guided walking tour features exposed campsites and buffalo bone deposits as deep as 20 feet below the surface. An off-road vehicle transports visitors from the Interpretive Center into the site area.

Hours: Guided tours daily 9-4, June 1-Labor Day; by appointment rest of year (weather permitting). **Cost:** $9; $8 (ages 65+); $5 (ages 6-12); free (ages 0-5). **Phone:** (406) 265-6417 or (406) 945-3503.

AMERICINN LODGE & SUITES OF HAVRE   (406)395-5000

Hotel $83-$152 **Address:** 2520 Hwy 2 W 59501 **Location:** On US 2, west side of town. **Facility:** 52 units. 2 stories (no elevator), interior corridors. **Parking:** winter plug-ins. **Terms:** cancellation fee imposed. **Pool(s):** heated indoor. **Activities:** hot tub, limited exercise equipment. **Guest Services:** valet and coin laundry.

BEST WESTERN PLUS GREAT NORTHERN INN
                                                (406)265-4200

Hotel
$90-$139

AAA Benefit: Members save 10% or more with Best Western!

Address: 1345 1st St 59501 **Location:** 0.7 mi e of town center on US 2. **Facility:** 74 units. 3 stories, interior corridors. **Pool(s):** heated indoor. **Activities:** hot tub, steamroom, exercise room. **Guest Services:** valet and coin laundry, area transportation. **Featured Amenity:** breakfast buffet.

TOWNHOUSE INN OF HAVRE   (406)265-6711

Hotel $85-$95 **Address:** 601 1st St W 59501 **Location:** Just w of town center on US 2. **Facility:** 102 units, some three bedrooms and kitchens. 2 stories (no elevator), interior corridors. **Parking:** winter plug-ins. **Terms:** cancellation fee imposed. **Pool(s):** heated indoor. **Activities:** sauna, hot tub. **Guest Services:** valet and coin laundry, area transportation.

HELENA (D-3) pop. 28,190, elev. 4,047'
• Restaurants p. 182

Helena succeeded the other gold camps of Bannack and Virginia City as the territorial capital in 1875. It became the state capital in 1889 after a hotly contested fight between "copper kings" William A. Clark and Marcus Daly. The city owes its existence to "The Georgians," four weary and discouraged Southern prospectors, who in 1864 stumbled down a gulch and grimly dubbed it "Last Chance Gulch," only to find gold where the city's main street now runs.

Later a more suitable name, Helena (He-LAY-na), was put to a vote. But the miners and the bullwhackers did not like the name's feminine ring. Consequently the emphasis was shifted to the first syllable, with the second "e" almost silent, and HEL-e-na became the accepted pronunciation. The gold rush faded quickly, and Helena settled down to become a trade center for the surrounding goldfields.

Reminders of the early days can be found in the architecture of the buildings that line Reeder's Alley off the 200 block of South Park Avenue in southwest Helena. The 1864 Pioneer Cabin at 210 Park Ave., said to be the oldest structure in Helena, is furnished with pioneer artifacts.

Marysville, a ghost town, is 25 miles northwest off CR 279. During the 1880s and '90s the town reigned as Montana's leading gold producer. The remnants of its saloons, shops and sidewalks still can be seen. Montana Military Museum, at Fort William Henry Harrison, serves as the state's official military repository with a rich collection of memorabilia, artifacts and archives; phone (406) 324-3550.

The ❦ Mount Helena Music Festival provides 2 days of blues, rock, reggae and zydeco. Held late June in downtown, the event also includes crafts, food and children's activities.

Helena Area Chamber of Commerce/Convention and Visitor Bureau: 225 Cruse Ave., Helena, MT 59601. Phone: (406) 442-4120 or (800) 743-5362.

Shopping areas: Once the quarters of miners, muleskinners and Chinese laborers during the gold rush, the buildings along Reeder's Alley, 100 S. Park Ave., now contain specialty shops as well as an 1864 cabin furnished with pioneer artifacts.

ARCHIE BRAY FOUNDATION FOR THE CERAMIC ARTS is at 2915 Country Club Ave. Educating artists who work in ceramics, the foundation was established in 1951 in a former brickyard by Western Clay Manufacturing Co. president and art patron Archie Bray. The 26-acre grounds, set among the Rocky Mountain foothills, feature hundreds of whimsical sculptures created by resident artists over the years. In summer, current residents exhibit their work in the Warehouse Gallery. Time: Allow 1 hour minimum. Hours: Mon.-Sat. 10-5, Sun. 1-5, June-Aug.; Mon.-Sat. 10-5, rest of year. Closed major holidays. Cost: Free. Phone: (406) 443-3502. ⛽

CATHEDRAL OF ST. HELENA is at the corner of Lawrence and Warren sts. This handsome Victorian Gothic structure was modeled after the Votive Church of the Sacred Heart in Vienna, Austria, and completed in 1914. Interior finishings are of Carrara marble, and the stained glass windows were made in Munich, Germany, by F.X. Zettler Co. An open-air sculpture gallery contains 29 statues of historical persons from the arts, sciences and religion.

Time: Allow 30 minutes minimum. Hours: Mon.-Fri. 7-6, Sat. 8:30-6:30, Sun. 7:30-6. Guided tours are given Tues.-Thurs. 1-3, late May-Labor Day; by reservation rest of year. Cost: Donations. Phone: (406) 442-5825.

HOLTER MUSEUM OF ART is at 12 E. Lawrence St. The museum features works of regional and national prominence. A permanent collection focuses on the cultural and artistic heritage of the Northwest. Hours: Tues.-Sat. 10-5:30, Sun. noon-4. Closed Jan. 1, Thanksgiving and Christmas. Cost: Donations. Phone: (406) 442-6400.

LAST CHANCE TOUR TRAIN departs from the Montana Historical Society Museum, Library and Archives at 225 N. Roberts St. This 1-hour jaunt makes a circuit through Helena's present and past on an automotive tour train. Passengers view such whimsical downtown architectural features as giant lizards, thumbprints and gargoyles; the Cathedral of St. Helena's splendid 230-foot-tall spires; Reeder's Alley; and the city's mansion district.

Hours: Tours depart Mon.-Sat. at 11, 1, 3 and 5:30, July-Aug.; at 11, 1 and 3, in June; at 11 and 3, Sept. 1-14. Cost: $7.50; $7 (senior citizens); $6 (ages 4-12). Phone: (406) 442-1023.

MONTANA HISTORICAL SOCIETY MUSEUM, LIBRARY AND ARCHIVES is across from the state capitol at 225 N. Roberts St. The history of Montana and the West is recounted through an extensive collection of Charles M. Russell's paintings and sculpture in addition to frequently changing exhibits. The Montana Homeland exhibition uses more than 2,000 artifacts, photographs and documents to trace Montana history from the end of the most recent ice age through World War II. A highlight is the display of "Big Medicine," a rare white bison with blue eyes and tan hooves born in 1933.

Hours: Mon.-Sat. 9-5 (also Thurs. 5-8). Closed major holidays. Cost: $5; $1 (ages 5-18); $12 (family, two adults and children ages 0-18). Phone: (406) 444-2694.

ORIGINAL GOVERNOR'S MANSION is at 304 N. Ewing St. Built in 1888, the Victorian mansion was the home of nine Montana governors 1913-59. The house is furnished in period. Time: Allow 30 minutes minimum. Hours: Guided tours are given Tues.-Sat. on the hour noon-3, May-Sept.; Sat. on the hour noon-3, rest of year. Closed major holidays. Cost:

$4; $1 (ages 5-18); $10 (family, two adults and children ages 0-18). **Phone:** (406) 442-3115 Apr.-Dec., or (406) 444-4789 rest of year for tour reservations.

STATE CAPITOL is at Sixth and Montana sts. Faced with sandstone and Montana granite, the capitol is topped by a dome of Montana copper. The cornerstone was laid July 4, 1899, and the building was dedicated July 4, 1902. Historical paintings and statues decorate the interior; prominent among these is Charles M. Russell's largest painting, the 12-by-25-foot "Lewis and Clark Meeting Indians at Ross' Hole," in the House of Representatives.

Time: Allow 45 minutes minimum. **Hours:** Mon.-Sat. 8-5. Guided tours are given on the hour Mon.-Sat. 9-2, May-Sept.; Sat. 10-2, Oct.-Dec. The Jan.-Apr. tour schedule in even-numbered years is Sat. 10-2; Mon.-Sat. 9-2 in odd-numbered years. Closed major holidays. Phone ahead to confirm schedule. **Cost:** Free. **Phone:** (406) 444-4789.

BARRISTER BED & BREAKFAST   (406)443-7330
Historic Bed & Breakfast $130-$145 **Address:** 416 N Ewing St 59601 **Location:** I-15 exit 192 (Prospect Ave), 1.5 mi sw via Prospect and Montana aves to 9th Ave, 0.8 mi w, then just s. Across from St. Helena Cathedral. **Facility:** The bedrooms in this 1874 Victorian mansion have ornate fireplaces. Common areas include a parlor, library, den and enclosed sun porch. 5 units. 3 stories (no elevator), interior corridors. **Parking:** winter plug-ins. **Terms:** check-in 4 pm, 4 day cancellation notice. **Guest Services:** complimentary laundry.

BEST WESTERN PREMIER HELENA GREAT NORTHERN HOTEL   (406)457-5500

Hotel
$159-$172

AAA Benefit: Members save 10% or more with Best Western!

Address: 835 Great Northern Blvd 59601 **Location:** I-15 exit 193 (Cedar St), 2 mi w, just w on Lyndale Ave, then just s on Getchell St; downtown. **Facility:** 100 units. 4 stories, interior corridors. **Parking:** winter plug-ins. **Amenities:** safes. **Dining:** Silver Star Steak Company, see separate listing. **Pool(s):** heated indoor. **Activities:** hot tub, exercise room. **Guest Services:** valet and coin laundry, area transportation. **Featured Amenity:** breakfast buffet.

COMFORT SUITES   (406)495-0505

Hotel
$115-$145
Address: 3180 N Washington St 59602 **Location:** I-15 exit 194 (Custer Ave), just e. **Facility:** 90 units, some efficiencies. 3 stories, interior corridors. **Parking:** winter plug-ins. **Amenities:** safes. **Pool(s):** heated indoor. **Activities:** hot tub, exercise room. **Guest Services:** valet and coin laundry, area transportation.

DAYS INN HELENA   (406)442-3280
Hotel $80-$250 **Address:** 2001 Prospect Ave 59601 **Location:** I-15 exit 192 (Prospect Ave), just w. **Facility:** 88 units, some kitchens. 2 stories (no elevator), interior corridors. **Parking:** winter plug-ins. **Amenities:** safes. **Activities:** hot tub, limited exercise equipment. **Guest Services:** valet and coin laundry.

FAIRFIELD INN & SUITES BY MARRIOTT   (406)449-9944
Hotel
$89-$129
AAA Benefit: Members save 5% or more!

Address: 2150 11th Ave 59601 **Location:** I-15 exit 192 (Prospect Ave), just sw. **Facility:** 58 units. 3 stories, interior corridors. **Parking:** winter plug-ins. **Pool(s):** heated indoor. **Activities:** hot tub, exercise room. **Guest Services:** valet and coin laundry.

Conveniently located just minutes from the State Capitol & Carroll College.

HAMPTON INN-HELENA   (406)443-5800
Hotel $99-$149 **Address:** 725 Carter Dr 59601 **Location:** I-15 exit 192 (Prospect Ave), just e. **Facility:** 81 units. 3 stories, interior corridors. **Parking:** winter plug-ins. **Terms:** 1-7 night minimum stay, cancellation fee imposed. **Pool(s):** heated indoor. **Activities:** hot tub, exercise room. **Guest Services:** valet and coin laundry, area transportation.

AAA Benefit: Members save up to 10%!

HELENA SUPER 8   (406)443-2450
Hotel $65-$75 **Address:** 2200 11th Ave 59601 **Location:** I-15 exit 192 (Prospect Ave) northbound; exit west business district southbound on US 12. **Facility:** 102 units. 3 stories, interior corridors. **Parking:** winter plug-ins. **Amenities:** safes. **Activities:** exercise room. **Guest Services:** valet and coin laundry.

HOLIDAY INN CONFERENCE CENTER DOWNTOWN   (406)443-2200
Hotel $119-$159 **Address:** 22 N Last Chance Gulch 59601 **Location:** Jct Park Ave and Broadway St. **Facility:** 71 units. 3 stories, interior corridors. **Terms:** 3 day cancellation notice, resort fee. **Pool(s):** heated indoor. **Activities:** hot tub, exercise room. **Guest Services:** valet and coin laundry, area transportation.

HOLIDAY INN EXPRESS HOTEL & SUITES   (406)442-7500
Hotel $99-$139 **Address:** 3170 N Sanders St 59602 **Location:** I-15 exit 194 (Custer Ave), just w, then just n. **Facility:** 87 units. 3 stories, interior corridors. **Parking:** winter plug-ins. **Pool(s):** heated indoor. **Activities:** hot tub, exercise room. **Guest Services:** valet and coin laundry.

JORGENSON'S INN & SUITES　　　(406)442-1770

◆◆◆ Hotel $70-$129 **Address:** 1714 11th Ave 59601 **Location:** I-15 exit 192 (Prospect Ave), just w of I-15 and US 287/12. Adjacent to the shopping mall. **Facility:** 114 units. 1-3 stories, interior/exterior corridors. **Parking:** winter plug-ins. **Terms:** cancellation fee imposed. **Dining:** Jorgenson's Restaurant & Lounge, see separate listing. **Guest Services:** valet and coin laundry, area transportation.

[icons]

LA QUINTA INN & SUITES HELENA　　(406)449-4000

◆◆◆ Hotel $94-$151 **Address:** 701 Washington St 59601 **Location:** I-15 exit 192 (Prospect Ave), just w. **Facility:** 74 units. 4 stories, interior corridors. **Parking:** winter plug-ins. **Pool(s):** heated outdoor. **Activities:** exercise room. **Guest Services:** valet and coin laundry.

[icons]

RED LION COLONIAL HOTEL　　　(406)443-2100

◆◆◆ Hotel $100-$150 **Address:** 2301 Colonial Dr 59601 **Location:** I-15 exit 192 (Prospect Ave) southbound; exit 192B northbound. **Facility:** 149 units. 2 stories, interior corridors. **Parking:** winter plug-ins. **Terms:** cancellation fee imposed, resort fee. **Pool(s):** heated indoor. **Activities:** hot tub, exercise room. **Guest Services:** valet and coin laundry, area transportation.

[icons]

RESIDENCE INN BY MARRIOTT　　　(406)443-8010

◆◆◆ **Extended Stay Hotel** $99-$169 **Address:** 2500 E Custer Ave 59602 **Location:** I-15 exit 194 (Custer Ave), just e. **Facility:** 91 kitchen units. 3 stories, interior corridors. **Parking:** winter plug-ins. **Pool(s):** indoor. **Activities:** hot tub, exercise room. **Guest Services:** valet and coin laundry, area transportation.

AAA Benefit: Members save 5% or more!

[icons]

THE SANDERS-HELENA'S BED & BREAKFAST　406/442-3309

◆◆◆ Historic Bed & Breakfast $140-$165 **Address:** 328 N Ewing St 59601 **Location:** 0.3 mi from Last Chance Gulch, 0.8 mi w of state capitol on 6th Ave, then just n. **Facility:** Restored 1875 mansion, located one block from the original Governor's Mansion, features period furnishings. 7 units. 3 stories (no elevator), interior corridors. **Parking:** winter plug-ins. **Terms:** check-in 4 pm. **Guest Services:** complimentary laundry.

[icons]

WINGATE BY WYNDHAM　　　(406)449-3000

◆◆◆ Hotel $99-$225

Address: 2007 N Oakes St 59601 **Location:** I-15 exit 193 (Cedar St), just sw. **Facility:** 100 units. 3 stories, interior corridors. **Parking:** winter plug-ins. **Amenities:** video games, safes. **Pool(s):** heated indoor. **Activities:** hot tub, exercise room. **Guest Services:** valet and coin laundry. **Featured Amenity:** full hot breakfast.

[icons]

Be a better driver.
Keep your mind on the road.

WHERE TO EAT

BENNY'S BISTRO　　　406/443-0105

◆◆ American Casual Dining $9-$21

AAA Inspector Notes: Whether you choose to dine here for lunch or dinner, you'll always be served delicious cuisine that's fresh and innovative. Focaccia bread is wonderful for any sandwich creation or as an accompaniment to an entree. Tapas are served Wednesday and Thursday evenings. There's live music on Friday and Saturday nights. **Features:** beer & wine. **Address:** 108 E 6th Ave 59601 **Location:** Center; in historic downtown; across from Chamber of Commerce. **Parking:** street only. [L] [D]

JADE GARDEN　　　406/443-8899

◆◆ Chinese. Casual Dining. $8-$19 **AAA Inspector Notes:** The traditional Chinese menu features Cantonese cooking and a wide selection of traditional favorites. The atmosphere is inviting and contemporary, and the service prompt and pleasant. It's extremely popular, which means possible long waits on weekend evenings. **Features:** beer & wine. **Address:** 3128 N Montana Ave 59602 **Location:** I-15 exit 194 (Custer Ave), 0.5 mi w. [L] [D]

JORGENSON'S RESTAURANT & LOUNGE

406/442-6380

◆◆ American Casual Dining $8-$22

AAA Inspector Notes: This family restaurant serves a variety of menu items, including seafood, beef and chicken entrees. Service is pleasant, casual and efficient. **Features:** full bar, patio dining, senior menu, Sunday brunch, happy hour. **Address:** 1720 11th Ave 59601 **Location:** I-15 exit 192 (Prospect Ave), just w of I-15 and US 287/12; in Jorgenson's Inn & Suites. [B] [L] [D]

LUCCA'S　　　406/457-8311

◆◆◆ Italian. Casual Dining. $22-$33 **AAA Inspector Notes:** Contemporary Italian fare in a relaxed atmosphere. Seafood risotto is just one of the specialties featured. Homemade desserts such as tiramisu and panna cotta are extremely popular. **Features:** full bar. **Reservations:** suggested. **Address:** 56 N Last Chance Gulch 59601 **Location:** Downtown; north end of Walking Mall. **Parking:** street only. [D] CALL

MACKENZIE RIVER PIZZA　　　406/443-0033

◆◆◆ Pizza. Family Dining. $8-$20 **AAA Inspector Notes:** Known for its eclectic Western decor, the restaurant lets patrons choose from several microbrews to accompany a specialty pizza or large, innovative sandwich. Pizza crusts are wonderful and offer the choice of sourdough, natural grain, deep dish or thin crust. **Features:** full bar. **Address:** 1110 Road Runner Dr 59602 **Location:** Just w of jct N Montana and E Custer aves. [L] [D] CALL

MEDITERRANEAN GRILL　　　406/495-1212

◆◆ Mediterranean. Casual Dining. $9-$27 **AAA Inspector Notes:** Patrons experience the tastes of the Mediterranean in the restaurant's large dining area, which is decorated in a villa style. Pizza dough is made in house. The large stone, gas-fired oven is a focal point. **Features:** beer & wine, patio dining, Sunday brunch. **Address:** 42 S Park Ave 59601 **Location:** From Montana State Capitol; 0.8 mi w on E 6th Ave, just s on N Jackson St, just w on Broadway St, then just s. **Parking:** street only. [L] [D]

ON BROADWAY　　　406/443-1929

◆◆ Italian. Casual Dining. $15-$30 **AAA Inspector Notes:** Guests may sit in the loft, overlooking the music stage, or in the intimate dining room. Either way, friendly, knowledgeable service is the norm. The menu changes seasonally, and the chef's creative and well-prepared offerings delight. On Thursdays, a jazz ensemble performs. **Features:** full bar. **Address:** 106 Broadway St 59601 **Location:** Jct Cruse St; center; in historic downtown. **Parking:** street only. [D]

SILVER STAR STEAK COMPANY   406/495-0677

▼▼▼ Steak. Casual Dining. $13-$58 **AAA Inspector Notes:** Located in a new multiuse development area, the diverse menu offers regional favorites such as bison steaks. **Features:** full bar. **Reservations:** suggested. **Address:** 833 Great Northern Blvd 59601 **Location:** I-15 exit 193 (Cedar St), 2 mi w, just w on Lyndale Ave, then just s on Getchell St; downtown; in BEST WESTERN PREMIER Helena Great Northern Hotel. **Parking:** street only.

L D CALL ⑤M

TOI'S THAI CUISINE   406/443-6656

▼▼ Thai. Casual Dining. $13-$21 **AAA Inspector Notes:** What big flavors are created in this small kitchen. The spices are bold and heat levels can be adjusted to your liking. Be sure to make a reservation, as this place has very limited seating and is very popular. **Reservations:** suggested. **Address:** 423 N Last Chance Gulch St 59601 **Location:** Center; in historic downtown. **Parking:** street only.

D

WINDBAG SALOON   406/443-9669

▼▼ American. Casual Dining. $10-$30 **AAA Inspector Notes:** Bustling at lunch and dinner, you'll be served comfort foods in a causal atmosphere. The old-time décor in this historic building is rustic and the ambience is charming. The crab cakes are a great starter. **Features:** full bar. **Address:** 19 S Last Chance Gulch 59601 **Location:** Jct Broadway St; center; in Walking Mall. **Parking:** street only. L D CALL ⑤M

HELENA NATIONAL FOREST (D-3)

Elevations in the forest range from 3,600 ft. at the gates of the Missouri River to 9,411 ft. on Red Mountain in the Lincoln district. Refer to AAA maps for additional elevation information.

In west-central Montana, Helena National Forest encompasses 976,000 acres. The forest straddles the Continental Divide and embraces the Big Belt and the Elkhorn mountains. The Missouri River passes through the Helena Valley near the center of the forest. Vegetation ranges from sagebrush and bunchgrass to Douglas fir, lodgepole pine and spruce.

There are more than 1,000 miles of trails and 1,600 miles of forest roads. Continental Divide National Scenic Trail passes through the forest. Ten campgrounds, picnic grounds, good hunting and fishing, historic sites, wilderness areas and several ghost towns are among the forest's attractions. For further information contact the Forest Supervisor, Helena National Forest, 2880 Skyway Dr., Helena, MT 59602; phone (406) 449-5201. *See Recreation Areas Chart.*

▼GEM **THE GATES OF THE MOUNTAINS RECREATION AREA** is 20 mi. n. of Helena via I-15 exit 209 to Gates of the Mountains Landing and is reached by boat or trails. In 1805, the members of the Lewis and Clark expedition were fortunate to gaze upon the majestic natural wonder that lay before them. Limestone walls towering 1,200 feet stood like rock sentries within the canyon where the Missouri River pushes through the Big Belt Range. Named by Meriwether Lewis as "gates of the mountains," the name stuck and today visitors continue to marvel at the splendor of the rock formations.

Wildlife that call the canyon home include bighorn sheep, mountain goats, deer, mountain lions, black bears, ospreys and falcons. The recreation area provides swimming, hiking, fishing and narrated boat trip opportunities. A dinner cruise also is available.

Hours: Narrated 2-hour boat trips, with stopovers at Meriwether picnic area, depart Mon.-Fri. at 9, 11, 1 and 3, Sat.-Sun. and holidays on the hour 10-4, in July; Mon.-Fri. at 11, 1 and 3, Sat.-Sun. on the hour 10-4, Aug. 1-Labor Day; Mon.-Fri. at 11 and 2, Sat.-Sun. and holidays at 10, noon, 2 and 4, Memorial Day-June 30; Wed.-Fri. at 11 and 2, Sat.-Sun. and holidays at 11, 1 and 3, day after Labor Day-Sept. 30. **Cost:** Narrated boat trip $16; $14 (ages 60+ and military with ID); $10 (ages 4-17). Dinner cruise $44. **Phone:** (406) 458-5241. ⊠ 🛇

HUNGRY HORSE pop. 826

- **Hotels & Restaurants map & index p. 168**
- **Part of Glacier National Park area — see map p. 163**

HISTORIC TAMARACK LODGE & CABINS   (406)387-4420 25

▼▼▼ Cabin $63-$320

Address: 9549 US 2 E 59919 **Location:** 1.6 mi n. **Facility:** 24 units, some cabins. 1 story, exterior corridors. **Parking:** winter plug-ins. **Terms:** 7 day cancellation notice-fee imposed, resort fee. **Activities:** fishing, cross country skiing, snowmobiling. **Featured Amenity: continental breakfast.**

🖫 🛜 ⊠ ☎ 🛢 🖳 🖵 / SOME UNITS ⓀC

MINI GOLDEN INNS MOTEL   406/387-4313 26

▼▼ Motel $86-$160

Address: 8955 US 2 E 59919 **Location:** East end of town. **Facility:** 38 units, some two bedrooms and efficiencies. 1 story, exterior corridors. **Parking:** winter plug-ins. **Terms:** 30 day cancellation notice-fee imposed. **Guest Services:** coin laundry. **Featured Amenity: continental breakfast.**

🖫 🍽 CALL ⑤M 🛜 / SOME UNITS 🛒 🛢 🖳 🖵

HUSON (C-2) pop. 210, elev. 3,015'

THE NINEMILE REMOUNT DEPOT AND RANGER STATION is off I-90 to exit 82, then 4 mi. n. on Remount Rd. A working ranger station on a 5,000-acre ranch features Cape Cod-style buildings. A self-guiding tour through the historic site reveals the daily life of the firefighting rangers 1930-53. Grand Menard Discovery Trail, 1.5 miles north of the station, features two .7-mile self-guiding tours through a pine forest. Tour and trail brochures are available.

Time: Allow 1 hour minimum. **Hours:** Site daily dawn-dusk. Ranger station Mon.-Fri. 8-4:30. Visitor center daily 9-5, Memorial Day-Labor Day. **Cost:** Donations. **Phone:** (406) 626-5201.

KALISPELL (B-2) pop. 19,927, elev. 2,956'
• Hotels & Restaurants map & index p. 168
• Part of Glacier National Park area — see map p. 163

Kalispell (KAL-is-pell) is in the Flathead Valley between Glacier National Park *(see place listing p. 163)* and Flathead Lake, a region noted for the production of sweet cherries. The area was known only to the Salish, who called it "the land between the mountains," until 1891 when the Great Northern Railroad laid track to this point. The nearby settlements of Demersville and Ashley were moved to create Kalispell.

Kalispell is circled by dense forests, lakes, rivers and mountains. To the east is the Swan Range of the Rocky Mountains, and to the west, the Kootenai Range. Flathead National Forest *(see place listing p. 156)* has its headquarters in the city.

Local parks include Woodland Park, with lagoons, formal gardens and picnicking. Three forks of the Flathead River drain into Flathead Lake, making the area an ideal place for fly fishing, white-water rafting, kayaking and sailing.

Flathead Convention & Visitor Bureau: 15 Depot Park, Kalispell, MT 59901-4008. **Phone:** (406) 756-9091 or (800) 543-3105.

Self-guiding tours: Information about walking tours of the historic district is available from Kalispell Chamber of Commerce; phone (406) 758-2800. For information about the greater northwestern Montana area contact Glacier Country at (800) 338-5072.

Shopping areas: The Kalispell Farmers Market, in the Kalispell Center Mall parking lot, offers more than 100 vendors selling homemade and homegrown products Saturdays from spring through fall.

[SAVE] **CONRAD MANSION MUSEUM** is 6 blks. e. of Main St. at Woodland Ave. and Fourth St. E. Built in 1895 for Kalispell's founder, Charles E. Conrad, who traded and freighted on the Missouri River, the 26-room mansion has been restored to its Victorian splendor and contains original furnishings. Visitors can take guided tours of the mansion and self-guiding tours of the gardens on the 3-acre site.

Time: Allow 1 hour minimum. **Hours:** Guided tours are given Tues.-Sun. on the hour 10-4, mid-June to mid-Oct.; Wed.-Sun. 10-4, mid-May to mid-June. Holiday tours are offered Thanksgiving weekend-late Dec. Phone ahead to confirm schedule. **Cost:** $10; $9 (ages 65+); $6 (ages 12-17); $4 (walking-age toddlers-age 11). **Phone:** (406) 755-2166.

[SAVE] **HOCKADAY MUSEUM OF ART** is at 302 Second Ave. E. Permanent and rotating exhibits showcase the art and culture of Montana, with special focus on Glacier National Park and the Northern Plains and Blackfeet Indians. **Time:** Allow 1 hour minimum. **Hours:** Tues.-Sat. 10-5. **Cost:** $5; $4 (ages 60+); $2 (college students with ID); free (students in grades K-12). **Phone:** (406) 755-5268.

NORTHWEST MONTANA HISTORICAL SOCIETY'S MUSEUM AT CENTRAL SCHOOL is at 124 Second Ave. E. Exhibits housed in a renovated 1894 school building cover such topics as Native American culture, the history of the Flathead Valley and the timber industry. Noteworthy is an exhibit about cowboy-turned-legislator Frank Bird Linderman, who documented northwest Montana's Native American culture through sculpture and writings.

Time: Allow 1 hour minimum. **Hours:** Mon.-Fri. 10-5. Closed major holidays. **Cost:** $5; $4 (ages 63+); free (ages 0-11 and students with ID). **Phone:** (406) 756-8381.

RECREATIONAL ACTIVITIES

Hot Air Ballooning

• **Fantasy Flights** departs from various locations in Flathead Valley. **Hours:** Hot air balloon trips depart daily at dawn, May-Oct. (weather permitting). **Phone:** (406) 755-4172.

AERO INN (406)755-3798 [46]

Hotel
$49-$104

Address: 1830 US 93 S 59901 **Location:** 1.3 mi s on US 93 from jct US 2. **Facility:** 61 units. 2 stories (no elevator), interior corridors. **Parking:** winter plug-ins. **Terms:** resort fee. **Pool(s):** heated indoor. **Activities:** sauna, hot tub. **Featured Amenity: continental breakfast.**

AMERICAS BEST VALUE INN (406)756-3222 [39]
Hotel $60-$135 **Address:** 1550 Hwy 93 N 59901 **Location:** 1.3 mi n on US 93 from jct US 2. **Facility:** 53 units. 2 stories (no elevator), interior corridors. **Parking:** winter plug-ins. **Terms:** cancellation fee imposed, resort fee. **Activities:** massage.

BEST WESTERN PLUS FLATHEAD LAKE INN & SUITES (406)857-2400

Hotel
$95-$230

AAA Benefit: Members save 10% or more with Best Western!

Address: 4824 Hwy 93 S 59901 **Location:** 7 mi s; jct SR 82. **Facility:** 59 units. 3 stories, interior corridors. **Parking:** winter plug-ins. **Terms:** 2-4 night minimum stay - seasonal. **Pool(s):** heated indoor. **Activities:** hot tub, exercise room. **Guest Services:** coin laundry. **Featured Amenity: full hot breakfast.**

(See map & index p. 168.)

COMFORT INN
(406)755-6700 **42**

▼▼▼ Hotel
$89-$239

Address: 1330 Hwy 2 W 59901 **Location:** 1 mi w on US 2 from jct US 93. **Facility:** 63 units, some two bedrooms. 2 stories (no elevator), interior corridors. **Parking:** winter plug-ins. **Pool(s):** heated outdoor. **Activities:** hot tub, exercise room. **Guest Services:** valet and coin laundry.

HAMPTON INN KALISPELL
(406)755-7900 **41**

▼▼▼ Hotel
$93-$239

AAA Benefit: Members save up to 10%!

Address: 1140 US 2 W 59901 **Location:** 0.9 mi w on US 2 from jct US 93. **Facility:** 120 units. 3 stories, interior corridors. **Parking:** winter plug-ins. **Terms:** check-in 4 pm, 1-7 night minimum stay, cancellation fee imposed. **Amenities:** video games. **Pool(s):** heated indoor. **Activities:** hot tub, exercise room. **Guest Services:** valet and coin laundry, area transportation.

HILTON GARDEN INN KALISPELL
(406)756-4500 **47**

▼▼▼ Hotel
$89-$259

AAA Benefit: Members save up to 10%!

Address: 1840 US 93 S 59901 **Location:** 1.4 mi s on US 93 from jct US 2. **Facility:** 144 units. 4 stories, interior corridors. **Parking:** winter plug-ins. **Terms:** 1-7 night minimum stay, cancellation fee imposed. **Dining:** Blue Canyon Kitchen & Tavern, see separate listing. **Pool(s):** heated indoor. **Activities:** hot tub, exercise room. **Guest Services:** valet and coin laundry, area transportation.

HOLIDAY INN EXPRESS & SUITES
(406)755-7405 **38**

▼▼▼ Hotel $99-$249 **Address:** 275 Treeline Rd 59901 **Location:** 3 mi n on US 93 from jct US 2, just w. **Facility:** 111 units. 3 stories, interior corridors. **Parking:** winter plug-ins. **Terms:** cancellation fee imposed, resort fee. **Amenities:** video games. **Pool(s):** heated indoor. **Activities:** hot tub, exercise room. **Guest Services:** valet and coin laundry.

KALISPELL/GLACIER INT'L AIRPORT AREA SUPER 8
(406)755-1888 **45**

▼▼ Hotel $53-$120 **Address:** 1341 1st Ave E 59901 **Location:** 1.2 mi s on US 93 from jct US 2. **Facility:** 74 units. 3 stories, interior corridors. **Parking:** winter plug-ins.

KALISPELL GRAND HOTEL
(406)755-8100 **44**

▼▼▼ **Historic Hotel** $85-$155 **Address:** 100 Main St 59901 **Location:** On US 93; jct 1st St; downtown. **Facility:** This historic property is one of the earlier modern hotels built in the area. After being allowed to deteriorate for years, the hotel has been lovingly restored and anchors a corner of the downtown area. 40 units. 3 stories, interior corridors. **Parking:** on-site and street. **Activities:** massage. **Guest Services:** valet laundry.

LA QUINTA INN & SUITES KALISPELL
(406)257-5255 **40**

▼▼▼◇ Hotel $94-$194 **Address:** 255 Montclair Dr 59901 **Location:** Jct US 93 and 2, 1 mi e. **Facility:** 71 units, some efficiencies. 2 stories, interior corridors. **Pool(s):** heated indoor. **Activities:** hot tub, exercise room. **Guest Services:** valet and coin laundry.

RED LION HOTEL KALISPELL
406/751-5050 **43**

▼▼▼◇ Hotel. Rates not provided. **Address:** 20 N Main St 59901 **Location:** Just s on US 93 from jct US 2; connected to Kalispell Center Mall. Adjacent to casino. **Facility:** 170 units, some efficiencies. 3 stories, interior corridors. **Parking:** winter plug-ins. **Terms:** check-in 4 pm. **Pool(s):** heated indoor. **Activities:** sauna, hot tub, exercise room. **Guest Services:** valet laundry.

WHERE TO EAT

THE ALLEY CONNECTION
406/752-7077 **38**

▼▼ Chinese. Casual Dining. $6-$18 **AAA Inspector Notes:** Guests dine on a variety of reasonably priced dishes with foundations of steak, seafood and poultry. Asian beef—a lemon grass-marinated fillet served with rice and stir-fried vegetables—proves to be a good choice. You can't go wrong no matter what you order at this restaurant that's been an institution in Kalispell since 1977. One of my favorites is the wonton soup. Chock-full of wontons, roasted pork and vegetables, it's a meal in itself. **Features:** beer & wine. **Address:** 22 1st St W 59901 **Location:** On US 93; jct 1st St; downtown.

BLUE CANYON KITCHEN & TAVERN
406/758-2583 **45**

▼▼▼ American. Casual Dining. $10-$26 **AAA Inspector Notes:** This casual restaurant is definitely upscale cowboy chic, constructed of large peeled log beams and braces. The walls are decorated with the ubiquitous Montana stuffed elk heads and antler chandeliers light the dining room. The chairs are unpeeled small log frames with upholstered seats and backs and the booths and benches are all finely upholstered. Ninety-eight percent of all the food coming out of the kitchen is made from scratch, and the in-house pastry chef produces all of their desserts. **Features:** full bar. **Reservations:** suggested. **Address:** 1840 US 93 59901 **Location:** 1.4 mi s on US 93 from jct US 2; in Hilton Garden Inn Kalispell.

BOJANGLES DINER
406/755-3222 **33**

▼▼ American. Family Dining. $4-$13 **AAA Inspector Notes:** The 1950s are fondly remembered via memorabilia that covers nearly every available space. Home-style choices include all-day breakfast items and soups and pies prepared in house. Don't pass up huckleberry sour cream pie, which is made from berries collected in the nearby mountains. **Address:** 1319 US 2 59901 **Location:** 1.1 mi w from jct US 93.

BONELLI'S BISTRO
406/257-8669 **37**

▼▼ Mediterranean. Casual Dining. $6-$10 **AAA Inspector Notes:** Through the use of fresh organic and local farmers' products, the kitchen creates the essence of Mediterranean cuisine. A nice touch is offering seasonal specials of soups, panini or Mediterranean wraps. Italian groceries line the display shelves and the pastry case spotlights tiramisu or limoncello cake. **Features:** patio dining. **Address:** 38 1st Ave E 59901 **Location:** Between E Center and 1st E sts; downtown. **Parking:** street only.

(See map & index p. 168.)

CISLO'S   406/756-7330 (31)

▼▼ ▼▼ American. Family Dining. $7-$18 **AAA Inspector Notes:** As it has for generations, the longtime family-owned favorite continues to serve no-nonsense home-style food to local families. The relaxed atmosphere evokes the feel of a home kitchen. **Address:** 2046 US 2 E 59901 **Location:** Just n of jct US 2 and SR 82.

[B] [L] [D]

GENKI   406/257-8889 (41)

▼▼ ▼▼ Asian Sushi. Casual Dining. $7-$17 **AAA Inspector Notes:** The convenient downtown restaurant centers its menu on sushi and sashimi. Those who prefer their fish cooked also can choose from a full array of traditional Asian dishes. **Features:** beer & wine. **Address:** 302 Main St 59901 **Location:** Downtown.

[L] [D]

HOPS DOWNTOWN GRILL   406/755-7687 (40)

▼▼▼ Western Burgers. Gastropub. $9-$20 **AAA Inspector Notes:** On the town's main street, the unassuming storefront location gives no hint of the delights to be found within the walls. Serving gourmet burgers and local brews, this place should be the destination of anyone seeking a satisfying dining experience in the Flathead Valley. Not surprisingly it is a favorite of locals and tourists alike. **Features:** beer & wine. **Reservations:** suggested. **Address:** 121 Main St 59903 **Location:** Downtown. **Parking:** street only. [D]

JULIE'S CENTER STREET CAFE   406/755-7171 (34)

▼▼ ▼▼ American. Family Dining. $6-$13 **AAA Inspector Notes:** This cozy family restaurant serves breakfast all day in addition to a variety of burgers, sandwiches, soups and salads. Made from a family recipe, the homemade sauerkraut, with or without a sandwich, is delicious. The biscuits and gravy are a local favorite. **Address:** 200 E Center St 59901 **Location:** Downtown. [B] [L]

THE MONTANA CLUB   406/260-4401 (44)

▼▼ ▼▼ Western Steak Seafood. Casual Dining. $8-$24 **AAA Inspector Notes:** This family-friendly spot with an adjacent casino has sister restaurants in Missoula and Butte. The building sports a wood interior with numerous historical pictures and menu items that include fresh Alaskan salmon, halibut and meats cut in house. Portions are plentiful. **Features:** full bar, happy hour. **Address:** 1301 S Main St 59901 **Location:** 1.3 mi s on US 93 from jct US 2.

[B] [L] [D] CALL [⅊M]

MONTANA COFFEE TRADERS   406/756-2326 (35)

▼▼ Coffee/Tea. Quick Serve. $6-$10 **AAA Inspector Notes:** This eclectic, popular restaurant roasts its own coffee beans for sale and specializes in espresso drinks. Service is limited, but the soups, salads and sandwiches are generous and well prepared. The in-house bakery produces some of the best dessert bars, muffins, scones and brownies in town. **Address:** 328 W Center St 59901 **Location:** Downtown. [B] [L]

NICKEL CHARLIE'S CASINO & EATERY   406/257-7756 (32)

▼▼ ▼▼ American. Casual Dining. $8-$24 **AAA Inspector Notes:** The food is served in large portions and attracts locals and tourists alike. Try the peppercorn steak or mesquite pork chops with apple compote and candied pecans. There's something for everyone. The staff provides service with a smile. Be sure to check out the vintage children's riding toys on the ceiling. **Features:** beer & wine. **Address:** 1275 US 2 E 59901 **Location:** 1.3 mi e of jct US 93.

[B] [L] [D]

RISING SUN BISTRO   406/755-7510 (36)

▼▼ ▼▼ French. Casual Dining. $7-$19 **AAA Inspector Notes:** This charming bistro is somewhat hidden away from the hustle and bustle of the downtown area. The menu offers something for every taste, and the dishes are well-prepared, fresh and tasty. **Features:** full bar, Sunday brunch. **Address:** 25 2nd Ave W 59901 **Location:** Jct 1st St W; downtown. [B] [L] [D]

SCOTTIBELLI'S RISTORANTE ITALIANO   406/890-7800 (39)

▼▼ ▼▼ Italian. Casual Dining. $10-$28 **AAA Inspector Notes:** Using recipes handed down from their Mama from Italy, this multi-generational family restaurant cooks up traditional favorites: pasta e fagioli soup, pasta carbonara, Margherita pizza and veal marsala are sure to please. For family-style dinners, large portion entrées are offered. One of the more popular dishes is the vongole marinate — clams sautéed in a garlic, lemon-wine sauce, topped with a seasoned dough, then baked till the dough gets crusty and billows with steam. **Features:** full bar. **Address:** 110 Main St 59901 **Location:** On US 93; jct 1st St; downtown. **Parking:** on-site and street.

[L] [D] CALL [⅊M]

SPENCER & CO   406/756-8941 (30)

▼▼ ▼▼ Steak. Casual Dining. $12-$29 **AAA Inspector Notes:** The classic steakhouse serves large, succulent cuts of beef on a sizzling platter. Although beef occupies the spotlight, chicken, seafood and pasta also have a place on the menu. **Features:** full bar. **Address:** 4010 US 93 N 59901 **Location:** 7.3 mi n from jct US 2.

[D]

THAI PALACE RESTAURANT   406/756-7956 (42)

▼▼ ▼▼ Thai. Casual Dining. $12-$22 **AAA Inspector Notes:** The casual storefront main street restaurant serves a variety of traditional Thai food as well as other Asian dishes. **Features:** beer & wine. **Address:** 319 Main St 59901 **Location:** Between 3rd and 4th sts; center. **Parking:** street only. [L] [D]

WHEAT MONTANA BAKERY & DELI   406/257-6530 (43)

▼▼ Deli. Family Dining. $5-$10 **AAA Inspector Notes:** Stop by for early-morning coffee and huge cinnamon rolls. Order sandwiches made with fresh baked breads to enjoy later. Breads and bagels are made from chemical-free flour freshly ground from Montana wheat. **Address:** 405 Main St 59901 **Location:** Downtown.

[B] [L]

KOOTENAI NATIONAL FOREST (A-1)

Elevations in the forest range from 1,862 ft. where the Kootenai River crosses into Idaho to 8,736 ft. on Snowshoe Peak. Refer to AAA maps for additional elevation information.

———

Kootenai National Forest is in the northwest corner of Montana, with a small section extending into Idaho. High, craggy peaks characterize the 2.2 million-acre region; portions of the Cabinet, Whitefish and Purcell mountains are the main ranges, attaining elevations as high as 8,700 feet. The area's climate is modified Pacific Maritime, and as a result Kootenai has an abundance of plant species more common to the Pacific Coast than to other parts of Montana.

There are diverse wildlife species including bear, elk, deer, mountain goats, big horn sheep and wolves. The forest also is home to many non-game species. Throughout the year bald eagles can be seen along the Kootenai River north of Libby; 205 species of birds have been recorded in the forest. Cabinet Mountains Wilderness has 85 small lakes; many are scenic, stocked with fish and reached by trail. Ski facilities are available northwest of Libby. The area has more than 50 campgrounds and 1,500 miles of hiking trails.

Ross Creek Cedars Scenic Area, off SR 56 southwest of Libby, and Ten Lakes Scenic Area, on the Canadian border northeast of Eureka, are reached by local and forest roads. Lake Koocanusa also is a popular recreational spot (see Libby p. 188).

For further information, write the Forest Supervisor, Kootenai National Forest, 31374 US 2, Libby, MT 59923; phone (406) 293-6211. *See Recreation Areas Chart.*

LAKESIDE (B-2) pop. 2,669, elev. 2,900'

On Flathead Lake's west shore, Lakeside offers summer and winter recreation, including boating, fishing, swimming, cross-country and downhill skiing, snowmobiling and ice fishing.

Lakeside-Somers Chamber of Commerce: P.O. Box 177, Lakeside, MT 59922. **Phone:** (406) 844-3715.

LAME DEER (E-7) pop. 2,052, elev. 3,380'

A popular destination for winter recreation, Lame Deer also is the headquarters for the Northern Cheyenne Indian Reservation. Activities on the reservation include the Sun Dance (dates vary) and a powwow in July. Cheyenne crafts, including moccasins, belts and jewelry, are available at the Northern Cheyenne Arts and Crafts Center at US 212 and Old Cemetery Rd.

LAUREL pop. 0,718

BEST WESTERN YELLOWSTONE CROSSING
(406)628-6888

Hotel
$96-$106

AAA Benefit: Members save 10% or more with Best Western!

Address: 205 SE 4th St 59044 **Location:** I-90 exit 434, just n, then just e. **Facility:** 60 units. 3 stories, interior corridors. **Parking:** winter plug-ins. **Amenities:** *Some:* safes. **Pool(s):** heated indoor. **Activities:** hot tub, exercise room. **Guest Services:** coin laundry.

LEWIS AND CLARK NATIONAL FOREST (B-3)

Elevations in the forest range from 4,000 ft. in the valley bottoms to 9,204 ft. on Scapegoat Mountain. Refer to AAA maps for additional elevation information.

Lewis and Clark National Forest is in west-central Montana. Consisting of 1,843,397 acres, the forest has two units. The Rocky Mountain Unit, which embraces about half of the acreage, lies along the eastern slope of the Continental Divide south of Glacier National Park. It includes portions of the Bob Marshall *(see Flathead National Forest p. 156)* and Scapegoat wildernesses.

The Rocky Mountain Unit rises sharply from grasslands to peaks between 7,000 and 8,000 feet in elevation. Access to the area is by a number of gravel roads off US 89 that connect with forest roads and trailheads and serve several campgrounds.

Southeast of Great Falls is the Jefferson Unit, scattered inland mountain ranges dotting the prairie, including the Little Belt, Castle, Highwoods, Big Snowy and Little Snowy mountain ranges and the north end of the Crazy Mountains. The Jefferson Division has short, dome-like mountains rather than jagged peaks.

The mountains are forest-covered and have moderate slopes that present less demanding hiking and riding trails than those found in the Rocky Mountain Unit. There are many streams but no large rivers or lakes.

Winter sports are available near Kings Hill Summit, some 40 miles north of White Sulphur Springs *(see place listing p. 214)*, Monarch and Neihart. For further information contact the Forest Supervisor, Lewis and Clark National Forest, 1101 15th St. N., Great Falls, MT 59405; phone (406) 791-7700. *See Recreation Areas Chart.*

LEWISTOWN (C-5) pop. 5,901, elev. 3,963'

Lewistown originally was a trading post on the Carroll Trail between Helena and Carroll. First called Reed's Fort, it later was renamed Lewistown after the military officer who established a fort nearby in 1876. Trading, only on a larger scale, continues to support the town, which is a market for the large cattle ranches and wheat farms of central Montana.

Lewistown Area Chamber of Commerce: 408 N.E. Main St., Lewistown, MT 59457. **Phone:** (406) 535-5436.

CENTRAL MONTANA MUSEUM is at 408 N.E. Main St. Area history is documented through collections of minerals, guns and Native American and Western artifacts. **Time:** Allow 30 minutes minimum. **Hours:** Daily 10-4, Memorial Day-Labor Day. **Cost:** Donations. **Phone:** (406) 535-3642.

B & B MOTEL
406/535-5496

Motel. Rates not provided. **Address:** 520 E Main St 59457 **Location:** Downtown. **Facility:** 36 units, some two bedrooms and efficiencies. 2 stories (no elevator), exterior corridors. **Parking:** winter plug-ins.

LEWISTOWN SUPER 8
(406)538-2581

Hotel $71-$125 **Address:** 102 Wendell Ave 59457 **Location:** West side of town, on US 87; near airport. **Facility:** 45 units. 2 stories (no elevator), interior corridors. **Parking:** winter plug-ins. **Guest Services:** coin laundry.

LIBBY (B-1) pop. 2,628, elev. 2,086'
• Hotels p. 188 • Restaurants p. 188

Natural resources have been the mainstay of Libby's economy since its settlement in the 1860s. Drawn by stories of gold in the north, prospectors first gathered in this region and named the town after the daughter of one of the men who discovered gold in a nearby creek. Mining, timber and tourism are the town's leading businesses.

Libby's environs contribute to the town's popularity as a recreational center. The nearby Kootenai National Forest *(see place listing p. 186)* provides extensive lands for public use, and anglers enjoy fishing in the Kootenai River and its tributaries.

Libby Area Chamber of Commerce: 905 W. 9th St., P.O. Box 704, Libby, MT 59923. **Phone:** (406) 293-4167.

HERITAGE MUSEUM is at 34067 US 2. A 12-sided log building contains exhibits about mining and forestry along with historical information about the Kootenai Indians, explorer David Thompson, local participation in World War II and the Civilian Conservation Corps (CCC). Wildlife displays, as well as rotating art, quilt and photography exhibits in the Tower Gallery, also can be seen. Outbuildings include an 1800s log cabin, a miner's cabin and the cookhouse from the Sylvanite Ranger Station. Archives are available by appointment. **Hours:** Mon.-Sat. 10-5, Sun. 1-5, first Sat. in June-Aug. 31; by appointment rest of year. Phone ahead to confirm schedule. **Cost:** Donations. **Phone:** (406) 293-7521.

LIBBY DAM is 13.5 mi. e. on SR 37, then 3.5 mi. n. on FR 228, following signs. Built 1966-72 to generate power and control flooding on the Kootenai River, the straight-axis dam is 422 feet high and 3,055 feet long. Its reservoir, Lake Koocanusa, extends 90 miles upstream and into British Columbia.

The Libby Dam Visitor Center, off FR 228, has interpretive displays and interactive exhibits about natural history, river navigation, flood control and electricity generation. A theater screens a 9-minute video describing the construction of the dam as well as a 10-minute video about Army Corps of Engineers dams on the Columbia River system.

Free ranger-led, 1-hour tours are available. *See Recreation Areas Chart.* **Hours:** Grounds daily dawn-dusk. Visitor center daily 9:30-6, mid-June to mid-Sept.; phone for schedule early May to mid-June; open by appointment rest of year. Tours are given daily at 10, noon, 2 and 4, mid-June to mid-Sept., when staff is available; by appointment rest of year. Phone ahead to confirm schedule. **Cost:** Free. **Phone:** (406) 293-5577 or (406) 293-7751, ext. 252.

SANDMAN MOTEL   406/293-8831
♥ Motel $55-$85 **Address:** 31901 US 2 59923 **Location:** Just w on US 2 from jct SR 37. Located in a quiet area. **Facility:** 16 units. 2 stories (no elevator), exterior corridors. **Parking:** winter plug-ins. **Terms:** 7 day cancellation notice-fee imposed.

VENTURE MOTOR INN   406/293-7711

Hotel
$75-$110

Address: 1015 W 9th St (US 2) 59923 **Location:** Just w on US 2 from jct SR 37. **Facility:** 71 units. 3 stories, interior corridors. **Parking:** winter plug-ins. **Dining:** Venture Inn Restaurant, see separate listing. **Pool(s):** heated indoor. **Activities:** hot tub. **Guest Services:** coin laundry. **Featured Amenity:** continental breakfast.

WHERE TO EAT

HENRY'S   406/293-7911
♥ American. Family Dining. $5-$12 **AAA Inspector Notes:** Traditional homemade fare is served at this informal coffee shop and adjoining dining room that sport antique-accented décor and some Western-themed items. The service staff's friendly demeanor adds a comfortably homey touch to the dining experience. The prices are good, too. **Address:** 405 W 9th St 59923 **Location:** Just w on US 2 from jct SR 37. [B] [L] [D]

THE LAST STRAW CAFE   406/293-4000
♥♥ American. Family Dining. $7-$17 **AAA Inspector Notes:** Serving breakfast all day, this restaurant also features emu and buffalo burgers along with awesome salads and more traditional meals. Try the extra-large hot biscuits. **Address:** 30890 US Hwy 2 59923 **Location:** 1 mi w of downtown; adjacent to Homesteader's Ranch & Feed store. [B] [L] CALL [&M]

VENTURE INN RESTAURANT   406/293-7711
♥♥ American. Casual Dining. $6-$16 **AAA Inspector Notes:** Ask anyone in Libby where to find a good salad bar and they'll tell you Venture Motor Inn. The potato and pasta salads are made in house as is the soup. The night I was here, I had a huge bowl of the rich and flavorful beef barley soup. I usually try to just taste the soup, as I don't want to fill up before my meal, but I couldn't help myself, it was that good. The salad bar has the requisite orange and green vegetables, all replenished regularly and kept clean of any stray drips or crumbs. **Address:** 1015 W 9th St (US 2) 59923 **Location:** Just w on US 2 from jct SR 37; in Venture Motor Inn. [B] [L] [D] CALL [&M]

LIMA (F-3) pop. 221, elev. 6,256'

RED ROCKS LAKES NATIONAL WILDLIFE REFUGE is off I-15 exit 0, then 28 mi. e. on a gravel road. Established as a refuge in 1935, this sanctuary with lakes, marshes, creeks and the isolation of the Centennial Valley has become one of North America's more important nesting areas for trumpeter swans and other wildlife. The prime viewing season is June through September. Primitive camping facilities are available. **Note:** The nearest fuel is in Lima. Inquire locally about road conditions. **Hours:** Refuge headquarters Mon.-Fri. 7:30-4. **Cost:** Free. **Phone:** (406) 276-3536.

LITTLE BIGHORN BATTLEFIELD NATIONAL MONUMENT (E-6)

The main entrance to Little Bighorn Battlefield National Monument is 15 miles southeast of Hardin via exit 510 off I-90, then a half-mile east via US 212. In the Valley of the Little Bighorn River in June 1876, Lt. Col. George Armstrong Custer and the 210 men of the 7th Cavalry Regiment under his command made their last stand against several thousand Lakota, Arapaho and Northern Cheyenne, many of whom were fleeing the restrictions of the reservation. Covering 1.2 square miles, the monument commemorates the dramatic climax of the Indian Wars by preserving the site of this Native American victory.

The monument embraces a national cemetery established in 1879, various monuments and memorials, and a historical museum with maps, photographs and dioramas depicting the battle. Just inside the entrance is a visitor center where park rangers provide tour information and self-guiding tour brochures.

Auto tour tapes with maps are available at the center and from Big Horn County Historical Museum and State Visitor Center *(see Hardin p. 178)* and other local outlets; phone (406) 665-1671.

Monument 8 a.m.-9 p.m., Memorial Day-July 31; 8-8, Aug. 1-Labor Day; 8-6, Apr. 1-day before Memorial Day and day after Labor Day-late Oct.; 8-4:30, rest of year. Visitor center daily 8-7:30. Closed Jan. 1, Thanksgiving and Christmas. Admission $10 (per private vehicle); $5 (per person arriving by other means). Cemetery free. Phone (406) 638-2621.

APSAALOOKE TOURS departs from the Little Bighorn Battlefield National Monument Visitor Center. Narrated van tours of the site of the Battle of the Little Bighorn are given by Native American guides. **Time:** Allow 1 hour minimum. **Hours:** Tours are given daily on the hour 10-3, Memorial Day-Labor Day. **Cost:** $8; $5 (ages 55+); $2 (ages 0-11). **Phone:** (406) 638-3139 or (406) 638-3114.

LIVINGSTON (E-4) pop. 7,044, elev. 4,501'
- **Restaurants p. 190**
- **Part of Yellowstone National Park area — see map p. 326**

The lush grasses of Paradise Valley were ideal for raising cattle, and the valley's warm chinook winds protected the area from bitter Montana winters. When the Northern Pacific Railroad laid tracks in 1882, both the cattle industry and Livingston flourished. Among the town's more memorable residents was Calamity Jane.

Livingston is at the head of Paradise Valley, through which flows the Yellowstone River and around which rise the Crazy Mountains and the Absaroka and Gallatin ranges of the Rockies. The area offers opportunities for wildlife viewing, hunting, fishing, rafting, backpacking, camping, skiing and snowmobiling.

A scenic drive, US 89, connects Livingston to Gardiner and the northern entrance to Yellowstone National Park *(see place listing p. 326)*. Livingston was the original entrance to Yellowstone.

Livingston Area Chamber of Commerce: 303 E. Park St., Livingston, MT 59047. **Phone:** (406) 222-0850.

Self-guiding tours: A brochure outlining a walking tour of the historic business district is available at Yellowstone Gateway Museum *(see attraction listing)* and the chamber of commerce.

LIVINGSTON DEPOT CENTER is at 200 W. Park St. Built in 1902, the restored Northern Pacific Railroad station was designed in the Italian Renaissance style by the original architects of New York's Grand Central Station. Featured is the exhibit Rails Across the Rockies: A Century of People and Places. Special events are scheduled throughout the year. **Hours:** Mon.-Sat. 9-5, Sun. 1-5, late May-early Sept. **Cost:** Free. **Phone:** (406) 222-2300.

YELLOWSTONE GATEWAY MUSEUM is off I-90 exit 333 at 118 W. Chinook St. Housed in a three-story, 1907 schoolhouse, the museum features a variety of local history exhibits, including Yellowstone National Park memorabilia and stage coaches once used within the park. Inside the Northern Pacific Railroad exhibit is a turn-of-the-20th-century caboose.

A map traces Meriwether Lewis' and William Clark's route through the area. Rounding out the museum's offerings are fossils, minerals and household items from area pioneers. **Time:** Allow 30 minutes minimum. **Hours:** Daily 10-5, Memorial Day-Sept. 30; Thurs.-Sat. 10-5, rest of year. **Cost:** $5; $4 (ages 55+); free (ages 0-18). **Phone:** (406) 222-4184.

BEST WESTERN YELLOWSTONE INN   (406)222-6110

Hotel
$100-$200

AAA Benefit: Members save 10% or more with Best Western!

Address: 1515 W Park St 59047 **Location:** I-90 exit 333, just n. **Facility:** 99 units, some kitchens. 3 stories, interior corridors. **Parking:** winter plug-ins. **Pool(s):** heated indoor. **Guest Services:** coin laundry.

LIVINGSTON COMFORT INN   (406)222-4400

Hotel $85-$100 **Address:** 114 Loves Ln 59047 **Location:** I-90 exit 333, just s on US 89, then just w. **Facility:** 49 units. 2 stories (no elevator), interior/exterior corridors. **Parking:** winter plug-ins. **Amenities:** safes. **Pool(s):** heated indoor. **Activities:** hot tub. **Guest Services:** coin laundry.

LIVINGSTON RODEWAY INN   (406)222-6320

Motel $120-$140 **Address:** 102 Rogers Ln 59047 **Location:** I-90 exit 333, just n on US 89, then just w. **Facility:** 44 units. 1 story, interior/exterior corridors. **Parking:** winter plug-ins. **Amenities:** safes. **Pool(s):** heated indoor. **Activities:** massage. **Guest Services:** coin laundry.

WHERE TO EAT

2ND STREET BISTRO   406/222-9463

WWWW Regional American. Casual Dining. $14-$28 **AAA Inspector Notes:** In a historic building, this bistro has antique oak chairs in the dining room and original art on the walls. Varying menu items are prepared with creative twists. Diners will find dishes prepared from only organic and specially purchased seafood, poultry, meats and game from local farms. A wide variety of house-specialty drinks, libations and wines from a wine cave complements meals. Homemade desserts change daily. **Features:** full bar. **Reservations:** suggested. **Address:** 123 N 2nd St 59047 **Location:** Jct E Park St; downtown; in Murray Hotel. **Parking:** on-site and street. D

GIL'S GOODS   406/222-4711

WW Pizza Breads/Pastries. Casual Dining. $6-$14 **AAA Inspector Notes:** Brought to you by the same owner as the 2nd St. Bistro, this eatery's concept is based on the European café, with a simple menu made from great ingredients. Try a specialty pizza with homemade dough topped with homemade sausage and fired in a brick oven, organic salad greens, homemade bakery items and sandwiches. **Features:** full bar, patio dining. **Address:** 207 W Park St 59047 **Location:** Jct N 2nd St; downtown; in Murray Hotel. **Parking:** street only. B L D CALL M

MONTANA'S RIB & CHOP HOUSE   406/222-9200

WW American. Casual Dining. $9-$28 **AAA Inspector Notes:** This restaurant's specialties include 24-hour marinated baby back ribs and an 8-ounce Montana tenderloin, hand-cut beef fillet. Diners also can sink their teeth into a variety of chicken, seafood and other steak entrées. Reservations are suggested at this bustling steakhouse. **Features:** full bar, patio dining, happy hour. **Reservations:** suggested. **Address:** 305 E Park Rd 59047 **Location:** Downtown; adjacent to Chamber of Commerce. L D

LOLO pop. 3,892

DAYS INN   (406)273-2121

WW Hotel $80-$110 **Address:** 11225 US 93 S 59847 **Location:** North edge of town. **Facility:** 40 units, some efficiencies. 2 stories (no elevator), interior/exterior corridors. **Parking:** winter plug-ins. **Terms:** 3 day cancellation notice-fee imposed. **Amenities:** safes. **Activities:** exercise room. **Guest Services:** coin laundry.

CALL M BIZ 📶 ✕ 🖥 🖨 🖵 /SOME UNITS 🔊 HS

LOLO NATIONAL FOREST (B-1)

Lolo National Forest is in western Montana. With boundaries stretching from the Swan Range in the northeast to the Idaho border, an area 120 miles long and 40 to 80 miles wide, the forest embraces about 2,100,000 acres. Although the Lolo is an important timber producer, many of its south-facing slopes are open and grassy. It also is one of the principal elk areas in western Montana.

Wilderness areas within the forest include the 33,000-acre Rattlesnake National Recreation Area and Wilderness as well as Welcome Creek and portions of Scapegoat.

Recreational opportunities abound on 3,500 miles of streams, including Rock Creek, a haven for trout-fishing enthusiasts. Approximately 485 species of fish and wildlife inhabit the forest, which has numerous camping and/or picnic sites and 1,780 miles of hiking trails; winter activities include downhill and cross-country skiing, snowmobiling along 360 miles of designated trails and ice fishing. Some recreation facilities are designed for handicapped access; inquire at a ranger station.

The forest has five offices: Ninemile Remount Depot and Ranger Station *(see Huson p. 183)*; the Lolo National Forest Supervisor's Office and Missoula Ranger District at Fort Missoula; and in the outlying districts of Seeley Lake, Superior and Plains/Thompson Falls.

For further information, write Lolo National Forest, Building 24, Fort Missoula, Missoula, MT 59804; phone (406) 329-3750. *See Recreation Areas Chart.*

MALTA (B-6) pop. 1,997, elev. 2,248'

Named for the island in the Mediterranean, Malta was the center of a cattle empire that reached from Glasgow to Havre and from the Missouri River to Canada during the late 19th century. Wheat and alfalfa have joined cattle as the area's leading products.

A large boulder at the intersection of US 2 and Sleeping Buffalo Resort looks like a sleeping buffalo. The Assiniboine Indians revered it, and the markings on it had a part in their tribal rituals.

The Little Rocky Mountains, called "island mountains" by early Native Americans, are 40 miles southwest on US 191. Gold was discovered in the mountains in 1884, and the historic remains set the scene for the mountain communities of Zortman and Landusky.

Notable Wild Bunch outlaws Butch Cassidy and Landusky resident Harvey "Kid Curry" Logan hid out in the area in 1901 after robbing a Great Northern passenger train, making off with around $60,000.

The Charles M. Russell National Wildlife Refuge, 60 miles south of Malta via US 191, sprawls across 1,100,000 acres around Fort Peck Reservoir. Drivers can access a scenic, 19-mile, self-guiding automobile tour route from two points along US 191. Signs along the way describe the area's history, geology and wildlife. Phone (406) 538-8706.

Malta Area Chamber of Commerce: 2 S. 1st St. E., P.O. Box 1420, Malta, MT 59538. **Phone:** (406) 654-1776.

BOWDOIN NATIONAL WILDLIFE REFUGE is 7 mi. e. on CR 2 following signs to 194 Bowdoin Auto Tour Rd. This 15,500-acre breeding and feeding area for migratory waterfowl, shorebirds and other wildlife, including deer, is one of the few northwestern nesting areas of the white pelican. The refuge can be seen via a 15-mile, self-guiding automobile tour (weather permitting); ideal viewing times are early fall and late spring. **Time:** Allow 1 hour minimum. **Hours:** Refuge open daily dawn-dusk. Headquarters open Mon.-Fri. 7:30-4. **Cost:** Free. **Phone:** (406) 654-2863.

GREAT PLAINS DINOSAUR MUSEUM & FIELD STATION is at 405 E. US 2. Guided tours offer visitors a glimpse into the world of dinosaurs and reveal fossil preparation techniques as well as the latest in dinosaur discoveries. **Time:** Allow 1 hour minimum.

Hours: Mon.-Sat. 10-5, Sun. 12:30-5, May-Oct.; by appointment rest of year. Closed major holidays. **Cost:** $5; $3 (ages 6-12). **Phone:** (406) 654-5300.

PHILLIPS COUNTY MUSEUM is at 431 E. US 2. The museum contains exhibits relating to the county's pioneer days, agriculture and mining. Visitors can see a large collection of Native American buckskins and beadwork, an outlaw display centered on local outlaw Harvey "Kid Curry" Logan and a 33-foot-long brachylophosaurus skeleton with photographs of the site where it was unearthed. **Time:** Allow 1 hour minimum. **Hours:** Mon.-Sat. 10-5, Sun. noon-5, May 1-Oct. 1; Tues.-Sat. 11-5, rest of year. **Cost:** $5; $3 (ages 5-18). **Phone:** (406) 654-1037.

EDGEWATER INN & RV PARK   406/654-1302
▼ **Motel** $80-$100 **Address:** 101 Hwy 2 W 59538 **Location:** Jct US 2 and 191 N. **Facility:** 32 units. 1 story, exterior corridors. **Parking:** winter plug-ins. **Pool(s):** heated indoor. **Activities:** sauna, hot tub, exercise room. **Guest Services:** valet and coin laundry, area transportation.

MALTANA MOTEL   406/654-2610
▼
Motel
$72-$85
Address: 138 S 1st Ave W 59538 **Location:** Just s of US 2 via US 191, just w; downtown. **Facility:** 19 units. 1 story, exterior corridors. **Parking:** winter plug-ins. **Terms:** cancellation fee imposed. **Guest Services:** area transportation.

GREAT NORTHERN HOTEL   406/654-2100
▼▼ American. Casual Dining. $4-$28 **AAA Inspector Notes:** For breakfast or lunch, visit the retro coffee shop setting in this hotel lobby. At dinner, you'll eat in a more formal, yet not stuffy, dining room. A separate lounge area invites relaxation. **Features:** full bar. **Address:** 2 S 1st Ave E 59538 **Location:** US 2, just s on US 191. **Parking:** on-site and street.

MANHATTAN pop. 1,520

LAND OF MAGIC   406/284-3794
▼▼ ▼▼ American. Casual Dining. $18-$35 **AAA Inspector Notes:** The Western-themed large dining room is where locals and travels alike gather. Choose from more than eight different cuts of steak or maybe try the Kansas ribs. A relish tray and dessert are included in the price. **Features:** full bar. **Address:** 11060 Front St 59741 **Location:** I-90 exit 283 (Logan Frontage Rd), just n, then 1 mi e.

SIR SCOTT'S OASIS   406/284-6929
▼▼ ▼▼ American. Casual Dining. $8-$67 **AAA Inspector Notes:** A true Montana steakhouse known for serving large, quality cuts of Montana beef. Other choices include seafood and fried chicken. All meals come with a vegetable tray, soup, salad and ice cream. Patio dining is offered, weather permitting. **Features:** full bar. **Reservations:** suggested. **Address:** 204 W Main St 59741 **Location:** I-90 exit 288, 1 mi n. **Parking:** on-site and street.

MARTINSDALE (D-4) pop. 64, elev. 4,819'

BAIR FAMILY MUSEUM is at 2751 SR 294. Charles M. Bair moved to Montana in 1883. He went into ranching and made his fortune in the Alaskan Gold Rush. The circa 1890s Bair ranch comprises antiques and paintings. Highlights include a collection of Paul Storr silver and an 18th-century British sideboard. **Time:** Allow 1 hour minimum. **Hours:** Daily 10-5, Memorial Day-Labor Day.; Wed.-Sun. 10-5, day after Labor Day-Oct. 31. Last tour begins 1 hour before closing. **Cost:** $5; $3 (ages 62+); $2 (ages 6-16). **Phone:** (406) 572-3314.

MARYSVILLE pop. 80

THE MARYSVILLE HOUSE   406/443-6677
▼ Steak. Casual Dining. $9-$60 **AAA Inspector Notes:** This very rustic, distinctive eatery in an old ghost town serves up T-bone steak, shrimp, oysters, grilled chicken, crab legs and lobster. A lively bar and down-home service staff round out the experience. **Features:** full bar. **Address:** 153 Main St 59640 **Location:** I-15 exit 200 (SR 279), 9.2 mi w, 6 mi s on Marysville Rd (from sign), then just n. **Parking:** on-site and street.

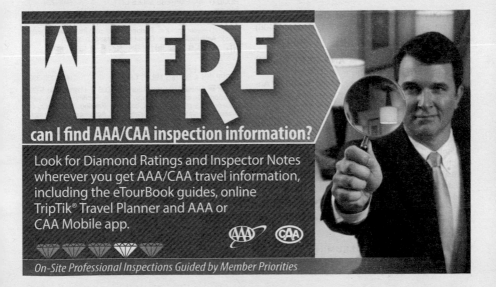

MEDICINE LAKE (B-8) pop. 225, elev. 1,951'

MEDICINE LAKE NATIONAL WILDLIFE REFUGE is 24 mi. n. on SR 16 to 223 N. Shore Rd. A nesting place for waterfowl and shorebirds, the 31,458-acre refuge houses about 230 species of birds at various times of the year. Fishing and hunting for waterfowl, upland game birds and deer are permitted in season; obtain maps and information at refuge headquarters, 1 mile south and 2 miles east of Medicine Lake. An automobile tour route runs from SR 16 along the northern boundary of the refuge to East Lake Highway. The condition of the gravel roads throughout the refuge is usually good but temporary closures may occur if rain or snow cause the roads to become hazardous. During hunting season (September 30 through January 1), a portion of the wildlife drive is closed to protect migratory birds, although you may still access the east section of the wildlife drive via East Lake Highway. **Hours:** Refuge open daily dawn-dusk. Headquarters open Mon.-Fri. 7-3:30. **Cost:** Free. **Phone:** (406) 789-2305. 🏕️

MILES CITY (D-7) pop. 8,410, elev. 2,364'

Miles City developed on the bottomland at the confluence of the Tongue and Yellowstone rivers. Gen. Nelson A. Miles arrived at the mouth of the Tongue River in August 1876 to force the Cheyenne and Sioux to return to the reservations. Miles built Fort Keogh at the site in 1877 and used it as a base for controlling the local tribes.

Main Street in times past was a block of saloons, gambling dens and brothels on the south, and banks, businesses and pawn shops on the north. Miles City has become a growing retail and service hub for eastern Montana and a center for cattle, sheep and crop farms.

Miles City Area Chamber of Commerce: 511 Pleasant St., Miles City, MT 59301. **Phone:** (406) 234-2890.

RANGE RIDERS MUSEUM AND BERT CLARK GUN COLLECTION is 1 mi. w. on US 10/I-94 Bus. Loop, across the Tongue River Bridge to 435 LP Anderson Rd. This 12-building complex features Western antiques and artifacts, archeological and geological specimens, and one of the Fort Keogh officer's quarters.

A detailed miniature replica of Fort Keogh is in the coach house. The Bert Clark gun collection comprises more than 400 pieces, including an elephant gun and a set of Belgian dueling pistols. **Time:** Allow 1 hour minimum. **Hours:** Daily 8-5, Apr.-Oct. **Cost:** $7.50; $5 (ages 62+); $3 (students in high school or college); $1 (students in elementary school). **Phone:** (406) 232-6146.

WATERWORKS ART MUSEUM is at 85 Water Plant Rd. Housed in a 1910 former water-treatment plant in a park overlooking the Yellowstone River, the center has two galleries featuring changing exhibits of Western, historical and contemporary art. **Hours:** Tues.-Sun. 9-5, May-Sept.; 1-5, rest of year. Closed major holidays. **Cost:** Free. **Phone:** (406) 234-0635.

BEST WESTERN WAR BONNET INN   (406)234-4560

Motel
$90-$160

AAA Benefit: Members save 10% or more with Best Western!

Address: 1015 S Haynes Ave 59301 **Location:** I-94 exit 138 (Broadus), 0.3 mi n. **Facility:** 53 units. 2 stories (no elevator), exterior corridors. **Parking:** winter plug-ins. **Pool(s):** heated indoor. **Activities:** sauna, hot tub, exercise room.

COMFORT INN MILES CITY   (406)234-3141

♦♦ **Hotel** $89-$135 **Address:** 1615 S Haynes Ave 59301 **Location:** I-94 exit 138 (Broadus), just s. **Facility:** 49 units. 2 stories (no elevator), interior corridors. **Parking:** winter plug-ins. **Pool(s):** heated indoor. **Activities:** hot tub. **Guest Services:** coin laundry.

GUESTHOUSE INTERNATIONAL INN & SUITES
          (406)232-3661

Hotel
$90-$120

Address: 3111 Steel St 59301 **Location:** I-94 exit 138 (Broadus), just s. **Facility:** 61 units, some two bedrooms and efficiencies. 2 stories (no elevator), interior corridors. **Parking:** winter plug-ins. **Terms:** cancellation fee imposed. **Pool(s):** heated indoor. **Activities:** hot tub, exercise room. **Guest Services:** coin laundry. **Featured Amenity:** breakfast buffet.

SLEEP INN & SUITES MILES CITY   (406)232-3000

♦♦♦ **Hotel** $75-$160 **Address:** 1006 S Haynes Ave 59301 **Location:** I-94 exit 138 (Broadus), 0.3 mi n. **Facility:** 90 units, some efficiencies. 3 stories, interior corridors. **Parking:** winter plug-ins. **Amenities:** safes. **Pool(s):** heated indoor. **Activities:** exercise room. **Guest Services:** coin laundry.

HOLIDAY INN EXPRESS MILES CITY   (406)234-1000

♦♦ **Hotel** $109-$169 **Address:** 1720 S Haynes Ave 59301 **Location:** I-94 exit 138 (Broadus), just s. **Facility:** 52 units. 2 stories (no elevator), interior corridors. **Parking:** winter plug-ins. **Pool(s):** heated indoor. **Activities:** hot tub. **Guest Services:** coin laundry.

WHERE TO EAT

MONTANA'S RIB & CHOP HOUSE   406/234-9200

♦♦ Regional American. Casual Dining. $8-$30 **AAA Inspector Notes:** This place features the winning formula of its other locations. Steaks, ribs, lamb and seafood are all served in a friendly atmosphere at an affordable price. **Features:** full bar, happy hour. **Address:** 3020 Stower St 59301 **Location:** I-94 exit 138 (Broadus), 1 mi n; jct Haynes Ave.

MISSOULA (D-2) pop. 66,788, elev. 3,223'
• Hotels p. 194 • Restaurants p. 196

Missoula lies astride the Clark Fork River, a tributary of the Columbia River named for William Clark. The town also occupies a valley that was once part of Glacial Lake Missoula, a prehistoric lake.

At the mouth of Hell Gate Canyon, Missoula straddles the route the Salish Indians traveled to reach the Great Plains hunting buffalo. Meriwether Lewis and William Clark later followed the same route through the canyon and camped approximately 9 miles southwest at Travellers Rest, near present-day Lolo. Many Native Americans died in the canyon, as the Blackfoot regularly ambushed the Salish, which prompted French-Canadian trappers to christen the site Porte de L'Enfer, "Gate of Hell."

One of the first lumber mills in the region began in Missoula. Lumber remains not only a major industry but also a major concern. The U.S. Forest Service maintains in Missoula its Region No. 1 headquarters, a research station devoted to forest fire research and the smokejumpers' training center. The University of Montana supports these studies with a 22,000-acre experimental forest in addition to conservation and wildlife research stations.

A short drive in any direction will lead into a national forest or a wilderness area. The Rattlesnake National Recreation Area and Wilderness, 6 miles north of downtown, has many small lakes, streams and trails.

The Museum of Mountain Flying is at the Missoula International Airport; phone (406) 721-3644. A Carousel for Missoula in Caras Park is a hand-carved 1918 merry-go-round created by volunteers. Rides are offered year-round; phone (406) 549-8382.

The ☙ International Wildlife Film Festival provides an opportunity for wildlife and conservation filmmakers, broadcasters, scientists, educators and students to network and share ideas relating to projects. The 8-day event takes place in spring.

The 3-day ☙ Humanities Montana Festival of the Book takes place in October. It is a literary celebration that features some 50 events showcasing more than 70 writers in a variety of demonstrations, exhibits, readings, receptions, signings and workshops.

Missoula Convention & Visitors Bureau: 101 E. Main St., Missoula, MT 59802. **Phone:** (406) 532-3250 or (800) 526-3465.

Self-guiding tours: Brochures outlining walking tours of public art and historical buildings in the downtown district are available from the convention and visitors bureau.

Shopping areas: Southgate Mall, US 93 and South Avenue, counts Dillard's, Herberger's, JCPenney and Sears among its 105 stores. The restored historic downtown, with a lighted riverfront nearby, also offers distinctive shopping opportunities.

GARNET GHOST TOWN, I-90 e. to exit 109, then 23 mi. e. on SR 200, after mile marker 22 turn s. on Bear Gulch Rd. and proceed 11 mi. on gravel road to parking lot. Lost in time, this intact mining town still reflects life as the community knew it at the end of the 19th century. Different from typical mining towns of the era, gold miners were encouraged to bring their families. After the 1930s, the town fell into disrepair and the last resident died in 1947. The remaining buildings, including the Wells Hotel, have been preserved.

Note: The gravel road is narrow and winding and not suitable for motorhomes and trailers. **Time:** Allow 2 hours minimum. **Hours:** Daily 9:30-4:45, Memorial Day-Sept. 30; Sat.-Sun. 11-3, rest of year. **Cost:** $3; free (ages 0-15). **Phone:** (406) 329-3914. 🅰

HISTORICAL MUSEUM AT FORT MISSOULA is s. on Reserve St. to South Ave., then 1 mi. w. following signs. The museum is at the center of what was Fort Missoula, established in 1877 at the height of the conflict with the Nez Perce under Chief Joseph. Galleries and exhibits depict the roles of the timber industry, forest management, the fort and early settlement in Missoula County history. Of the 21 historic structures and several original fort buildings that remain, 10 have been restored.

Guided tours are available by appointment. **Time:** Allow 1 hour minimum. **Hours:** Mon.-Sat. 10-5, Sun. noon-5, Memorial Day weekend-Labor Day; Tues.-Sun. noon-5, rest of year. Closed major holidays except Memorial Day, July 4 and Labor Day. **Cost:** $3; $2 (senior citizens); $1 (students with ID); $10 (family). **Phone:** (406) 728-3476.

MISSOULA ART MUSEUM is at 335 N. Pattee St. The museum is housed in the old public library and hosts more than 25 rotating exhibitions from local and international artists each year. Artworks reflect the culture of the American West with a focus on contemporary Montana artists. Free 20-minute guided tours are offered on Saturdays. **Time:** Allow 1 hour minimum. **Hours:** Tues.-Fri. 10-5, Sat.-Sun. noon-5. Closed major holidays. **Cost:** Free. **Phone:** (406) 728-0447.

SAVE **ROCKY MOUNTAIN ELK FOUNDATION/ELK COUNTRY VISITOR CENTER** is off I-90 exit 101, then .25 mile n. to 5705 Grant Creek Rd. The visitor center features conservation and hunting heritage exhibits and wildlife displays that include world-record elk. **Hours:** Mon.-Fri. 8-6, Sat.-Sun. 9-6, May-Dec.; Mon.-Fri. 8-5, Sat. 10-5, rest of year. Closed Jan. 1, Thanksgiving and Christmas. **Cost:** Donations. **Phone:** (406) 523-4545.

ST. FRANCIS XAVIER CHURCH is at 420 W. Pine St. Built in 1889, the church is noted for its 144-foot steeple, stained glass windows and paintings by Brother Joseph Carignano. Visitors may watch a 10-minute video explaining the paintings. **Time:** Allow 30 minutes minimum. **Hours:** Mon.-Sat. 8:30-5. **Cost:** Free. **Phone:** (406) 542-0321.

SMOKEJUMPERS BASE AERIAL FIRE DEPOT is 7 mi. w. to 5765 W. Broadway, next to Johnson-Bell Airport. Displays include dioramas, artifacts and photographs relating to the history of U.S. Forest Service firefighting. Service smokejumpers give guided tours of the base and offer firsthand accounts of firefighting and smokejumping. **Hours:** Daily 8:30-5, Memorial Day-Labor Day; by appointment rest of year. Tours are given at 10, 11, 1, 2, 3 and 4. **Cost:** Donations. **Phone:** (406) 329-4934.

RECREATIONAL ACTIVITIES

Skiing

- **Montana Snowbowl** is at I-90 Reserve St. exit. Other activities are offered in summer. **Hours:** Skiing available Wed.-Mon., late Nov. to mid-Apr.; otherwise varies. Hours vary; phone ahead. **Phone:** (406) 549-9777.

White-water Rafting

- **10,000 Waves Raft and Kayak Adventures** is at 1311 E. Broadway. Other activities are offered. **Note:** The attraction plans to relocate; phone ahead for updates. **Hours:** Rafting trips are offered daily, mid-Apr. to mid-Oct. Departure times vary; phone ahead. **Phone:** (406) 549-6670 or (800) 537-8315.

BROADWAY INN CONFERENCE CENTER   (406)532-3300
Hotel $70-$200 **Address:** 1609 W Broadway 59808 **Location:** I-90 exit 104 (Orange St), 0.5 mi s, then 1 mi w. **Facility:** 79 units. 2 stories, interior corridors. **Parking:** winter plug-ins. **Terms:** cancellation fee imposed. **Dining:** The Broadway Sports Bar, Grill & Casino, see separate listing. **Pool(s):** heated outdoor. **Activities:** hot tub, exercise room. **Guest Services:** valet and coin laundry, area transportation.

CAMPUS INN   406/549-5134
Motel $70-$150 **Address:** 744 E Broadway 59802 **Location:** I-90 exit 105 (Van Buren St), just s to Broadway, then just w. **Facility:** 78 units, some kitchens. 2 stories (no elevator), interior/exterior corridors. **Parking:** winter plug-ins. **Terms:** cancellation fee imposed, resort fee. **Pool(s):** heated indoor. **Activities:** hot tub, limited exercise equipment. **Guest Services:** coin laundry.

C'MON INN   (406)543-4600
Hotel $99-$139 **Address:** 2775 Expo Pkwy 59808 **Location:** I-90 exit 101 (Reserve St), just n. **Facility:** 119 units, some kitchens. 3 stories, interior corridors. **Parking:** winter plug-ins. **Amenities:** video games. **Pool(s):** heated indoor. **Activities:** hot tub, game room, exercise room. **Guest Services:** valet and coin laundry.

COMFORT INN - UNIVERSITY   (406)549-7600
Hotel $99-$179 **Address:** 1021 E Broadway 59802 **Location:** I-90 exit 105 (Van Buren St), just s, then just e. **Facility:** 95 units. 4 stories, interior corridors. **Parking:** winter plug-ins. **Terms:** check-in 4 pm. **Activities:** exercise room. **Guest Services:** valet and coin laundry.

DAYS INN/MISSOULA AIRPORT   (406)721-9776
Hotel **Address:** 8600 Truck Stop Rd 59808 **Location:** I-90 exit 96, just n. Adjacent to truck parking. **Facility:** 70 units, some kitchens. 2 stories (no elevator), interior corridors. **Parking:** winter plug-ins. **Activities:** playground, limited exercise equipment. **Guest Services:** coin laundry.

DAYS INN UNIVERSITY   (406)543-7221
Hotel $80-$100 **Address:** 201 E Main St 59802 **Location:** I-90 exit 104 (Orange St), 0.5 mi s to Broadway, 0.5 mi e to Washington St, just s to Main St, then just w. **Facility:** 50 units. 2 stories, exterior corridors. **Parking:** winter plug-ins. **Terms:** cancellation fee imposed. **Pool(s):** heated outdoor. **Activities:** limited exercise equipment.

ECONO LODGE
(406)542-7550

WWW Hotel $65-$100 Address: 4953 N Reserve St 59808 Location: I-90 exit 101 (Reserve St), just s. Facility: 67 units. 3 stories, interior corridors. Parking: winter plug-ins. Activities: hot tub. Guest Services: coin laundry.

FAMILY INN
406/543-7371

Motel
$70-$80

Address: 1031 E Broadway 59802 Location: I-90 exit 105 (Van Buren St), just s, then just e. Facility: 21 kitchen units. 2 stories (no elevator), exterior corridors. Bath: shower only. Parking: winter plug-ins. Terms: closed 9/1-5/1. Pool(s): heated outdoor. Guest Services: coin laundry. Featured Amenity: continental breakfast.

GUESTHOUSE INN & SUITES - MISSOULA
(406)251-2665

WWW Hotel $69-$109 Address: 3803 Brooks St 59804 Location: I-90 exit 101 (Reserve St), 5 mi s to Brooks St, then just w. Facility: 79 units. 3 stories, interior corridors. Parking: winter plug-ins. Activities: limited exercise equipment. Guest Services: valet and coin laundry.

HAMPTON INN
(400)549-1800

WWWW
Hotel
$99-$159

Hampton

AAA Benefit:
Members save up to 10%!

Address: 4805 N Reserve St 59808 Location: I-90 exit 101 (Reserve St), just s. Facility: 61 units. 4 stories, interior corridors. Parking: winter plug-ins. Terms: 1-7 night minimum stay, cancellation fee imposed. Pool(s): heated indoor. Activities: hot tub, exercise room. Guest Services: valet and coin laundry, area transportation. Featured Amenity: continental breakfast.

HILTON GARDEN INN MISSOULA AND MISSOULA CONFERENCE CENTER
(406)532-5300

WWWW Hotel $109-$239 Address: 3720 N Reserve St 59808 Location: I-90 exit 101 (Reserve St), just s. Facility: 146 units. 6 stories, interior corridors. Parking: winter plug-ins. Terms:

AAA Benefit:
Members save up to 10%!

1-7 night minimum stay, cancellation fee imposed. Amenities: video games. Dining: Blue Canyon Kitchen & Tavern, see separate listing. Pool(s): heated indoor. Activities: hot tub, exercise room. Guest Services: valet and coin laundry, area transportation.

HOLIDAY INN EXPRESS & SUITES
(406)830-3100

WWWW Hotel $113-$139 Address: 150 Expressway Blvd 59808 Location: I-90 exit 101 (Reserve St), just s. Facility: 82 units. 4 stories, interior corridors. Parking: winter plug-ins. Amenities: Some: video games. Pool(s): heated indoor. Activities: hot tub, game room, exercise room. Guest Services: valet and coin laundry, area transportation.

HOLIDAY INN MISSOULA-DOWNTOWN AT THE PARK
(406)721-8550

Hotel
$99-$199

Address: 200 S Pattee St 59802 Location: I-90 exit 104 (Orange St), 0.5 mi s to Broadway, just e to Pattee St, then just s. Facility: 200 units. 3 stories, interior corridors. Parking: winter plug-ins. Terms: check-in 4 pm, cancellation fee imposed. Pool(s): heated indoor. Activities: sauna, hot tub, exercise room. Guest Services: valet laundry, area transportation.

LA QUINTA INN MISSOULA
(406)549-9000

WWW Hotel $89-$164 Address: 5059 N Reserve St 59808 Location: I-90 exit 101 (Reserve St), just s. Facility: 80 units. 3 stories, interior corridors. Parking: winter plug-ins. Pool(s): heated indoor. Activities: hot tub, exercise room. Guest Services: valet and coin laundry.

QUALITY INN & SUITES
(406)542-0888

WWW Hotel $85-$165 Address: 4545 N Reserve St 59808 Location: I-90 exit 101 (Reserve St), 0.5 mi s. Facility: 52 units. 2 stories (no elevator), interior corridors. Parking: winter plug-ins. Amenities: safes. Pool(s): heated indoor. Activities: hot tub. Guest Services: valet and coin laundry.

RED LION INN
(406)728-3300

WWW Motel $89-$149 Address: 700 W Broadway 59802 Location: I-90 exit 104 (Orange St), just s, then just w. Facility: 76 units. 2 stories (no elevator), exterior corridors. Parking: winter plug-ins. Pool(s): heated outdoor. Activities: hot tub, exercise room. Guest Services: valet and coin laundry.

RUBY'S INN & CONVENTION CENTER
(406)721-0990

Hotel
$79-$125

Address: 4825 N Reserve St 59808 Location: I-90 exit 101 (Reserve St), just s. Facility: 125 units, some kitchens. 2 stories, interior/exterior corridors. Parking: winter plug-ins. Terms: 7 day cancellation notice-fee imposed. Pool(s): heated indoor. Activities: sauna, hot tub, exercise room. Guest Services: valet and coin laundry.

SLEEP INN BY CHOICE HOTELS
(406)543-5883

WWW Hotel $69-$140 Address: 3425 Dore Ln 59801 Location: I-90 exit 101 (Reserve St), 5 mi s, then just e on Brooks St. Facility: 59 units. 3 stories, interior corridors. Parking: winter plug-ins. Pool(s): heated indoor. Activities: hot tub. Guest Services: valet laundry.

STAYBRIDGE SUITES
(406)830-3900

WWW Extended Stay Hotel $99-$299 Address: 120 Expressway Blvd 59808 Location: I-90 exit 101 (Reserve St), just s. Facility: 101 units, some two bedrooms. 4 stories, interior corridors. Parking: winter plug-ins. Pool(s): heated indoor. Activities: hot tub, exercise room. Guest Services: complimentary and valet laundry.

STONECREEK LODGE (406)541-3600

   Extended Stay Hotel $91-$189 **Address:** 5145 Airway Blvd 59808 **Location:** I-90 exit 99 (Airway Blvd), just s. **Facility:** 101 units, some efficiencies. 3 stories, interior corridors. **Parking:** winter plug-ins. **Pool(s):** heated indoor. **Activities:** hot tub, exercise room. **Guest Services:** valet and coin laundry, area transportation.

SUPER 8-BROOKS ST (406)251-2255

Hotel $78-$87 **Address:** 3901 Brooks St 59804 **Location:** I-90 exit 101 (Reserve St), 5 mi s to Brooks St, then just w. **Facility:** 103 units. 3 stories (no elevator), interior corridors. **Parking:** winter plug-ins. **Guest Services:** coin laundry.

SUPER 8-RESERVE ST (406)549-1199

Hotel $73-$137 **Address:** 4703 N Reserve St 59808 **Location:** I-90 exit 101 (Reserve St), 0.4 mi s. **Facility:** 58 units. 3 stories, interior corridors. **Parking:** winter plug-ins. **Terms:** cancellation fee imposed. **Activities:** limited exercise equipment. **Guest Services:** coin laundry.

THUNDERBIRD MOTEL (406)543-7251

Motel $75-$95

Address: 1009 E Broadway 59802 **Location:** I-90 exit 105 (Van Buren St), just s to Broadway, then just e. **Facility:** 31 units, some two bedrooms. 2 stories (no elevator), interior/exterior corridors. **Parking:** winter plug-ins. **Terms:** cancellation fee imposed. **Pool(s):** heated indoor. **Activities:** hot tub, limited exercise equipment. **Guest Services:** coin laundry. **Featured Amenity:** continental breakfast.

Conveniently located off of the interstate. Close to the University of Montana.

VAL-U-INN (406)721-9600

Hotel. Rates not provided. **Address:** 3001 Brooks St 59801 **Location:** I-90 exit 101 (Reserve St), 5 mi s to US 93, then 0.7 mi e. Adjacent to shopping mall. **Facility:** 83 units. 3 stories, interior corridors. **Parking:** winter plug-ins. **Activities:** sauna, hot tub. **Guest Services:** valet and coin laundry.

WINGATE BY WYNDHAM (406)541-8000

Hotel $99-$195 **Address:** 5252 Airway Blvd 59808 **Location:** I-90 exit 99 (Airway Blvd), just s to E Harrier Dr. **Facility:** 100 units. 3 stories, interior corridors. **Parking:** winter plug-ins. **Terms:** check-in 4 pm. **Amenities:** video games, safes. **Pool(s):** heated indoor. **Activities:** hot tub, exercise room. **Guest Services:** valet and coin laundry, area transportation.

BAGELS ON BROADWAY 406/728-8900

Deli. Quick Serve. $2-$8 **AAA Inspector Notes:** In business since 1994, Bagels on Broadway tempts guests with dine-in or take-out options of New York-style bagels and other baked goods. **Address:** 223 W Broadway 59802 **Location:** I-90 exit 104 (Orange St), just s, then just e; downtown; across from courthouse. **Parking:** street only. **B** **L** CALL

BIGA PIZZA 406/728-2579

Pizza Natural/Organic. Casual Dining. $5-$19 **AAA Inspector Notes:** Here's a recipe for success: Jersey-born, bakes in a brick oven, uses organic/local ingredients and loves to eat. What do you get? A man who conjures up awesome pizza with signature combos such as house-made fennel marmalade, local bacon, Gouda cheese, mozzarella, garlic and olive oil. Sandwiches on homemade bread, salads and calzones also are offered and are just as creative. **Features:** beer & wine, patio dining. **Address:** 241 W Main St 59802 **Location:** Between Ryman and Woody sts; downtown. **Parking:** street only. **L** **D** CALL

BLUE CANYON KITCHEN & TAVERN 406/541-2583

American. Casual Dining. $12-$28 **AAA Inspector Notes:** This casual restaurant is definitely upscale "cowboy chic," constructed of large peeled log beams and braces. The walls are decorated with the ubiquitous Montana elk head mounts, and antler chandeliers light the dining room. The chairs are unpeeled, small log frames with upholstered seats and backs, and the booths and benches are all finely upholstered. Ninety-eight percent of all the food coming out of the kitchen is made from scratch, and the in-house pastry chef produces all desserts. **Features:** full bar, patio dining, happy hour. **Address:** 32720 N Reserve St 59808 **Location:** I-90 exit 101 (Reserve St), just s; in Hilton Garden Inn Missoula and Missoula Conference Center. **D**

THE BROADWAY SPORTS BAR, GRILL & CASINO 406/543-5678

American. Casual Dining. $9-$15 **AAA Inspector Notes:** In the Inn on Broadway, the restaurant has a large TV screen as well as smaller TVs positioned to enable diners in any seat to have a view. Sports is the watchword here, and the food—a large choice of snack foods, appetizers and finger foods, as well as full meals of meats, seafood and sandwiches—is familiar. Patrons meet, eat and cheer for their favorite team. **Features:** full bar, patio dining, happy hour. **Address:** 1609 W Broadway 59808 **Location:** I-90 exit 104 (Orange St), 0.5 mi s, then 1 mi w; in Broadway Inn Conference Center. **D**

CATALYST 406/542-1337

American. Casual Dining. $6-$11 **AAA Inspector Notes:** The menu choices change practically daily and utilize local produce when available. Fresh, creatively prepared homemade soups, sandwiches and salads are among the options, as are made-from-scratch cookies for dessert. You may want to visit the espresso bar. **Address:** 111 N Higgins Ave 59802 **Location:** Between Front and Main sts; downtown. **Parking:** street only. **B** **L**

CHINA BOWL RESTAURANT 406/721-9888

Chinese. Casual Dining. $7-$22 **AAA Inspector Notes:** Sit down to traditional and more creative Asian dishes at the comfortable family restaurant, conveniently located near shopping and theaters. A focal point of the décor is a large koi pond at the entrance of the dining room. **Features:** beer & wine. **Address:** 3445 American Way 59801 **Location:** I-90 exit 101 (Reserve St), 1 mi s. **L** **D**

CHINA GARDEN 406/721-1785

Chinese. Casual Dining. $9-$20 **AAA Inspector Notes:** In a small strip shopping center, the established, family-operated restaurant prepares traditional Cantonese and some Szechuan menu items for loyal locals and other guests. **Features:** beer & wine. **Address:** 2100 Stephens Ave 59801 **Location:** I-90 exit 104 (Orange St), 2.5 mi s to Stephens Ave; in Stephens Center. **Parking:** on-site and street. **L** **D**

CIAO MAMBO
406/543-0377

▼▼▼ Italian. Casual Dining. $11-$28 **AAA Inspector Notes:** Just like its sister restaurants, this family-owned place serves traditional and inventive dishes with a mambo twist. The marinara, with slivers of garlic, is fragrant and delicious. Have a seat at the counter and watch the chefs hand toss your pizza. Modern and contemporary décor surrounds guests adjacent to the open kitchen. **Features:** beer & wine. **Address:** 541 S Higgins Ave 59801 **Location:** Jct S 4th St W, s of bridge; downtown. **Parking:** street only. D

CURLEY'S BROILER
406/721-4133

▼▼ American. Casual Dining. $8-$26 **AAA Inspector Notes:** If you want such good comfort food choices as steaks, hot crab and French dip sandwiches, this is the best place to go. It has a very loyal local following and has been in operation for 40 years. Saturday and Sunday brunch is offered, but be sure to call for reservations. **Features:** full bar, Sunday brunch. **Address:** 2915 Brooks St 59801 **Location:** I-90 exit 101 (Reserve St), 5 mi s to US 93, then 0.7 mi e. L D

THE DEPOT
406/728-7007

▼▼ American. Casual Dining. $11-$39 **AAA Inspector Notes:** *Historic.* This historic railroad hotel offers casual dining either in the pub or the dining room and features fresh seafood, hand-cut steak, pasta and choice prime rib. The atmosphere is bustling and busy and the service prompt. Patio seating is available in season. The restaurant is just off the downtown area and is close to the railroad tracks. Seafood selections such as lobster and crab legs offer some variety. **Features:** full bar. **Reservations:** suggested. **Address:** 201 W Railroad St 59802 **Location:** I-90 exit 104 (Orange St), just s, e on Spruce St, then n on Ryman St. D CALL M

EL CAZADOR
406/728-3657

▼▼ Mexican. Casual Dining. $7-$15 **AAA Inspector Notes:** Brightly lit with colorful art-glass light shades, this convenient family-owned downtown restaurant has big windows perfect for people-watching. The freshly made salsa comes in a small glass pitcher to go with the hot chips. The wide variety of Mexican dishes is served by a very friendly staff. **Features:** beer & wine. **Address:** 101 S Higgins Ave 59801 **Location:** Downtown. **Parking:** street only. L D CALL M

FINN & PORTER
406/542-4660

▼▼▼ American. Fine Dining. $8-$40 **AAA Inspector Notes:** Guests can dine on Prime beef, fresh seafood and inventive specials in the sleek, modern dining room, which overlooks the Clark Fork River. Those in the mood for a lighter meal might try a specialty pizza from the wood-fired oven. **Features:** full bar, patio dining, Sunday brunch, happy hour. **Reservations:** suggested. **Address:** 100 Madison St 59802 **Location:** I-90 exit 105 (Van Buren St), just s, then just w on Front St; in DoubleTree by Hilton Hotel Missoula - Edgewater. B L D CALL M

IRON HORSE BREW PUB
406/728-8866

▼▼ American. Casual Dining. $8-$18 **AAA Inspector Notes:** This popular, lively watering hole serves a large selection of snacks, finger food and sandwiches. Enjoy their many specialty drinks, premium liquors and wide array of bottled and draft beers. During summer months, the deck is the place to be. **Features:** full bar, patio dining, happy hour. **Address:** 501 N Higgins Ave 59802 **Location:** Downtown. L D

IZA ASIAN RESTAURANT
406/830-3237

▼▼ Asian. Casual Dining. $9-$16 **AAA Inspector Notes:** Here you can sample authentic cuisines from Korea, Nepal, Malaysia, Japan, Indonesia and Thailand. For the uninitiated, the staff will explain all ingredients and recommend various condiments for each dish. The Asian theme of the restaurant is carried through to the clean lines of the decor; bamboo floors, wall accents and live plants complete the look. There's even traditional Japanese seating with footwells. Lunch values include bento boxes. **Features:** beer & wine. **Address:** 529 S Higgins Ave 59801 **Location:** Jct S 4th St W, s of bridge; downtown. **Parking:** street only. L D

THE KEEP
406/728-5132

▼▼▼ American. Fine Dining. $27-$40 **AAA Inspector Notes:** Take a short drive into a quiet residential area high on a hill overlooking the city. The building is a turreted faux castle structure with heavy stone/masonry construction and attractively landscaped grounds. A favorite with the locals, this landmark is often busy, so make a reservation to be safe. Dine in the elegant dining room or on the seasonal terrace. Steaks, seafood and salads are all made with flare. **Features:** full bar, patio dining. **Reservations:** suggested. **Address:** 102 Ben Hogan Dr 59803 **Location:** I-90 exit 101 (Reserve St), 5.4 mi s to 39th St, 1.2 mi e to High Park Way, 0.6 mi s to Whitaker Dr, 0.5 mi w to Ben Hogan Dr, then just s. D CALL M

THE MONTANA CLUB
406/543-3200

▼▼ Regional American. Casual Dining. $8-$30 **AAA Inspector Notes:** Inside a timbered building, this family-friendly eatery serves large portions of regional, house-cut meats and fresh Alaskan seafood. With the large menu, everyone will be happy. The restaurant has an adjacent casino, as well as sister locations in Kalispell, Great Falls and Butte. **Features:** full bar. **Address:** 2620 Brooks St 59801 **Location:** I-90 exit 101 (Reserve St), 5 mi s, then 1 mi e. B L D

THE MONTANA CLUB
406/541-8141

▼▼ Regional American. Casual Dining. $7-$28 **AAA Inspector Notes:** This family-friendly spot with an adjacent casino has sister restaurants in Kalispell, Butte and another in Missoula. The building sports a wood interior, and menu items include fresh Alaskan salmon, halibut and meats cut in house. Portions are plentiful. **Features:** full bar, senior menu, happy hour. **Address:** 4561 N Reserve St 59808 **Location:** I-90 exit 101 (Reserve St), just s. R L D

THE MUSTARD SEED ASIAN CAFE
406/542-7333

▼▼ Asian. Casual Dining. $6-$18 **AAA Inspector Notes:** In Southgate Mall, the cafe has a convenient private entrance. The blend of Pacific Rim cuisines is geared to American tastes. **Features:** full bar. **Address:** 2901 Brooks St 59801 **Location:** I-90 exit 101 (Reserve St), 5 mi s, 0.7 mi e, then just n; in Southgate Mall. L D CALL M

NARA KOREAN BAR-B-QUE & SUSHI
406/327-0731

▼▼ Asian Sushi. Casual Dining. $6-$25 **AAA Inspector Notes:** In a strip mall near major shopping and with easy freeway access, the lively restaurant presents an extensive menu of sushi and tempura, as well as a wide array of Korean specialties. **Features:** beer & wine. **Address:** 3075 N Reserve St, Suite K 59808 **Location:** I-90 exit 101 (Reserve St), 1.4 mi s; in Grant Creek Town Center. L D

PARADISE FALLS RESTAURANT, LOUNGE & CASINO
406/728-3228

▼▼ American. Casual Dining. $8-$18 **AAA Inspector Notes:** A lively sports bar, casino and restaurant featuring a wide array of appetizers, sandwiches and burgers as well as build-your-own pizzas and traditional entrées. **Features:** full bar, patio dining, Sunday brunch, happy hour. **Address:** 3621 Brooks St 59801 **Location:** I-90 exit 101 (Reserve St), 5 mi s, then just e. B L D

THE PEARL CAFE
406/541-0231

▼▼▼ Regional American. Fine Dining. $20-$38 **AAA Inspector Notes:** *Historic.* Self-described as country-French fare with a city flair, the owner-chef creates sumptuous savories like ginger scallops, chard ravioli and broiled lamb. Courses are served in a relaxed manner by a staff that is very knowledgeable of the ingredients that go into each dish. It started life as a café and bakery, and thank goodness the kitchen never stopped baking its own bread when the bakery in the name was dropped. The night I was there, I had sourdough and a white baguette in my basket. **Features:** beer & wine. **Address:** 231 E Front St 59802 **Location:** I-90 exit 104 (Orange St), 0.5 mi s, 0.3 mi e on W Broadway, just s on N Pattee St, then just e. **Parking:** street only. D

RED BIRD   406/549-2906
▼▼▼ American. Fine Dining. $25-$37 **AAA Inspector Notes:** This chef-owned, intimate hideaway is known for inventive seasonal cuisine served in quiet, architecturally dramatic surroundings. The menu consists of beef, chicken and seafood, along with appetizers such as wontons stuffed with Brie and candied pecans. Upon entry through the well-lighted alley just off the main downtown street, the dramatic restaurant grabs you with its bold architecture and Art Deco chandeliers. **Features:** beer & wine. **Reservations:** suggested. **Address:** 111 N Higgins Ave, Suite 100 59802 **Location:** I-90 exit 104 (Orange St), s to Broadway, e to Higgins Ave, then just s; in Florence Building. **Parking:** street only. [D] CALL [&M]

SA-WAD-DEE   406/543-9966
▼▼ Thai. Casual Dining. $8-$14 **AAA Inspector Notes:** Popular with locals, the family-run restaurant presents a menu of authentic fare. **Features:** beer & wine. **Address:** 221 W Broadway St 59802 **Location:** I-90 exit 104 (Orange St), just s, then just e; downtown; across from courthouse. **Parking:** street only. [L] [D]

SCOTTY'S TABLE   406/549-2790
▼▼▼▼ International. Fine Dining. $9-$33 **AAA Inspector Notes:** The stylish, jazz-infused bistro serves a mix of cuisines. The emphasis is heavy on rustic French and Italian, with a smattering of Greek, North African and other Mediterranean styles. **Features:** beer & wine, patio dining. **Reservations:** suggested. **Address:** 131 S Higgins Ave, Unit P3 59802 **Location:** Just n of Higgins Ave Bridge; downtown. **Parking:** street only. [L] [D]

SEAN KELLY'S, A PUBLIC HOUSE   406/542-1471
▼▼ Irish. Gastropub. $8-$20 **AAA Inspector Notes:** Where the Gaelic and garlic mix, the restaurant has the clubby atmosphere of a traditional Irish pub and food that transcends corned beef and cabbage (although that dish does make it onto the menu). **Features:** full bar, Sunday brunch. **Address:** 130 W Pine St 59802 **Location:** Downtown; near jct Higgins Ave. **Parking:** street only. [L] [D]

SEAN KELLY'S, THE STONE OF ACCORD   406/830-3210
▼▼ Irish. Gastropub. $8-$23 **AAA Inspector Notes:** Where the Gaelic and garlic mix, the restaurant has the clubby atmosphere of a traditional Irish pub and food that transcends corned beef and cabbage (although that dish does make it onto the menu). **Features:** full bar, Sunday brunch. **Address:** 4591 N Reserve St 59801 **Location:** I-90 exit 101 (Reserve St), just s. [B] [L] [D] CALL [&M]

THE SHACK CAFE 222   406/549-9903
▼▼ American. Casual Dining. $7-$20 **AAA Inspector Notes:** Innovative, freshly prepared foods, a multitude of vegetarian dishes and exceptional breakfast items are hallmarks here. Try the light Greek fettuccine, resplendent with olives, feta cheese and fresh spinach leaves. Patio seating is available in summer. Dinner is only offered seasonally. Phone ahead for days and hours. **Features:** beer & wine, patio dining. **Address:** 222 W Main St 59802 **Location:** Downtown. **Parking:** street only. [B] [L] [D]

THE SILK ROAD   406/541-0752
▼▼▼ International Small Plates. Casual Dining. $4-$9 **AAA Inspector Notes:** Just the name of the restaurant conjures up exotic smells and sounds. The owner hearkens to a time when you and your friends sat down to an array of appetizers and everyone shared in good food and conversation. The menu is not only global, but many of the items are chosen by you and me — everyone has a voice! Choices can be made on the restaurant's website, and suggestions are welcome. The restaurant specializes in using their own global spice blends. **Features:** beer & wine, Sunday brunch. **Address:** 515 S Higgins Ave 59801 **Location:** Jct S 4th St W, s of bridge; downtown. **Parking:** street only. [D]

SUSHI HANA   406/549-7979
▼▼ Japanese. Casual Dining. $6-$33 **AAA Inspector Notes:** This casual but stylish restaurant serves sushi, sashimi and teriyaki in a dining room infused with traditional Japanese koto music. Daily lunch and happy hour specials always are a delight to your taste buds. **Features:** beer & wine. **Address:** 403 N Higgins Ave 59802 **Location:** Downtown. **Parking:** street only. [L] [D]

VIETNAM GRILL   406/721-3410
▼▼ Vietnamese. Casual Dining. $8-$11 **AAA Inspector Notes:** A nice addition to the varied cuisine 'row' of Higgins Ave. This family run place has a menu full of home made Vietnamese 'street' food. I call it tasty comfort foods, especially the steaming bowl of fragrant Pho (soup). **Address:** 420 N Higgins Ave 59802 **Location:** Jct Pine St; downtown. **Parking:** street only. [L] [D]

VIETNAM NOODLE RESTAURANT   406/542-8299
▼▼ Vietnamese. Casual Dining. $8-$14 **AAA Inspector Notes:** In a small strip shopping center, this casual restaurant presents an extensive menu that includes a few Thai choices that are very popular with locals. The restaurant also has a small selection of Asian groceries for sale. **Address:** 2100 Stephens Ave, Suite 103 59801 **Location:** I-90 exit 104 (Orange St), 2.5 mi s to Stephens Ave; in Stephens Center. [L] [D]

MOIESE (C-2) elev. 2,600'

NATIONAL BISON RANGE is s.w. via SR 212. Up to 400 bison as well as herds of elk, pronghorn antelope, deer and bighorn sheep live on the 18,700-acre range. From mid-May to mid-October the refuge can be explored via a 19-mile self-guiding driving tour on a one-way gravel road. The tour takes about 2 hours. Only portions of the site are open the rest of the year.

Note: Two-wheeled vehicles are not allowed off the paved roads. Trailers and larger motor homes are restricted to shorter drives; check at the visitor center. The gravel and dirt roads present some long climbs and steep downgrades. Visitors must keep their vehicles on the tour road and must remain in or near them. **Hours:** Range open daily 7 a.m.-dusk. Visitor center open daily 9-6, mid-May to early Oct.; Mon.-Fri. 10-2, rest of year. Closed holidays early Oct. to mid-May. **Cost:** $5 (per private vehicle). **Phone:** (406) 644-2211.

MONIDA (F-3)

Monida is a former railroad town at the foot of Monida Pass and the Continental Divide. Scenic highway I-15 passes near town, offering views of the Centennial Mountains to the east and the Italian Peaks to the west. The name Monida is derived from the combination of Montana and Idaho.

MONTANA CITY pop. 2,715

ELKHORN MOUNTAIN INN   (406)442-6625
▼ Hotel $70-$90 **Address:** 1 Jackson Creek Rd 59634 **Location:** I-15 exit 187 (Montana City), just w. **Facility:** 22 units. 2 stories (no elevator), interior corridors. **Parking:** winter plug-ins. **Terms:** check-in 4 pm.
[11+] CALL [&M] [HS] 🛜 [✕] [▭] / SOME UNITS [🛏] [🔋] [🍽]

MONTANA CITY GRILL AND SALOON   406/449-8890
▼▼ American. Casual Dining. $8-$29 **AAA Inspector Notes:** Specialties of the house include slow-roasted prime rib, fresh seafood, homemade soup, chicken, pasta, charbroiled steak and huckleberry barbecued pork ribs. The atmosphere is casual with some booth seating; service is friendly and prompt. A good selection of microbrews and wines is offered. Breakfast is available on Sundays. **Features:** full bar, senior menu, happy hour. **Address:** 4 Hwy 518 59634 **Location:** I-15 exit 187 (Montana City), just w. [L] [D]

NEVADA CITY—See Virginia City p. 207.

OVANDO (C-2) pop. 81, elev. 4,100'

RECREATIONAL ACTIVITIES
Hunting
• **WTR Outfitters** is at 1200 Ed Rd. **Hours:** Hunting trips are offered in fall. Other activities are offered in summer. **Phone:** (406) 824-2471 or (406) 754-2471.

PABLO (C-2) pop. 2,254, elev. 3,085'

Pablo is home to the 1,317,000-acre Flathead Indian Reservation and the headquarters of the Confederated Salish and Kootenai Indian tribes. Approximately 3,700 tribal members live on or near the reservation and manage wildlife and natural resources.

THE PEOPLE'S CENTER is 1 mi. n. of the tribal complex at 53253 US 93. Exhibits focus on the history and culture of the Salish, Kootenai and Pend d'Oreille tribes. Art, photographs, oral histories and crafts are included in the collection. "Ed-Ventures," educational tours of nearby Flathead Reservation, are offered for an additional fee. **Hours:** Mon.-Fri. 9-5 (also Sat. 9-5, June-Sept.). Closed major holidays. Phone ahead to confirm schedule. **Cost:** $5; $3 (ages 55+ and students with ID); $10 (family). **Phone:** (406) 675-0160.

PHILIPSBURG (D-2) pop. 820, elev. 5,270'

In the heart of mineral-rich Flint Creek Valley, the town of Philipsburg emerged at the height of a silver mining boom in 1867 and was named for Philip Deidesheimer, a former Comstock engineer who built the area's first ore processing mill. The mill closed in 1869, marking the first of several mining busts and subsequent booms. The demand for manganese in steel production during World War I fueled a final ore producing period that lasted until the Great Depression.

The historic district, centered on Broadway, contains numerous late 19th- and early 20th-century structures. Outlying abandoned mines and ghost towns also attest to Philipsburg's mining legacy, although very few are still accessible. The surrounding Sapphire and Flint Creek mountain ranges attract a new breed of prospector, the rock hound, in search of gems and minerals.

Philipsburg is midway between Drummond and Anaconda on the Pintler Scenic Highway (SR 1). Broad views of Flint Creek Valley are available near mile markers 28 and 42.

Philipsburg Chamber of Commerce: P.O. Box 661, Philipsburg, MT 59858. **Phone:** (406) 859-3388.

GRANITE COUNTY MUSEUM & CULTURAL CENTER is at 135 S. Sansome St. An overview of a miner's life includes a mural depicting above-ground activities, an assay office and a reconstructed cabin. Exhibits include a sample of a real vein as well as tools, an ore car and mining memorabilia. **Hours:** Daily noon-5, Memorial Day-Sept. 30; by appointment rest of year. **Cost:** $4; free (ages 0-11). **Phone:** (406) 859-3020.

THE RANCH AT ROCK CREEK   406/859-6027
[fyi] Not evaluated. **Address:** 79 Carriage House Ln 59858 **Location:** 14 mi w on Rock Creek Rd (SR 348); 5.5 mi s on CR 102 (dirt road). Facilities, services, and décor characterize an upscale property. Find luxury accommodations in a Western setting. The all-inclusive ranch resort set on 6,000 acres offers horseback riding, bowling, a spa and a gourmet restaurant. The fly fishing is worth the trip.

WHERE TO EAT

DOE BROTHERS RESTAURANT   406/859-6676
American. Casual Dining. $6-$13 **AAA Inspector Notes:** Historic. Take a step back and enjoy this historic building dating from 1887. The soda fountain was built in 1920 and is still in use. There is an Italian marble front and other memorabilia from bygone eras. Try a vanilla phosphate or other ice cream treat. **Features:** beer & wine. **Address:** 120 E Broadway 59858 **Location:** Downtown. **Parking:** street only. B L D CALL 🔊M 🅐

POLARIS (E-2) elev. 6,355'

Polaris is the beginning point of the Pioneer Scenic Byway, which stretches for 32 miles to the Wise River and affords glimpses of such wildlife as antelope, deer and hawks. The route passes Crystal Park, a natural crystal mountain where visitors can dig for various crystals. Another stop along the drive is Elkhorn Hot Springs, a hot springs pool. This picturesque road is open until the first snowfall.

POLSON (C-2) pop. 4,488, elev. 2,931'
• Hotels p. 200 • Restaurants p. 200

Polson is in a natural amphitheater at the foot of Flathead Lake. During May and June water pours through the 200- to 500-foot perpendicular walls of the Flathead River Gorge at the rate of 500,000 gallons per second. Legend has it that Paul Bunyan dug the channel connecting the river and the lake.

Polson Area Chamber of Commerce: 418 Main St., Polson, MT 59860. **Phone:** (406) 883-5969.

FLATHEAD LAKE STATE PARK is just n. of Polson on US 93. This is the largest natural freshwater lake west of the Mississippi. Nearby points of interest include Big Arm, Finley Point, Wayfarers, West Shore and Yellow Bay units *(see Recreation Areas Chart)*; Somers Fish Hatchery; Montana University Biological Station; Station Creek Fish Hatchery; Wild Horse Island and Kerr Dam. **Cost:** $5 (nonresidents per private vehicle); $3 (nonresidents arriving by other means); free (residents). **Phone:** (406) 849-5256 for Big Arm, or (406) 887-2715 for Finley Point.

MIRACLE OF AMERICA MUSEUM is 2 mi. s. on US 93 to 36094 Memory Ln. This potpourri of Americana includes vintage automobiles, motorcycles, bicycles, jets, trains, tractors, steam engines and a 65-foot logging boat. Visitors also can see dolls and toys, historic logging and pioneer items, Native American artifacts, antique musical instruments and sheet music, and military collectibles. A pioneer village with more than 40 walk-in buildings and the Montana Fiddlers Hall of Fame also are on the grounds. Live History Days are held two days in July.

Hours: Daily 8-8, June-Aug.; Mon.-Sat. 8-5, Sun. 1:30-5, rest of year. Closed Easter and Christmas. **Cost:** $5; $2 (ages 3-12). **Phone:** (406) 883-6804.

POLSON-FLATHEAD HISTORICAL MUSEUM is at 708 Main St. Exhibits preserve the Native American and pioneer heritage of the surrounding area. Included are farm machinery, Native American artifacts, a chuck wagon, a stagecoach and a restored 1881 trading post. Marionettes created by puppeteer Blanche Harding are featured in an exhibit about the Lewis and Clark expedition. A model railroad is displayed. **Hours:** Mon.-Sat. 10-4, Memorial Day-Sept. 15. **Cost:** $5; free (ages 0-12). **Phone:** (406) 883-3049.

THE SHADOW **LAKE CRUISES** is on US 93E. Ninety-minute narrated tours of scenic Flathead Lake, the largest natural freshwater lake west of the Mississippi, are offered. Passengers enjoy views of the majestic Mission Mountains as well as 2,163-acre Wild Horse Island, inhabited by such wildlife as bighorn sheep, mule deer and wild horses Two-hour dinner cruises also are offered.

Hours: Ninety-minute tour requires a minimum of 6 people and departs daily at 1, 4 and 7:30, early spring-early winter. Dinner cruises depart Wed. and Sun. at 7. **Cost:** Ninety-minute tour $15; free (ages 0-5); $40 (family, two adults and two children). Dinner cruise $30. Reservations are recommended. **Phone:** (406) 883-3636.

RECREATIONAL ACTIVITIES
White-water Rafting
• **Flathead Raft Co.** is at 1305 US 93. Other activities are available. **Hours:** Rafting trips are offered daily, Memorial Day-early Sept. Departure times vary; phone ahead. **Phone:** (406) 883-5838 or (800) 654-4359.

AMERICAS BEST VALUE PORT POLSON INN   (406)883-5385
🏵️🏵️ **Motel** $59-$160 **Address:** 49825 US Hwy 93 E 59860 **Location:** Just s of downtown. **Facility:** 43 units, some efficiencies and kitchens. 2 stories (no elevator), interior/exterior corridors. **Parking:** winter plug-ins. **Terms:** cancellation fee imposed. **Guest Services:** coin laundry. (BIZ) 🛜 /SOME UNITS 🐾 🎬 🖥️ 🖨️

Plan complete trip
routings with the
TripTik® Travel Planner
on AAA.com/CAA.ca

BEST WESTERN PLUS KWATAQNUK RESORT
(406)883-3636

🏵️🏵️🏵️
Hotel
$80-$171

Best Western
PLUS

AAA Benefit: Members save 10% or more with Best Western!

Address: 49708 US Hwy 93 E 59860 **Location:** Just s of downtown. **Facility:** 112 units. 2-3 stories, interior corridors. **Parking:** winter plug-ins. **Terms:** 3 day cancellation notice-fee imposed, resort fee. **Pool(s):** heated outdoor, heated indoor. **Activities:** hot tub, marina. **Guest Services:** valet laundry, area transportation.

(SAVE) 🔋 🍽️ 🍸 CALL 📶 🐾
(BIZ) 🛜 ✖️ 🎬 🖥️ 🖨️ /SOME UNITS 🐾

WHERE TO EAT

HOT SPOT THAI CAFE   406/883-4444
🏵️ Thai. Casual Dining. $6-$18 **AAA Inspector Notes:** The casual restaurant serves Americanized dishes, though with authentic spices. A climb up the stairs to the second floor leads to dining with views of Flathead Lake. **Address:** 50440 US Hwy 93 E 59860 **Location:** Just s of downtown. (L) (D)

RICCIARDI'S ON MAIN   406/883-2900
🏵️🏵️ Italian. Casual Dining. $12-$30 **AAA Inspector Notes:** You're in for a taste treat at this place, where Italian dishes are the standout and clam chowder is out of this world. Made-in-house pasta, meatballs and marinara enhance several dishes. Overlooking Flathead Lake, the dining room has a fireplace and earth tones for a comfortable feel. **Features:** full bar, happy hour. **Address:** 101 Main St 59860 **Location:** Just e from jct US 93 (2nd Ave E). **Parking:** on-site and street. (D)

POMPEYS PILLAR NATIONAL MONUMENT (D-6)

Pompeys Pillar National Monument is 1 mi. n. of Pompeys Pillar off I-94 exit 23. William Clark carved his name on this huge sandstone formation in 1806; it is the only physical evidence of the Lewis and Clark expedition through the area. Clark named the rock after guides Charbonneau and Sacagawea's son, Baptiste, whom he nicknamed Pomp. The pillar also bears Native American pictographs and the names of early trappers, soldiers and settlers. Interpretive tours are available upon request at the visitor center.

Daily 9-6, early May-Sept. 30. The site is accessible the rest of the year only by a half-mile walk from a parking area. Admission $7 (per private vehicle). Phone (406) 875-2400 for the visitor center, or (406) 896-5013 for the Bureau of Land Management.

PRAY pop. 681

CHICO HOT SPRINGS LODGE   406/333-4933
(fyi) Not evaluated. **Address:** 1 Old Chico Rd 59065 **Location:** I-90 exit 333, 23 mi s on US 89, 1.2 mi e on Murphy Ln (flashing yellow light), 0.5 mi n on E River Rd, then 1 mi e. Facilities, services, and décor characterize an economy property.

WHERE TO EAT

CHICO HOT SPRINGS RESTAURANT   406/333-4933
▼▼▼▼ American. Fine Dining. $9-$55 **AAA Inspector Notes:**
Historic. The kitchen consistently delivers on quality and creativity
with dishes such as scallops in green curry with an apricot chutney,
and tender rack of lamb with homemade basil jelly. Signature dishes
include the pine nut encrusted halibut and the orange flambé dessert.
The setting, in the historic lodge is a relaxing throwback to a time
without TVs and smartphones. A breakfast buffet also is offered. **Features:** full bar. **Reservations:** suggested. **Address:** 1 Old Chico Rd
59065 **Location:** I-90 exit 333, 23 mi s on US 89, 1.2 mi e on Murphy
Ln (flashing yellow light), 0.5 mi n on E River Rd, then 1 mi e; in Chico
Hot Springs Lodge. (B) (D)

PRYOR (E-5) pop. 618, elev. 4,065'

CHIEF PLENTY COUPS STATE PARK is 1 mi. w.
off SR 416 following signs to 1 Edgar/Pryor Rd. A
museum features relics and interpretive displays
that describe Crow Indian culture and Chief Plenty
Coups, the tribe's last traditional chief. The Crow
leader is buried near his home at nearby Medicine
Spring.

Fishing opportunities are available. Day of Honor,
an event featuring speakers and cultural activities,
takes place Labor Day weekend. **Time:** Allow 1 hour
minimum. **Hours:** Park open daily 8-8, May-Sept.
Visitor center open daily 10-5, May-Sept.; by appointment rest of year. **Cost:** $5 (per motorized ve-
hicle); $3 (per person arriving by other means).
Phone: (406) 252-1289. 🏕

RED LODGE (F-5) pop. 2,125, elev. 5,548'

• **Restaurants p. 202**
• **Hotels & Restaurants map & index p. 336**
• **Part of Yellowstone National Park area — see
map p. 326**

At the base of the Beartooth Mountains, Red
Lodge is an all-year resort town. Winter sports include downhill and cross-country skiing, while
summer pursuits range from trout fishing and
boating to water skiing on Cooney Reservoir *(see
Recreation Areas Chart).*

Local legend attributes the town's name to a tribe
of Crow Indians called the Red Lodge Clan, who
covered their tepees with the local red clay. Coal-
mining operations later drew many Europeans to the
area.

**Red Lodge Area Chamber of Commerce and
Visitors Center:** 701 N. Broadway, P.O. Box 988,
Red Lodge, MT 59068. **Phone:** (406) 446-1718.

Self-guiding tours: A guide distributed by the
chamber of commerce features a walking tour of the
historic district and includes buildings that once
served as schools, jails, courthouses, banks and
hospitals.

▼▼ **BEARTOOTH SCENIC HIGHWAY** is US 212
ᴳᴱᴹ from Red Lodge to the northeastern entrance of Yellowstone National Park via Cooke City.
The Native Americans called the original Beartooth
Pass the "trail above the eagles." This 64-mile road
begins at 5,650 feet and rises to the Beartooth Plateau via a series of switchbacks.

After cresting the plateau at an elevation of almost 11,000 feet, where an unobstructed view of
more than 75 miles is possible, the road winds past
snowfields, small lakes and fields of flowers. Finally
it descends into a dense pine forest, passing tumbling waterfalls and streams interspersed with occasional jagged peaks.

Many scenic overlooks have been constructed.
Even in mid-summer, cool temperatures can be expected at higher elevations; a jacket or sweater is
recommended. **Time:** Allow 3 hours minimum.
Hours: The two-lane highway is usually open Memorial Day through mid-Oct. Phone ahead to confirm schedule. **Phone:** (800) 226-7623.

**CARBON COUNTY HISTORICAL SOCIETY & MU-
SEUM** is at 224 N. Broadway Ave. This local history
museum occupies two floors of the 1909 Labor
Temple, a three-story red brick building in Red
Lodge's historic business district. Among the exhibits on the museum's main floor are rodeo memorabilia, guns, Native American artifacts and a
stagecoach.

Simulated coal and hard rock mines on the lower
level help visitors imagine what working in the area's
coal mines was like at the turn of the 20th century.
Time: Allow 1 hour minimum. **Hours:** Mon.-Sat.
10-5, Sun. 11-3, Memorial Day-Columbus Day;
Thurs.-Fri. 10-5, Sat. 11-3, rest of year. **Cost:** $5; $3
(ages 6-17); $12 (family, two adults and children
ages 6-17 in the same household). **Phone:** (406)
446-3667.

RECREATIONAL ACTIVITIES

Fishing

• **Fly Fishing Only Adventures** offers fishing trips
on the Yellowstone River. **Hours:** Trips are available daily year-round. Departure times vary;
phone ahead. **Phone:** (406) 446-3819 or (406)
425-1761.

Skiing

• **Red Lodge Mountain Resort** is 6 mi. w. to 305
Ski Run Rd. **Hours:** Skiing available daily 8-5,
late Nov.-early Apr. **Phone:** (406) 446-2610 or
(800) 444-8977.

White-water Rafting

• (SAVE) **Adventure Whitewater Inc.** meets passengers on SR 78 at the red barn 1 mi. n. of Absa-
rokee. Other activities are offered. **Hours:** Rafting
trips daily at 10, 2 and 5:30, Memorial Day
weekend-Labor Day. **Phone:** (406) 446-3061 or
(800) 897-3061.

COMFORT INN OF RED LODGE   (406)446-4469 (21)
▼▼ ▼▼ Hotel $99-$185 **Address:** 612 N Broadway Ave 59068 **Location:** Jct US 212 and SR 78, north entrance. **Facility:** 55 units. 2
stories (no elevator), interior corridors. **Parking:** winter plug-ins.
Pool(s): heated indoor. **Activities:** hot tub, limited exercise equipment. **Guest Services:** coin laundry.
CALL 📞ⓜ 🛏 (BIZ) 📶 ⊠ 🅱 🅾 ⊇ / SOME UNITS 🔒

(See map & index p. 336.)

LU PINE INN   (406)446-1321 [24]
♥♥ Hotel $69-$149 **Address:** 702 S Hauser Ave 59068 **Location:** 0.4 mi s, just w of US 212. **Facility:** 46 units, some efficiencies. 2 stories (no elevator), interior corridors. **Parking:** winter plug-ins. **Terms:** resort fee. **Pool(s):** heated indoor. **Activities:** sauna, hot tub, exercise room. **Guest Services:** coin laundry.

🏊 BIZ 📶 ✕ 🖥 / SOME UNITS 🐾 📞 🎫

THE POLLARD   (406)446-0001 [22]
♥♥ Historic Hotel $75-$275 **Address:** 2 N Broadway Ave 59068 **Location:** US 212; downtown. **Facility:** A history room is among the common spaces at this 1893 inn. All guest rooms are supplied with robes. 39 units. 3 stories, interior corridors. **Parking:** plug-ins. **Terms:** check-in 4 pm, 14 day cancellation notice-fee imposed. **Dining:** The Pub at the Pollard, Vintage One Bistro, see separate listings. **Activities:** sauna, exercise room.

🍴 BIZ 📶 ✕ / SOME UNITS 🆓 🖥

ROCK CREEK RESORT   (406)446-1111 [25]

♥♥♥
Resort Hotel
$130-$390
Address: 6380 US Hwy 212 S 59068 **Location:** 5.8 mi s. Adjacent to a wilderness area. **Facility:** This resort at the base of the Beartooth Mountains offers townhouse, condominium and standard lodgings; only the main hotel building has an elevator. Many units overlook the rushing waters of Rock Creek. 87 units, some three bedrooms, efficiencies, kitchens, cabins and condominiums. 1-3 stories, interior/exterior corridors. **Terms:** 15 day cancellation notice-fee imposed, resort fee. **Amenities:** Some: safes. **Dining:** Old Piney Dell, see separate listing. **Pool(s):** heated indoor. **Activities:** sauna, hot tub, fishing, tennis, cross country skiing, bicycles, playground, exercise room. **Guest Services:** coin laundry. **Featured Amenity:** continental breakfast.

SAVE 🍴 🏊 BIZ 📶 ✕ 🎫 / SOME UNITS 🆓 📞 🍽

YODELER MOTEL   (406)446-1435 [23]
♥ Motel $60-$140 **Address:** 601 S Broadway Ave 59068 **Location:** Just s on US 212. **Facility:** 23 units, some two bedrooms and kitchens. 2 stories (no elevator), exterior corridors. **Parking:** winter plug-ins. **Terms:** cancellation fee imposed, resort fee. **Activities:** hot tub.

🍴 HS 📶 ✕ 📞 🍽 🖥 / SOME UNITS 🆓 🎫

WHERE TO EAT

BOGART'S   406/446-1784 [18]
♥♥ American. Casual Dining. $6-$17 **AAA Inspector Notes:** The local-favorite restaurant offers specialty pizzas, Mexican dishes and standard American cuisine amid Humphrey Bogart memorabilia, wild animal busts and varied antiques. Large portions of homemade sour cream chicken enchiladas, charbroiled burgers, pasta and surf and turf are served. **Features:** full bar, happy hour. **Address:** 11 S Broadway Ave 59068 **Location:** City Center. **Parking:** street only.

L D

BRIDGE CREEK BACKCOUNTRY KITCHEN & WINE BAR
                                                   406/446-9900 [20]
♥♥ American. Casual Dining. $10-$33 **AAA Inspector Notes:** The restaurant is a "must-go" spot for visitors to the town. Extensive, award-winning wine choices complement the chef's creative preparations. A menu staple is the "famous" clam chowder. **Features:** full bar. **Address:** 116 S Broadway Ave 59068 **Location:** Center. **Parking:** street only. L D CALL 📞M

CARBON COUNTY STEAKHOUSE   406/446-4025 [19]
♥♥♥ American. Casual Dining. $10-$30 **AAA Inspector Notes:** The in-house-cut organic steaks are the star attraction. The comfortable setting offers some al fresco dining in season. Lunch is served from Memorial Day to Labor Day. **Features:** full bar, patio dining, Sunday brunch. **Reservations:** suggested. **Address:** 121 S Broadway Ave 59068 **Location:** Center; in historic district. **Parking:** on-site and street. D

CHINA GARDEN   406/446-9909 [22]
♥♥ Chinese. Casual Dining. $8-$17 **AAA Inspector Notes:** Tasty food is served in a casual setting. The décor is contemporary rather than traditional. **Address:** 202 S Broadway Ave 59068 **Location:** Center. **Parking:** street only. L D

OLD PINEY DELL   406/446-1196 [23]
♥♥ American. Casual Dining. $17-$28 **AAA Inspector Notes:** Steak, seafood, veal and pasta entrees head up the list of eclectic selections served in this rustic, 1920s log cabin, adjacent to Rock Creek. **Features:** full bar, Sunday brunch. **Reservations:** suggested. **Address:** 6380 US Hwy 212 S 59068 **Location:** 5.8 mi s; in Rock Creek Resort. D 🎫

THE PUB AT THE POLLARD   406/446-0001 [17]
♥♥ English. Gastropub. $8-$11 **AAA Inspector Notes:** Historic. The English tradition is followed through at this pub. Of course, there are the Guinness, Beck's and other ales, but you'll also find less traditional libation options. Along with Scotch eggs, shepherd's pie, jacket potatoes and fish and chips, the menu features some regional foods such as bison and lamb. A game of darts is the norm while having a Guinness. **Features:** full bar, happy hour. **Address:** 2 N Broadway Ave 59068 **Location:** US 212; downtown; in The Pollard. **Parking:** on-site and street. D CALL 📞M

RED LODGE PIZZA CO.   406/446-3333 [21]
♥♥ Pizza. Family Dining. $7-$20 **AAA Inspector Notes:** Fresh ingredients line the nightly salad bar, and varied items go into creative pizzas or calzones made with homemade dough. Diners can get single slices or whole pies. A pizza bar is set up Monday and Tuesday. **Features:** full bar. **Address:** 115 S Broadway Ave 59068 **Location:** Center; in historic district. **Parking:** on-site and street.

L D CALL 📞M

VINTAGE ONE BISTRO   406/446-0001 [16]
♥♥♥
Regional American Casual Dining
$10-$32
AAA Inspector Notes: Historic. You may find bison rib-eye, elk medallions and in-house-smoked ribs and salmon. The intimate dining room is in a historic hotel. The décor includes Western art on the walls, wood accents and seats upholstered in leather. **Features:** full bar, patio dining. **Address:** 2 N Broadway Ave 59068 **Location:** US 212; downtown; in The Pollard. **Parking:** on-site and street. B D CALL 📞M

RED BOX CAR DRIVE-IN   406/446-2152
[fyi] Not evaluated. Popular with the locals, the summer drive-in is known for its burgers, hot dogs and shakes. Guests can relax on the patio next to Rock Creek. **Address:** 1300 S Broadway Ave 59068 **Location:** S on US 212.

RONAN (C-2) pop. 1,871

NINEPIPE AND PABLO NATIONAL WILDLIFE REFUGES are 4 mi. s. off US 93, and 3 mi. n. off US 93 then 1 mi. w. on Reservoir Rd., respectively. Each refuge covers more than 2,000 acres. Primarily of interest to bird-watchers, these areas are inhabited by ducks, geese and other water birds. A cooperative state, federal and tribal wildlife-viewing area is at Ninepipe National Wildlife Refuge.

Hours: Refuges are open daily dawn-dusk. Portions of Ninepipe are closed during hunting season (late Sept.-early Jan.) and nesting season (Mar. 1-July 15). The south and west sides of Pablo are closed to public use; the entire refuge is closed during hunting season. **Cost:** Free. **Phone:** (406) 644-2211.

STARLITE MOTEL   406/676-7000
♥ Motel. Rates not provided. **Address:** 18 Main St SW 59864 **Location:** Just w of jct US 93 and Main St. **Facility:** 15 units. 2 stories (no elevator), exterior corridors. **Parking:** winter plug-ins.

🍴 📶 📞 🖥 / SOME UNITS 🆓

ROUNDUP (D-5) pop. 1,788, elev. 3,226'

Renowned for the natural geographical design that made it ideal for herding livestock, Roundup features mountainous scenery and tree-lined streets. Fishing opportunities abound in the Musselshell River and at nearby Fort Peck Reservoir and Deadman's Basin.

MUSSELSHELL VALLEY HISTORICAL MUSEUM, 524 First St. W., houses a variety of items detailing Roundup's history, including fossils, Native American artifacts and paintings. Changing exhibits are featured in summer. On the grounds are a smithy, a print shop, a restored 1932 Pietenpol airplane and the 1884 NF Ranch house. **Hours:** Daily 1-5, May-Sept. **Cost:** Donations. **Phone:** (406) 323-1525 or (406) 323-1662.

BUSY BEE RESTAURANT & GIFT SHOP   406/323-2204

American Casual Dining $7-$25

AAA Inspector Notes: Both the Honeycomb and Fireside dining rooms at this restaurant are well suited to family dining. Selections include crisp chicken, tender beer-battered shrimp and homemade pie. Prime rib is offered weekend evenings. The 1950s style diner area also is a fun place to dine. **Features:** beer & wine. **Address:** 317 1st Ave W 59072 **Location:** South edge of city on US 12 and 87.

B L D

ST. IGNATIUS (C-2) pop. 842, elev. 2,940'

ST. IGNATIUS MISSION is .2 mi. s. on US 93 to sign, then .2 mi. e. to 300 Beartrack Ave. Established in 1854 by the Jesuit Fathers and Brothers, the 1891 brick church is decorated with 58 dry-fresco paintings executed about 1900 by Brother Joseph Carignano, the mission cook.

The missionaries' log cabin residence and chapel feature Native American and religious items. The first residence of the Sisters of Providence also is on the grounds. **Hours:** Mission daily 9-7, June-Aug.; 9-5, rest of year. Museum daily 10-4, Memorial Day-Labor Day. **Cost:** Donations. **Phone:** (406) 745-2768.

SUNSET MOTEL   406/745-3900

Motel $60-$80 **Address:** 333 Mountain View 59865 **Location:** Just s of downtown, exit US 93. **Facility:** 8 units. 2 stories (no elevator), exterior corridors.

ST. MARY

- Hotels & Restaurants map & index p. 168
- Part of Glacier National Park area — see map p. 163

TWO SISTERS CAFE   406/732-5535 (23)

American. Casual Dining. $13-$24 **AAA Inspector Notes:** Driving down the road from Glacier National Park, you can't miss the bright, multicolored café. This eatery, with its funky décor, serves up tasty twists on traditional favorites in a casual family-friendly setting. **Features:** full bar. **Address:** US 89 59411 **Location:** On US 89, 4.5 mi n. L D

ST. REGIS pop. 319

LITTLE RIVER MOTEL   (406)649-2713

Motel $45-$85

Address: 424 Little River Ln 59866 **Location:** I-90 exit 33, just n to flashing light, just w, then just sw. **Facility:** 11 units, some cottages. 1 story, exterior corridors. **Parking:** winter plug-ins. **Featured Amenity: continental breakfast.**

SUPER 8-ST. REGIS   (406)649-2422

Hotel $59-$93

Address: 9 Old Hwy 10 E 59866 **Location:** I-90 exit 33, just n. **Facility:** 53 units, some kitchens. 2 stories (no elevator), interior/exterior corridors. **Parking:** winter plug-ins. **Activities:** hot tub. **Guest Services:** coin laundry. **Featured Amenity: continental breakfast.**

SCOBEY (A-7) pop. 1,017, elev. 2,507'

DANIELS COUNTY MUSEUM AND PIONEER TOWN is at 7 W. County Rd. Some 40 buildings in this restored pioneer town portray early 20th-century homestead life. A collection of period antiques includes vintage vehicles. **Tours:** Guided tours are available. **Time:** Allow 1 hour, 30 minutes minimum. **Hours:** Daily 12:30-4:30, Memorial Day-Labor Day; Fri. 1-4 and by appointment, rest of year. **Cost:** $7; $4 (ages 5-12). **Phone:** (406) 487-5965.

SEELEY LAKE (C-2) pop. 1,659, elev. 4,028'
• Restaurants p. 204

Seeley Lake is a year-round recreation area tucked between the Mission Mountains and Swan Range on scenic SR 83. In summer visitors can indulge in camping, hiking, golf, fishing, swimming, boating, backpacking and horseback riding. Fewer than 10 miles from town are Placid Lake and Salmon Lake state parks (see Recreation Areas Chart); Seeley Lake itself has three Forest Service campgrounds, and at the north end of the lake is the 3.5-mile-long Clearwater Canoe Trail. Northeast of Seeley Lake is the 2.5-mile-long Morrell Falls National Recreation Trail, rated as "easy." Just east of the Morrell Falls trailhead access road is the Pyramid Pass Trail into Bob Marshall Wilderness. Head north to enjoy the 3.2-mile-long Holland Falls National Recreation Trail.

In the winter the average snow on the ground is about 3 feet. With a Nordic ski trail system for cross-country skiing and more than 300 miles of groomed snowmobile trails, the Seeley-Swan area provides good opportunities for winter recreation. Contact the Seeley Lake Ranger District office, 3 miles north of town on SR 83, for maps and brochures about access to trails and wildlife in the area; phone (406) 677-2233. Other local wintertime diversions include cultural presentations, ice fishing and dog sledding.

Seeley Lake Area Chamber of Commerce: 2920 SR 83 N., P.O. Box 516, Seeley Lake, MT 59868. **Phone:** (406) 677-2880.

LINDEY'S PRIME STEAK HOUSE   406/677-9229

Steak
Casual Dining
$22-$29

AAA Inspector Notes: Diners should be craving beef, because this menu features only flavorful, aged Prime sirloin and beef. Sharing is allowed. As a highlight during the summer, guests can enjoy thick "bayburgers," as they sit outside and overlook Seeley Lake. **Features:** full bar. **Address:** 3129 SR 83 59868 **Location:** Just s. D

SHELBY (B-3) pop. 3,376, elev. 3,276'

Shelby was one of the towns that the Great Northern Railroad left in its path as it pushed across the prairie. In its heyday, the town was paradise to cowboys after months on the range. A Saturday night might include carousing, horse racing, or—as once happened—holding up a passing opera troupe and making the train conductor do a clog dance to the rhythm of bullets.

Ranching, farming and the railroad supported the town until the 1922 discovery of oil in the Kevin-Sunburst fields. The area retains a few working oil pumps. Shelby's location on major transportation corridors established its right as an inland port for truck and rail shipping via the Northwest Express Transportation Authority.

Shelby Area Chamber of Commerce: 100 Montana Ave., P.O. Box 865, Shelby, MT 59474. **Phone:** (406) 434-7184.

MARIAS MUSEUM OF HISTORY AND ART is 4 blks. s. of US 2 at 206 12th Ave. N. Exhibits depicting highlights of Toole County history focus on the oil industry, homesteading, the 1923 Dempsey-Gibbons prize fight (which nearly bankrupted the community), barbed wire, and dinosaur and other fossil discoveries. **Time:** Allow 1 hour minimum. **Hours:** Mon.-Fri. 1-5 and 7-9, Sat. 1-4, June-Aug.; Tues. noon-4 or by appointment, rest of year. Closed major holidays. **Cost:** Donations. **Phone:** (406) 424-2551.

BEST WESTERN SHELBY INN & SUITES   (406)424-4560

Hotel
$100-$125

AAA Benefit: Members save 10% or more with Best Western!

Address: 1948 Roosevelt Hwy 59474 **Location:** I-15 exit 363, just w. **Facility:** 74 units. 3 stories, interior corridors. **Pool(s):** heated indoor. **Activities:** hot tub, exercise room. **Guest Services:** coin laundry, area transportation. **Featured Amenity:** breakfast buffet.

COMFORT INN OF SHELBY   (406)434-2212

Hotel
$83-$130

Address: 455 McKinley Ave 59474 **Location:** I-15 exit 363, just e, then just s. **Facility:** 128 units, some efficiencies. 3 stories, interior corridors. **Parking:** winter plug-ins. **Amenities:** *Some:* safes. **Pool(s):** heated indoor. **Activities:** sauna, hot tub, exercise room. **Guest Services:** coin laundry, area transportation. **Featured Amenity:** breakfast buffet.

O'HAIRE MANOR MOTEL   406/434-5555

Motel. Rates not provided. **Address:** 204 2nd St S 59474 **Location:** Just s of Main St via Maple St. **Facility:** 36 units. 2 stories (no elevator), interior/exterior corridors. **Parking:** winter plug-ins. **Guest Services:** coin laundry.

WHERE TO EAT

KOW LOON RESTAURANT   406/434-2030

Chinese. Casual Dining. $8-$13 **AAA Inspector Notes:** Tasty food, large portions and a weekday lunch buffet draw folks from all around. The décor is minimal and the staff is very friendly at this downtown location. **Features:** full bar. **Address:** 220 Main St 59474 **Location:** Center. **Parking:** street only. L D CALL

SHERIDAN pop. 642

IN-BACK STEAKHOUSE   406/842-7632

American. Casual Dining. $6-$25 **AAA Inspector Notes:** Diners can expect huge portions of hand-cut fries, big juicy burgers, well-prepared steaks and fish entrées at this casual eatery set in picturesque Ruby Valley. **Features:** full bar. **Address:** 102 Mill St 59749 **Location:** Center. B L D

SIDNEY (B-8) pop. 5,191, elev. 1,950'

Sidney is a marketing center for sugar beets and wheat and serves an active oil drilling and coal mining region. One of the larger auction houses in Montana, the Sidney Livestock Market Center on E. Main Street conducts cattle auctions every Wednesday. Local attractions include Fort Union, a late 1800s trapping and trading post, and horseback and wagon train rides.

Sidney Area Chamber of Commerce and Agriculture: 909 S. Central Ave., Sidney, MT 59270. **Phone:** (406) 433-1916.

MONDAK HERITAGE CENTER is at 120 3rd Ave. S.E. The museum's lower level houses a re-created pioneer town. Upper-level galleries feature local and national traveling art exhibits. **Time:** Allow 1 hour minimum. **Hours:** Tues.-Fri. 10-4, Sat. 1-4. Closed major holidays. **Cost:** Free. **Phone:** (406) 433-3500.

BEST WESTERN GOLDEN PRAIRIE INN & SUITES
(406)433-4560

Hotel
$130-$170

AAA Benefit: Members save 10% or more with Best Western!

Address: 820 S Central Ave 59270 **Location:** 1.8 mi n of jct SR 16 and 200. **Facility:** 72 units. 3 stories, interior corridors. **Pool(s):** heated indoor. **Activities:** hot tub, exercise room. **Guest Services:** coin laundry. **Featured Amenity: full hot breakfast.**

HOLIDAY INN EXPRESS & SUITES
(406)433-3200

Hotel $189-$209 **Address:** 251 W Holly St 59270 **Location:** Just nw of jct SR 16 and 200. **Facility:** 75 units. 4 stories, interior corridors. **Terms:** cancellation fee imposed. **Pool(s):** heated indoor. **Activities:** hot tub, limited exercise equipment. **Guest Services:** coin laundry.

MICROTEL INN & SUITES BY WYNDHAM SIDNEY
(406)482-9011

Hotel $116-$179 **Address:** 1500 S Central Ave 59270 **Location:** 1.3 mi n of jct SR 16 and 200. **Facility:** 76 units. 4 stories, interior corridors. **Pool(s):** heated indoor. **Activities:** hot tub, exercise room. **Guest Services:** coin laundry.

CALL

RICHLAND INN & SUITES
406/433-6400

Motel
Rates not provided

Address: 1200 S Central Ave 59270 **Location:** 1.5 mi n of jct SR 16 and 200. **Facility:** 86 units. 2 stories, interior corridors. **Parking:** winter plug-ins. **Activities:** hot tub, exercise room. **Guest Services:** coin laundry. **Featured Amenity: breakfast buffet.**

SILVER GATE (F-4) pop. 20, elev. 7,389'

Resembling an alpine village, Silver Gate is said to be the only municipality in the nation whose building codes mandate that all structures be made of logs and other materials native to the area.

The town is at the northeast entrance to Yellowstone National Park *(see place listing p. 326)*; nearby Cooke City *(see place listing p. 152)* also has access to the park. Silver Gate is an outfitting center for both cross-country skiing and snowmobiling. Fly fishing is excellent in nearby lakes and streams.

 BEARTOOTH SCENIC HIGHWAY—see Red Lodge p. 201.

STEVENSVILLE (D-2) pop. 1,809, elev. 3,524'

HISTORIC ST. MARY'S MISSION is at the w. end of Fourth St. at 315 Charlos St. The mission was established in 1841 by Father Pierre DeSmet. The present complex includes the 1880s-style restored chapel and a study, dining room and kitchen. Also restored is Father Anthony Ravalli's log house, which contains a pharmacy with a "ride-up" window. Chief Victor's cabin is a small museum that displays original furnishings and Native American and missionary artifacts.

Time: Allow 30 minutes minimum. **Hours:** Guided 1-hour tours are given Tues.-Sat. 10-4, Apr. 15-Oct. 15. **Cost:** $7; $6 (ages 60+); $5 (ages 7-17). **Phone:** (406) 777-5734.

BITTERROOT RIVER BED AND BREAKFAST   (406)777-5205

Bed & Breakfast $99-$139 **Address:** 501 South Ave 59870 **Location:** 1 mi s on Main St (SR 269), just w. **Facility:** 4 units. 2 stories (no elevator), interior corridors. **Terms:** 7 day cancellation notice-fee imposed, resort fee. **Activities:** fishing, bicycles.

SUPERIOR (C-1) pop. 812

RECREATIONAL ACTIVITIES
White-water Rafting

- **Pangaea River Rafting** departs from 11111 Mullan Rd. E. Other activities are available. **Hours:** Rafting trips are offered daily at 10:30, 12:30 and 4, Apr.-Sept. Phone ahead to confirm schedule. **Phone:** (406) 239-2392, or (877) 239-2392 for reservations.

- **ROW Adventures** departs from 62 Lynch Ranch Ln. **Hours:** White-water rafting trips depart daily at 9, July 8-Labor Day. **Phone:** (208) 765-0841 or (800) 451-6034.

- **Wiley E. Waters-Clark Fork** trips depart from 201 William Lloyd Ln. **Hours:** Full- and half-day rafting trips generally depart daily at 9 (PST), June 1-early Sept. Phone ahead to confirm schedule. **Phone:** (208) 457-1092, (509) 703-6564 or (888) 502-1900.

BIG SKY MOTEL   (406)822-4831

Motel $86-$96 **Address:** 103 4th Ave E 59872 **Location:** I-90 exit 47, just n. **Facility:** 24 units, some two bedrooms. 2 stories (no elevator), exterior corridors. **Parking:** winter plug-ins. **Terms:** cancellation fee imposed. **Guest Services:** coin laundry.

TERRY (D-7) pop. 605, elev. 2,253'

In the heart of agate country, Terry was the home of acclaimed photographer Evelyn Cameron. Many of the pictures she took 1894-1928 to chronicle the lives of Terry's early settlers were compiled in a book more than 50 years later, "Photographing Montana" by Donna Lucey.

Miles City Area Chamber of Commerce—Terry: 511 Pleasant St., Miles City, MT 59301. **Phone:** (406) 234-2890.

PRAIRIE COUNTY MUSEUM is at 101 S. Logan Ave. at jct. Laundre Ave. Housed in the Old State Bank of Terry building, the museum displays local memorabilia. A dentist's office, a barbershop, a schoolroom and hospital rooms are among the highlights. Area fossils also are featured.

Visitors also can see an unusual outhouse, a homestead shack, a depot and a caboose. The Evelyn Cameron Gallery features a collection of photographs that Cameron took of the area in the early 20th century. **Hours:** Mon. and Wed.-Fri. 9-3, Sat.-Sun. 1-4, Memorial Day weekend-Labor Day. **Cost:** Donations. **Phone:** (406) 635-4040.

THREE FORKS (E-3) pop. 1,869, elev. 4,061'

Three Forks was a favorite Native American hunting ground near the headwaters of the Missouri River. In 1805 Meriwether Lewis and William Clark documented their exploration of the beginning of the world's longest river system. Sacajawea (Sacagawea), the wife of one of their guides, lived in this area with the Shoshone until she was kidnapped and raised by the Minnetaree. A plaque in Sacajawea Park downtown commemorates her contribution to the success of the Lewis and Clark expedition.

The region supported several trading posts for trappers during the early 1800s; however, due to skirmishes with the Indians, their existence was short-lived. The first permanent non-native settlement was established nearby in 1864. As railroads and highways provided access to the area, settlers arrived, and Three Forks was founded in 1908. Excellent hunting and fishing opportunities continue to attract visitors today.

Three Forks Chamber of Commerce: 205 Main St., P.O. Box 1103, Three Forks, MT 59752. **Phone:** (406) 285-4753, or (406) 285-3011 (visitor center) Memorial Day weekend-Labor Day.

HEADWATERS HERITAGE MUSEUM is at 202 Main St. Life in the early 1900s is depicted through replicas that include a village blacksmith shop, railroad dispatcher's office, schoolhouse and millinery shop. Other rooms include a dental office, military display, kitchen and a beauty shop. An American-made anvil, found at the headwaters of the Missouri River and possibly the oldest of its kind in the United States, and the largest brown trout caught in Montana are displayed. Another exhibit features 571 types of barbed wire. **Hours:** Mon.-Sat. 9-5, Sun. 11-3, June-Sept.; by appointment rest of year. **Cost:** Donations. **Phone:** (406) 285-4778 in season, or (406) 285-3644 for appointments rest of year.

 LEWIS AND CLARK CAVERNS STATE PARK—see Whitehall p. 214.

MADISON BUFFALO JUMP STATE PARK is 5 mi. e. on I-90, then 7 mi. s. to 6990 Buffalo Jump Rd. As long as 2,000 years ago Native Americans hunted by driving buffalo off a cliff on this 618-acre site. Interpretive displays and hiking trails are offered. **Note:** Approach road is gravel; trailers are not recommended. **Time:** Allow 30 minutes minimum. **Hours:** Park open daily dawn-dusk. **Cost:** $5 (nonresidents per private vehicle); $3 (nonresidents arriving by other means); free (residents). **Phone:** (406) 994-4042. 🛖

MISSOURI HEADWATERS STATE PARK is 3 mi. e., then 3 mi. n. of US 10 to 1585 Trident Junction. Discovered July 27, 1805, by the Lewis and Clark expedition, the headwaters in this 527-acre park are formed by the joining of the Madison, Gallatin and Jefferson rivers. A scenic overlook and a campground are nearby. *See Recreation Areas Chart.* **Hours:** Park open daily dawn-dusk. **Cost:** $5 (nonresidents per private vehicle); $3 (nonresidents arriving by other means); free (residents). Camping fee $23 (nonresidents); $18 (nonresidents with a Montana State Park passport); $15 (residents). **Phone:** (406) 994-4042. 🅰 🖾 🐾 🛖

BROKEN SPUR MOTEL   406/285-3237

🔷 Motel $65-$125 **Address:** 124 W Elm (Hwy 2) 59752 **Location:** I-90 exit 278 westbound, 1.3 mi sw; exit 274 eastbound, 1 mi s on SR 287 to jct SR 2, then 3 mi se. **Facility:** 24 units, some efficiencies and cabins. 2 stories (no elevator), exterior corridors. **Parking:** winter plug-ins. **Featured Amenity: continental breakfast.**

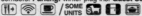

FORT THREE FORKS MOTEL & RV PARK   (406)285-3233

🔷 Motel $48-$109 **Address:** 10776 Hwy 287 59752 **Location:** I-90 exit 274, just n. **Facility:** 24 units. 2 stories (no elevator), exterior corridors. **Parking:** winter plug-ins. **Guest Services:** coin laundry.

SACAJAWEA HOTEL   406/285-6515

🔲 **Historic Hotel** Did not meet all AAA rating requirements for locking devices in some guest rooms at time of last evaluation on 02/18/2012. **Address:** 5 N Main St 59752 **Location:** I-90 exit 278, 0.5 mi s. Facilities, services, and décor characterize a mid-scale property. Rooms in this 1910 building have an old-fashioned ambience.

WHERE TO EAT

POMPEY'S GRILL   406/285-6515

🔷🔷🔷 Western American. Casual Dining. $16-$31 **AAA Inspector Notes:** *Historic.* Hand-cut Certified Angus steaks and specialty seafood are prepared to perfection. Pasta dishes and a Montana farm rack of lamb also are offered. The bar boasts reclaimed wood from the Lucin Cutoff railroad trestle, which once spanned the Great Salt Lake. Pompey was the name of Sacajawea's son. **Features:** full bar. **Reservations:** suggested. **Address:** 5 N Main St 59752 **Location:** I-90 exit 278, 0.5 mi s; in Sacajawea Hotel. **Parking:** street only. 🄳 CALL 🄼

TOWNSEND (D-3) pop. 1,878, elev. 3,813'

BROADWATER COUNTY MUSEUM, 133 N. Walnut St., features pioneer artifacts chronicling local history. **Time:** Allow 30 minutes minimum. **Hours:** Daily 1-5, mid-May to mid-Sept. Closed July 4. **Cost:** Free. **Phone:** (406) 266-5252.

TROY (B-1) pop. 938

Nestled between forested mountains on the banks of the Kootenai River, Troy is Montana's lowest-elevation town. Pioneers called the region Montana's Wilds, for its deep valleys, steep mountains and dense forests. Gold prospectors camped in the area in the mid-1880s, but the town wasn't permanently settled until the Great Northern established a freight yard here in 1892.

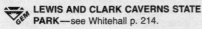

Ross Creek Cedars Scenic Area, 21 miles south on SR 56 then 4 miles west on Ross Creek Road, has a .9-mile interpretive nature trail that leads visitors through a 100-acre stand of old growth western red cedar. The lush woodland, with trees upwards of 8 feet thick and 175 feet tall, is a modified temperate rain forest.

Troy Chamber of Commerce: P.O. Box 3005, Troy, MT 59935. **Phone:** (406) 295-1064.

KOOTENAI FALLS is 5 mi. e. on US 2. The Kootenai River foams through a narrow, rocky gorge, forming a cataract that drops 300 feet over a distance of several hundred yards. Sacred to the Kootenai Indians, the area can be traversed via a network of trails.

Bridging the Burlington Northern Santa Fe mainline, a trail—the uppermost portion of which is paved and features an interpretive display and a picnic area—leads down through the forest to the edge of the gorge. Visitors can continue east to the falls or west to a swinging suspension bridge that connects to trails on the north side of the river. **Note:** A portion of the trail system lacks guardrails, is uneven and can be muddy in wet weather. **Time:** Allow 1 hour minimum. **Hours:** Daily dawn-dusk. **Cost:** Free.

ULM (C-3) pop. 738, elev. 3,346'

FIRST PEOPLES BUFFALO JUMP STATE PARK is off I-15 exit 270, then 3.5 mi. w. on Ulm-Vaughn Rd. The park preserves one of the largest known buffalo jump sites and interprets the buffalo culture. Exhibits depict how Native Americans hunted bison by stampeding them over the cliffs. Featured are a large mounted buffalo, implements fashioned from buffalo remains and a furnished tepee made of buffalo hides. Interpretive trails to the cliffs and grasslands are available.

Time: Allow 1 hour minimum. **Hours:** Daily 8-6, Apr.-Sept.; Wed.-Sat. 10-4, Sun. noon-4, rest of year. **Cost:** $5 (per private motorized vehicle); $3 (per person arriving by other means). **Phone:** (406) 866-2217.

VIRGELLE (B-4) elev. 2,560'

RECREATIONAL ACTIVITIES
Kayaking
- **Virgelle Merc & Missouri River Canoe Co.** is off US 87, then 7.5 mi. e. on a gravel road. Other activities are offered. **Hours:** Kayak and canoe trips are offered daily, mid-May to mid-Sept. Departure times vary; phone ahead. **Phone:** (406) 378-3110 or (800) 426-2926.

VIRGINIA CITY (E-3) pop. 190, elev. 5,822'

After fruitless panning along the Yellowstone River, six prospectors stumbled onto Alder Creek in May 1863, and their discovery of gold led to the establishment of a town. The settlement attracted thousands of miners and a band of renegades said to have committed more than 190 murders in 6 months. The miners formed a secret group called The Vigilantes, who captured and hanged 21 of the criminals, including the outlaws' leader, the sheriff.

One of the older cities in the state, Virginia City served as territorial capital 1865-75. More than 130 early buildings have been preserved; others have been reconstructed and can be visited. Among these are the state's first newspaper office, an equipped pharmacy of the period, the Wells Fargo Express Office, the Bale of Hay Saloon and general stores carrying 1860-80 merchandise. Boot Hill Cemetery contains the graves of road agents hanged by vigilantes in 1864.

Gold panning, hunting and fishing opportunities are available. A 1935 gold dredge can be seen at the River of Gold Mining Museum. All facilities are open Memorial Day through Labor Day.

Virginia City Visitor Information Center: 300 W. Wallace St., P.O. Box 338, Virginia City, MT 59755. **Phone:** (406) 843-5247 or (800) 829-2969.

GILBERT BREWERY is at Hamilton and Cover sts. Featured is "The Brewery Follies," a contemporary comedy variety show by the Brewery Players. Performances take place in a renovated 1860s brewery. **Note:** According to the attraction, "Due to mature content, parental guidance suggested." **Hours:** Brewery Follies performances are given daily at 4 and 8 p.m., late May-late Sept. **Cost:** Brewery Follies $18. Reservations are recommended. **Phone:** (406) 843-5218 or (800) 829-2969, ext. 3.

J. SPENCER WATKINS MEMORIAL MUSEUM is at 219 W. Wallace St. Displays chronicle the history of pioneer miners, ranchers and farmers. **Hours:** Daily 10-5, Memorial Day-Sept. 30. **Cost:** Donations. **Phone:** (406) 843-5500.

NEVADA CITY is 1.5 mi. w. on SR 287. The city sprang up with the discovery of gold in 1863. Some of Montana Territory's original buildings have been moved to this site and restored to form the Nevada City Museum. The Music Hall contains a collection of mechanical musical machines.

Time: Allow 1 hour minimum. **Hours:** Daily 10-6, mid-May to mid-Sept. **Cost:** Nevada City Museum or train ride $8; $6 (ages 6-16 and 55+). River of Gold $15 (per bucket). Combination tickets are available. **Phone:** (406) 843-5247 or (800) 829-2969.

Alder Gulch Shortline Railroad runs between Virginia City and Nevada City. The small, narrow-gauge train is pulled by a gasoline powered engine dubbed No. 8. A train pulled by a refurbished Baldwin 1910 steam locomotive, No. 12, also operates.

Time: Allow 1 hour minimum. **Hours:** No. 8 operates daily 10-5, May-Sept. **Cost:** Round-trip fare on No. 8 $8; $6 (ages 6-16 and senior citizens). River of Gold $15 (per bucket). Combination tickets are available. **Phone:** (406) 843-5247.

THOMPSON-HICKMAN MEMORIAL MUSEUM, 220 E. Wallace St., offers state and local memorabilia interpreting the history, geology and culture of 19th-century Virginia City. **Time:** Allow 30 minutes minimum. **Hours:** Daily 10-5, Memorial Day-Labor Day. **Cost:** Donations. **Phone:** (406) 843-5238.

VIRGINIA CITY OPERA HOUSE is at 338 W. Wallace St. Vaudeville and melodramas are performed in the style of the 19th-century touring companies that regularly stopped in this town. Three shows are performed during the season. **Hours:** Shows Wed. and Sat. at 2 and 7; Sun. and Thurs. at 2, Fri. and Tues. at 7, June 1-Labor Day. **Cost:** $16; $15 (senior citizens and military with ID); $10 (ages 0-17). Reservations are required. **Phone:** (800) 829-2969 for reservations.

WEST GLACIER (B-2) pop. 227, elev. 3,215'
- Hotels & Restaurants map & index p. 168
- Part of Glacier National Park area — see map p. 163

West Glacier is the western rail and highway entrance to Glacier National Park *(see place listing p. 163)*. White-water rafting, skiing, hiking and year-round camping are the area's most popular recreational activities. Fishing and golf also draw visitors in pursuit of outdoor fun. One golf course has rules that include: "do not throw clubs or balls at tame deer" and "players may move balls without penalty to avoid elk tracks."

KRUGER HELICOP-TOURS is 1 mi. w. of Glacier National Park on SR 2. Narrated 30-minute and 1-hour tours reveal breathtaking bird's-eye views of glaciers as you fly over Glacier National Park. Waterfalls and lakes rarely seen by park visitors are some additional highlights providing photographic opportunities. **Time:** Allow 30 minutes minimum. **Hours:** Departures require a minimum of four people. Daily 8-5, June-Sept. A 24-hour notice is required to cancel a tour reservation. **Cost:** Fares $120-$940 per person. **Phone:** (406) 387-4565, (406) 857-3893 in the off-season or (800) 220-6565.

RECREATIONAL ACTIVITIES
Backpacking
- **Glacier Guides** is 1.5 mi. w. on US 2. Other activities are offered. **Hours:** Backpacking trips are offered daily, May-Sept. Departure times vary; phone ahead. **Phone:** (406) 387-5555 or (800) 521-7238.

White-water Rafting
- **Glacier Raft Co.** is on Going-to-the-Sun Rd. at the west entrance to Glacier National Park. Other activities are offered. **Hours:** Rafting trips are offered daily, May-Sept. Departure times vary; phone ahead. **Phone:** (406) 888-5454 or (800) 235-6781.
- **Great Northern Whitewater Float Trips** is 1 mi. w. to 12127 US 2 E. Other activities are offered.

Hours: Rafting trips are offered daily, May 1 to mid-Sept. Departure times vary; phone ahead. **Phone:** (406) 387-5340 or (800) 735-7897.
- **Montana Raft Co.** is 1.5 mi. w. on US 2. Other activities are offered. **Hours:** Rafting trips are offered daily, May-Sept. Departure times vary; phone ahead. **Phone:** (406) 387-5555 or (800) 521-7238.
- **Wild River Adventures** is 1 mi. w. on US 2. Other activities are offered. **Hours:** Rafting trips are offered daily, late May to mid-Sept. Departure times vary; phone ahead. **Phone:** (406) 387-9453 or (800) 700-7056.

GLACIER RAFT COMPANY CABINS AT GLACIER OUTDOOR CENTER   (406)888-5454

Cabin
$126-$600

Address: 12400 US Hwy 2 E 59936 **Location:** On US 2, 0.5 mi w. **Facility:** 12 cabins. 1-2 stories (no elevator), exterior corridors. **Terms:** closed 10/16-4/30, check-in 4 pm, 45 day cancellation notice-fee imposed. **Activities:** fishing.

GLACIERS' MOUNTAIN RESORT, LLC   (406)387-5712
Cabin $119-$245 **Address:** 1385 Old Hwy 2 E 59936 **Location:** 6 mi sw on US 2, between MM 147 and 148, on west side of road to Old US 2, then just w. **Facility:** 5 cabins. 1 story, exterior corridors. **Parking:** winter plug-ins. **Terms:** check-in 4 pm, 2 night minimum stay - seasonal, 30 day cancellation notice-fee imposed.

SILVERWOLF LOG CHALETS   (406)387-4448

Cabin
$125-$179

Address: 160 Gladys Glen Rd 59936 **Location:** 6 mi sw on US 2; close to Coram, outside of park. Located in a quiet rural area. **Facility:** 10 cabins. 1 story, exterior corridors. *Bath:* shower only. **Terms:** closed 10/16-5/14, age restrictions may apply, 31 day cancellation notice-fee imposed. **Featured Amenity:** continental breakfast.

BELTON CHALET   406/888-5000
[fyi] Not evaluated. **Address:** 12575 US 2 E 59936 **Location:** US 2 E, at west entrance to Glacier National Park, just outside of the park. Facilities, services, and décor characterize a mid-scale property.

WEST YELLOWSTONE (F-4) pop. 1,271, elev. 6,667'
- Restaurants p. 211
- Hotels & Restaurants map & index p. 336
- Part of Yellowstone National Park area — see map p. 326

As its name suggests, West Yellowstone is at the west entrance to Yellowstone National Park *(see place listing p. 326)*. Due to this strategic location, the town's major industry is tourism. Numerous outfitters and rental operations supply visitors with various sports equipment, particularly snowmobiles and cross-country skis, for use in the park and in bordering national forest areas. Fly-fishing, hiking

(See map & index p. 336.)
and horseback riding can be enjoyed during summer.

Two miles north of West Yellowstone on US 287, the Interagency Aerial Fire Control Center provides tours explaining firefighting techniques daily 9-6 from mid-May to mid-October; phone (406) 646-7691.

For evening entertainment The Playmill Theatre at 29 Madison Ave. presents 2-hour musical comedy performances Monday through Saturday nights, with occasional Saturday matinees, mid-May through late August. Reservations are recommended. For more information and schedules contact the theater; phone (406) 646-7757.

West Yellowstone Chamber of Commerce: 30 Yellowstone Ave., P.O. Box 458, W. Yellowstone, MT 59758. **Phone:** (406) 646-7701.

 GRIZZLY & WOLF DISCOVERY CENTER is 1 blk. s. of the Yellowstone National Park west entrance at 201 S. Canyon St. in Grizzly Park. Grizzly bears and two gray wolf packs can be viewed in naturalistic habitats. Also offered are educational presentations, Yellowstone ranger talks, live birds of prey exhibits, safely in bear country demonstrations, films, an interactive bear museum, wolf enrichment, a Karelian Bear Dog and children's programs. **Time:** Allow 1 hour minimum. **Hours:** Daily 8-dusk. **Cost:** (valid for 2 consecutive days) $10.50; $9.75 (ages 62+); $5.50 (ages 5-12). **Phone:** (406) 646-7001 or (800) 257-2570.

MADISON RIVER CANYON EARTHQUAKE AREA is on US 287, 17 mi. n.w. of jct. US 191, in the Hebgen Lake Area. This 37,800-acre tract embraces Hebgen and Earthquake lakes. Traces remain of the 1959 earthquake, which blocked a river, moved huge boulders and tilted a lake bed. An observation room features a DVD presentation telling the story of the quake. The visitor center contains photographs of other devastating earthquakes.

Time: Allow 30 minutes minimum. **Hours:** Visitor center daily 10-6, Memorial Day-Labor Day. **Cost:** Free. **Phone:** (406) 682-7620 or (406) 823-6961.

YELLOWSTONE HISTORIC CENTER is at 104 Yellowstone Ave. Housed in a 1909 Union Pacific Railroad depot, the museum highlights the Yellowstone experience, from early tourism and railroad history to the 1988 fires and the rejuvenation of the park's ecosystems. Exhibits include early park stage coaches, a 1940s snow plane and a variety of films. Old Snaggletooth, a legendary grizzly bear, is prominently displayed among the wildlife specimens.

Time: Allow 1 hour minimum. **Hours:** Daily 9-9, late May-Labor Day; 9-6, early to late May and day after Labor Day through mid-Oct. **Cost:** $6; $5 (ages 60+ and active military with ID); $3 (ages 13-18); $2 (ages 4-12). **Phone:** (406) 646-1100.

YELLOWSTONE IMAX THEATER is at 101 S. Canyon St., adjacent to Yellowstone National Park's west entrance. A 45-minute IMAX film about the history, wildlife, geothermal activity and grandeur of America's first national park is shown on a six-story screen with stereo surround sound. **Hours:** Shows daily on the hour 10-9, June-Aug; 2-8, rest of year. Phone ahead to confirm schedule. **Cost:** $9; $8.50 (ages 60+); $6.50 (ages 3-12). **Phone:** (406) 646-4100 or (888) 854-5862.

ALPINE MOTEL   406/646-7544 43
Motel
$89-$169

Address: 120 Madison Ave 59758 **Location:** Just w of Canyon St (US 191) and Madison Ave; just nw of park entrance. **Facility:** 15 units, some kitchens. 1-2 stories (no elevator), exterior corridors. **Terms:** 7 day cancellation notice.

BEST WESTERN CROSS WINDS MOTOR INN
                                   (406)646-9557 36
Motel
$69-$199

AAA Benefit: Members save 10% or more with Best Western!

Address: 201 Firehole Ave 59758 **Location:** Just w of US 191 (Canyon St) and 287, on US 20 (Firehole Ave) at Dunraven St. **Facility:** 70 units. 2 stories (no elevator), exterior corridors. **Parking:** winter plug-ins. **Terms:** closed 3/18-4/17 & 10/21-12/19, check-in 4 pm. **Pool(s):** heated indoor. **Activities:** hot tub. **Guest Services:** coin laundry. **Featured Amenity: continental breakfast.**

BEST WESTERN DESERT INN   (406)646-7376 38
Hotel
$80-$248

AAA Benefit: Members save 10% or more with Best Western!

Address: 133 Canyon St 59758 **Location:** Jct US 191 (Canyon St) and 20 (Firehole Ave); 0.3 mi n of park entrance. **Facility:** 76 units, some kitchens. 3 stories, interior corridors. **Parking:** winter plug-ins. **Terms:** resort fee. **Pool(s):** heated indoor. **Activities:** hot tub. **Guest Services:** coin laundry.

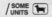

AAA/CAA travel information:

Available online, on the go

and in print!

(See map & index p. 336.)

BEST WESTERN WESTON INN (406)646-7373 [32]

Motel
$70-$300

AAA Benefit: Members save 10% or more with Best Western!

Address: 103 Gibbon Ave 59758 **Location:** On Canyon St (US 191), just n of Firehole Ave (US 20); 0.4 mi n of park entrance. **Facility:** 66 units, some kitchens. 3 stories (no elevator), interior/exterior corridors. **Terms:** closed 10/1-5/1. **Pool(s):** heated outdoor. **Activities:** hot tub.

BRANDIN' IRON INN 406/646-9411 [37]

Motel
$79-$169

Address: 201 Canyon St 59758 **Location:** At Firehole Ave (US 20) and Canyon St (US 191); 0.3 mi n of park entrance. **Facility:** 80 units, some kitchens. 2 stories (no elevator), exterior corridors. **Parking:** winter plug-ins. **Terms:** 3 day cancellation notice-fee imposed. **Activities:** hot tub. **Guest Services:** coin laundry. **Featured Amenity:** breakfast buffet.

Free expanded continental breakfast and hi-speed Internet

CITY CENTER MOTEL 406/646-7337 [42]

Motel
$69-$119

Address: 214 Madison Ave 59758 **Location:** At Madison Ave and Dunraven St; 0.3 mi nw of park entrance. **Facility:** 25 units, some two bedrooms. 1-2 stories (no elevator), exterior corridors. **Terms:** closed 11/2-3/31, 3 day cancellation notice-fee imposed.

Game room, communal kitchen and free Wi-Fi.

CLUBHOUSE INN (406)646-4892 [46]

Hotel $100-$260 **Address:** 105 S Electric St 59758 **Location:** Just sw of jct US 20/191/287; 0.4 mi w of park entrance. **Facility:** 77 units. 3 stories, interior corridors. **Parking:** winter plug-ins. **Terms:** closed 10/18-5/14, cancellation fee imposed. **Pool(s):** heated indoor. **Activities:** hot tub, exercise room. **Guest Services:** coin laundry.

DAYS INN WEST YELLOWSTONE (406)646-7656 [40]

Hotel
$100-$219

Address: 301 Madison Ave 59758 **Location:** Just w of Canyon St (US 191) at Madison Ave and Electric St; 0.5 mi nw of park entrance. **Facility:** 116 units. 3 stories, interior/exterior corridors. **Parking:** winter plug-ins. **Amenities:** Some: safes. **Pool(s):** heated indoor. **Activities:** hot tub, snowmobiling. **Guest Services:** coin laundry.

EVERGREEN MOTEL 406/646-7655 [34]

Motel $109-$125 **Address:** 229 Firehole Ave 59758 **Location:** On US 20 (Firehole Ave) at Electric St; 0.6 mi nw of park entrance. **Facility:** 17 units, some kitchens. 1 story, exterior corridors. **Parking:** winter plug-ins. **Terms:** cancellation fee imposed. **Activities:** picnic facilities. **Guest Services:** coin laundry.

GRAY WOLF INN & SUITES (406)646-0000 [50]

Hotel
$89-$259

Address: 250 S Canyon St 59758 **Location:** Just w of park entrance, just s. **Facility:** 103 units, some two bedrooms and kitchens. 3 stories, interior corridors. **Parking:** winter plug-ins. **Terms:** 3 day cancellation notice-fee imposed. **Pool(s):** heated indoor. **Activities:** sauna, hot tub. **Guest Services:** coin laundry. **Featured Amenity:** continental breakfast.

HOLIDAY INN WEST YELLOWSTONE (406)646-7365 [44]

Hotel
$119-$299

Address: 315 Yellowstone Ave 59758 **Location:** Just w of park entrance. **Facility:** 123 units, some two bedrooms. 3 stories, interior corridors. **Parking:** winter plug-ins. **Terms:** check-in 4 pm, 3 day cancellation notice-fee imposed. **Pool(s):** heated indoor. **Activities:** sauna, hot tub, exercise room. **Guest Services:** coin laundry.

KELLY INN (406)646-4544 [47]

Hotel $90-$260 **Address:** 104 S Canyon St 59758 **Location:** Just s of Canyon St (US 191) and Yellowstone Ave; 0.3 mi w of park entrance. **Facility:** 78 units. 3 stories, interior/exterior corridors. **Parking:** winter plug-ins. **Terms:** check-in 4 pm. **Pool(s):** heated indoor. **Activities:** sauna, hot tub. **Guest Services:** coin laundry.

LAZY G MOTEL 406/646-7586 [35]

Motel
$85-$105

Address: 123 Hayden St 59758 **Location:** Just s of Firehole Ave (US 20) and Hayden St; 0.8 mi w of park entrance. **Facility:** 15 units, some two bedrooms and efficiencies. 1-2 stories (no elevator), exterior corridors. **Parking:** winter plug-ins. **Terms:** closed 3/1-5/4 & 10/16-11/20, 2 night minimum stay - seasonal and/or weekends, 5 day cancellation notice-fee imposed. **Activities:** picnic facilities.

(See map & index p. 336.)

ONE HORSE MOTEL
406/646-7677 33

Motel
$79-$161

Address: 216 Dunraven St 59758 **Location:** Just w of jct US 191 (Canyon St) and 287; just n of US 20 (Firehole Ave) and Dunraven St. **Facility:** 19 units. 1 story, exterior corridors. **Terms:** closed 10/15-5/11, 7 day cancellation notice-fee imposed. **Guest Services:** coin laundry. **Featured Amenity:** continental breakfast.

STAGE COACH INN
(406)646-7381 41

Hotel
$69-$269

Address: 209 Madison Ave 59758 **Location:** Corner of Dunraven St and Madison Ave, just nw of park entrance. **Facility:** 84 units. 2 stories, interior corridors. **Terms:** cancellation fee imposed. **Activities:** sauna, hot tub, snowmobiling. **Guest Services:** coin laundry. **Featured Amenity:** continental breakfast.

SUPER 8
406/646-9584 31

Hotel
Rates not provided

Address: 1545 Targhee Pass Hwy (US 20) 59758 **Location:** 7.5 mi w of park entrance on Firehole Ave (US 20). **Facility:** 44 units. 2 stories (no elevator), interior corridors. **Activities:** playground, lawn sports. **Guest Services:** coin laundry. **Featured Amenity:** continental breakfast.

THREE BEAR LODGE
(406)646-7353 45

Hotel
$69-$229

Address: 217 Yellowstone Ave 59758 **Location:** Just w of park entrance. **Facility:** 70 units. 1-2 stories (no elevator), interior/exterior corridors. **Terms:** winter plug-ins. **Terms:** check-in 4 pm, cancellation fee imposed, resort fee. **Dining:** Three Bear Restaurant, see separate listing. **Pool(s):** heated outdoor. **Activities:** hot tub, snowmobiling, limited exercise equipment. **Guest Services:** coin laundry.

YELLOWSTONE LODGE
(406)646-0020 49

Hotel $69-$209 **Address:** 251 S Electric St 59758 **Location:** Just s of Yellowstone Ave and Electric St; 0.6 mi w of park entrance. **Facility:** 80 units. 3 stories, interior corridors. **Parking:** winter plug-ins. **Terms:** cancellation fee imposed. **Pool(s):** heated indoor. **Activities:** hot tub. **Guest Services:** coin laundry, area transportation.

YELLOWSTONE PARK HOTEL
(406)646-0255 48

Hotel
$89-$259

Address: 201 Grizzly Ave 59758 **Location:** Just w of park entrance. **Facility:** 66 units. 3 stories, interior corridors. **Parking:** winter plug-ins. **Terms:** closed 10/21-4/15, 2-3 night minimum stay - seasonal, 3 day cancellation notice-fee imposed. **Pool(s):** heated indoor. **Activities:** hot tub, limited exercise equipment. **Guest Services:** coin laundry. **Featured Amenity:** continental breakfast.

YELLOWSTONE WESTGATE HOTEL
(406)646-4212 39

Hotel $100-$270 **Address:** 638 Madison Ave 59758 **Location:** Just s of US 20 (Firehole Ave) at Iris St and Madison ave; 0.6 mi w of US 191 (Canyon St); 0.8 mi w of park entrance. **Facility:** 79 units, some kitchens. 3 stories, interior corridors. **Parking:** winter plug-ins. **Terms:** check-in 4 pm, cancellation fee imposed. **Pool(s):** heated indoor. **Activities:** hot tub. **Guest Services:** coin laundry.

WHERE TO EAT

BEARTOOTH BBQ
406/646-0227 31

Barbecue. Family Dining. $8-$15 **AAA Inspector Notes:** In-house-smoked meats and poultry make up the casual restaurant's menu. Those having a hard time deciding might consider a platter with any of a combination of ribs, brisket, chopped or sliced meats and smoked chicken with sauces made on site. **Features:** beer & wine. **Address:** 111 Canyon St 59758 **Location:** Center. **Parking:** street only.

BULLWINKLE'S SALOON & EATERY
406/646-7974 29

American. Casual Dining. $8-$28 **AAA Inspector Notes:** Even though the dining room is a large one, during the summer months you may find a wait for a table at this extremely popular place. **Features:** full bar. **Address:** 115 N Canyon St 59758 **Location:** Just n of park entrance. **Parking:** street only.

CAFE MADRIZ
406/646-9245 26

Spanish Small Plates. Casual Dining. $8-$30 **AAA Inspector Notes:** This is traditional Spanish comfort food such as meatballs in a savory broth, a fluffy potato and onion omelet and cold, cured meats and cheeses. The servings are a bit larger than tapas, so three dishes shared with two people should be enough. Seafood and chicken paella for two or four is on the menu, but allow 30 minutes, as it is cooked to order. **Features:** beer & wine. **Address:** 311 N Canyon St 59758 **Location:** 1 mi n from park entrance. **Parking:** street only.

THE GUSHER PIZZA AND SANDWICH SHOPPE
406/646-9050 33

American. Quick Serve. $8-$16 **AAA Inspector Notes:** The popular restaurant features pizza, sandwiches, burgers and steaks. Take-out and delivery are available. **Features:** beer & wine. **Address:** 40 Dunraven St 59758 **Location:** Corner of Madison and Dunraven sts.

KIWI' TAKEAWAY
406/640-0187 27

New Zealander. Quick Serve. $6-$11 **AAA Inspector Notes:** New Zealand-influenced cuisine is the mainstay at this casual restaurant. A varied menu lists homemade beef meat pies, curry chicken pies and buffalo meat pies as well as half-pound grilled beef or buffalo burgers, fresh soups and toasted sandwiches. **Address:** 237 Hwy 20 59758 **Location:** Just w of Canyon St (US 191); corner of Firehole Ave (US 20) and Electric St.

PETE'S ROCKY MOUNTAIN PIZZA & PASTA
406/646-7820 30

Pizza Sandwiches. Casual Dining. $8-$22 **AAA Inspector Notes:** This casual eatery offers a good selection of specialty pasta and pizza, including a build-your-own pizza. The breast of chicken and summer seafood salads are popular. Dinner is served only during the winter months. Vegetarian items and a children's menu are available. **Features:** beer & wine. **Address:** 112 Canyon St 59758 **Location:** Center; in Canyon Square. **Parking:** street only.

RED LOTUS
406/646-7002 32

Chinese. Casual Dining. $8-$19 **AAA Inspector Notes:** A newer decor with pretty bamboo accents are a few features at this restaurant. Open through the winter, a steaming bowl of fragrant hot and sour soup will hit the spot. **Address:** 19 Madison Ave 59758 **Location:** E on Madison Ave; downtown. **Parking:** street only.

(See map & index p. 336.)

RUNNING BEAR PANCAKE HOUSE   406/646-7703   28

American Family Dining
$6-$10

AAA Inspector Notes: These pancakes aren't the ones you usually make at home. An example: two huge pancakes loaded with walnuts and served with hot maple syrup. Among other specialties are the veggie omelet, taco salad and homemade cinnamon rolls. **Address:** 538 Madison Ave 59758 **Location:** 0.6 mi w of park entrance on Yellowstone Ave, just n on Hayden St. *Menu on AAA.com*

B L

SERENITY BISTRO   406/646-7660   35

Regional American. Casual Dining. $12-$38 **AAA Inspector Notes:** The casual bistro prepares more upscale food. The native Montanan chef turns out creative dishes that incorporate local and regional ingredients. This place is a nice alternative in a town full of pizza and burger joints. Open for breakfast during the summer months. **Features:** beer & wine. **Address:** 38 N Canyon St 59758 **Location:** 1 blk n of Grizzly Center; center. **Parking:** street only.

L D

THREE BEAR RESTAURANT   406/646-7811   36

American Casual Dining
$8-$25

AAA Inspector Notes: Varied dishes ranging from selections of beef and fish to sandwiches, soups and salads are likely to please just about anyone at this family restaurant. Home-baked pastries are mouthwatering treats. The décor is certainly Northwestern with a feel reminiscent of what it was like in Yellowstone's early days. The staff here makes you feel like a welcome guest. **Features:** full bar. **Address:** 205 Yellowstone Ave 59758 **Location:** Just w of park entrance; next to Three Bear Lodge. **Parking:** street only.

B D

WILD WEST PIZZERIA & SALOON   406/646-4400   34

Pizza. Casual Dining. $8-$25 **AAA Inspector Notes:** The pizzeria is a local favorite for its tasty pizzas, which are prepared from dough that's made here and then tossed by hand in the open kitchen. The finest cheese Wisconsin offers is brought in and grated in house. Live bands play on the weekends and karaoke is scheduled during the week. The décor is contemporary. **Features:** full bar. **Address:** 14 Madison Ave 59758 **Location:** E on Madison Ave; downtown. **Parking:** street only. L D CALL

WHITEFISH (B-2) pop. 6,357, elev. 3,033'

• Hotels & Restaurants map & index p. 168
• Part of Glacier National Park area — see map p. 163

Whitefish Lake borders Whitefish and extends 7 miles north. The area offers scenic vistas, fishing, swimming, boating and beach activities.

Restored to its 1927 chalet-like appearance, the Great Northern Railway Depot houses railroad artifacts and area memorabilia. On the grounds is the Great Northern Locomotive #181, one of only seven ever built.

Offering spectacular views of the Flathead Valley and Glacier National Park, the Whitefish Mountain Resort Scenic Lift carries passengers to the 7,000-foot summit; phone (406) 862-2900.

RECREATIONAL ACTIVITIES
Skiing

• **Whitefish Mountain Resort** is at 3840 Big Mountain Rd. Skiing and other activities are offered. **Hours:** Winter sports are available daily, early Dec. to mid-Apr. Summer activities are offered mid-June through Sept. 30. Hours vary; phone ahead. **Phone:** (406) 862-2900 or (800) 858-4157.

BAY POINT ON THE LAKE   (406)862-2331   17

Condominium $133-$211 **Address:** 300 Bay Point Dr 59937 **Location:** Waterfront. Jct US 93 and SR 487, 0.6 mi n on SR 487 to Skyles Pl, 0.3 mi w to Dakota Ave, 0.3 mi n, then just w. **Facility:** 34 condominiums. 2 stories (no elevator), exterior corridors. **Parking:** winter plug-ins. **Terms:** check-in 4 pm, 3 night minimum stay - seasonal, 30 day cancellation notice-fee imposed, resort fee. **Pool(s):** heated indoor. **Activities:** sauna, hot tub, limited beach access, marina, fishing, playground. **Guest Services:** coin laundry.

BEST WESTERN ROCKY MOUNTAIN LODGE
(406)862-2569   20

Hotel
$107-$210

AAA Benefit: Members save 10% or more with Best Western!

Address: 6510 Hwy 93 S 59937 **Location:** 1.3 mi s on US 93 from jct SR 487. **Facility:** 79 units. 2-3 stories, interior/exterior corridors. **Parking:** winter plug-ins. **Pool(s):** heated outdoor. **Activities:** hot tub, exercise room. **Guest Services:** coin laundry, area transportation. **Featured Amenity:** continental breakfast.

CHALET MOTEL   (406)862-5581   21

Motel
$60-$125

Address: 6430 US 93 S 59937 **Location:** 1 mi n on US 93 from jct SR 40. **Facility:** 34 units. 2 stories (no elevator), exterior corridors. **Parking:** winter plug-ins. **Terms:** cancellation fee imposed, resort fee. **Pool(s):** heated indoor. **Activities:** hot tub. **Guest Services:** coin laundry. **Featured Amenity:** continental breakfast.

GROUSE MOUNTAIN LODGE   406/862-3000   18

Hotel
Rates not provided

Address: 2 Fairway Dr 59937 **Location:** 1 mi w on US 93 from jct SR 487. **Facility:** 143 units. 3 stories, interior corridors. **Parking:** winter plug-ins. **Terms:** check-in 4 pm. **Dining:** Logan's Grill, see separate listing. **Pool(s):** heated indoor. **Activities:** sauna, hot tub, game room, exercise room, spa. **Guest Services:** valet and coin laundry, area transportation. **Featured Amenity:** full hot breakfast.

KRISTIANNA MOUNTAIN HOMES   406/862-2860   14

Vacation Rental Condominium. Rates not provided. **Address:** 331 Karrow Ave 59937 **Location:** Jct US 93 and SR 487, 2.4 mi n on SR 487, at flashing light go 5.2 mi on Big Mountain Rd, just n on Gelande St, then just w on Kristianna Close. Located in a quiet secluded area. **Facility:** This Swiss-style, two-story condo property is in a mountain setting. 8 condominiums. 2 stories (no elevator), interior/exterior corridors. **Parking:** winter plug-ins. **Terms:** check-in 4 pm. **Activities:** sauna, hot tub. **Guest Services:** coin laundry, area transportation.

(See map & index p. 168.)

THE LODGE AT WHITEFISH LAKE (406)863-4000 16

WWWW WWWW
Hotel
$115

Address: 1380 Wisconsin Ave 59937 **Location:** Waterfront. Jct US 93 and SR 487, 1.5 mi n on SR 487. **Facility:** Surrounded by mountains and wildlife preserves and on the shores of Whitefish Lake, this lodge offers amenities for all seasons, including skiing, boating, hiking and fishing. Glacier National Park is only 30 minutes away. Public areas have wrought iron chandeliers, animal mounts, and leather and wood accents. Some rooms provide balconies overlooking the lake. 101 units, some kitchens. 3 stories, interior/exterior corridors. **Parking:** on-site and valet. **Terms:** check-in 4 pm, 3 day cancellation notice. **Amenities:** safes. *Some:* video games. **Pool(s):** heated outdoor. **Activities:** sauna, hot tub, steamroom, limited beach access, marina, exercise room, spa. **Guest Services:** valet and coin laundry, area transportation.

SAVE ✈ ♨ 🛁 🍸 🏊 BIZ HS 🤖 ✕ 🎥
🖥 📷 📺

NORTH FORTY RESORT (406)862-7740 22

WWW WW **Cabin** $119-$289 **Address:** 3765 Hwy 40 W 59912 **Location:** 2.5 mi e on SR 40 from jct US 93. Located in a quiet secluded area. **Facility:** 22 cabins. 1 story, exterior corridors. **Parking:** winter plug-ins. **Terms:** check-in 4 pm, 2 night minimum stay - seasonal, 14 day cancellation notice-fee imposed, resort fee. **Activities:** sauna, hot tub.

BIZ 🤖 ✕ 🎥 📷 📺 📺 / SOME UNITS 🐕

PINE LODGE (406)862-7600 19

WWW WWW
Hotel
$79-$170

Address: 920 Spokane Ave 59937 **Location:** 1 mi s on US 93 from jct SR 487. **Facility:** 76 units, some kitchens. 3 stories, interior corridors. **Terms:** check-in 4 pm. **Activities:** hot tub, exercise room. **Guest Services:** valet and coin laundry, area transportation. **Featured Amenity:** continental breakfast.

SAVE ✈ CALL 📞M BIZ 🤖 ✕
🖥 📷 📺 / SOME UNITS 🐕

WHITEFISH MOUNTAIN RESORT 406/862-1960 15

WW WW **Vacation Rental Condominium.** Rates not provided. **Address:** 3889 Big Mountain Rd 59937 **Location:** Jct US 93 and SR 487, 2.4 mi n on SR 487, 5.2 mi n at flashing light. **Facility:** Guest rooms feature a fireplace, ski locker and ceiling fan, the perfect set up for ski enthusiasts. 147 units, some two bedrooms, three bedrooms, kitchens, houses and condominiums. 2-4 stories, interior/exterior corridors. **Parking:** winter plug-ins. **Terms:** off-site registration, check-in 4 pm. **Pool(s):** heated indoor. **Activities:** hot tub, downhill & cross country skiing, snowmobiling, recreation programs, bicycles. **Guest Services:** valet and coin laundry, area transportation.

✈ ♨ 🏊 🤖 ✕ 🖥 📷 📺 / SOME UNITS 🎥

WHERE TO EAT

AMAZING CRÊPES & CATERING 406/862-6002 15

W **Specialty. Quick Serve.** $6-$9 **AAA Inspector Notes:** Starting out from a humble food cart, the owners brought their savory and sweet creations to a more permanent location. The creative buckwheat crêpes are a treat for gluten-wary diners. **Address:** 123 Central Ave 59937 **Location:** Center. **Parking:** street only.

B L

BUFFALO CAFE 406/862-2833 19

WWW **American. Casual Dining.** $8-$25 **AAA Inspector Notes:** A longtime favorite among locals and skiers on their way to Big Mountain, this café serves hearty breakfasts, including breakfast pies and Mexican specialties. Also on the menu are a variety of salads, burgers and sandwiches. **Features:** beer & wine. **Address:** 514 3rd St E 59937 **Location:** Downtown. **Parking:** street only.

B L D

LOGAN'S GRILL 406/862-3000 14

WWWW **American. Fine Dining.** $9-$35 **AAA Inspector Notes:** Fine dining is the mode in this mountain resort atmosphere, which features a river rock fireplace and mounted big game heads. The menu supports wide-ranging taste temptations, including inventive burgers and sandwiches, all well prepared and made to order. Side dishes are varied and similarly tasty. **Features:** full bar, patio dining, happy hour. **Reservations:** suggested. **Address:** 2 Fairway Dr 59937 **Location:** 1 mi w on US 93 from jct SR 487; in Grouse Mountain Lodge. B L D CALL 📞M

LOULA'S 406/862-5614 17

WW WW **American. Casual Dining.** $6-$16 **AAA Inspector Notes:** This very popular, open and bright restaurant serves a full breakfast menu until 2 pm. Save room for the pies and other delicious desserts, all made in house in a dining room surrounded by dramatic landscape photos of the area. Handicap access is through the Lupfer Street entrance. **Features:** beer & wine. **Address:** 300 2nd St E 59937 **Location:** Jct Lupfer St; downtown. **Parking:** street only.

B L D

MAMBO ITALIANO 406/863-9600 16

WW WW **Italian. Casual Dining.** $11-$28 **AAA Inspector Notes:** Just like its sister restaurants, this family-owned establishment serves traditional and inventive dishes with a mambo twist. The marinara, with slivers of garlic, is fragrant and delicious. Have a seat at the counter and watch the chefs hand toss your pizza. Modern, contemporary decor surrounds guests adjacent to the open kitchen. **Features:** beer & wine, patio dining. **Address:** 234 2nd St E 59937 **Location:** Downtown. **Parking:** street only. D

THE NAKED NOODLE 406/862-6253 12

W **Noodles. Quick Serve.** $7-$12 **AAA Inspector Notes:** Diners choose pasta, soba, rice or spinach noodles, then decide from the many sauces, meats, vegetables, seafood and toppings in order to create a scrumptious meal. Can't decide? Choose one of the tried-and-true combinations posted on the board. For the most part, the restaurant is self-serve, but orders are taken by a patient and friendly staff. **Address:** 10 Baker Ave 59937 **Location:** Jct Railway St; downtown. L D CALL 📞M

THE SHAK 406/730-1070 20

W **Southern Barbecue. Family Dining.** $7-$16 **AAA Inspector Notes:** All your favorite Southern specialties can be found at this Cajun-type shack joint. Everything is smoked, even the potatoes. Slow-smoked meats results in the moistest brisket and the most flavorful pork that can be found anywhere, even in the South. Round out the meal with crisp hush puppies, aromatic smoked beans and sweet peach cobbler. **Address:** 669 Spokane Ave (US 93) 59937 **Location:** Just s of jct 2nd St. L D

TUPELO GRILLE AND WINE BAR 406/862-6136 13

WWWWWW
Continental
Casual Dining
$16-$36

AAA Inspector Notes: In keeping with the experience of the owners, who hail from the South, the menu's Continental dishes show hints of Southern Creole and Cajun influences. **Features:** beer & wine. **Address:** 17 Central Ave 59937 **Location:** Downtown. **Parking:** street only. D

(See map & index p. 168.)

WASABI SUSHI BAR & THE GINGER GRILL
406/863-9283   (18)

Asian
Casual Dining
$8-$45

AAA Inspector Notes: The menu centers on sushi and Asia-influenced dishes grilled with a contemporary flair. The lively, colorful dining room displays original artwork in oils, acrylics and fiber. **Features:** beer & wine. **Reservations:** suggested. **Address:** 419 E 2nd St 59937 **Location:** Downtown. **Parking:** street only. (D)

WHITEFISH LAKE RESTAURANT
406/862-5285   (11)

American
Casual Dining
$9-$39

AAA Inspector Notes: On one of the area's finest golf courses, the restaurant is housed in a structure made of logs from the surrounding forests. Guests dine on steak and seafood as well as inventive specials created nightly. **Features:** full bar, patio dining. **Reservations:** suggested. **Address:** 1200 US Hwy 93 N 59937 **Location:** 1 mi w on US 93 from jct SR 487. (L) (D)

WHITEHALL (E-3) pop. 1,038, elev. 4,351'

◆GEM◆ **LEWIS AND CLARK CAVERNS STATE PARK** is 7.3 mi. e. on SR 2 to 25 Lewis and Clark Rd. Dedicated in 1941, Montana's first state park includes a limestone cavern of vaulted chambers, intricate passageways and delicate, varicolored formations that make this one of the most beautiful caverns in the country. On the surface, 10 miles of hiking trails showcase the rugged site's 3,000 acres.

Note: The 2-hour guided cavern tours involve walking a total of 2 miles and require visitors to negotiate 600 (mostly descending) steps; full mobility is required and rubber-soled shoes are advised. Because the cavern temperature remains around 50 F, a jacket is recommended. Pets are not permitted in the cavern.

Hours: Park open daily 9-9, mid-Aug. to mid-Sept.; 9-5, rest of year. Cavern tours are given 9-6:30, mid-June to mid-Aug.; 9-4:30, May 1 to mid-June and mid-Aug. through Sept. 30. Candlelight cave tours are offered in late December; reservations are required. **Cost:** Park admission $5 (nonresidents per private vehicle); free (residents). Two-hour guided cavern tour $10; $5 (ages 6-11). **Phone:** (406) 287-3541. [icons]

WHITE SULPHUR SPRINGS (D-4)
pop. 939, elev. 5,100'

Nestled in the Smith River valley between the Little Belt Mountains in Lewis and Clark National Forest *(see place listing p. 187)* on the east and the Big Belt Mountains on the west, White Sulphur Springs offers numerous outdoor summer and winter recreational opportunities, including hunting, cross-country skiing, downhill skiing, snowmobiling, hiking and mountain biking. The Smith River and nearby Lake Sutherlin, Newlan Reservoir and several other lakes and reservoirs invite fishing, camping and water sports.

Reminders of frontier life can be found in Castle Town and Fort Logan.

CASTLE MUSEUM CARRIAGE HOUSE is 4 blks. n.e. off US 12/89 to 310 Second Ave. N.E., entered from the carriage house behind the castle. This restored Victorian house built in 1892 by B.R. Sherman, a cattleman and mine owner, sits on a hilltop overlooking the town. The gray stone structure, furnished in period, houses the Meagher County Historical Association Museum, which explores county history. **Time:** Allow 30 minutes minimum. **Hours:** Daily 10-6, mid-May to mid-Sept. Last tour begins 1 hour before closing. **Cost:** $5; $3 (ages 4-12 and 60+). **Phone:** (406) 547-2324 in season.

ALL SEASONS INN & SUITES   406/547-8888

[icon] Hotel $77-$165 **Address:** 808 3rd Ave SW 59645 **Location:** On US 89/12, south end of town. RV parking on premises. **Facility:** 32 units. 2 stories (no elevator), interior corridors. **Parking:** winter plug-ins. **Terms:** check-in 4 pm, cancellation fee imposed. **Activities:** hot tub. **Guest Services:** coin laundry.
[icons]

WIBAUX (C-8) pop. 589, elev. 2,634'

Wibaux has the distinction of being the first town to greet visitors entering Montana westbound on I-94. A statue of Frenchman Pierre Wibaux (WEE-bo), for whom the town is named, stands on the western edge of town.

Self-guiding tours: Brochures of a walking tour are available at the information center in The Pierre Wibaux Museum Complex.

THE PIERRE WIBAUX MUSEUM COMPLEX is at 112 E. Orgain Ave. It features the restored Pierre Wibaux office and house, built in 1892, and an adjoining barbershop with antique furnishings. A livery stable and a 1964 Montana Centennial Train railroad car are on the grounds. Displays include dinosaur fossils and homestead artifacts. **Hours:** Mon.-Sat. 10-6, Sun. 1-5, Memorial Day-Labor Day. **Cost:** Donations. **Phone:** (406) 796-9969.

WILLOW CREEK pop. 210

WILLOW CREEK CAFE AND SALOON   406/285-3698

[icon] Western American. Casual Dining. $10-$28 **AAA Inspector Notes:** *Historic.* Located in a historic building, this restaurant is well known for its fall-off-the-bone ribs and homemade desserts. Guests come from all around the region for dinner. **Features:** full bar. **Reservations:** suggested. **Address:** 21 Main St 59760 **Location:** I-90 exit 278, 6 mi s of Three Forks; follow signs. (D)

WISDOM pop. 98

THE CROSSING BAR & GRILL   406/689-3260

[icon] American. Family Dining. $7-$28 **AAA Inspector Notes:** After a day fishing, camping, hunting or sightseeing, thank goodness The Crossing Bar & Grill is open and serving up the best chow in the county. Huge burgers, perfectly cooked steaks, homemade soups, healthy salads and, of course, homemade desserts are offered. **Features:** beer & wine. **Address:** 327 Hwy 43 59761 **Location:** Center. (B) (L) (D) [icon]

WOLF CREEK (C-3) elev. 3,560'

Wolf Creek is a popular point for sports enthusiasts bound for Holter Lake *(see Recreation Areas Chart)*, 5 miles southeast of town. The result of one of a series of dams on the Upper Missouri River, the lake is bordered by the Sleeping Giant Wilderness, Beartooth Wildlife Management Area and Helena National Forest *(see place listing p. 183)*.

Almost all of the lake's recreational facilities are on its eastern shore. A particularly scenic drive begins at the junction of US 287 and SR 200 north of Wolf Creek, proceeds south on US 287 to the junction with I-15, then on to Helena, Butte and the Idaho border, passing some of Montana's most impressive mountains.

WOLF POINT (B-7) pop. 2,621, elev. 2,001'

While sustained mostly by agriculture, Wolf Point's economy also benefits from small manufacturing firms and Honeyland Inc., which maintains more than 4,000 bee colonies and produces about a half-million pounds of honey annually. Wolf Point also is the home of many Sioux and Assiniboine, who perform dances and observe celebrations June through August. The Wolf Point Wild Horse Stampede, said to be the state's oldest rodeo, takes place during the second week in July.

Wolf Point Chamber of Commerce & Agriculture: 218 Third Ave. S., Suite B, Wolf Point, MT 59201. **Phone:** (406) 653-2012.

WOLF POINT AREA MUSEUM is at 202 US 2. The museum exhibits clothing, arrowheads and other items used by the area's Native American and early settlers. Early radios and phonographs, military items, and sculptures and paintings by local artists also are on display. **Hours:** Mon.-Fri. 9-5, May 15-Sept. 15. Closed major holidays. **Cost:** Donations. **Phone:** (406) 653-1912.

 YELLOWSTONE NATIONAL PARK—See Wyoming p. 326.

Riding off into the Wyoming sunset

Wyoming

You could say that Wyoming is *Mecheweami-ing* to the max. The Delaware Indian word meaning "at the great plains" or "on the great plain"—helpfully simplified to the present state name—is certainly geographically apt. But Wyoming's mountains, grasslands, canyons, deserts and other natural attributes also are worthy of greatness.

The Continental Divide cuts a diagonal swath across this almost precisely rectangular state, bisecting it into the Missouri and Columbia and Colorado river basins. The divide winds northwest to southeast along the curved, jagged spine of the Rocky Mountains, and some of Wyoming's most scenic jewels can be found in this formidably mountainous territory.

Grand Teton National Park fully deserves gushing adjectives like "breathtaking" and "magnificent"; it was first photographed way back in 1872, and ever since shutterbugs

Bear crossing, Yellowstone National Park

have commemorated for posterity the region's sparkling blue lakes, impressive glaciers, mammoth snowfields and lush green stands of fir, pine and spruce. This awesome natural setting begat Jackson Hole, an outdoor recreation paradise offering thrill seekers a range of temptations from mountain climbing and windsurfing to skiing and whitewater rafting.

Yellowstone is the nation's first national park, and one of its most beloved. It's also a hot spot for geyser activity, the result of a volcanic eruption some 600,000 years ago. The thermal theatrics of Old Faithful receive top billing; this cone geyser shoots up to 8,000 gallons of boiling water some 150 feet in the air every 90 or so minutes, providing a spectacular show. But Yellowstone offers everything from the terrace-like formations of Mammoth Hot Springs and colorful hot clay bubbling from vivid paint pots to photographic encounters with the likes of grizzlies, black bears, elk, bison and bighorn sheep.

In Bighorn Canyon National Recreation Area, shared with neighboring Montana, canyon walls of sculpted rock rise up and encircle a 55-mile stretch of serene Bighorn Lake. Imposing Shell and Crazy Woman canyons punctuate the terrain of Bighorn National Forest. The Green River carved the backdrop of appropriately named Flaming Gorge National Recreation Area; as Creedence Clearwater Revival once observed in a song, you can kick your feet way down in shallow water and skip a flat rock across Green River.

Like a bad haircut, sagebrush crowns the massive monolith that is the centerpiece of Devils Tower National Monument. The remarkably well-preserved remains of fish, insects, reptiles, plants and birds at Fossil Butte National Monument provide compelling evidence that the region basked in a subtropical environment some 50 million years ago.

Rolling Westward

Wyoming's topographic highlights must have been eye-popping to the 19th-century pioneers who rumbled along the Oregon Trail in a series of wagon train processions, heading to a new life in California and the Pacific Northwest. Western lore is well documented at places like Fort Laramie National Historic Site, a fur-trading post established in 1834 that witnessed the unfolding drama of westward expansion as well as its varied cast: trappers, traders, missionaries, treasure seekers, homesteaders, cowboys and the Native American tribes that fiercely resisted the encroachments on their land.

Museums like The Nelson Museum of the West in Cheyenne, the Buffalo Bill Center of the West in Cody, the Wyoming Pioneer Memorial Museum in Douglas and the Wyoming Territorial Prison State Historic Site in Laramie all are repositories for this rich heritage. Cody not only pays tribute to its founder, Col. William "Buffalo Bill" F. Cody, but to Harry Longabaugh—or the Sundance Kid—who adopted his better-known moniker from the Wyoming town in which he once served time. And as fans of Paul Newman and Robert Redford know, that particular Wyoming legend was made into a pretty darn good movie.

Recreation

Wyoming lets you experience Wild West life without having to put up with Wild West hardships. Mount a trusty horse at the crack of dawn and head into the mountains, experience breathtakingly unspoiled wilderness and end the day relaxing around an open campfire. Outfitters offer everything from cattle herding adventures to overnight chuck wagon trips.

Yellowstone has more than 1,000 miles of hiking trails ranging from easy loops to strenuous treks; many visitors opt for a trail that ventures past at least one of the park's bubbling geysers. Yellowstone Lake is tops for boating; Shoshone Lake is a favorite for canoeing. If you're in the mood for a less demanding activity, the Togwotee Trail (US 26/287 through Fremont and Teton counties) offers scenery that is magnificent viewed from the passenger seat of a car.

A short skip south is Wyoming's *other* national park, Grand Teton. Extreme adventure enthusiasts will relish the challenge of climbing one of the park's four principal mountains—Grand Teton, Middle Teton, Buck Mountain and Mount Moran. Allow 2 days for a summertime ascent of Grand Teton; the Owen-Spaulding route, a 7-mile trek, is the most popular scramble to the top of this 13,770-foot peak.

There's another natural landmark in the state's opposite (northeastern) corner. Devils Tower, the nation's first national monument, soars 1,267 feet above the Belle Fourche River. Climbing the formation's fluted, nearly perpendicular heights is permitted, but most folks are content to hike the popular 1.3-mile Tower Trail that circles it.

White-water rafting in the vicinity of Jackson Hole has the bonus of spectacular mountain backdrops. The upper Snake River's relatively gentle water is well-suited for novices, but the lower Snake's white water will take you for a wild ride. And winter in Wyoming brings lots of snow and plenty of terrain for cross-country and downhill skiing; the packed powder typical of Snow King Mountain in Jackson Hole makes it a good spot for beginners.

Devils Tower National Monument and the Belle Fourche River

Historic Timeline

Year	Event
1807	John Colter, a member of the Lewis and Clark Expedition, spends months alone in a wilderness of mountains and geysers.
1834	Fur traders William Sublette and Robert Campbell establish a trading post at Fort Laramie.
1849	The United States buys Fort Laramie to use as a base to protect and supply travelers along the Oregon Trail.
1863	The Wyoming Territory's first newspaper, *The Daily Telegraph,* begins printing in Fort Bridger.
1869	Wyoming women become the first in the nation to obtain the right to vote.
1890	Wyoming becomes the 44th state.
1872	The wilderness area John Colter described as "Colter's Hell" is designated Yellowstone, the country's first national park.
1925	Nellie Tayloe Ross is sworn in as Wyoming's—and the nation's— first woman governor.
1958	The 4320th Strategic Missile Wing is established at F.E. Warren Air Force Base in Cheyenne.
1988	Wildfires in Yellowstone National Park scorch more than 1 million acres.
2010	Yellowstone receives nearly 1 million visitors in July, the most people ever to visit the park in a single month.

What To Pack

Temperature Averages Maximum/Minimum	JANUARY	FEBRUARY	MARCH	APRIL	MAY	JUNE	JULY	AUGUST	SEPTEMBER	OCTOBER	NOVEMBER	DECEMBER
Casper	33/14	37/16	43/21	56/31	66/40	77/49	87/56	85/55	74/45	61/36	44/23	37/18
Cheyenne	38/14	40/15	44/20	55/29	64/39	76/48	84/54	82/53	73/43	62/33	47/22	42/18
Evanston	29/10	34/12	42/19	52/26	61/33	72/40	79/46	78/45	68/37	57/28	40/18	32/10
Lander	31/8	36/12	45/20	56/31	66/40	76/48	86/55	84/54	73/45	60/34	43/19	35/12
Sheridan	34/9	36/11	43/19	56/31	67/40	75/48	87/56	86/53	74/43	62/33	46/21	39/14
Yellowstone NP	26/10	30/11	37/17	48/26	57/33	67/41	76/47	74/45	64/37	52/29	38/20	28/12

From the records of The Weather Channel Interactive, Inc.

Good Facts To Know

ABOUT THE STATE

POPULATION: 563,626.

AREA: 97,914 square miles; ranks 9th.

CAPITAL: Cheyenne.

HIGHEST POINT: 13,804 ft., Gannett Peak.

LOWEST POINT: 3,100 ft., Belle Fourche River Valley.

TIME ZONE(S): Mountain. DST.

GAMBLING

MINIMUM AGE FOR GAMBLING: 18.

REGULATIONS

TEEN DRIVING LAWS: No more than one passenger under the age of 18 is permitted (family members are exempt). Driving is not permitted 11 p.m.-5 a.m. The minimum age for an unrestricted driver's license is 16 and 6 months with driver's education course and 17 without driver's education course. Phone (307) 777-4800 for more information about Wyoming driver's license regulations.

SEAT BELT/CHILD RESTRAINT LAWS: Seat belts are required for driver and all passengers ages 9 and over. Children under age 9 are required to be in a child restraint in the rear seat, if possible. AAA recommends the use of seat belts and appropriate child restraints for the driver and all passengers.

CELL PHONE RESTRICTIONS: All drivers are banned from text messaging.

HELMETS FOR MOTORCYCLISTS: Required for riders under 18.

RADAR DETECTORS: Permitted.

MOVE OVER LAW: Driver is required to slow down and vacate a lane nearest police, fire and rescue vehicles stopped on the side of the road using audible or flashing signals.

FIREARMS LAWS: Vary by state and/or county. Contact the Wyoming Highway Patrol, 5300 Bishop Blvd., P.O. Box 1708, Cheyenne, WY 82009-3340; phone (307) 777-4301.

HOLIDAYS

HOLIDAYS: Jan. 1 ▪ Martin Luther King Jr. Day, Jan. (3rd Mon.) ▪ Washington's Birthday/Presidents Day, Feb. (3rd Mon.) ▪ Memorial Day, May (last Mon.) ▪ July 4 ▪ Labor Day, Sept. (1st Mon.) ▪ Veterans Day, Nov. 11 ▪ Thanksgiving, Nov. (4th Thurs.) ▪ Christmas, Dec. 25.

MONEY

TAXES: Wyoming's statewide sales tax is 4 percent, with local options for an additional increment up to 3 percent. Localities may also impose a lodging tax of up to 4 percent.

VISITOR INFORMATION

INFORMATION CENTERS: State welcome centers are on I-90 at 5th Street interchange east of Sheridan ▪ on I-90 exit 187 at Sundance ▪ on US 26/89/187 on north edge of Jackson ▪ 1 mile south of Cheyenne on I-25 at College Drive interchange ▪ on I-80 on east edge of Evanston ▪ on I-80 exit 401 south of Pine Bluffs ▪ and on I-80, 10 miles east of Laramie at Sherman Hill exit. The centers are open daily 8-6, Memorial Day-Labor Day, and daily 8-5, rest of year.

FURTHER INFORMATION FOR VISITORS:
Wyoming Travel and Tourism
5611 High Plains Rd.
Cheyenne, WY 82007
(307) 777-7777
(800) 225-5996

NATIONAL FOREST INFORMATION:
Rocky Mountain Region, U.S. Forest Service
740 Simms St.
Golden, CO 80401
(303) 275-5350
(877) 444-6777 (reservations)
Intermountain Region, USDA Forest Service
507 25th St.
Ogden, UT 84401
(801) 625-5306
(877) 444-6777 (reservations)
(877) 833-6777 (TTY)

FISHING AND HUNTING REGULATIONS:
Wyoming Game and Fish Department
5400 Bishop Blvd.
Cheyenne, WY 82006
(307) 777-4600

RECREATION INFORMATION:
Wyoming State Parks and Cultural Resources
Barrett Building
2301 Central Ave.
Cheyenne, WY 82001
(307) 777-6303

STATE PARK INFORMATION:
Division of State Parks and Historic Sites
Barrett Building
2301 Central Ave., 4th Floor
Cheyenne, WY 82002
(307) 777-6323

Wyoming Annual Events
Please call ahead to confirm event details.

JANUARY	FEBRUARY	MARCH
▪ Wild West Winter Carnival Riverton 307-856-4801 ▪ Sierra Madre Winter Carnival / Encampment 307-327-5501 ▪ Ice Fishing Derby Saratoga 307-326-8855	▪ Buffalo Bill's Birthday Celebration / Cody 307-527-5626 ▪ Donald E. Erickson Memorial Chariot Races Saratoga 307-326-8855 ▪ Casper Mountain Sled Dog Races / Casper 307-577-7162	▪ Jackson Hole Mountain Festival / Teton Village 307-733-2292 ▪ Children's Festival / Gillette 307-687-5211 ▪ World Championship Snowmobile Hill Climb Jackson 307-734-9653

APRIL	MAY	JUNE
▪ Big Wyoming Horse Expo Douglas 307-244-4922 ▪ Crawfish Boil / Gillette 307-680-6789 ▪ Western Spirit Art Show and Sale / Cheyenne 307-778-7290	▪ ElkFest and Antler Auction Jackson 307-733-3316 ▪ Cody's Wild West Days Cody 307-587-4221 ▪ Old West Days / Jackson 307-733-3316	▪ Cody Nite Rodeo / Cody 800-207-0744 ▪ Flaming Gorge Days Green River 307-778-3133 ▪ Woodchopper's Jamboree and Rodeo / Encampment 307-710-5558

JULY	AUGUST	SEPTEMBER
▪ Cheyenne Frontier Days Cheyenne 307-778-7222 ▪ Sheridan-Wyo-Rodeo Sheridan 307-672-9715 ▪ Green River Rendezvous Pinedale 307-367-4101	▪ Wyoming State Fair and Rodeo / Douglas 307-358-2398 ▪ Gift of the Waters Indian Pageant and Powwow Thermopolis 800-786-6772 ▪ Texas Trail Days in Pine Bluffs / Pine Bluffs 307-245-3746	▪ Fort Bridger Rendezvous Fort Bridger 435-213-5133 ▪ Jackson Hole Fall Arts Festival / Jackson 307-733-3316 ▪ Rendezvous Royale / Cody 307-587-5002

OCTOBER	NOVEMBER	DECEMBER
▪ Moonlight Madness Thermopolis 877-864-3192 ▪ Oktoberfest / Rock Springs 307-352-6789 ▪ Chili Cook-Off / Gillette 307-687-5213	▪ Christmas Opening and Parade of Lights / Worland 307-347-3226 ▪ Cheyenne Christmas Parade, Concert and Craft Show / Cheyenne 307-637-3376 ▪ Christmas Stroll / Sheridan 307-672-2485	▪ Lighted Christmas Parade Buffalo 307-684-5544 ▪ Mountain Man Christmas Parade / Pinedale 307-367-2242 ▪ Powell Country Christmas Powell 307-754-3494

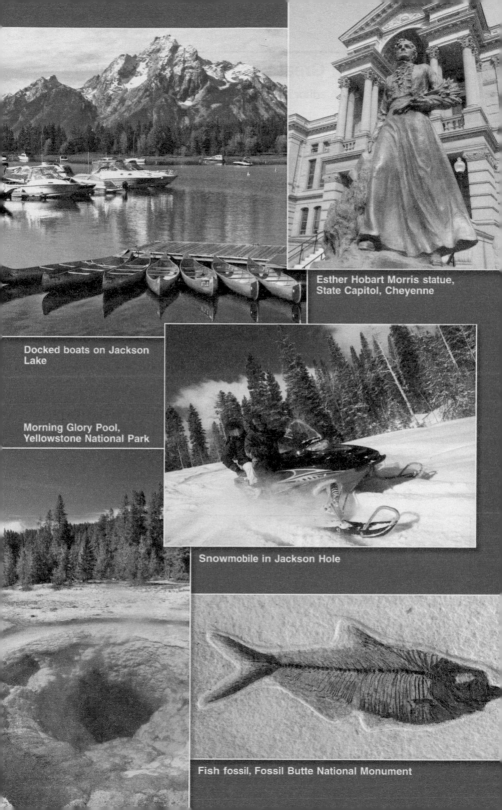

Esther Hobart Morris statue, State Capitol, Cheyenne

Docked boats on Jackson Lake

Morning Glory Pool, Yellowstone National Park

Snowmobile in Jackson Hole

Fish fossil, Fossil Butte National Monument

Index: Great Experience for Members

AAA editor's picks of exceptional note

Fort Laramie National Historic Site

Grand Teton National Park

Yellowstone National Park

Trail Town

Make the Most of Your Trip
with AAA eTourBook® Guides

Maximize your travel experience when you take along AAA eTourBook guides for your ereader or smartphone. Each of the more than 100 available digital titles is packed with:

- Destination details
- AAA Approved and Diamond Rated hotel and restaurant listings
- Attraction and event information
- Preplanned itineraries
- Editor's don't-miss picks

Download now at
AAA.com/ebooks

ROADS/HIGHWAYS
- INTERSTATE
- CONTROLLED ACCESS
- CONTROLLED ACCESS TOLL
- TOLL ROAD
- PRIMARY DIVIDED
- PRIMARY UNDIVIDED
- SECONDARY DIVIDED
- SECONDARY UNDIVIDED
- LOCAL DIVIDED
- LOCAL UNDIVIDED
- UNPAVED ROAD
- UNDER CONSTRUCTION
- TUNNEL
- PEDESTRIAN ONLY
- AUTO FERRY
- PASSENGER FERRY
- SCENIC BYWAY
- DISTANCE BETWEEN MARKERS
- EXIT NUMBER-FREE/TOLL
- INTERCHANGE FULL/PARTIAL
- WELCOME CENTER
- REST AREA/ SERVICE CENTER

BOUNDARIES
- INTERNATIONAL
- STATE
- COUNTY
- TIME ZONE
- CONTINENTAL DIVIDE

ROAD SHIELDS
- INTERSTATE/BUSINESS
- U.S./STATE/COUNTY
- FOREST/INDIAN
- TRANS- CANADA
- PROVINCIAL AUTOROUTE
- MEXICO
- HISTORIC ROUTE 66
- VT 41 REFERENCE PAGE INDICATOR

AREAS OF INTEREST
- INDIAN
- MILITARY
- PARK
- FOREST
- GRASSLANDS
- HISTORIC
- INT'L/REGIONAL AIRPORT
- INCORPORATED CITY

POINTS OF INTEREST
- TOWN
- NATIONAL CAPITAL
- STATE/PROVINCIAL CAPITAL
- AAA/CAA CLUB LOCATION
- FEATURE OF INTEREST
- COLLEGE/UNIVERSITY
- CAMPGROUND INFORMATION PROVIDED BY WOODALL'S®
- CUSTOMS STATION
- HISTORIC
- LIGHTHOUSE
- MONUMENT/MEMORIAL
- STATE/PROVINCIAL PARK
- NATIONAL WILDLIFE REFUGE
- SKI AREA
- SPORTS COMPLEX
- DAM

CITIES/TOWNS are color-coded by size, showing where to find AAA Approved and Diamond rated lodgings or restaurants listed in the AAA TourBook guides and on AAA.com:
- ● Red - major destinations and capitals; many listings
- ● Black - destinations; some listings
- ● Grey - no listings

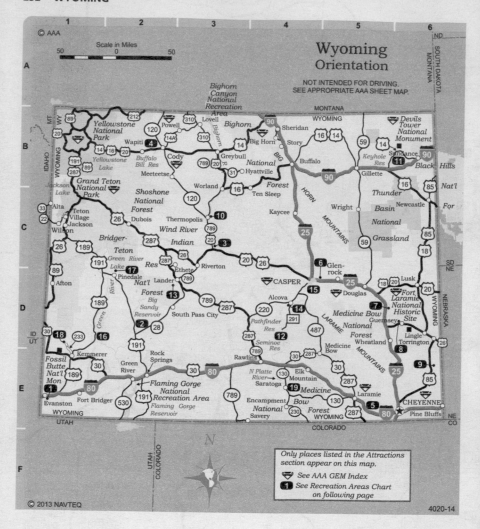

Wyoming
Orientation

NOT INTENDED FOR DRIVING.
SEE APPROPRIATE AAA SHEET MAP.

Only places listed in the Attractions section appear on this map.

⚘ See AAA GEM Index

🔳 See Recreation Areas Chart on following page

© 2013 NAVTEQ   4020-14

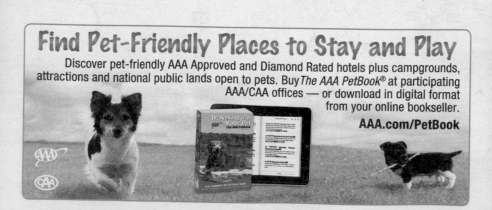

Recreation Areas Chart

The map location numerals in column 2 show an area's location on the preceding map.

	MAP LOCATION	CAMPING	PICNICKING	HIKING TRAILS	BOATING	BOAT RAMP	BOAT RENTAL	FISHING	SWIMMING	PETS ON LEASH	BICYCLE TRAILS	WINTER SPORTS	VISITOR CENTER	LODGE/CABINS	FOOD SERVICE
NATIONAL PARKS *(See place listings.)*															
Grand Teton (B-1) 485 square miles. Horse rental.		•	•	•	•	•	•	•	•	•	•	•	•	•	•
Yellowstone (B-2) 3,472 square miles. Horse rental.		•	•	•	•	•	•	•	•	•		•	•	•	•
NATIONAL FORESTS *(See place listings.)*															
Bighorn (B-4) 1,115,073 acres in north-central Wyoming. Horse rental.		•	•	•	•	•		•				•		•	•
Black Hills (B-6) 1,246,660 acres. Southwestern South Dakota and northeastern Wyoming.		•	•	•	•	•		•		•		•	•	•	•
Bridger-Teton (C-2) 3,439,809 acres in western Wyoming. Horse rental.		•	•	•	•	•		•	•	•	•	•	•	•	•
Medicine Bow (D-5) 1,093,618 acres in eastern Wyoming. Horse rental.		•	•	•	•	•		•		•	•	•	•	•	•
Shoshone (C-2) 2,466,586 acres in northwestern Wyoming.		•	•	•	•	•		•		•	•	•	•	•	•
NATIONAL MONUMENTS *(See place listings.)*															
Devils Tower (B-6) 1,347 acres.		•	•	•						•	•	•	•		
NATIONAL RECREATION AREAS *(See place listings.)*															
Bighorn Canyon (A-3) 120,000 acres in southern Montana and northern Wyoming.		•	•	•	•	•	•	•	•	•			•		•
Flaming Gorge (E-2) 207,363 acres. Cross-country skiing, horseback riding, hunting, ice fishing, parasailing, rafting, snowmobiling, water skiing.		•	•	•	•	•	•	•	•	•		•	•	•	•
STATE															
Bear River (E-1) 320 acres on I-80 near Evanston. *(See Evanston p. 259.)*	❶		•	•				•	•	•					
Big Sandy (D-2) 6,190 acres 6 mi. n. of Farson on US 191.	❷	•	•	•	•	•		•	•	•					
Boysen (C-3) 39,545 acres 14 mi. n.w. of Shoshoni off US 20. *(See Thermopolis p. 321.)*	❸	•	•	•	•	•	•	•	•	•			•		•
Buffalo Bill (B-2) 12,000 acres 9 mi. w. of Cody on US 14/16/20.	❹	•	•	•	•	•		•	•	•		•	•		
Curt Gowdy (E-5) 1,960 acres 26 mi. w. of Cheyenne off SR 210.	❺	•	•	•	•	•		•	•	•			•		•
Edness Kimball Wilkins (C-5) 315 acres 6 mi. e. of Casper off I-25.	❻		•	•				•	•	•			•		•
Glendo (D-5) 22,430 acres 4 mi. e. of Glendo off US 87.	❼	•	•	•	•	•	•	•	•	•			•		•
Guernsey (D-6) 8,638 acres 3 mi. w. of Guernsey off US 26.	❽	•	•	•	•	•		•	•	•			•	•	
Hawk Springs (E-6) 2,000 acres 39 mi. s. of Torrington off US 85.	❾	•	•	•	•	•		•	•	•					
Hot Springs (C-3) 1,034 acres in n.e. Thermopolis on SR 789 and US 20. *(See Thermopolis p. 322.)*	❿		•	•				•	•	•			•		•
Keyhole (B-6) 15,674 acres 7 mi. n. of I-90 between Moorcroft and Sundance.	⓫	•	•	•	•	•	•	•	•	•			•	•	•
Seminoe (D-4) 10,381 acres 35 mi. n. of Sinclair off I-80.	⓬	•	•		•	•		•	•	•			•		
Sinks Canyon (D-2) 600 acres 7.5 mi. s.w. of Lander on SR 131. *(See Lander p. 299.)*	⓭	•	•	•				•		•			•	•	
OTHER															
Alcova Reservoir (D-4) 3,400 acres 4 mi. s. of Alcova off SR 220.	⓮	•	•	•	•	•	•	•	•	•					•
Casper Mountain Park (D-4) 3,315 acres 7 mi. s. of Casper on SR 251. Cross-country and downhill skiing, snowmobiling; archery range, braille nature trail, bridle trails, horse rental.	⓯	•	•	•							•	•	•		•
Fontenelle Reservoir (D-2) 8,000 acres 35 mi. n. of Kemmerer via US 189.	⓰	•	•	•	•	•		•							
Fremont Lake (C-2) 5,000-acre lake 3.5 mi. n.e. of Pinedale off Fremont Lake Rd. *(See Pinedale p. 307.)*	⓱	•	•	•	•	•	•	•	•	•			•	•	•
Lake Viva Naughton (D-1) 1,375 acres 12 mi. n. of Kemmerer via SR 233.	⓲	•			•	•		•							
Saratoga Lake (E-4) 270-acre lake 1.5 mi. n. of Saratoga off SR 130.	⓳	•	•	•	•	•	•	•	•	•	•				

AFTON (D-1) pop. 1,911, elev. 6,267'

Mormon emigrants surveyed the already-settled site of Afton in 1896, using a carpenter's square, a rope and an almanac and taking their bearings from the North Star and the sun. An official survey made years later found the plot only about 5 feet off.

In addition to the arch of 3,011 elk antlers that spans Washington Street at the center of town, Afton is noted for Periodic Spring, a natural cold-water geyser. The spring is 5 miles east in Bridger-Teton National Forest *(see place listing p. 236).*

Afton lies in Star Valley along the scenic portion of US 89, which runs 255 miles between Mammoth Hot Springs in Yellowstone National Park *(see place listing p. 332)* and Geneva on the Idaho border.

Star Valley Chamber of Commerce: 150 S. Washington St., P.O. Box 190, Afton, WY 83110. **Phone:** (800) 426-8833.

LINCOLN COUNTY DAUGHTERS OF UTAH PIONEER MUSEUM is one-half blk. e. off US 89 at 46 E. 5th Ave. The museum displays artifacts chronicling Mormon history in southwestern Wyoming. **Hours:** Mon.-Fri. 1-5, June-Aug. **Cost:** Free. **Phone:** (800) 426-8833 for information.

LAZY B MOTEL   307/885-3187

Motel
$82-$110

Address: 219 S Washington St (US 89) 83110 **Location:** On US 89; center. **Facility:** 25 units. 1 story, exterior corridors. **Parking:** winter plug-ins. **Pool(s):** heated outdoor. **Guest Services:** coin laundry.

SAVE / SOME UNITS

ALCOVA (D-4) pop. 76, elev. 5,364'

Alcova lies in a small valley rimmed by rocky hills. In 1891 a group of Easterners bought a nearby site where hot springs flowed from the walls of a canyon. An analysis of the water showed a high concentration of minerals, but the $250,000 the syndicate planned to spend on improvements never materialized.

The water that finally proved important to the town is that impounded by Alcova Dam, 4 miles south of town off SR 220. The dam stretches 700 feet in length and rises 800 feet from the canyon riverbed. Reservoirs created by Alcova and nearby Pathfinder dams provide popular recreation sites for residents of Casper and other communities. *See Recreation Areas Chart.*

One of the more colorful local legends involves Ella "Cattle Kate" Watson, unpopular with townsfolk because of her freewheeling lifestyle and skill at raising cattle. She secretly married rancher Jim Averill so they could double their herd while she retained her homestead in her own name. Other

ranchers demanded that both leave town, but before they could make their getaway the two were hanged unceremoniously from a scrub pine. Cattle Kate's 1889 lynching made her the only woman to suffer this fate in Wyoming.

INDEPENDENCE ROCK STATE HISTORIC SITE is 25 mi. w. on SR 220. Called "The Great Register of the Desert," this well-known landmark is a 136-foot-high granite boulder with a base that covers more than 24 acres. Members of an expedition led by Robert Stuart, credited with the discovery of the Oregon Trail, first visited the rock in 1812. Since then more than 5,000 explorers, adventurers, missionaries and soldiers have carved their names on it.

Independence Rock was named during a celebration held July 4, 1830, by a party of fur trappers led by William Sublette. **Hours:** Daily dawn-dusk. **Cost:** Free.

ALPINE pop. 828

• Part of Jackson Hole Including Grand Teton National Park area — see map p. 293

ALPEN HAUS HOTEL RESORT   (307)654-7545

Hotel
$55-$150

Address: 46 W Hwy 26 83128 **Location:** Jct US 26 and 89. **Facility:** 23 units. 3 stories, interior corridors. **Terms:** cancellation fee imposed.

SAVE / SOME UNITS

WHERE TO EAT

FLYING SADDLE RESTAURANT   307/654-4422

Regional American. Casual Dining. $9-$29 **AAA Inspector Notes:** This casual eatery serves traditional American fare both in its dining room and on the summer patio. The chef takes care to buy seafood from Seattle, and the Kobe strip steak is butter-tender. **Features:** full bar, patio dining, happy hour. **Address:** 118878 Jct US 26 & 89 83128 **Location:** 0.5 mi e of jct US 26 and 89; in Flying Saddle Resort. D

ALTA (C-1) pop. 394, elev. 6,440'

• Part of Jackson Hole Including Grand Teton National Park area — see map p. 293

RECREATIONAL ACTIVITIES
Skiing
• **Grand Targhee Resort** is 12 mi. e. at 3300 E. Ski Hill Rd. Other activities are offered. **Hours:** Daily 9-4, Thanksgiving-early Apr. **Phone:** (307) 353-2300 or (800) 827-4433.

BIG HORN (B-4) pop. 490, elev. 4,081'

GEM SAVE THE BRINTON MUSEUM, 239 Brinton Rd., interprets the atmosphere of Western ranch life. The main house was built in 1892; businessman Bradford Brinton bought the property in 1923 and built several additions 1927-28. A large collection of Western art includes paintings, sculpture and etchings by John James Audubon, Edward Borein, Frank Tenney Johnson, Frederic Remington and Charles M. Russell.

Extensive collections of equipment, Plains Indian crafts, rare books and documents, and items pertaining to the history of the ranch are displayed in their original setting in the fully furnished ranch house and outbuildings. Changing exhibitions are presented in the reception gallery.

Time: Allow 1 hour minimum. **Hours:** Mon.-Sat. 10-5, Sun. noon-5. **Cost:** $5; $4 (ages 62+ and students with ID); free (ages 0-12). **Phone:** (307) 672-3173.

BIGHORN CANYON NATIONAL RECREATION AREA—See Montana p. 131.

BIGHORN NATIONAL FOREST (B-4)

Elevations in the forest range from 4,600 ft. in the northern section to 13,165 ft. at Cloud Peak. Refer to AAA maps for additional elevation information.

In the Bighorn Mountains of north-central Wyoming, the Bighorn National Forest encompasses 1,115,073 acres. The forest is traversed by US 14 (Bighorn Scenic Byway), which crosses 8,950-foot Granite Pass and winds through scenic Shell Canyon and Falls; US 14A (Medicine Wheel Passage), which passes by Medicine Mountain near the enigmatic Medicine Wheel; and US 16 (Cloud Peak Skyway), which crosses 9,677-foot Powder River Pass and threads through beautiful Ten Sleep Canyon.

Cloud Peak is the highest peak within the forest. Motorists pulling trailers should use caution on US 14/14A.

Backpacking and saddle and pack trips can be taken into 189,039-acre Cloud Peak Wilderness; horse and foot trails begin at trail heads accessible via gravel roads off US 14 and US 16. This scenic area has miles of streams and more than 200 lakes containing brook, cutthroat, golden and rainbow trout. Hunters come in search of deer and elk.

Throughout the forest are 30 campgrounds, 10 picnic grounds and a good trail network, including the Bucking Mule Falls National Recreation Trail.

Downhill skiing is available east of Worland (west of Buffalo); cross-country skiing can be pursued in all sections of the forest. Mountain climbing and snowmobiling also are popular.

Maps of the forest are available at the District Ranger's office in Sheridan at 2013 Eastside Second St., (307) 674-2600; in Lovell at 604 E. Main St., (307) 548-6541; and in Buffalo at 1415 Fort St., (307) 684-7806.

Two visitor centers offer nature trails, exhibits, maps and other information about the forest, recreational activities and nearby communities daily 9-5, Memorial Day weekend through Labor Day. Shell Falls Wayside Visitor Center is on US 14, 5 miles west of Burgess Junction. The Burgess Junction Visitor Center on US 14, 1.5 miles east of Burgess Junction, is closed until at least 2014; phone for updates.

For additional information contact the Forest Supervisor's Office, 2013 Eastside Second St., Sheridan, WY 82801; phone (307) 674-2600. *See Recreation Areas Chart.*

MEDICINE WHEEL is off US 14A on Medicine Mountain, about 27 mi. e. of Lovell. The pre-Columbian structure, a circular arrangement of stones 245 feet in circumference with 28 spokes extending from a central cairn, is believed to have been used for religious ceremonies or celestial observations. **Note:** The road to Medicine Wheel is closed to vehicular traffic. Visitors are required to walk 1.5 miles to the site. Exceptions can be made for elderly or physically impaired visitors.

SHELL CANYON AND FALLS is 30 mi. e. of Greybull on US 14. The site can be seen from the Shell Falls overlook on US 14. An interpretive trail provides views of the imposing limestone cliffs and deep granite gorge cut by Shell Creek. **Phone:** (307) 548-6541.

BLACK HILLS NATIONAL FOREST (B-6)

Elevations in the forest range from 3,300 ft. south of Hot Springs to 7,242 ft. at Harney Peak. Refer to AAA maps for additional elevation information.

In the scenic Black Hills of South Dakota and extending westward into Wyoming, the Black Hills National Forest covers more than 1.2 million acres. It was established in 1897. Stands of ponderosa pine, spruce and aspen are home to mountain lions, white-tailed and mule deer, elk and turkeys. Mountain goats and bighorn sheep are sometimes seen in the Harney Range area. Visitors should note that while summer days are warm, the nights can be quite cool.

Various routes make for a scenic drive. Peter Norbeck Scenic Byway creates a 70-mile loop via the Needles Highway, Iron Mountain Road—with its views of Mount Rushmore framed by tunnels—and the pigtail bridges. Norbeck Overlook, on Iron Mountain Road (US 16A south from Keystone, S.D.), offers a view of the Black Elk Wilderness.

The 20-mile Spearfish Canyon Scenic Byway along US 14A follows the pine- and spruce-covered banks of Spearfish Creek. Hiking trails to the canyon rims offer views of canyon walls and forests.

The 111-mile Centennial Trail runs the length of the Black Hills from Bear Butte State Park to Wind Cave National Park. With more than 30 access points, portions of the route are open to motorized vehicles, horseback riders and mountain bicycles.

The forest's visitor center at Pactola Reservoir, on US 385 west of Rapid City, S.D., provides information about the history and management of the forest, including wildlife, scenery and recreation areas. Maps and information also are available at the forest supervisor's office in Custer City, S.D., and at district rangers' offices in Custer City, Rapid City and Spearfish, S.D., and in Sundance and Newcastle, Wyo. Allow 30 minutes minimum. Visitor center open daily 8-7, Memorial Day weekend-Labor Day. Free.

Most of the forest's developed recreational facilities are in South Dakota, but the Wyoming segment does have four campgrounds with 76 sites. Entrance to the forest is free, but there are fees for day-use areas and camping. For further information contact the Forest Supervisor's Office, 1019 N. 5th St., Custer City, SD 57730; phone (605) 673-9200. *See Recreation Areas Chart.*

BRIDGER-TETON NATIONAL FOREST (C-2)

Elevations in the forest range from 5,660 ft. near Alpine to 13,804 ft. at Gannett Peak. Refer to AAA maps for additional elevation information.

Bordering Grand Teton (see place listing p. 266) and Yellowstone (see place listing p. 326) national parks, Bridger-Teton National Forest covers 3,439,809 acres in the Gros Ventre, Salt River, Teton, Wind River and Wyoming ranges. Within the forest are several live glaciers, an outstanding example of a geologic landslide and the state's highest mountain, Gannett Peak, shared by Shoshone National Forest (see place listing p. 318). Fishing, hunting, white-water rafting and winter sports attract visitors to the area.

The forest has three wilderness areas, all accessible only on foot or horseback. The Bridger Wilderness, 428,169 acres of scenic mountain country, lies on the west slope of the Continental Divide in the Wind River Range. More than 1,300 lakes, Gannett Peak and many glaciers highlight this rugged landscape, which is traversed by more than 500 miles of hiking and snowmobiling trails.

The Green River, beginning at the base of Gannett Peak, races through the Wind River Mountains before turning southward to join the Colorado River. The Teton Wilderness preserves 585,468 acres in

the northern section of the forest. Snow sometimes stays on the ground until early July in this barren alpine country of broad meadows, lakes, steep canyons, streams and waterfalls.

At Two Ocean Pass, Two Ocean Creek divides and sends one stream to the Pacific Ocean and another to the Atlantic; this geographic phenomenon supposedly exists nowhere else on the continent. The 287,000-acre Gros Ventre Wilderness, immediately east of Jackson, also is rugged, mountainous country ideally suited to backpacking, fishing and hunting.

Gros Ventre Slide is 5 miles east of Kelly on Gros Ventre Road. When the landslide occurred on the morning of June 23, 1925, this large earth movement dammed up the Gros Ventre (Big Belly) River. In a matter of minutes, trees and land fell from an elevation of 9,000 feet. Two years later part of the slide gave way, and the resulting wall of water, mud and rock destroyed the town of Kelly.

Scenic drives include Centennial National Scenic Byway from Dubois to Pinedale, the Green River Road from Pinedale north to the Green River Lakes, and the Skyline Drive from Pinedale northeast to Elkhart Park. Greys River Road leaves US 89 near Alpine and follows the river on its southward run; from its headwaters roads lead to US 89 near Geneva and to US 189 at Big Piney or Fontenelle reservoirs.

Pinedale (see place listing p. 307) and the resort town of Jackson (see place listing p. 274) are recreational activity centers. Near these two towns are the forest's three ski areas; trails for cross-country skiing also are available. Nearby hot springs include Granite Hot Springs, 35 miles southeast of Jackson on US 189, then 9 miles north. The Jackson Visitor Center, 532 N. Cache St., is open daily 8-7, June-Sept.; 9-5, rest of year.

For additional information contact the Forest Supervisor's Office, P.O. Box 1888, Jackson, WY; phone (307) 739-5500. *See Recreation Areas Chart.*

INSIDER INFO:
High-Altitude Health

Temples throbbing, gasping for breath and nauseated, you barely notice the scudding clouds or the spectacular view.

You might be suffering from Acute Mountain Sickness (AMS). Usually striking at around 8,000 feet (2,450 m) in altitude, AMS is your body's way of coping with the reduced oxygen and humidity of high altitudes. Among the symptoms are headaches, shortness of breath, loss of appetite, insomnia and lethargy. Some people complain of temporary weight gain or swelling in the face, hands and feet.

You can reduce the effect of high altitude by being in top condition. If you smoke or suffer from heart or lung ailments, consult your physician before your trip. Certain drugs will intensify the symptoms. To avoid Acute Mountain Sickness, adjust to elevations slowly; a gradual ascent with a couple days of acclimatization is best if you have time. For example, if you are planning a trip to the Rocky Mountains of

Colorado, you might want to spend the first night in a lower altitude city such as Denver as opposed to heading directly to an environment with extreme elevations.

On the way up, eat light, nutritious meals and stay hydrated by drinking a large amount of water, taking care to avoid caffeine, alcohol and salt. In addition, your doctor may be able to prescribe medication that can offset the effects of high-altitude.

If you develop AMS, you should stop ascending; you will recover in a few days. If the AMS is mild, a quick descent will end the suffering immediately.

Other high-altitude health problems include sunburn and hypothermia. Dress in layers to protect yourself from the intense sun and wide fluctuations in temperature.

Finally, after you lounge in the sauna or hot tub at your lodgings, remember to stand up carefully, for the heat has relaxed your blood vessels and lowered your blood pressure.

PERIODIC SPRING is about 5 mi. e. of Afton on FR 10211 (Swift Creek Rd.). In late summer the spring ceases to flow every 18 minutes, then gradually builds to a thundering, ice-cold torrent. This cycle occurs regularly for 9 months and fluctuates during the period of highest snow melt, from about mid-May to mid-August. A narrow dirt road leads to within half a mile of the spring; the last 200 yards of the hike are very steep. The road, not recommended for trailers, is closed during winter.

BUFFALO (B-4) pop. 4,585, elev. 4,645'
• Restaurants p. 239

Retaining the atmosphere and hospitality of the Old West, Buffalo is a ranching town on the eastern slope of the Bighorn Mountains. Many Native American battles took place in this area 1866-77, triggered by the presence of the Bozeman Trail and the forts built to protect it.

After the area was opened to settlement, Buffalo was founded in 1879. Buffalo became known as the "Rustlers' Capital," and by 1892 the tensions between the region's big cattlemen and farmers, or "nesters," had erupted into the Johnson County War. It took the U.S. Army to restore order.

The growth of sheep ranching in the late 1890s brought Basque herders, who were drawn to Buffalo because of the Bighorn Mountains' resemblance to their homeland in the Pyrenees. Basque descendants continue to practice their time-honored traditions.

Guided saddle trips and jeep tours of nearby scenic and historical attractions can be arranged through local operators. Sightseeing is most rewarding along the Cloud Peak Scenic Byway portion of US 16 that runs between Buffalo and Ten Sleep.

Hunters can visit the Hunters Information Station in the chamber of commerce building.

Buffalo Chamber of Commerce: 55 N. Main St., Buffalo, WY 82834. **Phone:** (307) 684-5544 or (800) 227-5122. *(See ad p. 238.)*

Self-guiding tours: Information about walking and driving tours is available from the chamber of commerce.

JIM GATCHELL MEMORIAL MUSEUM is at 100 Fort St. The museum, which honors a frontier pharmacist known for his friendship with and knowledge of the Plains Indians, houses more than 8,500 artifacts. Included in the displays are a variety of firearms, historical photographs depicting the early days of the West, Indian artifacts and pioneer items. **Hours:** Mon.-Sat. 9-6, Sun. noon-6, June-Oct.; Mon.-Fri. 9-4, in May. Closed Memorial Day, July 4, Labor Day and Columbus Day. Phone ahead to confirm schedule. **Cost:** $5; $3 (ages 6-16); $12 (family). **Phone:** (307) 684-9331. *(See ad p. 238.)*

MUSEUM OF THE OCCIDENTAL HOTEL is at 10 N. Main St. Founded in a tent in 1879, the Occidental quickly became one of the state's most renowned hotels. Guests included Buffalo Bill Cody, Teddy Roosevelt and Calamity Jane. Reputedly the only fully restored frontier hotel in Wyoming, antique furnishings and Old World ambience reflect its original grandeur. The lobby's embossed ceilings and the 1908 saloon's original back bar are particularly noteworthy. **Hours:** Daily 8-5. **Cost:** Donations. **Phone:** (307) 684-0451. [⏦]

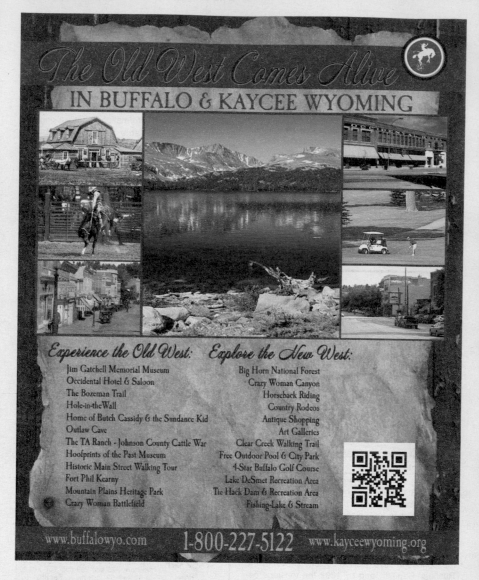

The Old West Comes Alive
IN BUFFALO & KAYCEE WYOMING

Experience the Old West:
- Jim Gatchell Memorial Museum
- Occidental Hotel & Saloon
- The Bozeman Trail
- Hole-in-the-Wall
- Home of Butch Cassidy & the Sundance Kid
- Outlaw Cave
- The TA Ranch - Johnson County Cattle War
- Hoofprints of the Past Museum
- Historic Main Street Walking Tour
- Fort Phil Kearny
- Mountain Plains Heritage Park
- Crazy Woman Battlefield

Explore the New West:
- Big Horn National Forest
- Crazy Woman Canyon
- Horseback Riding
- Country Rodeos
- Antique Shopping
- Art Galleries
- Clear Creek Walking Trail
- Free Outdoor Pool & City Park
- 4-Star Buffalo Golf Course
- Lake DeSmet Recreation Area
- Tie Hack Dam & Recreation Area
- Fishing-Lake & Stream

www.buffalowyo.com   1-800-227-5122   www.kayceewyoming.org

HAMPTON INN & SUITES   (307)684-8899

♦♦♦ **Hotel** $94-$170 **Address:** 85 US Hwy 16 E 82834 **Location:** I-90 exit 58, 1.6 mi w. **Facility:** 75 units. 3 stories, interior corridors. **Parking:** winter plug-ins. **Terms:** 1-7 night minimum stay, cancellation fee imposed. **Pool(s):** heated indoor. **Activities:** hot tub, exercise room. **Guest Services:** coin laundry.

AAA Benefit: Members save up to 10%!

[icons]

HISTORIC MANSION HOUSE INN   (307)684-2218

♦♦♦ **Historic Bed & Breakfast** $90-$185

Address: 313 N Main St 82834 **Location:** US 16; downtown. **Facility:** An original structure, built in 1903, houses the property's inn-style accommodations. Guests can relax or read in the second-floor sunroom. 7 units. 2 stories (no elevator), interior corridors. **Parking:** winter plug-ins. **Terms:** closed 1/1-1/31, 3 day cancellation notice-fee imposed. **Featured Amenity:** full hot breakfast.

[icons]

HOLIDAY INN EXPRESS HOTEL & SUITES   307/684-9900

♦♦♦ **Hotel.** Rates not provided. **Address:** 106 US Hwy 16 E 82834 **Location:** I-25 exit 299 (US 16), 0.5 mi e; I-90 exit 58, 1 mi w. **Facility:** 69 units. 3 stories, interior corridors. **Parking:** winter plug-ins. **Pool(s):** heated indoor. **Activities:** hot tub, exercise room. **Guest Services:** coin laundry.

THE OCCIDENTAL HOTEL   (307)684-0451

♦♦♦ **Historic Hotel** $75-$285

Address: 10 N Main St 82834 **Location:** Center. **Facility:** This historic property—consisting of a hotel, restaurant and bar—spans one city block. Most rooms are themed with Western characters, and the décor includes antiques and period pieces. 16 units, some two bedrooms, three bedrooms and kitchens. 2 stories (no elevator), interior corridors. **Parking:** street only. **Terms:** 14 day cancellation notice. **Dining:** The Virginian Restaurant, see separate listing. **(See ad p. 238.)**

[icons]

SUPER 8 OF BUFFALO   (307)684-2531

♦♦ **Hotel** $65-$105 **Address:** 655 E Hart St 82834 **Location:** I-25 exit 299 (US 16), just w; I-90 exit 58, 1.3 mi w. **Facility:** 48 units. 2 stories (no elevator), interior corridors. **Parking:** winter plug-ins.

WYO MOTEL   (307)684-5505

♦ **Motel** $49-$129 **Address:** 610 E Hart St 82834 **Location:** I-25 exit 299 (US 16), just w; I-90 exit 58, 1.3 mi w. **Facility:** 27 units, some efficiencies. 1 story, exterior corridors. **Parking:** winter plug-ins. **Terms:** cancellation fee imposed. **Pool(s):** heated outdoor. **Activities:** picnic facilities. **Guest Services:** coin laundry.

WHERE TO EAT

BOZEMAN'S TRAIL STEAKHOUSE   307/684-5555

♦♦ **American Casual Dining** $8-$28

AAA Inspector Notes: The steakhouse's varied menu lists not only burgers, buffalo steak and the house specialty baby back ribs but also shrimp dinners and a few Mexican items. The decor contributes to a Western and Plains Indian atmosphere. **Features:** full bar. **Address:** 675 E Hart St 82834 **Location:** I-25 exit 299 (US 16), just w. *Menu on AAA.com* [L] [D]

CHINA GARDENS   307/684-9208

♦♦ Chinese. Casual Dining. $7-$15 **AAA Inspector Notes:** The chef concentrates on Americanized Cantonese-style cooking at this spot using less oil and more flavorful spices in the sauces. There is a nice sampling of Thai dishes also available. **Address:** 386 N Main St 82834 **Location:** US 16; downtown. [L] [D]

CLEAR CREEK CANTINA   307/278-0043

♦♦ Tex-Mex. Casual Dining. $8-$24 **AAA Inspector Notes:** Stopping at this cantina is a must. It's colorful, cheerful and has great food. Menu items include a to-die-for green chili, terrific Tex-Mex cobb salad, Baja fish tacos, a variety of wraps and big burgers, slow-roasted and marinated pork tips, several selections of rib-eye dinners and their popular Two, Two n' Two lunch specials. I'd go back just for their refreshing margarita pie. Yum! **Features:** full bar. **Address:** 4 S Main St 82834 **Location:** I-25 exit 298 northbound; exit 299 southbound; downtown. **Parking:** street only. [L] [D]

THE VIRGINIAN RESTAURANT   307/684 6076

♦♦ Steak Seafood. Fine Dining. $18-$33 **AAA Inspector Notes:** *Historic.* The authentic, Old West décor is reminiscent of the 1890s. The specialty is locally grown, organic buffalo steak but the menu also features seafood, chicken and pasta. Table settings and the ambience are delightful. Request a seat in the cozy alcove. **Features:** full bar. **Address:** 10 N Main St 82834 **Location:** Center; in The Occidental Hotel. **Parking:** street only. [D]

WINCHESTER STEAK HOUSE   307/684-8636

♦♦ **Steak Casual Dining** $15-$38

AAA Inspector Notes: Voted as having the city's best steak and seafood, this family-run restaurant attracts folks from miles around for a casual dinner at a location convenient to both interstates and downtown. **Features:** full bar. **Address:** 117 US Hwy 16 E 82834 **Location:** I-25 exit 299 (US 16), 0.5 mi e; I-90 exit 58, just e. [D]

CARIBOU-TARGHEE NATIONAL FOREST—See Idaho p. 54.

CASPER (D-4) pop. 55,316, elev. 5,123'
• Hotels p. 241 • Restaurants p. 241

Casper's roots are buried in commerce. The town began as a ferry site on the Oregon Trail in 1847, when a group of Mormon immigrants who were camping realized that there was money to be made by boating travelers across the North Platte River. The idea caught on, and in the early 1850s a toll bridge was built; soon a military post was established to protect the span and its traffic.

The town's real asset, however, was not discovered until 1889, when the first well in the Salt Creek oil field was tapped; by 1915 the town was in an oil boom that matched the frenzy of the California, Colorado and Montana gold rushes.

The boom brought not only prosperity but also a national scandal over the nearby Teapot Dome oil field. In 1927 the U.S. Supreme Court handed down verdicts in the case, which included sentencing Secretary of the Interior Albert Fall to prison for secretly leasing the rich field to Mammoth Crude Oil Co. without taking competitive bids.

Casper is a major service and supply center for mineral, oil, natural gas, uranium and coal industries, as well as a center for many medical and financial services.

Stargazers can view astronomy-related programs throughout the year at Casper Planetarium, a half-mile north of I-25 exit 188B at 904 N. Poplar, phone (307) 577-0310. Along SRs 20/26 and 220, markers identify the California, Mormon, Oregon and Pony Express trails.

Casper Area Convention and Visitors Bureau: 139 W. Second St., Suite 1B, Casper, WY 82601. **Phone:** (307) 234-5362 or (800) 852-1889.

DAN SPEAS FISH REARING STATION is 10 mi. w. on SR 220, then 4.5 mi. w. on CR 308, following signs. The station is one of Wyoming's most productive fish hatcheries. Its use of a nearby spring, which promotes rapid fish growth, enables it to produce a 4-inch fish in 120 days. About 1.35 million fish are stocked annually. **Hours:** Daily 8-5. **Cost:** Free. **Phone:** (307) 473-8890.

FORT CASPAR MUSEUM AND HISTORIC SITE is .5 mi. n. of SR 220 off Wyoming Blvd. at 4001 Fort Caspar Rd. This site on the Oregon, California, Mormon, and Pony Express trails includes reconstructions of an 1847 Mormon Trail ferry, an 1859 Guinard bridge and an 1865 frontier Army fort. Museum exhibits recount the history of central Wyoming, from prehistory to the present.

Hours: Museum daily 8-6, June-Aug.; daily 8-5 in May and Sept.; Tues.-Sat. 8-5, rest of year. Reconstructed buildings daily 8:30-5:30, June-Aug.; 8:30-4:30 in May and Sept. **Cost:** $3; $2 (ages 13-18). **Phone:** (307) 235-8462.

HISTORIC TRAILS INTERPRETIVE CENTER is off I-25 exit 189, then 1 mi. n. to 1501 N. Poplar St. Seven galleries represent Western trail history through interactive and multimedia exhibits and dioramas. Visitors can sit in a covered wagon and view a simulated crossing of the North Platte River. A five-screen theater features an audiovisual presentation illustrating pioneer and Native American life. During the summer months, encampment reenactments take place and interpreters in period costume perform demonstrations.

Time: Allow 2 hours minimum. **Hours:** Tues.-Sun. 8-5, June-July; Tues.-Sat. 9-4:30, rest of year. Closed Jan. 1, Easter, Thanksgiving and Christmas. **Cost:** $6; $5 (ages 62+); $4 (students ages 16+ with ID). **Phone:** (307) 261-7700.

HISTORIC TRAILS WEST departs from Fort Caspar Museum and Historic Site, off Wyoming Blvd.; and from the Historic Trails Interpretive Center, 1501 N. Poplar St. The tour features a wagon train that travels along the actual ruts of the California, Mormon and Oregon trails. Visitors also can take an excursion where they ride horses as Pony Express riders did alongside the wagons. Historical accounts are given. Three- and 5-day expeditions also are available.

Hours: Daily, May-Oct. (weather permitting). **Cost:** Trips lasting 2 hours to overnight $45-$255. Trips lasting 3 to 5 days $795-$1,295. Reservations are recommended. **Phone:** (307) 266-4868.

INDEPENDENCE ROCK STATE HISTORIC SITE—see Alcova p. 234.

NICOLAYSEN ART MUSEUM AND DISCOVERY CENTER is at 400 E. Collins Dr. The center presents changing exhibits by national and regional artists. The Discovery Center offers informal hands-on and supervised programs, including a painting center, an image-rubbing table, a library and an art gallery. **Hours:** Tues.-Sat. 10-5, Sun. noon-4. Closed major holidays. **Cost:** $5; $3 (ages 5-17 and students with ID); free (on Sun.). **Phone:** (307) 235-5247.

PAINTED PAST LIVING HISTORY TOURS, 330 S. Center, Suite 414, offers three tours. The 1890s tour features Casper characters from the era; the Sand Bar murder mystery tour takes visitors back to the 1920s during Prohibition. The Casper the Friendly Ghost tour travels along the back alleys of downtown, where visitors will learn about historic buildings and past inhabitants. **Time:** Allow 1 hour, 30 minutes minimum. **Hours:** Tours offered June-Sept. Phone ahead to confirm schedule. **Cost:** $25. **Phone:** (307) 258-2585.

PLATTE RIVER RAFT N' REEL is at 1775 W. 1st St. Visitors can view wildlife during scenic float trips on the North Platte River. Fly-fishing trips on the river's Grey Reef stretch and white-water rafting trips also are offered. **Time:** Allow 1 hour minimum. **Hours:** Float trips daily, June-Aug. Phone ahead to confirm schedule. **Cost:** Float trips $35-$65. Reservations are required. **Phone:** (307) 267-0170.

[SAVE] **TATE GEOLOGICAL MUSEUM** is on the Casper College campus at 125 College Dr.; take Wolcott St./Casper Mountain Rd. s. Almost 3,000 fossil and mineral specimens are on display. You can tour a fossil preparation lab and meet "Dee," said to be one of the world's largest mounted Columbian mammoths. **Time:** Allow 1 hour minimum. **Hours:** Mon.-Fri. 9-5, Sat. 10-4. Closed major holidays. **Cost:** Donations. **Phone:** (307) 268-2447.

WERNER WILDLIFE MUSEUM is s. via Wolcott St. to 405 E. 15th St. The museum houses a pronghorn antelope diorama, a collection of Western birds and mounted specimens of wildlife native to Wyoming and other parts of North America. The Werner Trophy Room exhibits specimens from around the world. **Hours:** Mon.-Fri. 8:30-5. Closed Jan. 1, Thanksgiving and Christmas. Phone ahead to confirm schedule. **Cost:** Free. **Phone:** (307) 235-2108.

WYOMING VETERANS MEMORIAL MUSEUM is at 3740 Jourgensen Ave. at the Natrona County International Airport. Veterans are honored by displays of uniforms, military artifacts, historical documents and other memorabilia. The facility also creates oral and video recordings depicting the experiences of local and visiting veterans. **Time:** Allow 1 hour minimum. **Hours:** Tues.-Sat. 9-4. **Cost:** Free. **Phone:** (307) 472-1857.

BEST WESTERN RAMKOTA HOTEL   (307)266-6000

Hotel
$99-$119

AAA Benefit: Members save 10% or more with Best Western!

Address: 800 N Poplar St 82601 **Location:** I-25 exit 188B (N Poplar St), just ne. **Facility:** 230 units. 6 stories, interior corridors. **Parking:** winter plug-ins. **Terms:** 2-4 night minimum stay - seasonal and/or weekends. **Pool(s):** heated indoor. **Activities:** hot tub, game room, exercise room. **Guest Services:** valet and coin laundry, area transportation.

COURTYARD BY MARRIOTT CASPER   (307)473-2600

▼▼▼ Hotel $93-$170 **Address:** 4260 Hospitality Ln 82601 **Location:** I-25 exit 185, just s, then just w. **Facility:** 100 units. 4 stories, interior corridors. **Pool(s):** heated indoor. **Activities:** hot tub, exercise room. **Guest Services:** valet and coin laundry.

AAA Benefit: Members save 5% or more!

DAYS INN CASPER   (307)234-1159

▼▼ Hotel $90-$175 **Address:** 301 E 'E' St 82601 **Location:** I-25 exit 188A (Center St), just s, then just e. **Facility:** 121 units. 2 stories (no elevator), interior corridors. **Parking:** winter plug-ins. **Terms:** 3 day cancellation notice-fee imposed. **Pool(s):** heated outdoor. **Activities:** exercise room. **Guest Services:** valet and coin laundry.

HAMPTON INN & SUITES CASPER   (307)235-6668

▼▼▼ Hotel $129-$169 **Address:** 1100 N Poplar St 82601 **Location:** I-25 exit 188B (N Poplar St), just e. **Facility:** 100 units. 4 stories, interior corridors. **Parking:** winter plug-ins. **Terms:** 1-7 night minimum stay, cancellation fee imposed. **Pool(s):** heated indoor. **Activities:** hot tub, exercise room. **Guest Services:** valet and coin laundry, area transportation.

AAA Benefit: Members save up to 10%!

Visit your AAA/CAA Travel office to book a AAA Vacations® Disney package

HILTON GARDEN INN CASPER   (307)266-1300

▼▼▼ Hotel $99-$209 **Address:** 1150 N Poplar St 82601 **Location:** I-25 exit 188B (N Poplar St), just e. **Facility:** 121 units, some two bedrooms. 4 stories, interior corridors. **Parking:** winter plug-ins. **Terms:** 1-7 night minimum stay, cancellation fee imposed. **Pool(s):** heated indoor. **Activities:** hot tub, exercise room. **Guest Services:** valet and coin laundry.

AAA Benefit: Members save up to 10%!

HOLIDAY INN CASPER EAST AT MCMURRY PARK
(307)577-5000

▼▼▼ Hotel $129-$159 **Address:** 721 Granite Peak Dr 82609 **Location:** I-25 exit 182 (Hat Six Rd), just s, then just w. **Facility:** 120 units. 4 stories, interior corridors. **Terms:** cancellation fee imposed. **Pool(s):** heated indoor. **Activities:** hot tub, exercise room. **Guest Services:** valet and coin laundry, area transportation.

QUALITY INN & SUITES CASPER   (307)266-2400

▼▼ Hotel $86-$153 **Address:** 821 N Poplar St 82601 **Location:** I-25 exit 188B (N Poplar St), just e. **Facility:** 92 units, 2 stories (no elevator), interior corridors. **Parking:** winter plug-ins. **Amenities:** safes. **Activities:** exercise room. **Guest Services:** valet and coin laundry.

SUPER 8 CASPER WEST   (307)266-3480

▼▼ Hotel $95-$145 **Address:** 3838 CY Ave 82604 **Location:** I-25 exit 188B (N Poplar St), 1.5 mi s to CY Ave, then 1.7 mi w. **Facility:** 66 units. 3 stories (no elevator), interior corridors. **Parking:** winter plug-ins. **Activities:** picnic facilities. **Guest Services:** coin laundry.

MAINSTAY SUITES   307/472-7829

(fyi) Not evaluated. **Address:** 551 Granite Peak Dr 82609 **Location:** I-25 exit 182 (Hat Six Rd), just s, then just w. Facilities, services, and décor characterize a mid-scale property.

WHERE TO EAT

BOSCO'S ITALIAN RESTAURANTE   307/265-9658

▼▼ Italian. Casual Dining. $6-$24 **AAA Inspector Notes:** This casual, child-friendly restaurant is worth seeking out for create-your-own Alfredo dishes and traditional veal, chicken, shrimp and gnocchi preparations. Also on the menu are gluten-free items. **Features:** full bar, patio dining. **Reservations:** suggested, for dinner. **Address:** 847 E 'A' St 82601 **Location:** I-25 exit 188A (Center St), 0.4 mi s to E 'A' St, then 0.5 mi e. **Parking:** street only.

COTTAGE CAFE   307/234-1157

▼▼ American. Casual Dining. $9-$10 **AAA Inspector Notes:** This quaint little cottage serves healthy and delicious grilled panini and specialty sandwiches, wicked wraps, a popular tequila-lime chicken soup and a variety of fresh salads, including the Chinese chicken, grilled steak, Santa Fe, cucumber dill and more. The mild green chili quiche is served daily, as are the homemade breads. Sun porch dining is available. **Features:** Sunday brunch. **Address:** 116 S Lincoln St 82601 **Location:** I-25 exit 187, 0.4 mi s, just w, then just s. **Parking:** street only.

DSASUMO ASIAN BISTRO   307/237-7874

▼▼ Thai. Casual Dining. $11-$21 **AAA Inspector Notes:** The contemporary restaurant serves authentic Thai cuisine and features an extensive sushi menu. **Features:** full bar, patio dining. **Address:** 320 W 1st St 82601 **Location:** I-25 exit 188A (Center St), just s, then just w. **Parking:** on-site and street.

FIRE ROCK STEAK HOUSE   307/234-2333

▼▼▼ Seafood Steak. Casual Dining. $9-$38 **AAA Inspector Notes:** While this restaurant serves chicken, fish, pasta and a nice selection of sandwiches, the real reason to come here is for beef. The fine Mid-Western steaks are aged for 21 days, resulting in a great dining experience. **Features:** full bar, patio dining. **Address:** 6100 E 2nd St 82609 **Location:** I-25 exit 185, 0.5 mi s on Wyoming Blvd, then 1 mi e; in McMurry Business Park. [L] [D] CALL [M]

GOOSE EGG INN RESTAURANT   307/473-8838

◆◆ American. Casual Dining. $13-$27 **AAA Inspector Notes:** Just a little ways out of town, this historic and charming family restaurant offers entrees from the roost, from the pasture, off the hook and out of the net. Dinner includes a lovely relish tray, salad, potato and house-made bread of the day. Irene Brook doesn't use measuring cups for her delicious homemade desserts, which are baked the good old-fashioned way. This is a dining experience you will remember fondly. **Features:** full bar. **Reservations:** suggested. **Address:** 10580 Goose Egg Rd 82601 **Location:** I-25 exit 188B (N Poplar St), 1.7 mi s to CY Ave (CR 220), then 9.5 mi sw to Goose Egg Rd (south side of CR 220). [D]

J'S PUB & GRILL   307/472-3100

▼▼ New American. Casual Dining. $9-$29 **AAA Inspector Notes:** This nice atmosphere and fun eatery on the other side of Casper offers artistic and whimsical presentations. Menu items are creative, such as a chicken and waffle sandwich with onion petals, horseradish-encrusted filet mignon with lobster mashed potatoes and bananas Foster mini shakes served with chocolate Twinkies. **Features:** full bar, patio dining, happy hour. **Address:** 3201 SW Wyoming Blvd 82604 **Location:** I-25 exit 188B (N Poplar St), 1.5 mi s to CY Ave, then 1.8 mi w to SR 228. [L] [D] CALL [M]

LA COCINA   307/266-1414

▼▼ Mexican. Casual Dining. $7-$16 **AAA Inspector Notes:** This cozy eatery features popular daily specials, appetizers, sizzling fajitas and traditional Mexican fare. Favorites include pork chili soup, a variety of quesadillas, chicken or steak fajita salad, Santa Fe stir-fry and the ultimate combo plate. There may be a wait, but it's worth it. **Features:** full bar. **Reservations:** required. **Address:** 1040 N Center St 82601 **Location:** I-25 exit 188A (Center St), 1 mi e on Yellowstone Hwy (Center St); corner of N Center and K sts. [L] [D]

LIME LEAF ASIAN BISTRO   307/315-6888

▼▼▼ Asian. Casual Dining. $9-$19 **AAA Inspector Notes:** This cute building features attractive décor accents of wood, bamboo and live plants. The menu is lined with Chinese and Vietnamese specialties. The daily lunch special is popular with locals and travelers. **Features:** beer & wine. **Address:** 845 E 2nd St 82601 **Location:** I-25 exit 188A (Center St), 0.5 mi s, just e on E 1st St, just s on S Kimball St, then just e. [L] [D]

SILVER FOX STEAKHOUSE   307/235-3000

▼▼▼ American. Casual Dining. $9-$40 **AAA Inspector Notes:** Well-prepared dishes of prime rib and aged steaks are served in this relaxing setting that affords a nice mountain view in the main dining room. The filet mignon, fried green tomatoes and chicken pot pie are popular. Intimate booths also are available for a quieter dining experience. **Features:** full bar. **Reservations:** suggested. **Address:** 3422 S Energy Ln 82604 **Location:** I-25 exit 188B (N Poplar St), 4.2 mi sw on S Poplar St (SR 220). [L] [D] CALL [M] [✂]

SOUTH SEA CHINESE RESTAURANT   307/237-4777

▼▼ Chinese. Casual Dining. $8-$16 **AAA Inspector Notes:** The diverse menu here lists 102 budget-friendly choices of traditional Asian food, including the popular sizzling seafood combination platter. Uniformed servers are friendly. **Features:** beer & wine. **Address:** 3400 E 2nd St 82609 **Location:** I-25 exit 185, 0.3 mi s on Wyoming Blvd, then 0.5 mi w. [L] [D]

CHEYENNE (E-6) pop. 59,466, elev. 6,060'
• Hotels p. 244 • Restaurants p. 247

Cheyenne was named for the tribe of Plains Indians that once roamed southeastern Wyoming. In 1867 Union Pacific railroad chief engineer Maj. Gen. Grenville M. Dodge built a depot on the site, situated at the junction of several roads leading to military camps.

Before the track even reached town, it was overrun by gamblers, cowboys, speculators, shopkeepers and real estate salesmen, thus earning Cheyenne the nickname "Hell on Wheels." The town's reputation was so widespread that in 1868 a resident received a letter from Pennsylvania addressed simply "Cheyenne."

By 1869 Cheyenne had outgrown some of its cow-town adolescence to assume the more mature stature of territorial capital, an honor it retained when Wyoming became the 44th state in 1890.

Noted town residents include Nellie Tayloe Ross, the first woman governor in the United States; and Esther Morris, a pioneer for women's suffrage in Wyoming and former justice of the peace of South Pass City (see place listing p. 318). A statue honoring Morris is on Capitol Avenue. The Cowgirls of the West Museum, 205 W. 17th St., preserves the role of women in Western culture with exhibits of rodeo and ranching memorabilia including saddles, photographs and clothing; phone (307) 638-4994.

"Big Boy," one of the world's largest steam locomotives, is on permanent display in Holliday Park.

Since it was established in 1867 as a headquarters for the cavalry troops protecting pioneers and railroad construction workers, F.E. Warren Air Force Base has served various branches of the military, including the nation's first intercontinental ballistic missile group.

Happy Jack Road (SR 210) is a 38-mile scenic byway to Laramie that runs from rolling grasslands to the rocky foothills of the Pole Mountain Division of Medicine Bow National Forest. Equally interesting is a trip to Snowy Range, a region of fishing streams and mountain lakes.

In July ▼ Cheyenne Frontier Days recaptures the city's Wild West heritage with horse races, parades, nightly entertainment and what is claimed to be the world's largest outdoor rodeo.

Visit Cheyenne: 1 Depot Sq., 121 W. 15th St., Suite 202, Cheyenne, WY 82001. **Phone:** (307) 778-3133 or (800) 426-5009. *(See ad on inside front cover, p. 246.)*

Shopping areas: Frontier Mall, 1400 Dell Range Blvd., has more than 75 stores including Dillard's, JCPenney and Sears.

Self-guiding tours: A pamphlet describing a self-guiding walking tour of Cheyenne's historic downtown area is available at Visit Cheyenne.

CHEYENNE BOTANIC GARDENS, 710 S. Lions Park Dr., has a variety of themed gardens, including xeriscape, rose and rock gardens. A 6,800-square-foot solar-heated greenhouse conservatory houses tropical foliage, cacti, herbs and roses as well as a waterfall and a pond. Visitors can walk through a seven-circuit labyrinth; for blind and physically impaired visitors there are four stone benches inscribed with "finger labyrinths."

Kids learn about sustainability as they explore Paul Smith Children's Village. This LEED-certified site has a solar-powered discovery lab, a wetlands area, a tepee village, a secret garden and an amphitheater with seats made from recycled concrete. Special activities and events are offered.

Time: Allow 1 hour, 30 minutes minimum. **Hours:** Grounds daily dawn-dusk. Conservatory Mon.-Fri. 8-4:30, Sat. 11-3:30. Paul Smith Children's Village Wed.-Fri. 9-5, Tues. and Sat. 10-7, Sun. 10-5, June-Aug.; Tues.-Sat. 9-5, Sun. 10-4, rest of year. Closed major holidays. Phone ahead to confirm schedule. **Cost:** Free. **Phone:** (307) 637-6458. *(See ad on inside front cover.)* ⛲

CHEYENNE DEPOT MUSEUM is housed in the restored Union Pacific Railroad Depot at 121 W. 15th St. Regional railroad history is depicted through photographs, narratives, artifacts and a brief film presentation. Exhibits focus on the impact that Union Pacific Railroad operations had on the town and its residents. **Hours:** Mon.-Fri. 9-6, Sat. 9-5, Sun. 11-5, May-Sept.; Mon.-Sat. 9-5, Sun. 11-3, rest of year. Closed major holidays. **Cost:** $7; free (ages 0-12). **Phone:** (307) 632-3905. *(See ad on inside front cover.)*

◥◢ **CHEYENNE FRONTIER DAYS OLD WEST MUSEUM** is in Frontier Park at 4610 N. Carey Ave. The museum has some 60,000 artifacts, including a collection of more than 150 horse-drawn carriages and wagons, and classic Western and folk art. Also included is authentic clothing dating from the 1850s and an interactive children's gallery.

Hours: Daily 9-5, with extended hours during Cheyenne Frontier Days, June-Aug.; 10-5, rest of year. Closed Jan. 1, Thanksgiving and Christmas. **Cost:** $10; $8 (ages 65+ and military with ID); $5 (ages 13-18); free (ages 0-12 with adult). **Phone:** (307) 778-7290. *(See ad on inside front cover.)*

CHEYENNE STREET RAILWAY TROLLEY departs the Cheyenne Depot Square at 121 W. 15th St. Highlights of the 90-minute sightseeing tour include stops at the Cheyenne Frontier Days Old West Museum, State Capitol and Wyoming State Museum. **Hours:** Tours depart Mon.-Fri. at 10, 11:30, 1, 2:30 and 4, Sat. at 10, noon and 2, Sun. at noon and 2, early May-late Sept. **Cost:** $10; $5 (ages 2-12). **Phone:** (307) 778-3133 or (800) 426-5009. *(See ad on inside front cover, p. 246.)*

HISTORIC GOVERNORS' MANSION STATE HISTORIC SITE is at 300 E. 21st St. From 1905 to 1976 the site was the home of Wyoming's chief executives. Touch screens provide information about former governors and first ladies as well as the mansion's architecture. **Time:** Allow 1 hour minimum. **Hours:** Mon.-Sat. 9-5, Sun. 1-5, June-Sept.; Wed.-Sat. 9-5, Dec.-May. **Cost:** Free. **Phone:** (307) 777-7878.

◥◢ **THE NELSON MUSEUM OF THE WEST** is at 1714 Carey Ave. The museum celebrates the American West through exhibits of antique weapons, cowboy saddles, spurs, chaps, Native American beadwork, pottery, baskets and weavings. Cowgirl, outlaw and lawmen memorabilia is featured in addition to the "Cavalry in the West" exhibit. Mounted taxidermy from all continents also is highlighted. **Time:** Allow 1 hour minimum. **Hours:** Mon.-Sat. 9-4:30, June-Aug.; Mon.-Fri. 9-4:30, in May and Sept.-Oct. Closed major holidays. **Cost:** $4; $3 (ages 65+); free (ages 0-12). **Phone:** (307) 635-7670. *(See ad on inside front cover.)*

STATE CAPITOL is on Capitol Ave. between 24th and 25th sts. This neoclassic sandstone building, with a golden dome 50 feet in diameter, is architecturally uncommon for the region. Within the building are murals, woodwork, marble floors and displays of native wildlife. **Hours:** Mon.-Fri. 8-5. Closed major holidays. **Cost:** Free. **Phone:** (307) 777-7220. *(See ad on inside front cover.)*

TERRY BISON RANCH is accessed by taking I-80 to I-25S, then taking exit 2 off I-25S, then s. on Terry Ranch Rd. to ranch entrance. The historic working bison ranch has more than 3,000 bison. Fishing (no state license required), horseback rides and train tours are offered.

Hours: Bison tours daily dawn-dusk (weather permitting). **Cost:** Bison tours $12; $6 (ages 4-12). Horseback rides $40 per hour. Ages 0-7 are not permitted on horseback rides, but 15 minute pony rides are available for a fee. **Phone:** (307) 634-4171 or (800) 319-4171. *(See ad on inside front cover.)*

◥◢ **WYOMING STATE MUSEUM,** in the Capitol complex at 2301 Central Ave., features a variety of permanent and changing exhibits that allow visitors to delve into Wyoming's history.

The Drawn to This Land gallery catalogs the reasons people and businesses chose Wyoming as a place to flourish, and Swamped with Coal traces the development of the mining industry. Social history is the theme of the Living in Wyoming exhibition.

Visitors encounter a skeletal replica of a camptosaur—one of Wyoming's earliest inhabitants—in the R.I.P.-Rex in Pieces gallery; Wild Bunch focuses on other animals that have called the state home.

An interactive map pinpointing historical sites is the highlight of the Wyoming's Story collection;

guns, a cowboy diorama and Native American baskets and jewelry are just some of the items on display in the Barber Gallery. Designed for the little ones, the Hands-on History Room has a kid-size tepee, a chuck wagon and a curiosity cabinet.

Time: Allow 2 hours minimum. **Hours:** Mon.-Sat. 9-4:30. Closed major holidays. **Cost:** Free. **Phone:** (307) 777-7022. *(See ad on inside front cover.)*

BEST WESTERN PLUS FRONTIER INN   (307)638-8891

Hotel
$99-$299

AAA Benefit: Members save 10% or more with Best Western!

Address: 8101 Hutchins Dr 82007 **Location:** I-25 exit 367, just w. **Facility:** 74 units. 3 stories, interior corridors. **Amenities:** safes. **Pool(s):** heated indoor. **Activities:** hot tub, exercise room. **Guest Services:** valet and coin laundry. **Featured Amenity:** full hot breakfast.

[SAVE] [CALL] [&M] [≈] [BIZ] [(((•] [X]
[🚻] [📶] [💻] / SOME UNITS [S🐾] [HS]

CANDLEWOOD SUITES   (307)634-6622

[WVW] **Extended Stay Hotel** $109-$149 **Address:** 2335 Tura Pkwy 82001 **Location:** I-25 exit 9, just e on I-80 business loop/US 30, then just n. **Facility:** 86 efficiencies. 3 stories, interior corridors. **Parking:** winter plug-ins. **Activities:** picnic facilities, exercise room. **Guest Services:** complimentary and valet laundry.

[🚻] [CALL] [&M] [BIZ] [HS] [(((•] [X] [🚻] [📷] [💻]
/ SOME UNITS [S🐾]

DAYS INN CHEYENNE   (307)778-8877

[WVW] **Hotel** $90-$160 **Address:** 2360 W Lincolnway 82001 **Location:** I-25 exit 9, just e. **Facility:** 108 units. 2-4 stories, interior corridors. **Parking:** winter plug-ins. **Amenities:** safes. **Pool(s):** heated indoor. **Activities:** hot tub, exercise room. **Guest Services:** coin laundry.

[🚻] [≈] [BIZ] [(((•] [X] [🚻] [📷] [💻]
/ SOME UNITS [S🐾] [HS]

FAIRFIELD INN BY MARRIOTT CHEYENNE   (307)637-4070

[WVW] **Address:** 1415 Stillwater Ave 82001 **Location:** 1.2 mi e of jct Dell Range Blvd and Yellowstone Rd. Located on north side of airport. **Facility:** 60 units. 3 stories, interior corridors. **Parking:** winter plug-ins. **Pool(s):** heated indoor. **Activities:** hot tub, exercise room. **Guest Services:** valet laundry.

AAA Benefit: Members save 5% or more!

[🚻] [CALL] [&M] [≈] [BIZ] [(((•] [X] [🚻] [📷] [💻]

HAMPTON INN CHEYENNE   (307)632-2747

Hotel
$119-$179

AAA Benefit: Members save up to 10%!

Address: 1781 Fleischli Pkwy 82001 **Location:** I-25 exit 9, just e on I-80 business loop/US 30, then just n. **Facility:** 64 units. 3 stories, interior corridors. **Terms:** 1-7 night minimum stay, cancellation fee imposed. **Amenities:** video games. **Pool(s):** heated indoor. **Activities:** hot tub, exercise room. **Guest Services:** valet and coin laundry. **Featured Amenity:** continental breakfast.

[SAVE] [🚻] [CALL] [&M] [≈] [BIZ] [HS] [(((•] [X] [📷] [🚻]

[📷] [💻]

HOLIDAY INN CHEYENNE   307/638-4466

Hotel
Rates not provided

Address: 204 W Fox Farm Rd 82007 **Location:** I-80 exit 362, just s. **Facility:** 244 units. 6 stories, interior corridors. **Parking:** winter plug-ins. **Pool(s):** heated indoor. **Activities:** exercise room. **Guest Services:** valet and coin laundry.

[SAVE] [★] [🚻] [Y] [CALL] [&M] [≈]
[BIZ] [(((•] [💻] / SOME UNITS [🚻] [📷]

HOLIDAY INN EXPRESS HOTEL & SUITES   307/433-0751

[WVW] **Hotel.** Rates not provided. **Address:** 1741 Fleischli Pkwy 82001 **Location:** I-25 exit 9, just e. **Facility:** 76 units. 4 stories, interior corridors. **Amenities:** video games, safes. **Pool(s):** heated indoor. **Activities:** hot tub, exercise room. **Guest Services:** valet and coin laundry.

[🚻] [CALL] [&M] [≈] [BIZ] [HS] [(((•] [X] [📷] [🚻] [📷]
[💻]

LA QUINTA INN CHEYENNE   (307)632-7117

[WVW] **Hotel** $82-$140 **Address:** 2410 W Lincolnway 82009 **Location:** I-25 exit 9, just e. **Facility:** 105 units. 3 stories, interior corridors. **Pool(s):** heated outdoor. **Guest Services:** coin laundry.

[≈] [(((•] [💻] / SOME UNITS [🐾] [HS] [🚻] [📷]

LITTLE AMERICA HOTEL   (307)775-8400

Hotel
$99-$289

Address: 2800 W Lincolnway 82009 **Location:** I-25 exit 9, just w on US 30. Located in a quiet secluded area. **Facility:** 188 units. 1-3 stories (no elevator), interior/exterior corridors. **Terms:** cancellation fee imposed. **Amenities:** safes. **Dining:** Hathaway's Restaurant & Lounge, see separate listing. **Pool(s):** heated outdoor. **Activities:** regulation golf, playground, exercise room. **Guest Services:** valet and coin laundry. *(See ad p. 245.)*

[SAVE] [🚻] [🛎] [Y] [CALL] [&M]
[≈] [BIZ] [HS] [(((•] [X] [🚻]
[📷] [💻]

MICROTEL INN & SUITES BY WYNDHAM CHEYENNE   (307)634-3200

[WVW] **Hotel** $90-$140 **Address:** 1400 W Lincolnway 82001 **Location:** I-25 exit 9, 1.1 mi e. **Facility:** 56 units. 3 stories, interior corridors. **Parking:** winter plug-ins. **Activities:** exercise room. **Guest Services:** coin laundry.

[CALL] [&M] [(((•] [X] / SOME UNITS [🚻] [📷] [💻]

NAGLE WARREN MANSION B & B   (307)637-3333

Historic Bed & Breakfast
$158-$192

Address: 222 E 17th St 82001 **Location:** I-80 exit 362, 1.2 mi n on I-25 business loop/US 85/87 business route, then just e; jct House St; downtown. **Facility:** Handmade tiles adorn the fireplaces in most guest rooms at this Romanesque-style 1888 building. Furnishings include a variety of period antiques, and the architectural features throughout are fascinating. 12 units. 3 stories (no elevator), interior corridors. **Parking:** on-site and street. **Terms:** age restrictions may apply, 3 day cancellation notice-fee imposed. **Activities:** hot tub, bicycles, exercise room, massage. **Guest Services:** valet laundry, area transportation. **Featured Amenity:** full hot breakfast. *(See ad p. 245.)*

[SAVE] [★] [CALL] [&M] [(((•] [X] / SOME UNITS [S🐾]

▼ See AAA listing p. 244 ▼

▼ See AAA listing p. 244 ▼

OAK TREE INN CHEYENNE 307/778-6620

♦♦♦ **Hotel.** Rates not provided. **Address:** 1625 Stillwater Ave 82009 **Location:** I-25 exit 12, 0.8 mi se to Yellowstone Rd, 0.3 mi n to Dell Range Blvd, 1.2 mi e, then just se. Located on north side of airport. **Facility:** 30 units. 2 stories (no elevator), interior/exterior corridors. **Activities:** exercise room. **Guest Services:** coin laundry.

QUALITY INN OF CHEYENNE (307)638-7202

♦♦ **Hotel** $79-$129 **Address:** 2245 Etchepare Dr 82007 **Location:** I-25 exit 7, just w. **Facility:** 77 units. 2 stories, interior corridors. **Pool(s):** heated outdoor. **Activities:** exercise room. **Guest Services:** valet and coin laundry.

SPRINGHILL SUITES BY MARRIOTT (307)635-0006

♦♦♦ **Hotel** $129-$179

SPRINGHILL SUITES Marriott

AAA Benefit: Members save 5% or more!

Address: 416 W Fox Farm Rd 82007 **Location:** I-80 exit 362, just s, then just w. **Facility:** 92 units. 3 stories, interior corridors. **Pool(s):** heated indoor. **Activities:** hot tub, exercise room. **Guest Services:** valet and coin laundry.

SUPER 8 CHEYENNE (307)635-8741

♦♦ **Motel** $69-$179 **Address:** 1900 W Lincolnway 82001 **Location:** I-25 exit 9, 0.7 mi e. **Facility:** 60 units. 3 stories (no elevator), interior corridors. **Parking:** winter plug-ins. **Amenities:** Some: safes. **Guest Services:** coin laundry.

WINDY HILLS GUEST HOUSE 307/632-6423

♦♦♦ **Bed & Breakfast** $159-$310 **Address:** 393 Happy Jack Rd 82009 **Location:** I-25 exit 10B, 22 mi w on SR 210 (Happy Jack Rd), then 1 mi s on private gravel road. Located in a rural area. **Facility:** Adjacent to Curt Gowdy State Park, this beautiful property offers a B&B experience in the main house and well-thought-out options for vacation rentals and extended stays. 8 units, some efficiencies, kitchens, cabins and condominiums. 1-2 stories (no elevator), exterior corridors. **Terms:** check-in 4 pm, 3 day cancellation notice-fee imposed. **Activities:** sauna, hot tub, steamroom, boat dock, fishing, cross country skiing, lawn sports, picnic facilities, massage. **Guest Services:** complimentary laundry.

Download eTourBook guides
for top destinations at
AAA.com/ebooks

WHERE TO EAT

2 DOORS DOWN
307/634-6008

Burgers. Quick Serve. $8-$14 **AAA Inspector Notes:** Many locals claim this casual eatery offers the best burger in town. The juicy burgers, made from fresh ground beef, come straight up or topped with everything from pineapple and teriyaki sauce to bacon and cheddar. Other options include a salmon burger, grilled tuna burger, pot roast burger and a Philly cheesesteak. Entrée salads, a variety of soups and the heartier platters add some diversity to the menu. There are even vegetarian options. **Address:** 118 E 17th St 82001 **Location:** Jct Warren Ave and US 30, just n; downtown. **Parking:** street only. L D

THE ALBANY
307/638-3507

**American
Casual Dining
$8-$24**

AAA Inspector Notes: In business since 1942, this restaurant is in a large brick building and features high-back booths, wood floors and casual, friendly service. Serving steaks, seafood and chicken, the eatery is a good value at lunch and a bit more upscale at dinner. **Features:** full bar. **Address:** 1506 Capitol Ave 82001 **Location:** Jct Lincolnway, just s; downtown. L D

BREAD BASKET BAKERY & SANDWICH SHOPPE
307/432-2525

Breads/Pastries Sandwiches. Quick Serve. $4-$8 **AAA Inspector Notes:** The unassuming building of this bakery doesn't do justice to the delightful treasures waiting inside. The smell of freshly baked bread wafts through the air as patrons browse the bakery. Order a sandwich to go, or eat a meal at one of the small tables. Friendly staff members clearly enjoy their jobs. **Features:** patio dining. **Address:** 1819 Maxwell Ave 82001 **Location:** Between 18th and 19th sts; downtown. **Parking:** street only. B L

HATHAWAY'S RESTAURANT & LOUNGE
307/775-8400

American. Casual Dining. $7-$24 **AAA Inspector Notes:** Traditional elegance and style set this popular restaurant apart. Favorites include New York and filet mignon steaks, as well as pan-fried trout, seafood and pasta. The hostess offers a pleasant welcome as guests enter and a nice goodbye as they exit. Daily buffets line up with fresh fruits, baked goods and roasted meats cut to the diner's specifications. **Features:** full bar, patio dining, Sunday brunch. **Address:** 2800 W Lincolnway 82009 **Location:** I-25 exit 9, just w on US 30; in Little America Hotel. B L D CALL M

L'OSTERIA MONDELLO
307/778-6068

Italian. Casual Dining. $9-$16 **AAA Inspector Notes:** Upon entering this restaurant, patrons can see a fast food pizzeria. Offering a sit-down restaurant in the back, a full Italian menu features such entrées as pizza and pasta dishes including veal, chicken and scallops. **Features:** wine only. **Address:** 1507 Stillwater Ave 82009 **Location:** 1.2 mi e of jct Dell Range Blvd and Yellowstone Rd. L D

LUXURY DINER
307/638-8971

Breakfast. Casual Dining. $5-$14 **AAA Inspector Notes:** This is the place for breakfast in Cheyenne. The biscuits rate high and are either used for breakfast sandwiches or served with gravy. Omelets, French toast with almonds and huevos rancheros hint at some of the diversity on the menu. Lunch includes burgers, sandwiches, and hearty platters as well as homemade pie. Locals fill up the tables, but visitors are made to feel welcome. According to oral tradition, the main building used to be an operating trolley before becoming a diner in 1926. **Address:** 1401 W Lincolnway 82001 **Location:** I-25 exit 9, 1.1 mi e. B L

MORRIS HOUSE BISTRO
307/369-1378

Southern American. Fine Dining. $18-$31 **AAA Inspector Notes:** Located in an historic landmark—the former home of suffragette Esther Hobart Morris—the Victorian-inspired décor here creates a warm, inviting atmosphere. Inspired by South Carolina's Lowcountry, the seasonal menu features Southern cuisine virtually unknown in this area of the country. Examples include hush puppies stuffed with crab, shrimp with grits and Carolina fried flounder. Duck also makes an appearance on the menu and it would not be Wyoming without a cowboy rib-eye or other steak option. **Features:** full bar, patio dining, Sunday brunch. **Reservations:** suggested. **Address:** 2114 Warren Ave 82001 **Location:** Between 21st and 22nd sts; downtown. **Parking:** street only. D

PIZZERIA VENTI
307/433-1020

Pizza. Quick Serve. $3-$8 **AAA Inspector Notes:** Friendly staff members warmly greet patrons as they enter this restaurant—a nice touch for an otherwise fast food experience. The menu items feature a variety of hearty salads, baked pasta dishes and thin-crust pizza. **Address:** 112 E 17th St 82001 **Location:** Jct Warren Ave and US 30, just n, then just w; downtown. **Parking:** street only. L D

POOR RICHARD'S
307/635-5114

American. Casual Dining. $10-$28 **AAA Inspector Notes:** This eatery takes its name from Benjamin Franklin's Almanac, which he wrote under the pseudonym Poor Richard. The tasteful décor features antiques, replicas and general Americana from the Colonial era. The salad bar features an impressive array of fresh vegetables. Entrées include steaks, veal, chicken, lobster, king crab legs, salmon and shrimp. **Features:** full bar. **Address:** 2233 E Lincolnway 82001 **Location:** I-80 exit 364, just n on N College Dr (SR 212); 1.5 mi w on I-80 business loop/US 30. L D

SANFORD'S GRUB & PUB
307/634-3381

American. Casual Dining. $8-$22 **AAA Inspector Notes:** This casual, busily decorated restaurant presents a varied menu, which includes Cajun chicken, catfish and finger foods, as well as numerous beers. The Monte Cristo sandwich is a favorite. **Features:** full bar. **Address:** 115 E 17th St 82001 **Location:** I-80 exit 362, 1.2 mi n on I-25 business loop/US 85/87 business route, then just w. **Parking:** street only. L D

SENATOR'S RESTAURANT & BRASS BUFFALO SALOON
307/634-4171

**Steak
Casual Dining
$8-$40**

AAA Inspector Notes: Located in a rural area along the interstate frontage road and surrounded by various buildings, this spot resembles an old Western barn. The rustic pine dining room at this working ranch has dark wood walls and floors, basic tables with metal chairs and a casual décor. For those that do not opt for the specialty barbecued and grilled bison, there are other choices and a salad bar. The basic lunch menu lists sandwiches. The casually dressed staff provides friendly, yet adequate, service. **Features:** full bar, patio dining. **Address:** 51 I-25 Service Rd E 82007 **Location:** I-25 exit 2, just e, then 2.6 mi se on Terry Ranch Rd; in Terry Bison Ranch Resort. L D

SHADOWS PUB & GRILL
307/634-7625

American. Casual Dining. $8-$20 **AAA Inspector Notes:** Popular with locals and tourists alike, this pub is located inside a train depot and offers a variety of burgers, sandwiches, pizzas, steaks and traditional pub fare. Sports games are shown on 12 flat-screen TVs. **Features:** full bar. **Address:** 115 W 15th St, Suite 1 82001 **Location:** Jct Lincolnway and Central Ave, just se; downtown; in historic train depot. **Parking:** street only. L D

TWIN DRAGON
307/637-6622

Chinese. Casual Dining. $8-$16 **AAA Inspector Notes:** In a convenient downtown location, this restaurant is known for authentic food and friendly service from its staff, some of whom have been here for many years. **Features:** full bar. **Address:** 1809 Carey Ave 82001 **Location:** From center, 0.5 mi n. L D

CODY (B-2) pop. 9,520, elev. 5,095'

Founded by Col. William "Buffalo Bill" F. Cody in 1896, Cody is near the east and northeast entrances to Yellowstone National Park *(see place listing p. 326)*. Some of the state's most scenic areas, including Shoshone National Forest *(see place listing p. 318)*, Sunlight Basin, the Absaroka and Beartooth mountains and the Bighorn Canyon National Recreation Area *(see place listing p. 131)*, are nearby.

US 14/16/20, alternately known as the Buffalo Bill Cody Scenic Byway, has been called the most scenic 52 miles in America. Along the route are many unusual rock formations as well as the State of Wyoming Veterans Memorial Park (near Yellowstone Regional Airport), which honors those who served in World War II and the Korean and Vietnam wars. The highway runs 182 miles between Ranchester and Yellowstone National Park. Cody also is the northern terminus of the scenic section of SR 120 that travels 83 miles southeast to Thermopolis *(see place listing p. 321)*. Scenic US 14A heads 107 miles northeast to Burgess Junction.

Outfitters offer fishing, hayrides, horseback riding, hunting and pack trips and river float trips. Scenic flights overlooking the Bighorn Mountains and Grand Teton and Yellowstone national parks can be arranged through Choice Aviation, (307) 587-9262.

Of interest downtown are historic buildings dating from the beginning of the 20th century. Irma Hotel, 12th Street and Sheridan Avenue, has been a meeting place for local cattlemen, oilmen and shepherds since the early 1900s. Its $100,000 bar was a gift from Queen Victoria to Buffalo Bill in appreciation of his Wild West Show. Pahaska Tepee, Buffalo Bill's first hunting lodge, is at the east entrance to Yellowstone National Park.

Cody Chamber of Commerce: 836 Sheridan Ave., Cody, WY 82414. **Phone:** (307) 587-2297. *(See ad starting on p. 250, this page, p. 331.)*

BUFFALO BILL CENTER OF THE WEST is at 720 Sheridan Ave. The five museums that comprise the center are dedicated to the art, artifacts, crafts, cultures, traditions and history of the American West. In addition, a research library contains book and manuscript collections, historic photographs and an archive of Western songs and ballads.

Time: Allow 4 hours minimum. **Hours:** Daily 8-6, May 1 to mid-Sept.; daily 8-5, mid-Sept. through Oct. 31; daily 10-5, Mar.-Apr. and in Nov.; Thurs.-Sun. 10-5, rest of year. Closed Jan. 1, Thanksgiving and Christmas. **Cost:** (Valid for 2 consecutive days for all five museums) $18; $16 (ages 65+); $14 (students ages 18+ with ID); $10 (ages 6-17). **Phone:** (307) 587-4771. *(See ad starting on p. 250.)*

Buffalo Bill Museum is at 720 Sheridan Ave. at Buffalo Bill Center of the West. The museum displays belongings of the showman, scout and Pony Express rider, along with possessions of Annie Oakley and artifacts of the early West. Exhibits provide insight into the history of the American cowboy, conservation and dude ranching.

Hours: Daily 8-6, May 1 to mid-Sept.; daily 8-5, mid-Sept. through Oct. 31; daily 10-5, Mar.-Apr. and in Nov.; Thurs.-Sun. 10-5, rest of year. **Cost:** Included with Buffalo Bill Center of the West admission of $18; $16 (ages 65+); $14 (students ages 18+ with ID); $10 (ages 6-17). **Phone:** (307) 587-4771.

The Cody Firearms Museum is at 720 Sheridan Ave. at Buffalo Bill Center of the West. The museum is noted for its exhibits of American firearms, including the Winchester collection. The museum, featuring some 3,000 items, traces the development of firearms from the early 16th century. Examples range from centuries-old projectile arms to flintlocks and Gatling guns to modern sport rifles.

Hours: Daily 8-6, May 1 to mid-Sept.; daily 8-5, mid-Sept. through Oct. 31; daily 10-5, Mar.-Apr. and in Nov.; Thurs.-Sun. 10-5, rest of year. **Cost:** Included with Buffalo Bill Center of the West admission of $18; $16 (ages 65+); $14 (students ages 18+ with ID); $10 (ages 6-17). *(See ad starting on p. 250.)*

▼ See AAA listing this page ▼

(See map & index p. 336.)

The Draper Museum of Natural History is at 720 Sheridan Ave. at Buffalo Bill Center of the West. The museum features exhibits about the region's natural history and human influence from early explorers to ranchers. A highlight is a virtual expedition through mountain forests and valleys. **Hours:** Daily 8-6, May 1 to mid-Sept.; daily 8-5, mid-Sept. through Oct. 31; daily 10-5, Mar.-Apr. and in Nov.; Thurs.-Sun. 10-5, rest of year. **Cost:** Included with Buffalo Bill Center of the West admission of $18; $16 (ages 65+); $14 (students ages 18+ with ID); $10 (ages 6-17). **Phone:** (307) 587-4771. *(See ad starting on p. 250.)*

The Plains Indian Museum is at 720 Sheridan Ave. at Buffalo Bill Center of the West. The museum has an extensive collection of art, artifacts, ceremonial items and beadwork as well as dress and weaponry of the Arapaho, Blackfeet, Cheyenne, Crow, Shoshone and Sioux tribes. Exhibits depict the everyday existence of these Plains tribes. **Hours:** Daily 8-6, May 1 to mid-Sept.; daily 8-5, mid-Sept. through Oct. 31; daily 10-5, Mar.-Apr. and in Nov.; Thurs.-Sun. 10-5, rest of year. **Cost:** Included with Buffalo Bill Center of the West admission of $18; $16 (ages 65+); $14 (students ages 18+ with ID); $10 (ages 6-17). **Phone:** (307) 587-4771. *(See ad starting on p. 250.)*

Whitney Gallery of Western Art is at 720 Sheridan Ave. at Buffalo Bill Center of the West. The gallery houses a comprehensive collection of paintings, sculpture and prints depicting the West. Artists represented include Albert Bierstadt, George Catlin, Thomas Moran, Frederic Remington, Charles M. Russell and Joseph Henry Sharp. Reconstructed studios enable visitors to view artists' work areas.

Hours: Daily 8-6, May 1 to mid-Sept.; daily 8-5, mid-Sept. through Oct. 31; daily 10-5, Mar.-Apr. and in Nov.; Thurs.-Sun. 10-5, rest of year. **Cost:** Included with Buffalo Bill Center of the West admission of $18; $16 (ages 65+); $14 (students ages 18+ with ID); $10 (ages 6-17). **Phone:** (307) 587-4771. *(See ad starting on p. 250.)*

BUFFALO BILL DAM VISITOR CENTER is 6 mi. w. on US 14/16/20. In addition to a dam overlook, the visitor center has views of Shoshone Canyon, area wildlife displays and dinosaur and fossil exhibits. Self-guiding historical audio tours are available. **Time:** Allow 30 minutes minimum. **Hours:** Mon.-Fri. 8-7, Sat.-Sun. 9-5, June-Aug.; Mon.-Fri. 8-6, Sat.-Sun. 9-5 in May and Sept. **Cost:** Free. **Phone:** (307) 527-6076.

BUFFALO BILL-THE SCOUT STATUE is at the w. end of Sheridan Ave. The statue, by Gertrude Vanderbilt Whitney, represents young William Cody as a mounted Army scout signaling the discovery of enemy tracks.

THE CODY CATTLE COMPANY, 2.9 mi. w. on US 14/16/20, then .4 mi. n.w. to 1910 Demaris St., offers a chuck wagon supper and a live Western musical show. Dinner guests have the option of eating before or after the hour-long performance. Seating is in a large mess hall with a stage in front; special lighting and a backdrop create the illusion of being outdoors.

Time: Allow 1 hour minimum. **Hours:** Supper daily 5:30-8, June-Sept. Show daily at 6:30, June-Sept. **Cost:** Show only $13; $6.50 (ages 3-12). Dinner and show $26; $13 (ages 3-12). A combination ticket for the dinner, the show and admission to Cody Nite Rodeo *(see attraction listing p. 249)* is available most days June-Aug. and costs $41; $21 (ages 7-12); $13 (ages 3-6). Reservations are recommended. **Phone:** (307) 272-5770. 🍴

CODY CHAPEL MURALS INFORMATION CENTER is in Cody Chapel at Wyoming Ave. and 18th St. The center displays exhibits, artifacts, murals, paintings and sculpture relating to the Mormon colonization of the Big Horn Basin. Film presentations are given. **Tours:** Guided tours are available. **Hours:** Mon.-Sat. 9-7, Sun. 3-7, June 1-Sept. 15; by appointment rest of year. **Cost:** Free. **Phone:** (307) 587-3290.

CODY DUG UP GUN MUSEUM, 1020 12th St., has an extensive collection of guns and other weapons used during the American Revolutionary War, the Gold Rush era, the Civil War, the Indian Wars era, World War I, the 1920s and World War II. **Time:** Allow 1 hour minimum. **Hours:** Daily 9-9, May-Oct. **Cost:** Donations. **Phone:** (307) 587-3344.

CODY NITE RODEO is 2 mi. w. on US 14/16/20. The 2-hour rodeo features events like bronc riding, bull riding, team roping and barrel racing. Little ones can participate in the kids' calf scramble. **Hours:** Daily at 8 p.m., June-Aug. Special performances are held July 1-4 during Stampede Days. **Cost:** $18; $8 (ages 7-12). **Phone:** (307) 587-5155 or (800) 207-0744.

TECUMSEH'S OLD WEST MINIATURE VILLAGE AND MUSEUM is 2.5 mi. w. on US 14/16/20. The museum features displays of Native American and Old West artifacts, guns, other weaponry and wildlife. The history of Wyoming is characterized in miniature in a 66-scene display with moving trains and audio narratives. **Time:** Allow 1 hour minimum. **Hours:** Daily 9-7, June-Aug.; 9-5 in May and Sept.; by appointment rest of year. **Cost:** Free. **Phone:** (307) 587-5362.

TRAIL TOWN is 3 mi. w. on US 14/16/20. Featured is a group of historic buildings with indoor exhibits reassembled on the first site of the frontier town of Old Cody. Highlights include the grave of John "Jeremiah" Johnson and a log cabin used as a hideout by Butch Cassidy, the Sundance Kid and other members of the Wild Bunch.

CODY, WYOMING
THE WILDEST
WAY INTO YELLOWSTONE

BUFFALO BILL
CENTER
OF THE WEST

Always
Entertaining

Five museums.
Unlimited discovery.

Cody, Wyoming
centerofthewest.org

William F. "Buffalo Bill" Cody with Indian children, ca. 1915. Buffalo Bill Center of the West, Cody, Wyoming, USA. MS 6 William F. Cody Collection. P.6.243

(See map & index p. 336.)

The Museum of the Old West houses guns, carriages, clothing and many prehistoric and historic Plains Indian relics. **Hours:** Daily 8-7, May 15-Sept. 30. **Cost:** $8; $7 (ages 65+); $4 (ages 6-12). **Phone:** (307) 587-5302.

WILD SHEEP FOUNDATION is at 720 Allen Ave. The den-like educational area features audio and visual presentations, paintings, prints and mounted exhibits pertaining to wild sheep. A variety of bronzed bighorn sheep stand outside. **Time:** Allow 1 hour minimum. **Hours:** Mon.-Fri. 8-5. Closed major holidays. **Cost:** Donations. **Phone:** (307) 527-6261.

RECREATIONAL ACTIVITIES

White-water Rafting

- **Red Canyon River Trips** is at 1119 12th St. **Hours:** Trips depart daily at 9, 1 and 3, May 1 to mid-Sept. **Phone:** (307) 587-6988.

- **River Runners** is at 1491 Sheridan Ave. **Hours:** Two-hour and half-day trips run late May-late Aug. **Phone:** (307) 527-7238 or (800) 535-7238.

- **Wyoming River Trips** depart from 233 Yellowstone Ave. **Hours:** Trips offered several times daily, May-Sept. **Phone:** (307) 587-6661 or (800) 586-6661.

AMERICINN LODGE & SUITES OF CODY
(307)587-7716　67

Hotel
$99-$219

Address: 508 Yellowstone Ave 82414 **Location:** 1.9 mi w on US 14/16/20. **Facility:** 67 units. 2 stories (no elevator), interior corridors. **Parking:** winter plug-ins. **Terms:** cancellation fee imposed. **Amenities:** safes. **Pool(s):** heated indoor. **Activities:** sauna, hot tub. **Guest Services:** coin laundry. **Featured Amenity:** continental breakfast.

BEST WESTERN PREMIER IVY INN & SUITES
(307)587-2572　66

Hotel
$115-$290

AAA Benefit: Members save 10% or more with Best Western!

Address: 1800 8th St 82414 **Location:** 1 mi w on US 14/16/20. **Facility:** 70 units. 3 stories, interior corridors. **Amenities:** safes. **Dining:** 8th Street at the Ivy, see separate listing. **Pool(s):** heated indoor. **Activities:** hot tub, exercise room. **Guest Services:** complimentary and valet laundry.

BEST WESTERN SUNSET MOTOR INN
(307)587-4265　65

Motel
$185-$200

AAA Benefit: Members save 10% or more with Best Western!

Address: 1601 8th St 82414 **Location:** 0.8 mi w on US 14/16/20. **Facility:** 120 units. 1-2 stories (no elevator), exterior corridors. **Parking:** winter plug-ins. **Terms:** closed 11/1-5/22. **Pool(s):** heated outdoor, heated indoor. **Activities:** hot tub, playground, exercise room. **Guest Services:** coin laundry. **Featured Amenity:** continental breakfast.

BUDGET HOST INN　(307)587-4258　62

Motel $80-$140 **Address:** 1807 Sheridan Ave 82414 **Location:** 0.4 mi e. Located in a quiet area close to downtown. **Facility:** 23 units. 1 story, exterior corridors. **Terms:** closed 10/15-4/30, cancellation fee imposed. **Guest Services:** coin laundry.

BUFFALO BILL'S ANTLERS INN　307/587-2084　63

Hotel $50-$150 **Address:** 1213 17th St 82414 **Location:** Just e of jct US 14/16/20. **Facility:** 39 units. 2 stories (no elevator), interior corridors. **Terms:** closed 10/6-4/30.

BUFFALO BILL VILLAGE　(307)587-5544　61

Historic Cabin $89-$189 **Address:** 1701 Sheridan Ave 82414 **Location:** On US 14/16/20 and SR 120, just e of jct US 14 and SR 120; center. **Facility:** Despite being built between 1920 and 1923, this complex of closely-spaced log cabins offers today's modern conveniences. Check-in is handled at the extensive gift shop. 83 cabins. 1 story, exterior corridors. **Terms:** closed 10/1-4/30, 3 day cancellation notice-fee imposed.

THE CODY　(307)587-5915　68

Hotel $110-$285 **Address:** 232 W Yellowstone Ave 82414 **Location:** 2 mi w on US 14/16/20. **Facility:** 75 units. 3 stories, interior corridors. **Parking:** winter plug-ins. **Terms:** check-in 4 pm, cancellation fee imposed, resort fee. **Amenities:** safes. **Pool(s):** heated indoor. **Activities:** sauna, hot tub, bicycles, exercise room. **Guest Services:** coin laundry, area transportation.

(See map & index p. 336.)

CODY MOTOR LODGE   (307)527-6291 58

Motel
$99-$140

Address: 1455 Sheridan Ave 82414 **Location:** Just w on US 14/16/20 and SR 120. **Facility:** 31 units, some two bedrooms. 2 stories (no elevator), interior corridors. **Parking:** winter plug-ins. **Guest Services:** coin laundry. **Featured Amenity: continental breakfast.** *(See ad this page.)*

COMFORT INN AT BUFFALO BILL VILLAGE RESORT   (307)587-5556 59

Hotel $99-$199 **Address:** 1601 Sheridan Ave 82414 **Location:** US 14/16/20 and SR 120. **Facility:** 74 units. 2 stories (no elevator), interior corridors. **Parking:** winter plug-ins. **Terms:** 3 day cancellation notice. **Guest Services:** valet and coin laundry.

HOLIDAY INN AT BUFFALO BILL VILLAGE RESORT   (307)587-5555 60

Hotel $89-$239 **Address:** 1701 Sheridan Ave 82414 **Location:** US 14/16/20 and SR 120. **Facility:** 189 units. 2 stories (no elevator), interior corridors. **Parking:** winter plug-ins. **Terms:** 3 day cancellation notice-fee imposed. **Amenities:** video games. **Pool(s):** heated outdoor. **Activities:** exercise room. **Guest Services:** valet and coin laundry.

THE MAYOR'S BED & BREAKFAST INN   307/587-0887 56

Historic Bed & Breakfast $90-$215 **Address:** 1413 Rumsey Ave 82414 **Location:** Just n of Sheridan Ave at 14th St. **Facility:** Take a step back in time while staying here. This turn-of-the-century mansion was built to house Cody's first mayor. Many antiques and collectibles adorn this lovely house. 5 units, some cottages. 1-2 stories (no elevator), interior/exterior corridors. **Parking:** street only. **Terms:** cancellation fee imposed.

MOOSE CREEK LODGE & SUITES   307/587-2221 57

Hotel
Rates not provided

Address: 1015 Sheridan Ave 82414 **Location:** On US 14/16/20; downtown. **Facility:** 56 units. 1-2 stories (no elevator), interior/exterior corridors. **Pool(s):** heated indoor. **Activities:** limited exercise equipment. **Guest Services:** coin laundry. **Featured Amenity: continental breakfast.** *(See ad p. 254.)*

SKYLINE MOTOR INN   (307)587-4201 69

Motel
$69-$225

Address: 1919 17th St 82414 **Location:** 0.8 mi e on US 14/16/20 and SR 120. **Facility:** 46 units. 1-2 stories (no elevator), exterior corridors. **Parking:** winter plug-ins. **Terms:** closed 12/1-3/15. **Activities:** playground.

SUNRISE MOTOR INN   (307)587-5566 64

Motel
$50-$130

Address: 1407 8th St 82414 **Location:** 0.8 mi w on US 14/16/20. Next to Buffalo Bill Historical Center. **Facility:** 40 units. 1 story, exterior corridors. **Terms:** closed 10/15-4/30. **Pool(s):** heated outdoor. **Guest Services:** coin laundry. **Featured Amenity: continental breakfast.**

▼ See AAA listing p. 252 ▼

(See map & index p. 336.)

(See map & index p. 336.)

WHERE TO EAT

8TH STREET AT THE IVY
307/587-2572 ④④

♦♦♦♦
Western American Casual Dining
$8-$32

AAA Inspector Notes: This upscale dining experience features a Western-style décor with stone, wood and leather accents. Regionally available ingredients include lamb, steaks, elk and trout. **Features:** full bar, patio dining, Sunday brunch, happy hour. **Address:** 1800 8th St 82414 **Location:** 1 mi w on US 14/16/20; in BEST WESTERN PREMIER Ivy Inn & Suites.

B L D CALL ♿M

Fine Dining with Bar and Mountain View Patio Seating

ADRIANO'S ITALIAN RESTAURANT 307/527-7320 ④⓪
♦♦ Italian. Casual Dining. $8-$22 **AAA Inspector Notes:** The smells of authentic Italian pizza are what hit your nose as you enter Adriano's. Partake of the pizza or enjoy some of their other Italian entrees at this family style restaurant. **Features:** full bar. **Address:** 1244 Sheridan Ave 82414 **Location:** On US 14/16/20; downtown. **Parking:** street only. L D

BUBBA'S BAR-B-QUE RESTAURANT 307/587-7427 ④⑤
♦♦ Barbecue. Family Dining. $6-$14 **AAA Inspector Notes:** Texas meats are slow smoked over a hickory fire. Although spare ribs are the house specialty, guests also can try catfish with hush puppies, charbroiled steak or the popular sloppy Bubba sandwich. **Features:** beer & wine. **Address:** 512 Yellowstone Ave 82414 **Location:** US 14/16/20, 1.9 mi w. L D CALL ♿M

GEYSER BREWING CO. 307/587-5868 ④⑥
♦♦ American. Casual Dining. $14-$27 **AAA Inspector Notes:** Casual brewpub fare is offered in this cozy spot with low lighting and semi-partitioned rooms. **Features:** full bar, happy hour. **Address:** 525 W Yellowstone 82414 **Location:** From City Center, 2.5 mi w on US 14/16/20; next to rodeo grounds. D CALL ♿M

HERITAGE BAKERY & BISTRO 307/587-2622 ③⑨
♦♦ American. Casual Dining. $9-$25 **AAA Inspector Notes:** This cute little bistro is in a converted house. The owners take the time to do it right with a homey touch, from baking the bread for sandwiches to using local and fresh ingredients. Fresh-baked pie and cookies are for dessert. Breakfast is served on Saturday only. **Features:** beer & wine. **Reservations:** required, for dinner. **Address:** 1532 Wyoming Ave 82414 **Location:** From Sheridan Ave, just n on 16th St, just w. **Parking:** street only. L D

LA COMIDA 307/587-9556 ④②
♦♦ Mexican. Casual Dining. $8-$18 **AAA Inspector Notes:** The popular family-owned restaurant turns out inventive Mexican fare in good-size, attractively presented courses. Tasty margaritas complement the good food. Pleasant, expedient servers circulate through the relaxed setting and on the summer dining patio. **Features:** full bar. **Reservations:** suggested, weekends. **Address:** 1385 Sheridan Ave 82414 **Location:** On US 14/16/20; center. **Parking:** street only. L D

WYOMING'S RIB & CHOP HOUSE 307/527-7731 ④①
♦♦ American. Casual Dining. $8-$32 **AAA Inspector Notes:** This spot is popular, so reservations are a must. Famous for the ribs, the meat falls off the bone. Most dinners include an appetizer and a starch. Delicious steaks and burgers also are an option. The setting is cowboy casual and includes a lounge area. **Features:** full bar, happy hour. **Address:** 1367 Sheridan Ave 82414 **Location:** On US 14/16/20. **Parking:** street only. L D CALL ♿M

ZAPATA'S
307/527-7181 ④③

♦♦ ♦♦
Mexican Casual Dining
$8-$12

AAA Inspector Notes: Spices in the made-in-house sauces of New Mexican dishes are a bit more defined than those found in standard Tex-Mex fare. The mood is casual and the decor Mexican in the family-run spot. **Features:** full bar, patio dining. **Address:** 1362 Sheridan Ave 82414 **Location:** On US 14/16/20; center. **Parking:** street only. L D

DEVILS TOWER NATIONAL MONUMENT (B-6)

Devils Tower National Monument is accessible from SR 24, north off I-90 via US 14 or west from Belle Fourche, S.D.; from Alzada, Mont., SR 112 runs southwest off US 212. Occupying 1,347 acres in the area between Sundance and Hulett, the monument contains Devils Tower, the most conspicuous landmark in northeastern Wyoming.

The tower, a huge monolith resembling a colossal stone tree stump, rises 867 feet from its base and 1,267 feet above the Belle Fourche River. The 1.5-acre top has a growth of sagebrush and grass, and the almost perpendicular sides are fluted columns. The tower was formed when numerous sedimentary layers eroded from around a volcanic intrusion that had cooled in a teardrop formation.

About a half-mile from the entrance is a prairie dog colony. Near the monument's campground is an outdoor amphitheater. Ranger-naturalists conduct summer interpretive walks, talks and campfire programs.

The Tower Trail encircles Devils Tower. Climbing on the tower is permitted, but climbers must sign in before and after expeditions. **Note:** During the month of June, the National Park Service asks climbers to voluntarily refrain from climbing on the tower and hikers to voluntarily refrain from scrambling within the interior of the Tower Trail Loop out of respect for the Native American tribes that consider the tower a sacred site.

A visitor center about 3 miles from the park entrance contains geological specimens, artifacts and exhibits. Dogs, which must be leashed, are not permitted on the trails.

Allow 2 hours, 30 minutes minimum. The monument is open daily 24 hours. The visitor center is open daily 8-7, Memorial Day-Labor Day; 9-4, rest of year (weather permitting). Admission $10 per private vehicle; $5 per person arriving on foot, bicycle or motorcycle; free (ages 0-15). **Cards:** DS, MC, VI. Phone (307) 467-5283 Mon.-Fri. 8-4. *See Recreation Areas Chart.*

DIAMONDVILLE pop. 737

ENERGY INN 307/877-6901
♦ Motel. Rates not provided. **Address:** 3 US Hwy 30/189 83116 **Location:** Jct US 30 and 189. **Facility:** 41 units, some efficiencies. 1-2 stories (no elevator), interior/exterior corridors. **Parking:** winter plug-ins. 📶 🍴 🛒 📠

DOUGLAS (D-5) pop. 6,120, elev. 4,815'
• Restaurants p. 258

Known as Tent Town at its founding in 1886, Douglas served as a supply post for cattlemen and a distribution point for railroad consignments. The town's history is typical of the colorful, brawling days when cavalrymen, cowboys and railroad crews were opening the West, but in contrast to many other towns, few killings were recorded.

One of the town's rowdiest characters was George Pike, a cowhand whose rustling habits were so well-known that the cattle companies decided to hire him so he would at least benefit his current employer. One company thought so highly of Pike that at his death it erected an expensive tombstone with the following inscription:

Underneath this stone in eternal rest, Sleeps the wildest one of the wayward west. He was a gambler and sport and cowboy, too, And he led the pace in an outlaw crew. He was sure on the trigger and staid to the end, But was never known to quit on a friend. In the relations of death all mankind's alike, But in life there was only one George Pike.

Douglas also is said to be the original home of the "jackalope," a fanciful creation of Wyoming's taxidermists. Doubters are confronted with dozens of convincing mounted specimens of this animal—best described as a jackrabbit sporting antlers—displayed throughout the state. A 10-foot replica of the "hybrid" stands downtown in Centennial Jackalope Square at 3rd and Center streets and at the Douglas Area Chamber of Commerce, which is housed in a historic train depot.

Scenic River Path, running along the bank of the North Platte River in downtown, offers 2.5 miles of trails for walking, bicycling and observing nature. The river also provides opportunities for trout fishing, canoeing and float trips. Washington Park contains the burial monument of racehorse Sir Barton, the first triple crown winner in the United States.

The Wyoming State Fair, off I-25 adjacent to the town's business district, occurs for 8 days in mid-August. Visitors can enjoy livestock and horticultural exhibits as well as a demolition derby and rodeos; for information phone (307) 358-2398.

Douglas Area Chamber of Commerce: 121 Brownfield Rd., Douglas, WY 82633. **Phone:** (307) 358-2950. *(See ad p. 257.)*

AYRES NATURAL BRIDGE is in Ayres Park, 12 mi. w. on I-25, then 5 mi. s. on Natural Bridge Rd. La Prele Creek has worn a passageway through thick stone, leaving an arch 30 feet high and 50 feet wide surrounded by an amphitheater of red rock. **Hours:** Daily 8-8, Apr.-Oct. **Cost:** Free. *(See ad p. 257.)*

FORT FETTERMAN STATE HISTORIC SITE is 7 mi. n.w. via SR 93 off the North Douglas exit of I-25. The site preserves the fort's restored officers' quarters and an ordnance warehouse. Built in 1867, the fort was once a major Army supply post for the troops sent to subdue Indian uprisings. A museum contains exhibits depicting the history of the military and Fetterman City. Period rooms, weapons, artifacts and clothing are displayed.

Time: Allow 2 hours minimum. **Hours:** Daily 9-5, Memorial Day weekend-Labor Day. **Cost:** $4; free (ages 0-17). **Phone:** (307) 358-2864.

WYOMING PIONEER MEMORIAL MUSEUM is on the state fairgrounds off Center St. The museum began as a log structure in 1925 and has since enlarged to accommodate one of the largest displays of historic artifacts in the state. The museum contains an extensive collection of Wyoming pioneer items, military relics, Native American artifacts, maps, charts, newspapers and photographs from the late 1800s.

The Johnson Gallery houses the museum's Native American collection that includes such highlights as a 1964 Sioux-style teepee used in the movie "Dances with Wolves," numerous examples of decorative arts and multiple displays of Native American sculpture. Other museum highlights include clothing worn during Wyoming's territorial period, an art display with changing exhibits, a research library about Wyoming history and an 1885 one-room schoolhouse. **Hours:** Mon.-Fri. 8-5 (also Sat. 1-5, June-Sept.). **Cost:** Free. **Phone:** (307) 358-9288.

HOLIDAY INN EXPRESS & SUITES   (307)358-4500

Hotel
$149-$189

Address: 900 W Yellowstone Hwy 82633 **Location:** I-25 exit 140, 1 mi e. **Facility:** 76 units. 3 stories, interior corridors. **Parking:** winter plug-ins. **Amenities:** video games. **Pool(s):** heated indoor. **Activities:** hot tub, picnic facilities, exercise room. **Guest Services:** valet and coin laundry. **Featured Amenity:** continental breakfast.

SLEEP INN & SUITES   (307)358-2777

Hotel
$129-$179

Address: 508 Cortez Dr 82633 **Location:** I-25 exit 140, 0.5 mi e. **Facility:** 63 units. 3 stories, interior corridors. **Parking:** winter plug-ins. **Pool(s):** heated indoor. **Activities:** hot tub, picnic facilities, exercise room. **Guest Services:** valet and coin laundry. **Featured Amenity:** continental breakfast.

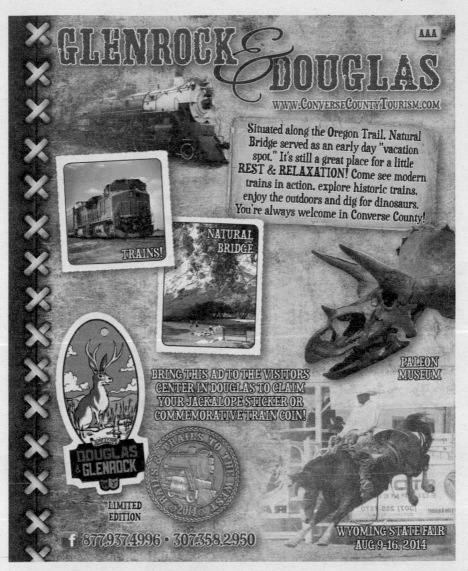

GLENROCK & DOUGLAS

WWW.CONVERSECOUNTYTOURISM.COM

Situated along the Oregon Trail, Natural Bridge served as an early day "vacation spot." It's still a great place for a little REST & RELAXATION! Come see modern trains in action, explore historic trains, enjoy the outdoors and dig for dinosaurs. You're always welcome in Converse County!

TRAINS!

NATURAL BRIDGE

PALEON MUSEUM

BRING THIS AD TO THE VISITORS CENTER IN DOUGLAS TO CLAIM YOUR JACKALOPE STICKER OR COMMEMORATIVE TRAIN COIN!

DOUGLAS & GLENROCK

LIMITED EDITION

TRAILS & TRAILS TO THE WEST 2014

877.937.4996 • 307.358.2950

WYOMING STATE FAIR AUG 9-16, 2014

WHERE TO EAT

CHUTES EATERY & SALOON 307/358-9790
▼▼▼ American. Casual Dining. $7-$29 **AAA Inspector Notes:** The contemporary Western atmosphere evident at this relaxed restaurant complements the array of menu selections. **Features:** full bar. **Address:** 1450 Riverbend Dr 82633 **Location:** I-25 exit 140, 0.8 mi e; in Douglas Inn & Convention Center. D

THE DEPOT RESTAURANT 307/358-9999
▼▼▼ American. Casual Dining. $9-$22 **AAA Inspector Notes:** This modern eatery offers a variety of appetizers, burgers, wraps and entrées including beef tenderloin, baby back pork ribs and some traditional Italian dishes. Call in advance for a boxed lunch to take on the road. **Features:** full bar, patio dining. **Address:** 100 E Walnut St 82633 **Location:** I-25 exit 140, 2 mi e to 2nd St, just n, then just w; downtown. L D CALL ⓖⓜ

DUBOIS (C-2) pop. 971, elev. 6,917'

Dubois grew from a rendezvous point for French, American and Indian trappers at the head of the Wind River Valley into a headquarters for cattle outfits, tie hack crews and river tie drives. From 1914 to 1946, stacked decks of railroad ties were floated down the Wind River from tie camps west of town to the railhead at Riverton. Dubois now is bordered by extensive cattle and dude ranching operations.

Northwest of Dubois is Union Pass, said to be the only place in the United States from which three rivers flow in different directions: Fish Creek is the source of the Columbia River, Jakeys Fork flows to the Mississippi, and Roaring Fork is part of the Colorado River drainage system.

Pack trips leave Dubois for Gannett Peak, Wyoming's highest peak, and the Fitzpatrick Wilderness, where there are 44 active glaciers.

Snowmobiling, dog sledding and cross-country skiing are popular at Union Pass and Togwotee Pass; both cross the Continental Divide west of Dubois.

Dubois Chamber of Commerce: 616 W. Ramshorn St., P.O. Box 632, Dubois, WY 82513. **Phone:** (307) 455-2556. *(See ad p. 330, p. 275.)*

DUBOIS FISH HATCHERY is 3 mi. e. on US 26/287, then 1.5 mi. s. at 5 Fish Hatchery Ct. Supplied by well and spring water, the station incubates and ships to other hatcheries nationwide up to 7 million eggs; it also rears nearly a half million fish yearly for stocking. Varieties include cutthroat, rainbow, grayling, brown and brook trout. **Hours:** Daily 8-5. **Cost:** Free. **Phone:** (307) 455-2431.

DUBOIS MUSEUM is at 909 W. Ramshorn St. The museum contains local artifacts depicting the industry, history, cultures and geology of Dubois and the Upper Wind River Valley. **Hours:** Daily 9-6, June-Aug.; Tues.-Sat. 10-4, rest of year. Hours may be extended during peak season. **Cost:** Free. **Phone:** (307) 455-2284.

NATIONAL BIGHORN SHEEP INTERPRETIVE CENTER is at 907 W. Ramshorn St. Through the use of dioramas, mounted animals, hands-on exhibits and DVDs visitors can learn about the history and biology of the bighorn sheep. "Sheep Mountain" replicates the bighorn's natural habitat. It focuses on predator-prey relationships, seasonal changes in habitat conditions, and plant and animal life with which bighorns interact.

Guided tours are available by reservation Nov.-Mar. **Time:** Allow 1 hour minimum. **Hours:** Mon.-Sat. 9-6, Sun. 9-5, Memorial Day weekend-Labor Day; Mon.-Sat. 9-5, rest of year. Closed Jan. 1, Thanksgiving and Christmas. Phone ahead to confirm schedule. **Cost:** $2.50; 75c (ages 0-12); $6 (family). **Phone:** (307) 455-3429 or (888) 209-2795.

THE LONGHORN RANCH LODGE AND RV RESORT
307/455-2337

Motel
$79-$149

Address: 5810 US Hwy 26 82513 **Location:** 3 mi e on US 26 and 287. **Facility:** 24 units, some two bedrooms, efficiencies and kitchens. 1 story, exterior corridors. **Parking:** winter plug-ins. **Terms:** closed 11/1-5/1, 3 day cancellation notice-fee imposed. **Activities:** fishing, playground. **Guest Services:** coin laundry. **Featured Amenity:** continental breakfast.
SAVE 🛜 ✕ 🅩 🖥 🖨 🖥 / SOME UNITS 🛏

ROCKY MOUNTAIN LODGE 307/455-2844
▼ Motel $60-$115 **Address:** 1349 W Ramshorn St 82513 **Location:** 1.6 mi w on US 26 and 287. **Facility:** 15 units, some kitchens. 2 stories (no elevator), exterior corridors. **Parking:** winter plug-ins. **Terms:** 3 day cancellation notice-fee imposed. **Activities:** fishing, picnic facilities.
🍽 🛜 ✕ 🅚 🖥 🖨 🖥 / SOME UNITS 🛏

TWIN PINES LODGE & CABINS 307/455-2600
▼▼ Historic Cabin. Rates not provided. **Address:** 218 W Ramshorn St 82513 **Location:** On US 26 and 287; center. **Facility:** Some rooms in the main lodge contain original furnishings. There also are some newer cabins available. Call ahead for reservations in the winter. 17 units, some cabins. 1-2 stories (no elevator), interior/exterior corridors. **Activities:** playground.
🍽 BIZ HS 🛜 ✕ 🅚 🖥 🖥 / SOME UNITS 🖨

WHERE TO EAT

COWBOY CAFE   307/455-2595
♦♦ ♦♦ American. Casual Dining. $6-$18 **AAA Inspector Notes:**
This casual café dishes up home-style cooking in hearty portions.
Coffee always is on and at least six to eight fruit and cream pies are
on hand daily, until they run out. Buffalo burgers and the cranberry
chicken sandwich are just a few favorites. **Features:** beer & wine,
patio dining. **Address:** 115 E Ramshorn St 82513 **Location:** On US
26 and 287; center. **Parking:** street only. [B] [L] [D]

NOSTALGIA BISTRO   307/455-3528
♦♦ ♦♦ American. Casual Dining. $8-$27 **AAA Inspector Notes:**
Turn-of-the-century decor will lure you in. Creative, expertly prepared
food will keep you coming back. The chef uses regional ingredients
and turns them into world-class cuisine with Asian and European
bents. Breads and desserts are homemade. When weather permits,
there's outdoor dining available. A new coffee shop adjoins the restaurant. **Features:** full bar, patio dining, happy hour. **Address:** 202 E
Ramshorn 82513 **Location:** Jct 1st St; downtown. **Parking:** on-site
and street. [L] [D] CALL [⑤M]

PAYA   307/455-3331
♦♦ Deli Pizza. Quick Serve. $6-$20 **AAA Inspector Notes:**
Homemade gluten-free pizzas hand stretched and cooked in a wood
oven are among choices on a menu that also lists deli favorites and
homemade soups and sausages. Homemade desserts end the meal
on the right note. Guests can eat in or sit on the covered deck. **Features:** beer & wine. **Address:** 112 E Ramshorn St 82513 **Location:**
Center. **Parking:** street only. [L] [D] CALL [⑤M] [Ⓚ]

RUSTIC PINE TAVERN   307/455-3989
♦♦ ♦♦ American. Casual Dining. $8-$22 **AAA Inspector Notes:**
A surprising find in a small town, this restaurant has a casually rustic
feel. The owners put their spin on Mexican comfort food along with
traditional Western fare such as steaks and hamburgers. **Features:**
full bar. **Reservations:** suggested. **Address:** 119 E Ramshorn St
82513 **Location:** 0.3 mi e on US 26 and 287; center.
[B] [L] [D] [Ⓚ]

ELK MOUNTAIN (E-4) pop. 191, elev. 7,240'

Elk Mountain, originally known as "The Crossing"
by pioneers who traversed the Overland Trail, is
noted for the wild game that take shelter on the
nearby refuge in the shadow of 11,156-foot Elk
Mountain. Both Elk Mountain Hotel and Garden
Spot Pavilion Dance Hall, next to the hotel, are on
the National Register of Historic Places.

Carbon County Visitors Council: 215 S. SR 70,
Riverside, WY 82325. **Phone:** (307) 324-3020 or
(800) 228-3547. *(See ad p. 309.)*

ENCAMPMENT (E-4) pop. 450, elev. 7,323'

Encampment takes its name from an Indian camp
where tribes gathered to hunt big game between the
Medicine Bow and Sierra Madre ranges. It was a
copper mining town from 1897 until the vein was ex-
hausted in 1908; a gold strike was reported as late
as 1937. Stock raising and lumbering are now the
principal industries.

Legend has it that Thomas Edison conceived of
the light bulb filament while looking at a frayed line
during a fishing trip near Encampment.

GRAND ENCAMPMENT MUSEUM is 2 blks. e.,
then 1 blk. s. of the post office. The museum houses
memorabilia recalling the area's Native American
encampment and copper mining days. The museum
complex also encompasses a pioneer village whose
14 buildings include a two-story outhouse and a

forest service lookout tower. A park next to the museum has picnic facilities and a playground.

Tours: Guided tours are available. **Time:** Allow 2
hours minimum. **Hours:** Daily 8-6, Memorial Day to
mid-Oct.; by appointment rest of year. **Cost:** Donations. **Phone:** (307) 327-5308.

ETHETE (C-3) pop. 1,553, elev. 5,354'

GAMBLING ESTABLISHMENTS
• **Little Wind Casino** is at 800 Blue Sky Hwy.
Hours: Daily 24 hours. **Phone:** (307) 438-7000.

EVANSTON (E-1) pop. 12,359, elev. 6,743'
• Restaurants p. 262

Designated the seat of Uinta County in 1870, Evanston lies in the center of the energy-rich Overthrust
Belt. It also is a departure point for trips into the Uinta
Mountains to the south. Depot Square Park is the
center of such summer activities as band concerts and
barbecues. Other recreational opportunities include
water sports at Woodruff Narrows Reservoir, north via
US 89, and cross-country skiing at Bear River State
Park *(see Recreation Areas Chart)*.

Bear River Information Center: 601 Bear River
Dr., Evanston, WY 82930. **Phone:** (307) 789-6540.

Evanston Wyoming Chamber of Commerce:
1020 Front St., Evanston, WY 82930. **Phone:** (307)
783-0370. *(See ad p. 260.)*

UINTA COUNTY MUSEUM is at 1020 Front St., in
the historic Carnegie Library building. The museum
features permanent and changing exhibits about
railroads, ranching and other aspects of the county's
history. **Hours:** Mon.-Fri. 9-5, Sat. 11-3 by appointment. **Cost:** Free. **Phone:** (307) 789-8248.

Chinese Joss House Museum, at 920 Front St.
adjacent to the Uinta County Museum, pays tribute
to Chinese immigrants who resided in the area circa
1870-1930. The building is a replica of an 1874 Chinese temple that burned down in 1922. Exhibits include archeological artifacts; historic photographs;
and items from the late 19th to early 20th centuries,
including pottery, paintings and other *objets d'art*.

Time: Allow 45 minutes minimum. **Hours:** Mon.-
Fri. 9-5, Sat. 11-3 by appointment. Closed major
holidays. **Cost:** Free. **Phone:** (307) 783-6320.

▼ See AAA listing p. 259 ▼

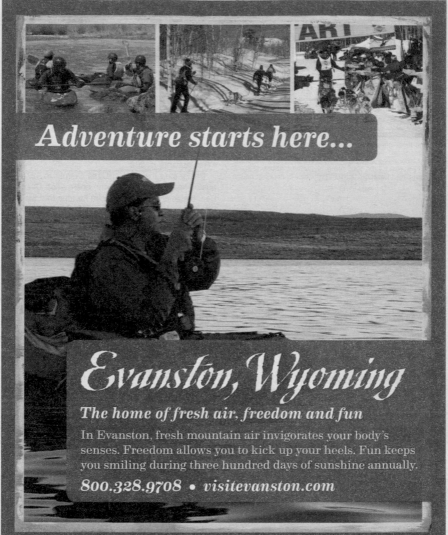

Adventure starts here...

Evanston, Wyoming

The home of fresh air, freedom and fun

In Evanston, fresh mountain air invigorates your body's senses. Freedom allows you to kick up your heels. Fun keeps you smiling during three hundred days of sunshine annually.

800.328.9708 • visitevanston.com

COMFORT INN
(307)789-7799

  Hotel $100-$145 **Address:** 1931 Harrison Dr 82930 **Location:** I-80 exit 3 (Harrison Dr), just n. **Facility:** 56 units. 2 stories (no elevator), interior corridors. **Parking:** winter plug-ins. **Pool(s):** heated indoor. **Activities:** hot tub, exercise room. **Guest Services:** valet and coin laundry.

HAMPTON INN
(307)789-5678

 Hotel $109-$159 **Address:** 101 Wasatch Rd 82930 **Location:** I-80 exit 3 (Harrison Dr), just n. **Facility:** 73 units. 4 stories, interior corridors. **Parking:** winter plug-ins. **Terms:** 1-7 night minimum stay, cancellation fee imposed. **Pool(s):** heated indoor. **Activities:** hot tub, exercise room. **Guest Services:** valet and coin laundry.

AAA Benefit: Members save up to 10%!

CALL

HOLIDAY INN EXPRESS HOTEL & SUITES
(307)789-7999

Hotel
$99-$169

Address: 1965 Harrison Dr 82930 **Location:** I-80 exit 3 (Harrison Dr), just n. **Facility:** 62 units. 3 stories, interior corridors. **Parking:** winter plug-ins. **Terms:** cancellation fee imposed. **Amenities:** video games. **Pool(s):** heated indoor. **Activities:** hot tub, exercise room. **Guest Services:** valet and coin laundry. **Featured Amenity:** full hot breakfast.

PRAIRIE INN
(307)789-2920

Motel
$59-$79

Address: 264 Bear River Dr 82930 **Location:** I-80 exit 6, 0.3 mi n. **Facility:** 30 units. 1 story, interior/exterior corridors. **Parking:** winter plug-ins. **Terms:** cancellation fee imposed. **Guest Services:** coin laundry. **Featured Amenity:** continental breakfast.

▼ See AAA listing p. 259 ▼

Know the Local Driving Laws When Traveling

Across the U.S. and Canada, visit **DrivingLaws.AAA.com** for local laws on speed limits, distracted driving, seat belts, trailers and towing, and traffic safety. Additional topics include driver licensing and motor vehicle fees and taxes.

DIGEST OF MOTOR LAWS

DrivingLaws.AAA.com

LEGAL TENDER RESTAURANT & LOUNGE
307/789-3770

American Casual Dining
$10–$30

AAA Inspector Notes: The salad bar at this restaurant beckons locals as well as being a favorite with guests. You can expect friendly service in a casual, relaxed atmosphere. Walls are adorned with some memorabilia of the original owner's career as an FBI agent. **Features:** full bar, early bird specials, senior menu. **Address:** 1601 Harrison Dr 82930 **Location:** I-80 exit 3 (Harrison Dr), just n; in BEST WESTERN Dunmar Inn. *Menu on AAA.com (See ad p. 261.)* B L D CALL M

EVANSVILLE pop. 2,544

CASPER C'MON INN
(307)472-6300

Hotel $120–$150 **Address:** 301 E Lathrop Rd 82636 **Location:** I-25 exit 185, just n to Lathrop Rd, then 0.5 mi e. **Facility:** 125 units, some kitchens. 3 stories, interior corridors. **Parking:** winter plug-ins. **Terms:** cancellation fee imposed. **Amenities:** video games. **Pool(s):** heated indoor. **Activities:** hot tub, exercise room. **Guest Services:** valet and coin laundry.

CALL M BIZ HS X H

SLEEP INN & SUITES CASPER EAST
(307)235-3100

Hotel $80–$119 **Address:** 6733 Bonanza Rd 82636 **Location:** I-25 exit 182, just n on Hat Six Rd. **Facility:** 80 units. 3 stories, interior corridors. **Parking:** winter plug-ins. **Pool(s):** heated indoor. **Activities:** hot tub, exercise room. **Guest Services:** valet and coin laundry.

HS X H / SOME UNITS

SUPER 8 CASPER EAST
(307)237-8100

Hotel $100–$134 **Address:** 269 Miracle St 82636 **Location:** I-25 exit 185, just n to Lathrop Rd, then just e. **Facility:** 57 units. 3 stories, interior corridors. **Parking:** winter plug-ins. **Pool(s):** heated indoor. **Activities:** hot tub, exercise room. **Guest Services:** valet and coin laundry.

CALL M BIZ H / SOME UNITS

FLAMING GORGE NATIONAL RECREATION AREA (E-2)

Reached by SR 530 or US 191 from I-80 in Wyoming or US 191 from Utah, Flaming Gorge National Recreation Area straddles the border between Wyoming and Utah. The area includes a 91-mile-long reservoir and the Flaming Gorge and Red canyons, which were carved through the Uinta Mountains by the Green River.

Lake Flaming Gorge is bounded primarily by Red Canyon to the south and by rolling hills and occasional abrupt cliffs and promontories to the north. Of geologic interest are the exposed strata in Firehole Canyon and the Sheep Creek Geological Loop.

Once belonging to Mexico, Wyoming's portion of the Flaming Gorge region was annexed to the United States after the Mexican War. John Wesley Powell, a one-armed Army major and professor, mapped the area on his way down the Green River in the late 1860s and early 1870s, naming Flaming Gorge and many other prominent landmarks.

I-80 is connected to SR 530 and US 191. In Utah, US 191 joins with SRs 43 and 44, which then link with SR 530 again, to form a complete 160-mile loop around the recreation area. Along the route are the

Flaming Gorge Dam and Visitor Center, off US 191 adjacent to the Bureau of Reclamation offices; the Red Canyon Visitor Center and Overlook, which offers a spectacular view from 1,400 feet above Red Canyon and Flaming Gorge Reservoir off SR 44; the Sheep Creek Geological Loop; and Flaming Gorge.

Known for its bountiful fishing waters, Lake Flaming Gorge also is a popular setting for swimming, boating and water skiing. Large boat ramps are found near campgrounds at convenient access points along the western and eastern sides of the lake.

The western shore, accessible from Buckboard, Wyo., and Lucerne Valley, Utah, has campsites and two marinas that provide boat rentals and supplies. Cedar Springs to the southeast is similarly equipped; the latter has a dock and marina. Other campgrounds are scattered throughout the Utah and Wyoming sections.

The reservoir contains a broad sampling of fish, including German brown, lake, rainbow and cutthroat trout; small-mouth bass; and kokanee salmon. Fishing is permitted all year. A license from either Utah or Wyoming is required.

Seasonal hunting is permitted except near public-use facilities. Cross-country skiing, snowmobiling and ice fishing are popular winter activities. For further information, contact the Flaming Gorge Ranger District, Flaming Gorge National Recreation Area, P.O. Box 279, Manila, UT 84046.

The recreation area is open all year, but most developed facilities are closed during the winter. The Red Canyon Visitor Center is open daily 10-5, Memorial Day weekend-Labor Day. The Flaming Gorge Dam Visitor Center is open daily 8-6, Memorial Day-Labor Day; daily 9-5, Apr. 1-day before Memorial Day and day after Labor Day-Oct. 14; Fri.-Mon. 10-4, rest of year. Guided tours of the dam depart from the visitor center daily 9-3, Memorial Day-Oct. 31; phone ahead to confirm schedule.

A use fee pass is required for all facilities. Passes are $5 (1-day), $15 (7-day) and $35 (annual), beginning from the date of purchase. America the Beautiful–National Parks and Federal Recreational Lands Pass holders enter free. Phone (435) 784-3445 for the ranger district, (435) 889-3713 for the Red Canyon Visitor Center, or (435) 885-3135 for the Flaming Gorge Dam and Visitor Center. *See Recreation Areas Chart.*

FLAMING GORGE DAM is off US 191 near Dutch John, Utah. The dam is a concrete arch structure rising 502 feet above bedrock. **Hours:** Guided 1-hour tours are offered daily 9-3, May 1 to mid-Oct. Phone ahead to confirm schedule. **Cost:** Free. **Phone:** (435) 885-3135.

JOHN JARVIE HISTORIC RANCH is about 8 mi. n.w. of Dutch John, Utah, on US 191, then 22 mi. e. on a gravel road, following signs to Browns Park. A haven for outlaws around the turn of the 20th century, Browns Park formerly was the site of a successful ranching operation started by Scottish immigrant John Jarvie in the 1880s. The ranch today includes a replica of the general store originally built in 1881, a blacksmith shop, a corral and a two-room dugout that was once Jarvie's residence.

A 15-minute orientation video is shown in a historical stone house that now serves as a museum. **Tours:** Guided tours are available. **Time:** Allow 1 hour minimum. **Hours:** Daily 10-5, Memorial Day-Labor Day; Wed.-Sat. 10-4:30, rest of year. **Cost:** Donations. **Phone:** (435) 885-3307 or (435) 781-4400. ⊞

FORT BRIDGER (E-1) pop. 345, elev. 6,670'

One of Fort Bridger's early residents was the renowned mountain man and scout Jim Bridger. Bridger, who hired himself out as a wilderness guide, was known for telling tall tales. According to popular lore, one of Bridger's most repeated stories was the one in which he tried to jump across a gorge in a petrified forest. The gorge turned out to be wider than he expected, but Bridger managed to escape death by remaining aloft on the gorge's petrified air.

Self-guiding tours: A driving tour atop an original hand-built roadbed of the Union Pacific begins 9 miles west of Fort Bridger at Leroy; from I-80 exit 24, follow CR 173 and SR 150. Utilize caution, as 22 miles of the route are unpaved. The tour continues past the abandoned town of Piedmont, several beehive-shaped charcoal kilns and the Uinta Mountains before entering Evanston *(see place listing p. 259).*

FORT BRIDGER STATE HISTORIC SITE is 3 mi. s. of I-80 exit 34. The fort was established in 1843 by Jim Bridger and Louis Vasquez. Visitors can see original buildings from the Army occupation 1858-90. Recent excavations have revealed the site of the original trading post, which has been reconstructed nearby. A museum offers exhibits tracing different periods of occupation.

Time: Allow 2 hours minimum. **Hours:** Grounds daily 8-dusk. Museum daily 9-5, May-Sept.; schedule varies rest of year based on staff availability. Phone ahead to confirm schedule. **Cost:** $4; free (ages 0-17). **Phone:** (307) 782-3842. ⊞

◆GEM FORT LARAMIE NATIONAL HISTORIC SITE (D-6)

Fort Laramie National Historic Site is off US 26, 3 miles southwest of the town of Fort Laramie. Near the confluence of the Laramie and North Platte rivers, the site covers 832 acres. From its founding as Fort William in 1834 and until 1849, the fort was an important fur-trading post. Purchased by the U.S. government in 1849 and renamed Fort Laramie, the fort served to aid in the migrations to Oregon and California. By 1890 the fort had outlived its usefulness and was abandoned, its land and buildings sold at public auction.

Eleven structures, including the 1874 cavalry barracks, have been restored and refurnished to recall the flavor of daily life at this post. A visitor center museum displays artifacts relating to civilian, military and Indian history on the northern Plains. From June to mid-August, staff members in period clothing demonstrate aspects of both military and civilian life in the 1870s. A vehicle for the physically impaired is available when the number of staff permits. An 1875 iron Army bridge that spans the North Platte River is 2 miles above the fort.

Grounds open daily dawn-dusk. Visitor center open daily 8-7, Memorial Day weekend-Labor Day; 8-4:30, rest of year. Visitor center closed Jan. 1, Thanksgiving and Christmas. Seven-day pass $3, free (ages 0-15); free (July 4). **Cards:** DS, MC, VI. Phone (307) 837-2221.

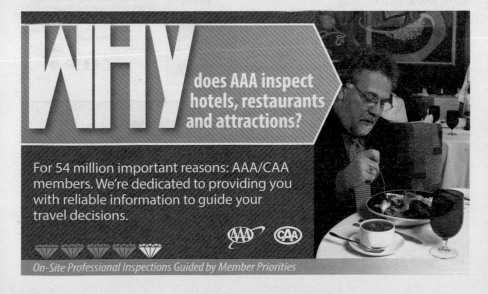

FOSSIL BUTTE NATIONAL MONUMENT (E-1)

Fourteen miles west of Kemmerer on US 30, Fossil Butte National Monument rises nearly 1,000 feet above the Twin Creek Valley. The buff-to-white beds of the Green River Formation contain one of the world's largest deposits of the fossils of freshwater fish that lived 50 million years ago. Fossils of mammals, reptiles, fish, insects and plants can be seen at the visitor center; a video presentation also is available.

A self-guiding hiking trail, 2.5 miles long, leads to the site of a historic fossil quarry, and a 1.5-mile trail takes visitors through an aspen tree grove. Interpretive programs are offered June through August.

Allow 2 hours, 30 minutes minimum. Grounds open all year but may be snow-covered Oct.-Apr. Visitor center daily 9-5:30, May-Sept.; 8-4:30, rest of year. Closed winter holidays. Free. Phone (307) 877-4455.

GILLETTE (B-5) pop. 29,087, elev. 4,538'

Gillette lies on a high plateau between the Black Hills and the Bighorn Mountains. The town's livestock industry dates from the early 1800s. Mule deer, pronghorns and buffalo graze on unspoiled land nearby.

Named for railroad surveyor Edward Gillette, the town was developed as a ranching area and became a hub for transporting livestock to market. Now coal and oil industries fuel Gillette's economy. During summer, coal mine tours can be arranged through the convention and visitors bureau. The bureau also offers an assistance program for hunters interested in the mule deer, pronghorn antelopes and elk populations in the area.

Campbell County Convention and Visitors Bureau: 1810 S. Douglas Hwy., Suite A, Gillette, WY 82718. **Phone:** (307) 686-0040.

ROCKPILE MUSEUM is 1 mi. from I-90 exit 124 at 900 W. Second St. (US 14/16E). The museum takes its name from a nearby rock formation. Local history is depicted through extensive displays that include firearms, pioneer and Native American artifacts and a restored sheep wagon. Next to the museum are two furnished rural schoolhouses. **Hours:** Mon.-Sat. 9-5. **Cost:** Free. **Phone:** (307) 682-5723.

BEST WESTERN TOWER WEST LODGE (307)686-2210

Hotel
$80-$230

 AAA Benefit: Members save 10% or more with Best Western!

Address: 109 N US Hwy 14-16 82716 **Location:** I-90 exit 124, just n. **Facility:** 189 units. 2 stories (no elevator), interior corridors. **Parking:** winter plug-ins. **Amenities:** video games. **Pool(s):** heated indoor. **Activities:** hot tub, exercise room. **Guest Services:** valet and coin laundry.

CANDLEWOOD SUITES (307)682-6100

Extended Stay Hotel $109-$169 **Address:** 904 Country Club Rd 82718 **Location:** I-90 exit 126, 0.5 mi s, then just e. **Facility:** 83 efficiencies. 3 stories, interior corridors. **Terms:** 7 day cancellation notice-fee imposed. **Activities:** picnic facilities, exercise room. **Guest Services:** complimentary and valet laundry.

COMFORT INN & SUITES OF GILLETTE (307)685-2223

Hotel
$89-$179

Address: 1607 W 2nd Ave 82716 **Location:** I-90 exit 124, 0.3 mi ne, then just se. **Facility:** 60 units. 3 stories, interior corridors. **Parking:** winter plug-ins. **Pool(s):** heated indoor. **Activities:** hot tub, exercise room. **Guest Services:** valet and coin laundry. **Featured Amenity: continental breakfast.**

COUNTRY INN & SUITES BY CARLSON (307)682-0505

Hotel
$89-$189

Address: 2597 S Douglas Hwy 82718 **Location:** I-90 exit 126, 0.6 mi s, then just e. **Facility:** 80 units. 3 stories, interior corridors. **Parking:** winter plug-ins. **Terms:** cancellation fee imposed, resort fee. **Pool(s):** heated indoor. **Activities:** hot tub, exercise room. **Guest Services:** valet and coin laundry. **Featured Amenity: full hot breakfast.**

FAIRFIELD INN & SUITES BY MARRIOTT   (307)682-1717

◆◆◆ Hotel $99-$259 Address: 2577 S Douglas Hwy 82718 Location: I-90 exit 126, 0.6 mi s, then just e. Facility: 80 units. 3 stories, interior corridors. Pool(s): heated indoor. Activities: hot tub, exercise room. Guest Services: valet and coin laundry.

AAA Benefit: Members save 5% or more!

[symbols] ✈ ⍾ CALL 🅼 ⛲ BIZ HS 🛜 ✕ 💻 / SOME UNITS 🅱 📺

HAMPTON INN   (307)686-2000

◆◆◆ Hotel $89-$199 Address: 211 Decker Ct 82716 Location: I-90 exit 124, just ne. Facility: 57 units. 3 stories, interior corridors. Terms: 1-7 night minimum stay, cancellation fee imposed. Pool(s): heated indoor. Activities: hot tub, exercise room. Guest Services: valet and coin laundry.

AAA Benefit: Members save up to 10%!

[symbols] ✈ ⍾ CALL 🅼 ⛲ BIZ 🛜 ✕ 💻 / SOME UNITS 🅱 📺

HOLIDAY INN EXPRESS & SUITES   (307)686-9576

◆◆◆ Hotel $134-$259 Address: 1908 Cliff Davis Dr 82718 Location: I-90 exit 126, just s to Boxelder Rd, then just e to Cliff Davis Dr. Facility: 83 units. 3 stories, interior corridors. Amenities: video games. Pool(s): heated indoor. Activities: hot tub, exercise room. Guest Services: valet and coin laundry.

[symbols] ⍾ ⛲ BIZ HS 🛜 ✕ 📹 🅱 📺 💻 / SOME UNITS 🛒

WINGATE BY WYNDHAM   (307)685-2700

◆◆◆ Hotel $99-$209

Address: 1801 Cliff Davis Dr 82718 Location: I-90 exit 126, just s to Boxelder Rd, then just e to Cliff Davis Dr. Facility: 84 units. 3 stories, interior corridors. Amenities: video games. Pool(s): heated indoor. Activities: hot tub, exercise room. Guest Services: valet and coin laundry. Featured Amenity: full hot breakfast.

SAVE ⍾ CALL 🅼 ⛲ BIZ HS 🛜 ✕ 📹 🅱 📺 💻

WHERE TO EAT

311 LOUNGE   307/685-8055

◆◆ American. Casual Dining. $12-$22 AAA Inspector Notes: Good food, mojitos, margaritas and martinis are creatively prepared at this lounge where the philosophy is eat, drink and unwind. Menu items include Mediterranean and Asian salads, baked Brie with honey and pecans, rosemary-infused and prosciutto-wrapped stuffed cherry peppers, salmon burger with lemon caper aioli, chicken satay sandwiches and a few tasty desserts. Watch out, the two mini burger sliders are addictive. Features: full bar, Sunday brunch, happy hour. Address: 311 S Gillette Ave 82716 Location: Downtown. Parking: street only. L D

THE CHOPHOUSE RESTAURANT   307/682-6805

◆◆◆ American. Casual Dining. $9-$60 AAA Inspector Notes: Prime beef cuts are cooked to the diner's liking in this upscale restaurant. The warm and inviting dining room's menu also is laden with made-to-order fresh fish and shellfish specialties and interesting interpretations of classic dishes. Gluten-free items are available. Features: full bar, early bird specials, happy hour. Address: 113 S Gillette Ave 82716 Location: I-90 exit 124, 0.3 mi n, then 1.5 mi e; at W 2nd St (US16) and Gillette Ave. Parking: on-site and street. L D CALL 🅼

HONG KONG RESTAURANT   307/682-5829

◆◆◆ Chinese. Casual Dining. $5-$15 AAA Inspector Notes: The restaurant presents traditional Chinese cuisine, including popular daily specials. Features: full bar. Address: 1612 W 2nd St 82716 Location: I-90 exit 124, just ne to US 14/16, then just e. L D CALL 🅼 🍴

LOS COMPADRES   307/682-1101

◆◆ Mexican. Casual Dining. $6-$15 AAA Inspector Notes: This little eatery offers great food, friendly service and a colorful atmosphere. Features: full bar. Address: 1700 W 2nd St 82716 Location: I-90 exit 124, just ne, then just se. L D

THE MAIN BAGEL COMPANY   307/687-1616

◆ Deli Coffee/Tea. Quick Serve. $6-$7 AAA Inspector Notes: At this family-owned and -operated eatery, bagels are boiled first, then baked, resulting in a chewy center and crunchy crust. Croissants, pizza, salads, sandwiches and wraps make up the menu. Daily soups are made in house. Features: patio dining. Address: 2610 S Douglas Hwy 82718 Location: I-90 exit 126, 0.5 mi s; in Power Basin Mall. B L

THE PRIME RIB RESTAURANT & WINE CELLAR   307/682-2944

American Casual Dining $9-$34

AAA Inspector Notes: This bustling upscale restaurant offers patrons many variations of well-prepared steaks, prime rib and seafood. An extensive selection of wine is kept in a state-of-the art, glass-enclosed wine case. Features: full bar, happy hour. Reservations: suggested. Address: 1205 S Douglas Hwy 82717 Location: I-90 exit 126, 0.5 mi n. *Menu on AAA.com*

L D CALL 🅼

GLENROCK (D-5) pop. 2,576, elev. 5,102'

Glenrock's hunting, fishing, hiking and mountain-climbing opportunities make it a hot spot for outdoor enthusiasts. Originally called Deer Creek Station, Glenrock was a stop along the Oregon Trail and the Pony Express National Historic Trail. The more than 350,000 settlers traversing the area from 1841 to 1869 would break at a certain rock situated in a nearby glen—hence the name that later was adopted by the town. The large, domelike Rock in the Glen, located just west of town off I-25, is inscribed with the names of some of the settlers.

Glenrock Area Chamber of Commerce: 506 W. Birch St., Glenrock, WY 82637. **Phone:** (307) 436-5652. *(See ad p. 257.)*

GLENROCK PALEONTOLOGICAL MUSEUM is at 506 W. Birch St. On display are a Triceratops skull, Oligocene mammal fossils and Tyrannosaurus rex teeth. Permanent exhibits include Sea Life in Wyoming: Devonian to Cretaceous Ages. **Time:** Allow 1 hour minimum. **Hours:** Tues.-Sat. 11-4, June-Aug.; Tues., Thurs. and Sat. 11-4, rest of year. Closed major holidays. Phone ahead to confirm schedule. **Cost:** Free. **Phone:** (307) 436-2667. *(See ad p. 257.)*

GRAND TETON NATIONAL PARK (B-1)

- Hotels p. 271 • Restaurants p. 271
- Attractions map p. 268
- Hotels & Restaurants map & index p. 295
- Part of Jackson Hole Including Grand Teton National Park area — see map p. 293

Elevations in the park range from 6,800 ft. at the valley floor to 13,770 ft. at Grand Teton Peak. Refer to AAA maps for additional elevation information.

Grand Teton National Park's southern entrance is north of Jackson on US 26/89/191; an eastern entrance is at Moran Junction on US 26/287. From this point US 89/191/287 heads north through the park into Yellowstone National Park *(see place listing p. 326)*. The park's 485 square miles include the major portion of Wyoming's Teton Range and the valley of Jackson Hole. Together the mountain range and valley frame a majestic landscape of eight large lakes and many smaller ones, glaciers, numerous snowfields and extensive pine, fir and spruce forests.

The Tetons are among the youngest mountains on the continent. The elevations established by the U.S. Geological Survey for the major peaks are Grand Teton, 13,770 feet; Mount Owen, 12,928 feet; Middle Teton, 12,804 feet; Mount Moran, 12,605 feet; South Teton, 12,514 feet; Teewinot Mountain, 12,325 feet; Thor Peak, 12,028 feet; Buck Mountain, 11,938 feet; Nez Perce Peak, 11,901 feet; Mount Wister, 11,490 feet; and Mount St. John, 11,430 feet.

Few mountain ranges have a greater variety of glaciated canyons than the Tetons. The fault-block mountains of this alpine park are rare in this country. Part of the park area lies above the tree line, which is at about 10,000 feet.

The Tetons were first photographed by William H. Jackson, a member of the Hayden Expedition sent by the government to survey the area in 1872.

General Information and Activities

The park is open all year, although most park facilities operate only from mid-May to mid-October. Visitor information is available at Colter Bay and Jenny Lake visitor centers and the Craig Thomas Discovery & Visitor Center in Moose. Free ranger-led activities in summer include hikes. Entrance stations and visitor centers distribute a schedule of activities.

More than 200 miles of trails afford short walks, strenuous hikes and overnight backcountry trips. Trail booklets can be found at some trail heads and at the visitor centers. Campsites along backcountry trails require a camping permit, available at the visitor centers and the Jenny Lake Ranger Station.

Game fish include brook, brown, cutthroat, Mackinaw, and rainbow trout, as well as whitefish. Fish can be taken with artificial flies during most of the summer and autumn, but the Mackinaw trout in Jackson and Jenny lakes are best caught by trolling with heavy tackle.

A Wyoming fishing license is required; a nonresident 1-day license is available for $14; a full-year permit is $92. Special fishing regulations apply in the park, and changes are made annually regarding limits and waters open to fishing; check the current regulations.

Mountain climbing is a popular summer pastime. Authorized guide services are available, and because of the difficulty of the Teton peaks, climbers are urged to use them. Prospective climbers should consult rangers for information about routes and appropriate equipment. The Jenny Lake Ranger Station is the park's climbing information center.

The usual alpine equipment is essential: ice axes, ropes and rubber-soled boots or climbing shoes. Two park-approved mountaineering schools offer lessons and guide service.

The climbing season in Grand Teton National Park ordinarily spans mid-June to mid-September, but conditions are best from July to early September. In most cases it is advisable to allow 2 days for an ascent of Grand Teton, Mount Owen or Mount Moran and 1 or 2 days for all the other peaks, depending upon your experience.

Riding on horses trained for mountain trails is another popular way to explore the park. From corrals at Colter Bay Village and Jackson Lake Lodge, the Grand Teton Lodge Company conducts daily guided 1- and 2-hour rides, half-day trail rides and wagon rides; phone (307) 543-2811.

Morning and evening horse or wagon rides with breakfast or dinner also are available for $39-$71. Guide fees vary according to trail, but all rates are regulated by the park and range from $33-$48. Restrictions apply to horseback riding.

CCInc. Auto Tape Tours allows drivers to set their own pace while a CD or cassette narrative describes the park's attractions and history. They are available at gift shops, RV campgrounds, Colter Bay Village, Jackson Lake Lodge, Jenny Lake, and by mail; phone (201) 236-1666.

If water levels allow, boat and canoe rentals, guided fishing trips and scenic boat trips can be arranged at the Colter Bay Marina at Colter Bay Village, the Bridge Bay Marina on Yellowstone Lake and the booking office at Jackson Lake Lodge. Canoe rentals are $17-$19 per hour, and boat rentals are $35 per hour or $175 per day (including gas).

Jackson Lake boat cruises lasting 1 hour, 30 minutes leave the Colter Bay Marina several times daily, if water levels allow. Daily trout breakfast cruises to Elk Island as well as Monday, Wednesday and Sunday evening dinner cruises also are offered. Cruise rates range from $30 to $62; $13 to $39 (ages 0-11). Contact the Grand Teton Lodge Co. for schedules and exact fares; phone (307) 543-3100.

Jenny Lake Boating Co. offers scenic cruises and shuttle service to the west shore of Jenny Lake. Round-trip shuttle service $12; $6 (ages 5-12). One-way shuttle service $7; $5 (ages 5-12). The

(See map & index p. 295.)

booking office is at the south end of Jenny Lake near the ranger station; phone (307) 734-9227, mid-May through September 30.

Motorboats can be operated on Jackson and Jenny lakes, but motors more than 10 horsepower cannot be used on Jenny Lake. Hand-propelled craft are permitted on Bearpaw, Bradley, Emma Matilda, Jackson, Jenny, Leigh, Phelps, String, Taggart and Two Ocean lakes and on the Snake River. Water skiing, jet skiing and windsurfing are permitted only on Jackson Lake.

Mandatory boating permits for both Grand Teton and Yellowstone national parks can be purchased at the visitor centers. Seven-day permits are $10 for nonmotorized craft and $20 for motorized craft; annual permits are $20 for nonmotorized craft and $40 for motorized craft.

Several companies offer scenic float trips on the Snake River from May through September (see attraction listings). Reservations for these relaxing excursions are recommended (and, in some cases, required).

Winter activities include cross-country skiing, snowshoe hikes and ice fishing. Marked trails for cross-country skiing also are provided.

Five campgrounds, Colter Bay, Gros Ventre, Jenny Lake, Lizard Creek and Signal Mountain, are open on a first-come, first-served basis. Opening dates vary from late April to early June; closing dates are from early September to mid-October. Rates are $21 per night and reservations are not accepted. See Recreation Areas Chart.

ADMISSION to the park is by private vehicle permit ($25 or $20 per motorcycle) and by single nonmotorized entry ($12), valid in both Grand Teton and Yellowstone national parks for 7 days; and by annual area permit ($50 for both parks) or annual permit ($80 for entrance to most federal sites). An Interagency Senior Pass for U.S. citizens ages 62+ is $10; an Interagency Access Passport for physically impaired U.S. citizens provides free admission.

PETS are permitted in the park only if they are on a leash or otherwise physically restricted at all times. They are not permitted on trails, in the backcountry or in any public building.

ADDRESS inquiries to Grand Teton National Park, P.O. Drawer 170, Moose, WY 83012; phone (307) 739-3300.

AMPHITHEATER LAKE TRAIL extends up the eastern slope of Disappointment Peak to two alpine lakes, Surprise and Amphitheater, both at altitudes of more than 9,000 feet. Amphitheater Lake occupies a protected glacial cirque, or steep hollow. An overlook, reached by several trails climbing 3,000 feet above the valley floor, offers a sweeping panorama of Jackson Hole and a view extending eastward 80 miles to the Wind River Mountains. A branch from the trail leads into Garnet Canyon. Trail conditions are available at the visitor centers. **Time:** Allow 6 hours minimum.

CASCADE CANYON TRAIL, 25 mi. n. of Jackson in the center of the park, explores the deepest recesses of the Tetons, passing through a broad, glacier-carved canyon with walls that rise thousands of feet on either side. Lake Solitude, near the head of the canyon at the tree line, is a pristine example of an alpine lake. **Time:** Allow 7 hours minimum.

CHAPEL OF THE TRANSFIGURATION is off Chapel of the Transfiguration Rd. near Moose. Above the altar of the 1925 log chapel is a large window framing a view of the Teton Range. Episcopal services are held during the summer; schedules are posted on a board outside the chapel and in park newspapers. **Time:** Allow 30 minutes minimum.

COLTER BAY VISITOR CENTER is near Jackson Lake. Videos featuring local wildlife and scenery are shown daily in the amphitheater. **Hours:** Daily 8-7, first Mon. in June-Labor Day; 8-5, early May-day before Memorial Day and day after Labor Day-early Oct. **Cost:** Free. **Phone:** (307) 739-3594.

CRAIG THOMAS DISCOVERY & VISITOR CENTER is across the street from the park headquarters in Moose. The center orients visitors to the unique natural and cultural history of the area and features stories about conservation and stewardship. Maps and permits are available. **Hours:** Daily 8-7, early June-Labor Day; 8-5, rest of year. **Cost:** Free. **Phone:** (307) 739-3399.

CUNNINGHAM CABIN HISTORIC SITE is 6 mi. s. of Moran Junction on US 26/89/191. The site was the base of pioneer Pierce Cunningham's Bar Flying U Ranch that once comprised some 560 acres. The site now contains the foundations of the house, barn, shed and outbuildings as well as the remains of a cabin. A leaflet outlining a self-guiding trail through the area also describes the life of the homesteader in Jackson Hole. **Time:** Allow 30 minutes minimum.

DEATH CANYON TRAIL, about 3 mi. s. of Moose, traverses the length of a canyon of profound depth and grandeur to broad meadows. No canyon better illustrates the contrasts of the Teton area. **Time:** Allow 6 hours minimum.

FLAGG RANCH INFORMATION STATION Hours: Daily 9-3:30, June 1-Labor Day.

HIDDEN FALLS AND INSPIRATION POINT TRAILS lead from the southern shore of Jenny Lake off Teton Park Rd. A boat ride to the trailhead is available in the summer. Ranger-guided tours to Hidden Falls and Inspiration Point depart the trailhead daily at 8:30 in season; departure time may vary. **Time:** Allow 2 hours minimum.

© 2013 NAVTEQ   © AAA

MOUNT BERRY
EL 8,951 FT

To Yellowstone National Park

WILDCAT PEAK
EL 9,693 FT

Conant Creek

Caribou-Targhee

Grand

Teton

National

Teton

Wilderness   Area

Creek

JOHN D. ROCKEFELLER JR. MEMORIAL PKY.

ROAD CLOSED
IN WINTER

Lizard
Creek

Jackson

RANGER PEAK
EL 11,355 FT

MOOSE
MOUNTAIN
EL 10,054 FT

National

EAGLES REST PEAK
EL 11,257 FT

Colter
Bay

Colter Bay

Two Ocean
Lake

Pacific

Colter Bay
Visitor Center

TRAIL

South Badger Creek

BIVOUAC PEAK
EL 10,825 FT

Grand Teton Lodge Company
Wild and Scenic Rafting Trips

Emma
Matilda
Lake

North Leigh Creek

TRIPLE
GLACIERS

Jackson Lake

GREEN MOUNTAIN
EL 9,614 FT

THOR PEAK
EL 12,028 FT

MT MORAN
EL 12,605 FT

Lake

Signal
Mountain

Signal
Mountain

Moran

Fork

Forest

National

River

Buffalo

Bridger-Teton

To Dubois

Leigh
Lake

Jenny
Lake

Cunningham
Cabin Historic
Site

Spread

Creek

MOUNT SAINT JOHN
EL 11,430 FT

PAINTBRUSH
TRAIL

Teton

CASCADE CANYON
TRAIL

Jenny
Lake

TETON PARKWAY

TETON GLACIER

GRAND TETON
EL 13,770 FT

NEZ PERCE
EL 11,901 FT

Jenny Lake
Visitor Center

Triangle X Ranch Float Trips

MIDDLE TETON
EL 12,804 FT

SOUTH TETON
EL 12,514 FT

AMPHITHEATER
LAKE TRAIL

MOUNT LEIDY
EL 10,326 FT

MOUNT WISTER
EL 11,490 FT

SCENIC BYWAY

BUCK MOUNTAIN
EL 11,938 FT

Chapel of the
Transfiguration

Menor's Ferry
Craig Thomas
Discovery and
Visitor Center

National

DEATH CANYON
TRAIL

FOSSIL MOUNTAIN
EL 10,916 FT

PROSPECTORS MTN
EL 11,241 FT

ROAD CLOSED
IN WINTER

Phelps
Lake

Moose

MOOSE-WILSON RD.

Lower Slide
Lake

HOUSETOP MTN
EL 10,537 FT

MOUNT
HUNT
EL 10,783 FT

Park

Kelly

Gros
Ventre

Gros
Ventre
Slide

TAYLOR
RANCH
RD.

Atherton
Creek

VENTRE

River

RD

GRANITE CANYON
TRAIL

GROS

National Elk

Gros Ventre
Slide

Jackson Hole
Mountain Resort

Teton
Village

Jackson
Hole
Airport
(JAC)

Forest

Jackson National
Fish Hatchery

Grand Teton
National Park
Attractions

To Idaho Falls, ID

390

Welcome
Center

National
Museum
of Wildlife
Art

Refuge

Platt

Creek

SHEEP MOUNTAIN
EL 11,239 FT

Scale in Miles

3.8   0   3.8

TETON PASS
EL 8,431 FT

22

Wilson

Jackson
Hole Hist
Society
& Mus.

Snake

MILLERS BUTTE
EL 6,775 FT

Curtis
Canyon

CAMPGROUND SITE WITHIN NAT'L.
PARK. INFORMATION PROVIDED
BY WOODALL'S ®.

2120-14

26 89 191 189

To Salt Lake City, UT

Jackson
Snow King Resort

Sands Whitewater
and Scenic River Trips

JACKSON PEAK
EL 10,741 FT

(See map & index p. 295.)

JENNY LAKE VISITOR CENTER is 8 mi. n. of Moose Junction on Teton Park Rd. The visitor center has exhibits about geology. **Hours:** Daily 8-5, mid-May to late Sept. **Cost:** Free. **Phone:** (307) 739-3392.

MENOR'S FERRY is near the Chapel of the Trans-figuration in Moose. The ferry is a reconstruction of the craft that was once the only means of crossing the Snake River in central Jackson Hole country. The original home of Bill Menor, one of the area's first settlers, is in the area; it contains historical objects and exhibits. **Time:** Allow 30 minutes minimum. **Hours:** Daily 10-4, early July-Aug. 31, weather and staff permitting. Phone ahead to confirm schedule.

PAINTBRUSH TRAIL starts near the outlet of Leigh Lake, follows the bottom of Paintbrush Canyon, crosses Paintbrush Divide and joins the Cascade Canyon Trail at Lake Solitude. The many wildflowers along this trail give the canyon its name. Wildlife, especially moose, can be seen near lakes and marshes. This trail affords several good views of Jackson and Leigh lakes. Since dangerous snow and ice remain on the divide until late in the year, check conditions at the visitor centers. Horses cannot be taken over the divide to Lake Solitude until late August.

SIGNAL MOUNTAIN is 3 mi. s. of Jackson Lake Junction on Teton Park Rd. The mountain affords a panorama of the valley, Jackson Lake, a portion of southern Yellowstone and the Teton, Gros Ventre and Hoback mountain ranges. A narrow, paved road that's 5 miles long leads to the summit. Trailers are not allowed on this road.

TETON CREST TRAIL traverses the Tetons from Teton Pass to Cascade Canyon. This high alpine country can be explored on foot or horseback.

VALLEY TRAIL runs parallel to the mountains from the e. shore of Leigh Lake s. to Teton Village. The trail is the point of origin of all trails into the Teton range. From this point, trails run westward into Cascade, Death, Granite, Open and Paintbrush canyons; others encircle String Lake, Jenny Lake and Hermitage Point on Jackson Lake. A popular hike follows the south shore of Jenny Lake to Hidden Falls.

Float Trips

Float Trips, on the Snake River through Grand Teton National Park, are conducted by experienced guides who thread rubber rafts down the river. These trips, which offer spectacular mountain scenery and opportunities to view native wildlife, are carefully supervised by the National Park Service.

Note: A minimum weight of 35-40 pounds is required for most float trips.

BARKER-EWING SCENIC FLOAT TRIPS depart from the float-trip parking lot at Moose Village; transportation from the parking lot to the launch area is provided. Scenic 10-mile trips are conducted entirely within the park's natural environment and provide opportunities to view wildlife and the Teton peaks. **Hours:** Trips depart several times daily, late May to mid-Sept. **Cost:** $70; $40 (ages 6-12). Fares may vary; phone ahead. Reservations are required. **Phone:** (307) 733-1800 or (800) 365-1800. *(See ad p. 268, p. 278.)*

DORNAN'S SNAKE RIVER SCENIC FLOAT TRIPS originate at Dornan's, on Moose St. in Moose. Lasting 3 to 3.5 hours, the 14-mile scenic float trips provide good opportunities for photography and for observing elk, bear and other wildlife. **Hours:** Trips depart daily at 8, noon and 4, mid-May to mid-Sept. (weather and water conditions permitting). **Cost:** $65; $55 (ages 0-11). Reservations are recommended. **Phone:** (307) 733-3699.

GRAND TETON LODGE COMPANY WILD AND SCENIC RAFTING TRIPS is 5 mi. n.w. of Moran Junction on US 89/191/287. The company offers 3- to 4-hour float trips as well as luncheon and dinner trips; transportation to and from the river is provided.

Hours: Three- to 4-hour float trips and luncheon trips run daily, late May-late Sept. Dinner trips run Tues., Thurs. and Sat., late May-late Sept. Phone ahead to confirm schedule. **Cost:** Three- to 4-hour float trip $62; $42 (ages 6-11). Luncheon trip $70; $50 (ages 6-11). Dinner trip $76; $55 (ages 6-11). Fares may vary; phone ahead. Ages 0-5 are not permitted. **Phone:** (307) 543-2811.

▼ *See AAA listing p. 271* ▼

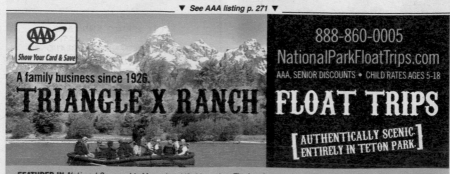

(See map & index p. 295.)

SIGNAL MOUNTAIN LODGE FLOAT TRIPS meets at Signal Mountain Lodge, on Inner Park Rd. in Moran; transportation to and from the Snake River is provided. A 10-mile scenic float ride down the river lasts 3.5 hours and features wildlife viewing opportunities. **Hours:** Trips depart daily at 7:30 and 5, mid-May to mid-Sept. (weather and water conditions permitting). **Cost:** $65; $40 (ages 6-12). Fares may vary; phone ahead. **Phone:** (307) 543-2831.

SOLITUDE FLOAT TRIPS departs the float-trip parking lot near the Moose Visitor Center. Ten-mile scenic trips are available. **Hours:** Trips are offered several times daily, May-Sept. (weather and water conditions permitting). **Cost:** $70; $45 (ages 6-12). Reservations are recommended. **Phone:** (307) 733-2871 or (888) 704-2800. *(See ad p. 279, p. 269.)*

(See ad p. 279, p. 269.)

SAVE **TRIANGLE X RANCH FLOAT TRIPS** meets in the float-trip parking lot across from the Craig Thomas Discovery & Visitor Center. Ten-mile float trips, an evening supper float, and sunrise and evening wildlife trips take visitors along the Snake River. **Hours:** Trips depart several times daily, May-Sept. **Cost:** Ten-mile float trip $59; $46 (ages 5-18). Fares may vary; phone ahead. Reservations are required. **Phone:** (307) 733-5500 or (888) 860-0005. *(See ad p. 269, p. 270.)*

(See ad p. 269, p. 270.)

(See map & index p. 295.)

HEADWATERS LODGE & CABINS AT FLAGG RANCH
307/543-2861   1

♦♦♦ **Resort Hotel.** Rates not provided. **Address:** Hwy 89 83013 **Location:** US 89 and 191; 2 mi s of Yellowstone National Park south entrance; 5 mi n of Grand Teton National Park north entrance. **Facility:** This property has a large log cabin exterior. The lodge rooms and cabins are nicely appointed and some offer views of the Grand Tetons. 92 units, some cabins. 1 story, exterior corridors. **Terms:** check-in 4 pm. **Activities:** fishing, recreation programs. **Guest Services:** coin laundry.

JACKSON LAKE LODGE
307/543-2811   2

♦♦♦ **Hotel.** Rates not provided. **Address:** US Hwy 89 83013 **Location:** 5 mi nw of Moran. **Facility:** 385 units. 1-3 stories, interior/exterior corridors. **Terms:** check-in 4 pm. **Amenities:** safes. **Dining:** 2 restaurants, also, The Mural Room, see separate listing, entertainment. **Pool(s):** heated outdoor. **Activities:** fishing, recreation programs, playground, trails. **Guest Services:** valet laundry, area transportation. *(See ad p. 271.)*

JENNY LAKE LODGE
307/733-4647   4

♦♦♦♦ **Cabin.** Rates not provided. **Address:** Jenny Lake Inner Park Rd 83012 **Location:** 3 mi off Inner Park Rd; jct N Jenny Lake. Located in a quiet area. **Facility:** This property, set in a pine-shaded location at the foot of the majestic Grand Tetons, offers hardwood floors, high beamed ceilings, willow and pine furnishings and upscale appointments. 37 units, some cabins. 1 story, exterior corridors. **Terms:** check-in 4 pm. **Amenities:** safes. **Dining:** Jenny Lake Lodge Dining Room, see separate listing. **Activities:** recreation programs, bicycles. **Guest Services:** valet laundry. *(See ad p. 271.)*

SIGNAL MOUNTAIN LODGE
307/543-2831   3

♦♦
Hotel
$162-$334

Address: 1 Inner Park Rd 83013 **Location:** Teton Park Rd, 2 mi s of US 89, 191 and 287. **Facility:** 79 units, some two bedrooms and cabins. 2 stories (no elevator), exterior corridors. **Terms:** closed 10/15-5/10, 7 day cancellation notice-fee imposed. **Dining:** The Peaks, see separate listing. **Activities:** marina, fishing, picnic facilities. **Guest Services:** coin laundry.

TOGWOTEE MOUNTAIN LODGE
307/543-2847   5

♦♦ **Hotel.** Rates not provided. **Address:** 27655 Hwy US 26 & 287 83013 **Location:** Jct US 26/287, 16.5 mi e of Moran. **Facility:** 88 units, some cabins. 1-3 stories (no elevator), interior/exterior corridors. **Terms:** check-in 4 pm. **Dining:** The Grizzly Grill, see separate listing. **Activities:** hot tub, fishing, snowmobiling, sledding, playground. **Guest Services:** coin laundry.

COLTER BAY VILLAGE & CABINS
307/543-2811

fyi Not evaluated. **Address:** US 89 and 287 83013 **Location:** 10 mi nw of Moran. Facilities, services, and décor characterize an economy property.

WHERE TO EAT

THE GRIZZLY GRILL
307/543-2847   4

♦♦ American. Casual Dining. $7-$28 **AAA Inspector Notes:** From high in the Grand Teton Mountain Range, comes tastes savored by cowboys and visitors alike. The ingredients used in many dishes are local, seasonal and when possible, organic. Seafood dishes meet the stringent sustainability practices of the Monterey Bay Aquarium Seafood Watch Program's "Best" or "Good Alternative" list. **Features:** full bar. **Address:** 27655 Hwy 26 & 287 83012 **Location:** Jct US 26/287, 16.5 mi e of Moran; in Togwotee Mountain Lodge.

JENNY LAKE LODGE DINING ROOM
307/733-4647   3

♦♦♦ Regional American. Fine Dining. $10-$85 **AAA Inspector Notes:** A visit to the upscale restaurant in Grand Teton National Park results in a memorable meal. Reservations are required for the gourmet breakfast and five-course dinner, but lunch is more relaxed and informal. Jackets are suggested, but sweaters are suitable for dinner. **Features:** full bar. **Reservations:** required. **Address:** Jenny Lake Inner Park Rd 83013 **Location:** 3 mi off Inner Park Rd; jct N Jenny Lake; in Jenny Lake Lodge.

THE MURAL ROOM
307/543-2811   1

♦♦♦ American. Casual Dining. $15-$41 **AAA Inspector Notes:** Murals depicting the history of Jackson Hole and wonderful views of the Tetons set the stage for your dining experience. The extensive menu features some game dishes. The wine list is extensive. **Features:** full bar. **Reservations:** suggested. **Address:** US Hwy 89 83013 **Location:** 5 mi nw of Moran; in Jackson Lake Lodge.

THE PEAKS
307/543-2831   2

♦♦
American
Casual Dining
$17-$35

AAA Inspector Notes: Situated on Jackson Lake with a great view of the Grand Tetons, this popular, contemporary rustic eatery, features a varied menu which includes roasted garlic soup, wild game sliders, pan-seared trout, organic risotto primavera, wild-caught salmon picatta and sautéed elk medallions. Expect a wait at peak times. **Features:** full bar. **Address:** 1 Inner Park Rd 83013 **Location:** Teton Park Rd, 2 mi s of US 89, 191 and 287; in Signal Mountain Lodge.

GREEN RIVER (E-2) pop. 12,515, elev. 6,082'

The northern gateway to the Flaming Gorge National Recreation Area *(see place listing p. 262)*, Green River developed as a stop along the Overland Trail in the mid-1800s. One prominent traveler was Maj. John Wesley Powell, who began his explorations of the Green and Colorado rivers in 1869. The town is a railroad center and the seat of Sweetwater County.

Green River Chamber of Commerce: 1155 W. Flaming Gorge Way, Green River, WY 82935. **Phone:** (307) 875-5711 or (800) 354-6743.

SWEETWATER COUNTY HISTORICAL MUSEUM is at 3 E. Flaming Gorge Way. The museum contains permanent and temporary exhibits about western American history, including a large collection of historical photographs of southwestern Wyoming. **Time:** Allow 30 minutes minimum. **Hours:** Mon.-Sat. 10-6. **Cost:** Free. **Phone:** (307) 872-6435.

HAMPTON INN & SUITES   (307)875-5300

▼▼▼▼ **Hotel** $109-$179 **Address:** 1055 Wild Horse Canyon Rd 82935 **Location:** I-80 exit 89, 0.4 mi s to Wild Horse Canyon Rd, then 0.5 mi n. **Facility:** 106 units. 4 stories, interior corridors. **Terms:** 1-7 night minimum stay, cancellation fee imposed. **Pool(s):** heated indoor. **Activities:** hot tub, picnic facilities, exercise room. **Guest Services:** coin laundry.

AAA Benefit: Members save up to 10%!

OAK TREE INN   (307)875-3500

▼▼ **Motel** $59-$69 **Address:** 1170 W Flaming Gorge Way 82935 **Location:** I-80 exit 89, 0.3 mi s. **Facility:** 80 units. 2 stories (no elevator), interior/exterior corridors. **Parking:** winter plug-ins. **Activities:** exercise room. **Guest Services:** coin laundry.

GREYBULL (B-3) pop. 1,847, elev. 3,788'

Greybull derives its name from a local Native American legend that claimed a great albino buffalo once roamed the area. The Native Americans revered the bull, considering it a sign from their Great Spirit. Indian arrowheads, fossils and semiprecious stones can be found around town. The site of widespread oil and mineral activity, Greybull recently has focused its attention on bentonite mining.

Scenic attractions in the vicinity include Shell Canyon and Falls *(see Bighorn National Forest p. 235)*, 24 miles east of US 14, and the drive over the Bighorn Mountains via scenic US 14 to Sheridan. Devil's Kitchen, a few miles northeast, and Sheep Mountain to the north are interesting geological formations.

Greybull Chamber of Commerce: 521 Greybull Ave., Greybull, WY 82426. **Phone:** (877) 765-2100.

GREYBULL MUSEUM is .2 mi. e. on US 14 at 325 Greybull Ave. The museum houses fossils, minerals, Indian artifacts and early Western memorabilia. Of interest are large ammonite fossils, which date from the Mesozoic era when the Greybull area was part of a large inland sea. **Hours:** Mon.-Fri. 10-8, Sat. 10-6, June 1-Labor Day; Mon.-Fri. 1-5, day after Labor Day-Mar. 31; Mon., Wed. and Fri. 1-4, rest of year. **Cost:** Free. **Phone:** (307) 765-2444.

BUDGET HOST WHEELS MOTEL   307/765-2105

▼▼▼ **Motel.** Rates not provided. **Address:** 1324 N 6th St 82426 **Location:** On US 14/16/20, north end of town. **Facility:** 29 units. 1 story, exterior corridors. **Parking:** winter plug-ins. **Guest Services:** coin laundry. (HS) 📶 /SOME UNITS

WHERE TO EAT

BEIJING GARDEN   307/765-9826

▼ Chinese. Casual Dining. $6-$12 **AAA Inspector Notes:** In a converted storefront building downtown, this restaurant offers a relaxed, casual dining experience. Asian dishes are well prepared and the service is friendly. **Address:** 510 Greybull Ave 82426 **Location:** 0.4 mi e on US 14. **Parking:** street only. L D

LISA'S   307/765-4765

▼▼▼ American Casual Dining $9-$40

AAA Inspector Notes: This spot offers up a mixture of Western and Southwestern courses as well as microbrewed beers. Locally raised beef is featured on the varied steak menu. Farmer's pasta, fajitas, chicken fried steak, shrimp and hot sandwiches also are available. Relax and unwind amidst stucco walls and an adobe fireplace. Closed on Sunday in the winter. **Features:** full bar. **Address:** 200 Greybull Ave 82426 **Location:** 0.4 mi e on US 14. *Menu on AAA.com* L D

GUERNSEY (D-6) pop. 1,147, elev. 4,361'
• Hotels p. 274

Just below the mouth of Platte River Canyon, Guernsey is in an area known for its limestone beds and a profusion of such artifacts as agricultural and war implements. Indians driven from their homes east of the Mississippi River and pioneers headed westward followed the river through this area.

During one of his expeditions in 1842, John C. Fremont camped near what is now the Oregon Trail Ruts State Historic Site *(see attraction listing)*. The small prairie next to the river (the present town site) impressed him as a good spot for a military installation because of its cottonwood trees, pines and abundant rock for building.

Prospectors discovered early that the rock formations around Guernsey were good for more than just building. Moss agate stone, unearthed from what is believed to be the first commercially developed deposit of moss agate in the nation, was found in the Guernsey-Hartville region and exported to Germany in the late 1800s. The additional discovery of copper led to the founding of nearby communities Hartville and Sunrise.

Guernsey Visitors Center: 90 S. Wyoming, P.O. Box 667, Guernsey, WY 82214. **Phone:** (307) 836-2715.

GUERNSEY STATE PARK MUSEUM is 1.2 mi. w. on US 26, then 2.7 mi. n. on SR 317 in Guernsey State Park *(see Recreation Areas Chart)*. Exhibits depict the natural and human history of the region. **Time:** Allow 30 minutes minimum. **Hours:** Daily 10-6, May-Sept. **Cost:** Park $6 (per private out-of-state vehicle); $4 (per private in-state vehicle). Museum free. **Phone:** (307) 836-2900.

OREGON TRAIL RUTS STATE HISTORIC SITE is 1 mi. s. on S. Wyoming Ave. from jct. US 26. The site presents well-preserved examples of mid-19th-century pioneer trails. Some of the ruts are 5 to 6 feet deep. Next to the ruts are footpaths used by muleteers and others who walked beside the wagons. Self-guiding trails provide an explanation of the site. No facilities are available. **Time:** Allow 30 minutes minimum. **Hours:** Daily dawn-dusk (weather permitting). **Cost:** Free. **Phone:** (307) 836-2334.

REGISTER CLIFF STATE HISTORIC SITE is 3 mi. s. on S. Wyoming Ave. from jct. US 26. The site contains a 100-foot cliff with the carved names of thousands of pioneers who journeyed past this point. Many of the inscriptions were made 1840-60. A walkway and an explanatory sign are at the base of the cliff.

BUNKHOUSE MOTEL   (307)836-2356

Motel
$80-$120
hot breakfast.

Address: 350 W Whalen St 82214 **Location:** On US 26; center. **Facility:** 32 units. 1 story, exterior corridors. **Terms:** cancellation fee imposed. **Activities:** picnic facilities. **Featured Amenity:** full

HULETT pop. 383

BEST WESTERN DEVILS TOWER INN   (307)467-5747

Hotel
$80-$190

AAA Benefit: Members save 10% or more with Best Western!

Address: 229 Hwy 24 82720 **Location:** Center. **Facility:** 40 units. 2 stories (no elevator), interior corridors. **Parking:** winter plug-ins. **Pool(s):** heated indoor. **Activities:** hot tub, exercise room. **Guest Services:** coin laundry.

HULETT MOTEL   (307)467-5220

Motel
$97-$130

Address: 202 Main St 82720 **Location:** On SR 24 (Main St), north end of town. **Facility:** 15 units, some two bedrooms and cabins. 1 story, exterior corridors. **Terms:** closed 12/1-3/31, check-in 4 pm.

WHERE TO EAT

PONDEROSA CAFE & BAR   307/467-5335
🔻🔻 American. Casual Dining. $7-$27 **AAA Inspector Notes:** The owner/chef at this local favorite hails from New Jersey, so patrons will find a few delicious Eastern specialties on the menu. However, he prepares Western cuisine like he has lived here all his life. Distinctive, local Western art is displayed in a rustic environment. **Features:** full bar, Sunday brunch. **Address:** 115 Main St 82720 **Location:** Center. **Parking:** street only. B L D ✎

HYATTVILLE (B-3) pop. 75, elev. 4,447'

Hyattville, which began as an isolated frontier cow town, is at the confluence of Medicine Lodge and Paint Rock creeks in a region that mixes rolling foothills with rugged canyons to create a series of caves, ledges and grassy knolls. The protective nature of this area is what lured its first inhabitants in prehistoric times.

Artifacts of early Paleo-Indian family groups were preserved in the layers of sediment beneath a sandstone cliff containing myriad petroglyphs and pictographs. Some of these can be seen at Medicine Lodge State Archeological Site, 6 miles northeast of town off SR 31 on Cold Springs Road; phone (307) 469-2234.

JACKSON (C-1) pop. 9,577, elev. 6,123'

• Hotels p. 280 • Restaurants p. 291
• Attractions map p. 268
• Hotels & Restaurants map & index p. 295
• Part of Jackson Hole Including Grand Teton National Park area — see map p. 293

The southern entrance to Grand Teton National Park *(see place listing p. 266)*, Jackson is on a scenic portion of US 89 that extends south 255 miles from Mammoth Hot Springs to Geneva, Idaho. It is the supply point and center of activity for ranchers and vacationers in Jackson Hole country. Recreation in the mountain-rimmed valley includes boating, fishing, hiking, horseback riding, mountain climbing, downhill and cross-country skiing, snowmobiling, white-water rafting and windsurfing on Jackson Lake.

Jackson's historic town square is the hub of activity, with plentiful dining and nightlife options. Visitors enjoy strolling amid a setting of Western architecture, with such accents as wooden sidewalks and elk antler arches. Shopping opportunities range from outdoor gear to trendy boutiques.

Live musical comedies are presented in summer at Jackson Hole Playhouse. The J.H. Rodeo also operates in the summer; phone (307) 733-7927. Gray Line of Jackson Hole offers tours of Grand Teton and Yellowstone national parks; for schedules and reservations phone (800) 443-6133.

While Snow King Scenic Chairlift provides uphill transportation for skiers in winter, summer passengers can enjoy scenic panoramas of Jackson Hole and the Tetons; phone (307) 733-5200 or (800) 522-5464.

(See map & index p. 295.)

(See map & index p. 295.)

Jackson Hole Chamber of Commerce: 112 Center St., P.O. Box 550, Jackson, WY 83001. **Phone:** (307) 733-3316.

BAR-T-5 COVERED WAGON COOKOUT & SHOW

is 1 mi. e. on Broadway, then .5 mi. s. on Redmond to 812 Cache Creek Dr. A Western-style dinner show begins with a covered-wagon ride. Mountain men, American Indians and Western musicians offer entertainment. **Hours:** Two shows nightly Mon.-Sat. and holidays at 5 and 6:30, mid-May to late Sept. **Cost:** $43; $36 (ages 5-12). Reservations are recommended. **Phone:** (307) 733-5386 or (800) 772-5386.

BRUSHBUCK GUIDE SERVICES, 400 US 89S,

picks up passengers from the Home Ranch parking lot in Jackson or the Stilson Ranch parking lot in Teton Village. With a knowledgeable guide in the driver's seat, visitors ride in a safari-style van through scenic Grand Teton National Park. Among the wildlife that may be seen on this 4-hour tour are bison, grizzly and black bears, eagles, elk, moose, wolves and pronghorn antelope. The tour includes snacks and beverages and the use of binoculars, spotting scopes, blankets and rain gear. Yellowstone National Park tours, multiday tours and private tours also are offered.

Note: The tour may include a walk through sagebrush flats; comfortable, durable clothing is recommended. **Hours:** Grand Teton tour departs daily at dawn (between 6 and 6:30) and dusk (between 4:30 and 5:15). Phone for other tour schedules. **Cost:** Grand Teton tour $125, plus $12 park entrance fee. Phone for other tour prices. Grand Teton tours require a minimum of two people. A 50 percent deposit is required for all tours. Reservations are required. **Phone:** (888) 282-5868.

🍴 ⛺

JACKSON HOLE HISTORICAL SOCIETY & MUSEUM, 225 N. Cache St., features exhibits about area history and sports and recreation. Firearms, tools and historical photographs are on display. Guided walking tours of Jackson's historical downtown area are available. **Time:** Allow 1 hour minimum. **Hours:** Tues.-Sat. 10-6, Sun. noon-5, Memorial Day weekend to mid-Sept. Schedule varies rest of year; phone ahead. **Cost:** $5; $4 (ages 60+ and students with ID); free (ages 0-11). **Phone:** (307) 733-2414.

JACKSON HOLE IDITAROD SLED DOG TOURS is

20 mi. s. on SR 191/189 at 11 Granite Creek; transportation to and from area hotels is provided. Sled dog trips in Bridger-Teton National Forest are offered. **Note:** Warm clothing is recommended. Meals

and supplemental clothing are provided. **Hours:** Full- and half-day trips mid-Nov. to mid-Apr. **Cost:** Full-day trip $325. Half-day trip $255. Reservations are required. **Phone:** (307) 733-7388 or (800) 554-7388.

JACKSON NATIONAL FISH HATCHERY is 4 mi. n.

on US 26/89/191 at 1500 Fish Hatchery Rd. The hatchery raises predominantly cutthroat trout. A public fishing pond is available to those with a fishing license. **Time:** Allow 30 minutes minimum. **Hours:** Daily 8-4. **Cost:** Free. **Phone:** (307) 733-2510.

NATIONAL ELK REFUGE is 1 mi. e. on Broadway

to Elk Refuge Rd. The 24,700-acre refuge is the winter home of 7,500 elk, one of the largest herds in North America. Elk can be seen November through April; during the summer they migrate to mountain meadows in Grand Teton and Yellowstone national parks and Bridger-Teton National Forest. The habitat also attracts other wildlife, including bighorn sheep and trumpeter swans.

The visitor center at 532 N. Cache St. offers exhibits and wildlife videotapes. **Hours:** Refuge open daily 24 hours. Visitor center open daily 8-7, Fri. before Memorial Day-Sept. 30; 9-5, rest of year. Closed Thanksgiving and Christmas. **Phone:** (307) 734-9378.

Sleigh Rides depart from the visitor center at 532 N. Cache St. Offered through Double H Bar, Inc., the 45-minute sleigh rides with knowledgeable guides provide up-close elk viewing. **Note:** Warm clothing is recommended. **Hours:** Daily 10-4, mid-Dec. through Mar. 31 (weather permitting). Closed Christmas. **Cost:** $18; $14 (ages 5-12). **Phone:** (307) 733-0277 or (800) 772-5386.

NATIONAL MUSEUM OF WILDLIFE ART is on

Rungius Rd. across from the National Elk Refuge. The museum is in a stone building wedged into a hillside so that it appears to be part of its surroundings. The collection includes more than 5,000 paintings, sculptures and photos of wildlife. Artists include Albert Bierstadt, George Catlin, John Clymer, Bob Kuhn, Georgia O'Keeffe, Carl Rungius, C.M. Russell and Conrad Schwiering.

Of note are the JKM Collection of big game animals and the American Bison exhibit. The museum also houses a children's discovery gallery, a library and changing exhibits. **Hours:** Daily 9-5, mid-May to mid-Oct.; Mon.-Sat. 9-5, Sun. 11-5, rest of year. Closed Columbus Day, Thanksgiving and Christmas. **Cost:** $12; $10 (senior citizens); $6 (ages 5-18 with adult); $30 (family, two adults and one child ages 5-18); $2 (each additional child ages 5-18). **Phone:** (307) 733-5771 or (800) 313-9553.

🍴

RIPLEY'S BELIEVE IT OR NOT! MUSEUM is n. of

jct. US 26/89/189/191 at 140 N. Cache St. The oddities of this collection include such weird wonders as a shrunken head, a jeweled horse, Annie Oakley's

(See map & index p. 295.)
pistol, a huge cigar and art created by using lint from the dryer. **Time:** Allow 1 hour minimum. **Hours:** Daily 9 a.m.-10 p.m., Memorial Day weekend-Labor Day; 10-6, rest of year. Closed Jan. 1 and Christmas. **Cost:** $11.99; $10.99 (senior citizens); $9.99 (ages 5-11). **Phone:** (307) 734-0000.

TETON EXPEDITIONS SCENIC FLOATS departs from 650 W. Broadway. Thirteen- and 21-mile trips allow passengers to view the scenic Grand Teton area and its wildlife, including bald eagles and moose. **Time:** Allow 3 hours minimum. **Hours:** Trips depart daily, May-Oct. **Cost:** Thirteen-mile trip $70; $60 (ages 4-12). Twenty-one-mile trip $125; $105 (ages 6-12). **Phone:** (800) 700-7238. 🍴

TETON WAGON TRAIN AND HORSE ADVEN-TURE offers trips along back roads between Grand Teton and Yellowstone national parks. The 4-day, 3-night guided wagon train trips, which stop at a different camp each night, include chuck wagon meals, evening entertainment, canoeing and horseback riding. Camping gear (including sleeping bags) is provided. **Hours:** Departures Mon. at 9, third week in June-third week in Aug. **Cost:** $895; $815 (ages 9-14); $765 (ages 4-8). Ages 0-3 are not permitted. Reservations are required. **Phone:** (307) 734-6101 or (888) 734-0101.

WAGONS WEST picks up passengers at the Antler Inn, 43 W. Pearl Ave. Tours traverse the Mt. Leidy Highlands in Jackson Hole. Two- and 4-day wagon treks, as well as hourly, 1-day and multiday horse pack rides, are available. Marshaled by a wagon master, a covered-wagon train carries passengers along scenic mountain trails. Chuck wagon meals and campfire entertainment are provided.

Hours: Wagon trips depart in Aug. Horseback rides June-Sept. Phone ahead to confirm schedule. **Cost:** Two-day wagon trip $470; $395 (ages 4-13). Four-day wagon trip $820; $725 (ages 4-13). Horseback rides $50-$90 depending upon duration of ride. Prices may vary; phone ahead. Reservations are required. **Phone:** (800) 447-4711.

WILDLIFE EXPEDITIONS OF TETON SCIENCE SCHOOLS picks up passengers in Jackson or at area hotels. Eight-passenger safari-style vehicles take passengers on half-, full- and multiday expeditions through Yellowstone and Grand Teton national parks. Led by local wildlife biologists, the expeditions focus on wildlife observation and natural history. **Time:** Allow 6 hours minimum. **Hours:** Tours daily. Phone ahead to confirm schedule. **Cost:** Half- and full-day expeditions $125-$300; $99-$240 (ages 6-12); free (ages 0-5). **Phone:** (307) 733-2623 or (888) 945-3567.

RECREATIONAL ACTIVITIES

Alpine Slides
- **Snow King Alpine Slide** is at 400 E. Snow King Ave. **Hours:** Daily, Memorial Day weekend and early June-Labor Day; Sat.-Sun., day after Labor Day-early Sept. (weather permitting). **Phone:** (307) 733-7680.

Hiking
- **Jackson Hole Llamas** departs from local trailheads. **Hours:** Trips daily, June-Sept. **Phone:** (307) 739-9582 or (800) 830-7316.

Mountain Biking
- **Teton Mountain Bike Tours** picks up riders from area hotels. **Hours:** Tours daily, mid-May to mid-Oct. **Phone:** (307) 733-0712 or (800) 733-0788.

Skiing
- **Snow King Resort** is at 400 E. Snow King Ave. Other activities are offered. **Hours:** Winter activities Tues.-Sat. 10-8, Sun.-Mon. 10-4, late Nov.-late Mar. (weather permitting). **Phone:** (307) 733-5200 or (800) 522-5464.

Snowmobiling
- **Jackson Hole Snowmobile Tours** picks up passengers from Jackson area accommodations. **Hours:** Tours offered Dec.-Mar. **Phone:** (800) 633-1733.

White-water Rafting
- **Barker-Ewing River Trips, Whitewater and Scenic Floats** meets at 945 W. Broadway. Other trips are offered. **Hours:** Trips depart daily, Memorial Day weekend to mid-Sept. **Phone:** (800) 448-4202.
- **Dave Hansen Whitewater and Scenic River Trips**
- **Jackson Hole Whitewater** is at 650 W. Broadway. Other activities are offered. **Hours:** Trips depart several times daily, May 15-Oct. 15. **Phone:** (307) 733-1007, or (800) 700-7238 out of Wyoming.
- **Lewis & Clark River Expeditions** is at 335 N. Cache Dr.; trips depart from 3 blks. n. of town square. Other activities are offered. **Hours:** Trips depart several times daily, mid-May to mid-Sept. **Phone:** (307) 733-4022 or (800) 824-5375.
- **Mad River Boat Trips** is at 1255 US 89S. Other activities are offered. **Hours:** Trips depart 15 times daily, mid-May to mid-Sept. **Phone:** (307) 733-6203 or (800) 458-7238. *(See ad p. 278.)*
- **Sands Whitewater and Scenic River Trips** is at 1450 US 89S. Other activities are offered. **Hours:** Trips depart daily, May 15-Sept. 30. **Phone:** (307) 733-4410 or (800) 358-8184.
- **Snake River Park Whitewater** is 12 mi. s. on US 89S. **Hours:** Trips depart four to five times daily, May 15-Oct. 15 (weather permitting). **Phone:** (307) 733-7078 or (800) 562-1878.

AAA/CAA travel information:

Available online, on the go and in print!

Excite Your Travel Senses

Get the interactive **Top Destinations travel guides** in the iPad version
AAA Mobile app with colorful photos, maps and "must do"
recommendations from AAA travel experts.

share

map

plan

The City
Is Chicago the American city? You won't get an argument from us.
Less intimidating than New York, more traditions than Los Angeles,
it's always had a can-do attitude and a work ethic t...

Fast Facts/Trivia

ALL ABOUT

Get the iPad version of the **AAA Mobile app** on iTunes.

(See map & index p. 295.)

49'ER INN AND SUITES   (307)733-7550 [37]

[fyi]
Motel
$99-$289

Under major renovation, scheduled to be completed July 2014. **Last Rated:** ♦♦♦ **Address:** 330 W Pearl St 83001 **Location:** Just w, just s of town square. **Facility:** 142 units, some two bedrooms and kitchens. 3 stories (no elevator), interior/exterior corridors. **Parking:** winter plug-ins. **Activities:** sauna, hot tub, exercise room. **Guest Services:** valet and coin laundry. Affiliated with Quality Inns. *(See ad p. 281.)*

[SAVE] [�11+] [BIZ] [📶] [🔒] [📷]
/ SOME UNITS [🐾] [HS] [📷]

ANGLER'S INN   (307)733-3682 [27]

Motel
$80-$210

Address: 265 N Millward St 83001 **Location:** Just nw of town square, n on Millward St or w on Mercill Ave from US 26/89/191. **Facility:** 28 units. 2 stories (no elevator), exterior corridors. **Parking:** winter plug-ins. **Terms:** 3 day cancellation notice-fee imposed. *(See ad this page.)*

[SAVE] [�11+] [📶] [✕] [🔒] [📷]
[☕]

4 WINDS MOTEL   307/733-2474 [29]

♦
Motel
$69-$139

Address: 150 N Millward St 83001 **Location:** Just w of town square, just n. Across from city park. **Facility:** 21 units. 2 stories (no elevator), exterior corridors. **Terms:** closed 10/16-4/30, check-in 4 pm, 3 day cancellation notice-fee imposed.

[SAVE] [�11+] [📶] [✕] [📷]

Great location, short walk to Town Square. Close to restaurants and shops. Across from city park.

ANTLER INN   (307)733-2535 [38]

♦♦
Hotel
$86-$275

Address: 43 W Pearl St 83001 **Location:** Just s of town square. **Facility:** 106 units, some two bedrooms and kitchens. 2 stories (no elevator), interior/exterior corridors. **Parking:** winter plug-ins. **Terms:** 4 day cancellation notice-fee imposed, resort fee. **Activities:** sauna, hot tub, exercise room. **Guest Services:** valet and coin laundry. *(See ad p. 283.)*

[SAVE] [�11+] [📶] [🔒] [📷]
/ SOME UNITS [🐾] [HS] [📷]

BUCKRAIL LODGE   307/733-2079 [44]

♦♦
Motel
$77-$166

Address: 110 E Karns Ave 83001 **Location:** 0.4 mi s of town square, just e. Located in a quiet residential area. **Facility:** 12 units. 1 story, exterior corridors. **Terms:** closed 10/16-5/10, 7 day cancellation notice-fee imposed. **Activities:** hot tub. *(See ad p. 282.)*

[SAVE] [BIZ] [📶] [✕] [📷] [🔒]
[📷] [☕]

▼ See AAA listing p. 280 ▼

(See map & index p. 295.)

COWBOY VILLAGE RESORT (307)733-3121 39

Cabin
$94-$284

Address: 120 S Flat Creek Dr 83002 **Location:** 0.4 mi w of town square to Flat Creek Dr, just s; downtown. **Facility:** 84 units, some cabins. 1 story, exterior corridors. **Parking:** winter plug-ins. **Terms:** resort fee. **Pool(s):** heated indoor. **Activities:** hot tub, exercise room. **Guest Services:** coin laundry, area transportation. (See ad p. 283.)

[SAVE] [🍴↑] [🏊] [BIZ] [📶] [✕] [🛗]
[🖨] [☕] / SOME UNITS [🐾]

ELK COUNTRY INN (307)733-2364 36

Motel
$76-$254

Address: 480 W Pearl St 83001 **Location:** Just w, just s of town square. **Facility:** 90 units, some kitchens and cabins. 1-2 stories (no elevator), interior/exterior corridors. **Parking:** winter plug-ins. **Terms:** 14 day cancellation notice, 10/1-5/31-fee imposed, resort fee. **Activities:** hot tub, playground, exercise room. **Guest Services:** valet and coin laundry. (See ad p. 283.)

[SAVE] [🍴↑] CALL [📶M] [BIZ] [📶] [✕]
[🛗] [🖨] [☕] / SOME UNITS [🐾] [🎿]

GOLDEN EAGLE INN 307/733-2042 34

Motel
$69-$160

Address: 325 E Broadway 83001 **Location:** 0.3 mi e of town square. Located in a quiet residential area. **Facility:** 23 units. 2 stories (no elevator), exterior corridors. **Parking:** winter plug-ins. **Terms:** closed 10/16-4/30, 3 day cancellation notice-fee imposed. **Pool(s):** heated outdoor.

[SAVE] [🏊] [📶] [✕] [🛗] [🖨]
[☕]

Golden Eagle Inn

Quiet residential neighborhood, short walk to Town Square. Large family rooms available. Clean & cozy.

Learn about inspections and Diamond Ratings at AAA.com/Diamonds

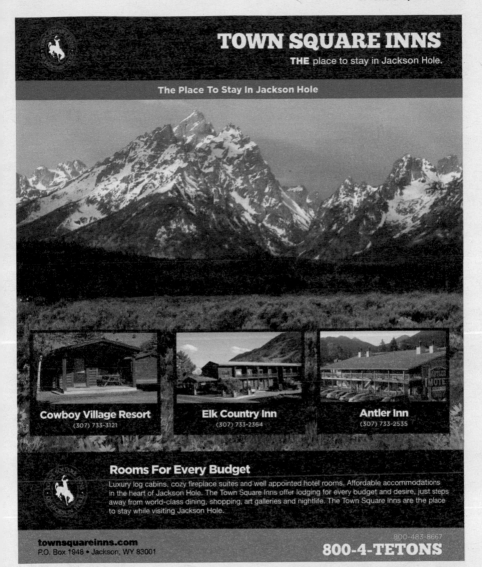

Get pet travel tips and enter the

photo contest at AAA.com/PetBook

(See map & index p. 295.)

HAMPTON INN JACKSON HOLE (307)733-0033 43

Hotel
$99-$339

AAA Benefit: Members save up to 10%!

Address: 350 S Hwy 89 83002 **Location:** 1.5 mi s on US 26/89/191. **Facility:** 87 units. 3 stories, interior corridors. **Parking:** winter plug-ins. **Terms:** check-in 4 pm, 1-7 night minimum stay, cancellation fee imposed. **Amenities:** safes. **Activities:** hot tub, exercise room. **Guest Services:** valet and coin laundry. *(See ad this page.)*

HOMEWOOD SUITES BY HILTON (307)739-0808 25

Extended Stay Hotel $119-$299 **Address:** 260 N Millward St 83001 **Location:** Just nw of town square, n on Millward St or w on Mercill Ave, from US 26/89/191. **Facility:** 41 kitchen units. 3 stories, interior corridors. **Terms:** 1-7 night minimum stay, cancellation fee imposed. **Amenities:** video games, safes. **Activities:** hot tub, bicycles, limited exercise equipment. **Guest Services:** complimentary and valet laundry.

AAA Benefit: Members save up to 10%!

Safety tip: Keep a current AAA/CAA Road Atlas in every vehicle

JACKSON HOLE LODGE (307)733-2992 33

Hotel
$89-$339

Address: 420 W Broadway 83001 **Location:** 0.3 mi w of town square. **Facility:** 59 units, some two bedrooms and kitchens. 3 stories (no elevator), exterior corridors. **Terms:** check-in 4 pm, 14 day cancellation notice-fee imposed. *(See ad p. 285.)*

THE LEXINGTON AT JACKSON HOLE HOTEL & SUITES
(307)733-2648 26

Hotel $109-$339 **Address:** 285 N Cache St 83001 **Location:** Just n on US 26/89/191; corner of N Cache St and Mercill Ave; downtown. **Facility:** 91 units, some efficiencies. 2-3 stories, interior/exterior corridors. **Parking:** winter plug-ins. **Terms:** check-in 4 pm, 3 day cancellation notice-fee imposed, resort fee. **Pool(s):** heated indoor. **Activities:** hot tub. **Guest Services:** valet and coin laundry.

(See ad p. 285.)

THE LODGE AT JACKSON HOLE (307)739-9703 42

Hotel
$119-$499

Address: 80 Scott Ln 83002 **Location:** 0.3 mi sw, just e of US 26/89/191. **Facility:** 153 units. 3 stories, interior corridors. **Parking:** winter plug-ins. **Terms:** check-in 4 pm, 7 day cancellation notice-fee imposed, resort fee. **Amenities:** video games, safes. **Pool(s):** heated outdoor, heated indoor. **Activities:** sauna, hot tub, exercise room. **Guest Services:** coin laundry, area transportation. **Featured Amenity:** breakfast buffet. *(See ad p. 286.)*

▼ See AAA listing this page ▼

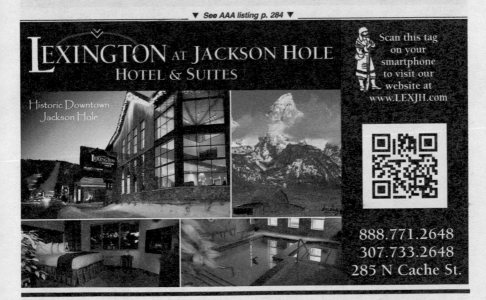
Discover free apps for mapping and more
at AAA.com/mobile or CAA.ca/mobile

▼ See AAA listing p. 284 ▼

(See map & index p. 295.)

PAINTED BUFFALO INN
(307)733-4340 **32**

Motel
$90-$240

Address: 400 W Broadway 83001 **Location:** Just w of town square. **Facility:** 137 units, some two bedrooms. 2 stories (no elevator), exterior corridors. **Parking:** winter plug-ins. **Terms:** check-in 4 pm, cancellation fee imposed, resort fee. **Pool(s):** heated indoor. **Activities:** sauna. **Guest Services:** coin laundry. **Featured Amenity: continental breakfast.** (See ad this page.)

  CALL
 / SOME UNITS

THE RUSTIC INN CREEKSIDE RESORT & SPA AT JACKSON HOLE
(307)733-2357 **24**

Cabin
$99-$459

Address: 475 N Cache St 83001 **Location:** 0.5 mi n on US 26/89/191. **Facility:** Log cabins with upscale décor are featured at this property on attractively landscaped, shaded grounds. The outdoor pool has a radiant heated deck. 155 cabins. 2 stories (no elevator), exterior corridors. **Terms:** check-in 4 pm, cancellation fee imposed, resort fee. **Pool(s):** heated outdoor. **Activities:** sauna, hot tub, exercise room, massage. **Guest Services:** valet and coin laundry, area transportation. **Featured Amenity: breakfast buffet.** (See ad p. 288.)

/ SOME UNITS

PARKWAY INN OF JACKSON HOLE   307/733-3143 **30**

 Motel. Rates not provided. **Address:** 125 N Jackson St 83001 **Location:** Just n of jct W Broadway Ave and Jackson St; 0.3 mi w of town square. **Facility:** 47 units. 2 stories, interior/exterior corridors. **Pool(s):** heated indoor. **Activities:** sauna, hot tub, exercise room. **Guest Services:** valet laundry.

    / SOME UNITS

RAWHIDE MOTEL   307/733-1216 **35**

 Motel. Rates not provided. **Address:** 75 S Millward St 83001 **Location:** Just s of US 26/89/191. **Facility:** 23 units. 2 stories (no elevator), exterior corridors.

RUSTY PARROT LODGE & SPA
(307)733-2000 **28**

Country Inn
$195-$470

Address: 175 N Jackson St 83001 **Location:** Just nw from town square. **Facility:** Featured at this modern lodge are pine-log beds, Southwestern-style décor and cooked-to-order breakfasts. A variety of spa treatments are available. 30 units. 3 stories (no elevator), interior corridors. **Parking:** on-site and valet, winter plug-ins. **Terms:** check-in 4 pm, 3 night minimum stay - weekends, 14 day cancellation notice-fee imposed, resort fee. **Amenities:** Come: safes. **Dining:** The Wild Sage, see separate listing. **Activities:** hot tub, spa. **Guest Services:** valet laundry.

▼ See AAA listing this page ▼

▼ See AAA listing p. 287 ▼

(See map & index p. 295.)

SNOW KING HOTEL   307/733-5200 45
▼▼▼ Resort Hotel. Rates not provided. Address: 400 E Snow King Ave 83001 Location: 0.4 mi s of E Broadway. Facility: Located at the foot of a mountain, this resort offers well-appointed guest rooms and a welcoming lobby. 245 units, some two bedrooms and condominiums. 7 stories, interior/exterior corridors. Terms: check-in 4 pm. Amenities: Some: safes. Pool(s): heated outdoor. Activities: sauna, hot tub, miniature golf, downhill & cross country skiing, snowboarding, ice skating, bicycles, trails, exercise room, massage. Guest Services: valet and coin laundry, area transportation.

[icons]

SPRING CREEK RANCH   (307)733-8833 23

▼▼▼
Resort Hotel
$180-$2250

Address: 1800 Spirit Dance Rd 83001 Location: 2 mi w on US 26/89/191, 0.5 mi w on SR 22, then 1 mi n on Spring Gulch Rd, follow signs. Located in a rural area. Facility: This activity-oriented ranch offers sweeping views of the mountains. Guest rooms are decorative and well coordinated; some are available with a balcony or patio. 108 units, some condominiums. 2-3 stories (no elevator), exterior corridors. Parking: winter plug-ins. Terms: check-in 4 pm, 22 day cancellation notice-fee imposed, resort fee. Dining: Granary, see separate listing. Pool(s): heated outdoor. Activities: hot tub, tennis, exercise room, spa. Guest Services: valet and coin laundry, area transportation.

[icons]

SUPER 8   (307)733-6833 46
▼▼ Hotel $60-$204 Address: 750 S US Hwy 89 83001 Location: Jct US 26/89/191, 0.5 mi s. Facility: 91 units. 3 stories (no elevator), interior corridors. Parking: winter plug-ins. Amenities: safes. Guest Services: coin laundry.

[icons]

VIRGINIAN LODGE   307/733-2792 41
▼▼▼
Motel
$59-$127

Address: 750 W Broadway 83001 Location: Just w. Facility: 170 units, some two bedrooms and efficiencies. 1-2 stories (no elevator), interior/exterior corridors. Parking: winter plug-ins. Terms: check-in 4 pm, cancellation fee imposed. Pool(s): heated outdoor. Activities: hot tub. Guest Services: coin laundry.

[icons]

THE WORT HOTEL   (307)733-2190 31
▼▼▼ ▼▼▼
Historic Boutique
Hotel
$129-$799

Address: 50 N Glenwood St 83001 Location: Center of downtown. Facility: Expect an authentic western lodging experience at this elegantly appointed boutique hotel with beautiful guest rooms and bathrooms with custom furnishings and amenities. 59 units. 2 stories, interior corridors. Parking: valet and street only. Terms: check-in 4 pm, 14 day cancellation notice-fee imposed, resort fee. Dining: Silver Dollar Grill, see separate listing. Activities: hot tub, exercise room, massage. Guest Services: valet laundry, area transportation. (See ad this page.)

[icons]

WYOMING INN OF JACKSON HOLE   (307)734-0035 40

▼▼▼ Hotel $130-$350 Address: 930 W Broadway 83001 Location: 0.5 mi s on US 26/89/191. Facility: 68 units. 1-3 stories, interior corridors. Terms: check-in 4 pm, 3 day cancellation notice, resort fee. Activities: exercise room, massage. Guest Services: complimentary and valet laundry. (See ad p. 290.)

[icons]

AMANGANI   307/734-7333
fyi Not evaluated. Address: 1535 NE Butte Rd 83001. Facilities, services, and décor characterize an upscale property. This luxury property sits on a hilltop.

▼ See AAA listing this page ▼

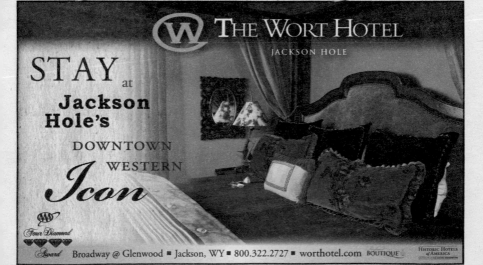

▼ See AAA listing p. 289 ▼

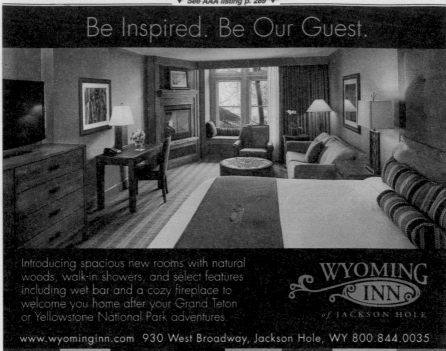

Be Inspired. Be Our Guest.

Introducing spacious new rooms with natural woods, walk-in showers, and select features including wet bar and a cozy fireplace to welcome you home after your Grand Teton or Yellowstone National Park adventures.

WYOMING INN *of* JACKSON HOLE

www.wyominginn.com   930 West Broadway, Jackson Hole, WY   800.844.0035

(See map & index p. 295.)

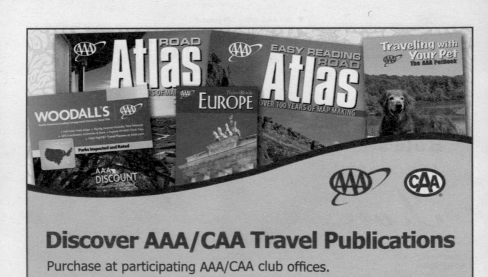

Discover AAA/CAA Travel Publications

Purchase at participating AAA/CAA club offices.

(See map & index p. 295.)

WHERE TO EAT

ATELIER ORTEGA   307/734-6400   54
Desserts. Quick Serve. $5-$15 **AAA Inspector Notes:** Pastry chef and master chocolatier Oscar Ortega, who was trained in Mexico City and Brescia, Italy, produces an extensive variety of hand-made chocolates, desserts and fine confections, which patrons can savor as they sip a fine artisan tea or espresso. Also offered are savory dishes, sweet or dessert crepes and homemade gelato. **Address:** 150 Scott Ln 83001 **Location:** 0.4 mi sw, just e of US 26/89/191. B L D CALL M

THE BLUE LION   307/733-3912   32
American. Fine Dining. $17-$39 **AAA Inspector Notes:** This casual, art-filled restaurant offers an intimate atmosphere in a refurbished older home. Menu selections include game, fresh fish, pasta, fowl, creative vegetarian dishes and the house specialty, rack of lamb with an addictive jalapeño mint dipping sauce. Homemade desserts are seasonal, delicious and can be shared. **Features:** full bar, patio dining, early bird specials. **Reservations:** suggested. **Address:** 160 N Millward St 83001 **Location:** US 26/89/191, just n; opposite Miller Park. **Parking:** street only. D

BON APPE THAI   307/734-0245   45
Thai. Casual Dining. $13-$24 **AAA Inspector Notes:** Just a few blocks from the Town Square, the restaurant serves made-from-scratch Thai fare in a casual and cozy dining room. **Features:** beer & wine. **Reservations:** suggested. **Address:** 245 W Pearl St 83001 **Location:** Just w, just s of town square. **Parking:** street only. L D

BUBBA'S BAR-B-QUE RESTAURANT   307/733-2288   44
Barbecue. Family Dining. $6-$15 **AAA Inspector Notes:** This popular, local favorite offers pit barbecue fare accented with homemade sauce. A good choice is the sloppy Bubba sandwich—barbecue turkey, pork and beef with a side of curly fries. Expect to sign-in and wait during busy periods. A salad bar is offered every day and 24-hour-dining takes place Friday and Saturday. **Features:** beer & wine. **Address:** 100 Flat Creek Dr 83001 **Location:** 0.5 mi w on US 26/09/191; jct Pearl St. B L D

THE BUNNERY, BAKERY & RESTAURANT   307/734-0075   36
American. Casual Dining. $6-$15 **AAA Inspector Notes:** Locals love the light meals, sandwiches and fresh all-natural bakery items, served in generous portions. The quaint interior boasts pine walls, large windows and artwork depicting local wildlife. Deck seating is available in summer. **Features:** beer & wine, patio dining. **Address:** 130 N Cache St 83001 **Location:** Just n of center. **Parking:** street only. B L D CALL M

CAFE GENEVIEVE   307/732-1901   42
Comfort Food Soul Food. Casual Dining. $12-$01 **AAA Inspector Notes:** Diners can discover inspired home cooking in this darling log cabin. Stop in for a Spanish frittata or fried chicken and waffles for breakfast. For lunch there are such sandwiches as grilled cheese, pulled pork or a Cuban. Dinner brings out broiled Idaho trout, caramelized day boat scallops or dry-aged pork chops with black-eyed peas and kale. Do not leave without trying the mouth-watering mixed green salad with candied pancetta and blue cheese. **Features:** full bar, patio dining, happy hour. **Address:** 135 E Broadway 83001 **Location:** Just e of Town Square. **Parking:** street only. B L D

CHINATOWN RESTAURANT   307/733-8856   53
Chinese. Casual Dining. $7-$15 **AAA Inspector Notes:** A favorite of the locals, this place has a large dining room, gilded tiled ceiling and friendly, efficient servers. **Features:** full bar. **Address:** 850 W Broadway 83001 **Location:** Just s on US 26/89/191; in Teton Plaza. L D CALL M

EL ABUELITO   307/733-1207   37
Mexican. Casual Dining. $7-$18 **AAA Inspector Notes:** Looking for consistently good Mexican cuisine? This is it. Locals frequent this place for tasty enchiladas, tacos and chimichangas. Huge portions at reasonable prices make this restaurant family friendly. A spacious dining room with wood accents is decorated with traditional Mexican art and colors. **Features:** full bar. **Address:** 385 W Broadway 83001 **Location:** 0.3 mi w on US 26/89/191. L D

E.LEAVEN RESTAURANT & BAKERY   307/733-5600   35
Sandwiches Breads/Pastries. Quick Serve. $8-$9 **AAA Inspector Notes:** Enjoy bagels, omelets, cold and hot sandwiches, fresh salads and seasonal soups at this casual eatery which is spacious and has lots of windows with stunning views. The tarragon chicken salad is a big hit. **Features:** beer & wine. **Address:** 175 W Center St 83001 **Location:** Just e of town square, just n. **Parking:** street only. B L

GRANARY   307/733-8833   28
Continental. Fine Dining. $8-$35 **AAA Inspector Notes:** In search of fine, upscale dining with a world-class view? You've found the right place. A favorite dish is the elk short loin. An extensive wine list featuring the finest California vintages, including Chalk Hill, is offered. **Features:** full bar, patio dining, happy hour. **Reservations:** suggested. **Address:** 1800 Spirit Dance Rd 83001 **Location:** 2 mi w on US 26/89/191, 0.5 mi w on SR 22, then 1 mi n on Spring Gulch Rd, follow signs; in Spring Creek Ranch. B L D

GUN BARREL STEAK & GAME HOUSE   307/733-3287   52
Regional Steak Wild Game. Casual Dining. $17-$36 **AAA Inspector Notes:** Enjoy aged beef from Texas, venison, buffalo and elk cooked to perfection on an open-fire pit grill. A former wildlife museum and taxidermy studio, many mounts of bison, wild boars, rattlesnakes and birds can be seen, as well as dioramas with bighorn sheep. Rough-hewn wood floors and hand-peeled lodge pole pine beams and tables set the décor along with a large river rock wood-burning fireplace. **Features:** full bar. **Address:** 862 W Broadway 83002 **Location:** Just s on US 26/89/191; in Teton Plaza. D CALL M

IGNITE GRILL   307/734-1997   51
Sushi. Casual Dining. $9-$19 **AAA Inspector Notes:** Tucked into a small strip mall, this restaurant has a modern and stylish ambience and a cool vibe. While sushi is the main attraction, flatbread pizza and specialty cocktails are quite popular. **Features:** full bar, happy hour. **Address:** 945 W Broadway 83001 **Location:** 1.2 mi w of town square. L D

THE KITCHEN   307/734-1633   33
New American. Casual Dining. $11-$29 **AAA Inspector Notes:** The chef here will please with innovative and creative dishes such as lobster sliders, truffled french fries and blue-corn-meal-encrusted trout. Ingredients are seasonally fresh and locally purchased when possible. The modern setting of the dining room is made inviting with a fireplace and deck seating when weather permits. **Features:** full bar, patio dining, happy hour. **Address:** 155 N Glenwood 83001 **Location:** Just off town square. **Parking:** street only. D

LOCAL: RESTAURANT & BAR   307/201-1717   39
Western Steak. Casual Dining. $12-$44 **AAA Inspector Notes:** The contemporary setting in this restaurant is the perfect backdrop to showcase the chefs' combined talents for creating house-cured charcuterie, in-house butchering of locally ranched game and meats and expertly prepared seafood. Brought to you by the same owners/chefs as Trio. **Features:** full bar, happy hour. **Address:** 55 N Cache St 83001 **Location:** Center; across from town square. **Parking:** street only. L D CALL M

THE MERRY PIGLETS MEXICAN GRILL AND CARRY-OUT   307/733-2966   34
Mexican. Family Dining. $7-$21 **AAA Inspector Notes:** Since 1969, this eatery has served fresh Mexican fare in a fun and lively setting. Regulars like to meet for a snack of nachos or quesadillas as well as dine on fire-roasted, mesquite-grilled fajitas. The con-queso and ranchero Tex-Mex sauces merit a thumbs-up. **Features:** full bar, happy hour. **Address:** 160 N Cache St 83001 **Location:** Just n of town square; next to Ripley's. **Parking:** street only. L D

(See map & index p. 295.)

NANI'S CUCINA ITALIANA
307/733-3888 (29)

◆◇◆
Italian
Casual Dining
$13-$33

AAA Inspector Notes: Dining here is an event—a trip to Italy right in Wyoming. A nice selection of pasta is available with home-made sauces and risotto with jumbo scallops. The thick, crusty bread is hard to stop eating. **Features:** full bar, patio dining. **Address:** 242 N Glenwood St 83001 **Location:** 0.3 mi n, turn n on Glenwood St or w on Mercill Ave from US 26/89/191. **Parking:** on-site and street. (D)

NIKAI ASIAN SUSHI BAR & RESTAURANT
307/734-6490 (30)

◆◇◆ Sushi. Casual Dining. $7-$18 **AAA Inspector Notes:** This popular eatery, located upstairs (elevator available), has an upscale décor and bamboo accents. Along with sushi and fresh fish flown in daily, the chef serves many Asian grilled items. **Features:** full bar. **Reservations:** suggested. **Address:** 225 N Cache St 83001 **Location:** Just n of town square. **Parking:** on-site and street. (D)

PEARL ST. MEAT & FISH CO.
307/733-1300 (46)

◇ Specialty. Quick Serve. $8-$21 **AAA Inspector Notes:** Gourmet and specialty foods line the shelves in the aisles of this market, and the meat case is loaded with all-natural beef and fish, specialty baked goods and specialty cheeses. Meals are served in the evening only; otherwise, lunches are ordered at the counter or salad and soup are dished from gourmet bars. **Address:** 40 W Pearl Ave 83001 **Location:** Just w, just s of town square. **Parking:** street only. (B) (L) (D)

PEARL STREET BAGELS
307/739-1218 (47)

◇ American. Quick Serve. $3-$8 **AAA Inspector Notes:** Crusty on the outside and chewy inside are the hallmarks of these New York-style boiled bagels. Luckily for us, we can find them here and at the Wilson, Wy., location. Other offerings include homemade chicken and tuna salad, cream cheese-lox spread and freshly roasted coffee. **Address:** 145 W Pearl Ave 83014 **Location:** Between S Millward and S Glenwood sts; just w of town square. **Parking:** street only. (B) (L)

RENDEZVOUS BISTRO
307/739-1100 (55)

◆◇◆ Regional American. Casual Dining. $13-$33 **AAA Inspector Notes:** This energetic bistro has a raw bar and prepares creative, imaginative and colorful appetizers, entrées, salads and desserts. Menu items may change seasonally and might include sage and sweet potato ravioli, braised organic chicken and kale, goose leg confit, seared scallops and a popular pork adobe. The desserts are glorious. Note some tables are close together. **Features:** full bar. **Reservations:** suggested. **Address:** 380 S Broadway 83002 **Location:** 1.7 mi w of town square. (D)

SILVER DOLLAR GRILL
307/733-2190 (38)

◆◇◆
American
Casual Dining
$10-$35

AAA Inspector Notes: This restaurant specializes in American-style chophouse cuisine, such as black Angus beef, seafood specialties and local wild game dishes. When the weather permits, al fresco meals are an option. Be sure to try the Kobe burger. **Features:** full bar, patio dining. **Reservations:** suggested. **Address:** 50 N Glenwood St 83001 **Location:** Center of downtown; in The Wort Hotel. **Parking:** street only. (B) (L) (D) CALL (L-M)

SNAKE RIVER BREWING CO RESTAURANT & BREWERY
307/739-2337 (50)

◇◇ American. Gastropub. $7-$15 **AAA Inspector Notes:** Wood-fired-oven pizza, calzones, bread, sandwiches, pasta and daily homemade soup fill the menu. Beer lovers will like the selection of ales and lagers. Patio seating is available outside this bustling eatery. **Features:** beer & wine, patio dining, happy hour. **Address:** 265 S Millward St 83001 **Location:** Just s of W Broadway. (L) (D)

SNAKE RIVER GRILL
307/733-0557 (41)

◆◇◆ Regional American. Fine Dining. $20-$40 **AAA Inspector Notes:** This restaurant affords views of Snow King Mountain. Lending to the décor are three-dimensional paintings on the ceiling, booths of tapestry and leather and a double-fireplace of moss-rock and log walls. Seasonal creations and artistic delights may include white gazpacho, bacon-wrapped Idaho trout, lamb chop lollipops and Prime steaks. **Features:** full bar, patio dining. **Reservations:** suggested. **Address:** 84 E Broadway 83001 **Location:** Jct King St; on town square. **Parking:** street only. (D)

SWEETWATER RESTAURANT
307/733-3553 (49)

◆◇◆ Regional American. Casual Dining. $8-$26 **AAA Inspector Notes:** *Historic.* Housed in a restored log cabin, the restaurant offers both indoor and outdoor seating. Attentive and well-trained staff members deliver out-of-the-ordinary daily specials, including fresh fish and steak, phyllo creations and vegetarian items. **Features:** full bar, patio dining. **Reservations:** suggested. **Address:** 85 S King St 83001 **Location:** Just se of town square; corner of King and Pearl sts. **Parking:** street only. (L) (D) (K)

TRIO
307/734-8038 (43)

◆◇◆ Regional American. Casual Dining. $13-$28 **AAA Inspector Notes:** Named for the local chefs who own the restaurant, this casual spot sports contemporary décor. Innovative cuisine is prepared with fresh ingredients. The restaurant usually is closed the first two weeks of April. **Features:** full bar. **Reservations:** suggested. **Address:** 45 S Glenwood St 83001 **Location:** Between Broadway and Pearl St; just sw of town square. **Parking:** street only. (D)

THE WILD SAGE
307/733-2000 (31)

◆◇◆
Regional
American
Fine Dining
$35-$46

AAA Inspector Notes: The restaurant is a favorite for upscale, intimate dining. Through the open kitchen, diners may glimpse at the chefs hard at work on their delectable meals. The seasonally changing menu might list New Zealand red deer, quail or squash soup. It's worth visiting often to sample the chef's specialties. Service is impeccable. **Features:** full bar. **Reservations:** required. **Address:** 175 N Jackson St 83001 **Location:** Just nw from town square; in Rusty Parrot Lodge & Spa. **Parking:** on-site and valet. ***Menu on AAA.com*** (D)

JACKSON HOLE INCLUDING GRAND TETON NATIONAL PARK

Visitors to the area often wonder exactly what "Jackson Hole" means. The "Hole" is actually a high mountain valley encompassed by the ranges of the Grand Tetons, bordered by the Teton Range on the west and the Gros Ventre Range on the east. Bisected by the Snake River, the valley is 80 miles long and 15 miles wide.

You'll rarely hear Jackson Hole Valley called anything other than Jackson Hole. Early trappers coined the term when they navigated the valley's steep slopes, which they likened to descending into an enormous hole. Although Jackson Hole is home to the town of Jackson and the Jackson Hole Mountain Resort, you'll notice that folks refer to both of these places as Jackson Hole, too—don't get confused since this isn't technically correct. The valley also boasts the pristine wilderness of Grand Teton National Park (including Moose and Moran) along with the small communities of Kelly, Teton Village and Wilson.

Mountain men sporting beaver hats started to explore this remote and rugged frontier in the early 1800s, as they trekked through the territory now known as Jackson Hole and Yellowstone on a quest to trap animals—in fact, the valley was named for David Jackson, a partner in a fur-trapping company. The Homestead Act eventually drew pioneers willing to take a chance on improving a free plot of land— Moran, Kelly and Wilson had a sprinkling of settlers by the 1890s. The harsh climate sent many packing, but those who stayed and toughed it out used the abandoned parcels to their advantage and developed large ranches.

By the late 1890s, the town of Jackson started to take root. A park, churches, bank, and shops sprang up, and ultimately a jail, saloons and rodeo added to the Old West intrigue. As the 20th century approached, residents made ends meet by hosting wealthy visitors at dude ranches and serving as guides for game-hunting and sport-fishing expeditions. The creation of Grand Teton National Park in 1929 launched Jackson Hole as a prime sightseeing destination and recreational paradise.

Outdoor enthusiasts flock to Grand Teton National Park to indulge in an enticing array of activities, including high-altitude hiking, float trips, wildlife viewing, boating and cross-country skiing. The park offers a habitat for many large mammals, while the rare trumpeter swan is among the resident bird life. Teton Park Road leads to Jenny Lake Lodge, campgrounds, fishing sites and many of the park's trails. East of the Snake River, Jackson Hole Highway (US 26/89/191) runs parallel to Teton Park Road between Moran and Moose and affords superb views of the Teton Range.

The town of Jackson retains vestiges of the Old West, yet manages to please the discriminating traveler. The old town square, adorned with elk horn

This map shows cities in Jackson Hole where you will find attractions, hotels and restaurants. Cities are listed alphabetically in this book on the following pages.

Jackson Hole
including
Grand Teton
National Park

© AAA

© 2013 NAVTEQ

6301-14

arches, is dotted with a mix of historic buildings, upscale eateries and boutiques. You can see many of Jackson's historic structures on a walking tour sponsored by the Jackson Hole Historical Society & Museum (see attraction listing). Teton Village serves as adventure hub to downhill skiers attempting the daring slopes of Jackson Hole Mountain Resort, or sightseers wishing to ride the gondola to lofty heights.

Grand Teton
National Park
Hotels & Restaurants

Grand Teton National Park

This index helps you "spot" where approved hotels and restaurants are located on the corresponding detailed maps. Hotel daily rate range is for comparison only. Restaurant price range is a combination of lunch and/or dinner. Turn to the listing page for more detailed rate and price information and consult display ads for special promotions.

GRAND TETON NATIONAL PARK

Map Page	Hotels	Diamond Rated	Rate Range	Page
❶ p. 295	Headwaters Lodge & Cabins at Flagg Ranch	◆◆	Rates not provided	272
❷ p. 295	Jackson Lake Lodge *(See ad p. 271.)*	◆◆◆	Rates not provided	272
❸ p. 295	**Signal Mountain Lodge**	◆◆	$162-$334 [SAVE]	272
❹ p. 295	Jenny Lake Lodge *(See ad p. 271.)*	◆◆◆◆	Rates not provided	272
❺ p. 295	Togwotee Mountain Lodge	◆◆	Rates not provided	272

Map Page	Restaurants	Diamond Rated	Cuisine	Price Range	Page
① p. 295	The Mural Room	◆◆◆	American	$15-$41	272
② p. 295	**The Peaks**	◆◆	American	$17-$35	272
③ p. 295	Jenny Lake Lodge Dining Room	◆◆◆	Regional American	$10-$85	272
④ p. 295	The Grizzly Grill	◆◆	American	$7-$28	272

WILSON

Map Page	Hotel	Diamond Rated	Rate Range	Page
❽ p. 295	Bentwood Inn	◆◆◆	$209-$350	324

Map Page	Restaurant	Diamond Rated	Cuisine	Price Range	Page
⑦ p. 295	Q Roadhouse	◆◆	Barbecue	$10-$29	324

TETON VILLAGE

Map Page	Hotels	Diamond Rated	Rate Range	Page
⓫ p. 295	**Four Seasons Resort Jackson Hole**	◆◆◆◆◆	$375-$6750 [SAVE]	320
⓬ p. 295	**Snake River Lodge & Spa**	◆◆◆◆	Rates not provided [SAVE]	320
⓭ p. 295	**The Alpenhof Lodge**	◆◆◆	$109-$459 [SAVE]	320
⓮ p. 295	**Teton Mountain Lodge & Spa**	◆◆◆◆	$129-$2999 [SAVE]	321
⓯ p. 295	**Hotel Terra Jackson Hole**	◆◆◆◆	$139-$3200 [SAVE]	320

Map Page	Restaurants	Diamond Rated	Cuisine	Price Range	Page
⑩ p. 295	**Westbank Grill**	◆◆◆◆	Regional American	$12-$36	321
⑪ p. 295	Gamefish	◆◆◆	Regional American	$9-$47	321
⑫ p. 295	**Alpenrose**	◆◆◆	Regional Swiss	$21-$34	321
⑬ p. 295	Teton Thai	◆◆	Thai	$14-$20	321
⑭ p. 295	Spur Restaurant & Bar	◆◆	Regional American	$14-$35	321
⑮ p. 295	IL Villaggio Osteria	◆◆◆	Italian	$11-$49	321
⑯ p. 295	Mangy Moose Restaurant and Saloon	◆◆	Regional American	$5-$37	321
⑰ p. 295	Masa Sushi	◆◆	Japanese	$10-$25	321

DRIGGS, ID

Map Page	Hotels	Diamond Rated	Rate Range	Page
⓲ p. 295	**Super 8 Driggs**	◆◆	$65-$182 [SAVE]	61
⓳ p. 295	**BEST WESTERN Teton West**	◆◆	$100-$120 [SAVE]	61
⓴ p. 295	Teton Valley Cabins	◆	$69-$99	61

Map Page	Restaurant	Diamond Rated	Cuisine	Price Range	Page
(20) p. 295	Teton Thai	◆◆	Thai	$9-$16	61

JACKSON

Map Page	Hotels	Diamond Rated	Rate Range	Page
(23) p. 295	**Spring Creek Ranch**	◆◆◆	$180-$2250 [SAVE]	289
(24) p. 295	**The Rustic Inn Creekside Resort & Spa at Jackson Hole** (See ad p. 288.)	◆◆◆	$99-$459 [SAVE]	287
(25) p. 295	Homewood Suites by Hilton	◆◆◆	$119-$299	284
(26) p. 295	The Lexington at Jackson Hole Hotel & Suites (See ad p. 285.)	◆◆◆	$109-$339	284
(27) p. 295	**Angler's Inn** (See ad p. 280.)	◆	$80-$210 [SAVE]	280
(28) p. 295	**Rusty Parrot Lodge & Spa**	◆◆◆◆	$195-$470 [SAVE]	287
(29) p. 295	**4 Winds Motel**	◆	$69-$139 [SAVE]	280
(30) p. 295	Parkway Inn of Jackson Hole	◆◆◆	Rates not provided	287
(31) p. 295	**The Wort Hotel** (See ad p. 289.)	◆◆◆◆	$129-$799 [SAVE]	289
(32) p. 295	**Painted Buffalo Inn** (See ad p. 287.)	◆◆	$90-$240 [SAVE]	287
(33) p. 295	**Jackson Hole Lodge** (See ad p. 285.)	◆◆	$89-$339 [SAVE]	284
(34) p. 295	**Golden Eagle Inn**	◆◆	$69-$160 [SAVE]	282
(35) p. 295	Rawhide Motel	◆	Rates not provided	287
(36) p. 295	**Elk Country Inn** (See ad p. 283.)	◆◆	$76-$254 [SAVE]	282
(37) p. 295	**49'er Inn and Suites** (See ad p. 281.)	[fyi]	$99-$289 [SAVE]	280
(38) p. 295	**Antler Inn** (See ad p. 283.)	◆◆	$86-$275 [SAVE]	280
(39) p. 295	**Cowboy Village Resort** (See ad p. 283.)	◆◆	$94-$284 [SAVE]	282
(40) p. 295	Wyoming Inn of Jackson Hole (See ad p. 290.)	◆◆◆	$130-$350	289
(41) p. 295	**Virginian Lodge**	◆	$59-$127 [SAVE]	289
(42) p. 295	**The Lodge at Jackson Hole** (See ad p. 286.)	◆◆◆	$119-$499 [SAVE]	284
(43) p. 295	**Hampton Inn Jackson Hole** (See ad p. 284.)	◆◆◆	$99-$339 [SAVE]	284
(44) p. 295	**Buckrail Lodge** (See ad p. 282.)	◆◆	$77-$166 [SAVE]	280
(45) p. 295	Snow King Hotel	◆◆◆	Rates not provided	289
(46) p. 295	Super 8	◆◆	$60-$204	289

Map Page	Restaurants	Diamond Rated	Cuisine	Price Range	Page
(28) p. 295	Granary	◆◆◆	Continental	$8-$35	291
(29) p. 295	Nani's Cucina Italiana	◆◆◆	Italian	$13-$33	292
(30) p. 295	Nikai Asian Sushi Bar & Restaurant	◆◆◆	Sushi	$7-$18	292
(31) p. 295	**The Wild Sage**	◆◆◆◆	Regional American	$35-$46	292
(32) p. 295	The Blue Lion	◆◆◆	American	$17-$39	291
(33) p. 295	the Kitchen	◆◆◆	New American	$11-$29	291
(34) p. 295	The Merry Piglets Mexican Grill and Carry-Out	◆◆	Mexican	$7-$21	291
(35) p. 295	E.Leaven Restaurant & Bakery	◆	Sandwiches Breads/Pastries	$8-$9	291
(36) p. 295	The Bunnery, Bakery & Restaurant	◆◆	American	$6-$15	291
(37) p. 295	El Abuelito	◆◆	Mexican	$7-$18	291
(38) p. 295	**Silver Dollar Grill**	◆◆◆	American	$10-$35	292

Map Page	Restaurants (cont'd)	Diamond Rated	Cuisine	Price Range	Page
㊴ p. 295	Local: Restaurant & Bar	▼▼▼	Western Steak	$12-$44	291
㊶ p. 295	Snake River Grill	▼▼▼	Regional American	$20-$40	292
㊷ p. 295	Cafe Genevieve	▼▼	Comfort Food Soul Food	$12-$31	291
㊸ p. 295	Trio	▼▼▼	Regional American	$13-$28	292
㊹ p. 295	Bubba's Bar-B-Que Restaurant	▼▼	Barbecue	$6-$15	291
㊺ p. 295	Bon Appe Thai	▼▼	Thai	$13-$24	291
㊻ p. 295	Pearl St. Meat & Fish Co.	▼	Specialty	$8-$21	292
㊼ p. 295	Pearl Street Bagels	▼	American	$3-$8	292
㊾ p. 295	Sweetwater Restaurant	▼▼	Regional American	$8-$26	292
㊿ p. 295	Snake River Brewing Co Restaurant & Brewery	▼▼	American	$7-$15	292
�51 p. 295	Ignite Grill	▼▼	Sushi	$9-$19	291
�52 p. 295	Gun Barrel Steak & Game House	▼▼	Regional Steak Wild Game	$17-$36	291
�53 p. 295	Chinatown Restaurant	▼▼	Chinese	$7-$15	291
�54 p. 295	Atelier Ortega	▼▼	Desserts	$5-$15	291
�55 p. 295	Rendezvous Bistro	▼▼▼	Regional American	$13-$33	292

VICTOR, ID

Map Page	Restaurants	Diamond Rated	Cuisine	Price Range	Page
㉓ p. 295	Scratch	▼▼	American	$8-$18	102
㉔ p. 295	The Knotty Pine Bar & Restaurant	▼▼	American	$8-$25	102
㉕ p. 295	Headwaters Grille	▼▼▼	Regional American	$7-$30	102

KAYCEE (C-4) pop. 263, elev. 4,660'

Kaycee Area Chamber of Commerce: 100 Park Ave., P.O. Box 147, Kaycee, WY 82639. **Phone:** (307) 738-2444. *(See ad p. 238.)*

HOOFPRINTS OF THE PAST MUSEUM is at 344 Nolan Ave. Exhibit topics highlight the Hole-in-the-Wall area's history and include the Bozeman Trail, Dull Knife Battlefield, Johnson County invasion and Fort Reno. Collections contain guns, historical pictures, utensils, Native American artifacts and time-lines. A jail, schoolhouse, cabin and tool shed are on the grounds. **Time:** Allow 1 hour minimum. **Hours:** Mon.-Sat. 9-5, Sun. 1-5, Fri. before Memorial Day-Oct. 31. **Cost:** Donations. **Phone:** (307) 738-2381. *(See ad p. 238.)*

KEMMERER (E-1) pop. 2,656, elev. 6,908'

One feature of the boom that followed the discovery of coal near Kemmerer in 1897 was the saloon of "Preaching Lime" Huggins, who maintained that he never sold a drink to a man already under the influence. Over the bar mirror hung such mottos as "Don't buy a drink before seeing that your baby has shoes." One of his patrons liked the establishment because he could do his repenting during his sinning and "get the whole thing over at once."

A nationwide retail chain originated in Kemmerer when James Cash Penney opened his first store, the Golden Rule, in 1902 with an initial investment of $500. The original home of the founder is now a museum at 107 JC Penney Dr.

Native fossils and historical artifacts are displayed at the visitor center in Herschler Triangle Park.

Kemmerer/Diamondville Area Chamber of Commerce: 921 Pine Ave., Kemmerer, WY 83101. **Phone:** (307) 877-9761 or (888) 300-3413.

FOSSIL COUNTRY MUSEUM is at 400 Pine Ave. Permanent exhibits in this museum include a replica of an underground coal mine and a moonshine still, mountain man artifacts, Union Pacific Railroad and World Wars I and II memorabilia, vintage clothing, fossils and a dinosaur footprint from a local coal mine.

Time: Allow 30 minutes minimum. **Hours:** Mon.-Sat. 9-5, Memorial Day-Labor Day; Mon.-Fri. 10-4, rest of year. Closed Jan. 1, July 4, Thanksgiving, day after Thanksgiving and Christmas. **Cost:** Donations. **Phone:** (307) 877-6551.

BEST WESTERN PLUS FOSSIL COUNTRY INN & SUITES
(307)877-3388

Hotel
$98-$118

AAA Benefit: Members save 10% or more with Best Western!

Address: 760 US 30/189 83101 **Location:** Jct US 30 and 189. **Facility:** 80 units. 3 stories, interior corridors. **Parking:** winter plug-ins. **Pool(s):** heated indoor. **Activities:** hot tub, picnic facilities, exercise room. **Guest Services:** coin laundry.

LANDER (D-3) pop. 7,487, elev. 5,372'

Lander began around 1869 when Camp Augur was built to protect the settlers and Shoshone Indians. In 1884 Lander became the seat of newly created Fremont County, which is as large as some Eastern states. The county covers 5,861,120 acres and is an important wildlife habitat for moose, elk, bighorn sheep, deer and pronghorn antelopes.

North of Lander is the vast Wind River Mountain Range. Part of this range is now the Wind River Indian Reservation. Farther northwest near Dubois is an area that was the site of a horse ranch operated by George Parker, alias Butch Cassidy. Cassidy frequently sold his stock in Lander, whose citizens maintained that he always had more to sell than he had raised.

SR 131 follows the middle fork of the Popo Agie River southwest of Lander to Sinks Canyon State Park *(see attraction listing)* and Shoshone National Forest *(see place listing p. 318)*. Lander contains the trailhead for the Continental Divide Snowmobile Trail.

Lander Area Chamber of Commerce: 160 N. 1st St., Lander, WY 82520. **Phone:** (307) 332-3892. *(See ad p. 330, p. 275.)*

SINKS CANYON STATE PARK is 7.5 mi. s.w. on SR 131. Moose, bighorn sheep and other wild game often can be sighted. The Popo Agie River disappears into the sinks of the Madison Limestone and reappears in a rise one-quarter of a mile down the canyon in a large trout pool.

The Sinks Canyon State Park Visitor Center provides information about natural features and recreational opportunities. *See Recreation Areas Chart.* **Hours:** Park open daily dawn-dusk. Visitor center daily 9-6, Memorial Day-Labor Day. Campground daily, May-Oct. **Cost:** Day use free. Camping $11. **Phone:** (307) 332-3077.

GAMBLING ESTABLISHMENTS

• **Shoshone Rose Casino** is at 5690 US 287. **Hours:** Daily 24 hours. **Phone:** (307) 335-7529.

BEST WESTERN THE INN AT LANDER
(307)332-2847

Hotel
$90-$130

AAA Benefit: Members save 10% or more with Best Western!

Address: 260 Grand View Dr 82520 **Location:** Jct US 287 and SR 789. **Facility:** 103 units. 2 stories (no elevator), interior corridors. **Parking:** winter plug-ins. **Pool(s):** heated outdoor. **Activities:** hot tub, exercise room. **Guest Services:** coin laundry.

HOLIDAY INN EXPRESS & SUITES LANDER (307)332-4005
Hotel $89-$139 **Address:** 1002 11th St 82520 **Location:** 1 mi w on US 287, just w on Lincoln St. **Facility:** 78 units. 3 stories, interior corridors. **Parking:** winter plug-ins. **Terms:** resort fee. **Pool(s):** heated indoor. **Activities:** hot tub, picnic facilities, exercise room. **Guest Services:** coin laundry.

HOLIDAY LODGE NATIONAL 9
307/332-2511

Motel
$65-$75

Address: 210 McFarlane Dr 82520 **Location:** Jct US 287 and SR 789. **Facility:** 39 units, some efficiencies. 2 stories (no elevator), exterior corridors. **Parking:** winter plug-ins. **Terms:** cancellation fee imposed. **Activities:** hot tub, picnic facilities. **Guest Services:** coin laundry. **Featured Amenity:** continental breakfast.

RODEWAY INN & SUITES/PRONGHORN LODGE
(307)332-3940

Motel
$70-$125

Address: 150 E Main St 82520 **Location:** Just n of jct US 287 and SR 789. **Facility:** 56 units, some efficiencies. 1-2 stories (no elevator), exterior corridors. **Parking:** winter plug-ins. **Dining:** The Oxbow Restaurant, see separate listing. **Activities:** hot tub, exercise room. **Guest Services:** valet and coin laundry. **Featured Amenity:** continental breakfast.

WHERE TO EAT

HITCHING RACK
307/332-4322
American. Casual Dining. $7-$33 **AAA Inspector Notes:** Dine on steak, seafood, chicken, pasta or prime rib, but leave room for one of the homemade desserts. There's an extensive soup and salad bar. Attentive service from a well-trained staff rounds out the experience. Plenty of microbrewed beers are offered. **Features:** full bar, patio dining. **Address:** 785 E Main St 82520 **Location:** 0.5 mi s on US 287.

THE MIDDLE FORK
307/335-5035
American. Casual Dining. $9-$19 **AAA Inspector Notes:** This eatery offers a serene and refreshing ambience, the perfect recipe for travelers. Expect colorful and thoughtful presentations. A few favorites include savory quiche, steak salad with greens and pork ragout. The creamy parsnip soup drizzled with white truffle oil is a home run. Seasonal desserts are decadent and made in house. **Features:** beer & wine, Sunday brunch. **Address:** 351 Main St 82520 **Location:** Just w of center. **Parking:** street only.

THE OXBOW RESTAURANT   307/332-0233

▼ American. Casual Dining. $6-$15 **AAA Inspector Notes:** Classic American dining here features casual, fast service with a smile. Daily specials include steak, pasta, chicken, seafood and ribs, in addition to the ample soup and salad bar. **Features:** full bar. **Address:** 170 E Main St 82520 **Location:** Just n of jct US 287 and SR 789; adjacent to Rodeway Inn & Suites/Pronghorn Lodge.

Ⓑ Ⓛ Ⓓ 🖫

LARAMIE (E-5) pop. 30,816, elev. 7,171'
• Restaurants p. 302

Although Native Americans roamed the Laramie Plains as early as 8000 B.C., Laramie's recorded history began in the early 19th century with the arrival of the area's first white man, Jacques LaRamie, a trapper for American Fur Co. In his steps followed mountain men, trappers, emigrants, soldiers and explorers, many tracing the old Cherokee Trail.

Fort Sanders, a short distance south, provided protection for the Overland Stage Line and for the Union Pacific. The railroad brought the bulk of Laramie's citizenry—including a sizable population of lawless riffraff who finally left town at the prompting of self-appointed vigilance committees. The first woman juror, Eliza Stewart, served in Laramie in March 1870. In the fall "Grandma" Louisa Swain became the first woman to vote in a general election.

Recreational opportunities abound nearby. Cross-country skiing is available east of Laramie, and downhill skiing and snowmobiling can be found in the Snowy Range of the Medicine Bow Mountains, west of the city on SR 130. Both regions are equally attractive to vacationers during the summer, with many camping and picnic areas.

Of geological interest is Sand Creek, a 6,000-acre natural landmark about 20 miles southwest of Laramie. Some of North America's finest examples of cross-bedded sandstone and "topple blocks" can be seen.

Laramie serves as the eastern end of a scenic portion of I-80, which runs 99 miles northwest to Walcott. Snowy Range Scenic Byway (SR 130), off the I-80 Snowy Range exit, offers a view of mountains, lakes and forests. At the summit, the Libby Flats Observatory and a viewing platform offer a panorama of the area.

Albany County Tourism Board Convention and Visitor Bureau: 210 E. Custer St., Laramie, WY 82070. **Phone:** (307) 745-4195 or (800) 445-5303. *(See ad this page.)*

Self-guiding tours: Brochures describing downtown and architectural walking tours are available at the Albany County Tourism Board Convention and Visitor Bureau.

ABRAHAM LINCOLN MEMORIAL MONUMENT is 10 mi. s.e. on I-80 exit 323, at the edge of a rest area. The 48.5-foot-tall monument, sculpted by Robert I. Russin, stands at an 8,640-foot summit off I-80 near Sherman Hill. The monument marks the highest point on this transcontinental route. I-80 follows the path of the first transcontinental railroad line.

AMES MONUMENT is 17 mi. s.e. on I-80, then 2 mi. s. on Ames Rd. The 60-foot granite pyramid honors Oliver and Oakes Ames, the two promoters of the transcontinental railroad. Built 1881-82, the monument marks the site of Sherman, a train inspection point before it became a ghost town with the relocation of the Union Pacific tracks. A plaque relates local history.

[SAVE] **LARAMIE PLAINS MUSEUM** is 1 blk. n. of I-80 and US 30 Business Loop at 603 E. Ivinson St. The museum is the restored 1892 Victorian mansion of Edward Ivinson, one of the city's

▼ *See AAA listing this page* ▼

original settlers. Period furnishings and thousands of artifacts from the area are displayed. The grounds include a carriage house and a one-room log schoolhouse. **Hours:** Guided tours are given Tues.-Sat. 9-4, Sun. 1-3, June-Aug.; Tues.-Sat. 1-4, rest of year. **Cost:** $10; $7 (senior citizens); $5 (students and military with ID); free (ages 0-5); $25 (family). **Phone:** (307) 742-4448.

UNIVERSITY OF WYOMING is between 9th and 30th sts. and Lewis and Grand aves. The university opened its doors in 1887. The 785-acre campus contains buildings of native sandstone. **Hours:** Cultural and fine arts programs and concerts are held year-round. **Phone:** (307) 766-4075.

American Heritage Center, 2111 Willett Dr. in the Centennial Complex, is a repository for manuscripts, special collections, rare books and the university's archives as well as a site for lectures, concerts, symposiums and exhibits. The center features changing displays from its collections including the art of Henry Farny, Alfred Jacob Miller and Frederic Remington. **Hours:** Mon.-Fri. 10-5 (also Mon. 5-9 when school is in session). Closed major holidays. **Cost:** Free. **Phone:** (307) 766-4114.

Anthropology Museum is at 12th and Lewis sts. It chronicles Wyoming's cultural history, including information about Northwest Plains Indians and other North American Indians. Collections include archeological and ethnological materials. **Hours:** Mon.-Fri. 8-5, Sept.-May; 7:30-4:30, rest of year. Closed major holidays. **Cost:** Free. **Phone:** (307) 766-5136.

Art Museum is at 22nd St. and Willett Dr. in the Centennial Complex. The museum contains more than 7,000 sculptures, prints, paintings and artifacts from many cultures and periods. Exhibitions focus on contemporary pieces, art of the American West and works from various countries that have influenced American artists. Artworks by established artists as well as traveling exhibitions are displayed. **Hours:** Mon.-Fri. 10-5 (also Mon. 5-9 when school is in session). Closed major holidays. **Cost:** Free. **Phone:** (307) 766-6622.

Geological Museum is in the e. wing of the S.H. Knight Building. The museum interprets the physical and historical geology of Wyoming through displays of rocks, minerals and fossils. Of interest is a mounted skeleton of a brontosaurus, purported to be one of only five exhibited in the world. Other dinosaur displays include an allosaurus, tyrannosaurus and triceratops. **Hours:** Tues.-Fri. 10-4, Sat. 10-3. Closed major holidays. **Cost:** Free. **Phone:** (307) 766-3386.

VEDAUWOO is 17 mi. s.e. via I-80 exit 329. The recreation area takes its name from the Arapaho Indian word meaning "earth born spirits." The picnic and camping areas are marked by rock formations developed during the ice age and rounded by weathering. Both expert and novice rock climbers practice their skills on the rocks. **Hours:** Daily 24

hours, May-Sept. (weather permitting). **Cost:** Day use/parking fee $5. Camping $10. **Phone:** (307) 745-2300.

WYOMING TERRITORIAL PRISON STATE HISTORIC SITE is at 975 Snowy Range Rd. at jct. I-80 exit 311. The site features a restored 19th-century prison, a warden's house, a prison industries building, a homestead ranch exhibit, a University of Wyoming experimental stock farm exhibit and special events. The 1872 Wyoming Territorial Prison is said to be the only prison in which outlaw Butch Cassidy was incarcerated.

Self-guiding museum and prison tours are available. Ghost tours are offered in October. **Time:** Allow 4 hours minimum. **Hours:** Daily 8-7, May-Oct. **Cost:** $5; $2.50 (ages 12-17). **Phone:** (307) 745-6161.

AMERICINN LODGE & SUITES OF LARAMIE   (307)745-0777

 Hotel $90-$189 **Address:** 4712 E Grand Ave 82070 **Location:** I-80 exit 316 (Grand Ave), just n. **Facility:** 59 units. 3 stories, interior corridors. **Parking:** winter plug-ins. **Pool(s):** heated indoor. **Activities:** hot tub, exercise room. **Guest Services:** valet and coin laundry.

BEST WESTERN LARAMIE INN & SUITES

(307)745-5700

Hotel
$89-$160

 AAA Benefit: Members save 10% or more with Best Western!

Address: 1767 N Banner Rd 82072 **Location:** I-80 exit 310 (Curtis St), just n. Located near truck stop. **Facility:** 61 units. 3 stories, interior corridors. **Pool(s):** heated indoor. **Activities:** hot tub, limited exercise equipment. **Guest Services:** coin laundry.

COMFORT INN LARAMIE   (307)721-8856

 Hotel $89-$125 **Address:** 3420 E Grand Ave 82070 **Location:** I-80 exit 316 (Grand Ave), 2.3 mi nw. **Facility:** 55 units. 2 stories, interior corridors. **Parking:** winter plug-ins. **Amenities:** safes. **Pool(s):** heated indoor. **Activities:** hot tub, exercise room. **Guest Services:** coin laundry.

DAYS INN   (307)745-5678

Hotel $91-$151 **Address:** 1368 N McCue St 82072 **Location:** I-80 exit 310 (Curtis St), 0.3 mi e, then just s. **Facility:** 53 units. 2 stories (no elevator), interior corridors. **Parking:** winter plug-ins. **Pool(s):** heated indoor. **Activities:** hot tub, exercise room. **Guest Services:** coin laundry.

FAIRFIELD INN & SUITES BY MARRIOTT   (307)460-2100

Hotel $109-$149 **Address:** 1673 Centennial Dr 82070 **Location:** I-80 exit 310 (Curtis St), just w, then just s. **Facility:** 82 units. 3 stories, interior corridors. **Pool(s):** heated indoor. **Activities:** hot tub, exercise room. **Guest Services:** valet and coin laundry.

AAA Benefit: Members save 5% or more!

HAMPTON INN   (307)742-0125

◆◆◆ Hotel $90-$169 **Address:** 3715 E Grand Ave 82070 **Location:** I-80 exit 316 (Grand Ave), 2.2 mi nw to Boulder Dr. **Facility:** 84 units. 3 stories, interior corridors. **Terms:** 1-7 night minimum stay, cancellation fee imposed. **Amenities:** video games. **Pool(s):** heated indoor. **Activities:** hot tub, exercise room. **Guest Services:** valet and coin laundry.

AAA Benefit: Members save up to 10%!

[icons]

HILTON GARDEN INN LARAMIE   (307)745-5500

◆◆◆ Hotel $109-$210 **Address:** 2229 Grand Ave 82070 **Location:** I-80 exit 316 (Grand Ave), 2.5 mi nw; at University of Wyoming Conference Center. **Facility:** 135 units. 5 stories, interior corridors. **Parking:** winter plug-ins. **Terms:** 1-7 night minimum stay, cancellation fee imposed. **Pool(s):** heated indoor. **Activities:** hot tub, exercise room. **Guest Services:** valet and coin laundry.

AAA Benefit: Members save up to 10%!

[icons]

HOLIDAY INN   (307)721-9000

◆◆◆ Hotel $139-$199 **Address:** 204 S 30th St 82070 **Location:** I-80 exit 316 (Grand Ave), 2.5 mi w to 30th St. **Facility:** 100 units. 4 stories, interior corridors. **Terms:** 14 day cancellation notice. **Amenities:** video games. **Pool(s):** heated indoor. **Activities:** hot tub, exercise room. **Guest Services:** valet and coin laundry.

[icons]

QUALITY INN & SUITES   (307)742-6665

◆◆◆ Hotel $88-$139 **Address:** 1655 Centennial Dr 82070 **Location:** I-80 exit 310 (Curtis St), just w, then just s. **Facility:** 72 units. 3 stories, interior corridors. **Amenities:** safes. **Pool(s):** heated indoor. **Activities:** hot tub, picnic facilities, exercise room. **Guest Services:** coin laundry.

[icons]

WHERE TO EAT

ALTITUDE CHOPHOUSE & BREWERY   307/721-4031

◆◆ American. Casual Dining. $8-$27 **AAA Inspector Notes:** In the historic downtown area, this restaurant offers a varying menu of Choice steak and shrimp, cedar-plank salmon, orange-braised pork loin and signature burgers and pizza. With several hand-crafted beers brewed on the premises, there is no shortage of sudsy choices here. In fact, a brewery sampling menu offers patrons the opportunity to experience the various creations available. The dessert menu changes monthly. **Features:** full bar. **Address:** 320 S 2nd St 82070 **Location:** I-80 exit 313, 1 mi n to Grand Ave, then just w.

[L] [D]

ANONG'S THAI CUISINE   307/745-6262

◆◆ Thai. Casual Dining. $9-$18 **AAA Inspector Notes:** Patrons can expect fresh ingredients and traditional Thai dishes at this popular restaurant. Choices include a variety of soups, salads, curries and noodle dishes including spicy kee mao noodles which comes highly recommended. **Features:** beer & wine. **Address:** 101 E Ivinson Ave 82070 **Location:** At 1st St and Ivinson Ave; downtown. **Parking:** street only. [L] [D]

JEFFREY'S BISTRO   307/742-7046

◆◆ New World. Casual Dining. $8-$21 **AAA Inspector Notes:** This popular eatery focuses on wholesome food and offers appetizers, seasonal soups and a nice variety of salads including sesame Thai carrot with baked tofu. Rounding out the menu are the tomato basil cheddar sandwich, grilled portobello with pesto and Brie, Thai curried chicken with bananas, and decadent desserts made in house. Vegan items are available. **Features:** beer & wine. **Address:** 123 E Ivinson Ave 82070 **Location:** I-80 exit 311 (Snowy Range Rd), 1.3 mi e to N 3rd St, just s to Ivinson Ave, then just w. **Parking:** street only. [L] [D]

NEW MANDARIN RESTAURANT   307/742-8822

◆◆ Chinese. Casual Dining. $7-$13 **AAA Inspector Notes:** This restaurant offers all of your favorite traditional foods like sesame chicken, egg rolls, fried won tons, pu pu platter, mu shu beef, chicken or pork and more. **Features:** beer & wine. **Address:** 1254 N 3rd St 82072 **Location:** I-80 exit 310 (Curtis St), 1.3 mi e to N 3rd St, then just s. [L] [D]

SWEET MELISSA VEGETARIAN CAFE   307/742-9607

◆◆ Vegan Vegetarian. Casual Dining. $6-$10 **AAA Inspector Notes:** This café features an eclectic assortment of vegetarian offerings, including soups, salads, sandwiches and pasta dishes. Chili tacos, lasagna and vegetable stir-fry with tofu are some of the flavorful offerings that please a diverse clientèle, vegetarian and meat-eater alike. Desserts are divine. Many gluten-free options are available. **Features:** full bar. **Address:** 213 S 1st St 82070 **Location:** Between Grand and Ivinson aves; downtown. **Parking:** street only. [L] [D]

LINGLE (D-6) pop. 468, elev. 4,171'

WESTERN HISTORY CENTER is 5 mi. w. at 2308 US 26. The center has displays about archeological excavations and the physical evidence left behind by the area's earliest citizens. In addition to a working lab, visitors can see fossils, mammoth bones and projectile points—items found in local digs that enable researchers to understand the lives of early residents of the Western plains.

Dig tours are available upon request. **Time:** Allow 1 hour minimum. **Hours:** Wed.-Thurs. and Sat. 10-4, Fri. 10-3, Sun. 1-4, Memorial Day-Labor Day; Mon. and Thurs.-Sat. 10-3, rest of year. Phone ahead to confirm schedule. **Cost:** Donations. Reservations are required. **Phone:** (307) 837-3052.

LITTLE AMERICA pop. 68
• Restaurants p. 304

LITTLE AMERICA HOTEL   (307)875-2400

◆◆ Motel $69-$124 **Address:** I-80, exit 68 82929 **Location:** I-80 exit 68, just n. **Facility:** 140 units, some two bedrooms. 1-2 stories (no elevator), interior/exterior corridors. **Terms:** cancellation fee imposed. **Amenities:** *Some:* safes. **Dining:** Little America Restaurant, see separate listing. **Pool(s):** heated outdoor. **Activities:** playground, exercise room. **Guest Services:** coin laundry. *(See ad p. 303.)*

[icons]

▼ See AAA listing p. 302 ▼

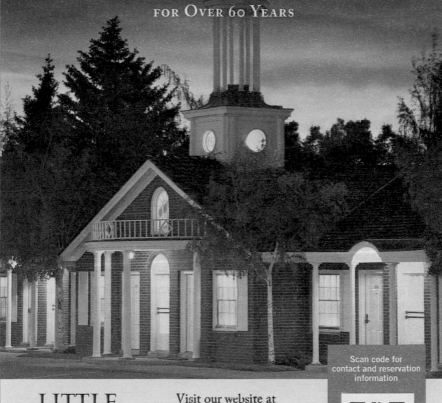

A FOUR SEASON HAVEN

EXCEPTIONAL SERVICE & HOSPITALITY
FOR OVER 60 YEARS

LITTLE AMERICA

WYOMING

Visit our website at
WYOMING.LITTLEAMERICA.COM
or call 888.709.9952
for more information.

Scan code for
contact and reservation
information

INTERSTATE 80, EXIT 68 · LITTLE AMERICA, WY 82929

WHERE TO EAT

LITTLE AMERICA RESTAURANT   307/875-2400
♦♦♦ ♦♦♦ American. Casual Dining. $6-$13 **AAA Inspector Notes:** Surrounded by beautifully groomed grounds, the restaurant offers a daily blue plate special and a good variety of entrees, such as fish and chips, roast turkey dinner, hot and cold sandwiches, a traditional Cobb or chef's deli salad, and a fresh fruit bowl. **Features:** full bar. **Address:** I-80, exit 68 82929 **Location:** I-80 exit 68, just n; in Little America Hotel. [B] [L] [D] CALL ⑤Ⓜ

Time: Allow 2 hours minimum. **Hours:** Trips depart Fri.-Sat. and holidays at 10 and 2, Memorial Day-Labor Day. Sunset dinner cruises depart Fri.-Sat. at 6:30 p.m. **Cost:** $40; $25 (ages 1-12). Phone for sunset dinner cruise fares. Recreation area admission $5 per private vehicle. Reservations are required. **Phone:** (307) 899-1401, or (307) 548-7230 for the marina. Ⓐ Ⓨ Ⓣ

LOVELL (B-3) pop. 2,360, elev. 3,837'

Lovell, founded by Mormons in 1900, serves as the southern gateway to Bighorn Canyon National Recreation Area *(see place listing p. 131)*. A recreation area visitor center offering interpretive displays and movies is at the junction of US 310 and scenic US 14A. Lovell is said to be the "Rose City" of Wyoming due to the exceptional climate for growing these flowers. Area recreational pursuits include camping, fishing, hunting, water sports, hiking, snowmobiling and trail riding.

Next to Bighorn Canyon is Pryor Mountain Wild Horse Range, a 38,000-acre refuge for wild horses and bighorn sheep.

Lovell Area Chamber of Commerce: 287 E. Main St., Lovell, WY 82431. **Phone:** (307) 548-7552.

HIDDEN TREASURE CHARTERS AND WYOMING ECO-TOURS departs from the Horseshoe Bend Marina, 1200 SR 37. Narrated boat rides on Bighorn Lake afford views of Bighorn Canyon National Recreation Area's wildlife and spectacular cliffs. Keep your eyes peeled for bighorn sheep and such birds as falcons, eagles, osprey, terns and swallows. Sunset dinner cruises also are available.

LUSK (D-6) pop. 1,567, elev. 5,014'

Named for an early settler, Lusk is a trading center for a ranching and dry-farming district that also is involved in some oil production. To the west are red-colored cliffs from which Native Americans obtained material for paint. Through this area ran the Cheyenne and Black Hills Stage Line, whose route is marked by two rows of white posts. Three miles east on US 20, a marker indicates the location of a segment of the Texas Trail. The trail was used to herd cattle from Texas to the open ranges of Wyoming, Montana and the Dakotas.

Niobrara Chamber of Commerce: 224 S. Main St., P.O. Box 457, Lusk, WY 82225. **Phone:** (307) 334-2950. *(See ad this page.)*

STAGECOACH MUSEUM is 322 S. Main St. The museum displays many relics of pioneer and Indian days, including an original Concord stagecoach, which was the last running stagecoach. The coach's Cheyenne-Deadwood running mate is in the Smithsonian Institution in Washington, D.C. **Hours:** Mon.-Sat. 10-4:30. **Cost:** $2; free (ages 0-12). **Phone:** (307) 334-3444. *(See ad this page.)*

AMERICAS BEST VALUE INN COVERED WAGON
(307)334-2836

Motel
$72-$155

Address: 730 S Main St 82225 **Location:** Just n of jct US 20/85. **Facility:** 51 units. 1-2 stories (no elevator), interior/exterior corridors. **Parking:** winter plug-ins. **Terms:** cancellation fee imposed. **Pool(s):** heated indoor. **Activities:** sauna, hot tub, playground, picnic facilities, limited exercise equipment. **Guest Services:** coin laundry.

BEST WESTERN PIONEER
(307)334-2640

Motel
$100-$190

AAA Benefit: Members save 10% or more with Best Western!

Address: 731 S Main St 82225 **Location:** Just n of jct US 20/85. **Facility:** 40 units. 1 story, exterior corridors. **Parking:** winter plug-ins. **Pool(s):** heated outdoor. **Activities:** bicycles, picnic facilities. **Guest Services:** coin laundry.

WHERE TO EAT

THE PIZZA PLACE   307/334-3000

Pizza. Quick Serve. $6-$12 **AAA Inspector Notes:** This small, family-owned and -operated eatery features a selection of pizza, subs, salads and calzones. Patrons can dine in or take-out. **Features:** beer only. **Address:** 218 S Main St 82225 **Location:** Just n of 3rd St; downtown. **Parking:** street only.

MEDICINE BOW (E-5) pop. 284, elev. 6,564'

Faced with no available lodgings when he arrived in Medicine Bow in 1885, American author Owen Wister was forced to spend his first night at the counter of the town's general store. Had he visited 26 years later, he could have slept at the Virginian Hotel, named after his well-known novel "The Virginian." Published in 1902, Wister's book became the inspiration for two stage plays, two silent films, a "talking" film and a television series in the 1960s.

Although Wister first described the modest town of Medicine Bow as a "wretched husk of squalor," he later wrote: "I don't wonder a man never comes back [East] after he has once been here a few years." Medicine Bow's still-operating Virginian Hotel now stands as a town landmark.

MEDICINE BOW MUSEUM is at 405 Lincoln Hwy. The museum is housed in a 1913 railroad depot. Local and traveling historical exhibits depict the history of Medicine Bow and the West. Among the displays are such Western items as cowboys' chaps and branding irons. A picnic area, restored caboose and Owen Wister's cabin are on the grounds. **Time:** Allow 30 minutes minimum. **Hours:** Mon.-Sat. 10-5, Memorial Day-Labor Day. **Cost:** Donations. **Phone:** (307) 379-2383.

MEDICINE BOW NATIONAL FOREST (D-5)

Elevations in the forest range from 5,000 ft. north of the Laramie River to 12,013 ft. at Medicine Bow Peak. Refer to AAA maps for additional elevation information.

In southeastern Wyoming, Medicine Bow-Routt National Forest consists of three separate districts that together cover 1,093,618 acres. Scenic SR 130 (closed in winter) crosses the Laramie and Brush Creek/Hayden districts, which extend northward from Colorado along the Snowy Range.

The Brush Creek/Hayden District spans the Continental Divide in the Sierra Madre Mountains west of Encampment. Douglas District, the northernmost section, is high in the rugged Laramie Mountains south of Douglas. Between Cheyenne and Laramie I-80 crosses the Pole Mountain Unit, noted for its unusual rock formations.

The Thunder Basin National Grassland *(see place listing p. 322)* lies in the energy-rich Powder River Basin north of Douglas. There also are four wilderness areas with 79,135 acres of forested land west of Laramie.

Opportunities for such winter sports as cross-country skiing and snowmobiling abound in the area. Camping, fishing, hiking and hunting also are available. For additional information contact the Forest Supervisor, 2468 Jackson St., Laramie, WY 82070. Phone (307) 745-2300. *See Recreation Areas Chart.*

MEETEETSE (B-2) pop. 327, elev. 5,798'
- **Restaurants p. 306**
- **Hotels & Restaurants map & index p. 336**
- **Part of Yellowstone National Park area — see map p. 328**

Meeteetse has retained so much of its original western flavor that you might feel like you've stepped onto a John Wayne movie set, but this is the real McCoy. Downtown's turn-of-the-20th-century buildings house 21st-century cafés and antique shops fronted by awning-covered wooden sidewalks. Horse-watering troughs and hitching posts complete the Old West feel.

Established in 1880, this is a town where Butch Cassidy once lived and Amelia Earhart and Will Rogers once visited, staying at a local dude ranch. Lying along the scenic portion of SR 120, which runs 83 miles between Cody and Thermopolis, Meeteetse is located in the midst of mountains, rivers and valleys. Grizzly bears, deer, bighorn sheep, elk, moose and mountain lions consider this area the perfect home, presenting great opportunities for wildlife photography. The picturesque surroundings also suit humans who enjoy boating, camping, fishing, water skiing, snowmobiling, cross-country skiing and hunting.

CHARLES J. BELDEN MUSEUM AND MEETEETSE MUSEUM is at 1947 State St. Two separate museums are located within the building. The

(See map & index p. 336.)

Charles J. Belden Museum features personal effects, sculpture and Western photography that led to Belden's fame. The far end of the building holds The Meeteetse Museum and includes artifacts gathered from local ranches and homesteads as well as a local wildlife collection.

Time: Allow 1 hour minimum. **Hours:** Mon.-Sat. 9:30-4, Sun. noon-4, May 1-early Nov.; Tues.-Sat. 10-3, Feb.-Apr. and early Nov.-Dec. 22. **Cost:** Free. **Phone:** (307) 868-2423. 🍴 🚻

MEETEETSE BANK ARCHIVES are at 1033 Park Ave. in a 1901 former bank building. Artifacts and records document local and regional history. **Time:** Allow 1 hour minimum. **Hours:** Mon.-Sat. 9:30-4, Sun. noon-4, May 1-early Nov.; Tues.-Sat. 10-3, Feb.-Apr. and early Nov.-Dec. 22. Closed Thanksgiving. **Cost:** Donations. **Phone:** (307) 868-2423.

OUTLAW STEAK AND RIB HOUSE　　307/868-2585　㊾
🍷 American. Casual Dining. $9-$24 **AAA Inspector Notes:** Known for its Captain Morgan's molasses and rum ribs and Jack Daniel's honey and whiskey ribs, this hometown café serves a variety of homemade dishes. Hand-tossed pizzas and thick sourdough sandwiches make for a hearty lunch. Fresh made-from-scratch pies round out the menu. Next door is the Cowboy Bar and Saloon, established in 1893—be sure to take a walk through and look at all the memorabilia. **Features:** full bar. **Address:** 1936 State St 82433 **Location:** Center. **Parking:** street only. Ⓛ Ⓓ 🐾 🎒

MOOSE
• **Part of Jackson Hole Including Grand Teton National Park area — see map p. 293**

THE LOST CREEK RANCH & SPA　　307/733-3435
fyi Not evaluated. **Address:** 1 Old Ranch Rd 83012 **Location:** 8 mi n. Facilities, services, and décor characterize an upscale property. Luxury is the mode at this all-inclusive ranch and spa.

NEWCASTLE (C-6) pop. 3,532, elev. 4,321'

Founded in 1889 when coal was discovered in the area, Newcastle was named after its sister community in England, Newcastle-Upon-Tyne. Mining is a continuing industry, along with ranching, lumbering and petroleum exploration. The yield of Newcastle's oil field is processed by its own refinery.

Newcastle Area Chamber of Commerce: 1323 Washington Blvd., Newcastle, WY 82701. **Phone:** (307) 746-2739 or (800) 835-0157.

Self-guiding tours: Brochures about driving tours are available from the visitor center at the junction of US 85 and US 16.

ANNA MILLER MUSEUM is 3 blks. w. of US 16/85 at 401 Delaware St. The museum displays wildlife, antique firefighting apparatus, pioneer articles, fossils, minerals and Native American artifacts.

Also at the site is the Jenney Cabin, built in 1875 by the expedition sent into the Black Hills area by the U.S. government to investigate reports of gold. The structure is best known as a way station on the Cheyenne-Deadwood stage line, which began in 1876. **Hours:** Mon.-Fri. 9-5 and by appointment. Closed major holidays. **Cost:** Free. **Phone:** (307) 746-4188.

PINES MOTEL　　　　　　　307/746-4334
💎💎 Motel　$59-$145

Address: 248 E Wentworth St 82701 **Location:** Just se of center, just ne from Summit Ave (US 16) and Wentworth St. Located in a residential area. **Facility:** 11 units, some two bedrooms and kitchens. 1 story, exterior corridors. **Parking:** winter plug-ins. **Terms:** 3 day cancellation notice-fee imposed. **Activities:** hot tub. **Featured Amenity:** continental breakfast.

SAGE MOTEL　　　　　　　(307)746-2724
💎 Motel　$65-$100
Address: 1227 S Summit Ave 82701 **Location:** 0.5 mi se of Main St on US 16 to Seneca Ave, then 0.3 mi e. **Facility:** 12 units. 1 story, exterior corridors. **Parking:** winter plug-ins. **Terms:** 3 day cancellation notice-fee imposed.

PAINTER
• **Hotels & Restaurants map & index p. 336**
• **Part of Yellowstone National Park area — see map p. 326**

HUNTER PEAK RANCH　　　　307/587-3711　㊾
🍷 Ranch $150-$220 **Address:** 4027 Crandall Rd 82414 **Location:** SR 296, 5 mi s of US 212; 40 mi n of SR 120. **Facility:** 8 units, some two bedrooms, three bedrooms, efficiencies, kitchens and cabins. 2 stories, exterior corridors. *Bath:* some shared. **Terms:** closed 11/1-4/30, check-in 4 pm, check-out 9 am, 91 day cancellation notice-fee imposed. **Activities:** beach access, fishing, lawn sports, picnic facilities. **Guest Services:** coin laundry.

PINE BLUFFS (E-6) pop. 1,129, elev. 5,047'

Pine Bluffs, named for the stunted pine trees on the bluffs overlooking the area, was once an important watering place along the Texas Cattle Trail. In 1871 more than 600,000 head of cattle were herded through the Pine Bluffs Crossroads, making it the largest cattle shipping point in the world.

Texas Trail Museum preserves historic treasures of the area; phone (307) 245-3713. The University of Wyoming Archaeological Dig presents a look into civilization 10,000 years ago through extracted nomadic Native American artifacts displayed at the University of Wyoming Archaeological Educational Center, Second and Elm streets. Also of interest is the Our Lady of Peace Shrine. Reputed to be one of the largest Marian statues in the United States, it can be seen from the north side of I-80.

Pine Bluffs Visitors' Center: Milepost 401 on I-80 (at the rest area), P.O. Box 486, Pine Bluffs, WY 82082. **Phone:** (307) 245-3695.

PINEDALE (D-2) pop. 2,030, elev. 7,176'

With the majestic Wind River Range as a backdrop, Pinedale serves as an outfitting point for recreation in the Bridger-Teton National Forest *(see place listing p. 236)*. Outdoor activities in the area include trout fishing and various water sports on nearby Fremont Lake, the second largest natural lake in Wyoming *(see Recreation Areas Chart)*. Fishing float trips originate on the Green River, while camping, climbing, backpacking and cross-country and downhill skiing also are available.

Eleven miles southwest of town, Father DeSmet Monument designates the site where the first Catholic Mass in Wyoming was held in 1840.

Upper Green River Rendezvous National Historic Landmark is 6 miles west of Pinedale on US 191. Native Americans from throughout the West and such legendary mountain men as Jim Bridger and William Sublette gathered each year during the 1830s to meet the supply caravans from St. Louis and barter, trade for furs and cavort.

Sublette County Chamber of Commerce/Visitors' Center: 19 E. Pine St., P.O. Box 176, Pinedale, WY 82941. **Phone:** (307) 367-2242. *(See ad p. 269.)*

Self-guiding tours: Information about the Pinedale Walking Tour and day trips in the area is available at the visitor center.

MUSEUM OF THE MOUNTAIN MAN is at 700 E. Hennick St. The museum contains exhibits

relating to the rugged individuals—Jim Bridger, Kit Carson, Thomas Fitzpatrick and William Sublette, to name a few—who opened the West to settlers. Displays focus on exploration, the fur trade, the Plains Indians and early settlement. Items of interest include Jim Bridger's rifle, a Shoshone sheep-horn bow and a collection of Rocky Mountain fur trade journals.

Time: Allow 30 minutes minimum. **Hours:** Daily 9-5, May-Sept.; Mon.-Fri. 10-4, in Oct.; by appointment rest of year. **Cost:** $5; $4 (ages 61+); $3 (ages 6-12). **Phone:** (307) 367-4101 or (877) 686-6266.

BAYMONT INN & SUITES (307)367-8300

Hotel
$59-$109

Address: 1424 W Pine St 82941 **Location:** 1 mi n on US 191. **Facility:** 82 units. 3 stories, interior corridors. **Parking:** winter plug-ins. **Pool(s):** heated indoor. **Activities:** hot tub, limited exercise equipment. **Guest Services:** coin laundry. **Featured Amenity:** continental breakfast.

SAVE ⓣ CALL &M 🚲 BIZ HS
📶 ✕ 🔒 📷 📺
/ SOME UNITS 🐾

BEST WESTERN PINEDALE INN (307)367-6869

 Hotel
$79-$139

 AAA Benefit: Members save 10% or more with Best Western!

Address: 864 W Pine St 82941 **Location:** 0.5 mi n on US 191. **Facility:** 84 units. 2 stories (no elevator), interior corridors. **Parking:** winter plug-ins. **Pool(s):** heated indoor. **Activities:** hot tub. **Guest Services:** coin laundry. **Featured Amenity:** full hot breakfast.

SAVE ⓣ 🚲 BIZ 📶 🔒 📷
📺 / SOME UNITS 🐾 HS

HAMPTON INN & SUITES (307)367-6700

 Hotel
$89-$149

 AAA Benefit: Members save up to 10%!

Address: 55 Bloomfield Ave 82941 **Location:** 1.5 mi n on US 191. **Facility:** 102 units. 3 stories, interior corridors. **Parking:** winter plug-ins. **Terms:** 1-7 night minimum stay, cancellation fee imposed. **Pool(s):** heated indoor. **Activities:** hot tub, picnic facilities, exercise room. **Guest Services:** valet and coin laundry. **Featured Amenity:** full hot breakfast.

SAVE 🚲 BIZ HS 📶 ✕ 🔒 📷 📺

THE LODGE AT PINEDALE 307/367-8800

Hotel $70-$110 **Address:** 1054 W Pine St 82941 **Location:** 0.7 mi n on US 191. **Facility:** 43 units. 3 stories, interior corridors. **Parking:** winter plug-ins. **Terms:** cancellation fee imposed. **Pool(s):** heated indoor. **Activities:** hot tub. **Guest Services:** coin laundry.

ⓣ 🚲 HS 📶 ✕ 🔒 📷 📺 / SOME UNITS 🐾

WHERE TO EAT

CHINA GOURMET 307/367-4788

Chinese. Casual Dining. $8-$17 **AAA Inspector Notes:** Diners can find an extensive menu full of Cantonese and Mandarin specialty items at this restaurant. There are also choices of some of the more well-known Thai dishes available. **Features:** beer & wine. **Address:** 44 W Pine St 82941 **Location:** Downtown. **Parking:** on-site and street. L D CALL &M

LAKESIDE LODGE RESTAURANT 307/367-3555

American. Casual Dining. $9-$34 **AAA Inspector Notes:** Diners can take in beautiful views of the glacial lake and mountain peaks beyond while sampling steaks, seafood and pasta dishes. Outdoor seating on the tiered deck is delightful, weather permitting. **Features:** full bar, Sunday brunch. **Reservations:** suggested, in summer. **Address:** 99 Forest Rd 111 82941 **Location:** 5 mi ne from US 191; on Fremont Lake; in Lakeside Lodge Resort & Marina. B L D 🎦

STOCKMENS RESTAURANT 307/367-4563

American Casual Dining $6-$17

AAA Inspector Notes: Succulent prime rib, large juicy prawns and Australian lamb are a few of the local favorites you can enjoy in an Old West atmosphere. Western hospitality comes with a smile. **Features:** full bar, Sunday brunch, happy hour. **Address:** 117 W Pine St 82941 **Location:** Center. *Menu on AAA.com*

B L D

WIND RIVER BREWING COMPANY   307/367-2337

WW WW American. Casual Dining. $10-$26 **AAA Inspector Notes:**
A concise step-by-step guide on the menu teaches you how to taste
handcrafted brews. You can't go wrong with the variety of mouthwatering appetizers, salads, sandwiches and steaks. A few standouts
are the "beer-b-q brisket" sandwich served with fried pickles, and a
pan-seared sesame encrusted ahi tuna with curried coconut fried
rice. **Features:** full bar, patio dining, happy hour. **Address:** 402 W
Pine St 82941 **Location:** Just e of center. **Parking:** on-site and
street. L D LATE

POWELL (B-3) pop. 6,314, elev. 4,365'

• **Hotels & Restaurants map & index p. 336**
• **Part of Yellowstone National Park area — see
map p. 326**

Native Americans from the Blackfoot, Crow and
Shoshone tribes inhabited the area exclusively until
explorer John Colter arrived in 1807. Following his
arrival came a stream of explorers, trappers and
miners. Powell, located about 75 miles from Yellowstone National Park's east entrance, was named
after Mayor John Wesley Powell, an early-day explorer. The town's proximity to the Bighorn, Pryor
and Absaroka mountain ranges makes it a recreational hot spot. A variety of wildlife inhabits the
area, and historic walking tours of the city are
available.

Powell Valley Chamber of Commerce: 111 S. Day
St., Powell, WY 82435. **Phone:** (307) 754-3494 or
(800) 325-4278.

**HEART MOUNTAIN INTERPRETIVE
CENTER,** 1539 Rd. 19, provides a glimpse
into the lives of Japanese-Americans interned at the
Heart Mountain Relocation Center following the
Pearl Harbor bombing. Designed to look like tar
paper barracks, the museum building features artifacts and interactive displays, a computer room, a
reflection room and a theater. A short interpretive
trail on the grounds offers eight stopping points.
Hours: Grounds daily 24 hours. Interpretive
Learning Center daily 10-5, Memorial Day weekend
to mid-Oct.; Wed.-Sun. 10-5, rest of year. **Cost:**
Grounds free. Interpretive Learning Center $7; $5
(ages 62+ and students with ID); free (ages 0-11).
Phone: (307) 754-8000.

HOMESTEADER MUSEUM is at 324 E.1st St. The
museum celebrates the area's homesteading history
and features a homestead cabin, a caboose and
displays focusing on farming, domestic life and such
notorious Western outlaws as Earl Durand. **Hours:**
Tues.-Fri. 10-5, Sat. 10-2, May-Sept.; Tues.-Fri.
10-4, Mar.-Apr. and Oct.-Dec. **Cost:** Free. **Phone:**
(307) 754-9481.

AMERICAS BEST VALUE INN   (307)754-5117 73

WW WW **Motel** $90-$175
Address: 777 E 2nd St 82435 **Location:** 0.3 mi e on US 14A. **Facility:** 49
units. 2 stories (no elevator), exterior
corridors. **Parking:** winter plug-ins.
Pool(s): heated outdoor. **Featured
Amenity:** continental breakfast.

SAVE 🛏 BIZ 📶 🔧 💻
/ SOME UNITS 🍽

RAWLINS (E-4) pop. 9,259, elev. 6,758'

• **Restaurants p. 310**

In traditionally wool- and hay-producing Carbon
County, Rawlins was a departure point for the Union
Pacific Railroad and for miners bound for the gold-rich Black Hills. Nearby mines produced the "Rawlins Red" pigment that was used on the Brooklyn
Bridge in 1874. The ruins of Fort Fred Steele, built
in 1868 to protect early railroads and settlers, are 12
miles east of town off I-80.

During the 1870s Rawlins was a wild town with
more than its share of outlaw activity. However, it
came to an abrupt halt by the end of the decade
when exasperated citizens employed vigilante tactics against one of the region's most notorious outlaws, Butch Cassidy and the Sundance Kid. After
the lynching of "Big Nose" George Parrot, warnings
were sent out to 24 other known outlaws, who left
town the next morning.

On the southern edge of the Sweetwater jade
fields and the eastern edge of the gem-riddled Red
Desert, Rawlins is noteworthy for its geological
features.

CARBON COUNTY MUSEUM is at 904 W. Walnut
St. Displays tell the story of Wyoming's first female
physician, Lillian Heath. Restored Western artifacts
include a sheepherder's wagon, an original Wyoming flag, a 1920 hook-and-ladder fire truck, a
1900s buggy, a horse-drawn sleigh and shoes made
from outlaw "Big Nose" George Parrot's skin.
Changing exhibits depict life in the West, Native
American lore, ranching and the Union Pacific Railroad. **Hours:** Tues.-Sat. 10-6, May-Sept.; Tues.-Sat.
1-5, rest of year. **Cost:** Donations. **Phone:** (307)
328-2740.

WYOMING FRONTIER PRISON is at 500 W.
Walnut St. The prison replaced the territorial prison
in Laramie in 1901 and operated until 1981. A 1-hour
guided tour includes three cell blocks, a cafeteria,
an exercise yard, visiting rooms, a gas chamber and
the death house. Three museums and a walking
path also are on the premises.
Hours: Tours daily 8:30-4:30, Memorial Day-Labor Day; Mon.-Thurs. at 10:30 and 1:30, rest of
year. Night tours are available by appointment.
Closed Jan. 1, Thanksgiving, Christmas Eve,
Christmas and day after Christmas. **Cost:** $8; $7
(ages 6-12 and 60+); $35 (family). Rates may vary;
phone ahead. **Phone:** (307) 324-4422.

BEST WESTERN COTTONTREE INN   (307)324-2737

WW WW **Hotel** $120-$160

 AAA Benefit: Members
save 10% or more with
Best Western!

Address: 2221 W Spruce St 82301 **Location:** I-80 exit 211, just n. **Facility:**
122 units. 2 stories (no elevator),
interior/exterior corridors. **Parking:**
winter plug-ins. **Terms:** 2-3 night
minimum stay - seasonal. **Pool(s):**
heated indoor. **Activities:** hot tub.

SAVE 📺 CALL M 🛏 BIZ 📶

🎥 🔧 🍴 💻 / SOME UNITS 🍽

COMFORT INN & SUITES (307)324-3663

Hotel
$100-$140

Address: 2366 E Cedar St 82301 Location: I-80 exit 215 (Cedar St), 0.3 mi w. Facility: 65 units. 3 stories, interior corridors. Pool(s): heated indoor. Activities: hot tub, exercise room. Guest Services: coin laundry.

FERRIS MANSION BED & BREAKFAST (307)710-3961

Historic Bed & Breakfast $110-$120 Address: 607 W Maple St 82301 Location: I-80 exit 211, 1.5 mi e to 7th St, just n, then just e; corner of W Maple and 6th sts. Facility: This beautifully restored mansion features front and side sitting decks and a baby grand piano in front of the grand oak stairway, which leads to spacious color-themed rooms that offer modern amenities. 4 units. 2 stories (no elevator), interior corridors. Terms: check-in 4 pm, cancellation fee imposed.

▼ See AAA listing p. 259 ▼

HAMPTON INN (307)324-2320

▼▼▼ **Hotel** $129-$179 **Address:** 406 Airport Rd 82301 **Location:** I-80 exit 215 (Cedar St), 0.8 mi nw. **Facility:** 78 units. 3 stories, interior corridors. **Terms:** 1-7 night minimum stay, cancellation fee imposed. **Amenities:** video games. **Pool(s):** heated indoor. **Activities:** hot tub, picnic facilities, exercise room. **Guest Services:** valet and coin laundry.

AAA Benefit:
Members save up to 10%!

CALL 🚗M 🛄 BIZ HS 🛜 ✕ 🎣 🖥 🖨 🖵 / SOME UNITS 🐾

PRONGHORN INN & SUITES (307)324-5588

▼▼▼
Hotel
$100-$175

Address: 812 Locust St 82301 **Location:** I-80 exit 214, 0.4 mi n on Higley Blvd, then just e. **Facility:** 59 units. 3 stories, interior corridors. **Parking:** winter plug-ins. **Terms:** cancellation fee imposed. **Guest Services:** coin laundry.

SAVE BIZ HS 🛜 🖥 🖨 🖵 / SOME UNITS 🐾

WHERE TO EAT

ANONG'S THAI CUISINE 307/324-6262

▼▼ Thai. Casual Dining. $9-$18 **AAA Inspector Notes:** This restaurant features reasonably priced Thai cuisine. Watch out, though, as some dishes can be very spicy! The dishes are authentic, very well prepared and very popular. **Address:** 210 5th St 82301 **Location:** Jct US 287; center. **Parking:** street only. L D

ASPEN HOUSE RESTAURANT 307/324-4787

▼▼ American. Casual Dining. $9-$27 **AAA Inspector Notes:** Unique dining choices reflect Eastern and Western influences. The friendly, willing staff serves fresh preparations of Szechuan, blackened and Cajun dishes, grilled steaks, stir-fries and seafood. **Features:** full bar. **Reservations:** suggested. **Address:** 318 5th St 82301 **Location:** Just s of center; corner of W Buffalo and 5th sts. **Parking:** street only. L D

RIVERTON (C-3) pop. 10,615, elev. 4,956'
• Restaurants p. 312

Once part of Wind River Indian Reservation, the lower Wind River Basin now supports 130,000 acres of farmland surrounding Riverton. Castle Gardens, a state historical monument 45 miles east, is a formation of knobs, pinnacles and spires rising abruptly 10 to 100 feet above the prairie. Petroglyphs depicting warriors, hunters and animals decorate the soft sandstone formations.

Riverton Area Chamber of Commerce: 213 W. Main St., Suite C, Riverton, WY 82501. **Phone:** (307) 856-4801 or (800) 325-2732. *(See ad p. 330, p. 275.)*

RIVERTON MUSEUM is at 700 E. Park Ave. The museum interprets the story of 20th-century homesteaders who brought the town to life in 1906. Displays include fixtures and merchandise from an early 20th-century general store, drugstore, school, beauty salon, dentist's office, church and post office. Northern Arapaho and Shoshone Indian artifacts also are exhibited.

An outdoor display features early 20th-century farm machinery. **Time:** Allow 1 hour, 30 minutes minimum. **Hours:** Tues.-Fri. noon-4, Sat. 10-1.

Closed major holidays. **Cost:** Free. **Phone:** (307) 856-2665.

WIND RIVER HERITAGE CENTER, 1075 S. Federal Blvd., displays 62 full-size mounts and 20-plus head mounts of bears, bighorn sheep, bison, deer, elk, moose, wolves and other animals. Other highlights include Native American art; an extensive collection of traps; and 50 period-dressed wax figures of such notable Westerners as Lewis and Clark, Jim Bridger, Big Nose George Parrot and Cattle Kate.

Tours: Guided tours are available. **Time:** Allow 1 hour minimum. **Hours:** Mon.-Sat. 10-4. Closed federal holidays. **Cost:** Free. **Phone:** (307) 856-0706.
🎣 🏛

GAMBLING ESTABLISHMENTS

• **Wind River Casino** is at 10269 SR 789. **Hours:** Daily 24 hours. **Phone:** (307) 856-3964. *(See ad p. 311.)*

COMFORT INN & SUITES (307)856-8900

▼▼▼ **Hotel** $101-$149 **Address:** 2020 N Federal Blvd 82501 **Location:** 1.5 mi ne on US 26/SR 789. **Facility:** 63 units. 3 stories, interior corridors. **Parking:** winter plug-ins. **Pool(s):** heated indoor. **Activities:** hot tub, exercise room. **Guest Services:** coin laundry.

CALL 🚗M 🛄 BIZ HS 🛜 🖥 🖨 🖵 / SOME UNITS 🐾

DAYS INN (307)856-9677

▼▼▼ **Motel** $80-$105 **Address:** 909 W Main St 82501 **Location:** 0.5 mi nw on US 26. **Facility:** 33 units. 2 stories (no elevator), exterior corridors. **Parking:** winter plug-ins. **Amenities:** Some: safes.

🍽️ BIZ 🛜 🖥 🖨 🖵 / SOME UNITS 🐾 HS

HAMPTON INN & SUITES RIVERTON (307)856-3500

AAA Benefit:
Members save up to 10%!

▼▼▼ **Hotel** $109-$159 **Address:** 2500 N Federal Blvd (US 26) 82501 **Location:** 2 mi ne on US 26/SR 789. **Facility:** 89 units. 3 stories, interior corridors. **Parking:** winter plug-ins. **Terms:** 1-7 night minimum stay, cancellation fee imposed. **Pool(s):** heated indoor. **Activities:** hot tub, exercise room. **Guest Services:** coin laundry. *(See ad p. 311.)*

CALL 🚗M 🛄 BIZ HS 🛜 ✕ 🖵 / SOME UNITS 🐾 🖥 🖨

HOLIDAY INN RIVERTON CONVENTION CENTER (307)856-8100

▼▼▼ **Hotel** $109-$169 **Address:** 900 E Sunset Dr 82501 **Location:** 0.8 mi ne on US 26/SR 789. **Facility:** 120 units. 2 stories, interior corridors. **Pool(s):** heated indoor. **Activities:** exercise room. **Guest Services:** valet and coin laundry.

  🍽️ 🍸 CALL 🚗M 🛄 BIZ 🛜 ✕ 🖥 🖨
🖵

SUPER 8 (307)857-2400

▼ **Motel** $65-$99 **Address:** 1040 N Federal Blvd 82501 **Location:** 1 mi ne on US 26/SR 789. **Facility:** 32 units. 2 stories (no elevator), interior corridors. **Parking:** winter plug-ins. **Terms:** 3 day cancellation notice.

🎣 🛜 🖥 🖨 🖵 / SOME UNITS

▼ See AAA listing p. 310 ▼

- **Free High-Speed Wireless Internet**
- **Hot on the House Breakfast**
- **Fitness Center, Hot Tub & Pool**

HAMPTON INN AND SUITES RIVERTON

2500 North Federal Blvd.
Riverton, WY 82501
307-856-3500

www.rivertonsuites.hamptoninn.com

▼ See AAA listing p. 312 ▼

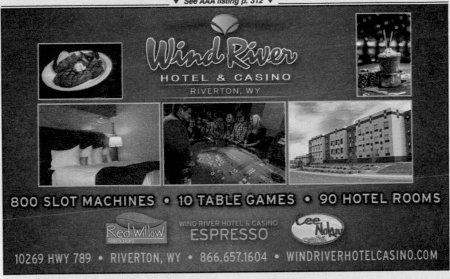

Wind River HOTEL & CASINO RIVERTON, WY

800 SLOT MACHINES • 10 TABLE GAMES • 90 HOTEL ROOMS

Red Willow RESTAURANT

WIND RIVER HOTEL & CASINO
ESPRESSO

Cee Nokuu cafe

10269 HWY 789 • RIVERTON, WY • 866.657.1604 • WINDRIVERHOTELCASINO.COM

WIND RIVER HOTEL & CASINO   307/856-3964

Hotel
$80-$149

Address: 10269 Hwy 789 82501 **Location:** 2 mi s from jct US 26. **Facility:** A colorful exterior depicts patterns from the Arapaho culture. A highlight of the lobby is the Discovery Room, a walk-through area depicting Arapaho history using pictures, artifacts and movies. 90 units. 3 stories, interior corridors. **Parking:** winter plug-ins. **Terms:** check-in 4 pm, resort fee. **Amenities:** safes. **Dining:** 2 restaurants, also, Red Willow, see separate listing. **Activities:** exercise room. **Guest Services:** coin laundry, area transportation. *(See ad p. 311.)*

WHERE TO EAT

THE BULL & BISTRO   307/240-1913

Steak Seafood. Casual Dining. $9-$29 **AAA Inspector Notes:** Guests can get a good value at lunch here with such sandwiches as oregano-rubbed roast beef and pesto turkey. The dinner menu features a variety of steak, lamb, pork chop and chicken dishes as well as a nice selection of seafood and pasta. When available, try the gingerbread cream puffs or chocolate pot de creme. **Features:** full bar. **Address:** 1100 W Main St 82501 **Location:** 1.5 mi ne of US 26/SR 789, 1 mi w. L D

RED WILLOW   307/856-3964

American. Casual Dining. $7-$28 **AAA Inspector Notes:** Diners receive incredible value in reasonably priced dishes of Maine lobster tail, Alaskan king crab and filet mignon, among others. No alcohol is served on the reservation. The staff carries out friendly service. **Address:** 10269 Hwy 789 82501 **Location:** 2 mi s from jct US 26; in Wind River Hotel & Casino. *(See ad p. 311.)*

B L D CALL

ROCK SPRINGS (E-2) pop. 23,036,
elev. 6,261'
• Restaurants p. 314

Rock Springs began in 1862 as a way station along the Overland Stage route. The Union Pacific also chose this route because of the area's rich coal deposits that fueled the railroad's locomotives. Mining and refining are still major industries, with resources expanding to include trona and natural gas. Some of the world's largest deposits of trona, used in the manufacture of glass, phosphates, silicates and soaps, lie 30 miles west of the city.

To the north and stretching more than 70 miles between the town of Eden and the Green Mountains is the Red Desert, an area of moving sand dunes second in size only to the Sahara Desert. Of archeological and geological interest, the Sands, as the region is known, has produced evidence of human habitation as far back as 5000 B.C.

Petroglyphs and pictographs adorn the walls of rock outcrops in Cedar, Pine and Killpecker canyons and White Mountain. Visitors also can see evidence of prehistoric Wyoming at Western Wyoming Community College, which maintains a collection of fossils.

Boars Tusk, a volcanic monolith, rises 400 feet above Killpecker Valley at the edge of the Sands.

The rock tower, 28 miles north of Rock Springs, is visible from US 191.

The Red Desert is home to one of the nation's largest herds of wild horses. To control the size of the herds, the Bureau of Land Management (BLM) conducts roundups; Mustangs captured by the BLM are kept at Rock Springs' Wild Horse Holding Facility, which conducts an Adopt-a-Horse program; phone (307) 352-0292. The Pilot Butte Wild Horse Scenic Loop provides views of these creatures; the dirt road has markers and covers some 23 miles.

Note: When traveling in desert areas, be sure to start with a full tank of gas and plenty of food and water. Off-road vehicles and cellular phones are recommended for travel in remote areas.

Rock Springs Chamber of Commerce: 1897 Dewar Dr., P.O. Box 398, Rock Springs, WY 82902. **Phone:** (307) 362-3771 or (800) 463-8637.

Self-guiding tours: A self-guiding walking tour of downtown Rock Springs covers sites related to the community's coal mining history. Brochures are available at the chamber of commerce.

COMMUNITY FINE ARTS CENTER is at 400 C St. The center contains a collection of more than 600 works by Wyoming and other Western artists as well as nationally and internationally known artists. Highlights include single works by Loren McGiver, Grandma Moses and Norman Rockwell. **Hours:** Mon.-Thurs. 10-6, Fri.-Sat. noon-5. **Cost:** Free. **Phone:** (307) 362-6212.

ROCK SPRINGS HISTORIC MUSEUM is at 201 B St. This museum describes area history, coal mining and the diverse nationalities that settled Rock Springs. The building was constructed in 1894 and restored in 1992. **Time:** Allow 1 hour minimum. **Hours:** Mon.-Sat. 10-5. Closed major holidays. **Cost:** Free. **Phone:** (307) 362-3138.

WESTERN WYOMING COMMUNITY COLLEGE NATURAL HISTORY MUSEUM is off I-80 exit 103, then 1 mi. s. to 2500 College Dr. The museum contains life-size replicas of dinosaurs, prehistoric fossil specimens and artifacts gathered from various formations around southwestern Wyoming. Exhibits, which are scattered throughout the student center, include reproductions of cave art from the Upper Paleolithic era and a 9-ton replica of an Easter Island statue. Maps are available at the entrance. **Time:** Allow 30 minutes minimum. **Hours:** Daily 9 a.m.-10 p.m., Aug.-May; Mon.-Thurs. 9 a.m.-10 p.m., rest of year. **Cost:** Free. **Phone:** (307) 382-1600.

AMERICAS BEST VALUE INN - THE INN   (307)362-9600

Hotel
$55-$165

Address: 2518 Foothill Blvd 82901 **Location:** I-80 exit 102 (Dewar Dr), just n. **Facility:** 147 units. 3 stories, interior corridors. **Parking:** winter plug-ins. **Amenities:** safes. **Pool(s):** heated indoor. **Activities:** limited exercise equipment. **Guest Services:** valet and coin laundry.

BEST WESTERN OUTLAW INN (307)362-6623

Hotel
$99-$159

AAA Benefit: Members save 10% or more with Best Western!

Address: 1630 Elk St 82901 **Location:** I-80 exit 104 (Elk St), 0.3 mi n. Next to a truck stop and gas station. **Facility:** 100 units. 1-2 stories (no elevator), interior/exterior corridors. **Dining:** Outlaw Inn Restaurant, see separate listing. **Pool(s):** heated indoor. **Activities:** exercise room. **Guest Services:** valet laundry. **Featured Amenity:** full hot breakfast.

(See ad this page.)

COMFORT INN & SUITES (307)362-9100

Hotel
$79-$199

Address: 2622 Commercial Way 82901 **Location:** I-80 exit 102 (Dewar Dr), just n to Foothills Blvd, then just e. **Facility:** 57 units. 3 stories, interior corridors. **Pool(s):** heated indoor. **Activities:** hot tub, exercise room. **Guest Services:** valet and coin laundry. **Featured Amenity:** full hot breakfast.

HAMPTON INN 307/382-9222

Hotel. Rates not provided. **Address:** 1901 Dewar Dr 82901 **Location:** I-80 exit 102 (Dewar Dr), 0.5 mi se. **Facility:** 70 units. 3 stories, interior corridors. **Parking:** winter plug-ins. **Amenities:** video games. **Activities:** hot tub, exercise room. **Guest Services:** valet and coin laundry.

AAA Benefit: Members save up to 10%!

HOLIDAY INN (307)382-9200

Hotel $129-$200 **Address:** 1675 Sunset Dr 82901 **Location:** I-80 exit 102 (Dewar Dr), just e, then 0.7 mi sw. **Facility:** 170 units. 4 stories, interior/exterior corridors. **Parking:** winter plug-ins. **Amenities:** *Some:* safes. **Pool(s):** heated indoor. **Activities:** hot tub, exercise room. **Guest Services:** valet and coin laundry.

HOLIDAY INN EXPRESS & SUITES (307)362-9200

Hotel $146-$200 **Address:** 1660 Sunset Dr 82901 **Location:** I-80 exit 102 (Dewar Dr), just e, then 0.5 mi sw. **Facility:** 79 units. 3 stories, interior corridors. **Parking:** winter plug-ins. **Terms:** cancellation fee imposed. **Pool(s):** heated indoor. **Activities:** hot tub, exercise room. **Guest Services:** valet and coin laundry.

HOMEWOOD SUITES BY HILTON (307)382-0764

◆◆ **Extended Stay Hotel** $99-$279 **Address:** 60 Winston Dr 82901 **Location:** I-80 exit 102 (Dewar Dr), 0.4 mi se, then just ne on Winston Dr. **Facility:** 84 efficiencies, some two bedrooms. 4 stories, interior corridors. **Parking:** winter plug-ins. **Terms:** 1-7 night minimum stay, cancellation fee imposed. **Pool(s):** heated indoor. **Activities:** hot tub, exercise room. **Guest Services:** valet and coin laundry.

AAA Benefit: Members save up to 10%!

[icons]

LA QUINTA INN ROCK SPRINGS (307)362-1770

◆◆◆ **Hotel** $94-$139 **Address:** 2717 Dewar Dr 82901 **Location:** I-80 exit 102 (Dewar Dr), just n. **Facility:** 129 units. 2 stories (no elevator), interior corridors. **Parking:** winter plug-ins. **Pool(s):** heated outdoor. **Activities:** picnic facilities, exercise room. **Guest Services:** valet and coin laundry.

[icons] / SOME UNITS

QUALITY INN (307)382-9490

◆◆ **Motel** $80-$140 **Address:** 1670 Sunset Dr 82901 **Location:** I-80 exit 102 (Dewar Dr), just e, then 0.5 mi sw. **Facility:** 103 units. 1 story, exterior corridors. **Parking:** winter plug-ins. **Amenities:** safes. **Pool(s):** heated outdoor. **Activities:** hot tub, exercise room. **Guest Services:** coin laundry.

[icons] / SOME UNITS

WHERE TO EAT

BONSAI 307/362-1888

◆◆ Asian. Casual Dining. $9-$21 **AAA Inspector Notes:** Expect an attentive staff, lovely presentations, a nice selection of soups, a variety of combination plates, standard and specialty rolls and small and large rolls at this simple eatery. **Features:** beer & wine. **Address:** 1996 Dewar Dr 82901 **Location:** I-80 exit 102 (Dewar Dr), 0.4 mi se. [L] [D]

COYOTE CREEK STEAKHOUSE & SALOON 307/382-4100

◆◆ Steak Seafood. Casual Dining. $15-$29 **AAA Inspector Notes:** Enjoy a cocktail at the bar before dinner and then feast on a nice house salad, an appetizer such as jumbo Gulf shrimp cocktail, a juicy steak, half rack of lamb or baby back ribs. The atmosphere is casual and the food is spot on. **Features:** full bar. **Address:** 404 N St 82901 **Location:** I-80 exit 102 (Dewar Dr) eastbound; exit 107 (US 30 BL/Pilot Butee Ave) westbound; corner of N St and Pilot Butte Ave; downtown. **Parking:** on-site and street. [L] [D]

FIESTA GUADALAJARA 307/382-7147

◆ Mexican. Casual Dining. $7-$16 **AAA Inspector Notes:** The colorful and festive décor inside this restaurant soon replaces the first impression of the shabby entry to an abandoned historic hotel. Quesadillas, nachos, steak and chicken fajitas, tamales, enchiladas and chile relleno are available and the mole is good enough to drink. A children's menu also is available. **Features:** full bar. **Address:** 19 Elk St 82901 **Location:** I-80 exit 102 (Dewar Dr), 2 mi e to Grant St, then just e; downtown. [L] [D]

OUTLAW INN RESTAURANT 307/362-6623

◆◆ American Casual Dining $13-$26

AAA Inspector Notes: Locals and tourists come together at this restaurant for choices that range from sandwiches and burgers to seafood, Angus beef, chops and cutlets, with prime rib and seafood specials offered every evening. In season, the Friday cioppino special (a hearty fish stew) merits consideration. Adventurous diners will appreciate the Rocky Mountain oysters appetizer, a great opportunity to prove the power of your palate. **Features:** full bar. **Address:** 1630 Elk St 82901 **Location:** I-80 exit 104 (Elk St), 0.3 mi n; in BEST WESTERN Outlaw Inn. *Menu on AAA.com*

[B] [L] [D]

TED'S SUPPER CLUB 307/362-7323

◆◆ Steak Seafood. Casual Dining. $14-$35 **AAA Inspector Notes:** For more than 45 years, locals have patronized this favorite spot for its steak, seafood and pasta dishes. **Features:** full bar. **Address:** 9 Purple Sage Rd 82901 **Location:** I-80 exit 99, just s, then just w; across from truck stop. [D] [icon]

WONDERFUL HOUSE 307/382-8800

◆◆ Chinese. Casual Dining. $8-$14 **AAA Inspector Notes:** This family-run restaurant is popular with the locals and serves authentic Chinese food made with fresh ingredients. **Features:** full bar. **Address:** 1676 Sunset Dr 82901 **Location:** I-80 exit 102 (Dewar Dr), just s, then just w. [L] [D]

SARATOGA (E-4) pop. 1,690, elev. 6,791'

Saratoga, named for Saratoga Springs, N.Y., is a supply center and access point for recreation on the North Platte River and in Medicine Bow National Forest *(see place listing p. 305)*. The 64 miles of the North Platte River between the Colorado border and Saratoga are a nationally designated blue-ribbon trout fishery and include a stretch of white water rated as high as 10 on the U.S. Forest Service scale.

Saratoga Hot Springs offers a natural hot springs pool open free to the public. Fishing areas are available on the Platte and golf facilities are nearby.

Saratoga-Platte Valley Chamber of Commerce: 210 W. Elm St., P.O. Box 1095, Saratoga, WY 82331. **Phone:** (307) 326-8855.

SARATOGA MUSEUM is at 104 Constitution Ave. The museum, in the 1917 Union Pacific Railroad depot on SR 130, contains historical and archeological artifacts depicting the settlement and growth of the Platte Valley. Geological displays and a sheep wagon also are included. **Time:** Allow 1 hour minimum. **Hours:** Thurs.-Mon. 10-4, Memorial Day weekend-Oct. 15; by appointment rest of year. **Cost:** Donations. **Phone:** (307) 326-5511.

SARATOGA NATIONAL FISH HATCHERY is 2.5 mi. n. on SR 130, then 1.5 mi. e. on a dirt road (CR 207), following signs. Constructed in 1915, the hatchery produces lake and brown trout eggs for export. **Time:** Allow 1 hour minimum. **Hours:** Daily 8-4. **Cost:** Free. **Phone:** (307) 326-5662.

RECREATIONAL ACTIVITIES

Fishing

- **Stoney Creek Outfitters** is at 216 E. Walnut St. **Hours:** Daily 7-7, May 1 to mid-Oct. Phone to verify off-season schedule. **Phone:** (307) 326-8750.

HACIENDA MOTEL 307/326-5751

[fyi] Not evaluated. **Address:** 1500 S 1st St 82331 **Location:** On SR 130, 0.4 mi s of center. Facilities, services, and décor characterize an economy property.

SAVERY (E-4) elev. 6,463'

LITTLE SNAKE RIVER MUSEUM is 1 blk. n. of SR 70 on CR 561. Until 1972, the main building of the museum was used as the Savery School. Exhibits pertain to the history of Little Snake River Valley, focusing on such subjects as area residents, outlaws, mountain men and cowboys. Also on the grounds is the Strobridge-Groshart-Hays House, built in 1888. The house has been restored to its original state since being donated to the museum site in 1993. **Time:** Allow 1 hour, 30 minutes minimum. **Hours:** Daily 11-5, Memorial Day-late Oct. **Cost:** Free. **Phone:** (307) 383-7262.

SHERIDAN (B-4) pop. 17,444, elev. 3,724'
• Restaurants p. 318

Sheridan is located halfway between the Mount Rushmore National Monument and Yellowstone National Park in the valley of the Little and Big Goose. Access through the Bighorn Mountains via US 14 (Bighorn Scenic Byway) or US 14A (Medicine Wheel Passage) offers spectacular sightseeing opportunities. The majestic Bighorn Mountains rise to the west and rolling plains slope to the east.

Sheridan is rich in Western history. In 1866 the area was part of unreserved Native American territory that was home for the Sioux, Cheyenne and Arapaho. Indian chiefs such as Dull Knife, Red Cloud and Crazy Horse fought battles to keep the white man from their precious hunting grounds.

The Bozeman Trail, a shortcut scouted by John Bozeman through eastern Wyoming, cut across Indian hunting grounds to the rich gold fields of Montana. The trail, which ran south of Sheridan along part of what is now US 87, was the scene of so many battles that it became known as the Bloody Bozeman. The U.S. Cavalry forbade trains of fewer than 100 wagons to take this trail.

The discovery of gold in the Black Hills brought a new influx of fortune seekers and further confrontations, culminating in the Battle of the Little Bighorn just north of Sheridan in southern Montana *(see Little Bighorn Battlefield National Monument in Montana p. 188)*.

Many battle sites are in the area, including those of the Wagon Box Fight and the Fetterman Massacre, near Fort Phil Kearny in Story *(see attraction listing p. 319)*; Dull Knife Battle, south of town; the Sawyer Fight, 20 miles north near Dayton; Rosebud Battle, north in Montana; and the Connor Battlefield in Ranchester, 15 miles north of Sheridan.

After the wars ended, Sheridan was incorporated and built up by the profitable businesses of cattle ranching, farming and coal mining. For today's outdoor enthusiast, recreational activities are nearly unlimited in the nearby Bighorn National Forest *(see place listing p. 235)* and include wildlife viewing, hiking, fishing, hunting, snowmobiling and cross-country and downhill skiing.

The town recaptures the flavor of the Old West during the Sheridan WYO Rodeo in mid-July; phone (307) 672-9715 for ticket information. In addition to several PRCA rodeo performances, highlights include a pancake breakfast, a carnival, concerts, parades and a golf tournament.

Sheridan Travel and Tourism: 1517 E. 5th St., P.O. Box 7155, Sheridan, WY 82801. **Phone:** (307) 673-7120. *(See ad p. 329.)*

Self-guiding tours: A walking tour of the city's historic Main Street District covers many original buildings from the late 1800s and early 1990s. A map is available from Sheridan Travel and Tourism.

THE BRINTON MUSEUM—see Big Horn p. 235.

FETTERMAN MONUMENT stands 20 mi. s. on US 87. On this site in 1866 Col. William J. Fetterman disobeyed orders to stay off the Bozeman Trail and took to the trail with only 81 men under his command. Crazy Horse and 2,000 warriors ambushed and killed the entire force. The site is near Fort Phil Kearny.

FORT PHIL KEARNY STATE HISTORIC SITE—see Story p. 319.

KING'S SADDLERY MUSEUM is at 184 N. Main St. This two-story facility highlights Western history and the life of cowboys. Native American artifacts, guns, photographs and leather saddles are displayed. **Time:** Allow 1 hour minimum. **Hours:** Mon.-Sat. 8-5. **Cost:** $2. **Phone:** (307) 672-2702 or (800) 443-8919.

TRAIL END STATE HISTORIC SITE is at 400 Clarendon Ave. The site is the former home of Sen. John B. Kendrick, the "Cowboy Senator." Set on 3.8 acres, the fully furnished 1913 Flemish-revival mansion has elaborate woodwork, stained-glass windows, chandeliers and hand-painted walls and ceilings. Exhibits reflect the period 1913-33. Self-guiding tours are available; guided tours also are available by appointment. **Time:** Allow 1 hour minimum. **Hours:** Daily 9-6, June-Aug.; 1-4, Apr.-May and Sept. 1-Dec. 14. **Cost:** $4; free (ages 0-17). **Phone:** (307) 674-4589.

WYO THEATER is at 42 N. Main St. The theater is an Art Deco structure built in 1923 and renovated in 1989. It is said to be the oldest operating vaudeville theater in the state. Musical entertainment, ballets and stage presentations are featured year-round. **Hours:** Box office open Mon.-Fri. noon-5. **Cost:** Varies depending on event. **Phone:** (307) 672-9084.

AMERICAS BEST VALUE INN   (307)672-9757

Motel
$59-$99

Address: 580 E 5th St 82801 **Location:** I-90 exit 23 (5th St), 0.4 mi w. **Facility:** 39 units. 2 stories (no elevator), exterior corridors. **Activities:** picnic facilities. **Guest Services:** coin laundry. **Featured Amenity:** breakfast buffet.

/ SOME UNITS

▼ See AAA listing p. 317 ▼

Best Western

SHERIDAN CENTER

WYOMING

EST⁰ 1962

612 N. Main St
Sheridan, WY
(307) 674-7421

- ♣ AAA Preferred hotel
- ♣ Minimum 10% discount off published rates
- ♣ FREE Best Western Rewards® program
- ♣ Complimentary hot breakfast
- ♣ Indoor pool and Spa
- ♣ Airport shuttle 24/7
- ♣ Full service restaurant and lounge with hi-def TVs
- ♣ Business Center
- ♣ Walking distance to downtown & tourist sites
- ♣ In-room dataports and high speed internet

AAA
Show Your Card & Save
Preferred Hotel

BEST WESTERN Sheridan Center
Located in historical downtown Sheridan, WY

www.SheridanCenter.com

▼ *See AAA listing this page* ▼

BEST WESTERN SHERIDAN CENTER (307)674-7421

Motel
$69-$189

AAA Benefit: Members save 10% or more with Best Western!

Address: 612 N Main St 82801 **Location:** I-90 exit 23 (5th St), 1 mi w, then just s. **Facility:** 139 units. 2 stories (no elevator), interior/exterior corridors. **Parking:** winter plug-ins. **Pool(s):** heated indoor. **Activities:** hot tub. **Guest Services:** coin laundry, area transportation. *(See ad p. 316.)*

BUDGET HOST INN (307)674-7496

 Motel $70-$129 **Address:** 2007 N Main St 82801 **Location:** I-90 exit 20, 0.7 mi s. **Facility:** 44 units. 1 story, exterior corridors. **Parking:** winter plug-ins. **Activities:** picnic facilities. **Guest Services:** coin laundry.

CANDLEWOOD SUITES (307)675-2100

 Extended Stay Hotel $90-$119 **Address:** 1709 Sugarland Dr 82801 **Location:** I-90 exit 25, just w, then just n. **Facility:** 71 units, some kitchens. 3 stories, interior corridors. **Parking:** winter plug-ins. **Activities:** picnic facilities, exercise room. **Guest Services:** complimentary and valet laundry.

HAMPTON INN SHERIDAN (307)673-2734

 Hotel $89-$199 **Address:** 980 Sibley Cir 82801 **Location:** I-90 exit 23 (5th St), just w. **Facility:** 65 units. 4 stories, interior corridors. **Parking:** winter plug-ins. **Terms:** 1-7 night minimum stay, cancellation fee imposed. **Pool(s):** heated indoor. **Activities:** hot tub, exercise room. **Guest Services:** coin laundry.

AAA Benefit: Members save up to 10%!

HOLIDAY INN ATRIUM & CONVENTION CENTER (307)672-8931

Hotel
$109-$159

Address: 1809 Sugarland Dr 82801 **Location:** I-90 exit 25, 0.3 mi nw. **Facility:** 212 units. 5 stories, interior corridors. **Parking:** winter plug-ins. **Terms:** cancellation fee imposed. **Dining:** Sugarland Mining Company, see separate listing. **Pool(s):** heated indoor. **Activities:** hot tub, game room, exercise room, massage. **Guest Services:** valet and coin laundry, area transportation.

MILL INN 307/672-6401

Historic Motel
$65-$135

Address: 2161 Coffeen Ave 82801 **Location:** I-90 exit 25, 0.3 mi w. **Facility:** A converted flour mill houses this property offering a nice selection of comfortably appointed guest rooms, some with mountain views. 44 units, some two bedrooms and kitchens. 2 stories, interior/exterior corridors. **Activities:** exercise room. **Guest Services:** coin laundry. **Featured Amenity:** continental breakfast. *(See ad this page.)*

WINGATE BY WYNDHAM (307)675-1101

◆◆◆ Hotel $83-$185 Address: 1950 E 5th St 82801 Location: I-90 exit 23 (5th St), just e. Facility: 66 units. 3 stories, interior corridors. Parking: winter plug-ins. Terms: cancellation fee imposed. Amenities: safes. Pool(s): heated indoor. Activities: hot tub, exercise room. Guest Services: valet and coin laundry.

🛬 🛱 BIZ HS 🛜 ✕ 🛏 🖥 🖨

WHERE TO EAT

JAVA MOON 307/673-5991

◆ Coffee/Tea. Quick Serve. $6-$15 AAA Inspector Notes: Although popular for its many coffee choices, the restaurant also offers delicious sandwiches and pastries. Features: patio dining. Address: 170 N Main St 82801 Location: Center. Parking: street only.

B L 🐾 🐾

SUGARLAND MINING COMPANY 307/672-8931

American
Casual Dining
$12-$28

AAA Inspector Notes: Tucked in a quiet area of the hotel, this intimate restaurant displays metal wall art depicting a mine and rail in addition to historical pictures of the city. Varied menu offerings include mahi mahi, lobster and steaks as well as such comfort foods as fried chicken. Features: full bar. Address: 1809 Sugarland Dr 82801 Location: I-90 exit 25, 0.3 mi nw; in Holiday Inn Atrium & Convention Center. D CALL 🔊

WYOMING'S RIB & CHOPHOUSE 307/673-4700

◆◆ American. Casual Dining. $7-$32 AAA Inspector Notes: Historic. Reservations are a must at this popular and casual chop house, where the meat falls off the bones of the succulent ribs. Also delicious are the steaks and burgers. Most dinners include an appetizer. Features: full bar. Reservations: required. Address: 847 N Main St 82801 Location: Jct 5th St; west end of town.

L D

SHOSHONE NATIONAL FOREST (C-2)

Elevations in the forest range from 4,600 ft. at Clarks Fork Canyon to 13,804 ft. at Gannett Peak. Refer to AAA maps for additional elevation information.

In northwestern Wyoming, the Shoshone National Forest was established by presidential proclamation in 1891 as the nation's first forest reserve. It occupies nearly 2.5 million acres. Its boundaries extend south from Montana and include parts of the Beartooth, Absaroka and Wind River mountains. The forest includes the state's highest mountain, Gannett Peak.

Forest watersheds and glacial runoff feed several rivers of the Missouri River Basin and serve as a major water source for many communities and ranches within or near the forest.

Scenic drives include Buffalo Bill Cody Scenic Byway (US 14/16/20) through the North Fork of the Shoshone River canyon en route to the east entrance of Yellowstone National Park (see place listing p. 326); the Wyoming Centennial Scenic Byway over Togwotee Pass on US 287/26 between Dubois and Moran Junction; the Beartooth Scenic Highway (US 212) over the Beartooth Plateau; and the Chief Joseph Scenic Highway (SR 296) from its junction with SR 120 to the junction of US 212. SRs 296, 291 and 131 also travel past spectacular mountain scenery.

Backcountry hiking, trail riding, fishing and primitive camping are available in the Fitzpatrick Wilderness, which has two of Wyoming's highest peaks and some of the nation's largest glaciers; the Popo Agie Wilderness, dotted by more than 200 lakes; the Absaroka-Beartooth Wilderness, containing many lakes and granite peaks; and the North Absaroka Wilderness, scored by steep canyons. Cross-country skiing also is available.

Information and maps (a fee is charged) can be obtained by writing the Forest Supervisor, 808 Meadow Ln., Cody, WY 82414-4516. Phone (307) 527-6241. See Recreation Areas Chart.

SOUTH PASS CITY (D-2) elev. 7,805'

When early travelers traversed South Pass, the gradual incline often left them unaware that they were crossing the Continental Divide. From 1840 to 1860 an estimated 300,000 settlers traveled through the gap.

Gold was discovered at a site about 12 miles north of the pass in 1842, but takings were not impressive at first. In 1867 the Carissa, a hard-rock lode, was found and a boom began. By 1871 South Pass City boasted 2,000 inhabitants and was the seat of Carter County, which encompassed a third of Wyoming.

William H. Bright, a South Pass City saloon keeper and Wyoming senator, introduced a bill granting women the right to vote, hold office and own property. With passage in 1869, Wyoming women became the first in the nation to participate in government, and Wyoming became nicknamed the "Equality State." One town citizen was Esther Hobart Morris, who in 1870 became the city's justice of the peace, the first woman in the country to hold any political office.

Despite its successes, South Pass City was not to escape the usual fate of boom towns: By 1875 the city was nearly deserted. The death of the mines did not, however, mean the end of South Pass City. In the 1950s a new boom came—one that involved not gold but iron ore. While the iron mines are now closed, the gold mines periodically operate, helping the town's economy. Tourism also has enabled the town to capitalize on its rambunctious past.

SOUTH PASS CITY STATE HISTORIC SITE encompasses the entire town; turn off SR 28 at Milepost 43 and follow signs. This ghostly reminder of South Pass City's mining era is being restored. Thirty-one log, frame and stone structures—including the Carissa Saloon, the South Pass Hotel, a jail, a livery stable, mill and a butcher shop—remain on 200 acres of land. A visitor center has interpretive displays depicting the town's past. Living-history programs also are offered. The site has a historic nature trail.

Time: Allow 2 hours minimum. Hours: Buildings open daily 9-6, May 15-Sept. 30. Cost: $4; free (ages 0-18). Phone: (307) 332-3684. 🎫

STORY (B-4) pop. 828, elev. 5,079'

Story took its name from Charles P. Story, an early mayor of nearby Sheridan who was related to Nelson Story, one of the first to drive Texas cattle over the Bozeman Trail into Montana in 1866. His northbound trip was the only significant use of the trail. Because the costs of maintaining the forts along the trail were immense in terms of both money and lives lost, the U.S. government eventually abandoned them and closed the Bozeman Trail.

Nestled at the base of the Bighorn Mountains in thick stands of Ponderosa pine and aspen, Story offers abundant recreational activities. Camping, hiking, fishing, hunting and horseback riding are readily available.

FORT PHIL KEARNY STATE HISTORIC SITE is reached by following signs from I-90 exit 44. The site preserves the remains of Fort Phil Kearny. Of the three forts built along the Bozeman Trail, Fort Phil Kearny suffered the worst. A visitor center houses displays and photographs. Markers identify the sites of the Fetterman interpretive trail and Wagon Box fights.

A self-guiding tour is available. **Time:** Allow 2 hours minimum. **Hours:** Visitor center open daily 8-6, May 15-Sept. 30; Wed.-Sun. noon-4, rest of year. Phone ahead to confirm schedule. **Cost:** $4; free (ages 0-17). **Phone:** (307) 684-7629 or (307) 684-7687. *(See ad p. 238.)*

THE STORY FISH HATCHERY is 2 mi. w. to end of SR 194. The hatchery was built 1907-08 and is the oldest operating fish hatchery in the state. The hatchery raises lake, rainbow and brook trout. Besides incubating and hatching fish eggs, the hatchery serves as a holding facility for fish and eggs destined for other stations throughout Wyoming. It includes an indoor hatchery and outdoor raceways and ponds. **Hours:** Daily 8-5. **Cost:** Free. **Phone:** (307) 683-2234.

WAGON BOX INN
307/683-2444

♦♦♦
American Casual Dining
$8-$50

AAA Inspector Notes: *Historic.* Worth the short drive off I-90, the restaurant was built in 1907 and has the feel of an old supper club decorated in a Western theme. Locals favor the steak and seafood along with the nightly special, and hot bread that melts in your mouth. **Features:** full bar. **Address:** 103 N Piney 82842 **Location:** I-90 exit 44 westbound, 7.2 mi nw on US 87 S; exit 33 eastbound, 7.2 mi sw on US 87 N. L D X N

SUNDANCE (B-6) pop. 1,182, elev. 4,750'

Sundance lies at the foot of Sundance Mountain, so named because the Sioux Indians held their councils and religious ceremonies at a place called Wi Wacippi Paha, or Temple of the Sioux. It is believed that Harry Longabaugh, better known as "The Sundance Kid," assumed his nickname in Sundance during his 18-month sentence in the Crook County jail for horse stealing.

Sundance is a convenient departure point for trips to nearby Devils Tower National Monument *(see place listing p. 255)* and Black Hills National Forest *(see place listing p. 235).* An 82-mile circle tour via US 14, SRs 24 and 111 and I-90 circles a portion of the national forest and offers opportunities to see the volcanic core of Devils Tower as well as pronghorns, wild turkeys and white-tailed deer.

Sundance Area Chamber of Commerce: P.O. Box 1004, Sundance, WY 82729. **Phone:** (307) 283-1000.

CROOK COUNTY MUSEUM AND ART GALLERY is on the lower level of the courthouse at 309 Cleveland St. The gallery contains more than 20,000 items from the Old West, including a re-creation of the original county courtroom. Photographs and legal papers of the Sundance Kid, who was incarcerated in the county jail for 18 months, also are displayed. Works by local artists are exhibited. **Hours:** Mon.-Fri. 8-4 (also Sat. 8-4, June-Aug.). **Cost:** Free. **Phone:** (307) 283-3666.

BEST WESTERN INN AT SUNDANCE   (307)283-2800

♦♦
Hotel
$80-$201

AAA Benefit: Members save 10% or more with Best Western!

Address: 2719 E Cleveland St 82729 **Location:** I-90 exit 189, just n, then just w; 1.5 mi ne of SR 585. **Facility:** 44 units. 2 stories (no elevator), interior corridors. **Parking:** winter plug-ins. **Pool(s):** heated indoor. **Activities:** hot tub. **Guest Services:** coin laundry.

TEN SLEEP (B-4) pop. 260, elev. 4,513'

Because Native Americans who traversed the Big Horn Basin of Wyoming reckoned time and distance in "sleeps," this midway point across the Big Horn Basin became known as Ten Sleep.

Range wars between cattle and sheep ranchers—quite common in the West during the 1890s and early 1900s—reached a climax with the Ten Sleep-Spring Creek Raid in 1909. This attack on the camp of an ex-cattleman who had brought a large herd of sheep into Big Horn Basin resulted in an investigation that eventually led to a peaceful arbitration.

Nearby Ten Sleep Canyon, on the western side of the Bighorn Mountains, is an outstanding feature of Bighorn National Forest *(see place listing p. 235).* Near the mouth of the canyon are a trout hatchery and a fish-rearing station; visitors are welcome at both stations. A scenic section of US 16 runs between Ten Sleep and Buffalo *(see place listing p. 237).*

TETON VILLAGE (C-1) pop. 330, elev. 6,329'

- **Attractions map p. 268**
- **Hotels & Restaurants map & index p. 295**
- **Part of Jackson Hole Including Grand Teton National Park area — see map p. 293**

Situated at the base of Jackson Hole Mountain Resort *(see attraction listing)*, Teton Village serves as a hub of activity during ski season. It is the site of many area lodgings and restaurants, and offers visitors the opportunity to browse in an assortment of specialty shops. An aerial tram in the village lifts passengers to the mountaintop, boasting one of North America's steepest and longest vertical drops.

Celebrate the joys of music at the Grand Teton Music Festival, which brings orchestra and chamber concerts in summer and winter months; phone (307) 733-1128 for ticket information.

RECREATIONAL ACTIVITIES

Skiing

- **Jackson Hole Mountain Resort** is 12 mi. w. via SRs 22 and 390. Other activities are offered. **Hours:** Daily 9-4, last Sat. in Nov.-first Sat. in Apr. **Phone:** (307) 733-2292 or (888) 333-7766.

THE ALPENHOF LODGE   (307)733-3242 🔢13

Hotel
$109-$459

Address: 3255 W Village Dr 83025 **Location:** Center. **Facility:** 42 units, some two bedrooms. 4 stories, interior corridors. **Terms:** closed 4/10-5/10 & 11/1-11/20, 10 day cancellation notice-fee imposed, resort fee. **Dining:** 2 restaurants, also, Alpenrose, see separate listing. **Pool(s):** heated outdoor. **Activities:** sauna, hot tub, downhill & cross country skiing, snowboarding, bicycles, massage. **Guest Services:** valet and coin laundry. **Featured Amenity:** full hot breakfast.

Alpenhof Lodge

European luxury located at the base of Jackson Hole Mountain Resort.

FOUR SEASONS RESORT JACKSON HOLE
(307)732-5000 🔢11

Resort Hotel
$375-$6750

Address: 7680 Granite Loop Rd 83025 **Location:** At base of Jackson Hole Mountain Resort. **Facility:** A ski concierge is along for every step at this ski-in/ski-out resort, where fine Western décor epitomizes rustic elegance. 124 units, some two and three bedrooms. 10 stories, interior corridors. **Parking:** on-site (fee) and valet. **Terms:** closed 4/10-4/30 & 11/1-11/24, check-in 4 pm, 30 day cancellation notice-fee imposed, resort fee. **Amenities:** safes. **Dining:** 3 restaurants, also, Westbank Grill, see separate listing. **Pool(s):** heated outdoor. **Activities:** sauna, hot tub, downhill & cross country skiing, recreation programs, game room, spa. **Guest Services:** valet laundry.

FOUR SEASONS RESORT *Jackson Hole*

Offering new heights of mountain luxury amidst the rugged wilderness of the American West.

HOTEL TERRA JACKSON HOLE   (307)739-4000 🔢15

Boutique Contemporary Hotel
$139-$3200

Address: 3335 W Village Dr 83025 **Location:** Center. **Facility:** Upscale and eco luxury best describe this full-service condo/hotel. Units feature bamboo furnishings, 100 percent organic cotton sheets and a hot tub. All bathrooms boast radiant heated floors. 132 units, some condominiums. 5 stories, interior corridors. **Parking:** on-site (fee) and valet. **Terms:** check-in 4 pm, 30 day cancellation notice-fee imposed, resort fee. **Amenities:** safes. **Dining:** IL Villaggio Osteria, see separate listing. **Pool(s):** heated outdoor. **Activities:** sauna, hot tub, steamroom, exercise room, spa. **Guest Services:** complimentary and valet laundry.

SNAKE RIVER LODGE & SPA   307/732-6000 🔢12

Resort Hotel
Rates not provided

Address: 7710 Granite Loop Rd 83025 **Location:** Center. **Facility:** Many luxuries are offered at this all-season resort set alongside the slopes for easy ski-in access. Guest rooms and baths are well appointed and some have a fireplace and/or balcony. 150 units, some condominiums. 5 stories, interior corridors. **Parking:** on-site (fee) and valet. **Terms:** check-in 4 pm. **Amenities:** safes. **Dining:** Gamefish, see separate listing. **Pool(s):** heated outdoor, heated indoor. **Activities:** sauna, hot tub, steamroom, downhill & cross country skiing, snowmobiling, snowboarding, bicycles, trails, exercise room, spa. **Guest Services:** valet and coin laundry, area transportation.

(See map & index p. 295.)

TETON MOUNTAIN LODGE & SPA   (307)734-7111   14

▼▼▼▼ ▼
Resort Hotel
$129-$2999

Address: 3385 W Cody Ln 83025 **Location:** Center. **Facility:** Nestled among the majestic Grand Tetons, this Western-style resort employs staff that caters to your every need. From the spa to the rooftop pool, you'll feel swept away at this retreat. 145 condominiums, some kitchens. 5 stories, interior corridors. **Parking:** valet and street only. **Terms:** check-in 4 pm, 30 day cancellation notice-fee imposed, resort fee. **Amenities:** safes. *Some:* video games. **Dining:** Spur Restaurant & Bar, see separate listing. **Pool(s):** heated outdoor, heated indoor. **Activities:** hot tub, steamroom, exercise room, spa. **Guest Services:** valet and coin laundry.

[SAVE] [⦿] [⎘] [Ⲩ] CALL [&M] [⚤] [BIZ] [HS] [📶] [✕]
[⊟] [▣] / SOME UNITS [S⊟] [⊡]

WHERE TO EAT

ALPENROSE   307/733-3242   12

▼▼▼
Regional
Swiss
Fine Dining
$21-$34

AAA Inspector Notes: A professional staff assists diners with the extensive wine list that features finer California and European varieties as well as a nice selection of after-dinner drinks. The atmosphere is European and offers a strong menu variety, including game dishes. **Features:** full bar. **Reservations:** suggested. **Address:** 3255 W Village Dr 83025 **Location:** 12.5 mi nw of Jackson, on SR 390, 7 mi n of SR 22; in The Alpenhof Lodge. [D]

GAMEFISH   307/732-6040   11

▼▼▼ Regional American. Fine Dining. $9-$47 **AAA Inspector Notes:** Windows on three walls afford views of the mountains in the upscale dining room, where guests savor expertly prepared game, meats and seafood. Creativity marks the desserts. **Features:** full bar, patio dining. **Reservations:** required. **Address:** 7710 Granite Loop Rd 83025 **Location:** Center; in Snake River Lodge & Spa. **Parking:** on-site (fee) and valet. [B] [L] [D]

IL VILLAGGIO OSTERIA   307/739-4100   15

▼▼▼▼ Italian. Fine Dining. $11-$49 **AAA Inspector Notes:** At this spot, I find it hard to decide between the home-made pizza with gourmet toppings or the grilled quail stuffed with pears, pine nuts and panettone. No matter what is on the plate, diners can enjoy great wines and beautiful scenery. Al fresco dining is available in season. Lunch is served only during the ski season. **Features:** full bar. **Address:** 3335 W Village Dr 83025 **Location:** Center; in Hotel Terra Jackson Hole. **Parking:** on-site and valet. [D]

MANGY MOOSE RESTAURANT AND SALOON
307/733-4913   16

▼▼ Regional American. Casual Dining. $5-$37 **AAA Inspector Notes:** Diners can watch village activity while eating prime rib, trout or beef stroganoff. The buffalo prime rib is a favorite but often goes quickly. This two-level dining room, which opens strictly for dinner, is covered with nostalgic items. Breakfast is in the casual cafe, while lunch and dinner are in the laid-back saloon. **Features:** full bar. **Address:** 1 McCollister Dr 83025 **Location:** Center of village.

[B] [L] [D]

MASA SUSHI   307/732-2962   17

▼▼ Japanese. Casual Dining. $10-$25 **AAA Inspector Notes:** Chef Masa Kitami delights guests with traditional sushi and sashimi as well as his own inventive creations such as the tasty Jackson Hole steak roll. The atmosphere is relaxing and scenic with great views of the surrounding mountains, skiers and tram. **Features:** full bar. **Reservations:** suggested. **Address:** 3345 W McCollister Dr 83025 **Location:** Center; in Inn at Jackson Hole. [D]

SPUR RESTAURANT & BAR   307/734-7111   14

▼▼▼▼ Regional American. Fine Dining. $14-$35 **AAA Inspector Notes:** This classic lodge-inspired restaurant specializes in seasonal creations, many grilled over an open fire. Among examples are molasses-seared elk chops, grilled venison, spec-wrapped Alaskan halibut or steak tartare with Peruvian chiles. For the forager, crispy portobello fries are a good choice. **Features:** full bar. **Address:** 3385 Cody Ln 83025 **Location:** Center; in Teton Mountain Lodge & Spa. [B] [L] [D]

TETON THAI   307/733-0022   13

▼▼ Thai. Casual Dining. $14-$20 **AAA Inspector Notes:** This family-run spot serves authentic Thai cuisine in a full-service setting. Space and seating is very limited. This restaurant has a sister location in Driggs, Idaho. **Features:** full bar. **Address:** 7342 N Granite Loop Rd 83025 **Location:** Center; west of ranch lot.

[L] [D]

WESTBANK GRILL   307/732-5000   10

▼▼▼
Regional
American
Fine Dining
$12-$36

AAA Inspector Notes: After a day skiing in the winter or white-water rafting in the summer, guests can savor a creatively presented, regionally influenced meal made all the more enjoyable by warmth from a massive stone fireplace. The grand dining room continues the resort's elegant rustic theme. Floor-to-ceiling windows offer a panoramic view of the slopes and the mountains. **Features:** full bar. **Reservations:** suggested. **Address:** 7680 Granite Loop Rd 83025 **Location:** At base of Jackson Hole Mountain Resort; in Four Seasons Resort Jackson Hole. **Parking:** on-site (fee) and valet.

[B] [L] [D] CALL [&M]

THERMOPOLIS (C-3) pop. 3,009, elev. 4,326'

• Hotels p. 322 • Restaurants p. 322

A treaty between the Shoshone and Arapaho nations and the United States specified that the waters of the hot mineral springs at Thermopolis would be available to everyone free of charge. The agreement continues to be honored at the State Bath House in Hot Springs State Park. Petroglyphs, 30 miles northwest of Thermopolis and about 8 miles off SR 120, are etched on a south-facing cliff at Legend Rock State Petroglyph Site.

Thermopolis is a favorite destination for hunters in search of pronghorn antelopes, game birds, elk and deer. South of Thermopolis on US 20 is Boysen Reservoir, with developed recreational facilities at Boysen State Park *(see Recreation Areas Chart)*.

Thermopolis provides access to two scenic highways—US 20 along Wind River Canyon and SR 120 traveling north to Cody.

Thermopolis-Hot Springs Chamber of Commerce: 220 Park St., P.O. Box 768, Thermopolis, WY 82443. **Phone:** (307) 864-3192.

HOT SPRINGS COUNTY MUSEUM AND CULTURAL CENTER is at 700 Broadway. The museum complex contains period rooms, a cherry-wood bar said to be visited by the Hole in the Wall gang, Native American artifacts, a restored country school, wildlife and mining exhibits, arts and crafts and geological, agricultural and oil industry displays. **Hours:** Mon.-Sat. 8-5, Memorial Day-Labor Day; Tues.-Sat. 9-4, rest of year. Closed Jan. 1, Thanksgiving and Christmas. **Cost:** $4; $2 (ages 6-12 and 60+). **Phone:** (307) 864-5183.

HOT SPRINGS STATE PARK is at the n.e. edge of town on US 20 and SR 789. The park contains mineral baths, pools, hot mineral springs, terraces and hot waterfalls, and is home to the state's bison herd. Of particular interest is Bighorn Hot Spring, which releases 3.6 million gallons daily and is one of the largest hot mineral springs in the world. Black Sulphur Springs and White Sulphur Springs are other springs within the park. *See Recreation Areas Chart.* **Hours:** Daily 6 a.m.-10 p.m. **Cost:** Free. **Phone:** (307) 864-2176.

WIND RIVER CANYON is 5 mi. s. via US 20. The canyon is a channel carved more than 2,000 feet deep by the rushing waters of the Wind River. Rock was blasted to create US 20, which tunnels through solid granite in three places. At the south end of the canyon is Boysen Dam.

Remarkable rock formations highlight the canyon walls, which are identified in terms of geological era and formation by strategically placed highway signs. One of the canyon's most prominent landmarks is Chimney Rock, about 10 miles south of Thermopolis.

WIND RIVER CANYON WHITEWATER is at 210 US 20S, Suite 5. Scenic float trips as well as whitewater, lunch and fishing trips are offered. **Hours:** Daily 7-5, Memorial Day-Labor Day. **Cost:** Scenic trip $39. Age requirements may vary depending on river conditions. Reservations and a deposit are required. **Phone:** (307) 864-9343 in season, or (888) 246-9343 year-round.

THE WYOMING DINOSAUR CENTER AND DIG SITES is at 110 Carter Ranch Rd. on the e. side of town. The 16,000-square-foot complex houses interpretive displays, dioramas and more than 30 full-size skeletons. Visitors may view the preparation lab, where bones are prepared for display, and take a 1-hour tour of the paleontological dig site.

Hours: Daily 8-6, May-Sept.; 10-5, rest of year. **Cost:** Museum $10; $5.50 (ages 4-12, ages 60+ and military veterans with ID). Dig site $12.50; $8.75 (ages 4-13, ages 65+ and military veterans with ID). Combination museum and dig site $18.50; $11.75 (ages 4-13, ages 60+ and military veterans with ID). **Phone:** (307) 864-2997.

BEST WESTERN PLUS THE PLAZA HOTEL

(307)864-2939

Historic Hotel
$122-$142

AAA Benefit: Members save 10% or more with Best Western!

Address: 116 E Park St 82433 **Location:** In Hot Springs State Park. **Facility:** There is a seasonal outdoor hot springs pool in the courtyard of this hotel. Guest rooms are beautifully appointed. 36 units. 2 stories (no elevator), interior corridors. **Parking:** winter plug-ins. **Pool(s):** heated outdoor. **Activities:** hot tub, massage.

DAYS INN HOT SPRINGS CONVENTION CENTER

(307)864-3131

Hotel $77-$159 **Address:** 115 E Park St 82443 **Location:** In Hot Springs State Park. **Facility:** 80 units. 2 stories (no elevator), interior/exterior corridors. **Parking:** winter plug-ins. **Terms:** cancellation fee imposed. **Dining:** The Safari Club Restaurant & Lounge, see separate listing. **Pool(s):** heated outdoor. **Activities:** sauna, hot tub, game room, exercise room, massage. **Guest Services:** coin laundry.

HOT SPRINGS SUPER 8

(307)864-5515

Hotel $68-$125 **Address:** Lane 5 Hwy 20 S 82443 **Location:** On US 20, just se. **Facility:** 52 units. 2 stories (no elevator), interior corridors. **Parking:** winter plug-ins. **Terms:** cancellation fee imposed. **Amenities:** video games, safes. **Pool(s):** heated indoor. **Activities:** sauna, hot tub, limited exercise equipment, massage. **Guest Services:** coin laundry.

WHERE TO EAT

FRONT PORCH BISTRO

307/864-3494

American. Casual Dining. $8-$15 **AAA Inspector Notes:** Gourmet sandwiches and hand-formed, made-in-house burgers on buns are just some of the reasons this place is recommended by locals. Travelers truly can enjoy cozy candlelight dinners. **Features:** full bar. **Address:** 536 Arapahoe St 82443 **Location:** Downtown. **Parking:** on-site and street.

THE SAFARI CLUB RESTAURANT & LOUNGE

307/864-3131

American. Casual Dining. $8-$36 **AAA Inspector Notes:** Hundreds of types of mounted fish, birds and animals decorate the restaurant and lounge, where house specials such as prime rib and pork chops are served in a fun, lively atmosphere. **Features:** full bar, patio dining, happy hour. **Address:** 115 E Park St 82443 **Location:** In Hot Springs State Park; in Days Inn Hot Springs Convention Center.

THUNDER BASIN NATIONAL GRASSLAND (C-5)

Thunder Basin National Grassland is in Campbell, Converse, Crook, Niobrara and Weston counties. Covering 1,800,339 acres, the national grassland was once a dust bowl. Settlers from the East, familiar only with the homesteading methods for a humid climate, met with disaster when they tried to establish farms in Wyoming's semiarid plains. Poor soil and recurrent droughts foiled attempts to cultivate the land, which soon deteriorated into dust bowls.

The grassland serves as an example of the regenerative use of land deemed unsuitable for cultivation. Sheep and cattle graze on the grassland's vast acreage, which also supports one of the world's largest herds of pronghorns. The Bozeman and Texas trails traverse a portion of the grassland.

The grassland lies within the Powder River Basin and contains a wealth of natural resources for energy development, including oil, gas and coal. The Black Thunder Mine, 9 miles from SR 59 on east SR 450, is one of the largest coal mines in the country. It operates on the grassland under a special state permit with forest service consent and produces more than 30 million tons of coal per year. For further information phone (307) 358-4690.

TORRINGTON (D-6) pop. 6,501, elev. 4,098'

Traversed by the Oregon, Mormon and California trails and the Overland Stage, Pony Express and overland telegraph lines, Torrington served as a Western gateway for pioneers. Named after settler William Curtis' hometown in Connecticut, Torrington is primarily a livestock exchange center, with cattle raising and agriculture as its main economic contributors.

Goshen County Chamber of Commerce: 350 W. 21st Ave., Torrington, WY 82240. **Phone:** (307) 532-3879.

HOMESTEADERS MUSEUM is s. on US 85 at 495 Main St. The museum is in the former Union Pacific depot and contains artifacts that depict the homestead period, which occurred from 1882-1929. **Hours:** Mon.-Wed. 9:30-4, Thurs.-Fri. 9:30-5, Sat. noon-4, June-Aug.; Mon.-Fri. 9:30-4, rest of year. **Cost:** Free. **Phone:** (307) 532-5612.

AMERICAS BEST VALUE INN   307/532-7118

Motel
Rates not provided

Address: 1548 S Main St 82240 **Location:** Just s of jct US 26 (W Valley Rd) and 85 (Main St). **Facility:** 57 units. 2 stories (no elevator), interior corridors. **Parking:** winter plug-ins. **Pool(s):** heated indoor. **Activities:** hot tub. **Guest Services:** coin laundry.

HOLIDAY INN EXPRESS & SUITES   307/532-7600

Hotel. Rates not provided. **Address:** 1700 E Valley Rd 82240 **Location:** On US 26 (E Valley Rd), 0.4 mi e of US 85 (Main St). Across from train tracks. **Facility:** 67 units. 2 stories, interior corridors. **Parking:** winter plug-ins. **Pool(s):** heated indoor. **Activities:** hot tub, exercise room. **Guest Services:** valet and coin laundry.

UCROSS

THE RANCH AT UCROSS   307/737-2281

Ranch. Rates not provided. **Address:** 2673 US Hwy 14 E 82835 **Location:** Jct US 14/16, 0.5 mi w. Located in a rural area. **Facility:** Big Horn Mountain scenery and a manicured lawn dotted with cottonwood trees create an appealing setting at this ranch, which offers annex rooms and four cabins. 31 units, some cabins. 1-2 stories (no elevator), interior/exterior corridors. **Pool(s):** heated outdoor. **Activities:** fishing, tennis, game room, limited exercise equipment.

WAPITI (B-2) elev. 5,641'

- **Hotels & Restaurants map & index p. 336**
- **Part of Yellowstone National Park area — see map p. 326**

The Wapiti Valley was popularized by William F. "Buffalo Bill" Cody. He brought guests to the area to enjoy the beauty of the valley and Yellowstone National Park. Wapiti Valley provides a scenic byway into or out of Yellowstone National Park *(see place listing p. 326)*. Among wildlife inhabiting the valley are elk, deer, buffalo, moose, bighorn sheep, bears, coyotes, bald and golden eagles, and even mountain lions.

Characterized by historic resorts, the valley also offers abundant recreational activities, including hiking, horseback riding, fishing, windsurfing, snowmobiling and skiing.

East Yellowstone Valley Chamber: P.O. Box 21, Wapiti, WY 82450. **Phone:** (307) 587-9595. *(See ad p. 332.)*

GREEN CREEK INN   307/587-5004   **76**

Motel $65-$180 **Address:** 2908 Northfork Hwy 82414 **Location:** 2.8 mi w on US 14/16/20; between Cody and Yellowstone National Park. Located in a quiet mountain valley. **Facility:** 17 units. 1 story, exterior corridors. **Terms:** closed 11/16-4/14, 7 day cancellation notice-fee imposed. **Guest Services:** coin laundry.

WHEATLAND (D-6) pop. 3,627, elev. 4,738'

Attracted by the cheap land and irrigation water that were made available by the Carey Act of 1894, settlers streamed into Platte County and transformed its dry landscape into productive farmland, dotted with such aptly named towns as Wheatland.

Wheat continues to be the region's principal crop, sustained in part by the Wheatland Irrigation Project, one of the largest privately owned enterprises of its type in the country. Wheatland also is the home of a white marble quarrying business and Laramie River Power Station, which supplies electric power to Wyoming and six neighboring states.

Recreational opportunities include camping and winter sports in nearby Medicine Bow National Forest *(see place listing p. 305)*. Grayrocks Reservoir, 16 miles northeast, is stocked with game fish and offers boating.

Platte County Chamber of Commerce: 65 16th St., Wheatland, WY 82201. **Phone:** (307) 322-2322.

LARAMIE PEAK MUSEUM is 2 mi. n. on 16th St. from exit 78 off I-25. The museum displays items relating to the early settlers of Platte County, the Oregon Trail and the cattle baron era. Some artifacts date from the late 1800s. **Time:** Allow 30 minutes minimum. **Hours:** Mon.-Fri. 10-5, Sat. 10-3, mid-May to mid-Sept.; by appointment rest of year. Closed major holidays. **Cost:** Donations. **Phone:** (307) 322-3765.

BEST WESTERN TORCHLITE MOTOR INN
    (307)322-4070

Motel
$100-$150

AAA Benefit: Members save 10% or more with Best Western!

Address: 1809 16th St 82201 **Location:** I-25 exit 80, just e, then 0.6 mi s. **Facility:** 50 units. 2 stories (no elevator), exterior corridors. **Parking:** winter plug-ins. **Terms:** check-in 4 pm. **Pool(s):** heated outdoor. **Activities:** hot tub, picnic facilities.

SUPER 8 (307)322-2224

WWW Hotel $75-$120 Address: 2401 16th St 82201 Location: I-25 exit 80, just e, then just s. Facility: 58 units. 2 stories (no elevator), interior corridors. Pool(s): heated indoor. Activities: hot tub, picnic facilities. Guest Services: coin laundry.

🔁 BIZ HS 🛜 ☒ 🔌 📷 💻

WILSON (C-1) pop. 1,482, elev. 6,152'
• Hotels & Restaurants map & index p. 295
• Part of Jackson Hole Including Grand Teton National Park area — see map p. 293

BAR J CHUCKWAGON SUPPER & WESTERN MUSIC SHOW, 1 mi. e. on SR 390 to 4200 W. Bar J Chuckwagon Rd., offers a chuck wagon supper and a live Western-style stage show. The Bar J Wranglers entertain guests with songs, stories and biscuit-baking and steak-grilling demonstrations. Time: Allow 4 hours minimum. Hours: Daily 5:30-10, Memorial Day-last Sat. in Sept. Cost: (Includes dinner and show) $22-$32; $12 (ages 4-12). Reservations are recommended. Phone: (307) 733-3370. 🍽

BENTWOOD INN (307)739-1411 🎱

WWWW Bed & Breakfast $209-$350 Address: 4250 Raven Haven Rd 83014 Location: 0.5 mi n on SR 390 (Moose Wilson Rd) from jct SR 22, then just e. Facility: A short drive from Jackson Hole, this beautiful log structure features a three-story river-rock fireplace offering a nice place to congregate in the living room. Guest rooms are tastefully decorated. 5 units. 2 stories, interior corridors. Terms: 2 night minimum stay - seasonal, 30 day cancellation notice-fee imposed. Activities: bicycles. 🛜 ☒ 🏊 🏋

WHERE TO EAT

Q ROADHOUSE 307/739-0700 ⑦

WW Barbecue. Casual Dining. $10-$29 AAA Inspector Notes: Another great eatery from the owner of Osteria and the Bistro, this place hones its focus on roadhouse fare. The eclectic menu ranges from lamb sliders to a hummus platter and wonderful, fragrant smoked meats. Buckets of peanuts on the table complete the roadhouse experience. Features: full bar, happy hour. Reservations: suggested. Address: 2550 Moose Wilson Rd 83014 Location: Jct SR 22 and 390 (Moose Wilson Rd), 1 mi ne. Ⓓ

WIND RIVER INDIAN RESERVATION (C-2)

Wind River Indian Reservation spans 2.2 million acres in western Wyoming; the tribal information office is at 15 North Ford Rd. in Fort Washakie. Of different linguistic stock and cultural background, the Shoshone and Arapaho tribes occupy different sections of the reservation. The graves of Chief Washakie and of Sacajawea, as well as the Shoshone Cultural Center, which offers displays and tours, are in Fort Washakie. Arapaho artifacts are displayed in the Arapaho Cultural Museum in Ethete.

Sun Dances are performed near Fort Washakie and Ethete for 3 days in July and August. Photography is prohibited. Powwows and rodeos are held throughout the summer. Christmas dances are performed Christmas Eve through Jan. 1. For further information write P.O. Box 217, Fort Washakie, WY 82514.

The information office is open Mon.-Fri. 8-4:45. Phone (307) 332-3040.

WORLAND (B-3) pop. 5,487, elev. 4,061'

Worland is in a rich farming and stock-feeding area in the center of Wyoming's Big Horn Basin. Sugar beets, beans, malt barley and hay are harvested on irrigated lands; local industries produce aluminum cans, soft drinks, beet sugar and cat litter.

On the grounds of the county courthouse is a 260-year-old Douglas fir that has been carved into a monument honoring Native Americans, part of sculptor Peter Toth's "Trail of the Whispering Giants." Among the city's nine parks is Pioneer Square, which has statues honoring the area's early settlers. A nearby drinking fountain offers artesian mineral water from the Bighorn Mountains.

The Bighorn Mountains are popular with campers, hikers, hunters, skiers and snowmobilers. Passing through the city is Bighorn River, offering abundant fishing opportunities.

Vestiges of a far earlier time are the Gooseberry Formations and Painted Desert west on SR 431. In this area of dramatically eroded formations were found the remains of eohippus (dawn horse), the earliest known equine. Wild horses still can be viewed north of town.

Worland-Ten Sleep Chamber of Commerce: 120 N. 10th St., Worland, WY 82401. Phone: (307) 347-3226. (See ad p. 334.)

SAVE WASHAKIE MUSEUM & CULTURAL CENTER is at 2200 Big Horn Ave.; a 25-foottall bronze mammoth greets visitors at the entrance. Fossils, mammoth bones and rock art are on display in The Ancient Basin, an exhibit that explores the archeology, geology and paleontology of the Big Horn Basin. The Last West exhibit chronicles area history, highlighting events like the Johnson County War, the Spring Creek Raid and the harsh winter of 1886-87.

Visitors can watch movies about cattle barons and global climate change, hear stories about the Old West and the railroad era, and use a touch screen to design their own cattle brand. Changing exhibits, special events and educational programs are offered throughout the year.

Time: Allow 1 hour minimum. Hours: Mon.-Fri. 9-5:30, Sat. 9-5, Sun. noon-4, mid-May to mid-Sept.; Tues.-Sat. 10-4, rest of year. Closed Jan. 1, Presidents Day, Easter, Thanksgiving and Christmas. Cost: $8; $7 (ages 62+); $6 (ages 7-12). Phone: (307) 347-4102.

COMFORT INN OF WORLAND   (307)347-9898

Hotel $95-$165 **Address:** 100 N Road 11 82401 **Location:** On US 16, 1.4 mi e. **Facility:** 50 units. 2 stories (no elevator), interior corridors. **Parking:** winter plug-ins. **Pool(s):** heated indoor. **Activities:** hot tub. **Guest Services:** coin laundry.

DAYS INN   (307)347-4251

Motel $94-$104 **Address:** 500 N 10th St 82401 **Location:** 0.5 mi n on US 20. **Facility:** 42 units. 1 story, exterior corridors. **Parking:** winter plug-ins. **Guest Services:** coin laundry.

WRIGHT   (C-5) pop. 1,807, elev. 5,121'

WRIGHT MUSEUM is at 104 Ranch Ct. Windmills, World War I artifacts, heavy mining equipment, wood-working implements and antique dishes are on display; there also are exhibits about oil drilling and coal mining. **Time:** Allow 30 minutes minimum. **Hours:** Mon.-Fri. 10-5, Sat. 10-2, Memorial Day-Oct. 1. **Cost:** Free. **Phone:** (307) 464-1222.

WRIGHT HOTEL   (307)464-6060

Hotel $129-$139 **Address:** 300 Reata Dr 82732 **Location:** Just w of jct SR 59 and 387. **Facility:** 71 units. 3 stories, interior corridors. **Parking:** winter plug-ins. **Terms:** 3 day cancellation notice. **Amenities:** safes. **Dining:** Open Range Steak House, see separate listing. **Guest Services:** coin laundry.

WHERE TO EAT

OPEN RANGE STEAK HOUSE   307/464-6161

Steak. Casual Dining. $9-$30 **AAA Inspector Notes:** Although Durham Ranch buffalo and certified Angus beef stand out on the menu of this popular steakhouse, diners also can order seafood, pasta, burgers and sandwiches. **Features:** full bar, patio dining. **Address:** 350 Reata Dr 82732 **Location:** Just w of jct SR 59 and 387; in Wright Hotel.

Get Your Car Vacation Ready!

Before setting out on vacation, have your car checked out by a dependable AAA/CAA Approved Auto Repair facility.

YELLOWSTONE NATIONAL PARK (B-2)

- Hotels p. 341 • Restaurants p. 341
- Attractions map p. 328
- Hotels & Restaurants map & index p. 336

Elevations in the park range from 5,314 ft. at the north entrance in Gardiner, Mont., to 11,358 ft. at Eagle Peak in the southeastern side of the park. Refer to AAA maps for additional elevation information.

Yellowstone National Park has five entrances: Gardiner, Mont. (north); West Yellowstone, Mont. (west); Jackson Hole via Grand Teton National Park (about 60 miles south); Cody (about 53 miles east); and Cooke City, Mont. (northeast).

The first national park, Yellowstone was established by an act of Congress in 1872. The region took its name from the dramatic gold-hued cliffs lining the river canyon, known by the Minnetaree Indians as *mi tse a-da-zi* (Yellow Rock River).

Though its mountain forests and meadows are beautiful in their own right, Yellowstone is unique for its geysers, hot springs, mud pools and fumaroles—the largest concentration of geothermal features in the world. The park sits atop one of the largest active volcanoes on earth, a "hot spot" that last erupted some 640,000 years ago, carving out a caldera 30 miles wide and 45 miles long. Heated by this vast subterranean magma chamber, the Yellowstone valley continues to steam and vent.

Fountains of scalding water burst high into the air from some geysers, while others bubble and spit in murky depths. Hot springs gleam in shades of emerald green and blue. Algae and bacteria withstand boiling temperatures to create these vivid colors; vigorous steam vents emit uncanny sounds and smells.

Miles of boardwalks, paved trails and driving loops allow visitors to come within close proximity of these active volcanic formations. Despite their cool

This map shows cities in Yellowstone National Park where you will find attractions, hotels and restaurants. Cities are listed alphabetically in this book on the following pages.

(See map & index p. 336.)

colors, mineral springs are boiling hot, and the solid-looking crusts around geyser formations can be remarkably fragile—keep a close watch over children while in these areas, and be sure to stay on boardwalks or formal paths.

In addition to its geologic wonders, Yellowstone National Park is also one of the most successful wildlife sanctuaries in the world. Grizzly and black bears can be sighted occasionally in the backcountry and sometimes from park roadways (a traffic situation known as "bear jam"). The park also has several thousand elk; many mule deer, pronghorn antelopes and moose; bands of bighorn sheep; and about 3,500 bison. Gray wolves were reintroduced to Yellowstone 1995-97, and several packs now roam the park and surrounding areas.

General Information

The park roads are open to automobile travel from May through October (weather permitting). The 60-mile road between the north entrance at Gardiner, Mont., and the northeast entrance at Cooke City, Mont., is open all year. During the off-season this road is accessible only from the north entrance near Gardiner, Mont.; the northeast entrance via Red Lodge, Mont., is usually open from Memorial Day weekend through September 30. The east entrance from Cody usually opens in mid-May and remains open as weather permits.

The approach to Cooke City, Mont., from Red Lodge, Mont., via the Beartooth Scenic Highway (US 212) negotiates Beartooth Pass at an elevation of almost 11,000 feet. From Cody the approach to Sylvan Pass follows US 14/16/20 through the carved red walls of Wapiti Valley.

The road between Canyon and Tower-Roosevelt runs over Dunraven Pass and along Mount Washburn and passes Tower Fall, where the spectacles of the gorge, the falls on Tower Creek and the palisades of rock high above the Yellowstone River can be viewed.

Although most of the park's 3,472 square miles lie in northwestern Wyoming, they also extend into Montana and Idaho. The central portion of the park is essentially a broad, elevated volcanic plateau that lies between 6,500 and 8,500 feet above sea level. On the south, east, north and northwest are mountain ranges with peaks and ridges rising between 2,000 and 4,000 feet above the enclosed tableland.

Most park facilities are open mid-May to mid-October, but food and lodging facilities are limited after October 1. During the off-season manned gas stations are available only at Gardiner and Cooke City, Mont. Unstaffed, credit card-only gas stations are available at developed locations when the roads are open. Interior park roads are open to guided snowcoach and snowmobile tours from mid-December through the first week in March. During the summer, rental cars are available at Cody and Jackson as well as at Billings, Bozeman, Livingston and West Yellowstone, Mont.

The roads through the park make many of the most prominent attractions readily accessible. During the summer travel season visitors may encounter slow traffic. Be especially alert for others stopped in the road to watch wildlife; if you must stop, pull well off the highway onto a marked wayside.

Note: According to National Park Service figures, about 80 percent of the park roads are "in a structurally deficient state...including narrow shoulders and rough surfaces." The roads are being gradually repaired under a 20-year program. For up-to-date road information phone (307) 344-2117.

The park headquarters is at Mammoth Hot Springs, 5 miles from the north entrance. The main post office is at Mammoth; ranger stations are at Old Faithful, Grant Village, Tower-Roosevelt, Mammoth Hot Springs, Lake, Madison, Bechler, Canyon and the south entrance. The Mammoth ranger station, open all year, is accessible by car in winter via the north entrance.

Park information can be received by tuning radios to 1610 AM. Low-powered transmitters broadcast from entrance stations.

From Memorial Day through Labor Day ranger-naturalists conduct geyser walks, natural- and living-history talks, photographic workshops and children's programs at Bridge Bay, Canyon, Fishing Bridge, Grant Village, Lake, Madison, Mammoth Hot Springs, Norris Geyser Basin, Old Faithful, West Thumb Geyser Basin and West Yellowstone. Free evening programs are given at most park campgrounds during the summer season.

ADMISSION to the park is by private vehicle permit ($25), motorcycle permit ($20) and single nonmotorized entry ($12), valid in both Yellowstone and Grand Teton national parks for 7 days; and by annual area permit ($50/both parks; free for active military and their dependents with ID) or an Interagency Annual Pass-National Parks and Federal Recreational Lands Pass ($80/entrance to most federal recreation sites). An Interagency Senior Pass for U.S. citizens ages 62+ is $10; an Interagency Access Pass for physically impaired U.S. citizens is free.

PETS are permitted in the park only if they are on a leash, crated or otherwise physically restricted at all times. They are not permitted more than 100 feet from the roads and parking areas, and are not permitted on trails, in the backcountry or in hydrothermal areas. It is illegal to leave pets unattended.

ADDRESS inquiries to the Superintendent, Yellowstone National Park, P.O. Box 168, Yellowstone National Park, WY 82190; phone (307) 344-7381. For lodging and guest service information write Yellowstone National Park Lodges, P.O. Box 165, Yellowstone National Park, WY 82190; phone (307) 344-7311 or (866) 439-7375.

Activities

Not all of Yellowstone's grandeur can be seen from the boardwalks. More than 1,000 miles of

© AAA

Yellowstone National Park
Attractions

⚑ CAMPGROUND SITE WITHIN NAT'L. PARK. INFORMATION PROVIDED BY WOODALL'S ®.

Scale in Miles
6.7   0   6.7

SCENIC BYWAY

(See map & index p. 336.)

backcountry trails lead to many of the park's less accessible attractions. A free backcountry use permit, obtainable from any area ranger station, is required for those who wish to camp in the backcountry. The permit can be obtained in person and no more than 48 hours in advance. Campsite reservations can be obtained by mail or at a backcountry office for a $20 fee.

There is no better way to explore the park than on horseback over the trails. Private stock can be ridden, or 1- or 2-hour guided rides are available at Mammoth Hot Springs, Tower-Roosevelt and

Canyon from Xanterra Parks & Resorts. Horses cannot be rented without a guide.

Motorboats and rowboats can be rented from Xanterra Parks & Resorts at the Bridge Bay Marina. Guided fishing trips also are available. A permit is required for all vessels (motorized and nonmotorized, including float tubes) and must be obtained in person. The fee is $10 for motorized vessels and $5 for nonmotorized vessels; the permits are valid for 7 days. Boat permits issued in Grand Teton National Park are honored in Yellowstone, but owners must register their vessel in Yellowstone and obtain a free Yellowstone validation sticker from a permit issuing station.

(See map & index p. 336.)

Jet skis, airboats, submersibles and similar watercraft are prohibited in Yellowstone National Park. All vessels are prohibited on park rivers and streams except the channel between Lewis and Shoshone lakes, where only hand-propelled vessels are permitted.

Guided snowcoach tours by Xanterra Parks & Resorts to the interior of the park are available mid-December to early March from Mammoth Hot Springs, near the north entrance; West Yellowstone, Mont., at the west entrance; Old Faithful; and Flagg Ranch, near the south entrance. Guided cross-country ski trips also are offered.

(See map & index p. 336.)

Most of the streams and lakes below the timberline contain one or more species of trout. Roadside streams and Yellowstone Lake offer some of the best fishing in the park. Fishing tackle is sold by Delaware North general stores located throughout the park.

Anglers ages 16+ are required to purchase a Yellowstone National Park fishing permit. A 3-day permit costs $18; a 7-day permit is $25. Children under 16 may fish without a permit under the direct supervision of an adult who has a valid park fishing permit, or they may obtain a free permit signed by an adult. For further information write the Chief Rangers Office, P.O. Box 168, Yellowstone National Park, WY 82190, or phone (307) 344-2107. Fishing regulations and permits can be obtained at any ranger station, visitor center or Yellowstone Park General Store. Fishing permits also are available at many businesses in the greater Yellowstone area. No state fishing license is required in Yellowstone National Park. The opening of the season varies from the Saturday of Memorial Day weekend to July 15 for different lakes and streams; it closes the first Sunday in November.

Check at visitor centers or ranger stations for season variations and legal limits. *See Recreation Areas Chart.*

Note: It is not only against park regulations but also dangerous to feed, touch or tease any wildlife.

Animals in the park are wild and should be viewed only from a safe distance. According to park regulations, you must stay at least 100 yards (the length of a football field) away from bears and wolves and at least 25 yards away from all other animals. The following items (whether new, used, clean, dirty, empty or full) may not be left unattended on picnic tables, in tents or tent trailers, in the back of pickups or in any other outdoor location at any time: food, beverage containers, cooking and eating utensils, stoves and grills, coolers and ice chests, cosmetics and toiletries, pet food and bowls, buckets and washbasins. All trash should be disposed of in bearproof garbage cans.

ALBRIGHT VISITOR CENTER & MUSEUM is at Mammoth Hot Springs. Housed in one of the original U.S. Cavalry buildings, the headquarters museum focuses on those who shaped the history of Yellowstone, including American Indians, mountain men, early explorers, the U.S. Army and the National Park Service. An art gallery displays the works of photographer William Henry Jackson and painter and explorer Thomas Moran. Films chronicle Moran's life and the park's development.

Hours: Daily 8-7, Memorial Day-Labor Day; 9-5, rest of year. Closed Thanksgiving and Veterans Day. Phone ahead to confirm schedule. **Cost:** Free. **Phone:** (307) 344-2263.

CANYON VISITOR EDUCATION CENTER is at Canyon Village. A room-size relief map illustrates

(See map & index p. 336.)

Yellowstone's volcanic activity, and a variety of inter-active exhibits describe the formation of geysers, hot springs and other geologic features here and around the world. A giant lava lamp demonstrates how magma rises with heat convection. Murals, di-oramas and panoramas show how glaciers and vol-canic eruptions have shaped the landscape. A 20-minute film explores the connection between the park's geological origins and its wildlife.

Hours: Daily 8-8, late May-Sept. 30; 9-5, rest of year. **Cost:** Free. **Phone:** (307) 242-2550.

FISHING BRIDGE MUSEUM AND VISITOR CENTER is 1 mi. off the main park road on the east entrance road. The 1931 stone-and-log building houses exhibits about biological life in the park. Mounted specimens include a regional collection of birds, as well as a grizzly sow and cubs and a family of river otters. **Hours:** Daily 8-7, late May-late Sept. **Cost:** Free. **Phone:** (307) 344-2450.

GRAND CANYON OF THE YELLOWSTONE is a section along the Yellowstone River between Canyon and Tower-Roosevelt. Noted for its spec-tacular yellow coloring, the deep river canyon offers striking views of the Yellowstone falls. Among the best vistas are Artist's Point on the south rim and In-spiration Point on the north rim. Lookout Point pro-vides the best view of the Lower Falls. Uncle Tom's Trail descends about halfway and ends at the base of the Lower Falls on the south side. The Upper Falls are visible from several trails and lookouts.

GRANT VILLAGE VISITOR CENTER is on the shore of the West Thumb of Yellowstone Lake. Ex-hibits depict fire's role in shaping the environment. The film "Ten Years After Fire" recounts the 1988 blaze that scorched 1.2 million acres. **Hours:** Daily 8-7, late May-late Sept. **Cost:** Free. **Phone:** (307) 344-2650.

LOWER AND MIDWAY GEYSER BASINS are n. of the Old Faithful area on the main park road. Cov-ering 12 square miles, this area features clusters of

(See map & index p. 336.)

thermal features including the Fountain Paint Pots. These boiling pools of red, yellow and brown mud change with the seasons and the water table. The 3-mile Firehole Lake Drive leads to Great Fountain Geyser, which erupts about twice a day from a beautiful travertine terrace.

Excelsior Geyser, one of the largest features in the Midway Basin, discharges thousands of gallons of water per minute into the Firehole River.

MAMMOTH HOT SPRINGS is near the park headquarters at the north entrance. The springs are characterized by terrace-like formations created by limestone deposits. Well-marked trails and boardwalks allow the safe viewing of the formations at close range. **Note:** Visitors must stay on the marked trails and boardwalks at all times, since in many places the thin crust is dangerous.

MUSEUM OF THE NATIONAL PARK RANGER is at the entrance to the Norris Campground. Housed in a 1908 soldier station, this small museum chronicles the role of national park rangers, from early military roots to today's specialized profession. A 25-minute film, "An American Legacy," traces the history of the National Park Service. **Hours:** Daily 9-5, late May-late Sept. **Cost:** Free. **Phone:** (307) 344-7353.

NORRIS GEYSER BASIN is just n. of Norris Junction on the main park road. Boardwalks and trails lead across this barren valley of steam vents and rainbow-colored pools. This is the oldest and hottest geothermal area in the park, with water temperatures above 200 degrees.

Steamboat Geyser, the world's tallest geyser, has reached heights of 300-400 feet but often remains quiet for months or years between major eruptions. Echinus Geyser was long considered the only predictable geyser at Norris, though its performance has fluctuated in the past decade. **Note:** Due to new seismic activity, some trails in this area may be closed.

NORRIS GEYSER BASIN MUSEUM is just off the main park road at Norris Junction. Exhibits describe the park's geothermal features, particularly in the active Norris area. **Hours:** Daily 9-6, late May-late Sept. **Cost:** Free. **Phone:** (307) 344-2812.

OLD FAITHFUL is on the main park road between Madison and West Thumb, just beyond the Old Faithful Inn. Though not quite as predictable as its name suggests, this 120-foot waterspout erupts every 80-90 minutes. A paved walkway and benches surround the cone geyser, keeping visitors about 300 feet away from the massive spray. Daily geyser predictions are posted at the Old Faithful Visitor Education Center and the lodge.

OLD FAITHFUL VISITOR EDUCATION CENTER is off the main park road between Madison and West

▼ See AAA listing p. 323 ▼

Soda Springs

RICH MEMORIES.
AFFORDABLE ADVENTURES.

Be it making waves or soaking up the sun, southeastern Idaho's Pioneer Country offers scenic vistas, secluded lakes and abundant outdoor recreational activities. Rejuvenate in hot pools, splash in the world's only captive geyser on your way to Yellowstone, or explore world-class mountain biking trails in Pocatello.

Historical and cultural attractions, such as the National Oregon/California Trail Center and the full size Fort Hall Replica offer a unique way to experience history. Contemporary accommodations and the natural beauty of this area enhance your experience on this trip of a lifetime.

(See map & index p. 336.)

Thumb, just beyond the Old Faithful Inn. Visitors can view Old Faithful through the center's massive front windows. Exhibits and films describe the park's geyser activity and Yellowstone history. Predictions are posted daily for eruptions throughout the park. **Hours:** Daily 8-8, Memorial Day-Sept. 30; 9-5, mid-Apr. through day before Memorial Day, mid-Oct. to mid-Nov. and mid-Dec. to mid-Mar. **Cost:** Free. **Phone:** (307) 344-2751.

UPPER GEYSER BASIN is on the main park road between Madison and West Thumb. The area surrounding Old Faithful Lodge contains the world's largest concentration of geysers, including the star of the show, Old Faithful. Other geysers such as Grand and Riverside are less frequent but equally spectacular. Boardwalks and paved trails allow visitors to walk within safe distance of geysers, fumaroles, hot springs and mud pots across the basin. **Time:** Allow 2 hours minimum.

YELLOWSTONE LAKE is e. and s. of the park road between West Thumb and Fishing Bridge. Covering 132 square miles at 7,733 feet above sea level, this lake is the largest body of water in North America at so high an altitude. It is also home to the continent's largest population of wild cutthroat trout. The mountain lake has 110 miles of shoreline and a maximum depth of more than 400 feet. Boating and fishing are popular summer sports, but because the water stays so cold, swimming is not advised; the lake freezes over completely in winter.

RECREATIONAL ACTIVITIES

Hiking

- **Adventure Yellowstone** picks up at area hotels. Other activities are offered. **Hours:** Trips depart daily. **Phone:** (406) 585-9041.

▼ See AAA listing p. 324 ▼

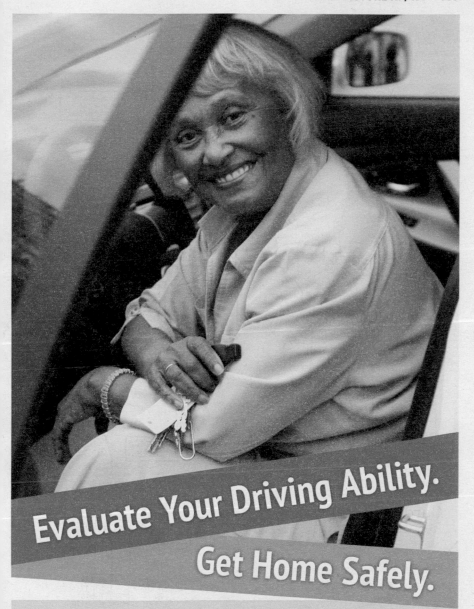

Evaluate Your Driving Ability.

Get Home Safely.

Assess your driving skills and
make adjustments before your next trip.

 AAA.com/DrivingEvaluation

© AAA

Yellowstone National Park

This index helps you "spot" where approved hotels and restaurants are located on the corresponding detailed maps. Hotel daily rate range is for comparison only. Restaurant price range is a combination of lunch and/or dinner. Turn to the listing page for more detailed rate and price information and consult display ads for special promotions.

YELLOWSTONE NATIONAL PARK

Map Page	Hotels	Diamond Rated	Rate Range	Page
1 p. 336	Shoshone Lodge	◆◆	$130-$200	341
2 p. 336	**Elephant Head Lodge** (See ad p. 329.)	◆◆	$150-$350 [SAVE]	341

Map Page	Restaurant	Diamond Rated	Cuisine	Price Range	Page
① p. 336	Mammoth Hot Springs Hotel Dining Room	◆◆	Regional American	$8-$28	341

EMIGRANT, MT

Map Page	Hotel	Diamond Rated	Rate Range	Page
5 p. 336	Mountain Sky Guest Ranch	◆◆◆◆	$720-$1146	155

BIG SKY, MT

Map Page	Hotels	Diamond Rated	Rate Range	Page
8 p. 336	The Lodge at Big Sky	◆◆◆	$130-$320	132
9 p. 336	Buck's T-4 Lodge	◆◆	$129-$169	132
10 p. 336	Rainbow Ranch Lodge	◆◆◆	$150-$450	132

Map Page	Restaurants	Diamond Rated	Cuisine	Price Range	Page
④ p. 336	The Cabin Bar & Grill	◆◆	Regional American	$10-$38	132
⑤ p. 336	Lotus Pad	◆◆	Thai	$14-$20	132
⑥ p. 336	Buck's T-4	◆◆◆	Regional American	$24-$32	132
⑦ p. 336	**The Corral Steakhouse**	◆◆	Steak	$9-$35	132
⑧ p. 336	Rainbow Ranch Lodge	◆◆◆	Regional American	$23-$41	132

GARDINER, MT

Map Page	Hotels	Diamond Rated	Rate Range	Page
13 p. 336	Yellowstone Basin Inn	◆◆	$95-$425	161
14 p. 336	Yellowstone Village Inn	◆◆	Rates not provided	162
15 p. 336	Comfort Inn Yellowstone North	◆◆	$95-$245	161
16 p. 336	**BEST WESTERN PLUS By Mammoth Hot Springs** (See ad p. 161.)	◆◆◆	$89-$219 [SAVE]	160
17 p. 336	Yellowstone Super 8-Gardiner	◆◆	$50-$210	161
18 p. 336	**Yellowstone River Motel**	◆	$65-$118 [SAVE]	161

Map Page	Restaurants	Diamond Rated	Cuisine	Price Range	Page
⑪ p. 336	The Antler Pub & Grill	◆◆	American	$9-$28	162
⑫ p. 336	**Yellowstone Mine Restaurant**	◆◆	American	$9-$22	162
⑬ p. 336	The Raven Grill	◆◆	American	$9-$26	162

RED LODGE, MT

Map Page	Hotels	Diamond Rated	Rate Range	Page
21 p. 336	Comfort Inn of Red Lodge	◆◆	$99-$185	201
22 p. 336	The Pollard	◆◆	$75-$275	202
23 p. 336	Yodeler Motel	◆	$60-$140	202
24 p. 336	Lu Pine Inn	◆◆	$69-$149	202
25 p. 336	**Rock Creek Resort**	◆◆	$130-$390 [SAVE]	202

Map Page	Restaurants	Diamond Rated	Cuisine	Price Range	Page
⑯ p. 336	**Vintage One Bistro**	◆◆◆	Regional American	$10-$32	202

Map Page	Restaurants (cont'd)	Diamond Rated	Cuisine	Price Range	Page
⑰ p. 336	The Pub at the Pollard	◆◆	English	$8-$11	202
⑱ p. 336	Bogart's	◆◆	American	$6-$17	202
⑲ p. 336	Carbon County Steakhouse	◆◆◆	American	$10-$30	202
⑳ p. 336	Bridge Creek Backcountry Kitchen & Wine Bar	◆◆	American	$10-$33	202
㉑ p. 336	Red Lodge Pizza Co.	◆◆	Pizza	$7-$20	202
㉒ p. 336	China Garden	◆◆	Chinese	$8-$17	202
㉓ p. 336	Old Piney Dell	◆◆◆	American	$17-$28	202

COOKE CITY, MT

Map Page	Hotel	Diamond Rated	Rate Range	Page
㉘ p. 336	Elk Horn Lodge	◆	$105-$125	152

WEST YELLOWSTONE, MT

Map Page	Hotels	Diamond Rated	Rate Range	Page
㉛ p. 336	Super 8	◆◆	Rates not provided [SAVE]	211
㉜ p. 336	BEST WESTERN Weston Inn	◆◆	$70-$300 [SAVE]	210
㉝ p. 336	One Horse Motel	◆	$79-$161 [SAVE]	211
㉞ p. 336	Evergreen Motel	◆	$109-$125	210
㉟ p. 336	Lazy G Motel	◆	$85-$105 [SAVE]	210
㊱ p. 336	BEST WESTERN Cross Winds Motor Inn	◆◆	$69-$199 [SAVE]	209
㊲ p. 336	Brandin' Iron Inn	◆◆	$79-$169 [SAVE]	210
㊳ p. 336	BEST WESTERN Desert Inn	◆◆	$80-$248 [SAVE]	209
㊴ p. 336	Yellowstone Westgate Hotel	◆◆◆	$100-$270	211
㊵ p. 336	Days Inn West Yellowstone	◆◆	$100-$219 [SAVE]	210
㊶ p. 336	Stage Coach Inn	◆◆	$69-$269 [SAVE]	211
㊷ p. 336	City Center Motel	◆	$69-$119 [SAVE]	210
㊸ p. 336	Alpine Motel	◆	$89-$169 [SAVE]	209
㊹ p. 336	Holiday Inn West Yellowstone	◆◆◆	$119-$299 [SAVE]	210
㊺ p. 336	Three Bear Lodge	◆◆◆	$69-$229 [SAVE]	211
㊻ p. 336	ClubHouse Inn	◆◆◆	$100-$260	210
㊼ p. 336	Kelly Inn	◆◆	$90-$260	210
㊽ p. 336	Yellowstone Park Hotel	◆◆◆	$89-$259 [SAVE]	211
㊾ p. 336	Yellowstone Lodge	◆◆	$69-$209	211
㊿ p. 336	Gray Wolf Inn & Suites	◆◆	$89-$259 [SAVE]	210

Map Page	Restaurants	Diamond Rated	Cuisine	Price Range	Page
㉖ p. 336	Cafe Madriz	◆◆	Spanish Small Plates	$8-$30	211
㉗ p. 336	Kiwi' Takeaway	◆	New Zealander	$6-$11	211
㉘ p. 336	Running Bear Pancake House	◆◆	American	$6-$10	212
㉙ p. 336	Bullwinkle's Saloon & Eatery	◆◆	American	$8-$28	211
㉚ p. 336	Pete's Rocky Mountain Pizza & Pasta	◆◆	Pizza Sandwiches	$8-$22	211
㉛ p. 336	Beartooth BBQ	◆◆	Barbecue	$8-$15	211
㉜ p. 336	Red Lotus	◆◆	Chinese	$8-$19	211
㉝ p. 336	The Gusher Pizza and Sandwich Shoppe	◆◆	American	$8-$16	211
㉞ p. 336	Wild West Pizzeria & Saloon	◆◆	Pizza	$8-$25	212

Map Page	Restaurants (cont'd)	Diamond Rated	Cuisine	Price Range	Page
㉟ p. 336	Serenity Bistro	◆◆	Regional American	$12-$38	212
㊱ p. 336	**Three Bear Restaurant**	◆◆	American	$8-$25	212

PAINTER

Map Page	Hotel	Diamond Rated	Rate Range	Page
㊾ p. 336	Hunter Peak Ranch	◆	$150-$220	306

CODY

Map Page	Hotels	Diamond Rated	Rate Range	Page
㊶ p. 336	The Mayor's Bed & Breakfast Inn	◆◆	$90-$215	253
㊷ p. 336	**Moose Creek Lodge & Suites** (See ad p. 254.)	◆◆	Rates not provided SAVE	253
㊸ p. 336	**Cody Motor Lodge** (See ad p. 253.)	◆	$99-$140 SAVE	253
㊹ p. 336	Comfort Inn at Buffalo Bill Village Resort	◆◆	$99-$199	253
㊿ p. 336	Holiday Inn at Buffalo Bill Village Resort	◆◆◆	$89-$239	253
㊶ p. 336	Buffalo Bill Village	◆	$89-$189	252
㊷ p. 336	Budget Host Inn	◆	$80-$140	252
㊸ p. 336	Buffalo Bill's Antlers Inn	◆	$50-$150	252
㊹ p. 336	**Sunrise Motor Inn**	◆	$50-$130 SAVE	253
㊺ p. 336	**BEST WESTERN Sunset Motor Inn**	◆◆	$185-$200 SAVE	252
㊻ p. 336	**BEST WESTERN PREMIER Ivy Inn & Suites**	◆◆◆	$115-$290 SAVE	252
㊼ p. 336	**AmericInn Lodge & Suites of Cody**	◆◆	$99-$219 SAVE	252
㊽ p. 336	The Cody	◆◆◆	$110-$285	252
㊾ p. 336	**Skyline Motor Inn**	◆	$69-$225 SAVE	253
㊿ p. 336	**Beartooth Inn of Cody**	◆◆	$60-$145 SAVE	252

Map Page	Restaurants	Diamond Rated	Cuisine	Price Range	Page
㊴ p. 336	Heritage Bakery & Bistro	◆◆	American	$9-$25	255
㊵ p. 336	Adriano's Italian Restaurant	◆◆	Italian	$8-$22	255
㊶ p. 336	Wyoming's Rib & Chop House	◆◆	American	$8-$32	255
㊷ p. 336	La Comida	◆◆	Mexican	$8-$18	255
㊸ p. 336	**Zapata's**	◆◆	Mexican	$8-$12	255
㊹ p. 336	**8th Street at the Ivy**	◆◆◆	Western American	$8-$32	255
㊺ p. 336	Bubba's Bar-B-Que Restaurant	◆◆	Barbecue	$6-$14	255
㊻ p. 336	Geyser Brewing Co.	◆◆	American	$14-$27	255

POWELL

Map Page	Hotel	Diamond Rated	Rate Range	Page
㉂ p. 336	**Americas Best Value Inn**	◆◆	$90-$175 SAVE	308

WAPITI

Map Page	Hotel	Diamond Rated	Rate Range	Page
㉄ p. 336	Green Creek Inn	◆	$65-$180	323

MEETEETSE

Map Page	Restaurant	Diamond Rated	Cuisine	Price Range	Page
㊾ p. 336	Outlaw Steak and Rib House	◆	American	$9-$24	306

YELLOWSTONE NATIONAL PARK
- Attractions map p. 328
- Hotels & Restaurants map & index p. 336

ELEPHANT HEAD LODGE   307/587-3980 ②

Historic Cabin
$150-$350

Address: 1170 Yellowstone Hwy 82414 **Location:** 11.7 mi e of Yellowstone National Park east gate on US 14/16/20. **Facility:** Cozy wilderness cabins, including three with lofts, are featured at this lodge. 15 cabins. 1 story, exterior corridors. **Terms:** closed 10/1-5/14, 30 day cancellation notice-fee imposed. **Activities:** fishing, recreation programs, playground. *(See ad p. 329.)*

SHOSHONE LODGE   (307)587-4044 ①
Cabin $130-$200 **Address:** 349 North Fork Hwy 82190 **Location:** 3.5 mi e of Yellowstone National Park east gate on US 14/16/20. Located in a quiet secluded area. **Facility:** 17 cabins. 1 story, exterior corridors. **Terms:** closed 10/2-5/19, 2 night minimum stay, 30 day cancellation notice-fee imposed. **Activities:** fishing. **Guest Services:** coin laundry.

CANYON LODGE   307/344-7311
Not evaluated. **Address:** Canyon Jct 82190. Facilities, services, and décor characterize an economy property.

LAKE LODGE & CABINS   307-344-7311
Not evaluated. **Address:** 1 Grand Loop Rd 82190 **Location:** 1.5 mi s of Lake Jct. Facilities, services, and décor characterize an economy property.

LAKE YELLOWSTONE HOTEL & CABINS   307-344-7311
Not evaluated. **Address:** 1 Grand Loop Rd 82190 **Location:** 1 mi s of Lake Jct. Facilities, services, and décor characterize an economy property.

MAMMOTH HOT SPRINGS HOTEL & CABINS   307-344-7311
Not evaluated. **Address:** Mammoth Hot Springs 82190. Facilities, services, and décor characterize an economy property.

OLD FAITHFUL INN   307-344-7311
Not evaluated. **Address:** West Thumb & Madison 82190 **Location:** Opposite Old Faithful Geyser; between West Thumb and Madison. Facilities, services, and décor characterize an economy property. This property is accessible from West Yellowstone, Flagg Ranch and Mammoth Hot Springs. You can stay in the Old Faithful Snow Lodge & Cabins 12/15-3/1.

WHERE TO EAT

MAMMOTH HOT SPRINGS HOTEL DINING ROOM   307/344-7901 ①
Regional American. Casual Dining. $8-$28 **AAA Inspector Notes:** This large dining room accommodates the many summer visitors that frequent this spot for fresh seafood and meats. Efficient, friendly staff members deliver well-prepared meals off a varied menu. For those visiting in spring and fall, phone for exact hours. **Features:** full bar. **Address:** Mammoth Hot Springs 82190 **Location:** In Mammoth Hot Springs Hotel & Cabins.

Disney's Art of Animation Resort

©Disney/Pixar

Disneyland® Resort Hotel

ENJOY A MAGICAL DISNEY VACATION

What's the best way to experience all the enchantment of a vacation to the *Walt Disney World*® Resort in Florida or the *Disneyland*® Resort in California? How do you squeeze the most magic out of the Theme Parks and the whimsically themed *Disney Resort* hotels? And how can you enjoy great savings and exclusive rewards not available anywhere else? By booking a *AAA Vacations*® package from AAA Travel, of course!

DISNEYLAND® RESORT, CALIFORNIA

- Stay just steps away from the magic at a *Disneyland*® Resort Hotel.

- **Now open!**
  Get ready to be floored—cruise into the amazing Cars Land at *Disney California Adventure*® Park.

WALT DISNEY WORLD RESORT, FLORIDA

- Stay in the middle of the magic at a *Walt Disney World* Resort hotel.

- **Now open!**
  New Fantasyland™—immersing you in Disney stories like never before at *Magic Kingdom*® Park.

New *Fantasyland*

Artist Rendering

©Disney/Pixar

Cars Land

WITH ENCHANTING AAA BENEFITS!

LET AAA BE YOUR GUIDE...

With a *AAA Vacations*® package, you can create the Disney vacation that fits your family, your taste and your budget. And not only will your AAA Travel professional help put everything (like accommodations, tickets and flights) together, you'll also get to enjoy great Disney benefits on top of the exclusive AAA benefits and savings once you get there! Then all you need to do is relax and have fun.

READY TO START MAKING MAGIC?
Then contact your **AAA Travel professional** today!

DISNEP PARKS

Offices

Cities with main offices are listed in **BOLD TYPE** and toll-free member service numbers in *ITALIC TYPE*.
All are closed Saturdays, Sundays and holidays unless otherwise indicated.
The addresses, phone numbers and hours for any AAA/CAA office are subject to change.
The type of service provided is designated below the name of the city where the office is located:

✛ Auto travel services, including books and maps, and on-demand TripTik ® routings.
● Auto travel services, including selected books and maps, and on-demand TripTik ® routings.
■ Books/maps only, no marked maps or on-demand TripTik ® routings.
▲ Travel Agency Services, cruise, tour, air, car and rail reservations; domestic and international hotel reservations; passport photo services; international and domestic travel guides and maps; travel money products; and International Driving Permits. In addition, assistance with travel related insurance products including trip cancellation, travel accident, lost luggage, trip delay and assistance products.
✪ Insurance services provided. If only this icon appears, only insurance services are provided at that office.
⬖ Car Care Plus Facility provides car care services.
▣ Electric vehicle charging station on premises.

AAA NATIONAL OFFICE: 1000 AAA DRIVE, HEATHROW, FLORIDA 32746-5063, (407) 444-7000

IDAHO

BOISE—AAA OREGON/IDAHO, 7155 W DENTON ST, 83704. WEEKDAYS (M-F) 8:00-5:30. (208) 342-9391, *(800) 999-9391.* ✛▲✪

COEUR D'ALENE—AAA WASHINGTON, 296 W SUNSET AVE #33, 83815. WEEKDAYS (M-F) 8:30-5:30. (208) 664-5868, *(800) 407-2020.* ✛▲✪

MERIDIAN—AAA OREGON/IDAHO, 2310 E OVERLAND STE 110, 83642. WEEKDAYS (M-F) 8:30-5:30. (208) 844-4222 ✛▲✪

POCATELLO—AAA OREGON/IDAHO, 1000 POCATELLO CRK RD #E5, 83201. WEEKDAYS (M-F) 8:30-5:30. (208) 237-2225, *(800) 574-4222.* ✛▲✪

TWIN FALLS—AAA OREGON/IDAHO, 1239 POLE LINE RD E #315, 83301. WEEKDAYS (M-F) 8:30-5:30. (208) 734-6441, *(800) 999-6441.* ✛▲✪

MONTANA

BILLINGS—AAA MOUNTAINWEST, 3220 4TH AVE N, 59101. WEEKDAYS (M-F) 8:30-5:30. (406) 248-7738, *(800) 391-4222.* ✛▲✪

BOZEMAN—AAA MOUNTAINWEST, 1530 N 19TH AVE STE B, 59718. WEEKDAYS (M-F) 8:30-5:30. (406) 586-6156, *(800) 391-4222.* ✛▲✪

GREAT FALLS—AAA MOUNTAINWEST, 1520 3RD ST NW STE G, 59404. WEEKDAYS (M-F) 8:30-5:30. (406) 727-2900, *(800) 391-4222.* ✛▲✪

HAMILTON—AAA MOUNTAINWEST, 1265 N 1ST ST UNIT B, 59840. WEEKDAYS (M-F) 8:30-5:30. (406) 363-3407 ✪

HELENA—AAA MOUNTAINWEST, 2100 11TH AVE, 59601. WEEKDAYS (M-F) 8:30-5:30. (406) 447-8100 ✛▲✪

KALISPELL—AAA MOUNTAINWEST, 135 HUTTON RANCH RD #106, 59901. WEEKDAYS (M-F) 8:30-5:30. (406) 758-6980, *(800) 391-4222.* ✛▲✪

MISSOULA—AAA MOUNTAINWEST, 1200 S RESERVE STE B, 59801. WEEKDAYS (M-F) 8:30-5:30. (406) 829-5500, *(800) 391-4222.* ✛▲✪

WYOMING

CHEYENNE—AAA MOUNTAINWEST, 2316 DELL RANGE BLVD #B, 82009. WEEKDAYS (M-F) 8:30-5:30. (307) 634-8861, *(800) 391-4222.* ✛▲✪

Metric Equivalents Chart

TEMPERATURE

To convert Fahrenheit to Celsius, subtract 32 from the Fahrenheit temperature, multiply by 5 and divide by 9.
To convert Celsius to Fahrenheit, multiply by 9, divide by 5 and add 32.

ACRES

1 acre = 0.4 hectare (ha)   1 hectare = 2.47 acres

MILES AND KILOMETRES

Note: A kilometre is approximately 5/8 or 0.6 of a mile.
To convert kilometres to miles multiply by 0.6.

Miles/Kilometres		Kilometres/Miles	
15	24.1	30	18.6
20	32.2	35	21.7
25	40.2	40	24.8
30	48.3	45	27.9
35	56.3	50	31.0
40	64.4	55	34.1
45	72.4	60	37.2
50	80.5	65	40.3
55	88.5	70	43.4
60	96.6	75	46.6
65	104.6	80	49.7
70	112.7	85	52.8
75	120.7	90	55.9
80	128.7	95	59.0
85	136.8	100	62.1
90	144.8	105	65.2
95	152.9	110	68.3
100	160.9	115	71.4

Celsius °		Fahrenheit °
100	BOILING	212
37		100
35		95
32		90
29		85
27		80
24		75
21		70
18		65
16		60
13		55
10		50
7		45
4		40
2		35
0	FREEZING	32
-4		25
-7		20
-9		15
-12		10
-15		5
-18		0
-21		-5
-24		-10
-27		-15

LINEAR MEASURE

Customary	Metric
1 inch = 2.54 centimetres	1 centimetre = 0.4 inches
1 foot = 30 centimetres	1 metre = 3.3 feet
1 yard = 0.91 metres	1 metre = 1.09 yards
1 mile = 1.6 kilometres	1 kilometre = .62 miles

LIQUID MEASURE

Customary	Metric
1 fluid ounce = 30 millilitres	1 millilitre = .03 fluid ounces
1 cup = .24 litres	1 litre = 2.1 pints
1 pint = .47 litres	1 litre = 1.06 quarts
1 quart = .95 litres	1 litre = .26 gallons
1 gallon = 3.8 litres	

WEIGHT

If You Know:	Multiply By:	To Find:
Ounces	28	Grams
Pounds	0.45	Kilograms
Grams	0.035	Ounces
Kilograms	2.2	Pounds

PRESSURE

Air pressure in automobile tires is expressed in kilopascals. Multiply pound-force per square inch (psi) by 6.89 to find kilopascals (kPa).

24 psi = 165 kPa   28 psi = 193 kPa
26 psi = 179 kPa   30 psi = 207 kPa

GALLON AND LITRES

Gallons/Litres			Litres/Gallons			
5	19.0	12	45.6	10	2.6	40	10.4
6	22.8	14	53.2	15	3.9	50	13.0
7	26.6	16	60.8	20	5.2	60	15.6
8	30.4	18	68.4	25	6.5	70	18.2
9	34.2	20	76.0	30	7.8	80	20.8
10	38.0	25	95.0	35	9.1	90	23.4

IDAHO
MONTANA
WYOMING
DRIVING DISTANCES
100 MILES IN US/KILOMETERS IN CANADA
2:00 AVERAGE TIME (EXCLUDING STOPS)

KILOMETERS IN CANADA

MILES IN U.S.

© 2013 NAVTEQ 3673-14

© AAA

Border Information

U.S. Residents Traveling to Canada

Border crossing requirements: Travelers are required to present proper travel documents in order to enter Canada and return to the U.S.

Air travel: A U.S. passport is required.

Land or sea travel: Proof of citizenship and proof of identity are required. Approved documents include a passport or passport card, Enhanced Driver's License or NEXUS trusted traveler program card. Visit the U.S. Department of State website travel.state.gov for the most current information on these requirements. Canadian citizens should refer to the Canada Border Services Agency website www.cbsa-asfc.gc.ca.

U.S. resident aliens: An Alien Registration Receipt Card (Green Card) as well as a passport from the country of citizenship is required.

Children: All children must provide their own travel documents. In lieu of a U.S. passport or passport card, children under 16 traveling to Canada by land or sea may present an original or copy of their birth certificate, a Report of Birth Abroad obtained from a U.S. consulate or a Naturalization Certificate. Minors must be accompanied by both parents; if one parent is absent, a notarized letter of consent from the absent parent giving permission to go on the trip is required.

Legal Issues: Persons with felony convictions, DUI convictions or other offenses may be denied entry into Canada.

Firearms: Canada has strict laws regarding the importing, exporting, possession, use, storage, display and transportation of firearms. These are federal laws that apply across the country. Firearms are divided into classes: non-restricted (most ordinary rifles and shotguns); restricted (mainly handguns) and prohibited (full and converted automatics and certain handguns, among others).

To bring a non-restricted or restricted firearm into Canada you must:
- Be 18 years of age or older
- Declare firearm(s) at the first point of entry
- Obtain an Authorization to Transport (ATT) from a provincial or territorial Chief Firearms Officer prior to arrival at the point of entry; contact the Canadian Firearms Centre at (800) 731-4000 for additional details.

Hunters may bring in, duty-free, 200 rounds of ammunition; a valid license or declaration to purchase ammunition is required. Those planning to hunt in multiple provinces or territories must obtain a hunting license from each one.

Firearms are forbidden in many of Canada's national and provincial parks, game reserves and adjacent areas. For additional information regarding the temporary importation and use of firearms consult the Canada Border Services Agency website.

Personal items: Clothing, personal items, sports and recreational equipment, automobiles, snowmobiles, cameras, personal computers and food products appropriate for the purpose and duration of the visit may be brought into Canada duty and tax-free. Customs may require a refundable security deposit at the time of entry.

Tobacco products: Those meeting age requirements (18 years in Alberta, Manitoba, Northwest Territories, Nunavut, Saskatchewan, Quebec and Yukon; 19 years in other provinces) may bring in up to 50

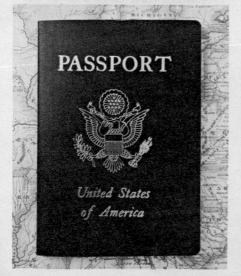

cigars, 200 cigarettes, 200 grams of tobacco and 200 tobacco sticks.

Alcohol: Those meeting age requirements (18 years in Alberta, Manitoba and Quebec; 19 years in other provinces and territories) may bring in limited alcoholic beverages: 40 ounces of liquor, 1.6 quarts of wine or 9 quarts of beer or ale (equivalent to 24 12-ounce bottles or cans).

- Amounts exceeding the allowable quantities are subject to federal duty and taxes, and provincial/territorial liquor fees.
- Provincial fees are paid at customs at the time of entry in all provinces and Yukon.
- It is illegal to bring more than the allowable alcohol quantity into the Northwest Territories or Nunavut.

Purchases: Articles purchased at Canadian duty-free shops are subject to U.S. Customs exemptions and restrictions; those purchased at U.S. duty-free shops before entering Canada are subject to duty if brought back into the United States.

Prescription drugs: Persons requiring medication while visiting Canada are permitted to bring it for their own use. Medication should be in the original packaging with a label listing the drug and its intended use. Bring a copy of the prescription and the prescribing doctor's phone number.

Gifts: Items not exceeding $60 (CAN) in value (excluding tobacco, alcoholic beverages and advertising matter) taken into or mailed to Canada are allowed free entry. Gifts valued at more than $60 are subject to regular duty and taxes on the excess amount.

Pets: You must have a certificate for a dog or cat 3 months and older. It must clearly describe the animal, declare that the animal is currently vaccinated against rabies and include a licensed veterinarian signature.

- Collar tags are not sufficient proof of immunization.
- Be sure the vaccination does not expire while traveling in Canada.
- The certificate is also required to bring the animal back into the U.S.

Exemptions: Service animals; healthy puppies and kittens under 3 months old with a health certificate signed by a licensed veterinarian indicating that the animal is too young to vaccinate.

Vehicles

- Vehicles entering Canada for leisure travel, including trailers not exceeding 8 feet 6 inches (2.6 m) in width, are generally subject to quick and routine entry procedures.
- To temporarily leave or store a car, trailer or other goods in Canada if you must leave the country, you must pay an import duty and taxes or present a valid permit. Canadian Customs officials issue vehicle permits at the point of entry.
- You are required to carry your vehicle registration document when traveling in Canada.
- If driving a car other than your own, you must have written permission from the owner.
- If driving a rented car, you must provide a copy of the rental contract.
- A valid U.S. driver's license is valid in Canada.
- In all Canadian provinces and territories except Alberta, British Columbia and Saskatchewan, it is illegal to use radar detectors, even if unplugged.
- Seat belt use is required for the driver and all passengers.

Financial Responsibility Laws in Canada: When an accident involves death, injury or property damage, Canadian provinces and territories require evidence of financial responsibility.

U.S. motorists should check with their insurance company regarding whether they are required to obtain and carry a yellow Non-Resident Inter-Province Motor Vehicle Liability Insurance Card (accepted as evidence of financial responsibility throughout Canada). Those not carrying proper proof may be subject to a substantial fine. If renting a vehicle, check with the rental car company.

U.S. Residents Returning to the U.S.

U.S. citizens returning to the U.S. from Canada by air must have a valid passport. Those returning by land or sea are required to present the appropriate travel documents outlined above.

Every individual seeking entry into the United States—foreign visitors, U.S. citizens or lawful permanent residents—must be inspected at the point of entry. Random searches may be conducted by U.S. Customs and Border Protection agents.

U.S. Exemptions for a Stay in Canada of 48 Hours or More

- Each individual may bring back tax- and duty-free articles not exceeding $800 in retail value.
- Any amount over the $800 exemption is subject to duty.
- The exemption is allowed once every 30 days.
- A family (related persons living in the same household) may combine purchases to avoid exceeding individual exemption limits.
- Exemptions are based on fair retail value (keep receipts of all purchases as proof).
- Exemptions apply to articles acquired only for personal or household use or as gifts and not intended for sale.
- The exemption may include 100 cigars, 200 cigarettes and 1 liter of liquor per person over age 21 (state liquor laws are enforced).
- All articles must accompany you on your return.

U.S. Exemptions for a Stay in Canada Less Than 48 Hours

- Each individual may bring back tax- and duty-free articles not exceeding $200 in retail value.
- The exemption may include no more than 50 cigarettes, 10 cigars, 5 fluid ounces (150 milliliters) of alcoholic beverage or 150 milliliters of perfume containing alcohol.
- A family may not combine purchases.
- If purchases exceed the $200 exemption, you forfeit the exemption and all purchases become subject to duty.
- All articles must be declared and accompany you upon return.

Gifts

- Gifts up to $100 fair retail value may be sent to friends or relatives in the United States provided no recipient receives more than one gift per day (gifts do not have to be included in the $800 exemption).
- Gifts of tobacco products, alcoholic beverages or perfume containing alcohol valued at more than $5 retail are excluded from this provision.
- Mark the contents, retail value and "Unsolicited Gift" on the outside of the package.

Prohibited: Narcotics and dangerous drugs, drug paraphernalia, obscene articles and publications, seditious or treasonable matter, lottery tickets, hazardous items (fireworks, dangerous toys, toxic or poisonous substances) and switchblade knives. Also prohibited are any goods originating in embargoed countries.

Canadian Residents Traveling to the U.S.

Canadian citizens entering the U.S. by air must have a valid passport. Canadian citizens entering the U.S. by land or sea are required to present the appropriate travel documents; refer to the Canada Border Services Agency website www.cbsa-asfc.gc.ca for the most current information on these requirements.

If traveling to the United States with a minor, carry documentation proving your custodial rights. A person under age 18 traveling to the United States alone or with only one parent or another adult must carry certified documentation proving that the trip is permitted by both parents.

U.S. Customs permits Canadian residents to bring—duty-free for personal use and not intended for sale—the following: clothing, personal items and equipment appropriate to the trip, up to 200 cigarettes, 50 cigars or 2 kilograms of tobacco, and 1 liter of alcoholic beverage.

Canadian Residents Returning to Canada

Canadian residents may bring back, free of duty and taxes, goods valued up to $400

(CAN) any number of times a year, provided the visit to the United States is 48 hours or more and all goods accompany the purchaser (a written declaration may be required).

You may claim a $50 (CAN) exemption on goods, excluding alcoholic beverages and tobacco products, if returning after an absence of less than 48 hours and not using any other exemption. If bringing back more than $50 worth of goods, the regular duty and tax rate is levied on the entire value. This exemption may apply any number of times in a year. No tobacco or alcohol may be brought back if returning from a visit of less than 48 hours.

If returning after 7 days or more (not counting the departure day from Canada)

you may claim up to a $750 (CAN) exemption. Goods other than alcohol and tobacco products need not accompany you (a written declaration may be required).

Permitted within the $400 and $750 exemptions: up to 50 cigars, 200 cigarettes, 200 tobacco sticks and 6.4 ounces of tobacco, and up to 40 ounces of liquor or 1.6 quarts of wine or 9 quarts of beer or ale (the equivalent of 24 12-ounce bottles or cans). You must meet the minimum age requirement of the province or territory entered to claim alcohol or tobacco products.

While AAA makes every effort to provide accurate and complete information, AAA makes no warranty, express or implied, and assumes no legal liability or responsibility for the accuracy or completeness of any information contained herein.

Points of Interest Index

Attractions appear at the top of each category
and offer a Great Experience for Members®.

Index Legend

EVENTS & FESTIVALS

HISTORIC SITES & EXHIBITS

OUTDOORS & SCIENCE

SHOPPING

SPORTS & RECREATION

TOURS & SIGHTSEEING

Photo Credits

Page numbers are in bold type. Picture credit abbreviations are as follows:
- (i) numeric sequence from top to bottom, left to right ■ (AAA) AAA Travel library.

- (Cover) Middle Fork of the Salmon River, Stanley, ID / © steve bly / Alamy
- **2** (i) © iStockphoto.com / vkbhat
- **2** (ii) © iStockphoto.com / codyphotography
- **2** (iii) © bikeriderlondon / Shutterstock.com
- **7** © Monashee Frantz / age fotostock
- **13** © iStockphoto.com / Adivin
- **18** (i) © iStockphoto.com / vkbhat
- **18** (ii) © iStockphoto.com / Adventure_Photo
- **19** © iStockphoto.com / Sportstock
- **20** (i) Courtesy of Wikimedia Commons
- **20** (ii) Courtesy of Wikimedia Commons
- **23** (i) © iStockphoto.com / vkbhat
- **23** (ii) © Gregory Johnston / Shutterstock.com
- **23** (iii) © iStockphoto.com / GMVozd
- **23** (iv) © iStockphoto.com / LUGO
- **23** (v) © iStockphoto.com / Silvrshootr
- **24** (i) © iStockphoto.com / thinair28
- **24** (ii) © iStockphoto.com / Wirepec
- **24** (iii) © Courtesy of The Discovery Center of Idaho
- **24** (iv) © Andre Jenny / Alamy
- **106** (i) © iStockphoto.com / aimintang
- **106** (ii) © iStockphoto.com / codyphotography
- **107** © iStockphoto / lmsvail99
- **108** (i) Courtesy of Wikimedia Commons
- **108** (ii) Courtesy of Wikimedia Commons
- **111** (i) © Andre Jenny / Alamy
- **111** (ii) © blickwinkel / Alamy
- **111** (iii) © iStockphoto.com / Saturated
- **111** (iv) © iStockphoto.com / domino99
- **111** (v) © Reimar Gaertner / age fotostock
- **112** (i) © spirit of america / Shutterstock.com
- **112** (ii) © iStockphoto.com / Decorah
- **112** (iii) © Carol Barrington / Alamy
- **112** (iv) © Dennis MacDonald / Alamy
- **216** (i) © Morales / age fotostock
- **216** (ii) © Tom Relchner / Shutterstock.com
- **217** © Tom Grundy / Shutterstock.com
- **218** (i) Courtesy of Wikimedia Commons
- **218** (ii) Courtesy of Wikimedia Commons
- **221** (i) © Megan Carley / Shutterstock.com
- **221** (ii) © EastVillage Images / Shutterstock.com
- **221** (iii) © Zack Frank / Shutterstock.com
- **221** (iv) © bikeriderlondon / Shutterstock.com
- **221** (v) © iStockphoto.com / hsvrs
- **222** (i) © Philip Eckerberg / Shutterstock.com
- **222** (ii) © Sharon Day / Shutterstock.com
- **222** (iii) © Boykov / Shutterstock.com
- **222** (iv) © Albert Pego / Shutterstock.com
- **347** © Garry Gay / Alamy
- **349** © image100 / age fotostock

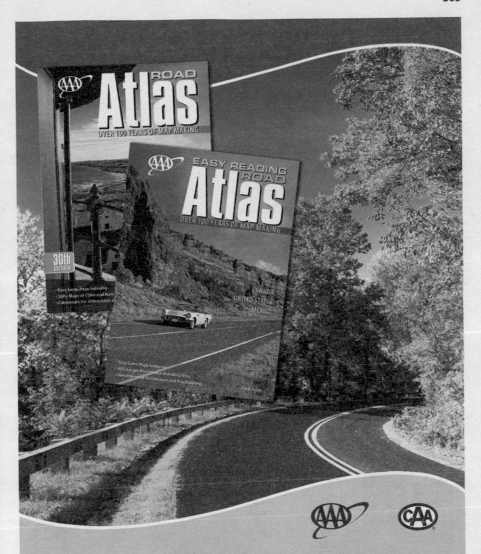

Find your way: AAA/CAA Road Atlases

Plan or change your driving route with up-close, up-to-date road maps.

Enjoy exceptional features like easy-to-read map text, same-page indexing, mileage and clearly identified exit numbers on major highways. Choose the standard version or the Easy Reading edition featuring 40 percent larger type.

Purchase at participating AAA/CAA club offices.

LET'S GET SOCIAL
Stay connected with #AAA

Visit with us on your favorite social media sites for the latest updates on hot discounts, cool destinations and handy automotive know-how.

Talk with us!

- Plus.google.com/+AAAnews
- Twitter.com/AAA_Travel
- YouTube.com/AAA
- Facebook.com/AAAFanPage
- Pinterest.com/AAA

Find Pet-Friendly Places to Stay and Play

Buy *The AAA PetBook*® at participating AAA/CAA offices — or download in digital format from your online bookseller.

- Pet-friendly AAA Approved and Diamond Rated hotels
- Campgrounds, attractions and national public lands that allow pets
- Handy tips and resources

Visit **AAA.com/PetBook** for information, travel tips and AAA PetBook Photo Contest details.

the
Choice
is yours.

Choose one or choose them all!

Get AAA/CAA travel information in the formats you prefer.

Whether you enjoy the convenience of ebooks and apps, the ease of 24/7 online resources or the fun of poring over guidebooks, the choice is yours.

Explore your options on AAA.com or CAA.ca, your app store, AAA.com/ebooks and club offices.